THE DIGITAL DICTIONARY

THE DIGITAL DICTIONARY

A Guide to Digital Equipment Corporation's
Technical Terminology

SECOND EDITION

REVISED AND EXPANDED

ROBERT E. MAROTTA, EDITOR

DECbooks

9 8 7 6 5

Printed in the United States of America.

Order number EY-3433E-DP

The manuscript for this book was created using generic coding and, via a translation program, was automatically typeset and paginated. Book production was done by Educational Services Development and Publishing in Bedford, MA.

The following are trademarks of Digital Equipment Corporation; this list should not be considered complete or exhaustive.

digital	DECservice	Professional
ALL-IN-1	DECsystem-10	RAINBOW
COS-310	DECSYSTEM-20	RSTS
DATATRIEVE	DECUS	RSX
DEC	DECwriter	UNIBUS
DECdirect	DIBOL	VAX
DECmail	LETTER PRINTER 100	VMS
DECmat	MASSBUS	VT
DECmate	PDP	Work Processor
DECnet	P/OS	

Library of Congress Cataloging in Publication Data

Main entry under title:

The Digital Dictionary.

Rev. ed. of: The DEC Dictionary. c1984.
1. DEC computers–Dictionaries. I. Marotta,
Robert E. II. Digital Equipment Corporation.
III. Title: DEC Dictionary.
QA76.8.D43D54 1986   004'.03'21   85-20466
ISBN 0-932376-82-7

CONTENTS

Appendix A

Readability/Translatability **617**

Appendix B

*The greatest problem in communication
is the illusion that it has
taken place.*

R.E.Marotta

INTRODUCTION

This Dictionary contains words used to describe Digital Equipment Corporation computer systems and related hardware and software products. It defines technical terms, lists common English words, expands acronyms, abbreviations, and mnemonics, and discusses guidelines for writing text that is easy to read and translate.

The Dictionary, therefore, provides a reference tool for people who communicate information about DIGITAL's computer systems and related products.

Structure

The Dictionary comprises two sections and two appendices:

- A Glossary of Technical Terms
- A list of Abbreviations, Acronyms, Mnemonics, and Expansions.
- Guidelines for Writing Readable and Translatable Text
- A list of Recommended Common English Words

The first section defines technical terms and distinguishes between meanings that apply to specific DIGITAL products and those that apply to DIGITAL products in general. This section also contains generic definitions of many terms that are used in DIGITAL's publications the same way that they are used throughout the computer industry.

The second section expands the abbreviations, acronyms, and mnemonics commonly used in DIGITAL publications.

The appendices present guidelines for writing easily readable and easily translatable text. It includes useful rules of grammar and syntax and suggests checklists for the processes of writing, editing, and translating technical communication. It also lists common English terms recommended for use in clear and concise writing.

Origin and Future

This Dictionary project combines earlier work done on the DEC Dictionary, the Software Glossary, and the First Edition of the DIGITAL Dictionary. In planning this book, the Dictionary Committee changed the format and focus of the book's ancestors and altered the guidelines for dealing with technical terms. The format helps distinguish between types of technical terms and makes the information accessible. With respect to technical vocabulary and language, the focus of the Dictionary has shifted from a prescriptive approach to a descriptive one. The definitions of technical terms in this Dictionary are based primarily on the glossaries found in DIGITAL's publications, describing how they are actually used and not prescribing any specific use.

As the source glossaries improve and grow to keep pace with expanding technical knowledge and new features of DIGITAL's products, this Dictionary will also grow. Periodic updates will keep this Dictionary current with the language used by the people who write about these systems and related products.

PRODUCTION AND PUBLICATION

Production

The Second Edition of the DIGITAL Dictionary is produced by DIGITAL's Publishing Services in Bedford, Massachusetts. Publishing Services is part of the Educational Services Development and Publishing group.

Publication

The DIGITAL Dictionary is published under the DECbooks imprint of Digital Press, a Digital Equipment Corporation book publishing group. The original edition was published in 1983 as a document for internal distribution. In 1984 Digital Press published a DECbooks edition for DIGITAL customers and for sale and use outside the Corporation. That edition contained the same terms and definitions as the internal edition.

This revised and expanded edition is produced for use by both DIGITAL employees and persons outside the Corporation. Improved communication is one expected, positive result of having a book that internally and externally helps establish common understanding of how a particular term is used. The success of any communication process is directly related to what the participants know in common. With this edition, DIGITAL persons and customers can move toward better, mutual communication about products and services.

The terms and definitions in this dictionary, except those labeled as generic, are from glossaries previously published by DIGITAL. Those definitions, therefore, have been verified for technical accuracy and completeness.

The abbreviations, acronyms, mnemonics, and their expansions, either DIGITAL-specific or generic, may not have been previously published in a reference list. Although all of the DIGITAL expansions have been verified for accuracy by the DIGITAL Dictionary Committee, some of the common or generic expansions have not been. The Committee has verified as many of those common and generic expansions as possible at various libraries and through other authoritative sources.

The Second Edition contains approximately 4,500 more entries than the First Edition. This revised edition comprises the number of entries, and their definitions or expansions, that were available up to the day of publication. However, some terms and abbreviations used to describe DIGITAL products may not be included because they were either not available to the Dictionary Committee at time of publication, or were so recently developed that the Committee did not have sufficient time before publication to verify their technical accuracy and completeness. The Dictionary Committee feels that the quality of the Second Edition, as in the First Edition, depends not on the number of entries but on the accuracy and completeness of the information therein.

The Dictionary Committee welcomes suggestions for new entries, corrections, and deletions from this book. A Reader's Comment page is provided at the back of this dictionary. You also may address suggestions to:

Digital Equipment Corporation
12 Crosby Drive
Bedford, MA 01730
ATTN: Chairperson
DIGITAL Dictionary Committee
BUO/E-95

The DIGITAL Dictionary Committee acknowledges the support of and contributions to this publication from many individuals and groups throughout DIGITAL.

The Committee especially acknowledges the support from the management of Educational Services Development and Publishing and Central Quality Group of Systems and Clusters Engineering.

SECTION I
GLOSSARY OF TECHNICAL TERMS

GLOSSARY OF TECHNICAL TERMS

Types of Technical Entries

Members of the Dictionary Committee, representing many areas throughout DIGITAL, submitted terms for consideration as entries into this Glossary. The Committee also solicited terms and definitions throughout the Corporation. Accepted entries were verified for technical accuracy and completeness within respective product areas.

The technical terms in this Glossary are in one of three categories:

- DIGITAL-specific
- product-specific
- generic

It is possible that a term may be used in all three categories. It may be used according to its DIGITAL-specific definition for some products, according to its product-specific definition for other products, and according to its generic definition for yet other DIGITAL products. The term itself was not the main consideration for placing it into one or more of the categories; the main criterion for labeling a term was how it is defined and used. It is NOT the purpose of this Glossary section to present a recommended definition and, therefore, a prescribed use of a term. The purpose is to show the varying uses of a term, historically and currently.

DIGITAL-specific terms are those that are defined or used the same way in four or more product or system areas and are different in meaning from industry-wide, generic use, even to the slightest degree.

Product-specific terms are those that are defined or used differently within DIGITAL in specific product, system, group, or language areas, and are different in meaning from industry-wide, generic use, even to the slightest degree. A term may have many product-specific definitions, depending on the number of different ways that the term is used throughout DIGITAL.

Generic terms are those that are defined or used the same way generally thoughout the industry.

A term and definition designated as specific to a product or products may be used that same way for other products, but not designated as such in this Glossary. The Dictionary Committee labeled terms and definitions according to the information available up to the time of publication.

Also, a product-specific definition, or definitions, may be given for a term, even though the term also has a DIGITAL-specific definition. This would indicate that although at least four areas use the term the same way, other product or system areas use it differently.

Generic terms are those that are commonly used the same way throughout industry. Generic terms and definitions not found in the DIGITAL Dictionary can be obtained from any of the standard glossaries or dictionaries, such as:

American National Dictionary for Information Processing, American National Standards Committee, 1977.

IEEE Standard Glossary of Software Engineering Terms, IEEE, Inc., 1983.

Standard Dictionary of Computers and Information Processing, Hayden Book Co., 1983.

The New American Computer Dictionary, Kent Porter. New American Library, New York, 1983.

DIGITAL-specific and Product-specific Terms and Definitions

The Glossary terms are listed in the order of alpha characters, letter by letter. All other characters, symbols, and spaces in a term were not considered for listing purposes.

The definitions are identified as generic, as DIGITAL-specific, or as related to one or more products, systems, groups, or languages. The following is a list of identification terms used in this dictionary. For classification convenience, we have combined some individual product, system, group, and language names to form composite terms, such as "VAX/RMS" and "VAX/VMS." Composite terms may have been used to identify a defined term as related to one or more of the individual components of the composite term. Any usage of an identification term in this dictionary should not be construed to be dispositive of the trademark usage to which Digital Equipment Corporation puts the product, system, group, or language name(s) generating the term, whether component, composite, or individual in nature.

Identification Terms

ACMS	DECSIM
ALL-IN-1	DECsystem-10
BASIC	DECSYSTEM-20
BASIC-PLUS-2	DECtype
BSE	DECWORD
COBOL-74	DIGITAL-specific
CDD	DSM-11
CTS-300	Ethernet*
DECmate II	FMS
DECnet	GAMMA

* Ethernet is a trademark of Xerox Corporation.

generic
GIGI
MACRO-11
MCS-10
Medical Systems
Memory Resident RT-11
MicroPower PASCAL
MICRO RSTS
MINC
MSG (SPETS)
PASCAL
PDP-11
PEARL
Publications
RAINBOW™
Rdb/ELN
RMS-11
Personal Computer Products
PRO/Communications
PRO/Diskette Systems
REAL
RGL/FEP

RSTS/E
RSX-11
RSX-11M
RSX-11M-PLUS
RSX-20F
RT-11
TDMS
TOPS-10
TOPS-20
USCF
VAX C
VAX COBOL
VAX Information Architecture
VAX-11
VAX DATATRIEVE
VAX DBMS
VAX PASCAL
VAX PL/I
VAX PSI
VAX/RMS
VAX/VMS
VT-11 GRAPHICS

abbreviated combined relation condition *n.*

DIGITAL-specific

The combined condition that results from the explicit omission of a common subject and common relational operator in a consecutive sequence of relation conditions.

abbreviation document *n.*

DECWORD and DECtype

Software that associates groups of words or short phrases with two-character abbreviations.

ABD *n.*

VAX/VMS

The abbreviation for ancillary control process buffer descriptor or ACP buffer descriptor. ABD is a data structure that is built by QI/O system services. The ABD and ACP I/O buffer packet (AIB) form the complex buffered I/O buffer. The ABD contains a description of the user data in P1 through P5 of the QI/O call. This data is passed to the ABD by QI/O system services. The only parameter that the user must supply is P1, the address of the file information block (FIB). Same as ancillary control process buffer descriptor and ACP buffer descriptor.

abnormal termination *n.*

VAX DBMS

A program stopped either through its own logic or by a system directive without issuing a FINISH to the database.

generic

The premature end of an image that occurs when the operating system detects a condition that prevents further successful execution.

abort *n.*

VAX/VMS

An exception that occurs in the middle of an instruction and sometimes leaves the registers and memory in an indeterminate state, such that the instruction cannot necessarily be restarted. See also exception.

absolute accuracy *n.*

MINC

A measure of the freedom from error, or the degree of exactness, determined from a specified reference or origin rather than from a relative point (as the difference value).

absolute address *n.*

generic

A binary identification number assigned to each permanent memory storage location.

absolute indexed mode *n.*

VAX/VMS

An indexed addressing mode in which the base operand specifier is addressed in absolute mode.

absolute loader *n.*

generic

A series of machine instructions designed to read programs and data into a permanent memory storage location for later execution.

absolute location *n.*

RGL/FEP

On a screen, a point whose x- and y-coordinates are based on its distance from the origin location. Its coordinates are measured as displacement from the (0.0) screen location, regardless of the location of the graphic cursor or text cursor. Same as absolute point.

absolute mode *n.*

VAX/VMS

A mode of address in which the program counter (PC) is used as the register in autoincrement deferred mode. The contents of the PC is the address of the location containing the actual operand.

absolute module *n.*

TOPS-10

A module whose program counters are set to absolute addresses only.

absolute point *n.*

VT-11 GRAPHICS

On a screen, a point whose x- and y-coordinates are based on its distance from the origin location; that is, its coordinates are measured as displacement from the (0.0) screen location, regardless of the location of the graphic cursor or text cursor. The coordinates' units are defined by the user. Same as absolute location.

absolute section *n.*

MicroPower PASCAL and RT-11

The portion of a program in which the programmer has specified physical memory locations of data items. An absolute section must reside in specific memory locations; it is not relocatable.

absolute shared region *n.*

VAX/VMS

A shared region that has the same virtual address in all processes that refer to it.

absolute time *n.*

VAX/VMS

Values expressing a specific date (month, day, and year) and time of day. Absolute time values are always expressed in the system as positive numbers.

DECSIM

The simulator clock value specified by a preceding vertical bar (|) in the DECSIM command language. The time value refers to simulation time 0 as opposed to an offset from the current simulator clock value.

absolute virtual address *n.*

TOPS-10

In user virtual address space, a fixed location that cannot be relocated by the software, but can be translated to a physical address by the hardware.

accelerated depreciation *n.*

BSE/generic

A method of depreciation that charges off more of the original cost of a fixed asset in the earlier years than in the later years of the asset's service life.

acceptance *n.*

USFC/generic

Refers to the equipment accepted by customer. This commences the lease and initiates lease payment.

access by record file address *n.*

RSX-11M

A unique way of identifying every record within a disk file. The record file address (RFA) remains valid only for that record for the life of the file. If a record is deleted, its RFA is not reused. See also record file address.

access control *n.*

DECnet

The process of screening inbound connect requests and verifying them against a local system account file. Access control is an optional session control function.

VAX/VMS

Validating connect, login, or file-access requests to determine whether or not they can be accepted. User name and password provide the most common means of access control.

access control list *n.*

FMS

A table that allows or denies users access to protected directories or objects. By maintaining such lists, users can restrict access to the data definitions stored in the dictionary.

VAX Information Architecture

A table that lists which users are allowed access to an object, and what kind of access.

VAX/VMS

A list that defines the kinds of access to be granted or denied to users of an object. Access control lists can be created for objects such as files, devices, and mailboxes. Each access control list consists of one or more entries known as access control list entries. Same as ACL.

access control list entry *n.*

VAX/VMS

An entry in an access control list. Access control list entries may specify identifiers and the access rights to be granted or denied the holders of the identifiers, default protection for directories, or security alarm details. Access control lists for each object can hold numerous entries, limited only by overall space and performance considerations. Same as ACE. (contrles ?) d'accs

access date *n.*

TOPS-10

The date on which a file on disk was last read or written. If a file has not been read or written since it was created, the creation date and the access date are the same.

access declaration *n.*

RSX-11M

At file opening, an indication of the record operations that a program will perform on the file.

access function *n.*

PEARL

A capability of defining where and in which way an object is accessed and the identifier that accesses the object.

accessibility character *n.*

TOPS-10

A character that indicates whether or not a tape volume is protected.

accessible *adj.*

CTS-300

Refers to records to which QUILL is authorized to have access.

access list *n.*

DECSIM

A list of one or more signal names, behavior internal states, element labels, or state variables used as arguments to commands in the command language.

access mode n.

generic

One of several ways that a program operates on a file's records.

VAX/VMS

Any of the four processor access modes in which software executes. Processor access modes are, in order from most to least privileged and protected: kernel (mode 0), executive (mode 1), supervisor (mode 2), and user (mode 3). When the processor is in kernel mode, the executing software has complete control of and responsibility for the system. When the processor is in any other mode, the processor is inhibited from executing privileged instructions.

DIGITAL-specific

The manner in which records in a record file will be read or written. The access modes are sequential, direct, or keyed sequential.

VAX DATATRIEVE and VAX/VMS

The method of retrieving and storing records in a file.

VAX DBMS

In the DBMS data manipulation language, that part of the READY statement's USAGE clause that describes what kind of processing to permit on the data in the realm ready. The access mode can be RETRIEVAL ("read only") or UPDATE ("read and write"). See also usage mode and allow mode.

access path n.

RSX-11M

The sequence of steps RMS-11 performs to transform the parameters in the user's record operation request into the requested record. Same as logical access path.

access privilege n.

generic

A characteristic that allows a file to be used only by a specific class of users.

access stream n.

DIGITAL-specific

A serial sequence of I-O operations on records in a sequential, relative, and indexed file.

access table n.

TOPS-10 and TOPS-20

A system table that lists the status of all files open for reading or writing in addition to the status of those files recently closed.

access time n.

generic

The time elapsed between asking for data and receiving the data.

access type n.

VAX/VMS

1. The way in which the processor accesses instruction operands. Access types are read, write, modify, address, and branch.

2. The way in which a procedure accesses its arguments. Same as record access type.

access violation n.

VAX/VMS

An attempt to reference an address that is either not mapped into virtual memory or not accessible by the current access mode.

account n.

DECWORD and RSTS/E

The allocation of RSTS/E or DECWORD facilities to each user. A user must have an account to use the system. Each user has a separate account, identified by a special account number and password.

VAX/VMS

A key to the system and a unit of system accounting. Each system user, including parts of the system itself, has an account. The system manager creates these accounts in the master file directory and assigns an account number to each. Individual users are identified by an account name as well. When you log in, you log in under a particular account name or number. This number informs the system where your files are and what kind of access to other files and system facilities you should be given.

User accounts are either privileged or nonprivileged. Privileged users have access to all system commands and to all parts of the system. Nonprivileged users are limited to everyday operations that do not threaten the integrity of the operating system.

DIGITAL-specific

A character-string name or number that identifies an individual user when the user logs in. That name or number informs the system where the user's files are and the type of access to other files and system facilities that the user should be given. See also UIC, UFD, account name, account number, member number, project number, and project programmer number.

accounting cycle *n.*

generic

The sequence of accounting procedures starting with journal entries for various transactions and events and ending with the financial statements.

accounting equation *n.*

generic

Assets = Liabilities - Owner's Equity

accounting manager *n.*

VAX/VMS

In the system process, a job controller function that writes accounting records to a system accounting log file to track job activity for user process termination, printer and batch jobs.

accounting period *n.*

generic

The period of time over which an income statement summarizes the changes in owner's equity. Usually the official period is one year, but income statements are also prepared for shorter, or interim, periods.

account name *n.*

DIGITAL-specific

A string that identifies a particular account used to accumulate data on a job's resource use. All user resources, except disk quotas, are charged to user account names. Disk quotas are charged to user UICs (user identification codes). See also account.

VAX/VMS

A string that identifies a particular account used to accumulate data on a job's resource use. This name is the user's accounting charge number, not the user's UIC.

account number *n.*

DIGITAL-specific

A number that identifies an authorized user logging into a system. The format of an account number is [number,number], where the first number is the project number and the second number is the programmer number. See also project number, account, member number, and programmer number.

generic

A discrete code that identifies system users.

account payable *n.*

generic

The amount that an entity owes to a creditor, usually a supplier; not evidenced by a promissory note.

account receivable *n.*

generic

An amount that is owed to an entity, usually by one of its customers as a result of the ordinary extension of credit.

account string *n.*

COBOL-74

A string of ASCII characters that identifies an account and can be used by the installation for downstream billing, reporting, charging, and so forth. The string can be broken into small data fields or be used as one field, depending on the needs of the installation.

accrual accounting *n.*

generic

Accounting for revenues in the period in which they are earned and for expenses in the period in which they are incurred. This is normal accounting practice.

accrued *adj.*

generic

Pertaining to a revenue that has been earned or an expense that has been recognized even though the related receivable/payable is not yet due.

accumulated depreciation *n.*

generic

An account showing the total amount of depreciation of an asset that has been accumulated to date. The difference is the asset's book value.

accumulation field *n.*

CTS-300

In the PRINT utility, a field in a record identified as containing data that is to be added (accumulated) from record to record for eventual printout.

accumulator *n.*

generic

A register or electrical circuit that stores data used for arithmetic or logic operations.

"a" character *n.*

VAX/VMS

Any character within a subset of ASCII characters consisting of uppercase characters A–Z, numerals 0–9, and the following special characters: ! '' '' % & ' ( ) * + , − . / : ; < = > ?

ACK0, ACK1 *n.*

DECnet

Affirmative acknowledgment replies in data-link escape (DLE) sequences in binary synchronous communications. These replies indicate that the previous transmission block was accepted by the receiver and that it is ready to accept the next block of the transmission. Use of ACK0 and ACK1 alternately provides sequential checking control for a series of replies. ACK0 is also an affirmative (ready to receive) reply to an initialization sequence (line bid) in point-to-point operation. See also affirmative acknowledgment.

ACL *n.*

VAX Information Architecture

The abbreviation for access control list. ACL is a table that lists which users are allowed access to an object, and the type of access allowed. Same as access control list.

AC mode (application control mode) *n.*

DECnet

A manner of protocol management in which programs interacting by means of the RSX-11M/SNA Protocol Emulator (PE) manage the SNA (systems network architecture) protocol. Such programs are said to be operating in the application control mode or AC mode. In AC mode, protocol emulator activity is restricted to managing certain transmission functions. A broader range of SNA protocol is available to programs operating in the AC mode than is available to programs operating in the emulator control (EC) mode. Same as application control mode.

ACMS *n.*

ACMS

The abbreviation for Application Control and Management System. ACMS is a software product, layered on VAX/VMS, used to define, run, and control online applications. Same as Application Control and Management System.

ACMS/AD *n.*

ACMS

The abbreviation for Application Control and Management System/Application Development. ACMS/AD is an optional software product for developing applications that run under the control of VAX-11 ACMS. ACMS/AD provides a task implementation method that uses high-level definitions to replace complex application code. Same as Application Control and Management System/Application.

ACMS central controller *n.*

ACMS

The ACMS process that serves as the central control point for the ACMS run-time system.

ACMSGEN *n.*

ACMS

The utility used to set ACMS system parameters. Similar to the VAX/VMS SYSGEN Utility.

ACMS operator *n.*

ACMS

An ACMS user authorized to control the daily operations of ACMS and/or its parts with the ACMS Operator commands.

ACMS operator command *n.*

ACMS

One of several DCL (DIGITAL Command Language) commands provided by ACMS to control the operations of the ACMS system software and ACMS applications.

ACMS user *n.*

ACMS

A VMS user authorized to access or control ACMS or its parts.

acoustic *adj.*

generic

Pertaining to the characteristics of sound.

acoustical *adj.*

generic

Pertaining to the characteristics that control sound waves.

acoustics *n.*

generic

The characteristics that control the direction of sound waves.

ACP *n.*

DIGITAL-specific

The abbreviation for ancillary control process. An ancillary control process is an interface operation between user software and an I/O driver. An ACP provides functions supplementary to those performed in the driver, such as file and directory management. Same as ancillary control process.

ACP buffer descriptor (ABD) *n.*

VAX/VMS

A data structure that is built by QI/O system services. The ABD and ACP I/O buffer packet (AIB) form the complex buffered I/O buffer. The ABD contains a description of the user data in p1 through p5 of the QI/O call. This data is passed to the ABD by QI/O system services. The only parameter that the user must supply is p1, the address of the file information block (FIB). Same as ABD.

ACP I/O buffer (AIB) *n.*

VAX/VMS

A data structure that points to the ABD (ACP buffer descriptor) and is part of the complex buffered I/O buffer. The AIB also contains some information about itself such as size, type, and length of packet header. Same as AIB. See also ACP buffer descriptor.

ACP queue header block (AQB) *n.*

VAX/VMS

A data structure that provides information to the QI/O system services and to the MTAACP process. It is created by the mount system program when the MTAACP is created. The AQB contains the AQB transaction queue that contains I/O request packets (IRPs) for the MTAACP, the process identification of the MTAACP process servicing the queue, and the number of volumes being serviced by the MTAACP. Same as AQB.

action item *n.*

ALL-IN-1

A personal memo the user enters on a daily basis, using Action Item Management, under the Desk Management Subsystem. ALL-IN-1 records these items for later display.

action routine *n.*

FMS

In the application program, a routine that is associated with a particular field or form and that is called when the operator signals completion of a field or form by pressing a terminator key. Same as user action routine.

active component *n.*

DECnet

A component whose operational state is other than OFF. The ACTIVE keyword can be used with the SHOW and LIST commands to display information about active lines, nodes, and logging.

VAX/VMS

A network component whose operational state is other than OFF. The ACTIVE keyword can be used with the NCP commands SHOW or LIST to display information about active lines, circuits, nodes, and logging.

active form *n.*

TDMS

The TDMS form, referenced in a request, that is used during a single programming request call. A conditional request can reference more than one form, but only one form can be active at any one time.

active lines *n.*

DECnet

Lines in the ON or SERVICE state.

active logging n.

DECnet

A state in which all known sink types are in the ON or HOLD state.

active page register n.

PDP-11 and VAX-11

A hardware register used by the operating system to map the virtual address space used by a task onto physical memory.

active search list n.

TOPS-10

An ordered list of file structures established for each job running on the system. See also passive search list.

active side n.

DECnet

In loopback tests, the node that controls a maintenance operation protocol.

active task n.

RSX-11M

A priority-ordered task that is in the list of all tasks resident in memory or checkpointed.

active task list n.

generic

A list of jobs or tasks, ordered by priority. The list sets the order in which jobs receive central processor time.

activity n.

PEARL

A function of PEARL performed by a language element of type TASK.

ACTLU n.

DECnet

The acronym for activate logical unit. An SNA (systems network architecture) session control request issued by the SSCP (system services control point). A successfully executed ACTLU causes the logical unit addressed in the command to be made available to the system. Same as activate logical unit.

ACTPU n.

DECnet

The acronym for activate physical unit. An SNA (systems network architecture) session control request issued by the SSCP (system services control point). A successfully executed ACTPU causes the physical unit addressed in the command to be made available to the system. Same as activate physical unit.

actual decimal point n.

DIGITAL-specific

The physical representation of the decimal point position in a data item.

actual parameter n.

PASCAL

A value or variable that is passed in a procedure or function call and is used during execution of the subprogram within a PASCAL program.

actual parameter list n.

MicroPower PASCAL and VAX PASCAL

The list of parameters specified in a subprogram call. The actual parameters must be in a specific sequence, separated by commas, and the list enclosed in parentheses.

adapter *n.*

generic

A connecting device that permits attachment of accessories or provides the capability to mount or link units.

adapter control block (ADP) *n.*

VAX/VMS

In the I/O data base, a structure that describes either a UNIBUS or MASSBUS adapter. Same as ADP.

ADB *n.*

VAX Information Architecture

Abbreviation for application database. ADB is a run-time database that contains information derived from application and task group definitions. Same as application database.

additive operator *n.*

DIGITAL-specific

An operator that performs addition (+) or subtraction (−). It performs the usual arithmetic conversions on its operands.

address *n.*

generic

A number or name that is unique to and identifies a thing such as a register or memory location.

VAX/VMS

A number used by the operating system and user software to identify a storage location. See also virtual address and physical address.

address access type *n.*

VAX/VMS

A type of operation in which the specified operand of an instruction is not directly accessed when the processor executes the instruction. The context of the address calculation is given by the data type of the operand.

addressing mode *n.*

VAX/VMS

The way in which an operand is specified; for example, the way in which the effective address of an instruction operand is calculated using the general registers. The basic general register addressing modes are: register, register deferred, autoincrement, autoincrement deferred, autodecrement, displacement, and displacement deferred. In addition, there are six indexed addressing modes (using two general registers) and a literal addressing mode. The PC (program counter) addressing modes are called: immediate (for register deferred mode using the PC), absolute (for autoincrement deferred mode using the PC), and branch.

address space *n.*

generic

The set of all possible addresses available to a process.

VAX/VMS

The set of all possible addresses available to a process. Virtual address space refers to the set of all possible virtual addresses. Physical address space refers to the set of all possible physical addresses sent out on the SBI.

add time *n.*

DIGITAL-specific

The minimum execution time for a binary ADD instruction excluding register-to-register operations.

ADE n.

RSTS/E, VAX/VMS

Refers to a software layered product. ADE was formerly the acronym for application development environment.

adjacent node n.

DECnet

A node connected to or removed from the executor node by a single physical line.

generic

A remote computer connected by a single physical line to a local computer in a large distributed computer network.

VAX/VMS

A network node removed from the local node by a single physical line.

adjusting entry n.

generic

An entry to update the balance originally recorded in an account so that it correctly reflects the revenue or expense of an accounting period.

adjustment n.

generic

A change in an account produced by an adjusting entry.

ADP n.

VAX/VMS

The abbreviation for adapter control block. ADP is a structure in the I/O data base that describes either a UNIBUS or MASSBUS adapter. Same as adapter control block.

ADT n.

DATATRIEVE

The abbreviation for application design tool. ADT is a DATATRIEVE utility that aids in creating domains, record definitions, and files by prompting with questions at each step in the process. Same as application design tool.

ADU n.

ACMS

The abbreviation for application definition utility. ADU is the primary tool for creating ACMS applications. ADU provides the commands and clauses for defining tasks, task groups, applications, and menus. Same as application definition utility.

advice n.

generic

Commands or information entered at one terminal that affect the actions occurring at another terminal.

affirmative acknowledgment (ACK0, ACK1) n.

DECnet

Affirmative acknowledgment replies in data-link escape (DLE) sequences in binary synchronous communications. These replies indicate that the previous transmission block was accepted by the receiver and that it is ready to accept the next block of the transmission. Use of ACK0 and ACK1 alternately provides sequential checking control for a series of replies. ACK0 is also an affirmative (ready to receive) reply to an initialization sequence (line bid) in point-to-point operation. Same as ACK0, ACK1.

after image *n.*

VAX DBMS

A copy of a database page that has been modified and is about to be written back to the database.

after-image journaling *n.*

VAX DBMS

The VAX DBMS utility with which the user can reconstruct a restored database up to the last successfully completed transaction. After-image journaling must be coordinated with backup and recover; the final quiet point on the database file must match the initial quiet point on the after-image journal.

AFTERWORD *n.*

DECWORD

The Gold AFTERWORD command that moves the cursor forward to the last character of a word instead of the first.

aged packet *n.*

DECnet

A packet that has exceeded the maximum number of visits for the recovering node.

aggregate *n.*

DIGITAL-specific

A collection of related data items that can be referred to individually or collectively. See also array and structure.

VAX/VMS

One of the derived types of array, structure, or union. An array has elements of the same data type, A structure has named members that can be of different data types. A union is a structure that has the length of its longest declared members and that contains the value of only one member at a time.

AIB *n.*

VAX/VMS

The abbreviation for ancillary control process I/O buffer or ACP I/O buffer. AIB is a data structure that points to the ACP buffer descriptor (ABD) and is part of the complex buffered I/O buffer. The AIB also contains some information about itself, such as size, type, and length of packet headers. Same as ACP I/O buffer. See also ACP buffer descriptor or ABD.

AID *n.*

DECnet

The abbreviation for attention identification. A code that is set in the 3270 display station when the operator takes an action that produces an I/O interruption. The character identifies to the host the action or key that caused the interrupt condition. The code is set when the operator presses a program access key or when selector lightpen attention occurs. The code is the first code received by the host program in the READ data stream. Same as attention identification character.

alarm *n.*

VAX/VMS

A message sent to operator terminals that are enabled as security operators. Security alarms are triggered by the occurrence of an event previously designated as worthy of the alarm because of its security implications. Same as security alarm.

algorithm *n.*

generic

A set of well defined processes for the solution of a problem using a limited number of steps.

%ALL *n.*

VAX Information Architecture

The parameter to a TDMS INPUT, OUTPUT, or RETURN request instruction that permits you to map data between all identically named form and record fields without specifying the individual fields. See also Implicit Mapping and explicit mapping. *

allocate *v.*

generic (computers)

To distribute computer resources.

generic (finance)

To spread a cost from one account to several accounts, products, or activities, or to several periods.

allocate a device *v.*

DIGITAL-specific

To reserve a device unit for exclusive use. A user process can allocate a device only when that device is not allocated by any other process.

allocation *n.*

DIGITAL-specific

The number of disk blocks associated with a file and normally assigned to a file when the file is created.

VAX PL/I

1. A specific unit of storage obtained for a based variable.

2. The activity of obtaining storage for a variable.

See also default extension quantity and extent.

allocation class *n.*

VAX/VMS

A unique number between 0 and 255 that the system manager assigns to a pair of hosts and the dual-pathed devices that the hosts make available to other nodes in the VAXcluster. The allocation class provides a way for users to access dual-pathed devices through either of the hosts. In this way, if one host of an allocation class set is not available, the user can gain access to a device specified by that allocation class through the other host of the allocation class.

allowance for doubtful accounts *n.*

generic

The amount of estimated bad debts that is included in accounts receivable.

allow declaration *n.*

RSX-11M

Part of the information a program provides when it opens a file. The allow declaration indicates the type of record operations that the program allows to be performed on the file by other programs.

allow mode *n.*

VAX DBMS

A part of the READY statement's USAGE clause in the DBMS data manipulation language. The allow mode describes the level of protection that users will provide for the data in the realms users want to ready. The allow mode can be BATCH, CONCURRENT, PROTECTED, or EXCLUSIVE. See also usage mode and access mode.

alpha characters *n.*

generic

A subset of the ASCII character set that contains the 26 letters, 10 digits, and certain special characters.

alpha field *n.*

generic

A field that contains characters defined as alpha characters.

alpha literal *n.*

generic

A constant string of alpha characters specified by the operator.

alphanumeric *adj.*

generic

A character set including letters, numbers, and other symbols such as punctuation marks and mathematical symbols.

alphanumeric character *n.*

VAX/VMS

An uppercase or lowercase letter, a dollar sign, an underscore, or a decimal digit.

alphanumeric UIC *n.*

VAX/VMS

A format of user identification code (UIC) that specifies the user's group and member in alphanumeric form rather than numeric form.

alphavariable *n.*

TOPS-10

An alphanumeric working item created by IQL (interactive query language) while generating a report. Names of alphavariables must start with A, can be up to thirty characters long and can contain a–z and 0–9. IQL creates an alphavariable when it sees an item name starting with A, does not find that name in the dictionary, and determines that the information is read and written to the same item. IQL makes the alphavariable as long as necessary to contain the longest amount of information.

alternate index *n.*

RSX-11M

A structure providing a secondary logical access path to records stored in an RMS-11 indexed file. Each alternate index is based on a related alternate key field in the user data record. See also primary index.

alternate key *n.*

RSX-11M

A series of bytes in a data record that can be used to identify the record for access. Alternate key value does not affect the position of the user data record in the file. See also segmented key.

VAX DATATRIEVE

A key, other than the primary record key, that can be used as a means of identifying a record for retrieval.

VAX/RMS

An optional key within the data records in an indexed file; used by VAX-11 RMS to build an alternate index. See also primary key and secondary key.

VAX/VMS

An optional key within the data records in an indexed file; used by VAX RMS to build an alternate index. See key (indexed files) and primary key.

alternate record key *n.*

DIGITAL-specific

A key, other than the primary record key, whose contents identify a record within a multikey indexed file.

alternate terminal *n.*

TOPS-10

A terminal that can receive transactions meant for another terminal.

ambient adj.

generic

On all sides.

American Standard Code for Information Interchange (ASCII) n.

VAX/VMS

A set of 8-bit binary numbers representing the alphabet, punctuation, numerals, and other special symbols used in text representation and communications protocol.

amortization n.

USFC/generic

The repayment of a loan by systematic installments.

ampersand (&) n.

VAX/VMS

The symbol used as a unary operator to compute the address of its operand. As a binary operator, it performs a bitwise AND on two operands, both of which must be of integral type. As an assignment operator (&=), it performs a bitwise AND of an expression with the value of the object referred to by the left-hand expression and assigns the result to that object. The double ampersand (&&), a binary operator, performs a logical AND on two operands. See also logical connective.

amplification n.

generic

An increase in the magnitude of a signal or flow of energy while other signal characteristics stay the same.

amplifier n.

generic

A device for making electrical signals stronger.

analog adj.

generic

Pertaining to the description of numerical quantities by means of physical variables, for example, voltage current; as contrasted with digital.

ancestor n.

DSM-11

Any node in an array on a higher level than a given node and on a direct path between that given node and the root of the array. For example, the nodes A(1), A(1,2), and A(1,2,5) are ancestors of the node A(1,2,5,6).

Common Data Dictionary

With respect to a CDD directory or object, a preceding dictionary or subdictionary directory in the CDD hierarchy. Ancestors have as descendants all related dictionary directories and objects that follow them in the hierarchy.

anchored choice n.

ALL-IN-1

Refers to a list of all the possible choices for an entry that the user has started when using the ALL-IN-1 function RECOGNITION.

anchored recognition n.

ALL-IN-1

Refers to the procedure of supplying the remainder of an entry that the user has started, when using the ALL-IN-1 function, RECOGNITION.

ancillary control process (ACP) n.

DIGITAL-specific

A process that acts as an interface between user software and an I/O driver. An ACP provides functions supplementary to those performed in the driver, such as file and directory management. Same as ACP.

ancillary peripheral *n.*

generic

Any device that is an auxiliary or accessory to the main computer.

annual percentage rate (APR) *n.*

USFC/generic

A percentage calculation of the finance charge portion of financing contract. NOTE: consumer lending terminology. Same as APR.

annular ring *n.*

Ethernet

An indicator (or ring) around the circumference of the coaxial cable every 2.5 meters (8.2 feet) to indicate a point where transceivers are to be connected. Same as transceiver attachment Mark.

ANSI *adj.*

generic

The acronym for American National Standards Institute, an organization that compiles and publishes computer industry standards.

ANSI-ASCII mode *n.*

TOPS-10

A data recording mode in which data is stored in 7-bit ASCII bytes (also called 7-bit mode). Data must be stored in this mode to meet ANSI standards.

answerback message *n.*

Rainbow™

A short message of up to 20 characters that the Rainbow 100 computer transmits upon receipt of an enquiry (ENQ) control character; generated by a <Ctrl/Break> from a remote computer or (optionally) upon first starting communications in terminal mode.

AP *n.*

VAX/VMS

The abbreviation for argument pointer. General register 12 (R12), which contains the address of the base of the argument list for procedures initiated by using the CALL instructions. Same as argument pointer.

aperture delay *n.*

MINC

The time between the instant an external HOLD command is received and the instant the sampled signal is actually being held by the hold circuits. Ideal time lapses would be zero, but actually are approximately 200 nanoseconds.

aperture uncertainty *n.*

MINC

The consistency with which the aperture delay repeats from command to command. Consistency is important in MINC if conversions are to be equally spaced in time.

application *n.*

generic

A set of procedures that performs a task or function.

ACMS

A set of tasks that are related in terms of the business activity they support and that are controlled as a single unit. An ACMS application is defined with the ACMS Application Definition Utility (ADU) and runs under the control of the ACMS run-time system.

application control (AC) mode *n.*

DECnet

A manner of protocol management in which programs interacting by means of the RSX-11M/SNA Protocol Emulator (PE) manage the SNA (systems network architecture) protocol. Such programs are said to be operating in the application control mode or AC mode. In AC mode, protocol emulator activity is restricted to managing certain transmission functions. A broader range of SNA protocol is available to programs operating in the AC mode than is available to programs operating in the emulator control (EC) mode. Same as AC mode.

Application Control and Management System (ACMS) *n.*

ACMS

A software product, layered on VAX/VMS, used to define, run, and control online applications. Same as ACMS.
(ACMS/AD)

Application Control and Management System/Application Development *n.*

ACMS

An optional software product for developing applications that run under the control of VAX-11 ACMS. It provides a task implementation method that uses high-level definitions to replace complex application code.

Application Database (ADB) *n.*

A run-time database that contains information derived from application and task group definitions. Same as ADB.

application definition utility (ADU) *n.*

ACMS

The primary tool for creating ACMS applications. The Application Definition Utility provides the commands and clauses for defining tasks, task groups, applications, and menus. Same as ADU.

application designer *n.*

VAX Information Architecture

A system user, often referred to as a system analyst, responsible for the overall specification and definition of an application and its parts.

application design tool (ADT) *n.*

DATATRIEVE

A DATATRIEVE utility that aids you in creating domains, record definitions, and files by prompting you with questions at each step in the process. Same as ADT.

application execution controller *n.*

ACMS

The ACMS component that controls task execution for all the tasks in an application. Each application has its own application execution controller.

application manager *n.*

generic

A system user responsible for the overall operation and maintenance of an application.

application program (or application package) *n.*

DIGITAL-specific

A program that performs a function specific to the needs of a particular end-user or class of end-users. An application program can be any program that is not part of the basic operating system. See also run-unit.

generic

A sequence of instructions and routines, not part of the basic operating system, designed to serve the specific needs of a user.

application programmer *n.*

generic

A system user responsible for creating and maintaining part or all of the programs for an application.

application programming services *n.*

ACMS

A set of subroutines, provided as part of the ACMS/AD product, that can be called from an application program.

applications processor *n.*

RSX-11M

An output despooler written by the user for a special purpose or specific job. Applications processors are treated like print processors in most cases.

applications task *n.*

RSX-11M

A task that performs a specific job for the user; it refers to any task that is not part of the operating system or of a programming language. Same as user task.

APR *n.*

USFC/generic

The abbreviation for annual percentage rate. A percentage calculation of the finance charge portion of financing contract. NOTE: consumer lending terminology. Same as annual percentage rate.

APT *n.*

generic

The abbreviation for automated product test. APT is a system used in the manufacturing environment for loading and monitoring of diagnostics and for production control. Same as automated product test.

AQB *n.*

VAX/VMS

The abbreviation for ancillary control process queue header block or ACP queue header block. AQB is a data structure that provides information to the QI/O system services and to the MTAACP process. It is created by the mount system program when the MTAACP is created. The AQB contains the AQB transaction queue that contains I/O request packets (IRPs) for the MTAACP, the process identification of the MTAACP process serving the queue, and the number of volumes being serviced by the MTAACP. Same as ancillary initial process queue header block or ACP queue header block.

arbitration *n.*

Rainbow™

A circuit in the Rainbow 100 computer that decides which event has priority.

arc *n.*

generic

A visible discharge of electricity.

arccosine *n.*

generic

The angle whose cosine is a specified value; the inverse function to the cosine.

arcsine *n.*

generic

The angle whose sine is a specified value; the inverse function to the sine.

arctangent *n.*

generic

The angle whose tangent is a specified value; the inverse function to the tangent.

area *n.*

RSX-11M

A portion of an indexed file treated independently by RMS-11 for initial allocation, extensions, placement, and bucket sizes.

VAX DATATRIEVE

In the database, a named subdivision that contains all record occurrences that have specified database key values that fall within the area's page range. Any number of record types can be stored within one area. In the data manipulation language (DML), area is referred to as a realm.

VAX DBMS

A named subdivision of the database that contains all record occurrences having database key values that fall within the area's page range. Area is synonymous with realm: realm is the term used in DML programs, and area is the term used in DDL.

VAX PL/I

A unit of storage in which based variables may be allocated.

VAX/RMS

A VAX-11 RMS-maintained region of an indexed file that is used for allocating buckets. An area consists of any number of buckets, and there may be from 1 through 255 areas in a file.

VAX/VMS

1. A region of an indexed file maintained by VAX RMS that allows a user to specify placement and/or specific bucket sizes for particular portions of a file. An area consists of any number of buckets; there may be form 1 to 255 area in a file.

2. A group of nodes in a network that can run independently as a subnetwork.

area *n.*

DIGITAL-specific

A subdivision of a database, named in the schema, that contains all records having the specified database key values in the area's page range.

area descriptors *n.*

RSX-11M

Data used by RMS-11 to maintain areas in an indexed file. RMS-11 stores this data in the file's prologue. See also key descriptors.

area identifier *n.*

VAX DBMS

A number defined in the schema DDL and used for internal communications with the database control system and uniquely identifying one area.

area router *n.*

VAX/VMS

A level 1 router.

33

area routing *n.*

VAX/VMS

A technique for grouping the nodes in a network into areas for routing purposes. Routing in a multiple-area network is hierarchical, with one level of routing within an area (called level 1 routing) and a second, higher level of routing between areas (called level 2 routing). Area routing permits DECnet to support configuration of very large networks.

argument *n.*

generic

A variable whose value determines the result of an operation or function.

FMS

In FMS, a variable or a value passed in a call to the Form Driver to specify the action of the call or to specify a variable to receive the results of an operation.

argument passing *n.*

VAX C

The mechanism by which the argument in a function call is associated with a parameter in the called function. In VAX C, all arguments are passed by value; that is, the parameter receives a copy of the argument's value.

argument pointer (AP) *n.*

VAX/VMS

General register 12 (R12) which contains the address of the base of the argument list for procedures initiated by using the CALL instructions. Same as AP.

arithmetic operation *n.*

generic

The process that results in a mathematically correct solution during the execution of an arithmetic statement or the evaluation of an arithmetic expression.

arithmetic operator *n.*

generic

An expression component that performs an arithmetic operation.

arithmetic type *n.*

generic

One of the integral data types, enumerated types, float, or double.

ARPANET *n.*

DECnet and TOPS-20

The acronym for Advanced Research Projects Agency Network. ARPANET is a resource-sharing network developed by Bolt Beranek and Newman Inc. This network provides for intercommunication, by means of common-carrier circuits, of dissimilar ARPANET computers at widely separated sites. Project Agency (ARPA) et reliant des ordinateurs.

array *n.*

DIGITAL-specific

A field that contains several elements referenced in a request by the same name and having the same characteristics (length, data type, and so on). Same as simple record array.

generic

Elements or data arranged in such a way that the system can examine and recover items with a specific subscript or key.

ascender *n.*

generic

A font value that specifies the greatest distance (in pixels) that the top of any character extends above the baseline.

ascending key *n.*

generic

A key whose values determine the ordering of data. Ascending order starts with the lowest key value and ends with the highest, according to the rules for comparing data items.

ascending order *n.*

generic

An order of sorting that starts with the lowest value of a key and proceeds to the highest value, in accordance with the rules for comparing data items.

ASCII *n.*

generic

The abbreviation/acronym for American Standard Code for Information Interchange. A set of 8-bit binary numbers representing the alphabet, punctuation, numerals, and other special symbols used in text representation and communications protocol.

ASCII stream file *n.*

RSTS/E

A file that stores ASCII characters sequentially in variable-length records. Each record consists of a line of text followed by a line terminator, which serves as the record delimiter. ASCII stream files are sequential access files.

ASECT *n.*

MicroPower PASCAL

The acronym for absolute addressed section. ASECT refers to that part of a program usually used for storing symbols. ASECTs must reside in specified memory locations and are not relocatable.

ASF *n.*

DECmate II

The abbreviation for automatic sheet feed. An accessory for the letter quality printer that feeds individual sheets of paper from two different trays to the printer. Same as automatic sheet feed.

aspect ratio *n.*

generic

The relationship of the width to height of an image displayed on a screen.

assemble *v.*

generic

To translate a program from symbolic language into a machine operation code.

assembler *n.*

VAX/VMS

A language processor that translates a source program containing assembly language directives and machine instructions into an object module.

assembly *adj.*

generic

Pertaining to the translation of a program from symbolic language into machine code.

assembly language *n.*

generic

A symbolic language that translates directly into machine language instruction.

VAX/VMS

A machine-oriented programming language. VAX MACRO is the assembly language for the VAX computer. See binary machine code.

assembly listing *n.*

generic

A detailed list showing coded and symbolic notations next to actual notations made by the assembly machine instruction.

asset *n.*

generic

An item of value and measurable cost owned or controlled by an entity.

assign a channel *n.*

DIGITAL-specific

To establish the necessary software link between a user process and a device unit that allows a user process to communicate with the device.

assignee *n.*

USFC/generic

A third-party funding source to whom the lease may be assigned.

assigning a device *n.*

DIGITAL-specific

The act or function of associating an I/O device to the user's job either for the duration of the job or until the user relinquishes control of the job.

generic

The establishing of the relationship of a device or memory to a running task, process, job, or program.

assignment *n.*

PEARL

A method of changing the value of an object.

USFC/generic

The transfer of the lease and equipment to a third-party funding.

assignment expression *n.*

VAX/VMS

An expression of the form: E1 asgnop E2, where E1 must be a 1 value, asgnop is an assignment operator, and E2 is an expression. The type of an assignment expression is that of its left operand. The value of an assignment expression is that of the left operand after the assignment has taken place. If the operator is of the form "op=", then the operation E1 op (E2) is performed, and the result is assigned to the object referred to by E1; E1 is evaluated only once.

assignment operator *n.*

VAX/VMS and VAX C

The combination of an arithmetic or bitwise operator with the assignment symbol (=); also, the assignment symbol by itself. These operators are used in assignment expressions.

assignment statement *n.*

VAX/VMS

The definition of a symbol name to use in place of a character string or numeric value. Symbols can define synonyms for system commands or can be used for variables in command procedures.

assign phase *n.*

FMS

A phase in which attributes, such as Must Fill or Response Required, are assigned to fields within a form.

associative *adj.*

generic

Referring to being independent of the way elements are combined in a statement or expression.

associative memory *n.*

generic

A memory where the storage locations are identified by their contents rather than their addresses.

associative storage *n.*

generic

Storage addressed by content rather than location.

assumed decimal point *n.*

generic

A decimal point position in a data item that is assumed; it has logical meaning but no physical representation and does not occupy a character position in the data item.

AST *n.*

DECnet

The abbreviation for asynchronous system trap. An RSX software interrupt that occurs as a result of an external significant event such as completion of an I/O request. On occurrence of the event, control passes to an AST service routine, and the AST is added to an Executive FIFO (first-in-first-out) queue for the program in which the service routine appears. Two types of ASTs are used by RSX application programs associated with the RSX-11/3271 Protocol Emulator (PE): application level ASTs and request level ASTs. Application level ASTs are specified with the QI/O attach (IO.ATA) option and are used for modifying the way the PE handles messages from the host. Request level ASTs are specified with any of the QI/O requests and are used to notify the application program of the completion of the requested QI/O operation. Same as asynchronous trap. See also asynchronous system trap.

VAX/VMS

The abbreviation for asynchronous system trap. A software-simulated interrupt to a user-defined service routine. ASTs enable a user process to be notified asynchronously with respect to its execution of the occurrence of a specific event. If a user process has defined as AST routine for an event, the system interrupts the process and executes the AST routine when that event occurs. When the AST routine exists, the system resumes the process at the point where it was interrupted. See also asynchronous trap.

asterisk (*) *n.*

VAX/VMS

A unary operator that treats its operand as an address and results in the contents of that address. As a binary operator, it multiplies two operands, performing the usual arithmetic conversion. As an assignment operator (*=), it multiplies an expression by the value of the object referred to by the left operand, and assigns the product to the object. The double asterisk (**) is an operator pair indicating two levels of indirection, not exponentiation.

37

ASTLVL *n.*

VAX/VMS

The abbreviation for asynchronous system trap level. A value kept in an internal processor register (ASTLVL) that is the most privileged access mode for which an AST is pending. The AST does not occur until the current access mode drops in privilege (rises in numeric value) to a value greater than or equal to ASTLVL. Thus, an AST for an access mode will not be serviced while the processor is executing in a more privileged access mode. Same as asynchronous system trap level.

asymptote *n.*

GAMMA

A line that is the limiting position of a tangent to a curve as its point of contact recedes indefinitely along an infinite branch of the curve.

asynchronous *adj.*

generic

Pertaining to events that are scheduled as the result of a signal asking for the event; pertaining to that which is without any spcified time relation.

MicroPower PASCAL and RT-11

Pertaining to the absence of regular time intervals; unexpected or unpredictable with respect to the execution of a program's instructions. In Micro-Power PASCAL, an asynchronous event does not operate in exact time coincidence and it occurs unpredictably in relation to instruction execution.

asynchronous call *n.*

Terminal Data Management System

A call to a TDMS (Terminal Data Management System) subroutine that begins, but does not necessarily complete, the requested operation before allowing a program to continue execution. At some time, the requested operation will complete and notify the program. In the meantime, a program and the requested operation can both proceed at the same time. See also synchronous call.

asynchronous record operation *n.*

VAX DATATRIEVE and VAX/VMS

A mode of record processing in which a user program can continue to execute after issuing a record retrieval or storage request without having to wait for the request to be fulfilled.

asynchronous system trap (AST) *n.*

generic

A system condition that results from an external event; system control passes to a service routine.

VAX/VMS

A software-simulated interrupt to a user-defined service routine. ASTs enable a user process to be notified asynchronously with respect to its execution of the occurrence of a specific event. If a user process has defined an AST routine for an event, the system interrupts the process and executes the AST routine when that event occurs. When the AST routine exits, the system resumes the process at the point where it was interrupted. Same as AST. See also asynchronous trap.

asynchronous system trap level (ASTLVL) *n.*

VAX/VMS

A value kept in an internal processor register (ASTLVL); it is the most privileged access mode for which an AST (asynchronous system trap) is pending. The AST does not occur until the current access mode drops in privilege (rises in numeric value) to a value greater than or equal to ASTLVL. Thus, an AST for an access mode will not be serviced while the processor is executing in a more privileged access mode. Same as ASTLVL.

asynchronous transmission *n.*

DECnet

Transmission in which time intervals between transmitter characters are not fixed. Transmission is controlled by start and stop elements at the beginning and end of each character. Same as start-stop transmission.

generic

The method of transmitting data one character at a time. Timing between bits is constant; timing between characters is variable.

asynchronous trap (AST) *n.*

DECnet

An RSX software interrupt that occurs as a result of an external significant event such as completion of an I/O request. On occurrence of the event, control passes to an AST service routine, and the AST is added to an Executive FIFO (first-in-first-out) queue for the program in which the service routine appears. There are two types of ASTs used by RSX application programs associated with the RSX-11/3271 Protocol Emulator (PE): application level ASTs and request level ASTs. Application level ASTs are specified with the QI/O attach (IO.ATA) option and are used for modifying the way the PE handles messages from the host. A request level AST can be specified with any of the QI/O requests and is used to notify the application program of the completion of the requested QI/O operation. Same as AST. See also asynchronous system trap.

at-end condition *n.*

COBOL-74

A programming condition reached:

1. during the execution of a READ statement for a sequentially accessed file

2. during the execution of a RETURN statement, when no next logical record exists for the associated sort or merge file, or.

3. during the execution of a SEARCH statement, when the search operation terminates without satisfying the condition specified in any of the associated WHEN phrases.

atom *n.*

generic

The smallest part of an element that has all characteristics of the element.

attach *v.*

DECnet and FMS

To dedicate a physical device unit for exclusive use by the task requesting the attachment. To use the RSX-11/3271 Protocol Emulator (PE) to communicate with the host, an RSX application program must attach to a pseudo device (TU unit) by issuing a QI/O attach request (IO.ATT, IO.ATA, or IO.ATT!1). See also channel.

generic

To assign an I/O device for the exclusive use of the computer program that is asking for it.

attached processor *n.*

VAX/VMS

The secondary processor in a VAX-11/782. See primary processor.

attach terminal *n.*

generic

To assign a terminal for exclusive use by the application program. Contrast with Detach Terminal.

attention *n.*

DECnet

An I/O interrupt generated by an IBM 3270 display station, usually as the result of an action taken by the operator of the device.

attention flag *n.*

VT-11 GRAPHICS

An indicator set by the VT-11 software to mark the occurrence of a graphic attention. The GRATTN subroutine reports the status of the attention flag and identifies the attention source (device). After the attention flag has been set, it is cleared by a call to an attention-handling subroutine (LPEN or KBC).

attention identification (AID) character *n.*

DECnet

A code that is set in an IBM 3270 display station when the operator takes an action that produces an I/O interruption. The character identifies to the host the action or key that caused the interrupt condition. The code is set when the operator presses a program access key or when selector lightpen attention occurs. The code is the first code received by the host program in the READ data stream.

attenuate *v.*

generic

To decrease the current, voltage, or power of a signal being sent between points.

attribute *n.*

DIGITAL-specific

A characteristic of a display field, as specified by the bit settings of a field's attribute character. The attributes of a field include: protected or unprotected (against modification by a display operator); alphanumeric or numeric only input control; displayed, nondisplayed, or display-intensified; selector-pen-detectable/nondetectable; and modified or not modified.

generic

A feature of an object or system.

VAX/VMS

In the security context, an attribute is a field of information maintained in the rights database that identifies a characteristic that may be accorded to a holder of the identifier. For example, if the holder and the identifier possess the resource attribute, the holder of that identifier can charge resources such as disk quota to that identifier.

attribute character *n.*

DIGITAL-specific

The first byte of each field of formatted display. The attribute character code defines the characteristics and location of the display field. The attribute character is not displayed.

attributes *n.*

generic

The collection of characteristics that define or distinguish a specified item.

FMS

Characteristics assigned to fields and forms. Must Fill, Response Required, Right Justified, and No Echo are attributes.

audible alarm *n.*

DECnet

A feature that causes a short, audible tone to be sounded automatically when a character is entered from an IBM 3277 keyboard into the next-to-last character position on the screen. It can also be sounded under program control by setting a bit in the write control character (WCC).

auditing *n.*

VAX/VMS

The act of noting the occurrence of an event that has security implications.

audit trail *n.*

ACMS

A monitoring tool that has a recording facility and a utility for generating reports. The recording facility gathers information about a running ACMS system and writes the information in the Audit Trail Log file.

Common Data Dictionary

A collection of the history list entries for a dictionary directory, subdictionary, or object, created with the /AUDIT qualifier. Same as history list.

generic

A reference accompanying an entry or posting; the reference is usually to an underlying source record or document.

authentication *n.*

VAX/VMS

The act of establishing the identity of users when they start to use the system. VAX/VMS (and most other commercial operating systems) use passwords as the primary authentication mechanism.

authorization file *n.*

VAX/VMS

A file containing an entry for every user that the system manager authorizes to gain access to the system. Each entry identifies the user name, password, default account, UIC, quotas, limits, and privileges assigned to individuals who use the system. Same as user authorization file.

auto-answerback *n.*

Rainbow™

A feature in the Rainbow computer that allows it to send its answerback message to a remote computer when communication is established between them.

auto-answer mode *n.*

PRO/Communications

On a modem, a setting that allows the modem to answer incoming calls without human intervention.

auto-bauding *n.*

RSX-20F

The process by which the terminal software determines the line speed on a dial-up line.

autocalling *n.*

RGL/FEP

The process used by the data plotting subroutines to automatically select the range of numeric values against which to plot data.

auto-create *adj.*

CTS-300

Pertaining to a method of creating an ISM (intermediate storage module) file that uses an indirect file rather than keyboard input to specify the parameters for the ISAM utility program ISMUTL.

autodecrement indexed mode *n.*

VAX/VMS

An indexed addressing mode in which the base operand specifier uses autodecrement mode addressing.

autodecrement mode *n.*

VAX/VMS

In autodecrement mode addressing, the contents of the selected register are decremented, and the result is used as the address of the actual operand of the instruction. The contents of the register are decremented according to the data type context of the register: 1 for byte; 2 for word; 4 for longword and F_floating; 8 for quadword, G_floating and D_floating; and 16 for octaword and H_floating.

autoincrement deferred indexed mode *n.*

VAX/VMS

An indexed addressing mode in which the base operand specifier uses autoincrement deferred mode addressing.

autoincrement deferred mode *n.*

VAX/VMS

An addressing mode in which the contents of the specified register is the address of a longword containing the address of the actual operand. The contents of the register are incremented by 4 (the number of bytes in a longword). If the PC is used as the register, this mode is called absolute mode.

autoincrement indexed mode *n.*

VAX/VMS

An indexed addressing mode in which the base operand specifier uses autoincrement mode addressing.

autoincrement mode *n.*

VAX/VMS

An addressing mode in which the contents of the specified register are used as the address of the operand, then the contents of the register are incremented by the size of the operand.

auto-job startup *n.*

CTS-300

A facility that causes a specified program to be run automatically once the run-time system program is loaded.

autoload *n.*

VAX/VMS

A method of loading overlay segments. The overlay run-time routines automatically load overlay segments when needed; they also handle any unsuccessful load request.

autoload vector *n.*

VAX/VMS

A transfer of control instruction generated by the task builder to resolve an up-tree reference to a global symbol.

automate *v.*

generic

To set up a process so that it can control itself.

automatic member *n.*

VAX DATATRIEVE

A record that implicitly becomes a member of a given set when the record is initially stored in the database.

VAX DBMS

A record inserted by the DBCS (data base control system) into a given set when the record is stored in the database. Automatic set membership is declared in the schema. See also manual member and manual set membership.

automatic pagination *n.*

DECtype

A print setting in which DECtype automatically divides a document into pages while it is printing.

automatic product test *n.*

Ethernet

A system used in the manufacturing environment for loading and monitoring of diagnostics and for production control. Same as APT.

automatic record locking *n.*

VAX/VMS

A VAX/RMS capability by which a user can have only one record in a specified file locked at any given time. The lock occurs on every execution of a $FIND or $GET macro instruction (unless the NLK bit is set in the record processing field). The lock is released when the next record is accessed, the current record is updated or deleted, the record stream is disconnected, or the file is closed.

automatic return *n.*

DECWORD

A carriage return automatically inserted by DECWORD. See also word wrap.

automatic set membership *n.*

VAX DBMS

A form of set membership (declared by the DBA using the schema DDL) established by DBMS when the record occurrence is stored.

automatic sheet feeder (ASF) *n.*

DECmate II

In the letter quality printer, an accessory that feeds individual sheets of paper from two different trays to the printer. Same as ASF.

automatic variable *n.*

VAX PL/I

A variable for which storage is allocated when the block that declares it is activated. The storage is released when the block is deactivated.

automatic volume recognition (AVR) *n.*

TOPS-10

A facility that automatically verifies label information when a tape is mounted, then assigns the tape to a waiting user. Same as AVR.

autorecovery *n.*

VAX DBMS

A mode of operation in which the DBCS automatically undoes changes made by a run unit that has terminated abnormally.

auto-repeat *adj.*

DIGITAL-specific

Pertaining to the terminal feature that causes the continuous transmission of the character for as long as the key for that character is pressed.

autoscaling *n.*

MINC

A MINC feature that automatically adjusts the axis units of a graph to the minimum and maximum numerical values of a set of data.

auto-screen blank *n.*

Rainbow™

A feature in the Rainbow 100 computer that turns off the display on the monitor after 30 minutes, leaving only a "phantom" blinking cursor.

autotab *n.*

FMS

A field attribute indicating that the Form Driver is to consider a field complete when the operator types the last character in the current field. Depending on the Form Driver call issued by the application program, the cursor can be moved immediately to the next field without requiring the operator to press a field terminator key.

autotab attribute *n.*

FMS

A field attribute indicating that the Form Driver is to consider a field complete when the operator types the last character in the current field.

auto-wraparound *n.*

DIGITAL-specific

The terminal feature that continues the current line on the next line when the end of the current line is reached.

Auto-XON/XOFF *n.*

Rainbow™

A feature in the Rainbow computer that automatically synchronizes it to a remote computer so as not to lose data.

auto-zeroing *n.*

MINC

A method to stabilize offset drift in an A/D converter. In a patented process used by the MINC A/D, auto-zeroing occurs at that stage in the A/D conversion at which a previously obtained sample voltage is held, and the A/D input circuits prepare to measure that voltage. Auto-zeroing can occur in either of two operation modes: single-ended mode and differential mode.

auxiliary keypad *n.*

DIGITAL-specific

The set of keys on the right of the keyboard. Some applications interpret these keys as special function keys; with other applications these keys have no purpose.

auxiliary run-time system *n.*

RSTS/E

Any run-time system built during RSTS/E system generation in addition to the primary run-time system, which controls system startup and shutdown.

available mode *n.*

VAX DBMS

A realm status condition that signifies the realm is potentially available to any run unit using a sub-schema that includes the realm. A realm goes from available mode to ready mode on the successful execution of a READY statement and returns to available mode only on the successful execution of a FINISH statement.

average cost method *n.*

generic

A method of finding cost of sales by using the average cost-per-unit of the beginning inventory plus purchases.

AVR *n.*

TOPS-10

The acronym for automatic volume recognition. A TOPS-10 facility that automatically verifies label information when a tape is mounted, then assigns the tape to a waiting user. Same as automatic volume recognition.

AWG *adj.*

generic

(Abbreviation for American Wire Gage.) Pertaining to a method of measuring the diameter of wire (the higher the number, the smaller the diameter).

axis *n.*

generic

1. A reference line from which or by which distances or angles can be measured.

2. A reference line about which an object or geometric turns or appears to turn.

Bachman diagram *n.*

DBMS

A graphic representation of the set relationships between owner and member records used to analyze and document a database design.

background processing *n.*

generic

The automatic execution of a low-priority computer program when higher priority programs are not using the system resources.

background program *n.*

RT-11

A low priority program operating automatically when a higher priority (foreground) program is not using system resources.

background text *n.*

FMS and Terminal Data Management System

The text on a run-time TDMS form that is displayed whenever the form is displayed. Such text cannot be modified by either the application program or the operator.

backplane *n.*

generic

The area of a computer or other equipment where many different logic and control elements are connected.

backplane interconnect *n.*

VAX/VMS

An internal processor bus that UNIBUS and MASSBUS adapters use to communicate with the central processor and main memory. The backplane interconnect (SBI) on the VAX-11/780 processor and is called the memory interconnect on the VAX-11/750 processor.

back up *v.*

DIGITAL-specific

1. To move the cursor backward, toward the top of a document. The BACK UP key moves the cursor back one character and causes the blue keys on the mini-keyboard to operate in the backward direction.

2. To make additional copies of documents or software for safekeeping, in case the original copy is accidentally damaged or destroyed.

backup *n.*

DIGITAL-specific

An additional copy or copies of documents or software made for safekeeping.

backup file *n.*

generic

A copy of an original file.

backup mode *n.*

FMS

In the Form Editor LAYOUT phase the mode that causes the Form Editor to perform operations in the backward direction, moving from the current cursor position to the left margin or top of the screen.

bad block *n.*

DIGITAL-specific

A damaged block on a disk that the system cannot access. Blocks become damaged from wear or abuse.

generic

A defective unit on a storage medium that software cannot read or write.

bad debt *n.*

generic

An account receivable that never will be collected. Sometimes called an uncollectable account.

balance *n.*

generic

The difference between the totals of the two sides of an account. An account has either a debit balance or a credit balance.

balanced tree *n.*

DSM-11

A graph that represents the structure of DSM arrays. Balanced trees are drawn like a family tree with the root (name) at the top and the nodes arranged below by their depth of subscripting. All nodes with one subscript are on the first level, all nodes with two subscripts are on the second level, and so forth. This tree structure is only a logical picture of an array; it does not reflect how DSM physically stores the array. For example, the tree structure shows all nodes that point to defined data nodes. DSM does not store such pointer nodes, but does recognize their logical existence.

balance forward *adj.*

generic

Describes an accounting method where payments and credits are made against a total outstanding balance rather than a specific invoice.

balance set *n.*

TOPS-20 and VAX/VMS

The set of all process working sets currently resident in physical memory. The process whose working sets are in the balance set have memory requirements that balance with available memory. The balance set is maintained by the system's swapper process.

balance sheet *n.*

generic

A financial statement that reports the assets and equities of a company at a particular time.

bandwidth *n.*

DIGITAL-specific

The range of frequencies assigned to a channel or system, that is, the difference expressed in Hertz between the highest and lowest frequencies of a band.

generic

The range of frequencies of a device, within which its operation follows a specified standard.

barrel connector *n.*

generic

A female-female connector used to connect two sections of coaxial cable.

base address *n.*

DIGITAL-specific

The lowest memory address into which a program is loaded. A base address is the basis for computing the value of some other relative address. It is the address of the first location of a program or data area. See also bottom address.

generic

A number or name used as a starting point address from which all other addresses may be modified.

based variable *n.*

VAX PL/I

A variable used to describe storage that is accessed by using a pointer.

baseline *n.*

generic

The line from which a graph is drawn. The baseline is the X axis on vertically oriented graphs, the Y axis on horizontal bar graphs, or the line representing zero if the data contains both positive and negative numbers; also, the imaginary line extending through a font and representing the line on which characters are aligned for printing. In conventional, alphanumeric fonts, the baseline is usually defined as the imaginary line touching the bottom of uppercase characters.

base operand address *n.*

VAX/VMS

The address of the base of a table or array referenced by index mode addressing.

base operand specifier *n.*

VAX/VMS

The register used to calculate the base operand address of a table or array referenced by index mode addressing.

base priority *n.*

generic

A number or name assigned to data indicating the order in which the data will be processed or transmitted.

VAX/VMS

The process priority that the system assigns a process when it is created. A base priority generally comes from the authorization file. The scheduler never schedules a process below its base priority. The base priority can be modified only by the system manager or the process itself. The base priority of a running process can be altered by any user with ALTPRI.

base register *n.*

DIGITAL-specific and VAX/VMS

A general register used to contain the address of the first entry in a list, table, array, or other data structure.

generic

A register whose content is added to or subtracted from the address section of a program instruction to create an actual address.

base segment *n.*

generic

The controlling part or section of an overlay program that can be loaded into main memory.

base type *n.*

MicroPower PASCAL

For a subrange, base type is the scalar type of which it is a subset. For a set, base type is the nonreal scalar type from which the elements of the set are chosen.

BASIC *n.*

generic

The acronym for Beginner's All-purpose Symbolic Instruction Code, a computer language used for timesharing and business applications.

batch processing *n.*

generic

A method of scheduling and executing programs in which the programs run with no programmer interaction.

VAX/VMS

A mode of processing in which all commands to be executed by the operating system (and, optionally, data to be used as input to the commands) are placed in a file or punched onto cards and submitted to the system for execution. Compare with command procedure.

batch stream *n.*

generic

A collection of commands and jobs that will be processed in the order that they are received.

battery *n.*

generic

A dc voltage source.

baud *n.*

generic

The speed at which data is transmitted over a data line; baud rates can be a measurement of bits per second, bytes per second, or characters per second.

BBI *n.*

DECnet

The abbreviation for begin bracket indicator. BBI is a bit in the request header that, when set, specifies that the accompanying transmission begins a bracket. Same as begin bracket indicator.

BCC *n.*

DECnet

The abbreviation for block check character. BCC is the result of a transmission verification algorithm accumulated over a transmission block, and normally appended at the end. An example of a transmission verification algorithm is the cyclic redundancy check (CRC) used by the RSX-11/3271 Protocol Emulator (PE). Same as block check character. problme ici, dans Ginguay, BCC = bloc check character. Plusieures personnes techniques ici m'ont dit la mme chose, mais Bob n'est pas l pour le moment pour confirmer.

BCUG *n.*

VAX PSI

The abbreviation for bilateral closed user group. An optional PSDN facility that restricts a pair of DTEs to communicating with each other. The basic BCUG also prevents this pair from accessing or being accessed by other DTEs. Additions to the BCUG facility allow one or both of the DTEs to access or be accessed by DTEs outside the group. These additions are known as BCUG with outgoing access and BCUG with incoming access respectively. Same as bilateral closed user group.

BDS *n.*

DECSIM

The abbreviation for behavioral DECSIM; BDS is the name of DECSIM's modeling behavior language. Same as behavioral DECSIM.

beam *n.*

generic

The unidirectional or almost unidirectional flow of energy or particles.

VT-11 GRAPHICS

A stream of electrons directed at a position on the display screen. Points, vectors, and other primitives are usually displayed relative to the current beam position. When a user initializes the display file, the beam points to the lower left corner of the viewing area of the screen (the point 0.,0.) in the default coordinate system.

bearing *n.*

generic

A mechanical part that supports a moving part, specifically a turning part, and allows it to move with little friction.

beep *n.*

generic

A short sound, such as that made by an electronic device, that functions as a signal or warning.

beeper *n.*

DECmate II

A warning tone produced by the word processor under certain conditions, such as when the printer stops.

before image *n.*

VAX DBMS

A copy of a database page before it is modified.

before-image journal *n.*

VAX DBMS

A file that contains images of records before they have been updated. DBMS uses before-image journaling to automatically undo updates to a database when a transaction is rolled back. Before-image journaling is also called recovery-unit journaling or short-term journaling.

begin block *n.*

PEARL

A begin block provides a means of structuring a PEARL program within the executable objects; TASK, PROCEDURE, and INTERFACE.

VAX PL/I

A sequence of statements headed by a BEGIN statement and terminated by a corresponding END statement. A begin block is entered when control flows into the BEGIN statement. When a begin block is entered, a block activation is created for it and for the variables declared within it.

begin bracket indicator (BBI) *n.*

DECnet

A bit in a request header that, when set, specifies that the accompanying transmission begins a bracket. Same as BBI.

beginning inventory *n.*

generic

The amount of inventory on hand and/or as recorded in the accounts at the beginning of the accounting period.

beginning-of-tape *n.*

generic

A special characteristic mark on a magnetic tape used to indicate the beginning of the magnetic recording area.

behavioral DECSIM (BDS) *n.*

DECSIM

Behavioral DECSIM is the name of DECSIM's modeling behavior language. Same as BDS.

behavioral simulation *n.*

DECSIM

A type of simulation that is performed from a high-level description of a machine and that does not necessarily consider actual data path or control signal implementation or timing.

behavior compiler *n.*

DECSIM

The DECSIM program that translates a behavioral model into BLISS code for execution during simulation. See SX.

behavior language *n.*

DECSIM

A functional modeling language for high-level DEC-SIM models used for defining the procedural models for interconnecting with gate models, or for simulating machines that run microcode.

behavior model *n.*

DECSIM

A model written in a procedural machine description language. The model is a functional or behavioral description, rather than a structural description.

BEHAVIOR subblock *n.*

DECSIM

Refers to the specific part of a model that is written in the DECSIM behavior language. It contains a functional description of the model.

bel *n.*

generic

The basic unit in a logarithmic scale for stating the ratio of two amounts of power or voltage.

benchmark *n.*

generic

A routine or program used in the evaluation of computer execution.

BETB *n.*

DECnet

The abbreviation for between brackets. BETB is an idle state in a session that uses brackets. A bracketed exchange has ended. Normal-flow data cannot be transmitted when a bracketed session is BETB. Same as between brackets.

bias *n.*

generic

The electrical, mechanical, or magnetic force applied to a relay, semiconductor, or other device to start an electrical or mechanical reference level for the operation of the device.

BID *n.*

DECnet

An SNA (systems network architecture) data flow control command used by the PLU (primary logical unit) to request permission to start a bracket.

bidirectional *adj.*

DECWORD

Capable of moving in opposite directions. Some letter quality printers can move paper forward or backward, and can print right-to-left and left-to-right.

bilateral closed user group (BCUG) *n.*

VAX PSI

An optional PSDN (packet switching data network) facility that restricts a pair of DTEs (data terminal equipment) to communicating with each other. The basic BCUG also prevents this pair from accessing or being accessed by other DTEs. Additions to the BCUG facility allow one or both of the DTEs to access or be accessed by DTEs outside the group. These additions are known as BCUG with outgoing access and BCUG with incoming access respectively. Same as BCUG.

VAX/VMS

An optional packet switching data network facility that restricts a pair of DTEs to communicating with each other.

bill of materials *n.*

generic

A list of specific types and amounts of direct materials expected to be used to produce a given job or quantity of output.

binary *adj.*

generic

Pertaining to a numbering system that uses a base of 2; a numbering system that uses only two digits, 1 and 0.

binary form file *n.*

FMS

A file containing a single form description in binary form. Its default file type is .FRM.

binary language representation (BLR) *n.*

Rdb/ELN

The first layer of protocol in the Digital Standard Relational Interface (DSRI). BLR is a procedural language that stores RCI requests in a densely-packed binary format. Same as BLR.

binary machine code *n.*

VAX/VMS

The internal instruction format actually used by the computer. It is called binary because only two characters – 0 and 1 – are used in this code.

binary operator *n.*

VAX C

An operator that performs a bitwise logical operation on two operands, which must be integral. The usual arithmetic conversions are performed. Both operands are evaluated. All bitwise operators are associative, and expressions using them may be rearranged.

binary search technique *n.*

RSX-11M

A searching technique applicable only to items ordered by the value in the search argument field. A binary search proceeds as follows:

1. locate an item at the middle of the items searched

2. divide the items into three parts: low part, high part, and the item found

3. if the item found does not satisfy the search, repeat this procedure on the low or high part depending on a comparison of the search value with the item found.

binary semaphore *n.*

MicroPower PASCAL

A global variable whose value varies from 0 to 1. Binary semaphores are managed by the kernel in response to requests from processes and interrupt service routines. Each binary semaphore can have a queue of waiting processes.

binary zero *n.*

generic

A byte with the value of binary zero (where all bits composing the byte are zeros).

bind *v.*

generic

To assign an address to a name in a program.

binding *n.*

VAX DBMS

A process that maps a record name to its physical location in the user work area (UWA) and notifies the DBCS (Database Control System) of the run unit's intention to use the database.

VAX/VMS

A process that comprises the following:

1. the resolution of external references between object modules used to create an image

2. the acquisition of referenced library routines, service entry points, and data for the image

3. the assignment of virtual addresses to components of an image.

See also linking

binding *n.*

Rdb/ELN

Invoking or opening a database to be accessed in a program module. With Rdb/ELN, this is done with the DATABASE statement.

bind session request *n.*

DECnet

An SNA (systems network architecture) session control request used to establish an LU to LU session. Parameters in the BIND command specify the protocol options and session Profile to be observed in the session. If parameters specified cannot be supported by the emulator (that is, if the several parameters do not conform with allowable options within a legitimate session Profile), the PE (protocol emulator) will reject the BIND by returning a negative response to the PLU (primary logical unit). If, in the course of the session, the applications do not abide by the rules specified in the BIND, the PE may cause the session to abort.

BIOS *n.*

Rainbow™

The abbreviation for Basic Input-Output System. BIOS is an element of both CP/M and DOS operating systems that is responsible for handling details of computer input and output data.

bipolar *adj.*

generic

Pertaining to NPN and PNP transistors having semiconductor material of both polarities (P and N); also applies to integrated circuits.

bisync *adj.*

generic

The acronym for bisynchronous, a two-part data original used as a control character within a communication system.

bit *n.*

generic

(From binary digit) The smallest part of information in a binary notation system; a binary digit (0 or 1).

bit complement *n.*

DIGITAL-specific

The result of exchanging 0s and 1s in the binary representation of a number. Thus the bit complement of the binary number 11011001 (217 sub 10) is 00100110. Bit complements are used in place of their corresponding binary numbers in some arithmetic computations. See also one's complement.

bit map *n.*

generic

A table describing each item in a related set of items.

bitmap *n.*

generic

A sequence of bytes representing a printing character.

bits per inch [or bits-per-inch (bpi)] *n.*

generic

The recording density of a magnetic tape; indicating how many characters can fit on one inch of the recording surfaces. See density.

bits-per-second *n.*

generic

A measure of serial data transmission speed.

bit string *n.*

VAX/VMS

A set of 0 to 32 contiguous bits located arbitrarily with respect to byte boundaries. A variable bit field is specified by four attributes: the address A of a byte; the bit position P of the starting location of the fit field with respect to bit 0 of the byte at address A, the size, in bits, of the bit field; an indication whether the field is signed or unsigned. Same as variable-length bit field (VBF).

bit stuffing *n.*

VAX PSI

A procedure used in bit-oriented link control protocols, whereby extra bits are inserted in the text of a packet, whenever the flag sequence occurs, in order to achieve transparency throughout the frame.

bitwise operator *n.*

VAX/VMS

An operator that performs a bitwise logical operation on two operands that must be integral. The usual arithmetic conversions are performed. All bitwise operators are associative, and expressions using them may be rearranged. The set comprises, in order of precedence, the single ampersand (bitwise AND), the caret ([^] bitwise exclusive OR), and the single bar ([|] bitwise inclusive OR).

blank fill attribute *n.*

FMS

A field attribute specifying that field values returned to the application program will contain ASCII spaces. See also character, PAD, and RIB.

BLISS *n.*

DIGITAL-specific

The acronym for Basic Language for Implementing System Software.

block *n.*

DECnet

A group of digits transmitted as a unit over which a coding procedure is applied for synchronization or error-control purposes. Same as frame.

generic

The smallest unit of space into which a mass storage device can be divided. Same as block data; a group of consecutive words, bytes, characters, or digits considered as a unit.

VAX/VMS

1. The smallest logically addressable unit of data that a specified device can transfer in an I/O operation (512 contiguous bytes for most disk devices).

2. An arbitrary number of contiguous bytes used to store logically related status, control, or other processing information.

block activation *n.*

VAX/VMS and VAX C

The run-time action of activating a block or function, in which local auto and register variables are allocated storage and, if they are declared with initializers, given initial values. (Static, extern, globaldef, and globalvalue variables are allocated and initialized at compile time.) The block activation precedes the execution of any executable statements in the function or block. Functions are activated when they are called. Internal blocks (compound statements) are activated when the program control flows into them. Internal blocks are not activated if they are entered by a GOTO statement, unless the GOTO target is the label of the block itself rather than the label of some statement within the block. If a block is entered by a GOTO statement, references to auto and register variables still are valid references, but the variables may not be properly initialized.

block align *v.*

FMS

To store forms in a Form Library file with each form starting on a block boundary. This technique requires more disk space, but provides faster access to the library at run time. See also disk block.

block-begin *n.*

PEARL

The start of a begin block.

block check character (BCC) *n.*

DECnet

The result of a transmission verification algorithm accumulated over a transmission block, and normally appended at the end. An example of a transmission verification algorithm is the cyclic redundancy check (CRC) used by the RSX-11/3271 Protocol Emulator (PE). Same as BCC.

block data *n.*

generic

A set of records that makes up one block. Same as block.

blocked I/O queue *n.*

VAX/VMS

A queue that records the I/O request packets (IRPs) that have failed to be processed due to virtual errors such as end-of-file or end-of-volume. The address of the blocked I/O queue is in the volume control block (VCB), created by the mount program at mount time.

block mode *n.*

DIGITAL-specific

A firmware feature that determines whether a terminal operates as an editing or interactive terminal. If BLOCK MODE is on, the terminal functions as a local editing terminal. If BLOCK MODE is off, the terminal functions as an interactive terminal.

blocked process *n.*

MicroPower PASCAL, TOPS-10, and TOPS-20

A process waiting for an event to occur (a specific semaphore signaled) before continuing execution. A blocked process is in the wait-active, wait-suspended, exception-wait-active, or exception-wait-suspended state. See also blocked task.

blocked record *n.*

TOPS-10 and VAX/VMS

A record contained in a file in which more than one record or segment can be contained in a block.

blocked task *n.*

RSX-11M

A task that cannot execute. Blocked tasks do not compete for central processor time, or memory, but they are still considered active. Most commonly a blocked task cannot execute because it is waiting for input or some other information from the system, such as an event flag, indicating that some event has occurred. See also task state, and blocked process.

block-end *n.*

PEARL

The end of a begin block.

blocking *n.*

DECnet

An undesirable condition that occurs when the memory storage of a node reaches its capacity and neighboring nodes cannot then empty into that node.

blocking AST *n.*

VAX/VMS

An AST that can be requested by a process using the lock management system services. A blocking AST is delivered to the requesting process when it is preventing another process from accessing a resource.

block I/O *n.*

VAX/VMS

A data-accessing technique in which the program manipulates the blocks (physical records) that make up a file, instead of its logical records; allows for the direct access to the blocks in a file without regard for the file organization or record format.

block I/O file *n.*

RSTS/E

A sequential or random access file that contains a series of numbered records. Each record in the file corresponds to one physical block on the storage device. The record size varies depending on the storage medium.

block size *n.*

generic

The volume of data items that determine the physical size of the block.

block spanning *n.*

RSX-11M

Specifying which records, if any, are allowed to span blocks when the user creates sequential files. If the user allows block spanning, records can cross block boundaries and are not restricted by block size. In relative and indexed files, records can automatically span blocks if a bucket contains more than one block; however, records cannot span buckets.

block step *n.*

ACMS

One of three kinds of steps used to define the work of a multiple-step ACMS task. A block step has three parts: attributes, work, and action.

BLR *n.*

Rdb/ELN

The abbreviation for binary language representation. BLR is the first layer of protocol in the Digital Standard Relational Interface (DSRI). It is a procedural language that stores RCI requests in a densely-packed binary format. Same as binary language representation.

bold *n.*

Publications/generic

Text printed extra dark. The BOLD key marks
text to be printed extra dark. DECtype produces
boldface by having the printer strike each character three times.

BOLT *n.*

PEARL

A synchronizer for controlling exclusive or shared
access to an object.

book inventory *n.*

generic

The amount of inventory shown in the accounting
records (which may be different from the amount
of inventory actually on hand).

book value *n.*

generic

The amount of an asset recorded in the accounts.

Boolean expression *n.*

generic

An expression composed of one or more relational
expressions; a string of symbols that specifies a
condition that is either true or false.

Boolean operators *n.*

generic

Symbols or words that enable you to join two or
more Boolean expressions. Boolean operators are
AND, OR and NOT.

Boolean valued expression *n.*

generic

An expression that will return a "true" or "false"
evaluation.

boot *n.*

generic

The short form of bootstrap; a technique or device
designed to bring itself into a desired state by
means of its own action. For example, one type
of boot is a routine whose first few instructions
are sufficient to bring the rest of itself into memory from an input device.

VAX/VMS

Short for bootstrap. A bootstrap is a technique or
device designed to bring itself into a desired state
by means of its own action, such as a routine
whose first few instructions are sufficient to bring
the rest of itself into memory from an input device.
Bringing a fresh operating system into memory is
called booting.

boot *v.*

generic

To bring a device or system to a defined state
where it can operate on its own. See also
bootstrap.

bootable volume *n.*

DIGITAL-specific

A disk containing a bootstrap loader program in
logical block 0.

boot name *n.*

VAX/VMS

The abbreviated name of the device being used
to boot software. For example, DUO is the boot
name for device DUA0.

bootstrap *n.*

generic

A procedure or device designed to bring itself into a needed state by action of itself only. Same as boot (n.).

bootstrap *v.*

generic

To cause an operating system to load itself and prepare itself. Same as boot (v.).

bootstrap *n.*

generic

A way or device designed to bring a system or device into a defined state by means of its own action, e.g., a machine routine whose first few instructions are enough to bring the rest of itself into the computer from an input device.

bootstrap block *n.*

VAX/VMS

A block in the index file of a system disk. It can contain a program that loads the operating system into memory.

bootstrap loader *n.*

generic

A routine whose first instructions are to load the remainder of itself into memory from an input device and to start a complex system of programs.

BOT *n.*

generic

(Acronym for beginning of tape marker.) A point indicating the beginning of the recording area of magnetic tape.

bottom address *n.*

generic

The lowest memory address into which a program is loaded. A bottom address is the basis for computing the value of some other relative address. It is the address of the first location of a program or data area. See also base address.

bottom line *n.*

generic

A colloquial term for net income.

bound *n.*

PASCAL, VAX PASCAL, and VAX PL/I

The upper or lower limit to the subscript values of a dimension of an array.

bound character *n.*

generic

A cell in the font that shares a bitmap with one or more other characters. The characters that share the bitmap appear the same in printing and in editing.

bpi *n.*

VAX/VMS

The abbreviation for bits per inch (or bits-per-inch). The recording d ensity of a magnetic tape, indicating how many characters can fit on one inch of the recording surface. See density.

bracket *n.*

DECnet

An uninterruptible unit of work; also an arbitrary period of activity during which all data exchanges are related. In EC (emulator control) and XEC (extended emulator control) modes, only the SLU (secondary logical unit) may begin a bracket or give permission to the PLU (primary logical unit) to begin the bracket. In EC mode, only the PLU may end a bracket. In AC mode, either application may begin or end a bracket. See also BID.

branch *n.*

DECsystem-10

The link between two or more nodes in a queue structure.

generic

A stop in the execution of sequential instructions and a jump to another instruction; also, a selection between two or more possible courses of action in a program's flow of control, based on some condition.

branch access type *n.*

VAX/VMS

An instruction attribute that indicates the processor does not reference an operand address, but that the operand is a branch displacement. The size of the branch displacement is given by the data type of the operand.

branch mode *n.*

VAX/VMS

An addressing mode in which the instruction operand specifier is a signed byte or word displacement. The displacement is added to the contents of the updated PC (which is the address of the first byte beyond the displacement), and the result is the branch address.

brand *n.*

MINC

A small, vertical line on a graph used to mark the exact horizontal location of data.

breach *n.*

VAX/VMS

A break in the system security that results in admittance of a person or program to an object.

break *v.*

DECWORD

1. To end a printed page and start a new one.

2. To hyphenate a word across two lines.

breaker *n.*

generic

(Short form of circuit breaker.) An electromechanical device designed to open a circuit under overload conditions thereby protecting the circuit from damage.

break field *n.*

CTS-300

In the PRINTU utility, a field identified as one that determines when accumulated data is printed.

break field *n.*

generic

A field that contains a value that allows records in a collection to be broken into subsets for the purpose of subtotaling and other operations.

breakin attempt *n.*

VAX/VMS

An effort made by an unauthorized source to gain access to the system. Since the first system access is achieved through logging in, breakin attempts primarily refer to attempts to log in illegally. These attempts focus on supplying passwords for users know to have accounts on the system, through informed guesses or other trial-and-error methods.

breaking hyphen *n.*

DECWORD, generic, and Publications

One of the four types of hyphens used in printing and publications. It is a hyphen used to join compound words that may be divided at the end of a line. See also hyphen.

breakpoint *n.*

generic

A point in a computer program, usually specified by an instruction, where its execution may be interrupted by external means or by a monitor program.

bridge *adj.*

generic

Pertaining to a type of rectifier circuit.

bridging fault *n.*

DECSIM

A fault in which two or more normally separate signal paths are connected together.

broadcast addressing *n.*

VAX/VMS

A special type of multicast addressing, in which all nodes are to receive a message.

broadcast circuit *n.*

VAX/VMS

A circuit on which multiple nodes are connected and on which exists a method for transmitting a message that will be received by multiple receivers.

brush *n.*

generic

A segment of copper used to conduct current from the turning part of a motor to the outside circuit.

bubble memory *n.*

generic

A type of computer memory using magnetic bubbles on a magnetic film to create memory locations.

bubble sort *n.*

generic

a sorting algorithm in which values are moved up into their correct places.

bucket *n.*

DIGITAL-specific and VAX/VMS

A storage structure of 1 to 32 disk blocks that is used to store and transfer units of data in files with a relative or indexed file organization. Unlike a block, a bucket can contain only entire records.

generic

The amount of data in a file that a program accesses for its use in any single input/output operation.

bucket header *n.*

RSX-11M

Seven bytes of control data that RMS-11 appends to every user data record in an indexed file. See also record header and record format overhead.

bucket locking *n.*

generic

A method that prevents access to any record within a bucket by more than one user until the user releases the bucket.

VAX DATATRIEVE

A means of preventing a second program or record access stream from accessing a record in a bucket until the first program or stream is finished adding to, modifying or deleting it. Bucket locking is used with relative and indexed files.

VAX/VMS

A facility that prevents access to any record in a bucket by more than one user until the original user releases the bucket.

bucket pointer *n.*

RSX-11M

A part of an index record that indicates the bucket whose high-key value is contained in the rest of the index record.

bucket size *n.*

RSX-11M

The number of blocks in a bucket. Bucket size is an attribute of a relative file or an indexed file area and cannot be changed for the life of the file.

bucket split *n.*

VAX/VMS

The result of inserting records into a full bucket. To minimize bucket splits, VAX RMS attempts to keep half of the records in the original bucket and transfers the remaining records to a newly created bucket.

bucket splitting *n.*

RSX-11M

The process of formatting a new bucket in the file and moving the high portion of the target bucket into the new bucket. Bucket splitting occurs when both of the following are true:

1. RMS-11 inserts a record into the target bucket to preserve ascending key value sequence or expand a record in the target bucket.

2. A record does not fit in the target bucket due to insufficient free space.

budget *n.*

generic

A financial plan that is used to estimate the results of future operations. Frequently used to help control future operations.

budgeted statements *n.*

generic

Statements prepared before the event or period occurs, using planned or projected data.

buffer *n.*

generic

A temporary storage space for data.

VAX/VMS

An internal memory area used for temporary storage of data records during input or output operations.

buffer control order *n.*

DECnet

A code that may be included in the WRITE data stream transmitted for a display station or printer. It provides additional formatting or definition of the WRITE data. See also order code.

buffered data path *n.*

VAX/VMS

A UNIBUS adapter data path that transfers 32 or 64 bits of data in a single SBI transfer.

buffered I/O *n.*

VAX/VMS

An I/O operation, such as terminal or mailbox I/O, in which an intermediate buffer from the system buffer pool is used instead of a process-specified buffer. Contrast with direct I/O. Same as system-buffered I/O.

buffer pointer *n.*

DIGITAL-specific

A position indicator located between two characters in an editing buffer, before the first character or after the last character in the buffer.

buffer ring *n.*

TOPS-10

A series of buffers used to overlap a program's execution and its I/O transfer.

buffer sweep *n.*

MINC

A sampling sweep that uses exactly one buffer for a data transfer. See also sweep. d'aprs ce qu'on m'a dit, dans le contexte de MINC, il s'agit plus d'un transfert que d'un balayage de donnes. donc: transfert par tampons ?

buffer underrun *n.*

MINC

A condition in which a data transfer requires a new buffer, but the device queue is empty because a number of buffers sufficient for the device queue has not been released.

bug *n.*

generic

An error or malfunction in a system, device, or program.

bugcheck *n.*

VAX/VMS

The operating system's internal diagnostic check. The system logs the failure and crashes the system.

Build Operation *n.*

TDMS

The execution of the BUILD LIBRARY command in the TDMS Request Definition Utility (RDU). This operation places in a VAX/VMS request library file the requests named in the request library definition and their associated form and record information. The program accesses this file at run time to execute a request.

built-in function *n.*

DIGITAL-specific

Prewritten routines, stored in the computer, that perform commonly used operations.

bundled *adj.*

generic

Pertaining to a software or hardware product that is included in the price of a computer system or product.

burst-mode sweep   *n.*

DIGITAL-specific

A sweep in which data is transferred from a particular device until the device queue is empty; the processor is not driven by interrupts. In addition, because a burst-mode sweep cannot be clock-driven, the time between samples is not constant.

bus   *n.*

DIGITAL-specific

A flat, flexible cable that consists of many transmission lines, or wires and that interconnects computer system components to provide communication paths for addresses, data, and control information.

generic

One or more conductors used as a path over which information is sent from one of many sources to one of many destinations.

Business Applications subsystem   *n.*

ALL-IN-1

A menu option provided in ALL-IN-1 Office Menu and Extended packages. A programmer can use this area to add in programs specific to a company or organization.

busy/not busy   *adj.*

DECnet

Pertaining to the status condition of a device as determined and stored by the IBM 3271 control unit. The control unit considers a device busy if it is performing an operation that was initiated by the control unit (namely, an ERASE-ALL-UNPRO-TECTED operation or print operation). A control unit may also find a device busy if it attempted to perform a command with the device but found the device busy executing a manually initiated operation (initiated from the keyboard, for example). See also status and sense bytes.

by descriptor   *n.*

VAX PL/I

A mechanism used to pass arguments to a subroutine. The arguments are declared with asterisk extents.

by immediate value   *n.*

VAX PL/I

A mechanism used to pass arguments to a subroutine. The arguments are declared with the VALUE attribute.

bypass   *n.*

generic

A parallel path around one or more elements of a circuit.

bypass label processing   *n.*

TOPS-10

The processing mode wherein the system ignores tape labels.

by reference   *n.*

DIGITAL-specific

A conventional PL/I method for passing arguments.

byte   *adj.*

generic

Pertaining to a binary character string made up of bits; the adjective, byte, is often used with a hyphen as in byte-addressable.

byte *n.*

generic

A binary character string made up of bits operated on as a unit and usually shorter than a computer word.

VAX/VMS

Eight contiguous bits starting on any addressable boundary. Bits are numbered 0 to 7 from right to left. Bit 0 is the low-order bit. When interpreted arithmetically, a byte is a two's complement integer with significance increasing from bits 0 through 6. Bit 7 is the sign bit. The value of the signed integer is in the range −128 to +127 decimal. When interpreted as an unsigned integer, significance increases from bits 0 through 7 and the value of the unsigned integer is in the range 0 to 255 decimal. A byte can be used to store one ASCII character.

byte expression *n.*

RGL/FEP

A data type indexed on single byte boundaries; that is, a data type that requires only 8 bits of storage.

byte manipulation *n.*

generic

The ability to process and list characters as one unit.

byte pointer *n.*

DIGITAL-specific

A hardware word format indicating the address, position, and length of a byte of information.

cache *v.*

DIGITAL-specific

To store blocks in memory for future use.

cache *n.*

generic

A very fast memory that can be used in combination with slower, large capacity memories.

cache cluster *n.*

RSTS/E and RSX-11M

A single- or multi-block unit of the RSTS/E data cache. The caching software imposes a grid of cache clusters on the logical structure of a disk. An I/O operation that reads blocks to be cached is broken into disk access requests by cache cluster. pouvoir s'appliquer qu' des terminaux)

cache cluster size *n.*

RSTS/E

The number of 512-byte blocks that can be stored in the RSTS/E data cache as one unit.

cache memory *n.*

DIGITAL-specific

A small, high-speed memory placed between slower main memory and the processor. A cache increases effective memory transfer rates and processor speed. It contains copies of data recently used by the processor, and fetches several bytes of data from memory in anticipation that the processor will access the next sequential series of bytes.

caching (cache) *n.*

DIGITAL-specific

The process of storing blocks in memory for future use; used to minimize physical transfer of data between mass storage devices and memory.

CAD/CAM *n.*

generic

The abbreviation for computer-aided design/computer-aided manufacturing. CAD/CAM refers to programs and software systems that increase the efficiency and accuracy of hardware design and manufacturing.

CALC mode *n.*

VAX DBMS

In DBMS, a way to calculate a record's storage address in the data base by using the value of one or more data items in the record. CALC mode is declared in the storage schema and can be used only with SYSTEM-owned sets.

calculation key (CALC key) *n.*

VAX DBMS

The data items defined in a record whose contents are used by the DBCS (Database Control System) to calculate a database key value when a record occurrence is stored.

calculation mode (CALC mode) *n.*

VAX DBMS

The location mode in which the user specifies that the storage location of a record occurrence is determined by a hash of the value specified data items.

Calendar Management *n.*

ALL-IN-1

A time-management, system selection in Desk Management that lets the user keep a personal calendar and schedule meetings.

calibrate *v.*

generic

To check a measuring device against a standard and adjust the device to that standard.

call *n.*

DIGITAL-specific

A transfer from one part of a program to another with the ability to return to the original program at the point of the call.

call *v.*

VAX PSI

To make (or attempt to make) a connection with a remote DTE (data terminal equipment) or establish a virtual circuit across a PSDN (packet switching data network) by sending Call Request packets.

VAX/VMS

To transfer control to a specified routine.

callable *adj.*

generic

Pertaining to a code that can be executed by another program.

callable DBQ *n.*

VAX DBMS

The abbreviated form of callable database query. A callable DBQ is a data manipulation interface to the database control system; it allows programs, written in any VAX language that conforms to the VAX calling standard, to access a database.

caller *n.*

generic

A program that executes another program or a subprogram.

call frame *n.*

VAX/VMS

A standard data structure built on the stack during a procedure call, starting from the location addressed by the frame pointer (FP) to lower addresses, and retrieved from (''popped off'') during a return from procedure. Same as stack frame.

calling program *n.*

VAX DATATRIEVE

A program that issues calls to other programs or subprograms to execute certain operations.

calling sequence *n.*

generic

The order in which instructions and data are transferred to other programs or subprograms.

call instruction *n.*

VAX/VMS

Refers to either of the processor instructions CALLG (call procedure with general argument list) or CALLS (call procedure with stack argument list).

call interface *n.*

VAX DATATRIEVE

A mechanism for a program to access components of a software product. For example, the VAX DATATRIEVE call interface is the part of DATATRIEVE that provides access to DATA-TRIEVE's data management services. There are three modes of access to DATATRIEVE's call interface:

- through the terminal server

- through the remote server

- from a calling program.

See also program interface.

call stack *n.*

VAX/VMS

The stack and conventional stack structure used during a procedure call. Each access mode of each process context has one call stack, and interrupt service context has one call stack.

cam *n.*

generic

A device used to transform rotary motion into linear motion. See also eccentric.

cancel session request *n.*

DECnet

A SNA (systems network architecture) session control request used to signal termination of a chain transmission, where the chain is to be discarded by the receiver. Upon receipt of CANCEL in EC mode, the protocol emulator (PE) discards buffered data and re-sets its buffer pointers for that session.

candidate key *n.*

Rdb/ELN

A field or set of fields that uniquely identifies the individual records of a relation.

canonic number *n.*

DSM-11

A number reduced to its simplest form. A canonic number contains only valid numeric characters and, optionally, a single decimal point. It has no leading zeros to the right of the integer or trailing zeros to the left of the decimal fraction.

capacitance *n.*

generic

The capability of an object to accept and store electric charges.

capacitor *n.*

generic

Two conductors separated by a dielectric and capable of assuming an electric difference of potential.

capacity planning *n.*

DIGITAL-specific

The act of collecting, archiving, and reporting on system capacity planning data for the purpose of determining the long-range hardware needs of a computer system such as physical memory, CPU, and disk.

capital investment *n.*

USFC/generic

Monies invested by an organization in fixed assets.

capstan *n.*

generic

A spindle of specific size that pulls the magnetic tape over the read/write head of a magnetic tape transport at a constant speed.

caption *n.*

FMS

Background text, associated with a field, that identifies the field. See also background text.

captive accounts *n.*

VAX/VMS

A type of VAX/VMS account that limits the activities of the user. Typically, the user is restricted to using certain command procedures and/or commands. The user may not be allowed to use the CTRL/Y key. (This type of account is synonymous with a turnkey or tied account.)

carbon ribbon *n.*

Publications/generic

A type of printer ribbon which may be used only once, as opposed to a cloth ribbon.

card deck *n.*

generic

An organized set of computer cards that contains data and/or instructions.

cardinality *n.*

DIGITAL-specific

The number of records in the table or relation.

careful writing *n.*

Rdb/ELN

The process of making multi-stage updates to the database in an order that guarantees that the database structure will never be inconsistent.

carriage return *n.*

Publications/generic

An invisible character that forces all following text to the next line.

carriage return key *n.*

generic

A key on the terminal keyboard that usually signals the end of user input. This also causes printing to start again at the far left margin, down one line.

carrier sense *n.*

VAX/VMS

A signal provided by the Physical layer of DECnet to indicate that one or more stations (nodes) are currently transmitting on the Ethernet channel.

carrier-sense multiple access with collision detection (CSMA/CD) *n.*

DECnet

A distributed channel allocation procedure in which every station can receive all other stations' transmissions. Each station awaits an idle channel before transmitting, and each station can detect overlapping transmissions by other stations. Same as CSMA/CD.

VAX/VMS

A link management procedure used by the Ethernet. Allows multiple stations to access the broadcast channel at will, avoids contention by means of carrier sense and deference, and resolves contention by means of collision detection and retransmission.

carrier transition *n.*

RSX-20F

A transition in the state of the carrier signal, either from "on" to "off", or vice versa.

carry *n.*

generic

That which results when the sum or product of two or more digits is equal to or bigger than the radix of the number system.

carrying cost *n.*

generic

The cost associated with holding items in inventory between the time of acquisition and the time of use.

cartesian product *n.*

Rdb/ELN

The simplest form of a join operation. Same as cross product.

case label *n.*

PASCAL

In the CASE statement, a constant of the same type as the case selector. A list of case labels, separated by commas and followed by a colon (:), precedes each statement that can be chosen for execution.

case selector *n.*

VAX PASCAL

In the CASE statement, the expression whose value determines the statement selected for execution. In choosing the statement to be executed, the CASE statement first evaluates the case selector. It then scans the case labels preceding each possible statement, and executes the statement that is labeled with the value of the case selector.

case sensitivity *n.*

generic

Refers to the ability to distinguish between uppercase (A–Z) and lowercase (a–z) letters.

Case Value *n.*

TDMS

A literal string in a TDMS request that determines whether a conditional request instruction executes at run time. TDMS checks that the case value matches the value in a control field. If there is a match, TDMS executes the request instructions associated with the case value.

cash *n.*

generic

Money, whether in currency or in a bank account.

cash budget *n.*

generic

A schedule of expected cash receipts and disbursements.

cash discount *n.*

generic

A reduction in sales or purchase price allowed for prompt payment.

cash flow *n.*

generic

The difference between cash receipts and cash disbursements during a period.

cast *n.*

VAX C

An expression preceded by a cast operator of the form "(type-name)". The cast operator forces the conversion of the evaluated expression to the given type.

catastrophe *n.*

generic

A large and sudden failure.

CBI *n.*

DIGITAL-specific

The abbreviation for computer based instruction. Instruction taken by reading displays on a computer screen and typing in responses when requested. Same as computer aided instruction.

CCB *n.*

VAX/VMS

The abbreviation for channel control block. A structure in the I/O data base created by the assign I/O channel system service to describe the device unit to which a channel is assigned. Same as channel control block.

CCITT *n.*

generic

Comite Consultatif International Telegraphique et Telephonique. An international consultative committee that sets international communications usage standards.

CCL *n.*

RSTS/E

The abbreviation for concise command language. A way to call a RSTS/E system program and provide it with input on a single command line. The system manager defines the CCL commands available on a particular RSTS/E system. Same as concise command language.

CDD *n.*

Common Data Dictionary, VAX DATATRIEVE, and VAX DBMS

The abbreviation for Common Data Dictionary. CDD is a central storage facility consisting of a hierarchy of directories that contain definitions used by VAX information architecture products. The CDD contains descriptions of data, not the data itself. CDD objects are stored hierarchically and are accessed by reference to dictionary path names.

CDD directories and subdictionaries contain objects such as:

* ACMS application, menu, and task group definitions

* ACMS/AD task and task group definitions

* DATATRIEVE domain, record, and procedure definitions

* DBMS schema, subschema, and storage schema definitions

* TDMS record and form definitions, requests, and request library definitions.

See also dictionary object.

CDDL *n.*

Common Data Dictionary and VAX DBMS

The abbreviation for common data definition language. CDDL is the data definition language utility that lets users insert record definitions into the CDD (Common Data Dictionary). Users create the data descriptions in a CDDL source file and compile the source file with the CDDL compiler. Same as common data definition language.

CDDV *n.*

Common Data Dictionary

The abbreviation for common data dictionary verification, usually expressed as dictionary verify/fix utility. CDDV is a common data dictionary utility that detects damaged dictionary files and repairs them. Same as dictionary verify/fix utility.

cell *n.*

generic

1. A basic unit of storage.

2. Any model designed as a component of an LSI or VLSI chip.

3. One of the individual elements that make up a font. Each cell typically contains the bitmap of a single printing character or, in the case of a bound character, the address of another bitmap

4. A single unit that is capable of changing some form of energy, such as chemical energy, radiant energy, or heat into electricity.

MSG (SPETS)

An element of the matrix representation of the gamma camera field of view. The analog-to-digital converters of GAMMA-11 transform the analog signals of the gamma camera into a digital matrix representation of this data. Each cell of the matrix represents the sum of the counts originating in a specific area of the gamma-camera crystal.

RGL/FEP

A major division of a graph's axis. A cell boundary is displayed as a long tickmark or a solid line across a graph. See also subcell.

center *v.*

Publications/generic

To position a line of text an equal distance from the left and right margins.

centering mark *n.*

DECmate II

An invisible character that forces the text that comes before it on the same line to be centered between the margins or at the centering point. A centering mark is also a line-end character. The cursor and any text following it moves to the beginning of the next line.

centering point *n.*

DECmate II

A point in a ruler, indicated by C, around which the text on that line is centered.

center point *n.*

Publications/generic

The position around which text is to be centered.

central processing unit (CPU) *n.*

generic

The main unit of a computer that contains the circuits controlling interpretation and execution of instructions; the central processing unit holds the main storage, arithmetic unit, and special registers. Same as central processor and CPU.

central processor *n.*

generic

(A short form of central processing unit.) The main unit of a computer that contains the circuits controlling the interpretation and execution of instructions. The part of a computer system that holds the main storage, arithmetic unit, and special registers; usually referred to as CPU. Same as CPU and central processing unit.

central site *n.*

DECsystem-10 and TOPS-10

The location of the central computer. Used in conjunction with remote communications to mean the location of the DECsystem-10 or TOPS-10 central processor as distinguished from the location of the remote station. Same as host site.

CEX *n.*

DECnet

The abbreviation for communications executive. CEX is a group of software modules and data bases that creates an environment within which data communications software, such as the PE (protocol emulator), can execute in cooperation with the RSX operating system. Same as communications executive.

chain *n.*

DECnet

A series of contiguous requests that form one logical message. Data transmitted in SNA (systems network architecture) is preceded by a transmission header (TH), and a request/response header (RH). The data itself is called the request/response unit (RU). A transmission in SNA, therefore, consists of one or more units, formatted as follows: TH RH RU. The RU (user-created data) cannot exceed 256 bytes. If a message consists of more than 256 bytes, it is sent in multiple TH/RH/RU segments, called chain elements. If an entire message is 256 bytes or less, it is transmitted in a chain consisting of one element. That element is marked OIC (only-in-chain); if an entire message is greater than 256 and no greater than 512 bytes, it is transmitted in two elements, the first of which is marked FIC (first-in-chain).

generic

A number of items connected in logical order so that each item points to the next item.

VAX DATATRIEVE

A series of interconnected single-member sets in which the sole member of one set is the owner of the next set.

VAX DBMS

A method of linking records within sets. A chain contains embedded pointers, within the owner and member records, that make up a set occurrence.

chain *v.*

generic

To start the execution of one program at the end of the execution of another.

chain mode *n.*

CTS-300

The mode in which a specified program is automatically executed upon the normal termination of another.

CHAIN mode *n.*

VAX DBMS

A way to link records sequentially using NEXT, PRIOR, and OWNER pointers. CHAIN mode is declared in the storage schema and cannot be used with sorted sets of CALC sets.

change key (characteristic) *n.*

RSX-11M

A flag associated with an alternate key. The flag indicates whether users allow the key field to change values during an update record operation. See also duplicate key, null key, and RSX-11M.

change mode *n.*

RSX-11M

In EDT (a text editor), a method of operating on text one character at a time. Change mode is the alternate to line mode, which operates on text one line at a time. Change mode is particularly suited to editing using a video terminal.

channel *n.*

DECnet

A logical communication path over which data can be sent. A continuous signal whose frequency, amplitude, or phase can be varied (modulated). See also attach.

generic

1. A path through which signals can be sent.

2. The part of a storage medium that is accessible to a given reading or writing site.

3. A band of frequencies used for communication.

VAX/VMS

1. A logical path connecting a user process to a physical device unit. A user process requests the operating system to assign a channel to a device so the process can communicate with that device. See also controller data channel.

2. A means of transmission over a packet switching data network. For VAX PSI, a logical path between a DTE and DCE over which data is transmitted. Each channel is identified by a unique reference number called a logical channel number (LCN).

channel control block (CCB) *n.*

VAX/VMS

A structure in the I/O data base created by the assign I/O channel system service to describe the device unit to which a channel is assigned. Same as CCB.

channel request block (CRB) *n.*

VAX/VMS

A structure in the I/O data base that describes the activity on a particular controller. The channel request block for a controller contains pointers to the wait queue of drivers ready to access a device through the controller. Same as CRB.

channel sweep *n.*

MINC

A sweep that transfers data between the REAL-11/MNC software and one or more analog-to-digital (A/D) converter channels or digital-to-analog (DA) converter channels. The results of a channel sweep consist of a collection of values each of which was transmitted over a separate channel.

character *n.*

generic

A letter, digit, punctuation mark, or other symbol used to organize, control, or represent data.

VAX/VMS

A symbol represented by an ASCII code. See also alphanumeric character.

character buffer *n.*

VAX/VMS

A temporary storage area used to store the last character deleted by an EDT delete character operation.

character editing *n.*

VAX/VMS

Editing text at the character level; an operational mode of EDT, entered through the CHANGE command.

character file *n.*

GIGI

A file that contains the definition of a character or group of characters.

characteristics *n.*

DECnet

Parameters that are generally static values in volatile memory or permanent values in a permanent data base. Characteristics can be set or defined and are usually operator controllable (for example, using NCP).

VAX/VMS

A display type for the NCP commands SHOW and LIST. It refers to static information about a component that is kept in either the volatile or permanent database. Such information may include parameters defined for that component by either the SET or DEFINE command.

character mode *n.*

MINC

The available features or characters that appear on the terminal screen.

character mode DTE *n.*

VAX PSI

A DTE (data terminal equipment) that is unable to handle data in packet form. This DTE must interface through a packet assembly/disassembly (PAD) facility to connect to a PSDN (packet switching data network).

character pattern *n.*

GIGI

The dot pattern contained in a character cell.

character pointer *n.*

RT-11

In a file, an indicator of the place where the next character typed will be entered. The character pointer is visible as a blinking cursor on VT-11 display hardware.

VAX/VMS

A contiguous set of bytes. A character string is identified by two attributes: an address and a length. Its address is the address of the byte containing the first character of the string. Subsequent characters are stored in bytes of increasing addresses. The length is the number of characters in the string.

character set *n.*

FMS

A set of 94 graphics corresponding to the printable characters.

character string descriptor *n.*

VAX PSI and VAX/VMS

A quadword data structure used for passing character data (strings). The first word of the quadword contains the length of the character string. The second word can contain type information. The remaining longword contains the address of the string. See also descriptor.

character transfer (CX) *n.*

DECWORD

A communication option that transfers one character at a time among the DECWORD keyboard, the DECWORD screen, stored documents, and another computer, called the host. CX can be used to make a DECWORD terminal act as though it were connected to the host. Character transfer is invoked by typing CX from the options menu. Same as CX.

character values *n.*

generic

Attributes that you set for the individual characters in a font: *HEIGHT*, *WIDTH*, and *OFFSET*.

charge off *n.*

generic

To record as an expense an amount that formerly was recorded as an asset.

chart of accounts *n.*

generic

A list of the names and numbers of the accounts included in an accounting system.

CHAR type *n.*

VAX PASCAL

A predefined scalar type that has the ASCII character set as constant values.

CHAS *n.*

generic

A chip-design data manager and system of software tools for VLSI engineers.

CHASE *n.*

DECnet

The SNA (systems network architecture) data flow control request used for synchronization between applications.

chassis *n.*

generic

The structure that holds and supports electronic components and their related circuitry.

checkpoint *n.*

generic

A point in a routine at which it is possible to store enough information to permit restarting computation or job run.

checkpoint *v.*

generic

To save the status of a program and data so that the program can be continued after a crash.

checkpointing *n.*

RSX-11M

The process by which the RSX-11 Executive makes memory space and processor time available to tasks according to their priority. If a higher-priority task is ready to run and no memory is available, then lower-priority tasks will be removed temporarily, or checkpointed, to make room for the higher-priority task. The lower-priority tasks are saved on the disk exactly as they were when interrupted. When memory is available, the tasks are returned to memory and proceed exactly where they left off. Also called rolling out.

check register *n.*

generic

A journal to record checks issued.

checksum *n.*

generic

A sum of digits or bits used to verify whether a number or an operation is valid.

child *n.*

Common Data Dictionary

Refers to a dictionary directory, subdictionary, or object in the CDD that immediately succeeds another directory or subdictionary in the CDD hierarchy. The preceding directory or subdirectory is called the parent. Each dictionary child has precisely one parent. For example, given CDD$TOP and CDD$TOP.MANUFACTURING, CDD$TOP is the parent and CDD$TOP.MANUFACTURING is the child. See also descendant and directory hierarchy.

children *n.*

DIGITAL-specific

Nodes in the queue structure on the branch logically below (schematically to the right of) the parent.

chunk *n.*

DECnet

Refers to 300 (octal) bytes of core memory in the DN20.

CICS/VS *n.*

DECnet

The abbreviation for customer information control system/virtual storage. A proprietary software product of IBM Corp. that serves as a data communications interface between transcription type applications and S/360 or S/370 operating systems. Same as customer information control system/virtual storage.

circuit *n.*

generic

1. A set of connected flip-flops, logic gates, and/or other electrical components that performs a specific set of functions.

2. A complete, closed-loop path for current to flow, usually including the source of electromotive force.

VAX PSI

A VAX PSI (packet switching interface) management component that contains records to identify PVCs (permanent virtual circuits) and specify parameters for these PVCs. See also virtual circuit.

VAX/VMS

Virtual communications paths between nodes or DTEs. Circuits operate over physical lines and are the medium on which all I/O occurs. X.25 circuits are virtual circuits.

circuit switching *n.*

generic

The creation of an electrical connection between calling and called sites in a communications network.

VAX PSI

A communications method in which a physical connection between a calling and called station is established on demand for exclusive use of the stations until the connection is released. Same as line switching.

circumference mode *n.*

Medical Systems

A closed-curve outline, and cells within the outline, defining an irregular ROI (region of interest).

classical fault *n.*

DECSIM

A fault type in which a digital signal is held in one of its binary states. Same as stuck-at fault.

clear *v.*

generic

To put a storage or memory device into a given state, usually zero.

clear character *n.*

FMS

A character appearing in empty data positions in a field. A blank is the default. An underscore (_) most closely duplicates the appearance of a paper form.

clear session request *n.*

DECnet

The SNA (systems network architecture) session control request used to purge outstanding requests and responses during error recovery or session termination.

clear-to-send *adj.*

generic

Pertaining to a signal which acknowledges, to the device that needs to transmit a signal, that the data communications channel is open and available.

CLI *n.*

RT-11

The abbreviation for command language interpreter. CLI is the program that translates a predefined set of commands into instructions that a computer system can interpret. Same as command language interpreter.

VAX/VMS

The abbreviation for command language interpreter. CLI is a procedure-based system code that executes in supervisor mode in the context of a process to receive, to check the syntax of, and to parse commands typed by the user at a terminal or submitted in a command file. Same as command language interpreter.

clip *v.*

generic

1. To limit the peaks of a waveform to a desirable level.

2. To drive an amplifier past its linear operating range.

clipper *n.*

generic

An electronic circuit that limits the peaks of a waveform by limiting the waveform to a desirable level.

clipping *n.*

generic

The discarding of pixels because of the limits of the Edit Buffer or the limits of a character cell.

RGL/FEP

A calculation used by the data plotting subroutines to cut off (make invisible) the data line of a graph at the data plotting window, and by the picture drawing subroutines to clip lines at the screen boundaries.

clock *n.*

generic

The source of timing signals in an electronic circuit.

MINC, PEARL, and RT-11

1. A device that counts external events.

2. A device that provides periodic signals to control the frequency of data transfers, such as A/D conversions.

clock-driven sweep *n.*

MINC

A sweep caused or driven by clock overflows. On each clock overflow, data is transferred. Clock-driven sweeps can take place at regular intervals, and the timing of the clock overflow can be specified through the parameters of the sweep program.

clock overflow *n.*

MINC

The condition that arises when the clock counter (an unsigned 16-bit integer) exceeds the largest value that it can hold.

clock preset *n.*

MINC

A parameter of the real-time clock that establishes the timing of clock overflows. This value is loaded into the clock counter when the clock is started or when a clock overflow occurs.

close *v.*

generic

To terminate all operations on a file.

closed curve sequence *n.*

GIGI

A series of locations that GIGI uses to interpolate a curve whose end points meet.

closed loop *adj.*

generic

Pertaining to a feedback control used to modify the input.

closed subroutine *n.*

TOPS-10

A subroutine that can be stored at one place and called from one or more calling routines.

closed user group (CUG) *n.*

VAX PSI and VAX/VMS

An optional PSDN (packet switching data network) facility that restricts two or more DTEs (data terminal equipment) in the same group to communicating with each other. The basic CUG (closed user group) also prevents these DTEs from accessing or being accessed by other DTEs outside the group. Additions to the basic CUG facility allow one or more DTEs to access or be accessed by DTEs outside the group. These additions are known as CUG with outgoing access and CUG with incoming access respectively. Same as CUG.

closing entries *n.*

Journal entries that transfer the balances in revenue and expense accounts to owner's equity.

cloth ribbon *n.*

Publications/generic

A type of printer ribbon that may be reused many times, as opposed to a carbon ribbon.

clunk *n.*

DIGITAL-specific

A colloquial expression referring to 100 nanoseconds as a "clunk" of time.

cluster *n.*

DIGITAL-specific

One or more contiguous disk blocks that the system treats as a unit when it creates or extends a file.

VAX/VMS

1. A set of contiguous blocks that is the basic unit of space allocation on a Files-11 disk volume.
2. A set of pages brought into memory in one paging operation.
3. An event flag cluster.
4. A configuration of VAX processors.

CLUSTERED VIA set option *n.*

VAX DBMS

A record placement option in which the Database Control System (DBCS) stores records on or near the page that contains the owner of the set. The CLUSTERED VIA option is declared in the storage schema. See also placement mode.

cluster size *n.*

DIGITAL-specific

The number of blocks in a cluster allocated contiguously on a disk.

generic

1. The primary address of groups of blocks on disk.
2. The memory size of a group of subroutines which are dedicated to the same task.

clutter *n.*

generic

Noise, or unusable data. Also see noise.

CMI *n.*

VAX/VMS

The abbreviation for computer memory interconnect. The part of the VAX-11/750 hardware that connects the processor, memory controllers, MASSBUS adapters, and the UNIBUS interconnect.

CMP *n.*

VAX/VMS

The compatibility mode bit in the hardware processor status longword.

coaxial *adj.*

generic

A two-conductor wire in which one conductor completely wraps the other with the two separated by insulation.

coaxial cable area *n.*

Ethernet

The actual area serviced by the Ethernet cable including horizontal displacement of drop cable on either side of the coaxial cable installed location.

coaxial cable connector *n.*

generic

A device used to connect two lengths of coaxial cable using a barrel connector or to attach a terminator at each end of a segment of coaxial cable.

COBOL *adj.*

generic

Acronym for Common Business Oriented Language.

CODASYL *n.*

generic

An acronym for the Conference on Data Systems Languages, the committee that designed the COBOL language and provided the guidelines used in the development of VAX-11 DBMS.

CODASYL-compliant *n.*

generic

Any database system that conforms to the guidelines set by the Conference on Data Systems Languages.

code *n.*

generic

A system of symbols used to represent information.

cold start *n.*

generic

A primary bootstrap of a system.

collate *v.*

generic

To merge two or more ordered sets of data or cards to produce one or more ordered sets that may or may not follow the original order.

collateral *n.*

generic

Assets pledged by a borrower.

collating sequence *n.*

generic

The sequence in which characters are ordered for sorting, merging, and comparing.

VAX/VMS

An order assigned to the characters of a character set (for example, ASCII, MULTINATIONAL, and EBCDIC) used for sequencing purposes.

collection *n.*

generic

A group of records that meet operator specified criteria.

VAX DATATRIEVE

A special type of record stream formed with the FIND command. The user can refer to a collection in subsequent statements until he can replace it with another collection, release it with the RELEASE command, finish the domain from which it derives, or exit DATATRIEVE. The user can also give a collection a name and then have several collections available at once. See also current.

collimator *n.*

GAMMA, Medical Systems, and MSG (SPETS)

A device that directs radiation in straight, parallel lines. A collimator has long, narrow tubes with absorbing or reflecting walls that permit the radiation to travel only in a direction parallel to the tubes' axis.

collision *n.*

VAX/VMS

Multiple network transmissions overlapping in the physical channel, resulting in garbled data and necessitating retransmission.

collision detect *n.*

VAX/VMS

A signal provided by the Physical layer of DECnet to its Data Link layer to indicate that one or more stations (nodes) are contending with the local station's transmission.

command n.

DIGITAL-specific

An instruction, generally an English word, typed
by the user at a terminal or included in a command procedure that requests the software monitoring a terminal or reading a command procedure
to perform some predefined operation.

generic

A character or group of characters that specifies
or causes an operation to be performed by a computer system.

VAX DATATRIEVE

An instruction, usually associated with Common
Data Dictionary (CDD) that performs data description functions. In DATATRIEVE, a command is
distinct from a statement. DATATRIEVE commands cannot be combined with each other and
cannot be used in statements. See also
statement.

VAX/VMS

An instruction, generally an English word, typed
by the user at a terminal or included in a command procedure that requests the software monitoring a terminal or reading a command procedure
to perform some well-defined activity. For example, typing the COPY command requests the system to copy the contents of one file into another
file.

command dispatcher n.

RSX-11M

The command dispatcher, MCR . . . , is a task that
takes commands typed at a terminal and passes
them to DCL (DIGITAL Command Language) or
MCR (monitor console routine) or to some other
CLI (command language interpreter) task that executes commands.

command file n.

VAX/VMS

A file containing commands and data that the
command interpreter can accept in lieu of the
user's typing the commands individually on a terminal. Thus, command procedures provide a
means of automatically passing commands to the
operating system. In addition, they permit users
to employ such programming techniques as loops,
counters, labels, and symbol substitution to set up
elaborate command sequences that can be
altered through user interaction. Command procedures can also be submitted to the system for
processing as batch jobs. Same as command
procedure and indirect command file.

command interpreter n.

RSX-11M and RSX-11M-PLUS

A system feature that makes it possible to communicate with the operating system from a terminal. RSX-11M and RSX-11M-PLUS provide two
CLIs: DCL (DIGITAL Command Language) and
MCR (monitor console routine).

VAX/VMS

A procedure-based system code that executes in
supervisor mode in the context of a process to
receive, to check the syntax of, and to parse commands typed by the user at a terminal or submitted in a command file.

command language n.

generic

A vocabulary of words and symbols used to direct
computer system operations.

command language interpreter (CLI) n.

generic

A program that translates a command or operation
code into machine code.

RT-11

The program that translates a predefined set of commands into instructions that a computer system can interpret. Same as CLI.

VAX/VMS

A procedure-based system code that executes in supervisor mode in the context of a process to receive, to check the syntax of, and to parse commands typed by the user at a terminal or submitted in a command file. Same as CLI.

command level *n.*

VAX/VMS

Input stream for the command interpreter. The initial input stream is always command level 0. Each subsequent execution of a procedure changes the command level.

command node *n.*

DECnet

The node where an NCP (network control program) command originates.

VAX/VMS

The node from which an NCP command is issued.

command parameter *n.*

VAX/VMS

The positional operand of a computer delimited by spaces, such as a file specification, option, or constant.

command procedure *n.*

VAX/VMS

A file containing commands and data that the command interpreter can accept in lieu of the user's typing the commands individually on a terminal. Thus, command procedures provide a means of automatically passing commands to the operating system. In addition, they permit users to employ such programming techniques as loops, counters, labels, and symbol substitution to set up elaborate command sequences that can be altered through user interaction. Command procedures can also be submitted to the system for processing as batch jobs. Same as Command file and indirect command file.

command process *n.*

ACMS

The process in the ACMS terminal control subsystem that handles user login and interaction between terminals and ACMS. See also agent.

command string *n.*

generic

generic

1. A command plus all the elements that comprise its argument.

2. Instructional words or signals that specify an operation to be performed by the computer.

RT-11

An input line that includes a command plus one or more qualifiers, and/or file specifications.

VAX/VMS

A line (or set of continued lines) containing a command and, optionally, information modifying the command. A complete command string consists of a command, its qualifiers, if any, and its parameters (file specifications, for example), if any, and their qualifiers, if any. A command string is normally terminated by pressing the RETURN key.

command string interpreter *n.*

generic

A software program that accepts a command and interprets that command into machine instructions.

comma operator *n.*

VAX C

A VAX C operator used to separate two expressions:

E1, E2

comment *n.*

generic

Optional text which is used to aid you in identifying a file. It is entered through the prompting screen and does not appear on the graph.

Publications/generic

Text displayed on the screen, but not printed with the document.

VAX C

A sequence of characters introduced by the pair /* and terminated by */. Comments are ignored during compilation. They may not be nested.

COMM EXEC *n.*

DECnet

A group of software modules and data bases that creates an environment within which data communications software can execute in cooperation with the RSX operating system. Same as communications executive (CEX).

commit *n.*

VAX DBMS

In DBMS, a function that terminates a recovery unit and makes permanent all database updates initiated by the recovery unit. In ACMS, an application definition utility keyword used when defining ACMS/AD tasks with recovery. See also retaining and rollback.

common *adj.*

generic

Pertaining to an area in memory that can be shared by one or more programs or subprograms.

VAX/VMS

A FORTRAN term for a program section that contains only data.

common carrier *n.*

VAX PSI

An organization that offers standard and consistent communications services within a country. For example, Western Union or the Bell System. See Postal, Telephone, and Telegraph Authority.

common costs *n.*

generic

Costs that are applicable to two or more cost objects and that must be allocated to those cost objects.

common data definition language (CDDL) *n.*

Common Data Dictionary and VAX DBMS

The data definition language utility that lets users insert record definitions into the CDD (Common Data Dictionary). Users create the data descriptions in a CDDL source file and compile the source file with the CDDL compiler. Same as CDDL. See also data definition language utility.

Common Data Dictionary (CDD) *n.*

Common Data Dictionary, VAX DATATRIEVE, and VAX DBMS

A central storage facility consisting of a hierarchy of directories that contain definitions used by VAX information architecture products. The CDD contains descriptions of data, not the data itself. CDD objects are stored hierarchically and are accessed by reference to dictionary path names.

CDD directories and subdictionaries contain objects such as:

- ACMS application, menu, and task group definitions

- ACMS/AD task and task group definitions

- DATATRIEVE domain, record, and procedure definitions

- DBMS schema, subschema, and storage schema definitions

- TDMS record and form definitions, requests, and request library definitions.

common event flag cluster *n.*

VAX/VMS

A set of 32 event flags that enables cooperating processes to post event notification to each other. Common event flag clusters are created as they are needed. A process can associate with one or two common event flag clusters.

commonly-used system program (CUSP) *n.*

RSTS/E and TOPS-10

A program included as part of the RSTS/E operating system. CUSPs perform common functions such as copying, deleting, and printing files. Same as CUSP.

common mode *adj.*

MINC

Pertaining to an input condition in which a signal component is common to both the sending and return terminals of a measuring device (such as an A/D converter). Some examples of its use are common mode noise, common mode rejection, and common mode interface.

communications control block (CCB) *n.*

DECnet

A data block used by the RSX-11/3271 Protocol Emulator (PE) and DECnet to manage and schedule communications processes for transfers of information between processes. Same as control buffer and CCB.

communications control character *n.*

DECnet

A functional character intended to control or facilitate transmission over data networks. Control characters, specified in ASCII or EBCDIC, form the basis for character-oriented communications control procedures. See also control character.

communications executive (CEX) *n.*

DECnet

A group of software modules and data bases that creates an environment within which data communications software can execute in cooperation with the RSX operating system. Same as COMM EXEC and CEX. See also executive.

communications port *n.*

PRO/Communications

The connector on the back of the system unit that is used to link the Professional with another Professional or a host computer, using either a cable or a telephone line.

communications region *n.*

RSX-20F

An area in KL memory that is used for coordinating status, preparing for byte transfer operations, and passing limited amounts of data. Both the KL and the PDP-11 have an owned communications region in which they alone can write.

communications servers *n.*

DECnet

Phase IV nodes that act as network front ends in off-loading certain communications functions from host nodes. Communications servers consist of router servers, terminal servers, and gateway nodes.

comparator *n.*

generic

A device that checks two items of data and indicates if they are the same.

comparison operator *n.*

VAX PL/I

One of the punctuation symbols ($>$, $<$, $=$, $\leq$, $\geq$, $\wedge$, $\wedge>$, or $\wedge=$) that states a relationship between two expressions and results in a 1-bit Boolean value indicating whether the relationship is true or false. Same as relational operator.

compatibility *adj.*

generic

Pertaining to the ability of a computer to execute programs written for another computer.

compatibility mode *n.*

VAX/VMS

A mode of execution that enables a VAX processor to execute nonprivileged PDP-11 instructions. The operating system supports compatibility mode execution by providing an RSX-11M execution environment for an RSX-11M task image. The operating system compatibility mode procedures intercept calls to the RSX-11M Executive and convert them to the appropriate operating system functions.

compilation *n.*

generic

The process of compiling a program.

compile *v.*

generic

To code from symbolic instructions written in a high-level source language.

compiler *n.*

generic

A program that translates a high-level source language into a language acceptable to a specific computer. A compiler is more powerful than an assembler because it adds instructions and subroutines to the original program.

VAX/VMS

A system component that translates a program written in a high-level language into an object module in binary machine code.

complement *n.*

generic

1. The difference between a number and the next larger power of the base or a number and the next larger power of the base minus one.

2. A transformation command for reversing the color of pixels drawn in a specified area in the Edit buffer.

MINC

The number of degrees added to an angle or arc to make it equal to 90 degrees.

complement number *n.*

generic

A part of the internal font name: a number naming a function that maps ASCII character codes to glyph codes. The font complement, thus, indicates which characters are available in a font and which character codes you must use in your text file to invoke the glyphs for those characteristics.

complement writing *n.*

GIGI and RGL/FEP

1. The writing mode in which the writing color is complemented. The writing is changed to the background color. The use of a pattern causes the background-colored part of the pattern to assume the writing color.

2. The writing mode in which GIGI complements the existing image as new images are written to the screen.

completion routine *n.*

generic

An instruction or set of instructions used as the final step in a programming operation.

complex buffered I/O buffer *n.*

VAX/VMS

Part of nonpaged dynamic memory allocated in system space for I/O processing. The complex buffered I/O buffer is built by the QI/O system service routines. It consists of the ACP I/O buffer packet (AIB) and the ACP buffer descriptor (ABD).

component *n.*

DECnet and PSI

An element in the network that can be controlled and monitored. Components include lines, nodes, logging, and objects. Components form part of the NCP command syntax.

VAX/VMS

In an array, record, or file, an individual data item. An array component is denoted by the array name and an index for each dimension. A record component (also called a field) is denoted by the record name followed by the field name.

composite *n.*

DECSIM

A group of model elements connected to form or define a more complex structure model that can be invoked as an element itself. A composite model is sometimes referred to as a building block model.

composite character *n.*

DECWORD, Publications/generic

A printed character produced by multiple striking of the same character in the same character space. Also called an overstruck character produced by pressing Gold DEAD key.

compound statement *n.*

PASCAL, VAX C, and VAX PASCAL

One or more PASCAL statements, bracketed by the reserved words BEGIN and END, that are executed sequentially as a unit.

compressed file pointer *n.*

DECsystem-10

An 18-bit pointer to the unit within the file structure and to the first super-cluster of the file. That
pointer is stored in the user file directory (UFD) for
each file in the UFD. It points to the retrieval
information block, which contains the information
necessary to access the desired file.

compute-bound *adj.*

generic

Pertaining to a slow system response caused by
the number of computations. See CPU-bound.

COMPUTED BY fields *n.*

VAX DATATRIEVE

Virtual fields that appear in a DATATRIEVE record
definition, but not in the physical record. Because
the value of a COMPUTED BY field is computed
as part of a statement, it occupies no space in
the record.

computer *n.*

generic

A device that processes information. A machine
that has input, output, storage, and arithmetic
devices plus logic and control units.

computer based instruction (CBI) *n.*

DIGITAL-specific

Instruction taken by reading displays on a computer screen and typing in responses when
requested. Same as CBI.

computer memory interconnect (CMI) *n.*

VAX/VMS

The part of the VAX-11/750 hardware that connects the processor, memory controllers, MASS-
BUS adapters, and the UNIBUS interconnect.

computer operator *n.*

generic

A person who runs the computer system console
and performs standard procedures such as loading tapes.

computer-output-microfilm *n.*

generic

A microfilm printer that will take output directly
from the computer thus substituting for line printer
or tape output.

concatenate *v.*

generic

To link multiple items into one; for instance, to join
two or more character strings to make a single
character string.

concatenated key *n.*

DIGITAL-specific

An index key made up of two parts; that is, the
key of one relation combined with the key of
another relation.

concatenation operator *n.*

DIGITAL-specific

A string operator used to combine two parts of an
arithmetic value expression or character string.

concealed device *n.*

VAX/VMS

An I/O device that has a logical name associated
with it; users thus see the logical name, rather
than the device name, displayed in most system
responses.

concise command language (CCL) *n.*

RSTS/E

A way to call a RSTS/E system program and provide it with input on a single command line. The system manager defines the CCL commands available on a particular RSTS/E system. Same as CCL.

concrete core drilling *n.*

generic

A procedure used for penetrating through poured cement (concrete) floors and walls for purposes of cable routing and distribution.

concurrency *n.*

VAX DBMS

The simultaneous use of a database by more than one user.

concurrent *adj.*

generic

Pertaining to the sharing of the CPU resource by cooperating processes whose life spans overlap; processes appear to execute simultaneously.

concurrent run unit *n.*

VAX DBMS

A program that is initiated during the time that another database accessing program is active.

concurrent update mode *n.*

VAX DBMS

The state of a realm in which its record can be modified by concurrent run units. See also shared update.

condition *n.*

VAX PL/I

An occurrence that causes the interruption of the program and initiates a search for a sequence of statements to be executed in response. See also ON condition.

VAX/VMS

An error state that exists when an exception is detected and declared by software. See also exception and condition handler.

conditional assembly *n.*

generic

The process of assembling parts of a symbolic program when certain conditions are given.

Memory Resident RT-11 and RT-11

An assembly of certain parts of a symbolic program that occurs only when conditions are met during the assembly process.

conditional branch *n.*

BASIC/generic

An instruction that causes the program to execute a statement or statements only when a specified condition is met.

conditional instruction *n.*

Terminal Data Management System

A Terminal Data Management System (TDMS) request instruction that executes only if certain conditions are true. TDMS executes a conditional instruction if the value in a control field matches the case value specified within the conditional instruction. See also conditional request and control field.

conditional operator *n.*

VAX C

The VAX C operator (?:), which is used in conditional expressions of the form:
E1 ? E2 : E3

conditional request *n.*

Terminal Data Management System

A request containing one or more conditional instructions. See also conditional instruction.

conditional sale *n.*

USFC/generic

A financing contract by which the customer does not receive clear title to the asset until completion of the contractual payments.

conditional statement *n.*

generic

A statement that determines the truth value of a condition. Subsequent program action depends on the truth value.

conditional variable *n.*

generic

A data item to which a condition-name applies.

condition codes *n.*

VAX/VMS

Four bits in the processor status word (PSW) that indicate the results of previously executed instructions.

condition handler *n.*

generic

A process by which the computer executes a specific routine when an exception condition occurs.

VAX/VMS

A procedure that the system must execute when an exception occurs. When an exception occurs, the operating system searches for a condition handler and, if found, initiates the handler immediately. The condition handler may perform some action to change the situation that caused the exception and continue execution for the process that incurred the exception. Condition handlers execute in the context of the process at the access mode of the code that incurred the exception. See also condition.

condition name *n.*

DIGITAL-specific

A user-defined word assigned to a specific value, set of values, or range of values, within the complete set of values that a conditional variable can possess; or the user-defined word assigned to a status of an implementor-defined switch or device.

VAX PL/I

A keyword associated with a specific ON condition and whose name suggests the nature of the condition.

condition value *n.*

VAX PL/I

A unique 32-bit number that identifies a specific operating system error, warning, or informational condition.

VAX/VMS

A 32-bit value that uniquely identifies the exception that caused the condition.

conductor *n.*

generic

A material that provides an easy path for the flow of energy in the form of heat, electricity, light, sound, and so forth.

conduit *n.*

generic

A metalic housing for wire and cable distribution throughout buildings and structures. There are many sizes and configurations of conduits.

configuration database *n.*

VAX/VMS

A database that contains files that provide information about networking components. Specifically, the files contain information about the local node, and all nodes, modules, circuits, lines, logging, and objects in the network. See also permanent database and volatile database.

configuration register *n.*

VAX/VMS

A control/status register for an adapter, for example, a UNIBUS adapter. It resides in the adapter's I/O space.

configure *v.*

generic

To arrange main components of a computer system such as a system processor, I/O devices, or memory, in some specific pattern; to set jumpers or switches, for example, on a module.

congestion *n.*

DECnet

The condition that arises when there are too many packets to be queued.

congestion control *n.*

DECnet

The transport component that manages buffers by limiting the maximum number of packets on a queue for a line. Also called transmit management.

congestion loss *n.*

DECnet

A condition where data packets are lost when transport is unable to buffer them.

VAX/VMS

A condition in which data packets transmitted over a network are lost when the DECnet-VAX Routing layer is unable to buffer them.

connect *n.*

DECnet

The process of creating a logical link.

connect (record operation) *n.*

RSX-11M

A condition by which RMS-11 makes the records of a file available to the user's program for a stream of operations.

connection *n.*

DECWORD

A link from DECWORD to another computer (such as another DECWORD system) enabling them to communicate with each other.

connector node *n.*

VAX/VMS

A node that serves as an X.25 gateway to permit VAX/VMS host nodes to access a packet switching data network.

connect password *n.*

DECnet

A one- to eight-character password used to validate access privileges between tasks on a network.

connect-to-interrupt *n.*

VAX/VMS

A function by which a process connects to a device interrupt vector. To perform a connect-to-interrupt, the process must map to the program I/O space containing the vector. See also page frame number mapping.

consecutive access *adj.*

generic

Pertaining to a method of sequential data access determined specifically by an I/O device.

console *n.*

generic

A part of a central processing unit that can control the remainder of the CPU.

VAX/VMS

The manual control unit integrated into the central processor. The console includes a serial line interface connected to a hard-copy terminal, which enables the operator to start and stop the system, monitor system operation, and run diagnostics.

console *n.*

generic

A part of a computer used for communication between the operator or maintenance engineer and the computer.

console support *n.*

Memory Resident RT-11

A memory resident RT-11 monitor function that provides character I/O to the terminal that is connected to serial line 1 on the MXV11 port.

console terminal *n.*

generic

A keyboard terminal used to start system operation and direct system activities between the computer operator and the computer system.

VAX/VMS

The hard-copy terminal connected to the central processor console.

consolidated balance sheet *n.*

USFC/generic

A balance sheet showing the financial condition of a corporation and all of its subsidiaries at a specific point in time.

consolidated statements *n.*

generic

Financial statements prepared for a corporate family as an entity. The family consists of a parent and those subsidiaries in which the parent owns more than 50% of the stock.

constant *n.*

generic

A value that does not change during the execution of the program.

contained program *n.*

generic

A contained program is a COBOL source program that is directly or indirectly contained in another COBOL source program.

container file *n.*

RSX-11M

A file on magnetic tape containing one or more RMS-11 files in backup format. When the output medium is tape, each command string to RMSBCK produces one container file.

contention *n.*

DECnet

A condition on a communications line when two or more stations attempt to transmit at the same time.

Rainbow™

A conflict between the two processors in the Rainbow 100 computer over a signal's validity.

generic

A conflict between two processors in the computer over a signal's availability.

context *n.*

MicroPower PASCAL

The set of data defining the environment, both hardware and software, in which a process executes. Hardware context includes the contents of the general registers, memory-mapping registers, floating-point registers, and processor status word. Software context includes the contents of various flags and pointers maintained by the kernel.

RSX-11M

The position of a record access stream within a file, consisting of current record and next record.

VAX/VMS

The environment of an activity. See also process context, hardware context, and software context.

context indexing *n.*

VAX/VMS

The ability to index through a data structure automatically because the size of the data type is known and used to determine the offset factor.

context switching *n.*

generic

The process of saving key registers and memory areas when temporarily stopping one job so the executive or monitor can execute another job. Key registers and memory areas are released when the original job is restored.

MicroPower PASCAL and RT-11

A procedure that saves the hardware and software environment of a process that has lost control of the CPU and establishes similar information.

VAX/VMS

Interrupting the activity in progress and switching to another activity. Context switching occurs as one process after another is scheduled for execution. The operating system saves the hardware context of the interrupted process in its PCB using the Save Process Context instruction, loads the hardware PCP of another process into the hardware context using the Load Process Context instruction, scheduling that process for execution.

context variable *n.*

Rdb/ELN

A dummy variable, declared in an Rdb/ELN record selection expression for the purpose of identifying the source of fields in a record stream.

contiguous area *n.*

VAX/VMS

A group of physically adjacent blocks.

contiguous file *n.*

generic

A file on a mass storage device whose blocks from beginning to end are next to each other.

continuation bucket *n.*

RSX-11M

An indexed file bucket containing part of a series of data records with the same key value. Duplicate series can exist only in level 0 buckets. When a duplicate series grows beyond a single bucket, RMS-11 continues it in a separate continuation bucket that is not represented by an entry in level 1. All records in a continuation bucket contain the same key value.

continuation character *n.*

VAX/VMS

A hyphen placed at the end of a command line, which allows the user to continue the command string on the next line after the RETURN key is pressed.

continued MFD *n.*

DECsystem-10

The master file directories (MFDs) on all file structures in the job's search list. See also MFD.

continued SFD *n.*

DECsystem-10

The subfile directories (SFDs) on all file structures in the job's search list that have the same name and path. See also SFD and subfile directory.

continued UFD *n.*

DECsystem-10

The user file directories (UFDs) for the same project-programmer number on all file structures in the job's search list.

continuous-form paper *n.*

Publications/generic

A long, continuous sheet of paper separated into pages by perforations. Same as fanfold paper.

continuous sweep *n.*

MINC

A condition in which a sweep proceeds indefinitely because the call for the sweep gives no provision for stopping the sweep. Same as indefinite sweep.

CONTROL *n.*

PEARL

An object that defines an operation to be applied to data during data transfer.

control and status register (CSR) *n.*

Memory Resident RT-11, MicroPower PASCAL, and RT-11

A peripheral interface that controls the operation of an I/O device, and monitors its status. Control information output to this register can enable interrupts, start operation, perform a desired function, and assume certain operating characteristics. Status information input from this register includes error and type of error, ready for or done operation, and other device-specific status information. Same as CSR.

control break *n.*

generic

A change in the value of a data item that is referenced in the CONTROL clause. More generally, a change in the value of a data item that is used to control the hierarchical structure of as report.

control break level *n.*

generic

The relative position within a control hierarchy at which the most major control break occurred.

control buffer *n.*

DECnet

A data block used by the RSX-11/3271 Protocol Emulator (PE) and DECnet to manage and schedule communications processes for transfers of information between processes. Same as communication control block (CCB).

control channel *n.*

PEARL

The channel of a DATAWAY along which controls are transferred.

control character *n.*

generic

A character whose purpose is to control an action such as linespacing, paging or termination of a job. Control characters do not usually print unless the operating system converts them for display.

DECnet

A character whose occurrence in a particular context initiates, modifies, or stops a control function. In the ASCII code, any of the 32 characters in the first two columns of the standard code table are control characters. In EBCDIC code there are also special characters used for control functions. See also communications control character.

control data item *n.*

generic

A data item, a change in whose contents may produce a control break.

control field *n.*

Common Data Dictionary

A program record field, also specified in a TDMS (Terminal Data Management System) request, whose value determines whether or not TDMS executes a conditional instruction. See also conditional instruction.

control file *n.*

TOPS-10 and TOPS-20

A file supplied by the user to define the operating parameters of a function to be performed by a utility.

control footing *n.*

generic

A report group that is presented at the end of the control group of which it is a member.

control heading *n.*

generic

A report group that is presented at the beginning of the control group of which it is a member.

control hierarchy *n.*

generic

A designated sequence of report subdivisions defined by the positional order of FINAL and the data-names within a CONTROL clause.

control key *n.*

VAX/VMS

The keyboard character that causes a control action. A control key is usually the combination of the CTRL key and an alphabetic key, for example, CTRL/Y.

control length *n.*

VAX DBMS

The length of the prefix portion of a record occurrence and all data items up to and including the last sort of CALC key item.

controller *n.*

DIGITAL-specific

A hardware line device that manages communications over a line. Controllers can be point-to-point, multipoint, or multiple line controllers (also called multiplexers). See also emulated control unit.

Ethernet

The implementation unit that connects a station to the Ethernet, typically comprising part of the physical layer, much or all of the data link layer, and appropriate electronics for interfacing to the station.

generic

A device that directs the operation of other devices connected to it.

controller data channel *n.*

VAX/VMS

A logical path to which a driver for a device on a multidevice controller must be granted access before it can activate a device.

controller name *n.*

DIGITAL-specific

All file structures residing on a specific controller. In particular, the names "DPA:" or "FHB:".

control level *n.*

GIGI

The level invoked after control keys are used. The control keys are ATTRIBUTE, ALTER, ENTER, and the key.

control link *n.*

DECnet and TOPS-20

Specific to ARPANET, the particular link between one Host and another used for communication between NCPs (network control processors).

control mode *n.*

DECnet

The situation that exists when the transmitter has ended transmission and has signaled line turnaround. In this condition the former receiver can now bid for control of the line.

control procedure *n.*

DECnet

The means used to control the orderly communication of information between stations on a data link. See also protocol.

control region *n.*

VAX/VMS

The higher-addressed half of process space (the P1 region). Control region virtual addresses refer to the process-related information used by the system to control processes such as the kernel, executive, and supervisor stacks; the permanent I/O channels; exception vectors; and dynamically used system procedures (such as the command interpreter). The user stack is normally found in the control region.

control region base register (P1BR) *n.*

VAX/VMS

The processor register, or its equivalent in a hardware process control block, that contains the base virtual address of a process control region page table.

control region length register (P1LR) *n.*

VAX/VMS

The processor register, or its equivalent in a hardware process control block, that contains the number of nonexistent page table entries for virtual pages in a process control region.

control section *n.*

generic

An identified, contiguous unit of software code which can be moved without damage to program logic.

TOPS-10

A unit of code (instructions and/or data) that is considered an entity and that can be relocated separately at load time without destroying the logic of the program. Control is passed properly from one control section to another regardless of their relative positions in user virtual address space. A control section is identified by a relocation counter and thus is the smallest unit of code that can be relocated separately.

control statement *n.*

CTS-300

An element (line or lines) of a control file. Each control statement has a prescribed syntax.

PASCAL and VAX PASCAL

The statement that directs the flow of control in a program, such as the IF-THEN-ELSE, FOR, WHILE, or CASE statements.

control station *n.*

DECnet

On a network, the station that supervises the network control procedures such as polling, selecting, and recovery. A control station is also responsible for establishing order on the line if contention or any other abnormal situation arises between any stations on the network. In the RSX-11/3271 Protocol Emulator (PE) environment, the host's transmission control unit (TCU) acts as a control station. See also tributary station.

VAX/VMS

The network node at the controlling end of a multipoint circuit. The control station controls the tributaries for that circuit.

control status register (CSR) *n.*

DECnet

A register containing a unique set of UNIBUS addresses to which a device controller responds. Same as CSR.

VAX/VMS

A register for the control/status of a device or controller. The CSR resides in the processor's I/O space. Same as CSR.

control structure *n.*

RSX-11M

A part of virtual memory used by RMS-11 routines to communicate with the program and with each other. See also I/O buffer and user buffer.

control variable *n.*

PASCAL

A scalar variable that takes on sequential values with each iteration of a FOR loop. After completion of the loop, the value of the control variable is undefined.

VAX PASCAL

A scalar variable that takes on sequential values with each iteration of a FOR loop. After normal completion of the loop, the value of the control variable is undefined.

VAX PL/I

A variable whose value is modified for each iteration of a DO-group and which may be tested to determine whether or not the statements in the DO-group are to be executed.

conversational *adj.*

generic

Pertaining to two-way communication.

conversion *n.*

VAX PL/I and VAX/VMS

The changing of a value from one data type to another. Conversions take place in assignments by changing the type of the right operand's result to that of the object referred to by the left operand; that type is also the type of the assignment expression itself. Conversions are also performed when arguments are passed to functions: CHAR and SHORT become INT; FLOAT becomes DOUBLE. Conversions can also be forced by means of a cast.

convert *v.*

RSX-11M

To use the RMSCNV utility to copy data from one file to another. Since the files may have different attributes, the data must be converted from its input form to the proper output form.

converter *n.*

generic

A device capable of changing power from one mode to another, such as analog to digital, parallel to serial, or ac to dc.

cooperating tasks *n.*

DECnet and VAX/VMS

Two tasks that communicate with each other in a task-to-task communication environment are called cooperating tasks. In particular, they must agree on optional user data to be passed, how they will send and receive messages to ensure that there is one transmit for each receive, and which task will disconnect the link.

coordinate *n.*

generic

A number used to specify the location or point on a line.

coordinate pair *n.*

generic

An x-coordinate and a y-coordinate that together define a location.

coordinates *n.*

generic

Parameters for specifying the location of a pixel by using an x-, y-pair to specify horizontal and vertical position or direction.

COPY field description statement *n.*

Common Data Dictionary

A CDDL (common data definition language) statement that inserts the field descriptions of existing records into the descriptions of new records.

copy-on-reference *n.*

VAX/VMS

A method used in memory management for sharing data until a process accesses it; the data is copied and made private before the access. Copy-on-reference allows sharing of the initial values of a global section whose pages have read/write access but contain pre-initialized data available to many processes.

core *n.*

generic

A configuration of magnetic material using an induced magnetic field for the purpose of storing data.

core common *n.*

RSTS/E

A data area in the RSTS/E user job's memory area that is used to exchange data between the monitor and the job or between programs running under the same job number. Same as common memory.

core memory *n.*

generic

A type of memory that stores data as magnetic fields on small iron rings.

co-routine *n.*

generic

One of two or more parts of the same program that appear to be running in the same place at the time. Co-routines run independently of each other.

corporate resolution *n.*

USFC/generic

A properly executed legal document that defines the authority of an Officer to obligate the Corporation.

cost *n.*

generic

A monetary measure of the amount of resources used for some purpose.

VAX/VMS

An integer value assigned to a circuit between two adjacent nodes. According to the routing algorithm, data packets are routed on paths with the lowest cost.

cost of capital *n.*

generic

The cost of using debt and equity capital; interest.

cost of sales *n.*

generic

The cost of merchandise sold or services performed.

co-tree *n.*

VAX/VMS

A unit of one or more secondary tree structures within a multiple tree overlay structure. When a co-tree's root segment contains code or data, the root segment of the co-tree is made resident in physical memory through calls to the overlay run-time routines.

counted string *n.*

VAX PSI

A data structure consisting of a byte-sized length followed by the string.

VAX/VMS

A character-string data structure consisting of a byte-sized length followed by the string. Although a counted string is not used as a procedure argument, it is a convenient representation in memory.

counter *n.*

BASIC

A variable for storing a value and allowing that value to be increased or decreased as directed by program instructions. A counter is often used to control the number of times a loop is executed.

generic

A register or storage location that records the number of times an event occurs.

counters *n.*

DECnet and VAX/VMS

Performance and error statistics kept for a component (e.g., line or node counters).

counting semaphore *n.*

MicroPower PASCAL

A global variable whose value varies between 0 and some number greater than 1. Counting semaphores are managed by the kernel in response to requests from processes. Each counting semaphore can have a queue of waiting processes.

CP/M® *n.*

Rainbow™

1. CP/M® is a registered trademark of Digital Research, Inc.

2. One of the operating systems used in many personal computers.

CP/OSS *n.*

ALL-IN-1

Charlotte Package/Office Systems Services. DIGITAL's original Office Automation System which was enhanced to become ALL-IN-1.

CPU *n.*

generic

The abbreviation for central processing unit. CPU is the main unit of a computer that contains the circuits controlling interpretation and execution of instructions. Same as central processing unit and central processor.

crash *adj.*

generic

Pertaining to a catastrophic failure of a computer system.

crash *n.*

generic

1. A catastrophic failure of a computer system.

2. In a disk drive, the heads touching the recording surface.

VAX/VMS

The system's response to an unstable condition, particularly if the system is corrupted. Rather than continuing to operate and possibly damaging itself, the system stops functioning. There is no concrete indication of a system crash at a user terminal; if the system has crashed, however, users will be unable to use their terminals. See also hanging.

CRB *n.*

VAX/VMS

The abbreviation for channel request block. A structure for the I/O database that describes the activity on a particular controller. The channel request block for a controller contains pointers to the wait queue of drivers ready to access a device through the controller.

CRC *n.*

DECnet and VAX/VMS

The abbreviation for cyclic redundancy check. An error detection scheme in which a receiver checks each block of data for errors. The check character is generated by taking the remainder after dividing all the serialized bits in a block of data by a predetermined binary number. The check character is compared with the transmitter-generated check character. If the check characters do not match, retransmission of the block of data is requested. See also cyclic redundancy check.

credit *v.*

generic

To make an entry on the right side of an account.

USFC/generic

Refers to an agreement to allow immediate use of goods and services with payment deferred until an agreed future date.

credit memorandum *n.*

generic

A document used by a seller to inform a buyer that the buyer's account receivable is being debited (reduced) because of errors, returns, or allowances.

creditor *n.*

generic

A party who lends money or extends credit to an entity.

critical section *n.*

MicroPower PASCAL

A portion of a process that must complete before a specific portion of another process can execute.

cross operation *n.*

Rdb/ELN

A procedure that selects a record from one relation, associates it with a record from another relation, and presents both as though they were part of a single record. Same as join operation.

cross product *n.*

The simplest form of a join operation. Same as cartesian product.

cross-reference listing *n.*

DIGITAL-specific

A printed listing that identifies all references to each specific symbol in a program. A cross-reference listing includes a list of all symbols used in a source program and the statements where they are defined or used.

cross-reference table or listing *n.*

generic

A printed table or listing that identifies all uses of addresses, registers or storage locations within a program.

crosstalk *n.*

generic

Communication or signals that are not wanted. See also noise and distortion.

CRT *n.*

VAX/VMS

Cathode ray tube. See also terminal.

CSMA/CD *n.*

DECnet

The abbreviation for carrier-sense multiple access with collision detection. A distributed channel allocation procedure in which every station can receive all other stations' transmissions. Each station awaits an idle channel before transmitting, and each station can detect overlapping transmissions by other stations. Same as carrier-sense multiple access with collision detection.

CSR *n.*

VAX/VMS

The abbreviation for control/status register. A register for the control/status of a device or controller. CSR resides in the processor's I/O space. Same as control/status register.

CUG *n.*

VAX PSI and VAX/VMS

The abbreviation for closed user group. An optional PSDN (packet switching data network) facility that restricts two or more DTEs in the same group to communicating with each other. The basic CUG also prevents these DTEs (data terminal equipment) from accessing or being accessed by other DTEs outside the group. Additions to the basic CUG facility allow one or more DTEs to access or be accessed by DTEs outside the group. These additions are known as CUG with outgoing access and CUG with incoming access respectively. Same as closed user group.

currency indicators *n.*

VAX DBMS

DBMS printers that serve as place markers in the database for the Database Control System (DBCS) and the run unit.

currency sign *n.*

VAX COBOL

The character "$" of the COBOL character set.

currency status indicators *n.*

VAX DBMS

Single-word registers that record the database of the record that is current-of-run unit, current-of-record, current-of-set, and current-of-area.

currency symbol *n.*

VAX COBOL

The character defined by the CURRENCY SIGN clause in the SPECIAL-NAMES paragraph. If there is no CURRENCY SIGN clause, the currency symbol is identical to the currency sign.

current *n.*

VAX DATATRIEVE and VAX DBMS

A command that:

1. in DBMS, identifies which database records or positions are being used as currency indicators

2. in DATATRIEVE, identifies the most recently formed collection.

See also collection.

current access mode *n.*

VAX/VMS

The processor access mode of the currently executing software. The current mode field of the processor status longword indicates the access mode of the currently executing software.

current assets *n.*

generic

Cash and assets that are expected to be converted into cash or used up in the near future, usually within one year.

current character *n.*

generic

The decimal value of the character you are editing or last edited.

Current Document block *n.*

ALL-IN-1

In the Document Processing Subsystem, the portion of the screen that displays a File Cabinet document that is available for work.

current liabilities *n.*

generic

Obligations that become due within a short time, usually one year.

current location counter *n.*

DIGITAL-specific

A counter kept by an assembler to determine the address assigned to an instruction or constant that is being assembled.

Current Message block *n.*

ALL-IN-1

In the Electronic Mail Subsystem, the portion of the screen that displays a File Cabinet message that is available for work.

current position *n.*

generic

A value that specifies the pixel location at which an editing operation occurs in the Edit Buffer.

current replacement cost *n.*

generic

The amount currently required to acquire an identical asset in the same condition and with the same service potential as the asset being replaced.

cursor *n.*

generic

A blinking line or figure on the screen that indicates where the next character the user types will appear.

CUSP *n.*

RSTS/E and TOPS-10

The abbreviation for commonly-used system program. A program included as part of the RSTS/E operating system. CUSPs perform common functions such as copying, deleting, and printing files. Same as commonly-used system program.

customer information control system/virtual storage (CICS/VS) *n.*

DECnet

A proprietary software product of IBM Corporation serving as a data communications interface between transcription applications and S/360 or S/370 operating systems. Same as CICS/VS.

customize *v.*

A-to-Z

To add features to an application that are unique to your own organization, such as a company header on a form.

cutoff *n.*

generic

The point of operation in a semiconductor device or a vacuum tube where current does not flow.

CX *n.*

DECWORD

The abbreviation for character transfer. CX is a communication option that transfers one character at a time among the DECWORD keyboard, the DECWORD screen, stored documents, and another computer, called the host. CX can be used to make a DECWORD terminal act as though it were connected to the host. Same as character transfer.

cycle (logarithmic) *n.*

RGL/FEP

The numbers in a single power of ten.

cycle time *n.*

generic

The time to read (and restore) a single word in main memory.

cyclic redundancy check (CRC) *n.*

DIGITAL-specific

An error detection scheme in which the receiver checks each block of data for errors. The check character is generated by taking the remainder after dividing all the serialized bits in a block of data by a predetermined binary number. The check character is compared with the transmitter-generated check character. If the check characters do not match, retransmission of the block of data is requested. Same as CRC.

cylinder *n.*

VAX/VMS

The tracks at the same radius on all recording surfaces of a disk.

DACTLU *n.*

DECnet

The acronym for deactivate logical unit. An SNA (systems network architecture) session control request issued by the SSCP (system services control point). SSCP is a command processor in the S/370 SNA access method that controls system resources. A successfully executed DACTLU terminates an SSCP-LU session and any LU-LU sessions in which the LU (logical unit) participates. The LU addressed in the command is then no longer available to the system. The characteristics of an SSCP-LU session are defined by the FM Profile 0, TS Profile 1 protocol set. Same as deactivate logical unit.

DACTPU *n.*

DECnet

The acronym for deactivate physical unit. An SNA (systems network architecture) session control request issued by the SSCP (system services control point). SSCP is a command processor in the S/370 SNA access method that controls system resources. A successfully executed DACTPU terminates an SSCP-PU session and all SSCP-LU and LU-LU sessions for the LUs (logical unit) controlled by the PU (physical unit). The PU addressed in the command is then no longer available to the system. The characteristics of an SSCP-PU session are defined by the FM Profile 0, TS Profile 1 protocol set. To SSCP, the protocol emulator is a physical unit. Same as deactivate physical unit.

damping *n.*

generic

The process of suppressing vibration or oscillation.

DAP *n.*

DECnet

The abbreviation for data access protocol. A set of standardized formats and procedures that facilitate the creation, deletion, transfer, and access of files between a user process and a file system in a network environment. Same as data access protocol.

Darlington amplifier *n.*

generic

A two-transistor amplifier having its collectors connected and the emitter of the input transistor connected to the base of the second transistor.

data *n.*

generic

Information that can be processed and/or produced by computers.

VAX/VMS

A general term referring to any representation of facts, concepts, or instructions in a form suitable for communication, interpretation, or processing.

DATA *n.*

generic

A statement that lists values to be assigned to READ statement variables.

data access protocol (DAP) *n.*

DECnet

In the network application layer of DNA (DIGITAL Network Architecture), the protocol used for remote file access and transfer. Same as DAP.

data base (or database) *n.*

generic

generic

A collection of interrelated data on one or more mass storage devices. The collection is organized to facilitate efficient and accurate inquiry and update.

VAX/VMS

1. All the occurrences of data described by a database management system.

2. A collection of related data structures.

database administrator (DBA) *n.*

generic

The person or group of people responsible for planning, designing, implementing, and maintaining a database. Same as DBA.

database control system (DBCS) *n.*

VAX DBMS

The DBMS component that, together with the VAX/VMS operating system, provides run-time control of database processing. Same as DBCS.

database declaration *n.*

Rdb/ELN

In a VAXELN Pascal program that accesses an Rdb/ELN database, the reference to the external file that contains the database.

database handle *n.*

Rdb/ELN

A variable name used in several EPILOG statements and clauses to uniquely identify a database.

database key (Dbkey) *n.*

VAX DBMS

In DBMS, a unique value that identifies a record in a database. The Database Control System assigns the value to a record when it is stored in the database. Although user run units cannot directly access database keys, they are used by the Database Control System whenever users store, retrieve, or manipulate a record. Same as Dbkey.

data base management *n.*

generic

A systematic approach to storing, updating, and retrieval of information stored as data items, usually in the form of records in a file, where many users, or even many remote installations, will use common data banks.

database management system (DBMS) *n.*

DIGITAL-specific

A system for creating, maintaining, and accessing a collection of interrelated data records that may be processed by one or more applications without regard to physical storage. VAX DBMS is a DIGITAL software product that complies with the standards for database management systems established by CODASYL. Same as DBMS.

generic

A software package that organizes and maintains a data base.

database pages *n.*

VAX DBMS

The structures used to store and locate data in a DBMS database. Database pages consist of one or more disk blocks of 512 bytes each. DBMS uses page-clustered I/O, a technique that retrieves groups of physically-related database pages, rather than an individual page, in response to a run-unit's request for data. See also page header.

database query (DBQ) *n.*

VAX DBMS

A DBMS utility that interprets data manipulation statements. DBQ provides access to data through both interactive and callable modes. Interactive DBQ is a DBMS query language. Callable DBQ provides access to the database for programs written in high-level languages. Same as DBQ. See also callable DBQ and interactive DBQ.

database remote interconnect (DRI) *n.*

Rdb/ELN

The outermost layer of the Digital Standard Relational Interface. DRI provides the protocol for dealing with interprocess and interprocessor communication. Same as DRI.

data bits per character *n.*

PRO/Communications

The number of bits a computer uses to represent a keyboard character. Computers that are exchanging information must use the same number of data bits per character.

data bucket *n.*

RSX-11M

A bucket in an indexed file that contains either user data records or SIDRs (secondary index data records). See also index bucket.

data cache *n.*

RSTS/E

The area of the extended buffer pool that stores information relating to RSTS/E read operations. Using the data cache reduces the number of data transfers from the disk.

data circuit-terminating equipment (DCE) *n.*

VAX PSI and VAX/VMS

A CCITT X.25 term referring to the network equipment that provides functions to establish, maintain, and terminate a connection and handle the signal conversion and coding between the data terminal equipment and the network. The switching exchange of the network to which DTEs (data terminal equipment) are connected. (In non-X.25 usage, the term is synonymous with "modem.") Same as DCE.

data clause *n.*

generic

A clause in a data description entry that describes an attribute of a data item.

data communication equipment (DCE) *n.*

DECnet

The equipment that provides the functions required to establish, maintain, and terminate a connection, the signal conversion, and coding required for communication between data terminal equipment and data circuit. The data communication equipment may or may not be an integral part of a computer. See also data terminal equipment and data link. Same as DCE.

Data Definition Languages (DDL) *n.*

DBMS

In VAX-11 DBMS, the languages used to describe schemas, subschemas, and storage schemas. Same as DDL.

data definition language utility *n.*

Common Data Dictionary and VAX DBMS

The VAX CDD (Common Data Dictionary) utility that lets users insert record definitions into the CDD. Users create the data descriptions in a CDDL (common data definition language) source file and compile the source file with the CDDL compiler. See also CDDL.

data file *n.*

generic

A file that contains information used in data processing.

datagram *n.*

DECnet

A unit of data passed between transport and the network services layer. When a route header is added, the datagram becomes a packet.

VAX PSI

A packet sent through a PSN (packet switching network) that is completely independent of all other packets so far as the network is is concerned, except possibly in respect to its order of transmission.

VAX/VMS

A unit of data sent over the network that is handled independently of all other units of data so far as the network is concerned. When a route header is added, a datagram becomes a packet.

data integrity *n.*

DIGITAL-specific

Preservation of data or programs by safeguarding against information loss due to hardware or software failures.

data item occurrence *n.*

VAX DBMS

One occurrence of a data item type. See also record instance, record occurrence, and data item type.

data item type *n.*

VAX DBMS

The smallest unit of defined data. A data item type can represent a single value or an array of one or more values. See also record instance, record type and data item occurrence.

data level *n.*

RSX-11M

The lowest level of an index, containing data buckets. See also index level and lowest index level.

data link *n.*

DECnet

A logical connection between two stations on the same channel. A multipoint line can have multiple data links. See also data communication equipment and data terminal equipment.

data-link control characters *n.*

DECnet

The characters used in the BSC (binary synchronous communication) protocol to control the transmission of data between stations.

data-link escape (DLE) *n.*

DECnet

A BISYNC control character sequence used exclusively to provide supplementary line-control signals. It is a two-character sequence where the first character is DLE. The second character varies according to the function desired and the code used. Same as DLE.

data-link layer *n.*

Ethernet

The highest of the two layers of the Ethernet specification that uses a medium-independent, link-level communication facility on top of the physical channel provided by the physical layers.

DECnet

The layer in which the modules create a communication path between adjacent nodes. Data-link modules ensure the integrity of data transferred across the path. Data-link modules for Ethernet local area networks, X.25 public data networks, and synchronous or asynchronous lines execute simultaneously and independently in this layer.

data link mapping (DLM) *n.*

VAX/VMS

Capability of using an X.25 virtual circuit as a DECnet data link.

data manipulation facility *n.*

VAX DATATRIEVE

The part of DATATRIEVE that parses, optimizes, and executes all commands and statements passed to DATATRIEVE.

Data Manipulation Language (DML) *n.*

DBMS

In DBMS, the statements that permit programs written in VAX-11 languages to access the database. Same as DML.

data mode *n.*

PRO/Communications

A setting on a modem that allows operators to use the modem to transmit data in the form of audio tones across a communications line.

data-name *n.*

VAX COBOL

A user-defined word that names a data item described in a data description entry. In general formats, "data-name" represents a word that must not be reference-modified, subscripted, indexed or qualified unless specifically allowed by rules of the format.

data overrun *n.*

MINC

A condition in which the system cannot process data at the requested rate. A data overrun is not detected until the processing of the data begins.

data pathway *n.*

PEARL

One or more DATA STATIONs (called DATIONs) optionally connected by INTERFACES. The data pathway enables a PEARL program to communicate with external (hardware) devices.

data phase *n.*

FMS

In the Form Editor, a phase in which named data items are associated with a form. Refer to named data.

data positions *n.*

FMS

Alterable character positions; within a field, the location denoted by a validation character where an operator can type data or an application program can display information. See also field length.

data processing *n.*

generic

The handling of information in a sequence of logical steps or operations.

data record *n.*

DIGITAL-specific

The record that a user program provides in its user buffer including RMS-11 overhead; the logical unit of data actively stored in a file. Same as user data record. See also index record.

dataset *n.*

PEARL

A collection of data items that travels along the
DATA CHANNEL of DATAWAY.

DATA STATION *n.*

PEARL

An object that defines an identifiable point in an
INPUT/OUTPUT network and that describes its
characteristics. It can be either PEARL-defined
(device) or user defined. Same as DATION.

data stream *n.*

DECnet

All data transmitted through a channel in a single
READ or WRITE operation to a display station or
printer.

data structure *n.*

VAX/VMS

Any table, list, array, queue, or tree whose format
and access conventions are well defined for reference by one or more images.

data terminal equipment (DTE) *n.*

DECnet

1. The equipment comprising the data source,
   the data sink, or both.

2. Equipment usually comprising the following
   functional units: control logic, buffer store, and
   one or more input or output devices or computers. It may also contain error control, synchronization, and station identification capability.

Same as DTE. See also data communications
equipment and data link.

VAX PSI

A CCITT term referring to the user's equipment
(computer or terminal) connected to a DCE on a
packet switching network for the purpose of sending and/or receiving data. Same as DTE.

VAX/VMS

An X.25 term referring to the user's equipment
(computer or terminal) connected to a DCE on a
packet switching data network for the purpose of
sending and/or receiving data.

data terminal ready (DTR) *n.*

DECnet

A control signal (applicable to the RS232) that
enters a modem from the data terminal or communications device that is using the modem. When
the signal is set, it informs the modem that the
data terminal equipment is ready to transmit and
receive data. When the signal is clear, the data
terminal equipment is not ready. Same as DTR.

data transmission *n.*

DECnet

The interchange of data messages from one point
to another over communications channels. See
also data communication.

DATATRIEVE *n.*

DIGITAL-specific

A data management language for manipulating, storing, and modifying records from VAX/RMS data files and VAX DBMS databases.

data type *n.*

DIGITAL-specific

A characteristic assigned to a field that determines the kind of data the field can contain. In TDMS (Terminal Data Management System), users determine the data type of a form field in the field identifiers and field validators of the form definition. Users determine the data type of a record field in the data type statement of a record definition.

generic

Referring to the classification of data as either alpha or decimal.

VAX PL/I

Class to which a data item belongs, for example, fixed-point decimal or character string. The data type of a variable determines the operations that can be performed on it.

VAX/VMS

In general, the way in which bits are grouped and interpreted. In reference to the processor instructions, the data type of an operand identifies the size of the operand and the significance of the bits in the operand. Operand data types include byte, work, longword, and quadword integer; floating and double-floating character string; packed decimal strings; and variable-length bit field.

DATAWAY *n.*

PEARL

One or more DATA STATION optionally connected by INTERFACEs. The DATAWAY enables the PEARL program to communicate with external (hardware) devices. Same as data pathway.

DATE$ *n.*

generic

A built-in function that returns a string containing the current day, month, and year.

DATION *n.*

PEARL

An object that defines an identifiable point in an input-output network and that describes its characteristics. It can be either PEARL-defined (device) or user-defined. Same as DATA STATION.

DBA *n.*

generic

The abbreviation for database administrator. DBA refers to the person or group of people responsible for planning, designing, implementing, and maintaining a database. Same as database administrator.

DBCS *n.*

VAX DBMS

The abbreviation for Database Control System. The portion of DBMS that, together with the host operating system, accesses the database. Same as Database Control System.

Dbkey *n.*

VAX DBMS

The abbreviation for database key. A key whose value is assigned by the Database Control System to uniquely identify a record within the database. Same as database key.

DBMS *n.*

DIGITAL-specific

The abbreviation for database management system. A system for creating, maintaining, and accessing a collection of interrelated data items that may be processed by one or more applications without regard to physical storage. In a database management system, logical relationships among records are established. Data is described independently of application programs, providing ease in application development, data security, and data visibility to management personnel. Same as database management system.

DBQ *n.*

VAX DBMS

The abbreviation for database query. A DBMS utility that interprets data manipulation statements. DBQ provides access to data through both interactive and callable modes. Interactive DBQ is a DBMS query language. Callable DBQ provides access to the database for programs written in high-level languages. Same as database query. See also callable DBQ and interactive DBQ.

DBR *n.*

VAX DBMS

The abbreviation for database recovery. In DBMS, the name of the process that performs database recovery. It is called by the monitor at restart. Same as database recovery.

DCE *n.*

VAX PSI and VAX/VMS

The abbreviation for data circuit-terminating equipment. A CCITT X.25 term referring to the network equipment that provides functions to establish, maintain, and terminate a connection and handle the signal conversion and coding between the data terminal equipment and the network. The switching exchange of the network to which DTEs (data terminal equipment) are connected. (In non-X.25 usage, the term is synonymous with "modem.") Same as data circuit-terminating equipment.

DCE *n.*

DECnet

The abbreviation for data communication equipment. The equipment that provides the functions required to establish, maintain, and terminate a connection, the signal conversion, and coding required for communication between data terminal equipment and data circuit. The data communication equipment may or may not be an integral part of a computer. Same as data communication equipment. See also data terminal equipment and data link.

VAX/VMS

The abbreviation for data circuit-terminating equipment. A CCITT X.25 term referring to the network equipment that provides functions to establish, maintain, and terminate a connection and handle the signal conversion and coding between the data terminal equipment and the network. The switching exchange of the network to which DTEs (data terminal equipment) are connected. (In non-X.25 usage, the term is synonymous with "modem.")

DCL *n.*

DIGITAL-specific

The abbreviation for DIGITAL Command Language. DCL is the standard command interface to DIGITAL's major operating systems. Same as DIGITAL Command Language.

DCL (DIGITAL Command Language) Server *n.*

DIGITAL-specific

One of two types of servers used to handle processing work for tasks. A DCL server handles images, DATATRIEVE commands, and DCL commands and command procedures.

DCL (DIGITAL Command Language) Server Image *n.*

DIGITAL-specific

The image, provided by ACMS, that is loaded into a DCL server process when the process is started by the execution controller.

VAX/VMS

The abbreviation for device data block. A structure that identifies the generic device/controller name, driver name, and location for a set of devices connected to a single controller.

DDCMP *n.*

DECnet

The abbreviation for Digital Data Communications Message Protocol. DDCMP is a formal set of conventions designed to provide error-free, sequential transmission of data over physical links. Same as Digital Data Communications Message Protocol.

DDL *n.*

VAX DBMS and VAX/VMS

The abbreviation for data definition languages. The languages used to describe schemas, subschemas, and storage schemas. Same as data definition languages. See also schema DDL, storage schema, and subschema.

DDL *n.*

DBMS

The abbreviation for data definition language. DDL is the language used to describe schemas, subschemas, and storage schemas in VAX-11 DBMS. Same as data definition language.

DDT *n.*

DIGITAL-specific

The abbreviation for DIBOL debugging technique. DDT is a program used for interactive dialog, control, and analysis of DIBOL program operations. Same as DIBOL debugging technique.

VAX/VMS

The abbreviation for driver dispatch table. DDT is a program used for interactive dialog, control, and analysis of DIBOL program operations. Same as DIBOL debugging technique.

deadlock *n.*

generic

A situation in which two or more processes request the same set of resources and there is no method for resolving the conflict.

debit *n.*

generic

The left side of an account or an amount entered on the left side.

debt *n.*

generic

An amount owed by an entity, usually evidenced by a document and usually with a specified payment date.

debtor *n.*

generic

A party who owes money to an entity.

debug *v.*

generic

To detect, find, and correct malfunctions in a program or computer system.

debugger *n.*

VAX/VMS

A program that aids a programmer in finding errors in other programs. Same as symbolic debugger.

decibel *n.*

generic

A measurement used to compare the power of two sounds.

decimal-aligned tab *n.*

generic

The column where the decimal point in a number will be aligned as it is typed.

decimal character *n.*

generic

A subset of the ASCII character set that contains the digits 0 through 9. When defined as decimal, the digits contain the value that they represent.

decimal field *n.*

generic

A field defined to contain only signed decimal data.

decimal overflow (DV) *n.*

VAX/VMS

A trap enable bit in the processor status word (PSW). Same as DV.

declaration *n.*

generic

The process of naming and describing units of information in a program. Units of information may include variables, constants, buffers, system library routines, etc.

PEARL

A definition of an object that sets up an access function for the object and allocates space for the object.

VAX PASCAL

A specification that lists one or more labels or associates an identifier with what it represents. With VAX PASCAL labels and identifiers for constants, types, variables, procedures, and functions must be declared.

VAX PL/I

An explicit or contextual specification of an identifier and its data type.

VAX/VMS

A statement that gives the characteristics (such as data type) of one or more variables.

declaration section *n.*

MicroPower PASCAL

A program specification that lists one or more labels or associates an identifier with the class of data types it represents. In PASCAL, labels and identifiers for constants, functions, procedures, types, and variables must be declared. The part of a program or subprogram block that contains the declarations is called the declaration section.

PASCAL

The part of a program or subprogram block the contains the declaration and definitions.

declare *v.*

generic

To name and describe a unit of information in a program.

DECmail *n.*

DIGITAL-specific

One of DIGITAL's Electronic Mail systems.

DECmate *n.*

DIGITAL-specific

A DIGITAL minicomputer standalone system that can be connected to other systems.

DECnet *n.*

DIGITAL-specific

The DIGITAL software facility that enables a user to access information on a remote computer via telecommunications lines.

DECnet *n.*

DIGITAL-specific

DIGITAL networking software that runs on nodes in both local and wide-area networks.

decoder *n.*

generic

A person or thing that changes information in code to a usable form.

decollate *v.*

generic

To separate one or more ordered sets from a larger ordered set.

decrement *v.*

generic

To decrease a numeric value by a specific amount; to decrease the numerical contents of a counter.

decryption *n.*

VAX/VMS

The process that restores encoded information to its original unencoded form.

DECtype *n.*

DIGITAL-specific

A DIGITAL word processing system.

dedicate *v.*

generic

To reserve a computer resource for the use of only one application program.

dedicated *adj.*

VAX/VMS

aPertaining to a system resource—an I/O device, image, or the entire system—that is assigned to a single application or purpose.

dedicated line *n.*

DECnet

A nonswitched communications channel permanently connected between two or more data stations.

deenergize (or de-energize) *v.*

generic

To remove power from a device.

DEF *n.*

generic

A statement that defines a single-line or multi-line function.

default *n.*

DIGITAL-specific

Information that the operating system assumes as input if the information is not explicitly provided.

generic

The value of an argument, field, or part of a command line assumed by a program if a specific value is not supplied by the user.

VAX/VMS

A value of operation that is automatically included in a command, unless the user specifies otherwise. In most cases, default settings will be what is "normal" or "expected."

USFC/generic

Failure to meet a lease obligation.

default dictionary directory *n.*

Common Data Dictionary

The CDD (Common Data Dictionary) directory assigned when users invoke an image that uses the CDD. This directory becomes the starting directory for path names. Users can define a directory as the default by assigning a path name to the VAX/VMS logical name CDD$DEFAULT. If a user does not, the default directory is CDD$TOP. The CDD dictionary management utility and some command qualifiers allow users to set temporary default directories. Users can also set the default directory with the DATATRIEVE SET DICTIONARY command.

VAX DATATRIEVE

The directory of the CDD (Common Data Dictionary) that the user is in at any one moment. The system assumes that directory as the default directory. The user can refer to the domains, records, tables, or procedures in the default dictionary directory by typing the simplest forms of their dictionary path names.

default directory *n.*

DECsystem-10 and FMS

The directory in which the monitor searches when a directory specification has not been given by the user.

default disk *n.*

VAX/VMS

The disk from which the system reads and to which the system writes (by default) all files that the user creates. The default is used whenever a file specification in a command does not explicitly name a device.

default extension *n.*

CTS-300

The device extension assigned by the system if no extension is specified by the user.

default extension quantity *n.*

RSX-11M

The number of blocks that RMS-11 requests the file processor to add to a file when RMS-11 must extend the file automatically to complete a record operation. See also allocation and extend.

default keyboard monitor *n.*

RSTS/E

The main keyboard monitor in which a user works. The user enters the default keyboard monitor after logging in. The system manager chooses the default keyboard monitor for a particular system.

defer *v.*

generic

To put off until a future time.

deferred echo *n.*

VAX/VMS

Refers to the fact that terminal echoing does not occur until a process is ready to accept input entered by type ahead.

deferred write *n.*

RSX-11M

An RMS-11 I/O write technique. RMS-11 does not write the data that is in an I/O buffer to disk until the system needs to use that buffer for other data.

defined variable *n.*

VAX PL/I

A variable declared with the DEFINED attribute that refers to all or part of another variable's storage.

definite response *n.*

DECnet

A positive or negative response returned to a request that specifies, by means of a setting in the request header, that a positive or negative response is to be returned.

deflection *n.*

generic

The change in direction of an electron beam in a CRT.

delayed control mode *n.*

DECnet

An SNA (systems network architecture) request mode in which multiple requests may be sent before a response is required.

delayed response mode *n.*

DECnet

An SNA (systems network architecture) request mode in which the receiver of a message may accept several requests before responding, and may return responses in any order.

delimit *v.*

generic

To separate, terminate, or organize the elements of a character string.

delimiter *n.*

generic

A character that separates elements of a program or data.

VAX/VMS

A character that separates, terminates, or organizes elements of a character string, statement, or program.

delta time *n.*

VAX/VMS

A time value expressing an offset from the current date and time. Delta times are always expressed in the system as negative numbers whose absolute value is used as an offset from the current time.

demand paging *n.*

TOPS-10 and TOPS-20

The operation in which all pages of a program are not resident in memory during execution. References to nonresident pages initiate the actions of moving in additional pages or replacing inactive pages.

demand zero page *n.*

VAX/VMS

A page, typically of an image stack or buffer area, that is initialized to contain all zeros when dynamically created in memory as a result of a page fault. This feature eliminates the waste of disk space that would otherwise be required to store blocks (pages) that contain only zeros.

density *n.*

generic

The number of bits per inch of magnetic tape. Typical values are 800 bpi and 1600 bpi. See bits per inch.

deposit region *n.*

RSX-20F

A region in KL memory that is accessed by the PDP-11 using protected deposits. See also relative address.

depreciable cost *n.*

generic

The difference between the cost of a long-term asset and its estimated residual value.

depreciable life *n.*

generic

The time period or units of activity (such as miles driven for a truck) over which depreciable cost is to be allocated.

depreciation *n.*

generic

The process of allocating the cost of an asset to the periods of benefit.

depreciation rate *n.*

generic

The percentage of the cost of an asset that is an expense each year.

depth *n.*

RSX-11M

The number of the root level in an index.

DEQUE *n.*

RSX-20F

The acronym for double-ended queue. The use of the acronym is product specific to RSX-20F. However, its expansion, double-ended queue, is used generically and means a variable-length list whose contents may be changed by adding or removing items at either end. Same as double-ended queue.

descendant *n.*

Common Data Dictionary

A name for a dictionary directory, subdictionary, or object in the CDD (Common Data Dictionary) that follows another directory or subdictionary in the CDD hierarchy. A dictionary directory or subdictionary owns all its descendants. CDD$TOP owns all the dictionary directories, subdictionaries, and objects, and they are all descendants or CDD$TOP. See also child, parent, and directory hierarchy.

DSM-11

For any array node (element), any other array node on a lower (deeper), subscript level that can be reached from that node and that shares the first n subscripts in common with that node. For example, the nodes A(1,2,2) and A(1,2) are descendants of A(1).

descender n.

FFE

A font value that specifies the greatest distance (in pixels) that the bottom of any character extends below the baseline.

descending adj.

DIGITAL-specific

Pertaining to a sorting order that starts with the highest value of a key and proceeds to the lowest in accordance with the rules for comparing data items.

descending order n.

VAX DBMS

An order of sorting that starts with the highest value of a key and proceeds to the lowest value, in accordance with the rules for comparing data items.

descriptor n.

DIGITAL-specific and VAX/VMS

A data structure used in calling sequences for passing argument types, addresses, and other optional information. See also character-string descriptor.

designated router n.

VAX/VMS

A routing node on the Ethernet selected to perform routing services on behalf of end nodes.

design file n.

A-to-Z

A Business Graphics file containing the description of how a graph looks.

despooler n.

DIGITAL-specific

A device that enables the orderly printing of files; the despooler is handled by the queue manager. The terms print processor, spooler, and despooler are used interchangeably.

DESQ n.

non-DIGITAL product*

A software integration program that enables you to move quickly from task-to-task at your computer, just as you might at your desk.

*   Copyright of Quarterdeck Office Systems.

detach v.

DIGITAL-specific

To free an attached physical device unit for use by other tasks.

generic

To place a job or process in a state where it is not under the control of any user.

detached job n.

DIGITAL-specific

A job that is not associated with a terminal on the RSTS/E operating system.

detached process n.

VAX/VMS

A process that has no owner. The parent process of a tree of subprocesses. Detached processes are created by either the job controller when a user logs on the system, when a batch job is initiated, or when a logical-link connect is requested. The job controller does not own the user processes it creates; these processes are therefore detached.

detached processing *n.*

DECWORD

1. A facility enabling DECWORD to perform different activities simultaneously. For example, a user can edit one document while DECWORD prints another.

2. A list-processing option, specified by DE from the list-processing menu, enabling DECWORD to perform the merging process, leaving the terminal free for other tasks.

detached program *n.*

DIGITAL-specific

A program that operates without a terminal. A detached program cannot communicate with the user until the program is attached to a terminal.

detach terminal *n.*

generic

A field attribute indicating that the application program can display a value on the screen for a particular field, but that the terminal operator cannot enter data there.

detail lines *n.*

CTS-300

Those lines of a QUILL report that output the data from individual records in a collection.

VAX DATATRIEVE

The lines containing data items in a report.

detectable field *n.*

DECnet

A display field that can be sensed by the selector lightpen.

detector *n.*

generic

A device or circuit that senses the presence of a condition or thing.

DEUNA *n.*

DIGITAL-specific

The abbreviation for DIGITAL Equipment UNIBUS Network Adaptor; DEUNA connects VAX and UNIBUS-based PDP-11 systems to the Ethernet. Same as DIGITAL Equipment UNIBUS Network Adapter.

device *n.*

generic

A component or assembly that is used for a specific purpose.

VAX/VMS

The general name for any peripheral hardware connected to the processor that is capable of receiving, storing, or transmitting data. Card readers, line printers, and terminals are examples of record-oriented devices. Magnetic tape devices and disk devices are examples of mass storage devices. Terminal line interfaces and interprocessor links are examples of communications devices. Devices are not necessarily hardware. See pseudo device.

device cluster *n.*

RSX-11M

A single- or multi-block unit of disk storage assignment; its size is characteristic of a device type.

device cluster size *n.*

RSTS/E

The cluster size, in blocks, that RSTS/E uses for a particular type of disk. For example, the device cluster size for an RX50 diskette is 1; the device cluster size for an RA81 disk is 16. The device cluster size for a disk type is the minimum cluster size that can be used for any file or directory on that kind of disk.

device controller *n.*

DIGITAL-specific

A hardware unit that electronically supervises one or more of the same device types. The device controller acts as a link between the CPU and the I/O devices. See also device handler.

VAX/VMS

The electronic circuits associated with each physical device in the system that serve as the interface between the processor and the device hardware.

device data block (DDB) *n.*

DIGITAL-specific and VAX/VMS

A structure that identifies the generic device/controller name, driver name, and location for a set of devices connected to a single controller. Same as DDB.

device datatype *n.*

Rdb/ELN

A VAXELN system datatype that represents a device interrupt connected to an interrupt service procedure.

Device Definition Utility *n.*

ACMS

The ACMS tool for defining which terminals have access to ACMS.

device designation *n.*

generic

A logical assignment or physical device name that identifies a specific device.

device driver *n.*

DECnet

The software that handles all I/O between the system and any of several devices connected to the system through a single controller unit.

generic

A program that provides communication between the device and the operating system.

VAX/VMS

The software associated with each physical device in the system that serves as the interface between the operating system and the device controller.

device handler *n.*

CTS-300, Memory Resident RT-11, MicroPower PAS-CAL, and RT-11

A software routine that services and controls the hardware activities of an I/O device.

DECnet

A protocol emulator (PE) that is responsible for servicing I/O requests routed to it by the RSX Executive QI/O processor. It is also responsible for the control and servicing of a hardware device (such as the DUP11 line interface). The RSX-11/3271 Protocol Emulator (PE) is a device handler. In the case of the PE, the device handler does not directly control the line interface hardware device but is used to communicate with the communications executive processes that directly control the device. Same as handler. See also device controller.

device independence *n.*

DIGITAL-specific

A characteristic of a program, file, or system that allows it to operate on/with any type of device.

generic

The ability to request an I/O operation regardless of device characteristics such as different cluster size or access speed.

device interrupt *n.*

VAX/VMS

An interrupt received on interrupt priority levels, 16 through 23. Device interrupts can be requested only by devices.

device media control language (DMCL) *n.*

VAX DATATRIEVE and VAX DBMS

The language used to define the relationship between physical files and database areas. DMCL is used to map logical page addresses to physical files and devices; it is also used as the name of the object file read by the DBCS to find and map data files. Same as DMCL.

device name *n.*

generic

A physical device name that identifies a particular hardware device; the name the operating system uses to refer to a hardware device.

VAX/VMS

The field in a file specification that identifies the device unit on which a file is stored. Device names also include the mnemonics that identify an I/O peripheral device in a data transfer request. A device name consists of a mnemonic followed by a controller identification letter (if applicable), followed by a unit number (if applicable), and ends with a colon (:).

device-oriented data structure *n.*

DIGITAL-specific

An I/O structure that provides information used by device-oriented components such as drivers, channel-control routines, and device-interrupt dispatchers.

device queue *n.*

MINC and VAX/VMS

A list of the buffers that have been released for use in a data transfer. MINC/REAL, the RLSBUF subprogram, is used to release buffers to the device queue so that other MINC/REAL subprograms can use the buffers in data transfers. See also spool queue.

device register *n.*

MicroPower PASCAL

A register associated with a particular hardware device. Device registers store information about the status and control of the associated device or exchange data with the device.

VAX/VMS

A location in device-controller logic used for requesting device functions (such as I/O transfers) and/or reporting status.

device unit *n.*

DIGITAL-specific

One of a set of similar peripheral devices (for example, disk unit 0, DECtape unit 1, and so forth).

generic

A single peripheral device selected from a set of peripheral devices.

VAX/VMS

One drive and its controlling logic, such as a disk drive or terminal. Some controllers have several device units connected to a single controller; for example, mass-storage controllers.

diagnostic *n.*

generic

A test that detects and isolates malfunctions.

VAX/VMS

A program that tests hardware, firmware, peripheral operation, logic, or memory and reports any faults it detects.

dial-up *adj.*

generic

Pertaining to telephone computer connections.

dial-up line *n.*

generic

A telephone line connected to a computer for use by terminals.

DIBOL *n.*

DIGITAL-specific

The acronym for DIGITAL Business Oriented Language. A COBOL-like language used to write business applications programs. It is the source language for CTS-300. Same as DIGITAL Business Oriented Language.

DIBOL debugging technique (DDT) *n.*

DIGITAL-specific

A program used on CTS-300 for interactive dialog, control, and analysis of DIBOL program operations. Same as DDT.

DIBOL instruction set (DIS) *n.*

DIGITAL-specific

A special set of hardware instructions supported by the DIBOL language on data system processors that support the DIS hardware. Same as DIS.

DICOMP *n.*

DIGITAL-specific

The compiler for the DIBOL language on the CTS-300 operating system.

dictionary *n.*

generic

A list that contains the information that describes the organization and format of a data file.

TOPS-20

A table stored by IQL (interactive query language) that describes a data file or data base. IQL refers to dictionaries when IQL generates reports and updates or searches through a data file. A dictionary stores the location of a data file or data base, as well as information about the individual data items in the file. Data-item entries in dictionaries contain information describing how the items are stored and cosmetic information anticipating printing (such as column titles and editing pictures).

VAX-11

The VAX-11 Common Data Dictionary. In the most general sense: an overall hierarchical storage facility that includes dictionary directories, subdictionaries, and objects.

dictionary directory *n.*

Common Data Dictionary and FMS

Locations that are analogous to parents in the hierarchy. They "own" other dictionary directories or dictionary objects, and they are labeled according to the paths through the hierarchy that lead to them.

dictionary management utility (DMU) *n.*

Common Data Dictionary and VAX DBMS

A utility of the Common Data Dictionary (CDD) that provides facilities for examining and maintaining the CDD contents. Same as DMU.

dictionary object *n.*

DIGITAL-specific

The basic named data definitions stored in the CDD (Common Data Dictionary), and that form the end points of the CDD hierarchy branches. Examples of objects include request definitions, form definitions, and record definitions. Same as objects. See also scalar.

dictionary verify/fix utility *n.*

Common Data Dictionary

A Common Data Dictionary utility (CDDV) that detects damaged dictionary files and repairs them. CDDV also compresses the data in dictionary files for more efficient use of storage.

die *n.*

generic

A single integrated circuit, exclusive of packaging.

dielectric *n.*

generic

The insulating medium between two plates of a capacitor.

differential mode *n.*

MINC

An input method in which the signal to be acted upon is defined as the instantaneous difference between input signal and return signal. In differential mode, the signals common to both terminals are not detected in the transmission. Therefore, "noise" in the transmission is effectively reduced.

digital *adj.*

generic

Pertaining to digits or to showing data or physical quantities by digits.

DIGITAL Command Language (DCL) *n.*

DIGITAL-specific

The standard command interface to DIGITAL's major operating system. Same as DCL.

VAX/VMS

A command interpreter in a VAX/VMS system. Contrast with monitor console routine.

Digital Data Communications Message Protocol (DDCMP) *n.*

DECnet

A protocol that ensures integrity and correct sequencing of messages between adjacent nodes. Same as DDCMP.

DIGITAL Equipment UNIBUS Network Adaptor (DEUNA) *n.*

DIGITAL-specific

The adapter that converts VAX and UNIBUS-based PDP-11 systems to the Ethernet. Same as DEUNA.

digital input module *n.*

MINC

A laboratory unit that provides the connection to the external devices that produce digital logic signals.

digital I/O (input/output) mask word *n.*

MINC

A 16-bit word of memory with selected bits set. The bit selection depends on the information elements (in a series of characters) to be selected or extracted.

DIGITAL Network Architecture (DNA) *n.*

DECnet

A set of protocols (rules) governing the format, control, and sequencing of message-exchange for all DIGITAL network implementations. The protocols are layered, and they define rules for data exchange from the physical link level up through the user interface level. DNA controls all data that travels throughout a DIGITAL network. DNA also defines standard network management and network generation procedures. Same as DNA.

digital output module *n.*

MINC

A laboratory unit that sends digital logic signals from the system to as many as 16 laboratory instruments (binary instruments).

Digital Standard Relational Interface (DSRI) *n.*

Rdb/ELN

The architecture defining how local and remote programs communicate with relational database management systems. Same as DSRI.

digital-to-analog (DA) conversion *n.*

MINC

The changing of discrete digital values (transferred from a digital computer) to analog voltages suitable for input to an analog laboratory instrument.

digital-to-analog (DA) converter *n.*

MINC

A laboratory module that performs digital-to-analog conversions; a laboratory module that translates digital values into the values of voltage. The MNC-series module that performs such conversions is the MNCAA.

digital transmission *n.*

generic

The action of sending information in units that are acceptable to a particular type of computer.

digitized speech *n.*

generic

Speech sounds that are recorded in digital form and output in analog form.

digit position *n.*

COBOL-74

The amount of physical storage required to store a single digit. This amount can vary depending on the usage of the data item describing the digit position. Further characteristics of physical storage are defined by the user.

generic

A position to be occupied by an alpha or a decimal character.

dimension (or DIM) *n.*

BASIC/generic

A statement that explicitly creates and names an array. If you specify a channel, BASIC creates a virtual array file.

PASCAL and VAX PASCAL

A range of values for one subscript or index of an array. An array can have any number of dimensions. See also multidimensional array.

VAX PL/I

A set of bounds describing one extent of an array.

diode *n.*

generic

An electronic device that allows current to flow in one direction only.

direct access *n.*

CTS-300, RT-11, and VAX DATATRIEVE

The use of hashing or some other random-access mode to retrieve or store records. See also random access.

generic

A method of addressing memory, a device or location by its actual value. Actual values are not translated or processed before they are used.

direct data path *n.*

VAX/VMS

A UNIBUS adapter data path that transfers 16 bits of data in a single SBI (synchronous backplane interconnect) transfer.

direct I/O *n.*

VAX/VMS

An input/output operation in which the system locks the pages containing the associated buffer in physical memory for the duration of the I/O operation. The I/O transfer takes place directly from the process buffer.

directive *n.*

DECSIM

A qualifier for the network description language and the behavior language. It controls selection of elements, timing modes, delay modes, arithmetic representation, etc.. A directive is enclosed in braces ({ }) and has an implicit effect on what it controls.

generic

An instruction or command in a program that controls the translation of that program.

RSX-11M

An RSX-11 request for a system function. See also system services and control point system services.

RT-11

Mnemonics in an assembly-language source program that are recognized by the assembler as commands to control a specific assembly process.

direct mapping cache *n.*

generic

A very fast semiconductor memory organized in such a way that only one address is needed to find any data stored there.

VAX/VMS

A cache organization (storing blocks in memory for future need) in which only one address comparison is needed to locate any data. Only one is needed because a block of main memory data can be placed in only one possible position in this cache.

direct mode *n.*

VAX DATATRIEVE

The allocation mode that allows access to a record through a database key value.

VAX DBMS

The location mode in which the user may specify a desired database page value to the DBCS (Database Control System) for use by the location mode algorithm.

directory *n.*

DIGITAL-specific

A group of files stored on a disk. See also user file directory.

generic

A list of files on a mass storage device.

VAX/VMS

A file that briefly catalogs a set of files stored on disk or tape. The directory includes the name, type, and version number of each file in the set, as well as a unique number that identifies the file's actual location and points to a list of its attributes. See also master file directory and UFD.

directory caching *n.*

RSTS/E and RSX-11M

A technique by which directory blocks are cached in memory to accelerate file processing and improve the performance of operations that involve the access of the disk directories.

directory cluster size *n.*

RSTS/E

The cluster size of a UFD (user file directory). The directory cluster size limits the size to which a directory can expand.

directory device *n.*

DIGITAL-specific

A storage-retrieval device, such as disk or DECtape, that contains file name descriptions and the layout of stored data (programs and other files). A directory device is randomly accessible.

generic

A storage device with a table of contents holding information about the files on that device.

directory hierarchy *n.*

Common Data Dictionary

The structure of Common Data Dictionary (CDD) directories. The hierarchy of dictionary directories, subdictionaries, and objects is similar to the hierarchy of relationships in a family tree. Each dictionary directory in the CDD tree may become a parent by owning other dictionary directories or dictionary objects. Dictionary objects are the terminal points of the hierarchy; they cannot be parents. See also child, descendant, and parent.

directory name *n.*

VAX/RMS and VAX/VMS

The field in a file specification that identifies the directory in which the file is listed. It begins with a left bracket or left angle bracket ([or <) and ends with a right bracket or right angle bracket (] or >). The brackets enclose either a group number and a user number separated by a comma, or an alphanumeric directory list.

directory path *n.*

DIGITAL-specific

The ordered list of directory names, starting with a UFD (user file directory) name, that uniquely specifies a directory without regard to a file structure. A file structure name, a path, and a filename and extension are needed to uniquely identify a file in the system. Same as path.

directory specification *n.*

DECsystem-10

A user's specification of the directory to the SCAN program typed within square brackets and having fields separated by commas. The first two fields, expressed in octal numbers, are the project and programmer numbers. They specify the particular UFD (user file directory). Additional fields are SFDs (system file directory) in order from the UFD down.

directory-structured *adj.*

DIGITAL-specific

Pertaining to a storage volume with a true volume directory (at its beginning) that contains information about all the files on the storage volume (file name, file type, length, and date-of-creation).

DIS *n.*

DIGITAL-specific

The abbreviation for DIBOL instruction set. DIS is a special set of hardware instructions supported by the DIBOL language on datasystem processors that support the DIS hardware. Same as DIBOL instruction set.

disable *v.*

DIGITAL-specific

To stop a terminal from sending input or receiving output.

disconnect *adj.*

DECnet

Pertaining to the process of closing a logical link.

disconnect (record operation) *v.*

RSX-11M

To terminate a stream of record operations, making the buffers assigned to the stream available for other operations.

disconnect abort *n.*

DECnet and VAX/VMS

An operation by which nontransparent tasks can deaccess a logical link without deassigning the channel. This form of disconnection indicates to the receiver that not all messages sent have been received.

discount *n.*

generic

Any deduction from a gross amount.

discrete *adj.*

generic

Pertaining to a single electronic component, not to integrated circuit devices.

discretionary controls *n.*

VAX/VMS

Security controls that are applied at the user's option, that is, they are not required. Access control lists are typical of such optional security features.

disk *adj.*

generic

Pertaining to a thin, round plate with a magnetic surface coating on which data can be stored by magnetic recording.

disk *n.*

generic

A thin, round plate with a magnetic surface coating on which data can be stored by magnetic recording.

disk-based system *n.*

DIGITAL-specific

A system, such as RSX-11M and RSX-11M-PLUS, in which the tasks and other functions that make up the operating system are stored on a disk and written into memory as they are needed.

disk directory *n.*

generic

A directory of the files on a disk.

diskette *n.*

generic

A small, flexible, magnetic disk used to store information. Same as floppy, floppy disk, floppy diskette.

disk file *n.*

generic

A file stored on a disk medium.

diskpack *n.*

generic

A set of thin circular recording surfaces mounted on a common hub and usually stored in a container.

disk-resident overlay (structure) *n.*

RSX-11M

1. A segment of a task that resides on disk until required by the memory-resident portion of the task.

2. The tree-like structure that relates the segments.

disk-resident overlay segment *n.*

VAX/VMS

An overlay segment that shares the same physical memory and virtual address space with other segments. The segment is read in from the disk each time it is loaded. See also memory-resident overlay segment.

disk scavenging *n.*

VAX/VMS

A method of obtaining information from a disk that the owner intended to discard. The information, although no longer accessible to the original owner by normal means, retains a sufficient amount of its original magnetic encoding so that it can be retrieved and used by one of the scavenging methods.

dismounting a file structure *n.*

TOPS-10

The process of deleting a file structure from a user's active search list but not necessarily physically removing the file structure from the system.

dispatcher *n.*

TOPS-20

The mechanism that selects processes to run from the set of runnable processes.

displaced indexed mode *n.*

VAX/VMS

An indexed addressing mode in which the base operand specifier uses displacement mode addressing. Same as displacement indexed mode.

displacement deferred indexed mode *n.*

VAX/VMS

An indexed addressing mode in which the base operand specified uses displacement deferred mode addressing.

displacement deferred mode *n.*

VAX/VMS

An addressing method in which the specifier extension is a byte, word, or longword displacement. The displacement is sign-extended to 32 bits and added to a base address obtained from the specified register. The result is the address of a longword that contains the address of the actual operand. If the PC (program counter) is used as the register, the updated contents of the PC are used as the base address. The updated contents of the PC is the address of the first byte beyond the specifier extension. Same as displacement mode.

displacement indexed mode *n.*

VAX/VMS

A method of indexed addressing in which the base operand specifier uses displacement mode addressing. Same as displaced indexed mode.

displacement mode *n.*

VAX/VMS

An addressing method in which the specifier extension is a byte, word, or longword displacement. The displacement is sign-extended to 32 bits and added to a base address obtained from the specified register. The result is the address of the actual operand. If the PC (program counter) is used as the register, the updated contents of the PC are used as the base address. The updated contents of the PC is the address of the first byte beyond the specifier extension. Same as displacement deferred mode.

DISPLAY *n.*

PEARL

A set of objects that jointly behave as an array or a structure.

display a ruler *v.*

DECWORD

To command DECWORD to show the current ruler on the screen and allow its settings to be changed. (Invoked by pressing Gold RULER.)

display field *n.*

DECnet

A group of contiguous characters in a formatted display image. The first character of a field is an attribute character defining the characteristics of the field. The remainder of the field consists of alphanumeric characters. The field continues to, but does not include, the next attribute character. See also input field, formatted display, and unformatted display.

display keys *n.*

DECWORD

The eleven blue keys on the mini-keyboard of a DECWORD terminal. When one of these keys is pressed, DECWORD advances or backs up through text the distance specified.

display-only attribute *n.*

generic

A field attribute indicating that the application program can display a value on the screen for a particular field, but that the terminal operator cannot enter data there.

dissipation *n.*

generic

Power used by a circuit or device.

distance key *n.*

DECmate II

Any one of the blue keys on the editing keypad that defines the distance the cursor can move in one key stroke.

distant Host *n.*

DECnet

Specific to ARPANET, a Host (a communications controlling computer) located more than 30 feet and less than 2000 feet from the IMP (interface message processor) that serves it. A distant Host requires IMP hardware in addition to the hardware required by the IMP of a local Host.

distributed *adj.*

DECnet

Pertaining to computer networks with decentralized network control where such functions as routing, formatting for transmission, and error-checking are equally distributed over all nodes.

distribution volume *n.*

RT-11

The disk, diskette, or tape cartridge on which RT-11 or MRRT software is sent to the user.

dividend *n.*

generic

A distribution of earnings to owners of a corporation.

division *n.*

COBOL-74

A set of zero, one, or more sections of paragraphs, called the division body, that are formed and combined in accordance with a specific set of rules. There are four divisions in a COBOL program: Identification, Environment, Data, and Procedure. See also division header.

PEARL

The basic constituent of a PEARL module. Two types of division exist: system division and problem division.

division header *n.*

COBOL-74

A combination of words followed by a period and a space that indicates the beginning of a division. See also division.

DKED *n.*

CTS-300

The abbreviation for DIBOL keypad editor. The DKED is similar in operation to the RT-11 K52 editor. Same as DIBOL keypad editor.

DLE *n.*

DECnet

The abbreviation for data-link escape. A BISYNC control character sequence used exclusively to provide supplementary line-control signals. It is a two-character sequence where the first character is DLE, and the second character varies according to the function desired and the code used. Same as data-link escape.

DLLOAD *n.*

DIGITAL-specific

A utility program that down-line loads a memory image from the host to the target system. See also down-line loading.

DMA *n.*

VAX/VMS

The abbreviation for direct memory access.

DMCL *n.*

VAX DATATRIEVE and VAX DBMS

The abbreviation for device/media control language. DMCL is the language used to define the relationship between physical files and database areas. DMCL is used to map logical page addresses to physical files and devices, it is also used as the name of the object file read by the DBCS (Database Control System) to find and map data files. Same as device/media control language.

DMCL object *n.*

VAX DATATRIEVE and VAX DBMS

The file of machine-language instructions that describes the physical structure of the database and provides buffer space for database pages.

DML *n.*

VAX DBMS

The abbreviation for data manipulation language. DML is a DBMS interface that permits user programs in another host language to interact with the database. Same as data manipulation language.

DML *n.*

DBMS

The abbreviation for data manipulation language. DML are statements that permit programs written in VAX-11 languages to access the database in DBMS. Same as data manipulation language.

DMU *n.*

Common Data Dictionary and VAX DBMS

The abbreviation for dictionary management utility. DMU is a utility of the Common Data Dictionary (CDD) that provides facilities for examining and maintaining the CDD contents. Same as dictionary management utility.

DN20 *n.*

DECnet

A DECnet communications front end.

DN200 *n.*

DECnet

A remote station, based on a PDP-11/34A, that can be connected over a synchronous line to a host system running TOPS-20. RJE-20 software can be loaded by DECnet V3.0, and the DN200 can then participate in a DECnet network as a full-routing node.

DNA *n.*

DECnet

The abbreviation for DIGITAL Network Architecture. DNA is a set of protocols (rules) governing the format, control, and sequencing of message-exchange for all DIGITAL network implementations. The protocols are layered, and they define rules for data exchange from the physical link level up through the user interface level. DNA controls all data that travels throughout a DIGITAL network. DNA also defines standard network management and network generation procedures. Same as DIGITAL Network Architecture.

DNLOAD *n.*

DECnet

A program that runs in the DECSYSTEM-20 and loads the communications front end with the DN64 software. It can also be used to dump the memory of the DN20.

DNMAC *n.*

DECnet

A program that is the cross assembler for PDP-11 macro source files.

document *n.*

BASIC/generic

Commentary in a program that explains what the various parts of the program do.

document destination *n.*

DIGITAL-specific

A print setting that defines which printer should print the designated document.

document number *n.*

DECWORD

A number DECWORD assigns to a new document when it is created. No two documents in an account have the same number.

Document Processing subsystem *n.*

ALL-IN-1

An ALL-IN-1 menu option that lets the user create and produce letters, memos, reports, and other documents.

DO-group *n.*

VAX PL/I

A sequence of statements headed by a DO statement and terminated with a corresponding END statement.

domain *n.*

generic

The set of values that an independent variable can have.

VAX DATATRIEVE

A DATATRIEVE data structure that associates a name with the relationship between a file and a record definition. Using the domain name gives access to information in the data file as interpreted by the record definition. For example, the domain PERSONNEL associates the file PERSON.DAT and the record definition PERSONNEL_REC.

domain-own *n.*

TOPS-20

A resource common to a domain across all processes using the domain. Typically, domain-own is used to refer to shared data.

doorbell *n.*

DECsystem-10

The software flag by which processors in a multiprocessing system interrupt each other.

dormant file structure *n.*

TOPS-10

A file structure that is physically mounted but has no current users (the mount count is zero).

dormant segment *n.*

TOPS-10

A sharable, high segment kept on a swapping space in core memory, which is in no user's addressing space.

dormant task *n.*

RSX-11M

A task that is installed but not yet requested to run. See also task state.

dot *n.*

GIGI, MSG (SPETS), and RGL/FEP

The density of one picture element; the smallest displayable unit on the monitor screen. See also pixel.

double-buffered I/O *n.*

generic

A method of transferring data that includes two storage areas to speed the process of transfer.

double entry system *n.*

generic

The system of recording transactions that maintains the equality of the accounting equation. Each entry results in recording equal amounts of debits and credits.

double floating data *n.*

VAX/VMS

Eight contiguous bytes (64 bits), starting on an addressable byte boundary, that are interpreted as containing a floating-point number. The bits are labeled from right to left, 0 to 63. An 8-byte, floating-point number is identified by the address of the byte containing bit 0. Bit 15 contains the sign of the number. Bits 14 through 7 contain the excess 128 binary exponent. Bits 63 through 16 and 6 through 0 contain a normalized 56-bit fraction with the redundant, most-significant fraction bit not represented. Within that fraction, bits of decreasing significance go from 6 through 0, 31 through 16, 47 through 32, then 63 through 48. Exponent values of 1 through 255 in the 8-bit exponent field represent true binary exponents of -128 to 127. An exponent value of 0 together with a sign bit of 0 represent a floating value of 0. An exponent value of 0 with a sign bit of 1 is a reserved representation; floating-point instructions processing this value return a reserved operand fault. The value of a floating data is in the approximate range $(+ \text{ or } -)$ 0.29×10 (-38 sup) to 1.7×10 (38 sup). The precision is approximately one part in 2 (55 sup) or 16 decimal digits.

double precision *n.*

VAX PASCAL

Precision of approximately 16 significant digits and a range from $10^{**}-38$ through $10^{**}38$, or 15 significant digits and a range from $10^{**}-308$ through $10^{**}308$ for a floating-point real number. The type DOUBLE provides double precision.

VAX/VMS

Precision of approximately 16 significant digits for a floating-point real number; the type DOUBLE provides double precision.

double type *n.*

PASCAL and VAX PASCAL

Predefined scalar type with double-precision real numbers as values.

down-line load *v.*

DECnet

To send a copy of a system image or other file over a line to the memory of a target node.

generic

To transfer a program from one computer to another computer for the second program to be executed.

down-line-load facility   (or DLL facility) *n.*

Memory Resident RT-11 and RT-11

Software that transmits the Memory Resident RT-11 (MRRT) operating system, user program(s), and data files from the host RT-11 system to one or more target SB11 systems.

down-line loading *n.*

DIGITAL-specific

Transmitting a program's memory image over a logical link, and loading and starting the program on a computer at another node. See also DLLOAD.

downline system load *n.*

VAX/VMS

A DECnet-VAX function that allows a remote target node to receive an operating system file image from another node.

downline task load *n.*

VAX/VMS

A DECnet-VAX function that allows a remote target node to receive an RSX-11S task from another node.

downtime *adj.*

generic

Pertaining to that time during which a computer is not operating.

DP *n.*

generic

The abbreviation for draft printer. A printer that produces drafts of documents. It is faster than the letter quality printer. Same as draft printer.

DPT *n.*

VAX/VMS

The abbreviation for driver-prologue table. The DPT is a table in the driver that describes the driver and the device type to the VAX/VMS procedure that loads drivers into the system. Same as driver-prologue table.

draft printer *n.*

generic

A printer that produces drafts of documents. It is faster than the letter quality printer. Same as DP.

drawing color *n.*

RGL/FEP

A shade of gray used for drawing graphic objects. If a color monitor is attached to a VT125, the gray shades map to colors.

DRI *n.*

Rdb/ELN

The abbreviation for database remote interconnect. DRI is the outermost layer of the Digital Standard Relational Interface. It provides the protocol for dealing with interprocess and interprocessor communication. Same as database remote interconnect.

drive *n.*

VAX/VMS

The electromechanical unit of a mass storage device system on which a recording medium (disk cartridge, disk pack, or magnetic tape reel) is mounted.

driver *n.*

VAX/VMS

The set of code in the kernel that handles the physical I/O to a device. This is implemented as a fork process.

driver-dispatch table (DDT) *n.*

DIGITAL-specific and VAX/VMS

A table in the I/O driver that lists the entry point addresses of standard driver routines and the sizes or diagnostic and error logging buffers for the device type. Same as DDT.

TOPS-20

A table containing the start I/O and unsolicited interrupt entry points for an I/O driver and the address of the function-decision table (FDT).

driver-fork level *n.*

VAX/VMS

The interrupt priority levels (IPLs) at which a driver fork processes executes, that is, IPLs 8 through 11. Every unit-control block indicates the driver fork level for its unit.

driver-prologue table (DPT) *n.*

VAX/VMS

A table in the driver that describes the driver and the device type to the VAX/VMS procedure that loads drivers into the system. Same as DPT.

driver start I/O routine *n.*

VAX/VMS

The routine in a device driver that is responsible for obtaining necessary resources (for example: the controller data channel) and for activating the device unit. Same as start I/O routine.

DSK *n.*

DECsystem-10

The general name of disk-like devices. The names "D:" and "DSK:" are predefined to be a set of structures following the job search list.

DSM-11 *n.*

DSM-11

The abbreviation for DIGITAL Standard MUMPS, Digital Equipment Corporation's implementation of ANSI Standard MUMPS for the PDP-11.

DSP *n.*

RSX-11M

The abbreviation for dynamic storage region-pool. DSP and DSR (dynamic storage region) are commonly called the pool. The pool is part of the Executive's partition in memory and contains the Executive's data base. Same as dynamic storage region-pool. See also secondary pool.

DSR *n.*

RSX-11M

The abbreviation for dynamic storage region. DSR and DSP (dynamic storage region-pool) are commonly called the pool. The pool is part of the Executive's partition in memory and contains the Executive's data base. Same as dynamic storage region. See also secondary pool.

DSRI *n.*

Rdb/ELN

The abbreviation for Digital Standard Relational Interface. DSRI is the architecture defining how local and remote programs communicate with relational database management systems. Same as Digital Standard Relational Interface.

DTE *n.*

DECnet and VAX/VMS

The abbreviation for data terminal equipment. DTE refers to the hardware interface between the main processor in a DECSYSTEM-2040, 2050, or 2060 and the PDP-11 processor in the DN20 communications front end. Same as data terminal equipment.

VAX PSI

The abbreviation for data terminal equipment. A CCITT term referring to the user's equipment (computer or terminal) connected to a DCE on a packet switching network for the purpose of sending and/or receiving data. Same as data terminal equipment.

DTL *n.*

DECnet

The abbreviation for DTE20 list. DTL is a list of the DTE-20 hardware interfaces. Same as DTE20 list.

DTR *n.*

DECnet

The abbreviation for Data Terminal Ready. DTR is a control signal (applicable to the RS232) that enters a modem from the data terminal or communications device that is using the modem. When the signal is set, it informs the modem that the data terminal equipment is ready to transmit and receive data. When the signal is clear, the data terminal equipment is not ready. Same as Data Terminal Ready.

dual display *n.*

Medical Systems

A data analysis process that displays two images of a static or dynamic study on the screen at the same time.

dummy *n.*

generic

An address, instruction, or data item that is not actual. It will be replaced by an actual address, instruction, or data during execution or revision of the code.

dummy *adj.*

generic

Pertaining to an address, instruction, or data item that is not actual, but will be replaced by an actual address, instruction, or data during execution or revision of the code.

dummy argument *n.*

DIGITAL-specific

A unique variable allocated by the compiler to contain a copy of an argument specified in a procedure invocation.

dump *n.*

generic

The listing or display of computer storage, often in response to an error condition. Usually identified by a preceding adjective (for example, crash dump).

duplex *adj.*

generic

Pertaining to the separate, two-way transmission of data at the same time.

duplicate key *n.*

CTS-300

A characteristic of having two or more records (within the ISAM file) with identical keys. See also change key.

RSX-11M

A flag associated with a primary or alternate key. The flag indicates whether or not the user allows more than one record in a file to contain the same value in a specific key field. See also change key or null key.

duplicate pointer array *n.*

RSX-11M

A series of record pointers stored in each SIDR (secondary index data record) for an alternate key where duplicates are allowed. Each pointer indicates a user data record containing the key value represented by the SIDR. See also pointer array.

DURATION *n.*

PEARL

A PEARL object used to represent time intervals.

DV *n.*

VAX/VMS

The abbreviation for decimal overflow. DV is a decimal overflow trap enable bit in the processor status word (PSW). Same as decimal overflow.

dyadic operator *n.*

PEARL

A PEARL operator that takes two operands.

dynamic *adj.*

generic

Continuously active or changing.

dynamic access *n.*

COBOL-74

An access mode in which specific logical records can be obtained from or placed into a mass storage file in a nonsequential manner (see random access), and obtained from a file in a sequential manner (see sequential access), during the scope of the same OPEN statement.

RSX-11M

The ability to change record access mode with each record operation.

VAX DATATRIEVE

The capability of switching between random and sequential access modes at will.

VAX/RMS and VAX/VMS

A technique in which a program switches from one record access mode to another while processing a file.

dynamic allocation *n.*

VAX DBMS

An option of the storage record entry that tells the DBCS (Database Control System) not to allocate space for a data item until a run unit attempts to perform a DML (data manipulation language) operation on that item and then to perform data compression on this item in the database. DYNAMIC allocation is declared in the storage schema. See also static allocation.

dynamic binding *n.*

TOPS-20

The act of binding names as execution progresses rather than at a separate linking time.

dynamic process *n.*

MicroPower PASCAL

A process that is not defined during target system initialization but created by action of another process during operation of the application.

dynamic storage region (DSR or DSRP) *n.*

Medical Systems

A patient file that contains up to 512 frames (matrix images) acquired at specified periods of time.

RSX-11M

A pool (DSR or DSRP are commonly referred to as pool) that is part of this Executive's partition in memory and that contains the Executive's data base. Same as DSR and DSRP. See also secondary pool.

D_floating datum *n.*

VAX/VMS

Eight contiguous bytes, starting on an addressable byte boundary, that are interpreted as containing a floating-point number.

D_floating point data *n.*

VAX/VMS

A double precision floating point number eight
bytes long having a range of +/− 2.9*10**−37 to
+/− 1.7*10**38 and a precision of approximately
sixteen decimal digits. Same as double floating
data.

e

earnings *n.*

generic

The amount by which total revenues exceed total expenses for an accounting period. Same as net income and profit.

earthing conductor *n.*

generic

Refers to the wire that is used to connect the coaxial cable shield connection point to a Network Earth Reference.

EBCDIC *n.*

generic

Acronym for Extended Binary Coded Decimal Interchange Code, an eight-bit character code made up of four zone bits and four numeric bits.

EBI *n.*

DECnet

The abbreviation for end-bracket indicator. EBI refers to a request header bit that, when set, indicates that the accompanying transmission ends a bracket. Same as end-bracket indicator.

echo *n.*

generic

A terminal handling characteristic in which the characters typed by the user on the terminal keyboard are also displayed on the screen or printer.

echo> *v.*

generic

To return to one who sends, without changes, what had been sent.

echo control *n.*

RSTS/E

An optional feature of the RSTS/E monitor that modifies the way the system handles terminal echo. Instead of echoing characters as a user types them, the system echoes characters only within a field that a program declares. Echo control is useful for forms-oriented data entry applications.

echo mode *n.*

DIGITAL-specific

The mode in which the characters being typed by the operator are reproduced on the screen.

EC mode *n.*

DECnet

The abbreviation for emulator control mode. An operating mode in which the management of SNA (systems network architecture) protocol is the exclusive concern of the protocol emulator (PE). Same as emulator control mode.

economic life *n.*

USFC/generic

The period over which one can expect to obtain the benefits of ownership and/or use of equipment.

economic order quantity (EOQ) *n.*

generic

A calculated optimal amount of stock to order when inventory is reduced to a level called the "reorder point."

EDDT *n.*

DECsystem-10

The abbreviation for executive dynamic debugging technique. EDDT is a version of DDT used for debugging programs (such as the monitor) in executive mode. Same as executive dynamic debugging technique.

EDI *n.*

RSX-11M

The mnemonic for Editor. EDI is a line text-editing utility. Same as Editor.

edit *v.*

generic

To bring an existing document to the screen in order to look at it, add new text, delete text, or make other changes.

edit buffer *n.*

FFE

In FFE, the buffer in which a bitmap is edited.

edit-directed stream I/O *n.*

VAX PL/I

Transmission of data between a program and an external input/output device for which the formatting and conversion of data are controlled by format specifications in a GET or PUT statement.

editing values *n.*

FFE

Attributes you set for FFE to have when you edit a character: current position, window position, and pen mode.

editing window *n.*

FFE

The upper left section of the FFE screen layout in which characters are displayed for editing.

editor *n.*

generic

A program that allows a user to create or modify text in a computer file.

Editor *n.*

RSX-11M

A line text-editing utility. Same as EDI.

VAX/VMS

A system image used for creating and altering text files.

editor menu *n.*

DECWORD

A menu containing options relevant to editing. Invoked by typing Gold MENU while creating or editing a document.

edit string *n.*

VAX DATATRIEVE

A character or group of characters that directs DATATRIEVE to format a field in a specified way.

EDT *n.*

DIGITAL-specific

The acronym for DEC Editor, DIGITAL's standard editing utility. Same as DEC Editor.

effective address *n.*

DIGITAL-specific and VAX/VMS

The hardware address obtained after deferred or indexing modifications are calculated.

EIA *n.*

DECnet

The abbreviation for Electronic Industries Association. EIA is a standards organization specializing in the electrical and functional characteristics of interface equipment. Same as Electronic Industries Association.

electrolyte *n.*

generic

The fluid in a storage battery that provides the process necessary for polarization.

electromagnetic *adj.*

generic

Having to do with force fields generated through electrical processes.

electromechanical *adj.*

generic

Pertaining to equipment having both electrical and mechanical components.

electron *n.*

generic

A particle with a negative charge that moves around the nucleus of an atom.

Electronic Industries Association (EIA) *n.*

DECnet

A standards organization specializing in the electrical and functional characteristics of interface equipment. Same as EIA.

electronic mail *n.*

generic

A paperless method of communicating and storing messages using a computer system.

Electronic Mail subsystem *n.*

ALL-IN-1

An ALL-IN-1 menu option that lets the user prepare, send, and receive messages on the ALL-IN-1 system.

element *n.*

generic

Any component of a network, such as a gate, register, memory, or processor.

elementary field *n.*

VAX DATATRIEVE

A record segment containing one item of information. It might contain a department number, a last name, or any other information a user may define as a single item. See also field.

elementary field description statement *n.*

Common Data Dictionary and VAX DATATRIEVE

A statement in a CDDL (common data definition language) or DATATRIEVE record definition that defines a field that is not subdivided into subordinate fields.

embed *v.*

DECWORD

To insert a ruler into a document, by pressing
RETURN after the ruler has been displayed.

embedded pointers *n.*

VAX DATATRIEVE

Pointers contained in the data records themselves
rather than a directory.

embedded ruler *n.*

DECmate II

A ruler that has been placed in a document by
pressing RETURN after the ruler has been
displayed.

emitter *n.*

generic

One of the three elements of a transistor; also, the
source of main carriers in semiconductor devices.

empty set *n.*

VAX DBMS

A set that does not contain any member records.

EMS destination *n.*

DIGITAL-specific

Electronic mail system destination. The name of
the computer node where an addressee can
receive mail messages.

emulated control unit *n.*

DECnet

A controller/line interface arrangement that
processes 3271 operations in conjunction with the
RSX-11/3271 Protocol Emulator (PE). Emulated
control units are assigned numbers for identification during generation of the PE. Each emulated
control unit appears to the host as an IBM 3271
control unit. For example, BU-0 (the name given
to the first controller of the BU device driver) is an
emulated control unit. See also controller.

emulation *n.*

DECnet

The use of a software/hardware combination that
enables a piece of equipment to be seen by an
IBM host as a 2780/3780-like remote station.

emulator *n.*

generic

A device or program that allows a program to run
on a type of computer other than the one for
which it was written.

RT-11

A hardware device that permits a program written
for a specific computer system to be run on a
different type of computer system.

emulator control mode *n.*

DECnet

A mode of operation in which management of
SNA (systems network architecture) protocol is
the exclusive concern of the protocol emulator
(PE). The protocol is transparent to the RSX-11M
application interacting in an EC session. Same as
EC mode.

enable *n.*

DIGITAL-specific

The ability to allow a terminal to send input or
receive output.

encryption *n.*

VAX/VMS

A process of encoding information so that its content is no longer immediately obvious to anyone who obtains a copy of it.

end-bracket indicator (EBI) *n.*

DECnet

A bit in the request header that, when set, indicates that the accompanying transmission ends a bracket. Same as EBI.

end communication layer *n.*

DECnet

The layer responsible for the system-independent aspects of creating and managing logical links for network users. End communication modules perform data flow control, end-to-end error control, and segmentation and reassembly of user messages. Same as network services layer.

end control *n.*

DECnet

The NSP (network services protocol) function that ensures the reliable, sequential delivery of NSP data messages. It consists of sequencing, acknowledgement, and retransmission mechanisms.

ending inventory *n.*

generic

The amount of inventory on hand at the end of an accounting period.

end node *n.*

DECnet

A topological description of a nonroutine node. Since a nonroutine node cannot perform route-through and supports only a single line, it must be an end node. However, it is also possible for a routing node with a single line to be an end node.

VAX/VMS

A node that can receive packets addressed to it and send packets to other nodes, but cannot route packets through from other nodes. Also called a nonrouting node.

end-of-file (EOF) *n.*

DIGITAL-specific

A character or record that, when accessed, indicates to the system that the end of the file has been reached. Same as EOF.

end of line *n.*

FMS

In the Form Editor, the rightmost screen position on a given horizontal line; not the rightmost character in a string of text.

end-of-line *n.*

FMS

Within the context of the Form Editor, the rightmost screen position on a given horizontal; not the rightmost character in a string of text.

end-of-procedure division *n.*

COBOL-74

The physical position in a COBOL source program after which no further procedures appear.

end of text *n.*

FMS

In the form editor layout phase, the rightmost character in a string of text.

end-of-text (ETX) *n.*

DECnet

An indicator that a message has ended. If multiple transmission blocks are contained in a message in BSC systems, ETX terminates the last block of the message. (ETB is used to terminate preceding blocks). The block check character is sent immediately following ETX. ETX requires a reply indicating the receiving station's status. Same as ETX.

end-of-transmission (EOT) *n.*

DECnet

A BISYNC data-link control character that indicates the end of a transmission; it may include one or more messages and it resets all stations on the line to control mode (unless that erroneously occurs within a transmission block). Same as EOT.

end-of-transmission block (ETB) *n.*

DECnet

A BISYNC data-link control character used during a message transfer operation to indicate to the receiving station that the BCC character follows and that another data block will be transmitted. When the RSX-11/3271 Protocol Emulator (PE) receives an ETB, it checks the BCC and then generates the appropriate response. Same as ETB.

end user *n.*

generic

The actual user of a computer system, not an original equipment manufacturer.

end-user module *n.*

DECnet

A module that runs in the user space of a network node and communicates with session control to obtain logical link service.

enlarged display *n.*

Medical Systems

A magnified image of a static or dynamic study.

E notation *n.*

MINC

A system of representing numbers that are greater than 999999 or less than 0.01. The letter E appears between the mathematical expression and the exponent; the letter E is used in place of the "x10" used in scientific notations.

ENQ *n.*

DECnet

The acronym for enquiry. ENQ is a BISYNC data-link control character used as a request for response to obtain an identification and/or an indication of station status. The RSX-11/3271 Protocol Emulator (PE) transmits an ENQ to request a reply from the host following a 3-second timeout, to request retransmission of the previous reply from the host, or as part of a temporary text delay (TTD) message signaling a transmitter abort sequence. Same as enquiry.

enqueue/dequeue *n.*

TOPS-10 and TOPS-20

A facility that ensures that resources such as files are shared correctly.

enquiry (ENQ) *n.*

DECnet

Used as a request for response to obtain identification and/or an indication of station status. In binary synchronous (BSC) transmission, ENQ is transmitted as part of an initialization sequence (line bid) in point-to-point operation, and as the final character of a selection or polling sequence in multipoint operation. Same as ENQ.

entity *n.*

DECnet

Major network management keywords such as CIRCUIT, LINE, LOGGING and NODE. Each entity has its own parameters and options. CIRCUIT, LINE, and NODE have counters also. Allowed plural forms are KNOWN and ACTIVE CIRCUITS, LINES, and NODES. NODES may also take the form LOOP NODES.

generic

The business concern, or other organization, for which a set of accounts is kept.

entry mask *n.*

VAX/VMS

A word whose bits represent the registers to be saved or restored on a subroutine or procedure call using the call and return instructions.

entry name *n.*

VAX PL/I

Identifier on a PROCEDURE or ENTRY statement that defines an entry point for that procedure.

entry point *n.*

DIGITAL-specific and VAX/VMS

A location that can be specified as the object of a call. It contains an entry mask and exception enables known as the entry point mask.

generic

The address at which any subroutine or subprogram will start execution.

enumerated type *n.*

VAX PASCAL and VAX/VMS

A type defined (with the enum keyword) to have an ordered set of integer values. The integer values are associated with constant identifiers named in the declaration. Although enum variables are stored internally as integers, they should be used in programs as if they had a distinct data type.

envelope *n.*

DECmate II

The space on a page reserved for one column, as defined in the control command. Used in multicolumn printing.

environment clause *n.*

COBOL-74

A clause that appears as part of an environment division entry.

EOF *n.*

DIGITAL-specific

The abbreviation for end-of-file. EOF is a character or record that, when accessed, indicates to the system that the end of the file has been reached. Same as end-of-file.

EOT *n.*

DECnet

The abbreviation for end-of-transmission. A BISYNC data-link control character that indicates the end of a transmission. It may include one or more messages, and it resets all stations on the line to control mode. Same as end-of-transmission.

EPILOG *n.*

Rdb/ELN

Rdb/ELN data manipulation language, used to store, retrieve, modify, and delete database entities.

EPROM *n.*

generic

The acronym for erasable programmable read-only memory. EPROM is a type of read-only memory that can be erased, thereby returning the device to a blank state. Same as erasable programmable read-only memory.

EPT *n.*

RSX-20F

The abbreviation for executive process table. EPT is the area in KL memory that is reserved for use in transmission of data between processors. See also relative address. Same as executive process table.

equality operator *n.*

VAX/VMS

One of the operators == (equal to) or ⊨ (not equal to). They are exactly analogous to the relational operators except that they are at the next lower level of precedence.

equijoin *n.*

Rdb/ELN

A join that involves matching values in a field from one relation with those in a corresponding field in another relation.

equity *n.*

generic

A general term for the difference between assets and liabilities.

equivalence name *n.*

VAX/VMS and VAX PL/I

A character string equated to a logical name such that, when a command or program refers to a file or device by its logical name, the system translates the logical name to its predefined equivalence name.

erasable programmable read-only memory (EPROM) *n.*

generic

A type of PROM that can be erased, thereby returning the device to a blank state. Same as EPROM.

erase mode *n.*

RGL/FEP

One of the writing modes; it removes previously drawn objects.

erase-on-allocate *n.*

VAX/VMS

A technique that applies an erasure pattern whenever a new area is allocated for a file's extent. The new area is erased with the erasure pattern so that subsequent attempts to read the area can only yield the erasure pattern and not some valuable remaining data. This technique is used to discourage disk scavenging.

erase-on-delete *n.*

VAX/VMS

A technique that applies an erasure pattern whenever a file is deleted or purged. This technique is used to discourage disk scavenging.

erasure pattern *n.*

VAX/VMS

A character string that can be used to overwrite magnetic media for the purpose of erasing the information that was previously stored in that area.

ergonomics *n.*

generic

The science of human engineering concerned with designing equipment, operating techniques, and work environments to maximize homan comfort and capabilities. It combines the study of human body mechanics and physical limitations with the psychological study of people in different working environments.

error *n.*

generic

Something that is incorrect or wrong.

error handler *n.*

BASIC/generic

A section of program code that tells BASIC what to do when an error occurs.

error interception *n.*

TOPS-10

An activity of the monitor in which it intercepts control of the program, examines location .JBINT, and transfers control to an error intercepting routine.

error log *n.*

DIGITAL-specific

A file that is used to record hardware and software failures and a selected amount of context of the failure.

error logger *n.*

VAX/VMS

A system process that empties the error log buffers and writes the error messages into the error file. Errors logged by the system include memory system errors, device errors and timeouts, and interrupts with invalid vector.

error message *n.*

DIGITAL-specific

Text displayed when an incorrect response is typed. Generally, one of four types of error message can be displayed: error, fatal error, user error, and warning.

generic

A message printed by the computer indicating a mistake or malfunction. An error message usually pinpoints the error and suggests how to correct it.

ersatz device *n.*

DECsystem-10

A disk-simulated library. Used like an ordinary device, it represents a particular project-programmer number.

escape *n.*

VAX/VMS

A transition from the normal mode of operation to a mode outside the normal.

escape character *n.*

VAX/VMS

The code that indicates the transition from normal to escape mode.

escape sequence *n.*

generic

A sequence of characters beginning with the ESCAPE character (ASCII-Decimal 27). ESCAPE sequences are used in loading, assigning, and invoking fonts. See also font load, font assignment and font invocation.

VAX/VMS

The set of character combinations starting with an escape character that the terminal transmits, without interpretation to the software setup, to handle escape sequences. An escape is a transition from the normal mode of operation to a mode outside the normal mode. An escape character is the code that indicates the transition from normal to escape mode.

ETB *n.*

DECnet

The abbreviation for end-of-transmission block. ETB is a BISYNC data-link control character used during a message transfer operation to indicate to the receiving station that the BCC character follows and that another data block will be transmitted. When the RSX-11/3271 Protocol Emulator (PE) receives an ETB, it checks the BCC and then generates the appropriate response. Same as end-of-transmission block.

etch *n.*

generic

The printed pattern used as a conductive path on a circuit board.

Ethernet *n.*

generic

A communications concept for local communication networks that employ coaxial cable as a passive communications medium to interconnect different kinds of computers, information processing products, and office equipment at a local business site without requiring switching logic or control by a central computer.

Ethernet communications system *n.*

Ethernet

Refers to the stations, cables controllers, and physical channel components and accessories as a whole in an operational Ethernet where data frames may be transmitted between any station pair. This includes the Ethernet physical channel and the stations.

Ethernet physical channel *n.*

Ethernet

The Ethernet communciations system, excluding the stations. The Ethernet physical channel includes the coaxial cable, coaxial cable connectors, barrel connectors, terminators, grounding components, transceivers, and transceiver drop cables. A local area network, specified jointly by Digital Eqipment Corporation, Intel Corporation, and Xerox Corporation.

Ethernet protocol *n.*

DECnet

In the data-link layer of DNA (DIGITAL Network Architecture), the protocol that implements the Ethernet data-link protocol for communication between adjacent nodes connected by an Ethernet local area network.

ETX *n.*

DECnet

The abbreviation for end-of-text. ETX is a BISYNC data-link control character indicating to the receiver the last (or only) block of a message. The RSX-11/3271 Protocol Emulator (PE) checks the BCC (block character check) character that follows and returns an appropriate response to the host. Contrast with ETB: ETX terminates the last block of a message; ETB terminates the first block or an intermediate block of a multiple-block transmission. Same as end-of-text.

evaluation order *n.*

DSM-11

The way in which DSM-11 evaluates expressions. Normally, DSM-11 evaluates all expressions in the following sequence:

1. all occurrences of indirection

2. all unary operators

3. all binary operators.

evasive action *n.*

VAX/VMS

A responsive behavior by VAX/VMS to discourage break in attempts (unauthorized use) whenever they seem to be in progress. VAX/VMS has a set of criteria it uses to detect the fact that break in attempts may be underway. Typically, once VAX/VMS suspects that an unauthorized user is attempting to log in, the evasive action consists of locking out all login attempts by the offender for a limited period of time.

event *n.*

DECnet

A network or system-specific occurrence for which the logging component maintains a record. See also event class and event type.

PEARL

A system action that is not dependent on time. When an event occurs a condition is set (true) and reset after the appropriate reaction has been initiated.

TOPS-10, TOPS-20, and VAX/VMS

A change in process status or an indication of the occurrence of some activity that concerns an individual process or cooperating processes. It is an incident reported to the scheduler that affects a process's ability to execute. Events can be synchronous with the process's execution such as a wait request, or they can be asynchronous such as I/O completion.

event class *n.*

DECnet and VAX/VMS

A particular classification of events. Generally, this follows the DNA (DIGITAL Network Architecture) architectural layers, with some layers possibly containing more than one event class. A class also includes the identification of system-specific events. See also event.

event code *n.*

TOPS-10

The octal code assigned to a particular event in the system event file.

event datatype *n.*

Rdb/ELN

A VAXELN system datatype that represents the state of an event used to synchronize processes.

event flag *n.*

FMS

A bit or word used as a signal. Typically the flag is zero, or clear, before a certain event occurs. After the event occurs, the flag is one, or set.

VAX/VMS

A bit in an event flag cluster that can be set or cleared to indicate the occurrence of the event associated with that flag. Event flags are used to synchronize activities in a process or among many processes.

event flag cluster *n.*

TOPS-20

A set of 32 event flags. Eight clusters are available to a process: two are process-local, two are common to cooperating processes within a group, and four are reserved for future use.

VAX/VMS

A set of 32 event flags used for event posting. Four clusters are defined for each process: two process-local clusters and two common event flag clusters. Of the process-local flags, eight are reserved for system use.

event logger protocol *n.*

DECnet

In the network management layer of DNA (DIGITAL Network Architecture), the protocol used for recording significant occurrences in lower layers. An event could result from a line coming up, a counter reaching a threshold, a node becoming unreachable, and so on.

event mark *n.*

Medical Systems

An occurrence or incident pulse. With the NCV-11 interface, an event mark is an external pulse noted in memory as a minus 1 in the sequential memory locations during the time that the incident (pulse) occurs.

event type *n.*

DECnet and VAX/VMS

A particular type of event, unique within an event class.

examine region *n.*

RSX-20F

A region in KL memory that is accessed by the PDP-11 using protected examines. See also relative address.

exception *n.*

DIGITAL-specific and VAX/VMS

An event detected by the hardware (other than an interrupt or jump, branch, case, or call instruction) that changes the normal flow of instruction or set of instructions. An exception differs from an interrupt in that an interrupt is caused by a system activity independent of the current instruction. There are three types of hardware exceptions; trips, faults, and aborts. Examples are: attempts to execute a privileged or reserved instruction, trace traps, compatibility mode faults, breakpoint instruction execution, and arithmetic traps such as overflow, underflow, and divide by zero. See also fault, trap, abort, and condition.

exception condition *n.*

DIGITAL-specific

An event, detected by hardware or software, that causes a change in the flow in instruction execution (caused by a condition other than an interrupt or execution of a jump, branch, case, or call instruction). An exception condition is associated with the execution of an instruction and occurs synchronously with process execution. Examples are arithmetic overflow or underflow, illegal address references, and trace traps.

exception dispatcher *n.*

VAX/VMS

An operating system procedure that searches for a condition handler when an exception condition occurs. If no exception handler is found for the exception or condition, the image that incurred the exception is terminated.

exception enables *n.*

VAX/VMS

Three bits of the PSW (processor status word) that control the processor's action on certain arithmetic exceptions. Same as trap enables.

exception response n.

DECnet

A negative response returned to a request which specifies, through a setting in the request header, that only exception responses be returned.

exception vector n.

VAX/VMS

A storage location known to the system that contains the starting address of a procedure to be executed when a given interrupt or exception occurs. The system defines separate vectors for each interrupting device controller and for classes of exceptions. Each system vector is a longword. Same as vector and interrupt vector.

exchange step n.

ACMS

One of three kinds of steps that define the work of a VAX-11 ACMS multiple-step task. An exchange step handles input and output between the task and the terminal user.

excluded-record string n.

generic

A string of characters used to mark records that cannot be assessed or processed.

exclusive update mode n.

VAX DBMS

The mode in which a run unit readies a realm when it must lock all other users out of the realm to perform updates.

executable image n.

VAX/VMS

An image that can be run in a process. When run, an executable image is read from a file for execution in a process.

executable section n.

PASCAL and VAX PASCAL

The part of a block delimited by BEGIN and END, containing the executable statements, that performs the actions of the block.

execution n.

generic

Performance of the instructions given by a program.

executive n.

DECnet

In an operating system, the controlling program or set of routines. See also communications executive.

generic

The set of programs, in an operating system such as I/O, resource allocation, and program execution that controls the running of routines.

executive adj.

generic

In software, pertaining to a program that controls other programs.

executive dynamic debugging technique (EDDT) n.

DECsystem-10

A version of DDT (dynamic debugging technique) used for debugging programs (such as the monitor) in executive mode. Same as EDDT.

executive mode n.

DIGITAL-specific and VAX/VMS

The second most privileged processor access mode (mode 1). The record management services (RMS) and many of the operating system's system service procedures execute in executive mode.

151

generic

The condition occurring when the system is running the part of a program that controls a set of internal routines.

executive process table (EPT) *n.*

RSX-20F

The area in KL memory that is reserved for use in transmission of data between processors. Same as EPT.

executor node *n.*

DECnet

The node where the active local network management function is running (the node actually executing the command); the active network node physically connected to one end of a line being used for a load, dump, trigger, or line loop test.

VAX/VMS

The node at which an NCP command actually executes.

exit *n.*

generic

A command that allows a user to quit a procedure or function or to finish execution of an image.

VAX/VMS

An image rundown activity that occurs when image execution terminates either normally or abnormally. Image rundown activities include deassigning I/O channels and disassociation of common event flag clusters. Any user-specified or system-specified exit handlers are called exits.

exit *v.*

A-to-Z

To proceed to the next screen or function.

exit handler *n.*

VAX/VMS

A procedure executed when an image exits. An exit handler enables a procedure that is not on the call stack to gain control and clean up procedure-owned data bases before the actual image exit occurs.

exit phase *n.*

FMS

In the form editor, a phase in which the current form may be saved and the form editor terminated.

exit status code *n.*

RSX-11M

The status-return code that all system tasks on the RSX-11M-PLUS systems, DCL and MCR commands, and utilities send when they have completed their operations.

expedited flow *n.*

DECnet

A transmission protocol in SNA (systems network architecture) that, when exercised, permits a request to be passed ahead of normal flow data.

expenditure *n.*

generic

The decrease in an asset or increase in a liability associated with the acquisition of goods or services.

expense *n.*

generic

Resources used up or consumed during an accounting period.

explicit mapping *n.*

Terminal Data Management System

The TDMS (Terminal Data Management System) request instructions (INPUT TO, OUTPUT TO, and RETURN TO) that specify mapping of data between form and record fields.

explicit prompt *n.*

RSX-11M

The three-letter prompt that identifies the command line interpreter or other system task. For example: DCL (DIGITAL Command Language), MCR (monitor console routine), and PIP (peripheral interchange program).

explicit scope terminator *n.*

generic

A reserved word that terminates the scope of a particular conditional statement.

exploded pie graph *n.*

generic

A pie graph in which one or more segments are broken away, or exploded, from the pie.

exponential decay *n.*

TOPS-20

An effect observed in which software that once worked has stopped working. Frequently the cause is that associated software has been improved.

exponential notation *n.*

DSM-11

A shorthand method of expressing very large or very small numeric quantities similar to scientific notation. The format for exponential notation is: number exponent. DSM-11 can interpret numeric literals or numeric data entered in exponential notation format; however, it does not produce the results of mathematical calculations in exponential notation format.

exponentiation *n.*

generic

The mathematical operation in which a number or a symbol is multiplied by itself one or more times.

expression *n.*

generic

1. A source language description or a logical or mathematical statement made up of operands and operations.

2. Any combination of variables and/or constants with arithmetic operators that the computer can evaluate to produce a result.

expression atom *n.*

DSM-11

A unit used to build expressions. An expression atom can consist of a single variable, literal, function, an expression atom preceded by a unary operator, or an expression in parentheses.

expression element *n.*

DSM-11

An expression element is the operand component of a DSM-11 expression. An expression element may be a constant, a simple variable, a literal, a local subscripted variable, a global variable, a function reference, or a subexpression.

extend (file operation) *n.*

RSX-11M

An RMS-11 request for the file processor to add blocks to a file's allocation. See also default extension quantity.

extended address *n.*

MicroPower PASCAL

Memory or device addresses in excess of 16 bits. Mapped memory systems use extended addresses in order to address more than 64KB address space.

extended argument block *n.*

DECsystem-10

A LOOKUP monitor call with at least six arguments and used only for disks.

extended attribute block (XAB) *n.*

VAX/VMS

An RMS user data structure that contains additional file attributes beyond those expressed in the file access block (FAB), such as boundary types (aligned on cylinder, logical block number, virtual block number) and file protection information. Same as XAB.

extended buffer pool (XBUF) *n.*

DIGITALspecific

1. A portion of a computer's physical memory that is reserved for use by the operating system. Message send/receive, the DECnet/E package, the RSTS/2780 package, the FIP buffering module, and the data caching module use this reserved memory; if none is available, they use small buffers. Same as XBUF.

2. An area of user memory reserved for extended buffers that can range in size from 32 words to the maximum size of the extended buffer pool. The extended buffer pool is used for data caching, directory caching, and other system functions.

extended diagnostic messages *n.*

RSX-11M

A feature of RMSBCK and RMSRST: The utility prints a detailed error message on the terminal, allowing the user to decide to continue processing or not. See also query mode.

extended emulator control mode (XEC mode) *n.*

DECnet

In sessions where management of SNA (systems network architecture) protocol is shared by the applications and a protocol emulator (PE), those sessions are said to be operating in extended emulator control (XEC) mode. Protocol options available in EC mode are also available in XEC mode. Same as XEC mode.

extended file *n.*

DECsystem-10

A file that has more than one RIB in which to record the retrieval pointers.

extended lookup *n.*

DECsystem-10

An undefined user operation (UUO) lookup with at least six arguments. This can be used only for disks.

extended mode *n.*

COBOL-74

The state of a file after execution of a OPEN statement with the EXTEND phrase specified for that file and before the execution of a CLOSE statement for that file.

extended precision *n.*

generic

Arithmetic operations on operands two or more word sizes in length.

extended RIBS *n.*

DECsystem-10

Additional retrieval information blocks (RIBs) required when the retrieval pointers in a file overflow the prime RIB. See also prime RIB.

extension *n.*

DIGITAL-specific

1. A three character string that helps to identify the type of a file. It immediately follows a period preceded by a file name.

2. The amount of space to be allocated at the end of a file each time a sequential write exceeds the allocated length of the file.

extent *n.*

RSX-11M

A portion of a file containing contiguous blocks that is not recognized by the file processor as being contiguous with other portions of the file. See also allocation.

VAX PL/I

The range comprising the low bound: high bound for one dimension of an array. Length of a string.

VAX/VMS

The contiguous area on a disk containing a file or a portion of a file. Consists of one or more clusters.

external data item *n.*

generic

A data item described as part of an external record in one or more programs of a run unit. An external data item can be referenced from any program in which it is described.

external data record *n.*

generic

A record described in one or more programs of a run unit. Its data items can be referenced from any program in which they are described.

external file *n.*

ACMS

A file that a main procedure opens but an external subroutine accesses.

PASCAL and VAX PASCAL

A file that exists outside the scope of a PASCAL program and therefore must be specified in the program heading.

external file connector *n.*

generic

A file connector that is accessible to one or more object programs in the run unit.

external key *n.*

VAX DATATRIEVE

A data item representing the key of a record that resides in an index with a pointer to the record, but does not reside in the record itself.

external page *n.*

RSX-20F

An area (4K) of real memory space (760000-777777) containing CPU and peripheral device control and status registers (also known as the I/O page).

external procedure *n.*

DIGITAL-specific

A procedure that is not contained in another procedure.

external storage *n.*

DIGITAL-specific

A storage medium other than main memory such as a disk or tape.

external subroutine *n.*

DIGITAL-specific

A subroutine callable by any program (if so linked) but that is not a part of the program.

external switch *n.*

VAX COBOL

A software device that indicates that one of two alternate states exists.

external symbol *n.*

DECsystem-10

A global symbol that is referenced in one module but defined in another module. The EXTERN statement in MACRO-10 is used to declare a symbol external. A subroutine name referenced in a CALL statement in a FORTRAN module is automatically declared external.

MicroPower PASCAL

A link between independently compiled or assembled program modules. An external symbol in one module represents a symbol globally defined in another module. See also global symbol.

external variable *n.*

DIGITAL-specific

A variable that is known in all blocks that declare it with the EXTERNAL attribute.

VAX/VMS

A variable that is defined externally to any function. External variables provide a means other than argument passing for exchanging data between the functions that compromise a C program.

F11ACP *n.*

VAX/VMS

Files-11 ancillary control process.

FAB *n.*

RMS-11, RSX-11M, and VAX/VMS

The abbreviation for file access block. FAB is an RMS user data structure that describes a particular file and contains file-related information needed for data operations such as OPEN, CLOSE, or CREATE. Same as file access block.

facility *n.*

TOPS-20

A collection of one or more modules that implement a set of related functions or services. A particular implementation of a facility could be either a process or a procedure. The interface to a facility is always in the form of a procedure call. Examples include record manager (a procedure-based facility), file manager (a process-based facility), and a compiler (a procedure-based facility).

VAX PSI

A service or mode of operation that a PSDN (packet switching data network) is able to provide for a user upon subscription and/or request, for example, fast select or reverse charging.

FAILSAFE *n.*

DECsystem-10

A utility program used to save the contents of the disk on magnetic tape and later restore the saved contents back onto disk.

fail-soft system *n.*

generic

A system that continues to process data despite the failure of parts of the system. Usually accompanied by a deterioration in performance.

failure exception mode *n.*

VAX/VMS

A mode of execution selected by a process indicating that it wants an exception condition declared if an error occurs as the result of a system service call. The normal mode is for the system service to return an error status code for which the process must test.

fair market value (FMV) *n.*

USFC/generic

The market value of the equipment. At the end of the lease, FMV is determined by the used equipment market place. Same as FMV.

FAL *n.*

DECnet

An abbreviation for file access listener. With DECnet, FAL is a program that resides on a DECnet host and acts as the target for requests made by the NFT programs residing on remote DECnet hosts. The FAL program is responsible for determining a user's access privileges to a requested file and the subsequent honoring or rejecting of the request. Same as file access listener.

MINC

An abbreviation for file access listener. FAL is an internode file utility that services local node requests to access remote node files. Same as file access listener.

fanfold paper *n.*

Publications/generic

A long, continuous sheet of paper separated into pages by perforations. Same as continuous-form paper.

fast select n.

VAX PSI

An optional PSDN (packet switching data network) facility that allows a DTE (data terminal equipment) to include a user data field of up to 128 bytes when setting up a virtual circuit.

fatal error n.

DIGITAL-specific

An error from which a process cannot recover. Fatal errors are those that cause the CPU to stop, or are disk write errors not caused by the disk drive being powered down or write-locked. Errors that a process can recover from are not fatal. Same as non-trappable errors.

fatal message n.

DIGITAL-specific

A message indicating that a fatal error condition has occurred. If the program does not abort automatically, the fatal message describes the error and requests corrective action.

fault n.

DECSIM

A real-life failure, modeled in fault simulation for scoring test patterns.

DIGITAL-specific

A hardware exception condition that occurs in the middle of an instruction. This condition leaves the registers and memory in a consistent state such that elimination of the fault and restarting the instruction gives correct results. See also exception.

fault collapsing n.

DECSIM

A partitioning of faults into equivalence classes to improve speed of test generation and simulation.

fault detection n.

DECSIM

The determination of a malfunction in a device under test by detecting incorrect response data at observation points (usually output pins of a chip or a module) during the execution of a test program.

fault dictionary n.

DECSIM

A list of elements in which each element consists of a fault signature associated with all the faults that cause the fault signature.

fault dropping n.

DECSIM

A technique that speeds up fault simulation by eliminating faults in the network dynamically as they are detected.

fault effect n.

DECSIM

Represents the value of a faulty network at any node where it differs from the good (unfaulted) network. (This term is unique to concurrent fault simulation.)

fault equivalence n.

DECSIM

Refers to two faults having an identical effect on a circuit.

fault signature n.

DECSIM

A set of values at network outputs or observation points used to determine what is bad in the network.

fault simulation *n.*

DECSIM

A process to determine the responses of a logic network to a given set of test patterns in the presence of a given set of faults, to score the test patterns, and to develop test programs.

fault simulator *n.*

DECSIM

A logic-level simulator that can simulate both faulty networks and good (unfaulted) networks.

fault source *n.*

DECSIM

A simulator's representation of a type of fault and its location.

fault tolerance *n.*

DECSIM

The capacity of a computer, subsystem, or program to withstand the effects of internal faults.

fault verification *n.*

DECSIM

A process that assures that a given circuit malfunction will be detected by a given test program.

FCB *n.*

DIGITAL-specific and VAX/VMS

The abbreviation for file control block. FCB in IAS and RSX-11M is a memory-resident structure used by the operating system to coordinate access to a file that is opened by an active task. Same as file control block.

FCP *n.*

RSX-20F and TOPS-20

The abbreviation for file control primitive. FCP is the mechanism that is used by the record managers for accessing a physical device. Same as file control primitive.

FCS *n.*

VAX PSI

The abbreviation for frame checking sequence. A 16-bit error check polynomial that checks that the bit content of a frame is the same before and after transmission. Where K = number of bits in the frame not including the flags and FCS itself and con = the contents of the frame not including the flags and the FCS itself. Same as frame checking sequence.

FMS

The abbreviation for file conversion system, an RSX-11M file management system. FCS is a set of routines that can be used in tasks to open and close files, read from them, write to them, and extend or delete them. Same as file conversion system.

RSX-11M

The abbreviation for file control services. FCS is a file management software product available on IAS and RSX-11M operating systems. Same as file control services. See also record management.

FDL *n.*

VAX/VMS

The abbreviation for file definition language. A special-purpose language used to write specifications for data files. These specifications are written in text files called FDL files; they are then used by VAX RMS utilities and library routines to create the actual data files.

FDT *n.*

DIGITAL-specific

The abbreviation for function decision table. FDT is a table located in a driver and used by QI/O to validate I/O requests. Same as function decision table.

VAX/VMS

Function decision table.

FDT routine *n.*

VAX/VMS

Driver routines called by the Queue I/O Request system service to perform device-dependent preprocessing of an I/O request.

FDU *n.*

TDMS

The abbreviation for form definition utility. FDU is a utility used to process form definitions and store them in the Common Data Dictionary (CDD). Same as form definition utility.

FDV *n.*

FMS

The abbreviation for Form Driver. FDV is the FMS run-time component that interacts with an application program to display forms on the VT100 or VT125 terminals and to accept data entered by the operators. Same as Form Driver.

FED *n.*

FMS

The abbreviation for Form Editor. FED is the FMS component used to create and modify forms through interactive sessions at a VT100 or VT125 terminal. During these sessions the forms are displayed on the screen. Same as Form Editor.

feedback *n.*

generic

The return of a sample of the output of a system or process to the input, often in such a way that the output is automatically kept within defined limits.

fence *n.*

TOPS-10

The boundary between the active and passive search lists.

ferric oxide *adj.*

generic

Pertaining to the chemical iron oxide, used in magnetic tape or disks.

ferrite *adj.*

generic

Pertaining to a type of magnetic material.

fetch *v.*

TOPS-10

To locate and load a quantity of data from storage.

FIB *n.*

VAX/VMS

The abbreviation for file information block. FIB is a data structure that is the first parameter (p1) used by the QI/O system service routines to build the I/O request packet (IRP) and the complex buffered I/O buffer (consisting of the ABD and the AIB). The FIB contains much of the information the user must pass to the MTAACP to perform a specific task. The information is supplied by the user. The FIB contains access control values (rewind, current position, read only, write, and so on), file identification, and wildcard context (maintains position for a wild card operation). Same as file information block.

fiber optic cable *n.*

generic

A transmission medium designed to transmit digital signals in the form of pulses of light. Fiber optic cable is noted for its properties of electrical isolation and resistance to electrostatic contamination.

DECnet

A cable made of glass fibers and designed to transmit digital signals in the form of pulses of light. Fiber optic cable is noted for its properties of electrical isolation and resistance to electrostatic contamination.

FIC *n.*

DECnet

The abbreviation for the first-in-chain. FIC refers to the first 256 bytes of data of a message consisting of more than 256 bytes, transmitted by an SNA (systems network architecture) program or by the protocol emulator in a session governed by the Profile 3 or 4 protocol set. That the chain element being transmitted is first-in-chain is specified by a setting in the chaining control field of the request header. In emulator control mode, the PE (protocol emulator) segments messages into 256 byte elements, and sets the chain indicators, as appropriate, in the request header, for messages flowing from RSX-11M to SNA. For messages flowing the other way in EC and XEC modes, SNA does the segmenting and sets the chain indicators. Same as first-in-chain.

FID *n.*

VAX/VMS

The abbreviation for file identifier. A 6-byte value used to uniquely identify a file on a Files-11 disk volume. The file number, file sequence number, and relative volume number are contained in the file identifier. Same as file identifier.

field *n.*

A-to-Z

A subdivision of an x value. Each x value may have up to eight fields.

FMS

On a form, a variable portion that can be modified by the operator and/or the application program; a field can contain field-marker characters, which cannot be modified. A field is defined by a contiguous string of field-marker and field-validation characters and cannot exceed one line in length.

generic

1. A specified subset of a storage area or a display area which is used for a specific class of data.

2. A place of work away from the central offices of an organization.

3. A segment of a data record.

VAX/VMS

A set of contiguous bytes in a logical record. See also variable-length bit field.

field attributes *n.*

FMS

Characteristics assigned to fields, such as must fill, right justified and echo.

generic

A description of the characteristics of the fields in a record.

field characters *n.*

FMS

Refers to both field definition characters and field marker characters.

field-definition characters *n.*

FMS

Characters that define data positions within a field and describe valid input for that position. The field-definition characters and the valid input associated with each are:

    A - Alphabetic
    C - Alphanumeric
    N - Signed numeric
    X - Any character
    9 - Numeric

See also field marker character.

field description *n.*

DIGITAL-specific

A collection of data in a data dictionary that describes a field in the file. A field description contains the name, length, type, and starting position of the field it describes.

field description statement *n.*

Common Data Dictionary

The statement that defines field characteristics in CDDL (common data definition language) source files. The four types of field description statements are ELEMENTARY, STRUCTURE, COPY, and VARIANT.

field identifiers *n.*

TDMS

The characters specified in a TDMS form definition that determine the location, length, and picture-type of a field.

field initialization *n.*

DECnet

The process of assigning to the field the attributes that were specified to the preprocessor, filling the field with the initial value (if one was specified) or the filler character, and clearing the indicator that the field contains master duplication data.

field-marker characters *n.*

FMS

Punctuation characters that are displayed within a field but which cannot be modified by the operator; used for clarity and readability of data in a field, Examples of field-marker characters are hyphen (-) and slash (/). See also field-definition characters.

field mode *n.*

FMS

In the Form Editor Layout phase, the mode that lets you create and modify fields in a form. Only field-validation characters or field-marker characters can be entered in field mode. Contrast with text mode.

field name *n.*

DIGITAL-specific

In a field, the heading enclosed by angle brackets (<>). The field name is a label enabling both the user and the system to identify a particular field. For example, if the field name is <name>, the contents of that field will be a name.

generic

A six character alpha string that names a field.

FMS

A field attribute identifying each field within a form. Names are 1 to 32 characters long; the first character must be alphabetic.

VAX DATATRIEVE

A record segment containing one item of information. Same as elementary field.

field picture *n.*

FMS

The appearance of a field as specified by its field characters. The picture describes both the valid contents of a field and its screen format.

Terminal Data Management System

A group of one or more field identifiers in a TDMS (Terminal Data Management System) form definition that determines the location, length, and picture-type of a field. For example, 99999 is a field picture that indicates that up to five numeric characters can be entered in that field. See also Picture-Type.

field reset *n.*

DECnet

A field is reset by filling it with the initial value, if one was specified, or the filler character, and clearing the indicator that the field contains master duplication data. Field reset is identical to field initialization except that the fields current attributes are not altered.

field terminator code *n.*

DECWORD

A value that corresponds to the manner in which input is terminated in a field.

generic

A value that represents a key that can be struck to complete input to a field.

field terminator key *n.*

generic

A key pressed by the operator to signal the completion of data entry to a field or a form.

field tree *n.*

VAX DATATRIEVE

A hierarchical model of the fields in a DATATRIEVE record, based on the record definition stored in the Common Data Dictionary.

field-validation characters *n.*

generic

Characters that define data positions within a field and that describe valid input for that position.

Field Validator *n.*

TDMS

A special field attribute that requires the terminal operator's input to be within a specified range, match an item from a specified list, or meet one or more other conditions.

field value *n.*

DECWORD

In a field, the piece of information following the field name. The field value, the actual content of a field, can vary in every record.

FMS

The contents of a field as known by the Form Driver and not including any field-marker characters. Field values are always stored as ASCII characters and not as binary numeric values.

FIFO *n.*

generic

First in, first out. A method used for processing and recovery of data in which the oldest item is processed or recovered first.

VAX/VMS

First-in/first-out; the order in which processing is performed. For example, processing on a FIFO queue would be on a first-come, first-served basis. See also LIFO.

FIFO (First-In, First-Out) method *n.*

generic

A method for finding the cost of sales, using the assumption that the oldest goods (those first in) were the first to be sold (first out).

figurative constant *n.*

generic

A compiler-generated value that a program can refer to with specific reserved words. Also, a symbolic character.

FILDDT *n.*

DECWORD

An Executive DDT (dynamic debugging technique). FILDDT is a version of DDT used for examining and changing a file on disk instead of in core memory. This program is used to examine a monitor for debugging purposes.

file *n.*

generic

A collection of related records treated as a unit and usually referenced by a logical name.

VAX/VMS

A set of data elements arranged in a structure significant to the user. A file is any named, stored program or data, or both, to which the system has access. Access can be of two types: read-only, meaning the file is not to be altered, and read-write, meaning the contents of the file can be altered. See also volume.

file access block (FAB) *n.*

RMS-11, RSX-11M, and VAX/VMS

An RMS user data structure that describes a particular file and contains file-related information needed for data operations, such as OPEN, CLOSE, or CREATE. Same as FAB.

file access listener (FAL) *n.*

DECnet

A program that resides on a DECnet host and acts as the target for requests made by the NFT programs residing on remote DECnet hosts. The FAL program is responsible for determining a user's access privileges to a requested file and the subsequent honoring or rejecting of the request. Same as FAL.

MINC

An internode file utility that services local node requests to access remote node files. Same as FAL.

file allocation *n.*

DIGITAL-specific

The assigning of the placement of a file on a volume.

file attributes *n.*

RSX-11M

Characteristics of a file stored in the file directory and prologue. They include elements such as file organization and record format.

File Cabinet *n.*

ALL-IN-1

The computer storage area where all documents created or received are retained for later use: the user's personal data-base.

file cluster *n.*

RSX-11M

A single- or multi-block unit of disk storage assignment. File cluster is the minimum unit used by the file processor during file allocation and extension. File cluster size is a file attribute.

file component *n.*

PASCAL and VAX PASCAL

An accessible unit of a file variable. A file component can be of any type except a file type or a structured type with components of a file type.

file constant *n.*

VAX PL/I

A name declared with the FILE attribute but not the VARIABLE attribute.

file control block (FCB) *n.*

DIGITAL-specific

In IAS and RSX-11M, a memory-resident structure used by the operating systems to coordinate access to a file that is opened by an active task. Same as FCB.

file control primitive (FCP) *n.*

RSX-11M

The mechanism that is used by the record manager for accessing a physical device. Same as FCP.

file control service (FCS) *n.*

RSX-11M

A file management software product available on IAS and RSX-11M operating systems. Same as FCS.

file conversion system *n.*

FMS

An RSX-11M file management system. FCS is a set of routines that can be used in tasks to open and close files, read from them, write to them, and extend or delete them. Same as FCS.

file daemon *n.*

DECsystem-10

The monitor calls the file daemon (if FTFDAE=1) every time that someone tries to access a file that has a 4, 5, 6, or 7 code in the owner's protection field and the access failed due to a protection error.

file definition language (FDL) *n.*

VAX/VMS

A special-purpose language used to write specifications for data files. These specifications are written in text files called FDL files; they are then used by VAX RMS utilities and library routines to create the actual data files.

file description attribute *n.*

VAX PL/I

One of the PL/I attribute keywords that can be specified in the declaration of a file constant or used in an OPEN statement. The file description attributes indicate the properties of the file and the manner in which a file will be used.

file extension *n.*

TOPS-10

A string of 1 to 3 alphanumeric characters, usually to describe the kind of information in a file. The file extension must be separated from the filename by a period.

File Folders *n.*

ALL-IN-1

An optional category the user can include in a document's header information to specify a certain file grouping.

file generation number (or file generation) *n.*

DIGITAL-specific xD

A number supplied by the user to distinguish separate "runs" of a program or procedure. The number is used to specify a particular generation of a file; otherwise, the latest generation is used.

file generation version *n.*

DIGITAL-specific

A number supplied by the system to distinguish separate instances of a particular generation. File generation version allows the rerunning of a particular generation until it is correct.

file header *n.*

DIGITAL-specific

Each file has an associated file header block that includes information needed by the file system to find and use the file. Some of the information in the file header block is displayed by the DCL DIRECTORY command. See also block header.

VAX/RMS and VAX/VMS

A block in the index file that describes a file on a FILES-11 disk. Every file residing on the disk has at least one file header, which provides the location of the file's extents.

file-ID (file-identification) *n.*

RSX-11M

An identifying notation optionally returned when a file is created or opened by file specification.

file-identification (file-ID) number *n.*

RSX-11M

A number in the form (mmm,nnn) that is displayed by the DCL DIRECTORY command and that is used by the file system to locate files on FILES-11 disk volumes. In some commands, the file-ID number can be substituted for a file specification, but in general that number is used only by the system.

file identifier (FID) *n.*

VAX/VMS

A 6-byte value used to uniquely identify a file on a Files-11 disk volume. The file number, file sequence number, and relative volume number are contained in the file identifier. Same as FID.

file information block (FIB) *n.*

VAX/VMS

A data structure that is the first parameter (p1) used by the QI/O system service routines to build the I/O request packet (IRP) and the complex buffered I/O buffer (consisting of the ABD, ancillary control buffer descriptor, and the AIB, ancillary control process I/O buffer). The FIB contains much of the information the user must pass to the MTAACP to perform a specific task. The information is supplied by the user. The FIB contains access control values (rewind, current position, read only, write, and so on), file identification, and wildcard context (maintain position for a wild card operation). Same as FIB.

file maintenance *n.*

DIGITAL-specific

The activity of keeping a mass storage volume and its directory up to date by adding, changing, or deleting files.

file management system *n.*

DIGITAL-specific

A set of VAX/VMS operating system procedures that programs can call to process files and records within files. VAX/RMS lets program issued GET and PUT requests at the record level (record I/O) as well as read and write blocks (block I/O). RMS is an integral part of the VMS system software and is used by high-level languages, such as VAX/VMS, COBOL and BASIC, to implement their input and output statements. DATATRIEVE uses VAX/RMS to create, define, store, and maintain files and records within files. See also record management services (RMS).

file name *n.*

DIGITAL-specific

A string of up to six characters that names a file. It may immediately follow a device name and immediately precede an extension.

file-name (or filename) *n.*

DIGITAL-specific

A user-defined word that names a file described in a file description entry or a sort-merge file description entry within the file section of the data division.

generic

A title assigned to a group of related records in computer memory or on a mass storage device.

VAX/VMS

The field preceding a file type in a file specification that contains a 1- through 39-character name for a file.

file name extension (or filename extension) *n.*

DIGITAL-specific

One to three alphanumeric characters usually chosen by the program to describe the class of information in a file. The extension is separated from the filename by a period.

VAX/VMS

The field in a file specification that consists of a period (.) followed by a 0- to 39-character type identification. By convention, this field identifies a generic class of files that have the same use or characteristics, such as compiler and assembler listing files, binary object files, and so on. Same as file type.

file number *n.*

Medical Systems

A channel number associated with a file; the number is used when referring to the file within a program.

file organization *n.*

VAX/VMS

The particular file structure used as the physical arrangement of the data comprising a file on a mass storage medium. The RMS file organizations are sequential, relative, and indexed.

file-oriented data structure *n.*

DIGITAL-specific

An I/O structure that provides information used by file-oriented components.

file page *n.*

TOPS-20

The data that is between two form feeds or before the first or after the last form feed of a file.

file position *n.*

PASCAL

The position immediately following the file component that was last read or written. Only the component at the current file position can be accessed.

file processor *n.*

RSX-11M

1. A component of the operating system that maintains the structure and integrity of data storage on file-structured devices.

2. In RSTS/E, the file processor.

See also FILES-11 ancillary control processor.

file reference *n.*

VAX PL/I

The use of an identifier declared as a file constant, a scalar reference to a variable with the FILE attribute, or a function that returns a file value.

files *n.*

generic

Information that has been collected in such a way that it can be stored in a computer.

FILES-11 *n.*

RSX-11M and VAX/VMS

The name of the on-disk structure used by the RSX-11, IAS, and VAX/VMS operating systems.

VAX/VMS

The name of the disk structure used by the RSX-11, and VAX/VMS operating systems. Refer also to Files-11 Structure Level 1 and Files-11 Structure Level 2.

FILES-11 ancillary control process (FILES-11 ACP) *n.*

RSX-11M, TOPS-20, and VAX/VMS

The interface process that is the file manager for the FILES-11 on-disk structure. Same as FILES-11 ACP.

Files-11 Structure Level 1 *n.*

VAX/VMS

The original Files-11 structure used by IAS, RSX-11M, IAS, and VAX/VMS operating systems. Refer also to Files-11 Structure Level 2. Same as On-Disk Structure Level 1 (ODS-1).

Files-11 Structure Level 2 *n.*

VAX/VMS

The second generation disk file structure supported by VAX/VMS. Same as On-Disk Structure Level 2 (ODS-2).

file section *n.*

TOPS-10

That part of a file recorded on any one volume. The sections of a file do not have sections of other files interspersed.

VAX/VMS

A file section is the part of a file that contains the user data and that is delimited by the header and trailer labels. Only one section of a given file can be written on any one volume. Multiple sections of a file or other file sections cannot be interspersed within a file section.

file set *n.*

TOPS-10

A collection of one or more files recorded consecutively on a volume set.

file sharing *n.*

VAX DATATRIEVE

The process of allowing two or more independent programs to use the data in a file concurrently. The kind of access allowed is dependent on file organization.

VAX/VMS

The capability of a particular relative or indexed file to allow access to more than one process.

file specification   (filespec) *n.*

DIGITAL-specific

The unique identification of a file that gives its physical location and an indication of its contents. All files are specified in the following form: ddnn:[g,m]filename.typ;version, where ddnn is the device name. Same as filespec.

generic

A string of characters that comprises the device name, file name, and extension for a file.

TOPS-10 and TOPS-20

A unique identification of a file or a mass storage medium (such as a disk). It describes the physical location of the file (node, device, and directory) and identifies the file name, file type, and file version number.

VAX/VMS

A unique name for a file on a mass storage medium. It identifies the node, the device, the directory name, the file name, the file type, and the version number under which a file is stored.

file specification area *n.*

TOPS-10

The area of core in which SCAN stores the result of scanning the user's file specification. This instructs WILD as to the files to select.

file structure *n.*

DIGITAL-specific

The logical arrangement of blocks (which are normally 128 words long) on one or more physical input/output device units of the same type to form a collection of named files.

generic

The organization of files within directories on a mass storage medium.

VAX/VMS

The way in which the blocks forming a file are distributed on a disk or magnetic tape to provide a physical accessing technique suitable for the way in which the data in the file is processed.

file structure abbreviation *n.*

TOPS-10

A short form of the name of one or more file structures. This refers to all those structures in the ALL search list whose names match the short form. For example, if there were structures "PRIV." and "PACK:", "P" would refer to both structures but "PR:" would mean just "PRIV:".

file-structured *adj.*

generic

Pertaining to a device where data is stored by filename.

file-structured device *n.*

DIGITAL-specific

A device on which data is given names and arranged into files; the device also contains directories of these names. Usually synonymous with directory device.

file structure owner *n.*

TOPS-10

The user whose project-programmer number is associated with the file structure in the administrative file STRLST.SYS. The REACT program is used to enter or delete this project-programmer number or any of the other information that is contained in an STRLST.SYS entry.

file structure search list *n.*

TOPS-10

For each job, a list that specifies the order in which the file structures that user can access are to be searched when device DSK: is specified. Same as job search list.

file system *n.*

VAX/VMS

A method of recording, cataloging, and accessing files on a volume.

file transfer (FLX) *n.*

RSX-11M

A utility used to convert various core image formats. Same as FLX.

file type *n.*

DIGITAL-specific

The alphanumeric character string assigned to a file either by an operating system or a user. It can be read by both the operating system and the user. System-recognizable file types are used to identify files having the same format or type. If present in a file specification, a file type follows the file name in a file specification, separated from the file name by a period. A file type has a fixed maximum length that is system-dependent.

generic

The field in a file specification that is made up of a period followed by 0 and 3 characters. The file type provides more information on possible contents of the file.

VAX/VMS

The field in a file specification that consists of a period (.) followed by a 0- to 39-character type identification, by convention, this field identifies a generic class of files that have the same use or characteristics, such as compiler and assembler listing files, binary object files, and so on. Same as file name extension.

file variable *n.*

PASCAL and VAX PASCAL

The named sequence of components of the same type used in I/O operations. A file can have any number of components; they may be of any type except a file type or a structured type containing components of a file type.

file version number *n.*

TOPS-20

Numeric component of a TOPS-20 file specification. As a file is updated and changed, the file's version number is updated with each successive copy.

fill character *n.*

DIGITAL-specific

A specific character selected to be stored in the remaining data positions of a field that is not completely occupied. See also zero fill, blank fill, RIB, attribute and PAD.

filling *n.*

CTS-300

A user option that allows space in a group to be left unused. This is space which is unused after the number of records are chosen for the group. Filling prevents partial records from exiting within a group and prevents records from extending across group (and possible block) boundaries. Filling creates a file in which records are more quickly accessed at the expense of some wasted space. Same as fill to end-of block.

DECWORD

The act of storing the data or document on disk.

fill mode *n.*

Medical Systems

An irregular ROI (region of interest) that is defined by filled cells.

fill number *n.*

RSX-11M

The number of bytes that a user wants and that are in an indexed file bucket used to store records. Data level and index level fill numbers can be set for each index in the file, but are honored by RMS-11 only during operations that so request. By default, RMS-11 uses all free bytes in a bucket to store records.

fill to end-of-block *n.*

CTS-300

A user option, called filling, that allows space in a group to be left unused. This space that is unused after the number of records are chosen for the group. Filling prevents partial records from existing within a group and prevents records from extending across group (and possibly block) boundaries. Filling creates a file in which records are more quickly accessed at the expense of some wasted space. Same as filling.

filter *n.*

DECnet

A set of on/off states for a logging event class that indicates whether or not each event type in that class is to be recorded.

Financial Modeling *n.*

generic

A computerized program that lets the user create charts and graphs for analysis and manipulation of accounts and records.

findlist *n.*

TOPS-10

A findlist is a qualifying argument of an immediate mode command that instructs IQL (interactive query language) to apply the command to selective records in the data file.

finished goods inventory *n.*

generic

Goods that have been completely manufactured but not yet shipped.

finite state machine *n.*

DECnet

1. A model of a system that has a finite number of input states and output states in which the output state at any time depends upon the present input and internal state.

2. Specific to ARPA, the finite state machine diagrammed and outlined in this document and in other ARPA literature concerns connection states. The finite state machine for connections provides the implementation for the network control program and is also referred to as the "NCP finite state machine."

firmware *n.*

generic

Software that is stored in a fixed (wired-in) or 'firm' way, usually in a read-only memory; a set of instructions designed to help hardware perform its assigned functions.

first *n.*

VAX DBMS

A set-ordering criterion that requires that the new record occurrences be positioned first in the series of record occurrences.

first character *n.*

FFE

A font value that specifies the character with the lowest decimal value in the font.

first-in-chain (FIC) *n.*

DECnet

FIC refers to the first 256 bytes of data of a message consisting of more than 256 bytes, transmitted by an SNA (systems network architecture) program or by the protocol emulator in a session governed by the Profile 3 or 4 protocol set. That the chain element being transmitted is first-in-chain is specified by a setting in the chaining control field of the request header. In emulator control mode, the PE (protocol emulator) segments messages into 256 byte elements, and sets the chain indicators, as appropriate, in the request header, for messages flowing from RSX-11M to SNA. For messages flowing the other way in EC and XEC modes, SNA does the segmenting and sets the chain indicators. Same as FIC.

first normal form *n.*

Rdb/ELN

The state of a relation when all repeating groups have been removed from it.

fiscal period *n.*

generic

An accounting period.

fixed asset *n.*

generic

Refers to property, plant, and equipment.

fixed control area *n.*

VAX DATATRIEVE

The fixed-length header portion of a variable-with-fixed-control record. It is fixed in size by the programmer. One use of the header is to identify related records.

VAX PL/I

A data area associated with a record that is maintained separately from the data portion of the record and that can be read or written in an I/O operation.

VAX/RMS

An area, prefixed to a variable-length record, containing additional information about the record that may have no bearing on the other contents of the record. For example, the fixed control area may contain line numbering or carriage control information.

fixed cost *n.*

generic

A cost element that does not vary with the volume of activity.

fixed decimal *n.*

FMS

A field attribute indicating that a field is signed or unsigned numeric and has a single decimal point (.) as a field-marker character. Data typed by an operator is justified and formatted in a special way.

fixed-length control area *n.*

VAX/VMS

An area, prefixed to a variable-length record, containing additional information about the record that may have no bearing on the other contents of the record. The fixed-length control area may be used, for example, to contain line numbering or carriage-control information.

fixed-length record format *n.*

VAX DATATRIEVE and VAX/VMS

A file format in which all records are the same size. See also variable with fixed-control, variable length, record format and stream.

fixed-length records *n.*

generic

A file in which all the records have the same length.

fixed line numbers *n.*

VAX/VMS

Numbers fixed to lines of text in a file. EDT maintains a record of them during the editing sessions in which the files are used; they are copied to the file when the editing session ends.

fixed member *n.*

VAX DBMS

In DBMS, a record occurrence that, upon becoming a member of a set occurrence of a set type, must remain a member of that set until the record occurrence is erased from the database. Fixed set membership is specified in a schema DDL entry. See also mandatory member, optional member, and retention class.

fixed-point *adj.*

generic

Pertaining to a type of computation with integers only and without any decimal point or decimal remainders.

fixed-point binary *n.*

VAX PL/I

Data type for integer values.

fixed-point decimal *n.*

VAX PL/I

A data type for decimal data with a fixed number of fractional digits.

fixed spacing *n.*

FFE

One of two kinds of spacing in LN01 font files: fixed and variable. In a fixed space font, all the cells have the same width regardless of the width of the glyphs in the cells.

flag *n.*

DIGITAL-specific

An indicator that signals the occurrence of a condition (commonly a 1 in a specific bit).

generic

A character, bit position, or circuit that indicates a specific condition.

MicroPower PASCAL and RT-11

A variable or register used to record the status of a program or device.

VAX/VMS

A bit that can be set to invoke the execution of a particular sequence of instructions; frequently, an indicator used to tell some later part of a program that a certain condition occurred earlier.

flag *v.*

generic

To identify a specific condition by means of a character, bit position, or circuit.

flag sequence *n.*

VAX PSI

A series of ones and zeros that indicates the start and end of a frame.

flange *n.*

generic

A raised segment of a part, often used to attach the part to another part or to limit movements.

flash mode *n.*

VT-11 GRAPHICS

The mode in which a picture or part of a picture on the display screen blinks on and off. This mode can be selected by specifying a positive integer value for the display parameter (included in many subroutine called) or by using the FLASH subroutine. When the user initializes the display file, the flash mode is disabled.

flat file *n.*

VAX DATATRIEVE

A two-dimensional array of data items.

flicker *n.*

VT-11 GRAPHICS

An unsteadiness in the displayed image. This is caused in refreshed displays when the display processor does not have enough time to complete one frame before the phosphor at the beginning of the frame begins to fade out.

flip-flop *n.*

generic

An electronic circuit having two stable output states.

floating (point) data *n.*

VAX/VMS

Four contiguous bytes (32 bits) starting on an addressable byte boundary. The bits are labeled from right to left from 0 to 31. A 4-byte floating_point number is identified by the address of the byte containing bit 0. Bit 15 contains the sign of the number. Bits 14 through 7 contain the excess 128 binary exponent. Bits 31 through 16 and 6 through 0 contain a normalized 24-bit fraction with the redundant most significant fraction bit not represented. Within the fraction, bits of decreasing significance go from bit 6 through 0, then 31 through 16. Exponent values of 1 through 255 in the 8-bit exponent field represent true binary exponents of −128 to 127. An exponent value of 0 together with a sign bit of 0 represents a floating value of 0. An exponent value of 0 with a sign bit of 1 is a reserved representation; floating-point instructions processing this value return a reserved operand fault. The value of a floating data is in the approximate range (+ or −) 0.29×10 (-38 sup) to 1.7×10 (38 sup). The precision is approximately one part in 2(33 sup) or 7 decimal digits. Same as F_floating-point data.

floating point *n.*

DIGITAL-specific

A number system in which the position of the radix point is indicated by the exponent part and another part represents the significant digits or fractional part (for example, 5.39×10 (sub 8) – Decimal; 137.3×8 (sub 4) – octal; 101.10×2 (sub 13) – binary).

generic

A number that may be positive or negative but that has a whole (integer) portion and a fractional (decimal) portion; an arithmetic operation in which the decimal point is not fixed, but placed automatically in a correct position in a computer word.

VAX PL/I

Data type used for very small or very large numbers. A floating-point value has a mantissa and an optionally signed integer exponent.

floating-point *adj.*

generic

Pertaining to arithmetic operations in which the location of the decimal point will automatically be placed in its correct position.

floating-point expression *n.*

RGL/FEP

An expression that requires real (decimal) numbers; the decimal point is required part of the number.

floating-point notation *n.*

DIGITAL-specific

Representation of real number data in the mantissa, fraction format, followed by a positive or negative component. The exponent is introduced by the letter E for a single-precision number, as in 7.321E02; by the letter D for a double-precision number, as in 9.345D10; and by the letter Q for a quadruple-precision number as in 6.307Q04.

floating-point operation *n.*

DIGITAL-specific

An operation on data of type floating or double floating.

floating type *n.*

VAX/VMS

One of the data types float or double, representing a single- or double-precision floating-point number.

floating underflow *n.*

VAX/VMS

A trap enable bit in the processor status word (PSW).

flood study *n.*

Medical Systems

An image of a uniform radiation source that the camera acquires.

floppy *adj*

generic

Pertaining to a small, flexible, magnetic disk used to store information.

floppy disk (or floppy) *n.*

generic

A small, flexible, magnetic disk used to store information. Same as diskette, floppy, floppy diskette.

floppy diskette *n.*

generic

A small, flexible, magnetic disk used to store information. Same as diskette, floppy, floppy disk.

flowchart *n.*

generic

A graphic description of the events that occur in the solution of a program, usually shown as a series of decisions and resulting operations.

flow control *n.*

DECnet

The NSP (network services protocol) function that coordinates the flow of data on a logical link in both directions, from transmit buffers to receive buffers to ensure that data is not lost, to prevent buffer deadlock, and to minimize communications overhead.

VAX PSI

The mechanism that keeps traffic within limits acceptable by the end-receiver or any intermediate receiver. At the terminal level, the flow control mechanism must guarantee that the flow of characters will stop if the buffer fills up.

flow control parameter negotiation *n.*

VAX PSI

An optional PSDN (packet switching data network) facility that permits selection of maximum packet sizes and window sizes in each direction of a particular virtual circuit.

flush *n.*

RSX-11M

A record operation that writes all I/O buffers to a file if they haven't already been written.

flux *n.*

generic

1. A resin material used in soldering electrical connections.

2. The component lines of the magnetic field coming from a magnet or electrical conductor by which the density of the field is described.

FLX *n.*

RSX-11M

The acronym for file transfer. FLX is a utility used to convert various core image formats. Same as file transfer.

flying *adj.*

generic

Pertaining to read/write heads in magnetic disk systems that do not usually touch the disk surface.

FM *n.*

DECnet

The abbreviation for function management. FM is one of the Profiles of an SNA (systems network architecture) session. The FM Profile is concerned primarily with data-flow control and the manner in which data is presented to the receiving NAU (network addressable unit). Same as function management. See also Profile.

FMS *n.*

FMS

The abbreviation for Forms Management System. FMS is a set of software tools to simplify the development and maintenance of application programs involving formatted I/O to video terminals. Same as Forms Management System.

FMS-2 *n.*

FMS

A short form of FMS level II routines. FMS-2 are DEC-supplied routines and services used in an application program that:

- reads and executes the instruction in request or library definitions

- writes/reads text on the reserved message line on the terminal

- opens/closes input and output paths between terminals and programs

- traces run-time request action.

FMU *n.*

FMS

The abbreviation for Form Management Utility. FMU is the FMS component that manages form descriptions by creating form libraries, form summaries, object modules, COBOL data declaration statements, and library directions. In FMS version 1, the abbreviation FUT (form utility) was used; in subsequent versions, FMU is used. Same as Form Management Utility. See also FUT and form utility.

FMV *n.*

USFC/generic

The abbreviation for fair market value. FMS is the market value of the equipment. At the end of the lease, FMV is determined by the used equipment market place. Same as fair market value.

FOB (free on board) *n.*

generic

The abbreviation for free on board; FOB at a specified location means that the seller or shipper pays transportation costs to that location.

follow-the-index *n.*

RSX-11M

The procedure that RMS-11 uses when it must start at the Root and read down an index to a specific record location.

font *n.*

generic

A specific representation of text characters. The attributes of a font are typeface, typesize, and rendition.

font assignment *n.*

FFE

An ESCAPE sequence that associates the internal font name and a number that is used to invoke a font within a text file.

font family *n.*

generic

The design or style of a font, such as Triumvirate, Times, Souvenir, and so on.

font file *n.*

generic

A file that contains the definition of a character or group of characters.

font invocation *n.*

FFE

An ESCAPE sequence, containing a number, inserted in the text file to be printed.

font load *n.*

FFE

A single sequence of data that contains all the specified input font files.

font name *n.*

FFE

A font value that specifies an internal text-string, used by other LN01 software in loading fonts.

font values *n.*

generic

Attributes you set for the entire font, such as orientation and line spacing.

footer *n.*

generic

Text that appears in the bottom margin of printed pages, such as a document title, page number, or date.

footing area *n.*

generic

The position of the page body adjacent to the bottom margin.

forced job startup *n.*

CTS-300

A feature that allows a program to be started, and control transferred to it, upon execution of a statement from within another program.

forecast *n.*

generic

An estimate or projection of costs, revenues, or both.

foreground *n.*

generic

The part of the operating system that executes high priority programs. Data acquisition occurs in the foreground.

foreground *adj.*

generic

Pertaining to the condition in which a program or task with the highest priority is executed first.

foreground processing *n.*

DIGITAL-specific

High-priority processing, usually resulting from real-time entries, given precedence by means of interrupts over lower-priority, "background" processing.

foreground program *n.*

CTS-300 and RT-11

A program having the highest priority for system resources. A program operating in the foreground partition of the RT-11 foreground/background architecture. A foreground program has priority over a background program.

foreign key *n.*

Rdb/ELN

A key that does not uniquely identify records in its own relation, but is used as a link to matching fields in other relations.

foreign volume *n.*

VAX/VMS

Any volume that is not a FILES-11 formatted volume whether it is file-structured or not.

fork *n.*

generic

1. The point at which division into branches occurs.

2. Any of the branches.

fork block *n.*

VAX/VMS

That portion of a unit control block that contains a driver's context while the driver is waiting for a resource. A driver awaiting the processor resource has its fork block linked into the fork queue.

fork dispatcher *n.*

VAX/VMS

A VAX/VMS interrupt service routine that is activated by a software interrupt at a fork interrupt priority level (IPL). Once activated, it dispatches driver fork processes from a driver fork queue until no processes remain in the queue for that IPL.

fork process *n.*

DIGITAL-specific

A resident process that executes at software interrupt level entirely within the system address space, and runs to completion without entering a wait state. Fork processes have minimal context, I/O drivers are fork processes.

MicroPower PASCAL

A process on the fork queue. A fork process is created with the FORK request by an interrupt service routine. See also fork queue.

VAX/VMS

A minimal context process that executes code under a series of constraints: it executes at raised interrupt priority levels; it uses R0 through R5 only (other registers must be saved and restored); it executes in system virtual address space; it is only allowed to refer to and modify static storage that is never modified by higher interrupt priority level code. VAX/VMS uses software interrupts and fork processes to synchronize executive operations.

fork queue *n.*

MicroPower PASCAL

A queue set up in the kernel to allow processes special sequential access to the processor. Although lower than interrupt priorities, the fork queue priority is higher than any process priority, expediting the execution of processes placed on the fork queue. For example, interrupt-handling routines placed on the fork queue will execute before other processes in the application. This method ensures quick attention to interrupts.

VAX/VMS

A queue of driver fork blocks that is awaiting activation at a particular interrupt priority level (IPL) by the VAX/VMS fork dispatcher.

form *n.*

ALL-IN-1

The text that ALL-IN-1 displays on the screen to request and provide information. There are three types of forms in ALL-IN-1: menu, entry, and text.

generic

A preselected terminal screen image used to display and collect information.

FMS

A collection of structured information displayed on a terminal screen. An FMS form consists of no more than one screen of information; on or more forms can occupy a screen at once. See also paper form.

PRO/Diskette System

A request for information that is displayed on the Professional screen when P/OS requires information that the user provides.

formal parameter n.

MicroPower PASCAL and VAX PASCAL

A name, declared in the heading of a procedure or function, that represents an actual parameter to be passed when that procedure or function is invoked.

TOPS-20

Procedure parameters that the caller can specify.

formal parameter list n.

VAX PASCAL

A list of formal parameter declarations that appears in the heading of a procedure or function. The entries in the list are separated by semicolons and the list is enclosed in parentheses.

formant n.

generic

Natural spectral peaks of the vocal tract that aid in the recognition of speech sounds.

form application aids n.

FMS

The multifunction FMS component that does the following:

- Converts binary form files to form descriptions

- Creates COBOL data declaration files

- Converts binary forms to object modules for use as memory-resident forms

- Provides form descriptions and library file directory listings

- Creates vector modules for user action routines

format n.

generic

A specific arrangement of data on a form, file, or printout.

format item n.

VAX PL/I

A character code (and possibly associated value or values) indicating input or output data representation and formatting.

format list n.

VAX PL/I

A list of format items corresponding to variable references or output data items for edit-directed stream I/O.

format string n.

generic

A string of characters that shows how decimal data is to be formatted when it is output.

formatted device *n.*

generic

An external storage device which has been prepared to accept data from a specific program.

form attributes *n.*

FMS

Characteristics assigned to an entire form. Examples of form attributes are first line to clear, last
line to clear, screen width, and so forth.

form context *n.*

FMS

The information associated with a form definition
including the content of its fields and the video
characteristics of the form and its fields.

form definition *n.*

FMS and Terminal Data Management System

Description of a screen form created in the FDU
(form definition utility. It includes names and data
types of form fields; used for entering data which
is mapped to the program buffers.

Form Definition Utility (FDU) *n.*

TDMS

The TDMS utility used to process (create, modify,
replace, or copy) form definitions and to store
them in the Common Data Dictionary (CDD).

form description *n.*

FMS

The collection of attributes and information
needed to display a form on a screen or to produce a form summary for subsequent printing on
a hard-copy device. A form description can be
stored in source format in a source form file or in
binary format in a binary form file or library.

Form Development *n.*

ALL-IN-1

An ALL-IN-1 subsystem that lets the user create
and modify entry forms for use in the ALL-IN-1
system.

form document *n.*

DECtype

In the DECtype List Processing application, the
document that contains text to be printed.

DECWORD

A label DECWORD uses to associate the type of
printer and the style of printing required for a document. Use the form setting in the print menu to
specify a form name.

form driver (FDV) *n.*

FMS

A set of subroutines that interact with an application program to display forms on video terminals
and to accept data entered by operators. Same
as FDV.

form editor (FED) *n.*

FMS

The FMS utility you use to create and modify
forms through interactive sessions at a video terminal and during which the forms are displayed on
the screen. Same as FED.

form feed (British: page throw) *n.*

generic

The calibrated movement of paper or printing
medium through a printing device by varyious
means such as roller pressure or synchronization
of paper holes with tractor teeth on the printing
paten.

VAX/VMS

In EDT, the movement of the cursor position to the start of a new page; one of the default word delimiters; the default page delimiter.

form field attribute *n.*

Terminal Data Management System

A condition or characteristic, specified in a TDMS (Terminal Data Management System) form definition, that applies to a field in a form. For example, a field attribute can require that an operator enter data into a field. Certain field attributes, such as video characteristics, assigned in the form definition can be overridden by a request. The form definer assigns field attributes or accepts default attributes during the assign phase.

form field constant *n.*

Terminal Data Management System

A character or embedded space that is displayed in a field on a TDMS (Terminal Data Management System) form at run time. For example, users can use a hyphen as a field constant in a field that represents a telephone number.

form field validator *n.*

Terminal Data Management System

A special TDMS (Terminal Data Management System) field attribute that requires the terminal operator's input to be within a specified range, match an item from a specified list, or meet one or more other conditions. The form definer assigns field validators during the assign phase.

form language *n.*

FMS

The grammar for defining forms as an alternative method to using the form editor. Also the name of the language in which the forms are defined.

Form Language *n.*

FMS

The component of FMS that provides a syntax and grammar for defining forms as an alternate method to using the Form Editor. The Form Language does not display forms interactively on the screen, nor does it require a VT100 terminal for creation and modification of forms.

form librarian *n.*

FMS

The FMS component that creates and manipulates form libraries.

form library *n.*

FMS

A file containing an organized collection of one or more form descriptions in binary format.

Form Management Utility (FMU) *n.*

FMS

The FMS component that manages form descriptions by creating form libraries, form summaries, object modules, COBOL data declaration statements, and library directories. Same as FMU. See also BUS and form utility.

Forms Management System (FMS) *n.*

FMS

A set of software tools to simplify the development and maintenance of application programs involving formatted I/O to video terminals. Same as FMS.

form snapshot *n.*

FMS

A file containing a representation of the current screen image; it is produced by the Form Driver at the request of a running application program, for subsequent printing. A form snapshot consists of background text, clear characters, field-marker characters, and any information displayed by the program or data entered by the operator.

form summary *n.*

FMS

A file produced by the Form Management Utility for subsequent printing that completely describes a form. The summary consists of the form attributes, form image, video attributes map, fields and their attributes, and the named data associated with the form.

form tester *n.*

FMS

The FMS component that provides a means of testing a form without first having to write an application program or put the form in a library.

formula mode *n.*

ALL-IN-1

In Desk Calculator, the operating state that lets the user perform algebraic functions.

form upgrade utility (FUU) *n.*

FMS

The FMS component that converts FMS Version 1 form descriptions into Version 2 form descriptions. Same as FUU.

form utility (FUT) *n.*

FMS

The term used in FMS Version 1, superceded in subsequent versions by the term 'Form Management Utility' (FMU). Both refer to the FMS component that manages form descriptions by creating form libraries, form summaries, object modules, COBOL data declaration statements, and library directories. See also FMU and Form Management Utility. Same as FUT.

FORTRAN *n.*

generic

An abbreviation for FORmula TRANslator, a programming language used primarily for scientific applications.

fount *n.*

generic

The British word for font, referring to the assortment of printing characters, usually of the same size and design. Same as font.

four-byte signed integer (key) *n.*

RSX-11M

A key data type that can represent the decimal integer values −2,147,483,648 through +2,147,483,647. See also two-byte signed integer, two-byte unsigned binary, four-byte unsigned binary, packed decimal key, signed integer and string.

four-byte unsigned binary (key) *n.*

RSX-11M

A key data type that can represent the decimal integer values 0 through +4,294,967,295. See also two-byte unsigned binary, two-byte signed integer, four-byte signed integer, packed decimal key and string.

FP *n.*

VAX/VMS

The abbreviation for frame pointer. FP in VMS is general register 13; it contains the address of the base of the last CALL rack frame. Same as frame pointer.

FPD *n.*

VAX/VMS

First part (of an instruction) done.

fragment *n.*

VAX DBMS

The part of a record occurrence that is contained within one page of the database.

fragmentation *n.*

TOPS-10

The state existing when swapped segments cannot be allocated in the contiguous set of blocks on the swapping space and therefore must be allocated in separate sections.

frame *n.*

DECnet

A group of digits transmitted as a unit, over which a coding procedure is applied for synchronization.

DIGITAL-specific

A data structure built on the stack in conformance with the VAX-11 procedure call standard. Same as frame.

GAMMA and MSG (SPETS)

An image representing an organ over a finite amount of time, similar to a frame of a movie or one photograph.

generic

The binary digits across the width of magnetic or paper tape.

TOPS-10

The smallest data aggregate on a magnetic tape. It consists of 8 bits (on a 9-track tape) or 6 bits (on a 7-track tape), plus a parity bit.

VAX PSI

A unit delimited by flags and that includes a header; it is used by the link level to exchange packets and control-and-error information between the DTE (data terminal equipment) and the DCE (data circuit-terminating equipment).

VT-11 GRAPHICS

The picture created by one pass of the display processor through the active display list.

frame checking sequence (FCS) *n.*

VAX PSI

A 16-bit error check polynomial that checks that the bit content of a frame is the same before and after transmission. Where K = number of bits in the frame not including the flags and FCS itself and con = the contents of the frame not including the flags and the FCS itself. Same as FCS.

frame pointer (FP) *n.*

TOPS-20 and VAX/VMS

General register 12 in TOPS-20; it contains the address of the base of the last CALL stack frame. Same as FP.

framing *n.*

DECnet

The DDCMP (Digital Data Communication Message Protocol) component that synchronizes data at the byte and message level.

free (record operation) *n.*

RSX-11M and VAX DATATRIEVE

In RMS-11, releasing of buckets locked by a record access stream. See also bucket locking.

free blocks *n.*

DIGITAL-specific

Unused blocks on a file structured device.

free space *n.*

generic

A section of the page that grows and shrinks as changes are made to the database. See also database page.

free space page *n.*

DIGITAL-specific

In a database file, fixed-length pages that point to other pages in the database file that are not assigned to any relation. Free space pages can be thought of as "space management" pages.

freeze *n.*

DECnet

To suspend a process in such a way that it can be continued. A process may be directly frozen by an explicit request of its superior process or indirectly frozen because its superior has been frozen.

front end processor (or front-end processor) *n.*

DECnet

A communications computer associated with a host computer. It may perform line control, message handling, code conversion, error control, and applications functions such as control and operation of special-purpose terminals.

FSM *n.*

DECnet

The abbreviation for finite state machine. FSM refers to a system of connection states that provide implementation for the NCP (network control program)

FU *n.*

VAX/VMS

Floating underflow trap enable bit in the processor status word.

full duplex *n.*

DECnet and RT-11

1. In communications, a simultaneous, two-way, independent transmission in both directions.

2. A communications line or terminal capable of full duplex transmission.

generic

A communications system in which there is a capability for 2-way transmission and acceptance between two sites at the same time.

full duplex (or full-duplex) *adj.*

DECnet, TOPS-10, and RT-11

In communications, pertaining to a simultaneous, two-way independent, "asynchronous" transmission (transmission in both directions).

generic

Pertaining to a communications method in which data can be transmitted and received at the same time.

full-duplex channel *n.*

DECnet

A channel that services concurrent communications in both directions (to and from the station).

full path *n.*

TOPS-10

The ordered list that uniquely identifies a specific disk file. It is the sequence of directories from the UFD (user file directory) to the directory containing the specific file, plus the filename and extension of the file.

full path name *n.*

Common Data Dictionary

A unique designation that identifies a dictionary directory, subdictionary, or object in the CDD (Common Data Dictionary) hierarchy. The full path name is a concatenation of the given names of directories and objects, beginning with CDD$TOP, ending with the given name of the object or directory the user wants to specify, and including the given names of the intermediate subdictionaries and directories. The names of the directories and objects are separated with periods. See also path name, relative path name, and given name.

full-payment lease *n.*

USFC/generic

A lease by which the lease payments will return to the lessor the purchase price of the equipment, the cost of financing, administration costs, and an expected profit.

full process *n.*

DIGITAL-specific

A process defined by hardware general registers, a hardware PCB (process control block), a software PCB, and a process header.

full routing node *n.*

DECnet

A node that allows communication between non-adjacent nodes. If all nodes in a network are full routing nodes, then each node can communicate with each other node in the network.

fully associative cache *n.*

generic

A fast semiconductor memory organized so data can be recovered by content instead of by address. See direct mapping cache.

VAX/VMS

A cache organization in which any block of data from main memory can be placed anywhere in the cache. Address comparison must take place against each block in the cache to find any particular block.

fully connected network *n.*

generic

A computer network in which each system is directly linked with every other system in the network.

function *n.*

generic

A function is a subroutine that returns a value to the main program.

functional fault *n.*

DECSIM

A fault type that can be described by a change in function (operation) of some identifiable portion of a system.

functionality *n.*

generic

A computer industry term for what the hardware or software can do.

functional test *n.*

DECSIM

A test intended to exercise an identifiable function of a system.

function call n.

DIGITAL-specific

A primary expression followed by parentheses. The parentheses contain a comma-separated list of expressions that are the actual arguments to the function.

function code n.

VAX/VMS

A 6-bit value specified in a Queue I/O Request system service that describes the particular I/O operation to be performed. Same I/O function code.

function decision table (FDT) n.

VAX/VMS

A table in the drive that lists all valid function codes for the device and lists the addresses of I/O preprocessing routines associated with each valid function.

function designator n.

VAX PASCAL

The use of a function name and actual parameter list in an executable statement to invoke the function.

function diagram n.

MINC

A symbolic diagram on the top of each NMC-series module that shows the function of the module and its key interconnection lines to other modules.

function heading n.

VAX PASCAL

The specification, in a function declaration, of the name, formal parameter list, and result type of a function.

function key n.

PRO/Diskette System

A PRO/operating system type of key on the Professional keyboard that, when pressed, instructs P/OS or a P/OS application to do something specific.

function keys n.

ALL-IN-1

The keys on the minikeypad that perform special operations in ALL-IN-1. These keys have different uses depending on the current system or subsystem the user is accessing.

function level n.

GIGI

The operational level in effect after using a function key. The function keys are LINE key, BOX key, CIRCLE key CURVE key, and ERASE key.

function management (FM) n.

DECnet

One of the Profiles of an SNA (systems network architecture) session. The FM Profile is concerned primarily with data-flow control and the manner in which data is presented to the receiving NAU (network addressable unit). Same as FM. See also Profile.

function mode n.

In Desk Calculator, the operating state that lets the user perform any simple mathematical operations.

function modifier n.

DECnet and VAX/VMS

A 10-bit value specified in a Queue I/O Request system service that modifies an I/O function code. Same as I/O function modifier.

function reference *n.*

PASCAL

The function name and actual parameter list in an executable statement used to invoke the function.

VAX PL/I

The name of a user-written (or built-in) function in a PL/I statement.

fundamental frequency *n.*

generic

The frequency of repetition of a complex wave; in speech, the pitch of the vocal chord vibrations.

fundamental type *n.*

VAX/VMS

The set of arithmetic data types plus pointers. The fundamental types in C programs comprise those data types that can be represented naturally on a particular machine; usually, this means integers and floating-point numbers (of various machine-dependent sizes) and machine addresses.

FUT *n.*

FMS

The abbreviation for form utility, a term used in FMS Version 1 and superceded in subsequent versions by the term for management utility (FMS). FUT refers to the FMU component that manages form descriptions by creating forms libraries, form summaries, object modules, COBOL data declaration statements, and library directories. Same as form utility. See also FMU and Form Management Utility.

FUU *n.*

FMS

The abbreviation for form upgrade utility. FUU is the FMS component that translates V1, V1.1, and V1.5 form descriptions into V2. form descriptions. It can translate one binary form file to another binary form file, or one Form Library to another Form Library. Same as form upgrade utility.

F_floating datum *n.*

VAX/VMS

Four contiguous bytes starting on an addressable byte boundary. The bits are labeled from right to left 0 to 31. A two-word floating-point number is identified by the address of the byte containing bit 0. Bit 15 contains the sign of the number. Bits 14 through 7 contain the excess −128 binary exponent. Bits 31 through 16 and 6 through 0 contain a normalized 24-bit fraction with the redundant, most significant fraction bit not represented. Within the fraction, bits of decreasing significance go from bit 6 though 0, then 31 through 16. Exponent values of 1 through 225 in the 8-bit exponent field represent true binary exponents of −128 to 127. An exponent value of 0 together with a sign bit of 0 represents a floating value of 0. An exponent value with a sign bit of 1 is a reserved representation; floating-point instructions processing this value return a reserved operand fault. The value of a floating datum is in the approximate range of (+ or −) 0.29×10 (sup −38) to 1.7×10 (sup 38). The precision is approximately one part in 2 (sup 23), or seven decimal digits. Same as floating (point) datum.

F_floating-point data *n.*

VAX/VMS

Four contiguous bytes (32 bits) starting on an addressable byte boundary. The bits are labeled from right to left from 0 to 31. A 4-byte floating_point number is identified by the address of the byte containing bit 0. Bit 15 contains the sign of the number. Bits 14 through 7 contain the excess 128 binary exponent. Bits 31 through 16 and 6 through 0 contain a normalized 24-bit fraction with the redundant most significant fraction bit not represented. Within the fraction, bits of decreasing significance go from bit 6 through 0, then 31 through 16. Exponent values of 1 through 255 in the 8-bit exponent field represent true binary exponents of −128 to 127. An exponent value of 0 together with a sign bit of 0 represents a floating value of 0. An exponent value of 0 with a sign bit of 1 is a reserved representation; floating-point instructions processing this value return a reserved operand fault. The value of a floating data is in the approximate range (+ or −) 0.29×10 (-38 sup) to 1.7×10 (38 sup). The precision is approximately one part in 2(33 sup) or 7 decimal digits. Same as floating (point) data.

gain *n.*

generic

1. Any increase in power when a signal is transmitted from one point to another.

2. The ratio between the output signal and input signal of a device.

3. The numerical ratio by which the amplitude of an electrical signal is multiplied.

4. The excess of the amount over the book value of an asset realized from the sale of fixed assets.

GALAXY *n.*

TOPS-10

A batch system (part of the TOPS-10 operating system) that runs unattended jobs concurrently with timesharing jobs. The GALAXY system contains the programs QUASAR (system scheduler and queue manager); SPRINT (input spooler); BATCON (batch controller), and LPTSPL and SPROUT (output spoolers).

gamma camera interface *n.*

GAMMA and MSG (SPETS)

The hardware that takes the data from the gamma camera, digitizes it, and transfers it to the computer. The NCV-11 is the gamma camera interface; Gamma-11 also supports the NC-11A gamma camera interface.

gap *n.*

generic

1. The space on a magnetic tape or disk that separates records, files, or sectors from other records, files or sectors.

2. The space between the poles of a magnetic recording head.

garbage *n.*

generic

Unacceptable and unusable information.

gate *n.*

generic

A signal used to pass or control one or more other signals in a circuit.

gate array *n.*

generic

A geometric pattern of logic gates contained in a single chip. During manufacturing, it is possible to interconnect the gates to perform a complex function that can be used as a standard production. A gate array programmed to perform a specific task is often referred to as a custom gate array.

gate-level model *n.*

generic

A model of a digital network made up of basic low-level primitives such as gates and flip flops.

gate-level simulation *n.*

generic

A detailed level of logic simulation that includes timing analyses (both minimum and maximum rise/fall propagation delays) and race analyses (dynamic design rule checking), as well as provisions for undefined and high impedance states.

gateway *n.*

DECnet and VAX PSI

The connection between two individual packet switching networks. The connection provides a link through which a DTE (data terminal equipment) can communicate with a DTE on a different network.

general expenses *n.*

generic

Expenses other than cost of sales and selling expenses. In some entities, general expenses include interest expenses and administrative expenses.

general identifier *n.*

VAX/VMS

One of three possible types of identifiers that specify one or more groups of users. The general identifier is alphanumeric and typically is a convenient term that symbolizes the nature of the group of users. For example, typical general identifiers might be PAYROLL for all users allowed to run payroll applications, RESERVATIONS for operators at the reservations desk, or CHEM224 for students in the CHEMISTRY 224 class, and so forth.

general ledger *n.*

generic

The name for the formal ledger containing all of the financial statement accounts. It has equal debits and credits as evidenced by the trial balance.

general process *n.*

MicroPower PASCAL

In mapped target systems, a process without special access to kernel- or device-register areas of memory.

general purpose financial statements *n.*

generic

Financial statements prepared for the use of investors and other outside parties. These statements must be prepared in accordance with generally accepted accounting principles. Contrast with financial statements that are prepared for management, to which the generally accepted accounting principles need not apply.

general register *n.*

VAX/VMS

Any of the sixteen 32-bit registers used as the primary operands of the native-mode instructions. The general registers include 12 general purpose registers, which can be used as accumulators, as counters, and as pointers to locations in main memory, and the FP, AP, SP, and PC.

generation *n.*

DIGITAL-specific

Refers to the creation of a different version of a file each time the file is changed by editing or by some other activity. Same as file generation.

generation number *n.*

DIGITAL-specific

A number, associated with a file within the file directory, that is incremented each time the file is changed by editing or by some other activity. Same as file generation number.

generation version *n.*

DIGITAL-specific

The file derived from another file and containing edits or changes made to that other file. The new generation version retains the same filename with an incremented generation number. Same as file generation version.

generic device name *n.*

DIGITAL-specific

A device name that identifies the type of device but not a particular unit; a device name in which the specific controller and/or unit number is omitted.

generic

A mnemonic that identifies a type of device but not a specific unit.

TOPS-10

The name of a class of physical units in an abbreviated form. The abbreviation is usually three characters. For example, DTA is the generic name for DECtapes.

ghost hyphen *n.*

DECWORD

A character (Gold PRINT HYPH) that tells DECWORD where it may automatically hyphenate a word that must be divided at the end of a line. See also hyphen.

GIGI *n.*

GIGI

The acronym for graphics image generator and interpreter. GIGI is a text and graphics terminal that also contains a local BASIC interpreter in its microcode. The GIGI graphics interpreter uses ReGIS (remote graphics instruction set), and the BASIC interpreter can be controlled locally or remotely from a host processor.

gimbal *n.*

generic

A mechanical frame having two connecting axes of revolution at right angles.

given name *n.*

FMS

Each directory and object has a given name assigned to it. The root directory, having only descendants but no ancestor, has been assigned the name CDD$TOP. The names of all other directories and objects are assigned by the user creating them. The given name of an object is also called the "object name."

GLOB *n.*

DECsystem-10

A system utility program used to read collections of relocatable binary modules that have been loaded together (from both library files and separate files). This utility generates an alphabetical, cross-referenced list of all the global symbols encountered.

global *n.*

DSM-11

A tree-structured data file stored in the common data base on the disk. Globals comprise an external system of symbolically referenced systems.

generic

A symbol, label, or value defined in one program module and referenced by one or more other programs or modules.

RT-11

A value defined in one program module and used in others. Globals are often referred to as entry points in the module in which they are defined and as externals in the other modules that use them.

VAX/VMS

Affecting the entire file, the entire system, or the entire image, depending on context. A global substitution in a test file would be to change all instances of a particular string to something else, for example, changing "fall" to "autumn."

GLOBAL *n.*

PEARL

A PEARL object that is capable of being accessed anywhere within a PEARL program.

global attribute *n.*

DIGITAL-specific

A field that can occur in any number of relations in the database, and is defined so its value will have the same meaning.

global cross-reference *n.*

DIGITAL-specific

A list of global symbols, in alphabetical order, accompanied by the name of each referencing module.

global field *n.*

DIGITAL-specific

A field that can occur in any number of relations in the database, and is defined so its value will have the same meaning.

global filter *n.*

DECnet

A filter that applies to all entities within an event class and type.

global identifier *n.*

PASCAL and VAX PASCAL

An identifier that is declared in a block at an outer level and therefore can be used inside the current (inner-level) block without redeclaration.

global name *n.*

generic

A user-defined name that is declared in only one program but may be referenced from that program and from any program contained within that program.

global page table *n.*

VAX/VMS

The page table containing the master page table entries for globally-available (shared) I-sections.

global search-and-replace *n.*

DECmate II

A feature that locates every occurrence of a word or phrase defined by the user, deletes it, and in its place inserts new text also defined by the user.

global section *n.*

VAX/VMS

A data structure or sharable image section potentially available to all processes in the system. Access is protected by privilege and/or group number of the UIC (user identification code).

global section descriptor *n.*

DIGITAL-specific

A table maintained and used by memory management to interpret the image file of a global section. Each global section has an entry in the global section table.

global section table *n.*

DIGITAL-specific

A table maintained by memory management to interpret the contents (I-sections) of a linkable image section.

global symbol *n.*

MicroPower PASCAL

A link between independently compiled or assembled program modules. A global symbol is defined in one module and can be referenced from other modules. An identifier is an example of a global symbol.

RSX-11M

A global symbol is a value defined in one object module that can be used in other object modules. Many global symbols are defined in the system library. Global symbols are identified and defined by the Task Builder. See also local symbol.

TOPS-10

A symbol that is accessible to modules other than the one in which it is defined. The value of a global symbol is placed in the loader's global symbol table when the module containing the symbol definition is loaded.

VAX PL/I

An external static variable declared with the GLOBALDEF or GLOBALREF attribute. Global symbols may also have the VALUE attribute; symbols so declared are constants that do not occupy any storage, but whose values are resolved at link time.

VAX/VMS

1. A symbol defined in a module that is potentially available for reference by another module. The linker resolves (matches references with definitions) global symbols.

2. A command language symbol that is accessible at all command levels.

global symbol table (GST) *n.*

DIGITAL-specific and VAX/VMS

In a library, an index of defined global symbols used to access the modules defining the global symbols. The linker also puts global symbol tables into an image. For example, the linker appends a global symbol table to executable images that are intended to run under the symbolic debugger, and it appends a global symbol table to all sharable images. Same as GST.

global variable *n.*

DSM-11

A named reference to data on storage media. A global variable can be either simple (a variable name that references a single datum) or subscripted (a variable name that references an array). Global variables are not unique to a user; they can be examined or changed by any authorized user.

glyph *n.*

generic

The pictorial representation of a font character, represented internally by a bitmap.

Gold key *n.*

DECWORD

A key labeled with the word GOLD and that has an effect only when it is pressed before another key. On the main keyboard, gold lettering on the front of the keys indicates what these keys will do if pressed after the Gold key. For instance, if a user presses the Gold key, and then the MENU key, DECWORD will display the main menu or the editor menu on the screen.

VAX/VMS

The upper-left key on the terminal keypad, which enables alternate keypad functions.

gradient *n.*

generic

The rate at which a variable quantity increases or decreases.

graph *n.*

generic

A pictorial representation of information.

graphic array *n.*

VT-11 GRAPHICS

A collection of values stored in an array and plotted as points on the x- or y-axis by the XGRA or YGRA subroutines. Graphic arrays can also be plotted as sets of long vectors with the FIGR subroutine.

graphic attention *n.*

VT-11 GRAPHICS

An event created when the light pen is pointed at a primitive on the display screen that has been made light-pen sensitive, or an event created by a keystroke on the terminal keyboard.

graphic cursor *n.*

GIGI and RGL/FEP

A blinking, diamond-shaped cursor that indicates that the terminal is operating in graphic mode. Same as graphics cursor.

graphic-display subsystem *n.*

VT-11 GRAPHICS

The required hardware for running programs that use the VT-11 graphics subroutines. It consists of a VT-11 display processor, a CRT display scope with light pen, and a cable connecting the CRT with the processor board.

graphic memory *n.*

MINC

The area of a MINC terminal that preserves graphic data. The graphic memory allows users to display the same data in more than one graphic format.

graphic mode *n.*

GIGI and RGL/FEP

A terminal operating mode in which the ReGIS interpreter is enabled.

graphic object *n.*

RGL/FEP

Any portion of a picture that is perceived as an entity. Examples are a line, circle, or a message written in graphic text. There are two types of graphic objects: picture objects and graphic text.

graphic program *n.*

MINC

A program that computes data and constructs diagrams for the display of that data on graphic display terminals.

graphic routine *n.*

MINC

A statement that performs a routine task associated with graphic display.

graphics *n.*

generic

The use of lines, figures, shapes, and shaded areas to display information.

graphic screen *n.*

RGL/FEP

The screen to which the terminal writes when it is in graphic mode. See also VT-100 screen.

graph region *n.*

MINC

The portion of the terminal screen reserved for graphic display. MINC has three graphic regions: upper, lower, and full screen.

graph type *n.*

generic

The style of a graph (such as bar, pie, line, or scatter graph).

gray scale *n.*

GIGI and RGL/FEP

Eight levels of intensity GIGI uses on black and white monitors.

grid *n.*

A-to-Z

The lines that are "behind" the graph and outline around the graph. Such lines add perspective to the graph and help users compare the data with the number on the axes.

gross *adj.*

generic

Pertains to an amount before deductions.

gross margin *n.*

generic

The difference between sales revenue and cost of sales.

gross profit *n.*

generic

Another term for gross margin.

ground *n.*

generic

A voltage reference point in a system that has a zero voltage potential.

grounding *n.*

generic

Hardware units used to implement the electrical connection between the coaxial cable shield and the building grounding electrode. The components include the earthing conductor, the coaxial cable ground clamp, the barrel connector or coaxial cable connector used as the coaxial cable shield connection point, and the hardware necessary to make a connection with the network earth reference point.

grounding electrode *n.*

generic/Ethernet

Wire or conductor extending from a building's electrical service entrance panel to a site, used as the earth reference for the building electrical power system.

ground potential difference *n.*

generic/Ethernet

The voltage (potential) that is measured between either a Network Earth reference point and a building grounding electrode; or, between two network earth references in a multi-building site.

group *n.*

CTS-300

A user-defined division of an ISAM (indexed sequential access method) file. A group contains records or index entries. Once specified, group size is constant throughout all parts of an ISAM file.

generic

1. A set of users who have identical access privileges.

2. A number of persons or things that are together in one location.

3. A number of persons or things put together because of like qualities.

TOPS-10

A contiguous set of disk clusters allocated as a single unit of storage and described by a single retrieval pointer.

TOPS-20 and VAX/VMS

1. A set of users who have special access privileges to each other's directories and files within those directories (unless protected otherwise), as in the context system, owner, group, world, where group refers to all members of a particular owner's group.

2. A set of jobs (processes and their subprocesses) with access to a group's common event flags and logical name tables.

group data item *n.*

COBOL-74, VAX DBMS and VAX DATATRIEVE

A named sequence of one or more data items.

group dictionary *n.*

DECWORD

A special dictionary stored in a group account. If a user account does not contain a personal dictionary, DECWORD looks in the group account for a group dictionary named WORDS.WPS. A group dictionary is used when several people want to use the same vocabulary. For example, users in a finance department could create a group dictionary containing financial words. See also dictionary.

group field *n.*

Terminal Data Management System and VAX DATATRIEVE

A record segment containing one or more elementary fields.

group item *n.*

generic

A data item that contains subordinate data items.

group number *n.*

VAX/VMS

The first number in a user identification code (UIC). See also project number.

group record array *n.*

Terminal Data Management System

A record array whose elements contain other fields. Each of these fields has the same characteristics (length, data type, and so on), and each field is referenced in a request by the same name, but with a unique subscript. In request instructions, include the group array field name to make each field name unique.

GST *n.*

VAX/VMS

The abbreviation for global symbol table. GST, in a library, is an index of defined global symbols used to access the modules defining the global symbols. The linker also puts global symbol tables into an image. For example, the linker appends a global symbol table to executable images that are intended to run under the symbolic debugger, and it appends a global symbol table to all sharable images. Same as global symbol table.

guard band *n.*

generic

The area on a disk that separates the data recording area from the rest of the disk.

G_floating data *n.*

VAX/VMS

An extended range floating point number 8 bytes long having a range of $+/-$ 0.56*10**$-$308 to */$-$ 0.9*10**308 and a precision of approximately 15 decimal digits.

G_floating datum *n.*

VAX/VMS

A G_floating datum is 8 contiguous bytes on an arbitrary byte boundary. The precision of a G_floating datum is approximately one part in 2 (sup 52), typically a decimal digit.

h

half duplex *n.*

generic

A communication system in which two-way communication is possible, but only one way at a time.

half-duplex *adj.*

generic

Pertaining to a communications system in which data can be either transmitted or received but only in one direction at one time.

half-duplex channel *n.*

generic

A channel that permits two-way communications, but in only one direction at any instant.

half-duplex contention *n.*

DECnet

A transmission mode in which a session between cooperating applications may operate. In the half-duplex contention mode, one application (specified in the BIND request) wins contention when both try to send at the same time.

half-duplex flip-flop *n.*

DECnet

A transmission mode in which a session between cooperating applications may operate. In the half-duplex flip-flop mode, the application that controls the change direction indicator (CDI) field of the RH, can use its send capability. The other application must supply a receive buffer for incoming data. Control over the CDI is application-determined. The half-duplex flip-flop mode is not available to EC-sessions.

half line *n.*

DECWORD

A space between lines that is half the normal vertical space.

half-sine *n.*

generic

180 degrees of a sine wave.

half word *n.*

DECsystem-10

A contiguous sequence of bits or characters that comprises half of the computer word and may be addressed as a unit. On the KL-10, bits 0 through 17 comprise the left half word and bits 18 through 35, the right half word. Each half word is 18 bits long.

generic

A group of bits including either the first or last half of the complete computer word.

halt *v.*

DECWORD

To cancel some Gold-key functions by pressing Gold HALT.

handle *n.*

Rdb/ELN

A name used to uniquely identify a database, request, or transaction.

handler *n.*

CTS-300, Memory Resident RT-11, MicroPower PASCAL, and RT-11

A software routine that services and controls the hardware activities of an I/O device. It allows user programs to perform data transfers without specific knowledge of the device characteristics. Same as device handler and device driver.

DECnet

A protocol emulator that is responsible for servicing I/O requests routed to it by the RSX Executive QI/O processor. It is also responsible for the control and servicing of a hardware device (line interface such as DUP11). Same as device handler and device controller.

handshaking (or handshaking sequence) *n.*

DECnet and VAX/VMS

The exchange of logical link connection information between two tasks. This exchange enables the successful completion of a logical link connection.

hanging *n.*

VAX/VMS

The extremely slow response of the system. When, during an interactive session, the terminal appears to be going nowhere or doing nothing, it is said to be hanging. When the system hangs, users might think that it has crashed.

hanging cursor position *n.*

generic

The place on the screen occupied by the cursor when it is one character position to the right of the end of a field. This is the initial position of the cursor for a right-justified field.

hard copy *n.*

generic

Computer output printed on paper.

hard-copy terminal *n.*

DIGITAL-specific and VAX/VMS

A terminal that prints on paper rather than displaying on a screen.

hard error *n.*

TOPS-10

A non recoverable error.

hard return *n.*

DECmate II and DECWORD

A return or carriage return, inserted by pressing RETURN. See also word-wrap return.

hardware *n.*

generic

The physical part or parts of a computer system.

hardware address *n.*

VAX/VMS

For an Ethernet device, the unique Ethernet physical address associated with a particular Ethernet communications controller (usually in read-only memory) by the manufacturer.

hardware bootstrap *n.*

DIGITAL-specific

A bootstrap that is inherent in the hardware and need only be activated by specifying the appropriate load and start address.

hardware context *n.*

VAX/VMS

The values contained in the following registers while a process is executing: the program counter (PC); the processor status longword (PSL); the 14 general registers (R0 through R13); the four processor registers (POBR, POLR, P1BR and P1LR) that describe the process virtual address space; the stack pointer (SP) for the current access mode in which the processor is executing; and the contents to be loaded in the stack pointer for every access mode other than the current access mode. While a process is executing, its hardware context is continually being updated by the processor. While a process is not executing its hardware context is stored in its hardware PCB (process control block).

hardware PCB (or hardware process control block) *n.*

DIGITAL-specific

Twenty-four longwords of hardware-maintained process information.

VAX/VMS

A data structure known to the processor that contains the hardware context when a process is not executing. A process's hardware PCB resides in its process header.

hardwired *adj.*

generic

Pertaining to the state of being directly connected and not changing.

hardwired connection *n.*

DIGITAL-specific

A permanent, as opposed to switched, physical connection between two computers for the purpose of transmitting data.

hashing *n.*

VAX DATATRIEVE and VAX DBMS

The changing of a data value (for example, a key value) into a fixed-length form using a special algorithm. Hashed key values are used as physical pointers to database record occurrences.

HASP *n.*

generic

The acronym for Houston Automatic Spooling Program. An IBM 360/370 O/S software front end that performs job spooling and controls communications between local and remote processors and remote job entry (RJE) stations. Same as Houston Automatic Spooling Program.

head *n.*

generic

A device that reads, records, or stores data on a storage medium.

header *n.*

DECnet and VAX PSI

The control information prefixed in a message text, such as source or destination code or message type.

generic

Text that appears in the top margin of printed pages, such as a document title, page number, or date.

DECWORD

Text that appears in the top margin of printed pages, such as a document title, page number, or date. Use a printer control block to create headers.

TOPS-20

1. The initial part of a message containing control characters used to determine subsequent handling of the text or data that follows.

2. Specific to ARPANET, an extension of the header containing the leader, the byte size used in the message, the length of the message, and possibly filler fields.

VAX/VMS

That portion of a task image that contains the task's characteristics and status. Shared regions, although built like a task, do not have a header.

header information *n.*

ALL-IN-1

Data that uniquely identifies a document or mail message in the user's File Cabinet. A document name and creation date are examples of header information.

heading *n.*

DECnet

The control information prefixed in a message text such as source or destination code or message type. Same as header and leader.

PASCAL and VAX PASCAL

Specification that precedes a block and defines the block's name and parameters.

heap *n.*

MicroPower PASCAL

An area of memory in the MicroPower PASCAL application for dynamic allocation of pointer objects. Processes' stacks are allocated from the heap.

heartbeat *n.*

generic

A signal generated by the H4000 Transceiver and transmitted on the collision pair of the transceiver cable. This signal indicates that a packet was sent and is used to verify that the collision detection circuitry is functional.

height *n.*

generic

A character value that specifies the vertical size (in pixels) of the character.

help key *n.*

DIGITAL-specific

A key the user can press to obtain explanatory messages about the subsystem, form, or field the user is currently in.

help messages *n.*

generic

Explanatory messages to help users to understand the system or to correct a problem.

help user action routine *n.*

generic

A user-written routine activated when the operator presses HELP.

help word *n.*

TOPS-10

A key word that the user submits to IQL (interactive query language) for a display of explanatory help text. HELP is used as an IQL assistance command to display a list of the help words.

hexadecimal *adj.*

generic

Pertaining to a number system using the base 16.

hibernate state *n.*

RSTS/E

An RSTS/E job state in which the job is detached and its execution suspended until a user attaches to it from a terminal.

hibernation *n.*

TOPS-10 and VAX/VMS

A state in which a process is inactive, but known to the system with all of its current status. A hibernating process becomes active again when a wake request is issued. It can schedule a wake request before hibernating, or another process can issue its wake request.

hierarchical database *n.*

DIGITAL-specific

A type of database that organizes the relationships between record types as a tree structure. Related records are stored on the same branch of the tree to make data retrieval efficient.

hierarchical data structure *n.*

VAX DATATRIEVE

A data structure in which each element may be related to any number of elements at a level below it, but to only one element above it in the hierarchy. Hierarchical structure shows interset relationships. See also tree data structure.

hierarchical design *n.*

generic

Pertaining to the description of a system or model of a system; the design is created in terms of more detailed models.

hierarchical network *n.*

DECnet

A computer network in which processing control functions are performed at several levels by computers specially suited for the functions performed such as in a factory or for laboratory automation.

hierarchical simulation *n.*

generic

Simulation of a model created by using a hierarchical design.

hierarchy *n.*

DIGITAL-specific

A ranked series of Common Data Dictionaries, directories, and objects analogous to the relationships in a family tree. Each dictionary directory in the CDD tree may become a parent by owning other dictionary directories or dictionary objects. Ancestors are those directories that precede the directories and objects they are related to in the tree. Ancestors have as descendants all related dictionary directories and objects that follow them in the schema.

generic

Two or more elements arranged in a graded series.

high bound *n.*

VAX PL/I

The upper limit of one dimension of an array.

highest index level *n.*

RSX-11M

The highest level in an index called the root. The root is a single-bucket entry point to the index for random accesses using the associated keys.

highest possible key value *n.*

RSX-11M

A logical maximum whose form depends on key data type. RMS-11 uses the highest possible key value to mark the logical end of an index level.

high-key value *n.*

RSX-11M

The key value of the last record in an indexed file bucket wherein the last record in a bucket has an equal or higher key value than any other record in the bucket. The last record in a bucket has a lower key value than the first record in the next bucket in the chain, neglecting continuation buckets, if present. Both data and index buckets have high-key values. The key value used in the primary level 0 is the primary key value.

high-level language *n.*

DIGITAL-specific

A language for specifying computing procedures or organization of data within a digital computer. Higher-level languages are distinguished from assembly and machine languages by the omission of machine specific details required for direct execution on a given computer. These languages frequently allow direct expression of abstract concepts important to an area of computer applications. Programs written in a higher-level language require a translation system (usually an interpreter or a compiler) to have the desired effect on a given computer system.

generic

A computer programming language designed for certain applications and not needing a specific computer.

highlight *v.*

generic

1. To draw attention to something, in a drawing or on a screen.

2. To center, underline, bold, or capitalize text in a document.

high-order bit *n.*

generic

The most significant bit of a computer word that can define a number to be negative or positive.

high-order byte *n.*

RT-11

The most significant byte in a word. The high-order byte occupies bit positions 8 through 15 of a PDP-11 word and is always an odd address.

high-order end *n.*

DIGITAL-specific

The leftmost character of a string of characters.

high portion *n.*

RSX-11M

Those records in an indexed file bucket with key values higher than the record being inserted or updated. During a bucket split, the high portion of the data is moved to a newly created bucket.

high segment *n.*

TOPS-10

A part of the user's addressing space that is used to contain pure code that can be shared by other users. This segment's contents usually are write-protected.

high voltage *n.*

generic

An electrical difference of potential that can cause danger to life.

highwater marking *n.*

VAX/VMS

A technique for discouraging disk scavenging. In the truest sense, the system tracks the furthest extent that the owner of a file has written into the file's allocated area. It then prohibits any attempts at reading beyond the written area, on the premise that any information that exists beyond the currently written limit is information some user had intended to discard. VAX/VMS accomplishes the goals of highwater marking with its erase-allocate strategy.

histogram *n.*

generic

A graphic description of one or all parameters showing distribution, mean-value failure limits, and sample log sizes.

historical cost *n.*

generic

The cost incurred for an asset at the time the asset was acquired.

history list *n.*

Common Data Dictionary

An optional record, or audit trail, maintained by the CDD (Common Data Dictionary) to monitor the processing and use of dictionary directories, sub-dictionaries, or objects. See also audit trail.

holder *n.*

VAX/VMS

A user who possesses a particular identifier. The user is said to be the holder of an identifier if he or she possesses that identifier. The right database is the place where the system associates users and the identifiers they hold.

hold state *n.*

DECnet

A logging state in which the sink is temporarily unavailable and events for it should be queued.

Hollerith *adj.*

generic

Pertaining to a special type of code or card with holes in it using 12 rows per column an usually 80 columns per card.

home block *n.*

TOPS-10

The block written twice on every unit that identifies the file structure the unit belongs to and its position on the file structure. This block specifies all the parameters of the file structure along with the location of the MFD (master file directory). The home block appears in the HOME.SYS file.

VAX/RMS and VAX/VMS

A block in the volume's index file that contains information pertaining to the volume as a whole, such as volume label and protection.

home cursor position *n.*

FMS

The character position indicated when the cursor appears at the upper left corner of the screen.

home position *n.*

generic

The upper left corner of the screen.

hop *n.*

DECnet

Relative to the transport layer, hop is the logical distance between two adjacent nodes in a network. See also path length.

VAX/VMS

The logical distance between two nodes. One hop is the distance from one node to an adjacent node.

hopper *n.*

generic

A device that holds something to be fed into a machine.

horizontally indexed field *n.*

FMS

A field with multiple occurrences across a line of a form; the second and subsequent occurrences of the field have the same name as the initial occurrence, and they are accessed by index value rather than by name. Note that the concept of horizontally indexed fields has changed from Version 1 of FMS to Version 2.

host *n.*

DIGITAL-specific

1. The primary or controlling computer in a multiple computer network.

2. As used by ARPANET (appears always Host or HOST), a Host is a computer, connected to a node, that is either a provider or user of ARPANET services.

3. A complete computer facility with a central processor, mass storage devices (such as disks), peripherals (such as printers), and a monitor command routine (MCR) or command decoder.

See also local host and distant host.

host *adj.*

generic

Pertaining to the primary or controlling computer in a multiple computer network.

host-based PAD *n.*

VAX PSI

A Packet Assembly/Disassembly Facility situated at the host node and not within the PSDN (packet switching data network).

host development environment *n.*

DIGITAL-specific

A VAX/VMS of MicroVMS system where applications are designed, developed, and debugged.

Host/Host protocol *n.*

DECnet

1. The specific level of protocol that allows hosts to initiate and maintain communication between processes running on distributed computers.

2. As used by ARPANET, the second-level protocol implemented by the network control program. Host/Host protocol provides the ground rules for establishing and maintaining logical connections between processes running on different Hosts.

host interface *n.*

DECnet

The interface between a communications processor and a host computer.

host language *n.*

VAX DATATRIEVE and VAX DBMS

A programming language used with the data manipulation language to perform actions on the database. The host language actually manipulates data once it is in memory.

host language statement *n.*

DIGITAL-specific

A statement written in the language of the application.

host node *n.*

DECnet

The node that provides services for another node (for example, during a down-line task load).

VAX/VMS

1. For DECnet, a node that provides services for another node (for example, the host node supplies program image files for a downline load). For VAX PSI, a node that accesses a packet switching data network by means of an X.25 multihost connector node.

2. The node that makes a device available to other nodes in the VAXcluster. A host node can be either a VAX that adds the device to the MSCP-server database or an HSC50.

host operating system *n.*

VAX DATATRIEVE

The operating system that controls the execution of a program, service, or application.

host processor *n.*

MicroPower PASCAL

A computer, running an RT-11 operating system, on which MicroPower PASCAL application programs are developed.

RT-11

The processor on which program development, system generation, and run-time system building is done. In MRRT-11 applications, the host processor is a PDP-11 or an LSI-11 having system resources that are not directly available to the SB11 system(s); for example, file-structured peripherals.

host-satellite system *n.*

VT-11 GRAPHICS

A hardware/software configuration in which graphic processing is distributed between a large host computer and a satellite graphic terminal driven by a smaller satellite computer. The satellite computer in such a system closely resembles a stand-alone system, except that the display subsystem is connected to the host computer by a serial data link rather than by the UNIBUS.

host system *n.*

VAX/VMS

The system on which a task is built.

host/target relationship *n.*

RT-11

A complementary relationship between a host and a target computer in which software is developed on a host RT-11 system and then transferred to a target SB11 for execution.

hot start *n.*

DIGITAL-specific

The on-line recovery and continuation of the system.

Houston Automatic Spooling Program (HASP) *n.*

DECnet

An IBM 360/370 O/S software front end that performs job spooling and controls communications between local and remote processors and remote job entry (RJE) stations. Same as HASP.

hyphen (-) *n.*

DECWORD

DECWORD uses four kinds of hyphens:

1. An ordinary hyphen, produced by pressing the normal hyphen key on the keyboard.

2. Gold PRINT HYPH, called a ghost hyphen. A character that tells DECWORD where it may automatically hyphenate a word if that word falls at the end of a line.

3. Gold-1-PRINT HYPH, called a breaking hyphen. A hyphen used to join compound words that may be divided at the end of a line.

4. Gold-2-PRINT HYPH, known as breaking words without hyphens. A way of dividing a word between two lines without using a hyphen (typically used in mathematical equations).

hyphen pass *n.*

DECWORD

A Gold command that directs DECWORD to search the document for ends of lines that contain more than a specified number of spaces. The user can then enter hyphens as necessary.

hysteresis *n.*

MINC

1. The phenomenon of a response of a system unit lagging behind an increase or decrease in the strength of a signal.

2. The tendency of certain binary devices to show different threshold values when changing from 0 to 1 than when changing from 1 to 0.

H_floating data *n.*

VAX/VMS

An extended range floating point number 16 bytes long having a range of $+/- *.84*10**-4932$ to $+/- 0.59*10**4932$ and a precision of approximately 33 decimal digits.

H_floating datum *n.*

VAX/VMS

An H_floating datum is 16 contiguous bytes starting on an arbitrary byte-boundary.

IC *n.*

generic

The abbreviation for integrated circuit. An IC is a combination of connected circuit elements always linked on or in a continuous material. Same as integrated circuit.

icon *n.*

generic

A graphic or picture representation of a function displayed on a terminal screen.

ICP *n.*

DECnet

The abbreviation for installation checkout package. ICP is a program that demonstrates that the basic operation of the VAX PSI software is correct. Same as installation checkout package.

IDB *n.*

DIGITAL-specific and VAX/VMS

The abbreviation for interrupt dispatch block. An IDB is a structure in I/O data base that describes the characteristics of a particular controller and points to devices attached to that controller. Same as interrupt dispatch block.

identification *n.*

generic

The set of characteristics by which something is known or recognized.

identifier *n.*

DSM-11

A name consisting of one to eight alphanumeric characters. The first character must be either an alphabetic character or the percent (%) symbol. Identifiers are used as names for variables, routines, and globals. The percent symbol must be used as the first character of a library routine or global name.

PEARL

A sequence of letters and digits that is used to name or identify a PEARL object.

VAX PASCAL

One or more alphanumeric characters that denote a variable, constant, type, procedure, function, or other item that is not a reserved word. Although an identifier can be any length, PASCAL treats only the first 31 characters as significant.

VAX PL/I and VAX/VMS

A user-supplied name of from 1 to 31 characters that denotes the name of a variable, statement label, entry point, or file constant. The name is a sequence of letters and digits; the underline (_) and dollar sign ($) are considered letters. The first character of an identifier must be a letter.

idle segment *n.*

TOPS-10

A sharable segment that is being used by one or more swapped out jobs, but not by any jobs currently in memory.

idle time *n.*

generic

The time when a CPU is inactive.

TOPS-10

That part of uptime in which no job could run because all jobs were halted or waiting for some external action such as I/O.

IEEE bus *n.*

MINC

A cable of 16 wires, or bus lines, that MINC and all instruments on the bus lines share. The IEEE bus enables MINC to communicate with IEEE-standard instruments.

IFAB *n.*

DIGITAL-specific

The abbreviation for internal file-access block. IFAB is a block, within another block, that is required for each open file. IFAB is used by RMS-32 (record management system). Same as internal file-access block.

image *n.*

generic

1. Duplicate information or data copied from one medium to another.

2. Programs or data sections output by a linker.

3. A statement in some programming languages or utilities that describes the format in which data is to be displayed or stored.

VAX/VMS

Procedures and data bound together by the linker. There are three types of images: executable, shareable, and system.

image activator *n.*

VAX/VMS

A set of system procedures that prepares an image for execution. The image activator establishes the memory management data structures required both to map the image's virtual pages to physical pages and to perform paging.

image exit *n.*

VAX/VMS

An image rundown activity that occurs when image execution terminates either normally or abnormally. Image rundown activities include deassigning I/O channels and disassociation of common event flag clusters. Any user-specified or system-specified exit handlers are called exits. See exit.

image file *n.*

VAX/VMS

A file containing the information necessary to establish an incarnation of a user program in a process including the memory image.

image header *n.*

VAX/VMS

The first part of an image file created by the linker. Variable in length, it contains all information for the image activator and memory management to control mapping and page faulting. See also image section descriptor.

image I/O segment *n.*

VAX/VMS

That portion of the control region that contains the RMS internal file-access blocks (IFAB) and I/O buffers for the image currently being executed by a process.

image memory *n.*

GIGI

A bit map GIGI uses to maintain and display images on the screen.

image mode n.

DIGITAL-specific

A mode of data transfer in which each byte of data is transferred without any interpretation or data changes.

generic

A method of data transfer in which each byte is transferred without change.

image name n.

generic

The name of the file in which an image is stored.

image privileges n.

VAX/VMS

The privileges assigned to an image when it is installed. See also process privileges.

image section (ISECT) n.

VAX/VMS

A group of program sections (PSECTs) with the same attributes (such as read-only access, read/write access, absolute, relocatable, etc.) that is the unit of virtual memory allocation for an image. For VAX/VMS, ISECT is the same as image section. ISECT is listed for VAX/VMS with the same definition as image section elsewhere in this section. Same as ISECT.

image section descriptor n.

VAX/VMS

Block of longwords describing mapping information for an image section, contained in the image header. See also image header.

immediate control mode n.

DECnet

An SNA (systems network architecture) request mode in which a program issues a request and then must wait for a response before it can issue another request.

immediate mode n.

MINC

A manner in which a computer executes statements. In immediate mode, the computer executes statements as soon as the user types them.

TOPS-10

An operation mode in which the IQL (interactive query language) processes a command when the user enters the command. The user can display selected items from a data file on the terminal and edit them.

VAX/VMS

A type of autoincrement mode addressing in which the PC (program center) is used as the register.

immediate mode addressing n.

TOPS-10

The interpretation of certain instructions in which the effective address of the instruction is used as the value of an operand (rather than the address of an operand).

immediate response mode n.

DECnet

An SNA (systems network architecture) request mode in which responses are returned in the same sequence in which the related requests were received.

immortal MPP *n.*

MCS-10

A program (for processing messages) that cannot be terminated by MCS-10. The program can be stopped by the operator.

IMP *n.*

DECnet and TOPS-20

The acronym for the interface message processor. The IMP, developed for ARPANET, is the minicomputer interface between the ARPANET and a Host computer. Messages from Host A destined for Host B, go first to the Host A IMP, travel through the IMP subnet to the Host B IMP, and from the Host B IMP to Host B. The IMP serves to insulate the Hosts from such problems as routing, flow control, and data validity. Same as interface message processor.

impact printer *n.*

generic

A printer in which printing is the result of mechanical parts pressing the copy medium.

IMP/Host protocol *n.*

DECnet and TOPS-20

Specific to ARPANET, the first-level protocol that provides the operating rules for the passage of messages between Hosts and IMPs in order to create virtual communication paths between Hosts. The IMP/Host protocol also serves to optimize one Host's use of communications capacity without denying use of capacity by other Hosts.

implementor-name *n.*

COBOL-74

A system name that refers to a particular feature available on that implementor's computing system.

implicit job startup *n.*

CTS-300

A feature that allows control to be passed to a specified program upon execution of a statement from within another program, similar to forced job startup. With this feature, a request can be made to start the specified program if it is not already running.

implicit mapping *n.*

Terminal Data Management System

An instruction (OUTPUT %ALL, INPUT %ALL, or RETURN %ALL) in a TDMS (Terminal Data Management System) request that lets users map data between all identically named form and record fields without specifying the individual fields. If the request definition utility finds an error in an implicit mapping, it does not include that mapping when it stores the request in the CDD (Common Data Dictionary). At run time, TDMS performs only the correct mappings. See also explicit mapping.

implicit prompt *n.*

RSX-11M

The right angle-bracket prompt (>) is called the implicit prompt. It indicates that a command line interpreter is ready to receive input.

implicit scope terminator *n.*

VAX COBOL

- A separator period that ends the scope of any preceding unterminated statement

- A phrase of a statement that, by its occurrence, ends the scope of any statement in the preceding phrase

IMP subnet *n.*

DECnet and TOPS-20

Specific to ARPANET, a completely autonomous communications system (transparent to the user) with the essential task of transferring bits reliably, quickly, and relatively free of errors, from a source to a specific destination. The Host is specifically prohibited from changing the logical characteristics of the IMP. The IMP can continue its task on behalf of other Hosts even if its Host is down. It is not dependent on its Host for either buffering or program loading.

impure code *n.*

generic

A section of program code that is modified each time it is executed.

TOPS-10

The code that is modified during the course of a run (such as data tables).

IMS/VS *n.*

DECnet

The abbreviation for information management system/virtual storage. A proprietary IBM software product that provides data communication and data-base management facilities for use by S/370 application programs. Same as information management system/virtual storage.

inactive display list *n.*

VT-11 GRAPHICS

A list of graphic instructions and data residing in the display file but not included in the current frame by the display processor.

inbound connection *n.*

DECnet

The term inbound refers to the fact that a task receives logical link connection requests.

VAX/VMS

Logical link connection requests that a task receives.

Inbox *n.*

DIGITAL-specific

In Electronic Mail, the storage area where messages received are held until you read them.

incarnation *n.*

VAX DATATRIEVE

A resource that is automatically allocated on a call or a recursive call.

incarnation-own *n.*

VAX DATATRIEVE

A resource that is unique to the particular incarnation (embodiment) of a domain within a process but that is preserved from call to call.

incarnation-temporary *n.*

VAX DATATRIEVE

A resource that is automatically allocated on a call or recursive call and disappears upon return.

INCLUDE file *n.*

VAX PL/I

The external file from which the compiler reads source text during the compilation of a PL/I program.

income *n.*

generic

The difference between revenue and expense.

income statement *n.*

generic

A statement of revenues and expenses, and the difference between them.

income tax *n.*

generic

A tax that is levied as a percentage of taxable income.

increment *n.*

generic

An amount added to a value.

incremental compiler *n.*

generic

A program that translates a code into machine language by taking the data from each source statement and processing it before moving on to the next source statement.

incremental reorganization *n.*

RSX-11M

The process of inserting each data record where it logically belongs in level 0 and updating the upper levels of an index.

indefinite sweep *n.*

MINC

A condition in which a sweep continues indefinitely because the call for the sweep gives no condition for stopping the sweep. See also continuous sweep.

index *n.*

DECWORD

1. A display that lists all the documents stored in a user account. For each document, the index shows a document name and number.

2. A list of topics in a document. To select entries for an index, use the Gold INDEX function while entering or editing text in a document. While the document is printing, DECWORD places the index entries into a new document. The user can then use list processing to sort the index into alphabetical order.

DIGITAL-specific

The structure that allows retrieval of records in an indexed file by key value. See key (indexed files).

generic

1. A table used to access data directly.

2. The number that refers to a single element in an array.

index bucket *n.*

RSX-11M

A bucket in an indexed file that contains index records. See also data bucket.

index data item *n.*

COBOL-74

A data item in which the value associated with an index-name can be stored in a form specified by the implementor.

index data-name *n.*

COBOL-74

An identifier that is composed of a data-name followed by one or more index-names enclosed in parentheses.

index descriptor *n.*

RSX-11M

A memory-resident copy of a key descriptor's fields required for normal operations.

indexed address *n.*

TOPS-10, TOPS-20, and VAX/VMS

An address that is formed by adding the content of an index register to the content of an address field prior to or during the execution of a computer instruction.

indexed addressing mode *n.*

VAX/VMS

An addressing mode in which two registers are used to determine the actual instruction operand: an index register and a base operand specified. The contents of the index register are used as the index (offset) into a table or array. The base operand specifier supplies the base address of the array (the base operand address or BOA). The address of the actual operand is calculated by multiplying the contents of the index register by the size (in bytes) of the actual operand and adding the result to the base operand address. The addressing modes resulting from index mode addressing are formed by adding the suffix "indexed" to the addressing mode of the base operand specifier: register deferred indexed, autoincrement indexed, autoincrement deferred indexed (or absolute indexed), autodecrement indexed, displacement indexed, and displacement deferred indexed.

indexed field *n.*

FMS

Referring to one of two types of form fields: a horizontally indexed field and a vertically indexed field. See also horizontally indexed field or vertically indexed field.

generic

In a form, a field with multiple occurrences, all having the same name and being accessed by index value in addition to name. Indexed fields do not have to appear in a vertical or a horizontal direction.

indexed file *n.*

VAX DATATRIEVE

A file that contains records and a primary key index (and optionally one or more alternate key indices) used to process the records sequentially by index or randomly by index.

indexed file load *n.*

RSX-11M

An RMS-11 utility that bypasses normal access methods to load an Indexed file with records from a file that the user designates.

indexed file organization *n.*

DIGITAL-specific

A file organization that allows random retrieval of records by key value and sequential retrieval of records within the key of reference. See also indexed file, key, segmented key, and sequential file organization.

VAX DATATRIEVE and VAX/VMS

A file organization in which a file contains records and a primary key index (and optionally one or more alternate key indices), used to process the records sequentially by index or randomly by index.

indexed form array *n.*

Terminal Data Management System

A list of elements on a TDMS (Terminal Data Management System) form, all of which have the same name and the same characteristics (length, data type, and so on). The form definer specifies how many elements the array contains.

indexed organization *n.*

COBOL-74

The permanent logical file structure in which each record is identified by the value of one or more keys within that record.

indexed register *n.*

TOPS-10, TOPS-20, and VAX/VMS

A register whose contents may be added to the operand address prior to or during the execution of a computer instruction. On the KL-10, accumulators 1 through 17 (octal) may be used as index registers (accumulator 0 may not be used as 1). Same as index register.

indexed sequential access method *n.*

DIGITAL-specific

The abbreviation for indexed sequential access method. A method of file organization, storage, and access. Records are stored and accessed on the basis of the contents of a specified field called a key field. An index is used to determine a position from which a short sequential search is made for the desired entry. Same as ISAM. See also indexed sequential file and indexed file organization.

indexed sequential file *n.*

VAX PL/I

A record file in which each record has one or more data keys embedded in it. Records in the file are individually accessible by specifying a key associated with a record.

index file *n.*

CTS-300

In an ISAM file, the section of the total file that contains both the index entries and the overflow area.

VAX/VMS

The file on a Files-11 volume that contains the access information for all files on the volume and enables the operating system to identify and access the volume.

index file bit map *n.*

VAX/VMS

A table in the index file of a FILES-11 volume that indicates which file headers are in use.

index key *n.*

Rdb/ELN

A field in a record that is used to define an index. Rdb/ELN can locate records in the relation directly, without searching sequentially.

VAX DATATRIEVE

A field of a record in an indexed file that determines the order of search and retrieval. An indexed file has one primary key and optionally one or more alternative keys. In DATATRIEVE, an index key is a field from a record definition named in the DEFINE FILE command.

index level *n.*

RSX-11M

The higher levels (1+) of an index, containing index buckets. See also data level, lowest index level.

index mode *n.*

VAX DBMS

A DBMS data structure within a hierarchical index that provides additional speed of access. See also index mode set.

index mode set *n.*

VAX DBMS

A sorted set in which a tree-structured index is used to access specific records quickly. Index mode is declared in the storage schema definition language. See also index node and sorted mode.

index-name *n.*

COBOL-74

A user-defined word that names an index associated with a specific table.

index number *n.*

VAX PL/I

The key field to which a key specified in a given I/O operation applies. An indexed file can have multiple keys each of which has an index. The first, or primary, index is always zero.

index page *n.*

Rdb/ELN

In an Rdb/ELN database file, fixed-length pages that contain the B-tree structures on which an index is built. See also index root page.

index record *n.*

RSX-11

A record maintained by RMS-11 in levels 1+ of all indexes. The record contains a high-key value for a bucket in the next lower level and a pointer to that bucket. See also data record and user data record.

index register *n.*

generic

A storage device whose contents may be used to modify an address during the execution of computer instructions.

TOPS-10, TOPS-20, and VAX/VMS

A register whose contents may be added to the operand address prior to or during the execution of a computer instruction. On the KL-10, accumulators 1 through 17 (octal) may be used as index registers (accumulator 0 may not be used as 1). Same as indexed register.

index root page *n.*

Rdb/ELN

In an Rdb/ELN database file, a fixed-length page that contains the first-level entry for the index to a relation.

indirect address *n.*

DIGITAL-specific

An address file containing commands that are processed sequentially but that could have been entered interactively at a terminal.

generic

An address pointing to another address.

RT-11, TOPS-10, and TOPS-20

An address that indicates a storage location where the address of the referenced operand (or another indirect address) is to be found.

indirect command file *n.*

generic

A file that holds commands to be executed.

VAX/VMS

A file containing commands and data that the command interpreter can accept in lieu of the user's typing the commands individually on a terminal. Thus, command procedures provide a means of automatically passing commands to the operating system. In addition, they permit users to employ such programming techniques as loops, counters, labels, and symbol substitution to set up elaborate command sequences that can be altered through user interaction. Command procedures can also be submitted to the system for processing as batch jobs. Same as command file and command procedure.

indirect cost n.

generic

A cost element that relates to more than one cost object.

indirection n.

DSM-11

A means of using the value of an expression instead of the expression itself. Indirection is denoted by the at (@) sign followed by an element that evaluates to an expression atom. Whenever DSM finds an occurrence of indirection, it substitutes the value previously given the expression atom for the occurrence of indirection. This allows DSM to execute the same segment of code repeatedly for different values of the expression atom.

indirect reference n.

DSM-11

An indirect reference is a language feature that permits a string variable to represent a command's argument or argument list. In operation, the string value of the variable is taken as the argument or argument list.

infile n.

RSX-11M

A convention for the term "input file specification".

infix operator n.

VAX PL/I

An operator that is positioned between two operands in an expression to define the operation.

information bit n.

DECnet

A bit that is generated by the data source and that is not used for error control by the data transmission system. See also overhead bit.

information management n.

generic

The handling (management) of the internal and external data available to all the entities and users within an enterprise, plus the tools and support service to make the data easily accessible and easy to use.

information management system/virtual storage (IMS/VS) n.

DECnet

A proprietary IBM software product that provides data communication and data base management facilities for use by S/370 application programs. Same as IMS/VS.

information type n.

DECnet

One of CHARACTERISTICS, COUNTERS, EVENTS, or SUMMARY, used with the NCP command SHOW to control the type of information returned. Each entity parameter and counter is associated with one or more information types.

initialization *n.*

DIGITAL-specific

The process of preparing a new disk for use with a computer or to erase a used disk in preparation for a new use. Initialization sets up an empty file directory on a disk.

initialization procedure *n.*

DATATRIEVE

A fixed sequence of DATATRIEVE commands, statements, clauses, or arguments that are created, named, and stored in the Common Data Dictionary. See also procedure.

initialize *v.*

CTS-300

1. To format a volume in a particular file-structured format in preparation for use by an operating system.

2. To set counters, switches, or addresses to some starting value.

DECWORD

To prepare a new disk or diskette for use. Initializing a disk or diskette erases any documents that were stored there.

DIGITAL-specific

The process by which the computer prepares an additional disk for handling user information. This process erases any information that was on the disk.

generic

To prepare to start.

RT-11

To set counters, switches, or addresses to starting values at prescribed points in the execution of a program, particularly in preparation for re-execution of a sequence of code. To format a volume in a particular file-structured format in preparation for use by an operating system.

TOPS-10

To set counters, switches, or addresses to zero or other starting values at prescribed points in the execution of a computer routine, particularly in preparation for re-execution of a sequence of code.

initializer *n.*

VAX/VMS

The part of a declaration that gives the initial value(s) for the preceding declarator. An initializer consists of an equal sign (=) followed by either a single expression or a comma-separated list of one or more expression in braces.

initial MicroPower PASCAL (initial MPP)

DECsystem-10

One or more copies of a message processing program that will be started by MCS-10 when it is started.

INITS *n.*

DECnet

The acronym for initiate self. An SNA (systems network architecture) network service request used by an SLU to request a session with a specific PLU. Same as initiate self.

input *n.*

generic

1. Information that is read by a computer.

2. Anything such as power, energy, or data entered into a device or system in order to produce a result or output.

3. Information that is introduced into a program for use in processing.

input *adj.*

generic

1. Pertaining to a device, process, or channel involved in acquisition of data.

2. Pertaining to anything such as power, energy, or data entered into a device or system in order to produce a result or output.

input device *n.*

DIGITAL-specific

Hardware that allows the user to communicate with the CPU. Often abbreviated as I/O. See also I/O device.

input field *n.*

DECnet

An unprotected field in which data can be entered, modified, or erased. See also display field.

input mode *n.*

COBOL-74

The state of a file after execution of an OPEN statement with the INPUT phrase specified, and before the execution of a CLOSE statement for that file.

input/output device *n.*

DIGITAL-specific

Hardware that allows the user to communicate with the CPU. Often abbreviated as I/O.

input/output operation *n.*

DIGITAL-specific

The actual transfer of data between memory and disk, involving the positioning of the disk heads and the electrical flow of data. Same as physical I/O operation.

input/output request packet (IRP) *n.*

DIGITAL-specific

An I/O data structure that is constructed by the Queue I/O Request system service. This service optionally returns a status code, number of bytes transferred, and device and function dependent information in an IOSB. Not returned from the service call, but filled in when the I/O request completes. Same as IRP.

input-output section *n.*

COBOL-74

The section of the Environment Division that names the files and the external media required by an object program, and that provides information required for transmission and handling of data during execution of the object program.

input/output status block *n.*

DIGITAL-specific

A quadword data structure associated with the Queue I/O Request system service. This service optionally returns a status code, number of bytes transferred, and device and function dependent information in an IOSB. Not returned from the service call, but filled in when the I/O request completes.

input procedure *n.*

COBOL-74

A set of statements that is executed each time a record is released to the sort file.

PASCAL

Procedure that reads data into a program. PASCAL provides three predeclared input procedures: READ, READLN, and GET.

input process *n.*

DIGITAL-specific

The process of transmitting data from peripheral equipment, or external storage, back to internal storage.

input stream *n.*

VAX/VMS

The source of commands and data. It is either the user's terminal, the batch stream, or a command procedure.

insertion class *n.*

VAX DBMS

An attribute of member records that describes how and when members are added to sets. See also automatic member and manual member.

insert mode *n.*

DIGITAL-specific

An input mode that causes typed characters to be placed at the current cursor location.

FMS

The mode in the Form Editor LAYOUT phase that causes typed characters to be placed at the current cursor location. It moves the cursor to the right, shifting other characters on the line to the right also. The mode in the Form Driver that is the default for right-justified fields.

installation checkout package (ICP) *n.*

DECnet

A program that demonstrates that the basic operation of the VAX PSI software is correct. Same as ICP.

installation procedure *n.*

DECnet

DECnet installation is the process of setting up the DECnet software and modifying several system files to include DECnet-related jobs. DECnet installation occurs after DECnet configuration.

installation verification procedure *n.*

DIGITAL-specific

A procedure to verify that both the LAT-11 server and LAT (local area transport) node systems are working properly. Same as IVP.

installed task *n.*

RSX-11M

An installed task is one that is named in the system task directory (STD), a list of task control blocks (TCBs) which contain information about each task. Taking a task out of the STD is called removing it. Users automatically install and remove their tasks through the RUN command.

installment *n.*

generic

Payment of a debt or an accounts receivable in several amounts at periodic intervals rather than in one sum.

instantiation instance *n.*

DECSIM/generic

A usage or call of a previously defined MODEL, or MACRO. The instance also specifies how connections are to be made to a MODEL.

instruction *n.*

generic

A unique set of characters that specifies computer operation.

instruction buffer *n.*

VAX/VMS

An 8-byte buffer in the processor used to contain bytes of the instruction currently being decoded and to prefetch instructions in the instruction stream. The control logic continuously fetches data from memory to keep the 8-byte buffer full.

inswap *n.*

TOPS-20

The act of restoring a process's working set to the balance set from secondary storage.

integer *n.*

COBOL-74

An nonnegative numeric literal or a numeric data item that does not include any character positions to the right of the assumed decimal point. Where the term 'integer' appears in general formats, integer must not be a numeric data item, and must not be signed or zero, unless explicitly allowed by the rules of that format.

generic

A whole number that may be positive or negative but that does not have a fractional part.

integer operation *n.*

DIGITAL-specific

An arithmetic operation on data of type byte, word, longword, or quadword.

integer type *n.*

DIGITAL-specific

Predefined scalar type that has the integers as values.

integer variable *n.*

DIGITAL-specific

A variable representing only whole numbers within the range of −32767 to +32767.

integral type *n.*

VAX/VMS

One of the data types CHAR or INT (all sizes, signed or unsigned).

integrated circuit (IC) *n.*

generic

An IC is a combination of connected circuit elements always linked on or in a continuous material. Same as IC.

integrator *n.*

generic

A circuit in which the output is proportional to the total of the changes at the input over a period of time.

integrity *n.*

generic

The ability to ensure that database record relationships and the contents of data items are not adversely affected by concurrent processes.

intensity *n.*

VT-11 GRAPHICS

The apparent brightness of objects on the display screen.

interactive adj.

generic

Pertaining to the switching of information and control between a user and a computer process or between computer processes.

interactive adj.

generic

Refers to an environment in which an operator and a program can communicate mutually.

interactive DBQ n.

VAX DBMS

In DBMS, a data manipulation interface to the database control system that allows low-volume, interactive access to a database. The user can use Interactive DBQas a tool to test and debug program logic. When used on a VT100 terminal, interactive DBQ uses a split screen to show a user's current position in a subschema after each DML statement is executed. See also database query and callable DBQ.

interactive processing n.

DIGITAL-specific

A mode of computer operation in which the commands and data that control the actions of the computer are entered by a person at a terminal rather than by a programmed script.

interactive system n.

VAX/VMS

A computer system in which the user and the operating system communicate directly by means of a terminal. The operating system immediately acknowledges and acts upon requests entered by the user at the terminal.

interactive terminal n.

DIGITAL-specific

A standard hardware terminal with a keyboard from which a user can type commands or responses to prompts.

interchange record separator (IRS) n.

DIGITAL-specific

In binary synchronous communications, a control character for the IBM 3780 communications terminal. In the 3780 record format, each record within a block terminates with an IRS character if the terminal is not in transparent mode. Same as IRS.

interconnectable behavior model n.

DECSIM

A modeling approach based on structurally interconnected behavior models. Structural (or gate level) models may be included in the network; the network may be configured in either a hierarchical or a single-level style.

interest n.

generic

The income earned (or cost incurred) for the use of money.

interface *n.*

DIGITAL-specific

1. A shared boundary defined by common physical interconnection characteristics, signal characteristics, and meanings of interchange signals.

2. A device or equipment making possible interoperation between two systems, e.g., a hardware component or a common storage register.

3. A shared logical boundary between two software components.

generic

A common connection that is used for sending and/or accepting information and control between programs, machines, and persons.

INTERFACE *n.*

FMS

A boundary with functional properties enabling the exchange of control or information.

PEARL

An object whose content is executable code used to transform data during conditions in which the format required by two linked DATIONs is different.

INTERFACE BEGIN *n.*

PEARL

The head of an interface that contains information on the use of the interface.

INTERFACE BODY *n.*

PEARL

A number of nested blocks that perform the functions of an interface.

interface message processor (IMP) *n.*

DECnet and TOPS-20

The interface message processor, developed for ARPANET, is the minicomputer interface between the ARPANET and a Host computer. Messages from Host A destined for Host B, go first to the Host A IMP, travel through the IMP subnet to the Host B IMP, and from the Host B IMP to Host B. The IMP serves to insulate the Hosts from such problems as routing, flow control, and data validity. Same as IMP.

interjob dependency *n.*

TOPS-10

The technique by which a batch job is kept from running until after the running of another job.

interlace *n.*

DIGITAL-specific

The display of every other horizontal line of pixels in order to reduce flicker on low-resolution monitor screens.

interlacing *n.*

MINC

A feature of the MINC terminal by which additional scan lines are placed between the normal lines in the terminal's screen. This feature reduces the amount of undefined space within each character; it is useful, for example, when photographing the screen.

interleaving *n.*

generic

The alternating of two or more operations or functions through the use of computer subsystems at the same time.

TOPS-10

The process of configuring the memory addressing so that consecutive addresses are not stored in the same memory module. This allows the possibility of increasing memory speed by overlapping part of the operation of different memory modules.

VAX/VMS

The process of assigning consecutive physical memory addresses alternately between two memory controllers.

interleaving unit *n.*

VAX DBMS

The duration for which a run unit retains the data base exclusively.

intermediate text block (ITB) *n.*

DECnet

In binary synchronous communications, a control character used to terminate an intermediate block of characters. A block check character is sent immediately following ITB, but no line turnaround occurs. Same as ITB.

intermodule reference *n.*

MicroPower PASCAL

A reference made in one module to a symbol defined in another module.

internal file *n.*

PASCAL

A file that exists only within the scope of a block and is deleted when execution of that block ends.

internal file-access block (IFAB) *n.*

DIGITAL-specific

A block, within another block, that is required for each open file. IFAB is used by RMS-32 (record management system). Same as IFAB.

internal file connector *n.*

VAX COBOL

A file connector that is accessible to only one object program in the run unit.

internal procedure *n.*

VAX PL/I

A procedure that is contained within another procedure.

internal storage *n.*

DIGITAL-specific

Addressable high-speed storage directly controlled by the central processing unit.

internal symbol *n.*

TOPS-10

A global symbol located in the module in which it is defined. In a MACRO-10 program, a symbol is declared internal with the INTERN or ENTRY pseudo-op. These pseudo-ops generate a global definition that is used to satisfy all global requests for the symbol.

internal variable *n.*

VAX PL/I

A variable whose value can be referenced within the block that declared it or referenced within any block contained within the block that declared it.

internet *n.*

generic

A network in which DIGITAL computers are connected to those of another manufacturer.

interpreter *n.*

CTS-300

A program that translates and executes each source language statement before translating and executing the next statement. In CTS-300 the compiler (DISCOMP) does the translation and the run-time system program interprets the translated code for execution.

DECsystem-10

A computer program that translates and executes each source language statement before translating and executing the next. AID (attention identification) is an interpreter on the DECsystem-10.

DSM-11

A part of the DSM-11 operating system that translates DSM commands and statements into machine instructions and executes the specified operations. The interpreter translates a DSM routine each time it is run.

generic

A computer program that translates and executes each source language statement before translating and executing the next statement.

interprocess communication *n.*

TOPS-10 and TOPS-20

The mechanism that allows messages to be sent between processes in the system.

interprocess communication facility (IPCF) *n.*

TOPS-10, TOPS-20, and VAX/VMS

A common event flag cluster, mailbox, or global section used to pass information between two or more processes. Same as IPCF.

interrecord gap *n.*

generic

1. The space between records on magnetic tape caused by delays in starting and stopping tape motion.

2. A signal of an end of a record or a block of records.

TOPS-10, TOPS-20, and VAX/VMS

A blank space deliberately placed between data records on the recording surface of a magnetic tape. Same as IRG.

interrupt *v.*

generic

To cause a break in the usual flow of a system or program to perform an external task.

interrupt *n.*

generic

A break in the usual flow of a program to process an external request.

VAX/VMS

1. An event other than an exception or a branch, jump, case, or call instruction that changes the normal flow of instruction execution. Interrupts are generally external to the process executing when the interrupt occurs. See also device interrupt, software interrupt, and urgent interrupt.

2. A packet, sent through a packet switching data network, that bypasses normal flow control procedures used by data packets.

interrupt, pseudo *n.*

DECnet

As used by TENEX, a synonym for software interrupt. See also interrupt (software).

interrupt data block (IDB) *n.*

VAX/VMS

A structure in the I/O data base that describes the characteristics of a particular controller and points to devices attached to that controller. Same as IDB.

interrupt dispatch block *n.*

DIGITAL-specific

A device-oriented data structure that contains the CSR (communication status register) address for a controller and a list of associated units. Used to associate an interrupt with the correct UCB (unit control block).

interrupt-driven *adj.*

generic

Pertaining to software that uses interrupt service routines to process external requests.

RT-11

Pertaining to software that uses the interrupt facility of a computer to handle I/O and respond to user requests. RT-11 is such a system.

interrupt-driver I/O *n.*

RT-11

Asynchronous data transfers controlled by the peripheral that notifies the central processing unit (CPU),when the transfer is complete.

interrupt masking *n.*

PEARL

The method of defining whether a specified interrupt is ignored.

interrupt message *n.*

DECnet

A high-priority message used to inform another task of some significant event.

VAX/VMS

A user-generated message sent outside the normal exchange of data messages during nontransparent task-to-task communication. This use of the term interrupt is contrary to the normal usage, which means to designate a software or hardware interrupt mechanism.

interrupt priority level (IPL) *n.*

VAX/VMS

The interrupt level at which a software or hardware interrupt is generated. There are 31 possible interrupt priority levels: IPL 1 is lowest, 31 is highest. The levels arbitrate contention for processor service. For example, a device cannot interrupt the processor if the processor is currently executing at an interrupt priority level equal to or greater than the interrupt priority level of the device's interrupt service routine. Same as IPL.

interrupt procedure *n.*

DIGITAL-specific

A procedure that is invoked in response to an external event.

interrupt service routine (ISR) *n.*

generic

That software that processes external requests that cause interrupts.

MicroPower PASCAL

A routine designed to execute when a particular device signals the processor with an interrupt. The processor locates ISRs in memory, using an address vector supplied by the interrupting device.

MINC

A set of instructions that interrupts the normal sequential execution of program statements by the computer. With this routine, the computer is directed to execute an alternate set of instructions that enables communication between the computer and a calling peripheral device. In most cases, the ISR keeps track of the state of the computer prior to its being interrupted, and restores the computer to that state when it has finished using the computer to execute its own set of instructions.

VAX/VMS

The routine executed when an interrupt occurs. Same as ISR.

interrupt (software) *n.*

DECnet

An interrupt that has been activated to occur under specific conditions, been assigned specific priorities, and has been provided with a specific processing routine

interrupt stack (IS) *n.*

VAX/VMS

The system-wide stack used when executing in interrupt service context. At any time, the processor is either in a process context executing in user, supervisor, executive or kernel mode, or in system-wide interrupt service context operating in kernel mode, as indicated by the interrupt stack and current mode bits in the PSL (process status longword). The interrupt stack is not context switched. Same as IS.

interrupt stack pointer *n.*

VAX/VMS

The stack pointer for the interrupt stack. Unlike the stack pointers for process context stacks, which are stored in the hardware PCB, the interrupt stack pointer is stored in an internal register. Same as ISP.

VAX/VMS

A storage location known to the system that contains the starting address of a procedure to be executed when a given interrupt or exception occurs. The system defines separate vectors for each interrupting device controller and for classes of exceptions. Each system vector is a longword. Same as exception vector, vector, and interrupt vector address.

interrupt vector address *n.*

generic

An indirect address that points to the starting address of an interrupt service routine.

VAX/VMS

A storage location known to the system, that contains the starting address of a procedure to be executed when a given interrupt or exception occurs. The system defines separate vectors for each interrupting device controller and for classes of exceptions. Each system is a longword. Same as vector, exception vector, and interrupt vector.

interstimulus-interval (ISI) mode *n.*

MINC

A method of time-data sampling by which the elapsed times between successive firings of the Schmitt-Trigger 2 (ST2) are measured and stored.

intra-record data structure *n.*

generic

The entire collection of group and elementary data items from a logical record.

invalid definition *n.*

FMS

The request definition or library definition that is marked invalid because RDU (request definition utility) has attempted to validate the definition but found incorrect external references, or the definer created the definition in NOVALIDATE mode.

invalid key condition *n.*

COBOL-74

A condition at object time caused when a specific value of the key associated with an indexed or relative file is determined to be invalid.

invalid key condition *n.*

generic

At run time, a condition caused when the value of the key associated with an indexed or relative file is determined to be invalid.

inventory *n.*

generic

Goods being held for sale including partially finished products and raw materials associated with those goods.

inventory turnover *n.*

generic

A ratio that indicates how many times inventory was totally replaced during the year.

inverted file *n.*

VAX DATATRIEVE

A file that stores the record identifiers (or keys) for all records with a given attribute (or value) for a data item field. For example, in a personnel file, an inverted file for marital status "single" would contain the attribute "single" and a key or pointer to each record with the value "single".

investment tax credit *n.*

USFC/generic

Proportion of a company's new capital investment that can be used to reduce its taxes.

invisible character *n.*

DECWORD

A character which instructs DECWORD to format or highlight text, such as a word wrap or underlining. When the user presses gold VIEW, DECWORD displays the invisible characters.

invisible hyphen *n.*

DECmate II and DECtype

An invisible character that tells the system where it may hyphenate a word if necessary.

invoice *n.*

generic

A document prepared by the seller describing the items sold and the amount the buyer owes for them.

I/O *n.*

generic

Refers to input and output functions.

I/O bound *adj.*

generic

Pertaining to the condition in which a computer program is waiting for an input/output device before the program can continue to execute.

I/O buffer *n.*

DIGITAL-specific

A portion of a task's virtual address space used to store data intended for or arriving from peripheral devices. See also control structure and user buffer.

I/O channel *n.*

DIGITAL-specific

The logical connection between a user program and a file or device.

I/O control *n.*

DIGITAL-specific

The name of an Environment Division paragraph in which object program requirements are specified for specific input-output techniques, rerun points, sharing of same areas by several data files, and multiple file storage on a single input-output device.

I/O data base *n.*

VAX/VMS

A collection of data structures that describes I/O requests, controllers, device units, volumes, and device drivers in a VAX/VMS system.

I/O driver *n.*

VAX/VMS

The set of code in the kernel that handles the physical I/O to a device. This is implemented as a fork process. Same as driver.

I/O function *n.*

DIGITAL-specific and VAX/VMS

An I/O operation interpreted by the operating system and typically resulting in one or more physical I/O operations.

I/O function code *n.*

VAX/VMS

A 6-bit value specified in a Queue I/O Request system service that describes the particular I/O operation to be performed (e.g., read, write, rewind). Same as function code.

I/O function modifier *n.*

VAX/VMS

A 10-bit value specified in a Queue I/O Request system service that modifies an I/O function code. Same as function modifier.

I/O lockdown *n.*

VAX/VMS

The state of a page when it cannot be paged or swapped out of memory.

I/O mode *n.*

DIGITAL-specific

The state of a file after execution of an OPEN statement, with the input-output phrase specified for that file, and before the execution of a close statement for that file.

ion *n.*

generic

An atom or a group of atoms with either positive or negative electrical charges.

I/O operation *n.*

DIGITAL-specific

The process of requesting a transfer of data from a peripheral device to memory (or vice versa), the actual transfer of the data, and the processing and overlaying activity to make both of those happen.

I/O pending *n.*

DECnet

The condition of a remotely attached display station that results in a response to a polling operation.

I/O request packet (IRP) *n.*

VAX/VMS

A data structure constructed by the QI/O (Queue I/O) system service to describe a user's I/O request to the device driver. If the I/O request involves a file-structured magnetic tape device, the request will be queued to the appropriate MTAACP. The IRPs are queued according to the priority of the requesting process. Same as IRP.

I/O rundown *n.*

VAX/VMS

An operating system function in which the system cleans up any I/O in progress when an image exits.

IOSB *n.*

DECnet

The abbreviation for I/O status block. IOSB is a two-word array associated with a QI/O request in which a code is returned on completion of the requested I/O operation. Same as I/O status block.

DIGITAL-specific and VAX/VMS

A data structure associated with the Queue I/O Request system service. This service optionally returns a status code, number of bytes transferred, and device/function-dependent information in an I/O status block. It is not returned from the service call, but filled in when the I/O request completes.

I/O space *n.*

VAX/VMS

The region of physical address space that contains the configuration registers, device control/status, and data registers. These regions are not physically contiguous.

I/O status block (IOSB) *n.*

DECnet

A two-word array associated with a QI/O (Queue I/O) request in which a code is returned on completion of the requested I/O operation. Same as IOSB.

DIGITAL-specific and VAX/VMS

A data structure associated with the Queue I/O Request system service. This service optionally returns a status code, number of bytes transferred, and device/function-dependent information in an I/O status block. It is not returned from the service call, but filled in when the I/O request completes.

I/O unit *n.*

RSX-11M

The data moved in and out of a task during an I/O operation. For disk sequential files, the I/O unit is one or more blocks, depending on the MCB (module control block) value; for relative and indexed files, the I/O unit is the bucket. See also multiblock count.

IPCF *n.*

DECnet

The abbreviation for interprocess communication facility. IPCF is a module within the TOPS-20AN monitor that provides for the passing of information between processes within the system. Processes send and receive information in the form of packets. Same as interprocess communication facility.

DIGITAL-specific

The abbreviation for interprocess communication facility. IPCF is a facility that allows communication among jobs and system processes. Same as interprocess communication facility.

VAX/VMS

The abbreviation for interprocess communication facility. IPCF is a common event flag cluster, mailbox, or global section used to pass information between two or more processes.

IPL *n.*

VAX/VMS

The abbreviation for interrupt priority level. IPL is the interrupt level at which a software or hardware interrupt is generated. There are 31 possible interrupt priority levels: IPL 1 is lowest, 31 is highest. Same as interrupt priority level.

IRG *n.*

DIGITAL-specific

The abbreviation for interrupt masking interrecord gap. IRG is a blank space deliberately placed between data records on the recording surface of a magnetic tape. Same as interrecord gap.

VAX/VMS

The abbreviation for interrecord gap. A blank space deliberately placed between data records on the recording surface of a magnetic tape.

IRP *n.*

DIGITAL-specific and VAX/VMS

The acronym for I/O request packet. IRP is a data structure constructed by the QI/O (Queue I/O) system service to describe a user's I/O request to the device driver. If the I/O request involves a file-structured magnetic tape device, the request will be queued to the approximate MTAACP. The IRPs are queued according to the priority of the requesting process. Same as I/O request packet.

irregular ROI *n.*

Medical Systems

A region of interest (ROI) that is defined as any size or shape within the boundaries of the matrix.

IRS *n.*

DECnet and RSX-11M

The abbreviation for interchange record separator. In binary synchronous communications, IRS is a control character for the IBM 3780 communications terminal. In the 3780 record format, the IRS character is the last character of each record within a block, if the terminal is not in transparent mode. Same as interchange record separator.

IS *n.*

VAX/VMS

The abbreviation for interrupt stack. IS is the system-wide stack used when executing in interrupt service context. At any time, the processor is either in a process context executing in user, supervisor, executive or kernel mode, or in system-wide interrupt service context operating in kernel mode, as indicated by the interrupt stack and current mode bits in the PSL (process status longword). The interrupt stack is not context switched. Same as interrupt stack.

ISAM *n.*

DIGITAL-specific and VAX/VMS

The abbreviation for the indexed sequential access method. A method of file organization, storage, and access. Records are stored and accessed on the basis of the contents of a specified field called a key field. An index is used to determine a position from which a short sequential search is made for the desired entry. In many applications ISAM has considerable advantage over random or sequential methods. Same as indexed sequential access method. See also indexed sequential file and indexed file organization.

ISD *n.*

TOPS-20

The abbreviation for image section descriptor. A block of longwords, contained in the image header, describing information for an image section. Same as image section descriptor.

ISECT *n.*

VAX/VMS

ISECT is a group of program sections (PSECTS) with the same attributes (such as read-only access, read/write access, absolute, relocatable, etc.); the group is the unit of virtual memory allocation for an image. Same as image section.

ISECT, I-section *n.*

TOPS-20

Sections that comprise executable image files and linkable image files produced by the linker. Each ISECT or I-section contains program sections and relocation information. They contain either read/write or read-only code and data. See also image section.

ISMUTL *n.*

CTS-300

The CTS-300 utility program used to create and maintain ISAM files.

ISO reference model *n.*

DECnet

The International Standards Organization Reference Model for Open System Interconnection, ISO draft proposal DP7498. A proposed international standard for network architectures which defines a seven layer model, specifying services and protocols for each layer.

isotope *n.*

Medical Systems

A species of matter atoms containing the same number of protons as some other species, but a different number of neutrons. The atomic numbers of isotopes are identical, but the mass numbers (atomic weight) differ.

MSG (SPETS)

A stable element that emits electromagnetic radiations.

ISP *n.*

VAX/VMS

The abbreviation for interrupt stack pointer. The stack pointer for the interrupt stack. Unlike the stack pointers for process context stacks, which are stored in the hardware PCB, the interrupt stack pointer is stored in an internal register.

ISR *n.*

MicroPower PASCAL

The abbreviation for interrupt service routine. ISR is a routine designed to execute when a particular device signals the processor with an interrupt. The processor locates ISRs in memory, using an address vector supplied by (or elicited from) the interrupting device. ISRs are also called interrupt-handling routines or interrupt handlers. Same as interrupt service routine.

MINC

The abbreviation for interrupt service routine. ISR is a set of instructions that interrupts the normal sequential execution of program statements by the computer. With this routine, the computer is directed to execute an alternate set of instructions that enable communication between the computer and a calling peripheral device. In most cases, the ISR keeps track of the state of the computer prior to its being interrupted, and restores the computer to that state when it has finished using the computer to execute its own set of instructions. Same as interrupt service routine.

VAX/VMS

The abbreviation for interrupt service routine. ISR is the routine executed when an interrupt occurs. Same as interrupt service routine.

ISW block *n.*

DECsystem-10

A disk block written by the refresher that contains the bit map for the initial storage allocation table for sweeping. Any bad regions are marked as already in use. The ISW block appears in the HOME.SYS file.

233

ITB *n.*

DECnet

The abbreviation for intermediate text block. ITB is a control character in binary synchronous communications used to terminate an intermediate block of characters. A block check character is sent immediately following ITB, but no line turnaround occurs. Same as intermediate text block.

item *n.*

TOPS-10

An item is a symbolic term used in TOPS-20 to indicate a data item, alphavariable, or numeric variable.

item-list *n.*

VAX PSI

A sequence of items in memory. Each item has a two-word header containing the length of the item (in bytes, including the header) and a type field. The type field contains an entry that indicates the meaning of an item. The header may be followed by an arbitrary amount of data whose format is determined by the 'type' field.

iteration *n.*

RT-11

The repetition of a group of instructions.

iteration factor *n.*

VAX PL/I

An integer constant written in parentheses that specifies the number of times to use a value in the initializing of array elements, or the number of times to use a given format item or picture specification.

IV *n.*

VAX/VMS

Integer overflow trap enable bit in the processor status word.

IVP *n.*

DIGITAL-specific

The abbreviation for installation verification procedure; IVP verifies that both LAT-11 server and LAT (local area transport) node systems are working properly. Same as installation verification procedure.

JACCT program *n.*

DECsystem-10

A program running with the JACCT privilege bit. This is set by the monitor for special system programs such as LOGIN. This bit gives the caller full file access allowing the caller to LOOKUP and READ any file in the system regardless of the file's protection code.

jack *n.*

generic

A socket that accepts a plug at one end and attaches to electric circuits at the other.

jam *n.*

generic

The result of hardware malfunctions usually created by careless control of paper.

jelly bean *n.*

generic

A discrete circuit component such as a resistor, capacitor, or a DIP (dual in-line packaging).

jitter *n.*

generic

A signal condition not stable in its amplitude or phase.

job *n.*

generic

A unit of work performed by a computer.

VAX/VMS

The accounting unit equivalent to a process and its subprocesses, if any, and all subprocesses that they create. Jobs are classified as batch and interactive. For example, the job controller creates an interactive job to handle a user's requests when the user logs onto the system, and it creates a batch job when the symbiont manager passes a command input file to it.

RSTS/E

The unit that RSTS/E uses to keep track of users during a terminal session. When the user logs in, the system creates a job and assigns a job number. The system uses the job number to keep track of everything done during the terminal session.

job controller *n.*

VAX/VMS

The system process that establishes a job's process context, starts a process running the LOGIN image for the job, maintains the accounting record for the job, manages symbionts, and terminates a process and its subprocesses.

job cost sheet *n.*

generic

A schedule showing actual or budgeted inputs for a special order.

job data area (JOBDAT) *n.*

DECsystem-10

The first 140 octal locations of a user's virtual address space. This area provides storage for certain data items used by both the monitor and the user's program. Same as JOBDAT.

job information block (JIB) *n.*

VAX/VMS

A data structure associated with a job that contains the quotas pooled by all processes in the job.

job keyboard monitor *n.*

RSTS/E

The RSTS/E keyboard monitor that manages a job. The job keyboard monitor is the default keyboard monitor, unless the user changes it with a specific command.

job-order costing *n.*

generic

A system of cost accounting in which costs are accumulated for individual jobs.

job search list *n.*

TOPS-10

For each job, a list that specifies the order in which the file structures that a user can access are to be searched when device DSK: is specified. Same as file structure search list.

job slot *n.*

TOPS-10

An independent process under the control of the MSC-10 (mass storage control) job scheduler.

job step *n.*

DECsystem-10

A serial or parallel sequence of executing instructions such as a transfer of control to another section of the program.

join operation *n.*

Rdb/ELN

A procedure that selects a record from one relation, associates it with a record from another relation, and presents both as though they were part of a single record. Same as cross operation.

It is possible to join more than two relations. Further, a record from one relation might match several records in another relation. For example, a record in the EMPLOYEES relation would be joined with several records in the SALARY_HISTORY relation to produce a complete salary history for each employee.

journal *n.*

generic

A record in which transactions are recorded in chronological order.

journal entry *n.*

generic

A recording of a transaction in a journal with an explanation of the transaction, if needed.

journal file *n.*

generic

A database file that contains all records modified by a run unit, usually chronologically ordered.

VAX DATATRIEVE and VAX DBMS

A file, containing all records or pages modified by a run unit, that allows reconstruction of the data in the case of database contamination due to system or program failures.

journaling *n.*

generic

1. The process of recording all system transactions into a file.

2. An option that enables you to retrieve edits from an editing session that ends abnormally.

VAX/VMS

The recording of input during an EDT editing session.

joystick *n.*

Medical Systems

The control device to move and mark the position of the crosshairs on the color video monitor. The H3060 joystick assembly includes the joystick and the joystick interrupt buttons (JB).

JSYS trap *n.*

DECnet and TOPS-20

A user-accessible mechanism, specific to TENEX and BBN (Bolt Beranek and Newman Inc.), enabling one process to control the execution environment of another process inferior to it. The monitoring process is notified when an inferior process attempts to execute one of a predefined set of monitor calls. It can then make one of three choices: perform the call itself on behalf of the trapped process; allow the trapped process to perform the call; or modify the parameters of the call, then allow the trapped process to perform the call. See also monitor call intercept facility.

jump *n.*

DIGITAL-specific

1. A departure from the normal sequence of executing instructions.

2. A transfer of control to another section of the program.

generic

An instruction that causes the next instruction to be selected from a specified storage location instead of the next sequential address.

jumper *n.*

generic

A short length of wire used to complete a circuit temporarily, or to bypass a circuit.

junction record *n.*

DIGITAL-specific

A record inserted between two records of the same type.

VAX DBMS

A record that relates two records to each other. Using a junction record is one way to define a recursive or many-to-many relationship between two records.

justify *v.*

DECWORD

To print a document with a straight right margin, so that the last character on each line falls in the same column. If J appears in the ruler instead of R, DECWORD adds spaces between words or characters to justify the document while printing. The document will not appear justified on the screen. See also semijustified margin.

generic

To print a document with an even right or left margin, or both.

K *n.*

VAX/VMS

A unit for measuring the size of memory or similar resources. K is short for kilo and is used roughly to mean 1000, although K is equal to 2**10, or 1024.

KDP *n.*

DECnet

A DECnet term that refers to a combination of a KMC11 (controller) and one of four DUP11s. With the KMC11, the DUP11 functions as a direct memory access device. The interface to the network is synchronous.

keeplist *n.*

DIGITAL-specific

A list of database keys used by a run unit to lock records for later reference.

VAX DBMS

A list of record identifiers used to recall their associated records. Identifiers are placed on and removed from keeplists at the direction of a DML (data manipulation language) operation.

kernel *n.*

DIGITAL-specific

The irreducible minimum of the executive; the core of the operating system. The kernel runs in kernel mode which has no hardware protection at all and no restrictions on machine use.

generic

The most privileged processor access mode.

MicroPower PASCAL

A set of software modules supplied by DIGITAL for inclusion in the MicroPower PASCAL target system that provides basic real-time control and service functions for all processes in the target system. Kernel components include the system scheduled and dispatcher and a large number of service functions that can be invoked by the user.

VAX/VMS

The mechanism modules in the executive that implement the controls over the ability of processes to access various system resources such as memory and devices. Same as protection kernel.

kernel executive *n.*

Rdb/ELN

The layer of software that lies between the raw hardware and the system software in a VAXELN system. Its function is to control sharing of system resources and to synchronize communication among the various programs in the system.

kernel instruction set *n.*

VAX-11

The subset of the VAX-11 instruction set that is always present in all processors on the VAX-11 family.

kernel mode *n.*

TOPS-10

The executive submode on the KL-10 processor in which I/O and system-wide functions operate. Code executed in kernel mode can access and alter all of memory.

DSM-11

The hardware mode in which the operating system normally executes. In this mode, all machine instructions can be executed.

RSX-11M, TOPS-20, and VAX/VMS

The most privileged processor access mode (mode 0). The operating system's most privileged services, such as I/O drivers and the pager, run in kernel mode.

key *n.*

COBOL-74

A data item that identifies the location of a record, or a set of data items that serve to identify the ordering of data.

CTS-300

In an ISAM file, the field of a stored record that uniquely identifies that record. The key is used as the basis of both storage and access.

DECnet

A data item used to locate a record in a random access file system.

generic

1. A specific device or switch that is manually operated to record or input data.

2. One or more characters used to identify or find a record or word.

RSX-11M

An identifier for a record during random record operations, used especially for indexed files. A key is the contents of one or more specific portions of each user data record; the combination of these portions is called a key field. For each key defined for a file, RMS-11 constructs an index in the file. See also segmented key.

VAX DATATRIEVE

The value of a data item that identifies a record.

VAX DBMS

The value of a data item that identifies the location of a record or the ordering of data. The data item can be part of a user-defined record, as a CALC key or sort key, or it can be part of the system-defined prefix.

VAX PL/I

1. A value used in I/O statements to specify a particular record in a file.

2. A data item embedded within a record in an indexed sequential file, or the relative record number of a record in a relative file.

VAX/RMS

A string or numeric data that specifies a particular record that is accessed randomly. A key for indexed files is different than a key for relative files. See also primary key, alternate key, and random access by key (indexed files) and relative record number (relative files).

VAX/VMS

Indexed files: A character string, a packed decimal number, a 2- or 4-byte unsigned binary number, or a 2- or 4-byte signed integer within each data record in an indexed file. The user defines the length and location within the records; VAX RMS uses the key to build an index. See primary key, alternate key, and random access by key value.

Relative files: The relative record number of each data record in a data file; VAX RMS uses the relative record numbers to identify and access data records in a relative file in random access mode. See relative record number.

In Sort Utility: The data field in a record that contains the information by which the user wants to sort the records.

keyboard *n.*

DIGITAL-specific

In DIGITAL documentation, the generic term keyboard refers to the entire board, consisting of either the main keypad or the main keypad and the auxiliary keypad combined.

keyboard interaction *n.*

DIGITAL-specific

An optional interactive feature available on all operating systems. The subroutine KBC reads the ASCII values of keyboard characters and can interpret the characters to represent program branches, menu items, or graphic functions.

keyboard monitor *n.*

DIGITAL-specific

The portion of the resident monitor that provides the interface between the user at a terminal and an operating system.

generic

A program that checks and verifies the command level input from the terminal user to the operating system.

RSTS/E

The part of a run-time system that accepts and analyzes user commands. Each RSTS/E keyboard monitor has an identifying prompt that it displays when it expects command input.

keyboard overlay *n.*

DIGITAL-specific

A plastic cover for the keyboard that lets users relabel the keys.

key characteristics *n.*

RSX-11M

Features of individual keys in an indexed file, including duplicates, changes, and null keys.

key data type *n.*

RSX-11M

A feature of a key indicating to RMS-11 how to interpret the data in the associated key field. Supported types include string, 2- and 4-byte binary integer and packed decimal.

key descriptors *n.*

RSX-11M

Data used by RMS-11 to maintain keys in an indexed file. RMS-11 stores this data in the file's prologue. See also area descriptor.

keyed access *n.*

VAX DATATRIEVE and VAX PL/I

A type of random access that uses an index to retrieve or store data records. The index relates the contents of the record's key field to a location in the file. See also random access.

key field *n.*

DECnet

The position of the key within the record, for direct and indexed files. See also position of key in record.

RSX-11M

The concatenation of one or more portions of a user data record. The key field contains the value for the associated key. See also segmented key.

VAX DATATRIEVE

A data field within a record whose contents can be used to identify the record for retrieval.

key match *n.*

VAX DATATRIEVE

The relationship between the key value specified in an operation and the contents of the key field of the record retrieved. There are three kinds of key matches: an exact match indicates that the key field of the record accessed must exactly match the key value specified in the operation; an approximate match means that the contents of the key field of the record accessed may be equal to or greater than the specified key value; in a generic key match only an initial portion of the key value is specified, and the record accessed is the first such occurrence of a record whose key field begins with those characters. The generic and approximate key matches may be combined.

key of reference *n.*

COBOL-74

The key, either prime or alternate, currently being used to access records within an indexed file.

RSX-11M

A number indicating the index RMS-11 should follow during a random record operation. A key of reference of 0 indicates the primary index, while a key of reference of 1, 2, and so on, indicates the first alternate index, second alternate index, and so on.

keypad *n.*

generic

A set of special keys, as on a terminal, in addition to the main keyboard.

keypad application mode *n.*

DIGITAL-specific

The mode of certain terminals in which all keys on the terminal's keypad generate special control sequences that can be defined by application software.

keypad numeric mode *n.*

generic

A mode in which keys on the terminal's keypad generate the ASCII codes for the symbols printed on standard keycaps; the ENTER key generates the same code as the RETURN key on the main keyboard. In this mode, application software cannot distinguish between numeric characters typed on the main keyboard and numeric characters typed on the auxiliary keypad.

key search *n.*

VAX DATATRIEVE

The process of locating a record by matching a key value. See key match.

key sequence *n.*

VAX DATATRIEVE

The collating sequence of data records, determined by the value of the key field in each of the data records. May be the same as, or different from, the entry sequence of the records.

key sort *n.*

CTS-300

A sort that is done using only record key values and corresponding record addresses.

key value *n.*

RSX-11M

The value of the data in the field associated with the key.

VAX DATATRIEVE

The value supplied in an operation to identify a specific record for retrieval. See primary key and alternate key.

VAX DBMS

The value(s) supplied in a DML operation to identify a specific record for retrieval.

KEYWORD *n.*

DECWORD

A command name. For example, a KEYWORD in a printer control command instructs DECWORD to perform a specific function. See also printer control keyword.

keyword or (key word) *n.*

DIGITAL-specific

A reserved word whose presence is required when the format in which the word appears is used in a source program.

generic

A word used in information retrieval to group information together or to retrieve it.

PEARL

A word that has a predefined meaning in PEARL. A keyword cannot be used as an identifier, nor can it be redefined.

VAX DATATRIEVE

A word reserved for use in certain specified syntax formats, usually in a command or a statement.

VAX DBMS

A reserved word that is required in a DDL, COBOL, FORTRAN, or DML statement. By convention, the keywords are generally underlined in the syntactical expressions

VAX PL/I

An identifier that has a specific meaning to PL/I when used in the appropriate context.

VAX/VMS

A word (series of characters) that is reserved by the C language and cannot be used as an identifier. Keywords identify statements, storage classes, data types, and the like. Function names are not C keywords; they may be redefined by the user.

kill *v.*

generic

To stop a job.

Klatt synthesizer *n.*

generic

A practical implementation of a format speech synthesizer developed by Dennis Klatt at the Massachusetts Institute of Technology. The Klatt synthesizer is used in DECtalk.

kludge *n.*

DIGITAL-specific

An ill-assorted collection of poorly matched parts that form a poorly constructed entity.

known *n.*

DECnet

The classification for one or more of the same components. Known includes all active and interactive occurrences of the component type.

known component *n.*

VAX PSI

A VAX PSI management component that exists in the data base. A known component includes all active and inactive occurrences of the component type.

VAX/VMS

The classification for one or more of the same components. This classification includes all active and inactive occurrences of the component type. For example, known nodes include all active and inactive nodes in the network.

known lines *n.*

DECnet

All lines addressable by network management in the appropriate data base (volatile or permanent) on the EXECUTOR node. All lines may not be in a usable state.

KSP *n.*

VAX/VMS

Kernel Mode Stack Pointer.

KT11 *n.*

RSX-20F

A hardware memory management option.

label *n.*

generic

1. Information that uniquely identifies a group of data.

2. The logical name assigned to a statement or series of statements.

VAX/VMS

A record that identifies and delimits a magnetic tape volume or file section.

label group *n.*

VAX/VMS

A collection of one or more contiguous label sets. See also label set.

label identifier *n.*

VAX/VMS

The three initial characters of a label name that identify one or more labels within a label set. These three initial characters will always be the same, such as HDR, which are used to identify header labels within a header label set. See also label set.

label number *n.*

VAX/VMS

A digit that indicates the sequence of a label within a label set. For ANSI labels, label number one is always present if the label set exists. See also label set.

label set *n.*

VAX/VMS

A collection of one or more contiguous labels with the same three initial characters. These three characters are called the "label identifier". See also label identifier.

LAN *n.*

DECnet

A privately owned data communications system that offers high-speed communications channels optimized for connecting information processing equipment. The geographical area is usually limited to a section of a building, an entire building, or a group of buildings. Same as local area network.

landscape *n.*

generic

One of two kinds of orientation: landscape and portrait. In landscape orientation, lines of text are printed parallel to the long dimension of the paper. Conceptually, the characters in a landscape font are aligned "sideways"—that is, each character in the font is rotated 90 degrees counterclockwise.

LAP *n.*

VAX PSI and VAX/VMS

The abbreviation for link access protocol. LAP is a set of procedures used for link control. Two sets of procedures have been defined:

1. LAP procedure—The DTE/DCE interface is defined as operating in two-way simultaneous asynchronous response mode (ARM) with the DTE (data terminal equipment) and DCE (data circuit-terminating equipment) containing a primary and secondary function.

2. LAPB procedure—The DTE/DCE interface is defined as operating in two-way asynchronous balanced mode (ABM).

Same as link access protocol.

large data buffer (LDB) *n.*

DECnet

Buffers used for intermediate storage of incoming and/or outgoing messages. Same as LDB.

large-scale integration *n.*

generic

The accumulation of a large number of circuits on a single chip or semiconductor.

last *n.*

VAX DBMS

A set-ordering criterion that places new record occurrences last in the series of records.

last character (LC) *n.*

FFE

A font value that specifies the character with the greatest decimal value in the font. Same as LC.

last-in-chain (LIC) *n.*

DIGITAL-specific

The last segment of a message whose entire length exceeded 256 bytes, transmitted by an SNA (systems network architecture) application or by the protocol emulator (PE) to the SNA side of the network, in a session governed by Profile 3 or 4 protocol set. That the element being transmitted is last-in-chain, is specified by a setting in the chaining control field of the request header. In EC (emulator control) and XEC (extended emulator control) modes, the PE sets the chain indicator in messages it is transmitting to SNA. For messages flowing the other way, SNA sets the chain indicator. Same as LIC.

LAT *n.*

generic

The abbreviation for local area transport; LAT is a communications protocol used in a local area network.

LAT (local area network) control program (LCP) *n.*

generic

The program that provides the function to control and obtain information from the LTDRIVER (LAT port driver). Same as LCP.

LAT-11 Server *n.*

DIGITAL-specific

The PDP-11 based terminal server that runs the LAT-11 software.

latency *n.*

DIGITAL-specific

1. The time from initiation of a transfer operation to the beginning of actual transfer; that is, verification plus search time.

2. The delay while waiting for a rotating memory to reach a given location as desired by the user. The average latency is one half the revolution time plus one half the block time.

generic

1. The time between issuing a command to read/write information and the beginning of the read/write operation.

2. The time needed for a request data word on a disk storage unit to appear under the read head.

3. The time needed to set up access to a specific storage location.

LAT node (local area transport node) *n.*

generic

A system connected to the same Ethernet as the LAT-11 Server, providing users of the server with network services.

layer *v.*

generic

To set a separate price on a hardware or software package.

layered environment services (LES) *n.*

VAX PSI

A communications executive that coordinates the operation of independent protocol-handling modules. These modules, called protocol processing images (PPIs), operate the different layers of the communications protocols. LES coordinates the interaction between PPIs and device drivers and user processes, and also provides an interface to the host operation system. Same as LES.

layout *n.*

generic

A planned arrangement.

LBN *n.*

VAX/VMS

The abbreviation for logical block number. LBN is a volume-relative address of a block on a mass storage device. The blocks that form the volume are labeled sequentially starting with logical block 0. See also typical block number. Same as logical block number.

LC *n.*

FFE

The abbreviation for last character. LC is a font value that specifies the character with the greatest decimal value in the font. Same as last character.

LCN *n.*

VAX PSI

The abbreviation for logical channel number. A unique reference number that identifies a logical channel. A data terminal equipment (DTE) recognizes a virtual circuit by its associated LCN. Same as logical channel number.

LCP *n.*

generic

The abbreviation for LAT (local area transport) control program. LCP provides the functions to control and obtain information from the LTDRIVER (LAT port driver). Same as LAT control program.

LDB *n.*

DECnet

The abbreviation for large data buffer. LDBs are buffers used for intermediate storage of incoming and/or outgoing messages. Same as large data buffer.

leader *n.*

DECnet

1. The control information prefixed in a message text, such as source or destination code on message type. Same as header, heading.

2. Specific to ARPANET, the area heading a packet that specifies control information and other elements distinct from the message to be transferred. The leader specifies a Host field, a message type, a link number and specific flags. The Host field contains the address of the receiving Host when the message is from Host to IMP (interface message processor), or IMP to IMP, and the sending Host when the message is from IMP to Host. The "old type" leader is 32 bits long and is used by TOPS-20AN. The "new type" leader is 96 bits long.

generic

That part of the tape that precedes the beginning of tape mark.

TOPS-10

A blank section of tape at the beginning of a reel of magnetic tape or the beginning or end of a stack of paper tape.

leading spaces *n.*

generic

Spaces used to fill out the length of a right-justified field.

leaf *n.*

MCS-10

A node that terminates a branch. A leaf has no nodes to the right of it and is the place in the queue where incoming messages are stored.

leaf input name *n.*

MCS-10

The name of a leaf that is used when the leaf is accepting input transactions. The leaf must always have an input name.

leaf output name *n.*

DECsystem-10

The name of a leaf that is used when the leaf is accepting output transactions. The leaf will not have an output name unless one was generated for it. If no output name was generated, the leaf input name is used as the output name.

leakage *n.*

generic

The unacceptable flow of electricity over or through an insulator.

leased line *n.*

generic

A communications line reserved for the use of a single customer and with permanent connection points at specified locations.

VAX PSI

A line reserved for the exclusive use of a leasing customer without interchange switching arrangements. Same as private line. See also non-switched line.

lease rate *n.*

USFC/generic

The annualized percentage rate on the lease payment stream, exclusive of advance payments or purchase options.

least-recently-used *adj.*

TOPS-20

Pertaining to a type of memory management that removes the page that was most recently least-used in order to free space for inserting a new page into the working set. Same as LRU.

least significant bit (LSB) *n.*

MINC

With MINC, the least significant bit is the value associated with the last bit of the A/D input word. In a 12-bit A/D converter, this value is 1/4096 of the full-scale range. In the case of MINC A/D, this translates to 1.5 mV. Same as LSB.

least significant byte *n.*

RSX-11M

The last byte examined when RMS-11 performs key value comparisons. Key data type determines whether the lowest-addressed byte (binary and integer data types) or highest-addressed byte (string and packed decimal data types) is the least significant.

least significant digit *n.*

generic

The digit of a number on the far right.

LED *n.*

generic

The abbreviation for Light Emitting Diode. A source of light on an indicator panel. Same as Light Emitting Diode.

ledger *n.*

generic

A group of accounts. Entries are posted to the ledger from the journal.

left-justified attribute *n.*

generic

A field attribute specifying that the data entered is to be aligned with the leftmost data position.

left side bearing *n.*

FFE

A font value that specifies, in portrait orientation, the number of pixels each character is translated (shifted) within its cell for reasons of appearance or legibility.

legend *n.*

generic

The box that appears below a graph, identifying the fields of the graph.

LES *n.*

VAX PSI

The abbreviation for layered environment services, a communications executive that coordinates the operation of independent protocol-handling modules. These modules, called protocol processing images (PPIs), operate the different layers of the communications protocols. LES coordinates the interaction between PPIs and device drivers and user processes, and also provides an interface to the host operation system. Same as layered environment services.

LES process descriptor (LPD) *n.*

VAX PSI and VAX/VMS

A short form for layered environment services process descriptor. It is an extended interrupt request packet of variable length. LPDs are used by the communication operating environment (LES) to pass data between the protocol processing images (PPIs). Same as LPD.

letter quality printer (LQP) *n.*

generic

The printer used to produce final copies of documents. It produces typing comparable in quality to that of a typewriter. Same as LQP.

letter-to-sound rules *n.*

generic

A set of formal statements that convert orthographic text (written text) into phonemes (functional sounds) in a given language.

level *n.*

RSX-11M

A chain of buckets in an indexed file. All buckets in a level have the same conceptual function: level 0 buckets contain data records, either user data records or sides; level 1 buckets contain index records that point to level 0 buckets and indicate their high-key values; level 2 buckets contain index records that point to level 1 buckets and indicate their high-key values; and so on to the single-bucket level called the root.

level 1 router *n.*

VAX/VMS

A node that can send and receive packets, and route packets from one node to another, only within a single area.

level 2 router *n.*

VAX/VMS

A node that can send and receive packets, and route packets from one node to another, within its own area and between areas. Also known as an area router.

level indicator *n.*

COBOL-74

Two alphabetic characters that identify a specific type of file or a position in a hierarchy.

level number *n.*

COBOL-74 and VAX DBMS

A user-defined word, expressed as a one- or two-digit number that indicates the hierarchical position of a data item or the special properties of a data description entry,

VAX PL/I

An integer constant that defines the relationship of a name within the hierarchy of a structure with respect to other names in the structure.

leveraged lease *n.*

USFC/generic

A lease in which the lessor finances part of the cost of the asset with debt secured by the total value of the equipment.

lexical function *n.*

VAX/VMS

A command language construct that the command interpreter evaluates and substitutes before it parses a command string. Lexical functions return information about the current process and about character strings.

lexical scope *n.*

Rdb/ELN

The range of a user-defined variable, such as a context variable or request handle, based on the order of the statements in the program, not the order in which Rdb/ELN executes the statements.

liability *n.*

generic

The legal claim of a creditor.

LIBOL *n.*

TOPS-10

The COBOL object time system.

librarian *n.*

VAX/VMS

A program that allows the user to create, update, modify, list, and maintain object library, help library, text library, and assembler macro library files.

library *n.*

generic

An organized group or set of routines and subroutines stored in a file as part of a computer program.

LIBRARY area *n.*

DIGITAL-specific

An area that stores files that users need to reference frequently.

library definition *n.*

FMS

A binary object in the CDD (Common Data Dictionary) that lists all the request definitions that a particular FMS Level II application uses.

library definition file *n.*

FMS

A VAX/VMS file containing the library definition text.

library definition text *n.*

FMS

The series of instructions which identify the request definitions an application program uses. RDU (request definition utility) translates this library definition text into a library definition.

library document *n.*

DECWORD

A document in which frequently used phrases and paragraphs are saved.

generic

A document containing paragraphs of text, with a name for each paragraph.

library file *n.*

MicroPower PASCAL

A file containing one or more relocatable object modules used to incorporate other programs. These program modules might be used repeatedly in a program or by more than one program. Library files are merged or linked with source program modules during MicroPower PASCAL development.

VAX/VMS

A direct access file containing one or more modules of the same module type.

library module *n.*

MicroPower PASCAL

A program module from a library file.

library-name *n.*

COBOL-74

A user-defined word that names a COBOL library used by the compiler for compilation of a given source program.

library search mode n.

TOPS-10

The mode in which a module (one of many in a library) is loaded, if one or more of its declared entry points satisfy an unresolved global request.

library text n.

COBOL-74

A sequence of character-strings and/or separators in a COBOL library.

LIC n.

DECnet

The abbreviation for last-in-chain. The last segment of a message whose entire length exceeded 256 bytes transmitted by an SNA (systems network architecture) application or by the protocol emulator to the SNA side of the network, in a session governed by Profile 3 or 4 protocol set. Same as last-in-chain.

lifetime n.

PEARL

The total time during which an object or block exists.

LIFO n.

generic

Last-in/first-out; the order in which processing is performed. For example, a LIFO queue would process data on a last-come, first-served basis. See also FIFO.

LIFO (Last-In, First-Out) method n.

generic

A method of finding the cost of sales, using the assumption that the goods most recently purchased (those last in) were the first to be sold (first out).

ligature n.

generic

Two or more characters included in a single cell to improve appearance or readability.

light button n.

VT-11 GRAPHICS

A name of an item in a menu. The item is usually a character string that has been made sensitive to the lightpen. The keyboard can also select light buttons, whether or not they are sensitive to the lightpen.

light emitting diode n.

generic

A source of light on an indicator panel. Same as LED.

light event n.

Medical Systems and MSG (SPETS)

An oscilloscope flash.

lightpen n.

generic

A solid-state, light-detecting device consisting of a photosensitive diode. It is used to input information to a CRT display.

lightpen (or light-pen) adj.

generic

Pertaining to a solid-state, light detecting device used to input information to a CRT display.

light-pen hit *n.*

VT-11 GRAPHICS

An event, or graphic attention, created when the lightpen is pointed at a primitive or subpicture on the display screen that has been made light-pen sensitive. A hit is internally recognized as an interrupt from the light-pen device.

light-pen sensitivity *n.*

VT-11 GRAPHICS

A characteristic of a primitive or subpicture that allows a graphic attention to occur when a user points to the object with the pen.

limit *n.*

VAX/VMS

The size or number given items requiring system resources (such as mailboxes, locked pages, I/O requests, and open files) that a job is allowed to have at any one time during execution. See also quota.

line *n.*

DECnet

Refers to a physical path. In the case of a multi-point line, each tributary controller on the line (each RSX-11/3271 Protocol Emulator (PE) line) is treated as a separate line. See also multipoint line.

generic

1. The length from the leftmost position on the screen to the rightmost position on the screen along a given horizontal.

2. A series of characters or words terminated by a tab or line feed.

VAX/VMS

The network management component that provides a distinct physical data path.

linear predictive coding *n.*

generic

A technique for digitizing a signal that takes advantage of the signal's repetitive nature.

line buffer *n.*

VAX/VMS

A storage area used to store the last line deleted by an EDT delete line operation.

line characteristics *n.*

PRO/Communications

The operational features of a communications line, such as transmission speed. On the Professional, users can choose these features to suit their particular communications needs.

line cost *n.*

DECnet

An arbitrary positive integer value assigned to a physical path. Because the routing algorithm selects the least-cost path to a destination, an operator can dynamically affect the path to be taken by changing line costs.

line feed *n.*

generic

A signal or code which causes the printer to advance the paper a specified number of lines or a display to advance the cursor a specified number of lines.

VAX/VMS

Moving the cursor position down one line; one of the default word delimiters in EDT. In keypad character editing, a line feed deletes the characters from the cursor position to the left word delimiter.

line identification *n.*

DECnet

Refers to the device, controller, and unit assigned to a line.

line index *n.*

VAX DBMS

A dynamic page of a database section that acts as a directory to records or fragments on the database page. See also database pages.

line label *n.*

DSM-11

An optional name at the beginning of a routine line that identifies the line within that routine, A line label should have no more than eight alphanumeric characters.

line level *n.*

generic

The print position of a line of text. Subscripts are printed below line level; superscripts are printed above line level.

line level loopback test *n.*

DECnet and DECsystem-10

Testing a specific data link by sending a message directly to the data link layer and over a wire to a device that returns the message to the source. See also line loopback.

line loopback *n.*

DECnet

Used to test a specific data link by sending a repeated message over a hardware path to a device that returns the message to the source. The RSX-11/3271 Protocol Emulator (PE) provides the line loopback test program (LBK) for loopback testing. With this feature, a line may also be looped in the modem to test the modem. See also line level loopback test.

line number *n.*

generic

A number that identifies a line.

VAX/VMS

A number used to identify a line of text in a file processed by a text editor.

line of credit *n.*

generic

An agreement with financial institutions for short-term borrowing on demand.

line pattern *n.*

GIGI

An eight-dot pattern which GIGI uses to write.

RGL/FEP

The sequence of dots and dashes used in drawing a line.

line printer *n.*

VAX/VMS

An output device that prints files one line at a time. It is used for printing large amounts of output that would otherwise tie up a slower device. Almost every system has a device designated as the line printer. In some cases, the "line printer" will actually be a high-speed terminal.

line reference *n.*

DSM-11

A reference to a line within a DSM-11 routine. A line reference can be a line label or a line label and offset.

line spacing *n.*

FFE

A font value that specifies the distance (in pixels) between lines in printing. It is sometimes defined as the distance between baselines.

line switching *n.*

DECnet

A method of transmission in which a switch forms an electrical circuit between lines, forming a "copper path." Same as circuit switching.

line type *n.*

VT-11 GRAPHICS

The type of line used to display vectors on the screen. There are four line types: solid line, long-dash line, short-dash line, and dot-dash line.

linguistics *n.*

generic

The scientific study of language. A broad field encompassing acoustic and articulatory phonetics, phonology, morpho-syntax, semantics, first and second language acquisition, dialectology and a number of other sub-fields.

link *n.*

CTS-300

The information at the end of each ISAM (indexed sequential access method) group that identifies the characteristics of that group and the location of the next logical group.

DECnet

1. Any specified relationship between two nodes (points) in a network.

2. A communications path between two nodes.

See also data link.

DECsystem-10

A program that provides automatic loading and relocation of binary programs, produces an optional storage map, and performs loading and library searching. The program also loads and links relocatable binary programs and generates a symbol table in core for execution under DDT.

link *v.*

CTS-300

To join two or more object module routines to form one executable program.

generic

To produce executable code from object code.

linkable image *n.*

DIGITAL-specific

An image that has its internal references resolved but they must be bound to an executable image in order to execute.

link access protocol (LAP) *n.*

VAX PSI and VAX/VMS

A set of procedures used for link control. Two sets of procedures have been defined:

1. LAP procedure—The DTE/DCE interface is defined as operating in two-way simultaneous asynchronous response mode (ARM) with the DTE (data terminal equipment) and DCE (data circuit-terminating equipment) containing a primary and secondary function.

2. LAPB procedure—The DTE/DCE interface is defined as operating in two-way asynchronous balanced mode (ABM).

Same as LAP.

linkage *n.*

RT-11

In programming, code that connects two separately coded routines and passes values and/or control between them.

linkage section *n.*

COBOL-74

The section in the Data Division of the called program that describes data items available from the calling program. These data items can be referred to by both the calling and called program.

linked file *n.*

generic

A file whose contents are connected with an instruction or a reference address that passes control between sections of the file.

RT-11

A file whose blocks are joined together by references rather than by consecutive locations.

linker *n.*

generic

A program that reads object files and produces image files that can be executed by the system.

VAX/VMS

A system program that creates an executable program, called an image, from one or more object modules produced by a language compiler or assembler. Programs must be linked before they can be executed.

linker loader *n.*

generic

A single program that loads, relocates, and links compiled and assembled programs, routines, and subroutines into tasks. Same as linking loader.

linking *n.*

DIGITAL-specific and VAX/VMS

The resolution of external references between object modules used to create an image, the acquisition of referenced library routines, service entry points, and data for the image, and the assignment of virtual addresses to components of an image. See also binding.

MicroPower PASCAL

A process that converts object modules to a format suitable for loading and executing. The linking of object modules:

1. assigns absolute addresses

2. produces a load map and creates a symbol table

3. relocates the program sections within the object modules

4. resolves global symbols that are defined in one module and referenced by external symbols in another

5. searches library files to locate unresolved global symbols.

linking loader *n.*

generic

A single program that loads, relocates, and links compiled and assembled programs, routines, and subroutines into tasks. Same as linker loader.

link management *n.*

DECnet

The DDCMP (Digital Data Communications Message Protocol) component that controls transmission and reception on links connected to two or more transmitters and/or receivers in a given direction.

link map *n.*

RT-11

A memory address map produced by the linker listing the locations of program segments as they will be loaded into memory.

liquid asset *n.*

generic

Cash or an asset that can quickly be turned into cash.

list applications *n.*

DIGITAL-specific

The process by which you can see a list of the applications you have installed on the system.

list-directed stream I/O *n.*

VAX PL/I

The transmission of data between a program and an input/output device, for which PL/I provides automatic data conversion and formatting.

list document *n.*

DECWORD

In list processing, the document that contains the variable information to be merged with the form document.

DIGITAL-specific

A file that contains records to be used in list processing; such files contain the records that have information that changes on each form document.

list-element *n.*

DIGITAL-specific

One item specified with the LIST command; a list-element may be _<RETURN_>, a dictionary field, or a temporary field.

listing *n.*

DIGITAL-specific

The printed copy generated by a line printer or terminal.

generic

Optional copy generated by a compiler that lists data items and contents of a specified program.

VAX PL/I

An output file created by the compiler that lists the statements in the source program, the line numbers it has assigned to them, the names of variables and constants referenced in the program, and additional optional information.

list processing *n.*

DIGITAL-specific

A word processing function by which many copies of a single document are output with certain information changing from one copy to the next.

list study *n.*

Medical Systems

A file that contains a collected list of the counts (events) in the order that they occurred.

literal *n.*

COBOL-74

A character-string whose value is implied by the ordered set of characters constituting the string.

CTS-300

An element of a programming language used for the explicit representation of a character or of character strings. In DIBOL-11, a literal is enclosed in quotes to denote that the character or string is to be taken literally and not evaluated.

DSM-11

A string of characters delimited by double quotation marks that occurs within the context of a routine and that never changes value from one execution of the routine to another. DSM recognizes two types of literals: numeric literals and string literals.

generic

1. A specific symbol that can not be modified during the translation of a program.

2. A value expression representing a constant. A literal is either a character string, enclosed in quotation marks, or a number.

PEARL

The explicit representation of the value of an object.

TOPS-10

Any string of characters enclosed in quotes and used by IQL (interactive query language) exactly as specified, Users can set off a literal with either single (') or double (" ") quotes.

TOPS-20

A source representation for a constant value.

VAX DBMS

A value expression representing a constant. A literal is either a character string, enclosed in quotation marks, or a number.

literal mode *n.*

VAX/VMS

An addressing mode in which the instruction operand is a constant whose value is expressed in a 6-bit field of the instruction. If the operand datatype is byte, word, longword, quadword, or octaword, the operand is zero-extended and can express values in the range 0 through 63 (decimal). If the operand data type is F_floating, D_floating, G_floating, or H_floating, the 6-bit field is composed of two 3-bit fields, one for the exponent and the other for the fraction. The operand is extended to floating or double floating format.

LMT *n.*

DECnet

The abbreviation for LOGON mode table. LMT is a set of SNA (systems network architecture) session rules that have been defined to the S/370 SNA access method, and assigned to a one- to eight-character name that may be specified to the PE (protocol emulator) in the connect block, and subsequently by the PE in the INITS request to SNA. Same as LOGON mode table.

load *v.*

CTS-300 and DECnet

To transmit data into main storage

DECsystem-10

To produce a core image and/or a saved file from one or more relocatable binary files (REL files) by transforming relocatable addresses to absolute addresses. This operation is not to be confused with the GET operation, which initializes a core image from a saved file.

generic

To enter a program or data into memory.

Medical Systems and RT-11

To store a program or data in memory; to place a volume on a device unit and put the unit on line.

load device n.

VAX/VMS

The drive that holds the distribution media during software installation.

loader n.

generic

A program that takes data from another program or storage device and enters it in main memory at a specified location.

load map n.

CTS-300, MicroPower PASCAL, and RT-11

A table, produced during creation of a MicroPower PASCAL application program, that provides information about the load module's (memory image's) characteristics; for example, the transfer address, the global symbol values, and the low and high address limits of the relocated code.

generic

A map listing the locations of storage addresses and entry points.

load module n.

CTS-300, MicroPower PASCAL, and RT-11

A program in a format ready for loading and executing (relocated, with references to labels and identifiers resolved). A completed memory image file is the load module for an application.

generic

A routine that has been translated and cross referenced into a program that can be stored in main memory and is ready for loading and executing.

load request n.

DECnet and DECsystem-10

The message sent by the remote station ROM to a host. It asks the host to load the remote station and can specify the route for loading over the network.

local area network n.

DECnet

A privately owned data communications system that offers high-speed communications channels optimized for connecting information processing equipment. The geographical area is usually limited to a section of a building, an entire building, or a group of buildings. Same as LAN.

local area transport (LAT) n.

generic

A communications protocol used in a local area network. Same as LAT.

local disk n.

VAX/VMS

A disk drive in a CI environment that is independent of HSC control.

local DTE n.

DECnet and VAX PSI

A frame of reference; the DTE at which the user is located.

local field n.

DIGITAL-specific

A field that has meaning only in the relation in which it appears, even if the field name appears in more than one relation.

local Host *n.*

DECnet and TOPS-20

Specific to ARPANET, a Host that is close enough to the IMP (interface message processor) to allow for a connection by means of a 30-foot cable.

local identifier *n.*

PASCAL and VAX PASCAL

An identifier that is declared within a block and is unknown (and therefore inaccessible) outside that block.

locality *n.*

VAX/VMS

A characteristic of a program that indicates how close or far apart the references to locations in virtual memory are over time. A program with a high degree of locality does not refer to many widely scattered virtual addresses in a short period of time. Same as program locality.

local network services protocol (local NSP) *n.*

DECnet

Refers to the network services protocol executing in the local node.

local node *n.*

DECnet

1. From the user's standpoint: a relative term indicating the node at which a terminal is logged in.

2. From network management's standpoint: the node at which a requested task is executing.

generic

The node at which the user is virtually located.

VAX/VMS

The network node at which the user is physically located.

LOCAL object *n.*

PEARL

An object declared in a procedure, task, interface, or begin block.

local peripherals *n.*

TOPS-10

The I/O devices and other data processing equipment (excluding the central processor and memory) located at the central site.

Local repeater *n.*

Ethernet

An Ethernet repeater designed to link Ethernet cable segments separated by not more than 80 meters.

local symbol *n.*

TOPS-10

A symbol known only to the module in which it is defined. Because the local symbol is not accessible to other modules, the same symbol name with different values can appear in more than one module. These modules can be loaded and executed together without conflict. Local symbols are primarily used when debugging modules.

VAX/VMS

1. A symbol meaningful only to the module that defines it. Symbols not identified to a language processor as global symbols are considered to be local symbols. A language processor resolves (matches references with definitions) local symbols. They are not known to the linker and cannot be made available to another object module. They can, however, be passed through the linker to the symbolic debugger. Contrast with global symbol.

2. A command language symbol name that is accessible only at the current command level and subsequently invoked levels. It is deleted when the command level at which it is defined exits.

local task n.

DECnet

A task executing at a local node.

local variable n.

DSM-11

A variable that exists only in memory. Local variables are unique to a user and can usually be inspected and/or changed only by that user.

generic

A programming symbol used to communicate values inside the part of the program that is executed (as opposed to global variable).

locate mode n.

VAX/VMS

A record access technique in which a program records in an RMS block buffer, working storage area to reduce overhead. See also move mode or program locality, and record transfer mode.

location n.

CTS-300 and RT-11

An address in storage or memory where a unit of data or an instruction is (or can be) stored.

generic

A place in memory identified by an address where a unit of data may be stored.

GIGI and RGL/FEP

A point defined by the x- and y-coordinate pair.

location mode n.

VAX DATATRIEVE

The access method by which the database control system determines the database key values associated with record occurrences. See also DIRECT mode, CALC mode, VIA mode and Record Location mode.

VAX DBMS

The method used for determining record storage. The location mode can be DIRECT using the unique identifier assigned by DBMS, CALC based on the CALC keys in each record, or VIA set (according to the relationships established for the records in the set declaration).

locator-qualified adj.

VAX PL/I

Pertaining to a pointer reference and punctuation symbol ($\rightarrow$) that associates a storage location with a based variable.

locator-qualified reference n.

VAX PL/I

The specification of a based variable by means of a pointer or offset value that indicates the location of the variable.

lock, locking n.

generic

An association between a job and a resource.

VAX COBOL

The VAX COBOL facilities that allow concurrent use of a database or a sequential, relative, or indexed file without corrupting their records.

VAX DBMS

The VAX DBMS facilities that allow concurrent use of a database without allowing two users to modify the same record at the same time. VAX DBMS maintains locks on individual records, entire realms, or both.

locked adj.

RT-11 and TOPS-10

Pertaining to routines or jobs in memory that are not presently (and may never be) candidates for swapping or transferring.

locked job   *n.*

DECsystem-10

A job in core that can never be a candidate for swapping or transferring.

locked password   *n.*

VAX/VMS

A password that cannot be changed by the account's owner. Only system managers or users with the SYSPRV privilege can change locked passwords.

locking a page in memory   *v.*

VAX/VMS

Making a page within a process ineligible for either paging or swapping. A page stays locked in physical memory until VAX/VMS specifically unlocks it.

locking a page in the working set   *v.*

VAX/VMS

Making a page within a process ineligible for paging out of the working set for the process. The page can be swapped when the process is swapped. A page stays locked in a working set until it is specifically unlocked.

lock mode   *n.*

VAX/VMS

A value associated with a request to the lock management system services, indicating the compatibility of the requested lock with other locks.

lockout   *n.*

generic

Stopping the use of the files in timesharing computers.

lock value block   *n.*

VAX/VMS

An optional block of data associated with a lock-status block. the lock value block can be used to communicate information among processes sharing a resource.

log   *n.*

VAX/VMS

A record of performance.

log file   *n.*

DIGITAL-specific

A file used to store information that is normally output to a terminal.

DECWORD

Any file in which everything that happens during processing is recorded.

TOPS-10 and TOPS-20

A file into which batch writes a record of an entire job. This file may be printed as the final step in the batch processing of a job.

VAX DATATRIEVE

A file containing an account of all transactions (changes, additions, deletions) applied to the data in the database, usually chronologically ordered. It allows reconstruction of the data to prefailure conditions in case of database contamination due to hardware errors, etc.

logged-in user file directory (logged-in UFD)   *n.*

TOPS-10

The user file directory (UFD) that corresponds to the project-programmer number under which the user is logged in.

logger *n.*

TOPS-20

Specific to ARPANET, the process within a Host that listens to log in requests.

logging *n.*

DECnet

Recording information from an occurrence that has potential significance in the operation and/or maintenance of a network in a potentially permanent form where it can be accessed by persons and/or programs to aid them in making immediate or long-term decisions. See also logging console and logging monitor.

VAX/VMS

The network management component that routes event data to logging sinks such as a console or file.

logging console *n.*

DECnet

A logging sink that is to receive a human-readable record of events. This can be a terminal or a user-specified file. See also logging and logging monitor.

VAX/VMS

A logging sink that is to receive a record of events in a form that is comprehensible to system users. Typically, a logging console is a terminal or a user-specified file.

logging event type *n.*

DECnet

The identification of a particular type of event; for example, a line restarted or a node down.

logging file *n.*

DECnet

A logging sink that is to receive a machine-readable record of events for later retrieval.

VAX/VMS

A logging sink that is to receive a machine-readable record of events for later retrieval. The logging file is user defined.

logging identification *n.*

DECnet

The sink type associated with the logging entity (file, console, or monitor).

logging in *n.*

VAX/VMS

The identification of a user to the operating system. When users log in, they type an account name and password in response to the appropriate prompts from the system. If the name and password match an account on the system, the user will be permitted access to that account.

logging monitor *n.*

DECnet and VAX/VMS

A logging sink that is to receive a machine-readable record of events for purposes of making immediate decisions. This is a user-oriented program. See also logging, logging console.

logging out *n.*

VAX/VMS

Issuing the DCL command LOGOUT, which informs the operating system that the user has finished using a particular terminal.

logging sink flags *n.*

DECnet

A set of flags in an event record that indicate the sinks on which the event is to be recorded. See also sink.

logging sink node *n.*

DECnet

A node to which logging information is directed.

logging source process *n.*

DECnet

A process that recognizes an event.

logic *n.*

generic

A set of circuit elements used to perform a discrete operation.

logical access path *n.*

RSX-11M

The sequence of steps RMS-11 performs to transform the parameters in the user's record operation request into the requested record. Same as access path.

logical addresses *n.*

VAX/VMS

The actual addresses that the task can access.

logical block *n.*

generic

A fixed number of contiguous bytes used for data transfer. Also see virtual block, physical block, logical block and physical record.

VAX DATATRIEVE

An arbitrarily-defined fixed number of contiguous bytes that is used as the standard I/O transfer unit throughout an operating system. The commonly-used logical block in VAX systems is 512 bytes long.

logical block number *n.*

DIGITAL-specific

A number used to identify a block on a mass storage device. The blocks that comprise the volume are labeled sequentially starting with logical block number 0. A logical block number is volume-oriented rather than device-oriented or file-oriented. See also physical block, virtual block number, and logical structure.

VAX/VMS

A volume-relative address of a block on a mass storage device. The blocks that form the volume are labeled sequentially starting with logical block 0. See also physical block number. Same as LBN.

logical channel *n.*

VAX PSI and VAX/VMS

A logical link between a DTE (data terminal equipment) and its DCE (data circuit-terminating equipment). The physical communications line between a DTE and DCE is divided into a set of logical channels.

logical channel number (LCN) *n.*

VAX PSI and VAX/VMS

A unique reference number that identifies a logical channel. A DTE recognizes a virtual circuit by its associated LCN. Same as LCN.

logical connective *n.*

VAX/VMS

One of the binary operators && (logical AND) and I (logical OR).

logical connectivity *n.*

DECnet

The ability of nodes to communicate with each other.

logical device name n.

CTS-300, DECsystem-10, and RT-11

An alphanumeric name a user chooses to represent a physical device. This name can be used synonymously with the physical device name in all references to the device. Logical device names allow device independence in that the most convenient physical device can then be associated with the logical name at run time. Logical names take precedence over physical names.

generic

An alphanumeric name created and assigned to a physical device.

logical expression n.

DIGITAL-specific

An expression that has a true or false value.

VAX/VMS

An expression made up of two or more operands separated by logical connectives. Each operand must be of a fundamental type or must be a pointer or other address expression, but do not have to be of the same type. Logical expressions always return 0 or 1 type (1NT) to indicate a false or true value, respectively. Logical expressions are always evaluated from left to right, and the evaluation stops as soon as the result is known.

logical I/O function n.

VAX/VMS

A set of I/O operations (for example, READ and WRITE logical block) that allow restricted direct access to device level I/O operations using logical block addresses.

logical link n.

DECnet

1. A carrier of a single stream of full-duplex traffic between two user-level processes.
2. A virtual data path connection between two network programs.

VAX/VMS

1. A communication path between programs on two network nodes. Contrast with physical link.

2. A carrier of a single stream of full-duplex traffic between two user-level processes.

logical name n.

VAX/VMS

A user-specified name for any portion or all of a file specification. For example, the logical name INPUT can be assigned to a terminal device from which a program reads data entered by a user. Logical name assignments are maintained in logical name tables for each process, each group, and the system.

logical name table n.

VAX/VMS

A table that contains a set of logical names and their equivalent names for a particular process, a particular group, or for the system.

logical node n.

DECnet

The node to which the system sends a user's queued output. At login time, the logical node is the same as the physical node. The user may specify a logical node by using the SET LOCATION command from TOPS-20 command level.

logical operation *n.*

DIGITAL-specific

A Boolean operation on data of type, byte, word, or longword.

logical operator *n.*

COBOL-74

One of the reserved words AND, OR, or NOT. In the formation of a condition, both or either of AND and OR can be used as logical connectives. NOT can be used for logical negation.

DSM-11

An operator that produces a truth-valued result based on the truth value of its operand or operands.

PASCAL

A reserved word or symbol that specifies a logical test. The logical operators in PASCAL include AND, OR, and NOT.

VAX PL/I

One of the punctuation symbols ($^\wedge$, &, !, or !) that performs a logical operation on bit-string values.

logical record *n.*

COBOL-74

The most inclusive data item. The level-number for a record is 01. See also report writer logical record.

generic

A set of data units or items arranged and recorded by contents, function, and use.

TOPS-10

A collection of related items stored together. With TOPS-10, it is possible to have:

1. several logical records stored in a single physical record

2. each logical record stored in a single physical record

3. each logical record occupy one or more physical records

4. logical records span several physical records, and at the same time, have more than one logical record in a single physical record.

VAX DATATRIEVE

A unit of data within a file whose length is defined by the user and whose contents have significance to the user. A group of related fields treated as a unit.

VAX DBMS

The most inclusive data item; it is also called a record type, because it describes the structure of many record occurrences. The level-number for a record type is 01. A record type may be either an elementary item or a group item.

VAX/VMS

A group of related fields treated as a unit.

logical screen coordinates *n.*

GIGI

User-defined screen coordinates.

logical structure *n.*

RSX-11M

A method of making the file processor device-independent. Each disk is considered to be composed of a logically contiguous series of data units called blocks. The disk driver translates the logical block number to a physical location.

logical unit (LU) *n.*

DECnet

Logical unit is a non-specialized network addressable unit (NAU) corresponding to an application type program in an SNA (systems network architecture) network. Same as LU.

logical unit number (LUN) *n.*

DECnet and RSX-11M

A number associated with a physical device unit during a task's I/O operations. Each task in the system must establish its own correspondence between logical unit numbers and physical device units. An RSX user application program that uses the RSX-11/3271 Protocol Emulator (PE) for communications associates each TU (tape unit) device (station-controller arrangement) with a logical unit number. When issuing QI/O requests, the program specifies the logical unit number of the associated TU device to be serviced by the requested I/O operation. Same as LUN.

generic

A number or set of numbers used by peripheral units during system loading or system generation which is not primarily assigned to a specific physical device.

logical unit status (LUSTAT) *n.*

DECnet

LUSTAT is an SNA (systems network architecture) data flow control request used to transfer status information that is not directly related to communications. Same as LUSTAT.

logic simulator *n.*

generic

A tool that helps verify that a logic design is functioning properly or as designed.

log in *v.*

generic

To gain access to an operating system as an authorized user.

login *adj.*

generic

Referring to the procedure that lets a user gain access to and communicate with the computer.

login file *n.*

VAX/VMS

A command procedure that is automatically executed at login and at the beginning of a batch job.

LOGO *n.*

generic

A symbol, graphic design, or combination of characters, usually representing a company, organization, or product.

LOGON mode table (LMT) *n.*

DECnet

A set of SNA (systems network architecture) session rules that have been defined to the S/370 SNA access method, and assigned to a one- to eight-character name that may be specified to the PE (protocol emulator) in the connect block, and subsequently by the PE in the INITS request to SNA. Same as LMT.

logout *adj.*

generic

Referring to the procedure to terminate communication with the computer.

log out or log off *v.*

generic

To terminate a process or job on the system.

long vector *n.*

VT-11 GRAPHICS

A vector stored in long-vector format, occupying two words. A long vector may not exceed 1023 rasters in length.

longword *n.*

FMS

Four bytes used to score integers.

VAX/VMS

1. A 32-bit word (A VAX word).

2. Four contiguous bytes starting on an addressable byte boundary. Bits are numbered from right to left 0 through 31. The address of the longword is the address of the byte containing bit 0. When interpreted arithmetically, a longword is a two's complement integer with significance increasing from bit 0 to bit 230. When interpreted as a signed integer, bit 31 is the sign bit.

loop *n.*

DIGITAL-specific

A sequence of instructions that is executed repeatedly until a terminal condition is satisfied.

generic

A branch that directs the computer to repeat program statements until specified conditions are met.

loop *v.*

generic

1. To repeat the same sequence of instructions.

2. To continuously repeat a computer operation.

loopback *n.*

DECnet

The process of systematically testing a link by sending a signal part way down the link and returning it. This method is used to verify the operation of devices along a communications link. See also line level loopback test.

loopback node *n.*

DECnet

A special name for a node that is associated with a line for loopback testing purposes (the SET NODE LINE command sets the loopback node name). A loopback node is treated as if it were a remote node; all traffic to the loopback node is looped over the associated line.

loop body *n.*

PASCAL and VAX PASCAL

A statement or group of statements that are executed repetitively under the control of a FOR, REPEAT, or WHILE statement.

looping *n.*

generic

A state in which a program repeats the same sequence of instructions.

loop node *n.*

DECnet

A special name for a node that is associated with a line for loop testing purposes. The NAP SET NODE LINE command sets the loopback node name. All traffic to the loop node is sent over the associated line.

VAX/VMS

A local node associated with a particular line and treated as if it were a remote node. All traffic to the loop node is sent over the associated line.

loss *n.*

generic

An excess of cost over net proceeds for a single transaction; negative income for a period.

lost time *n.*

DECsystem-10

The time that the null job was running, while at least one other job waited to run but could not because one of the following was true:

1. The job was being swapped out.

2. The job was being swapped in.

3. The job was on disk waiting to be swapped in.

4. The job was momentarily stopped so devices could become inactive in order to shuffle job in core.

low bound *n.*

VAX PL/I

The lower limit of one dimension of an array.

lowercase *adj.*

DECWORD

The small letters that are typed without first pressing the SHIFT or CAPS LOCK keys.

lowest index level *n.*

RSX-11M

The chain of index buckets whose entries point to data buckets. Same as level 1. See also data level and index level.

low-order byte *n.*

RT-11

The least significant byte in a word. The low-order bytes occupies bit positions 0 through 7 in a PDP-11 word and is always an even address.

low-order end *n.*

COBOL-74

The rightmost character of a string of characters.

low segment *n.*

DECsystem-10

The segment of user virtual address space beginning at zero. It contains the job data area and I/O buffers. The length of the low segment is stored in location .JBREL of the job data area. When writing two-segment programs, it is advisable to place data locations and impure code in the low segment.

LPD *n.*

VAX PSI and VAX/VMS

The abbreviation for layered environment services process descriptor. An extended interrupt request packet of variable length. LPDs are used by the communication operating environment to pass data between the protocol processing images. Same as layered environment services process descriptor.

LQP *n.*

generic

The abbreviation for letter quality printer. LQP is the printer used to produce final copies of documents. It produces typing comparable in quality to that of a typewriter. Same as letter quality printer.

LRU *adj.*

VAX/VMS

The abbreviation for least-recently-used. Pertaining to a type of memory management that removes the page that was the most recently least-used in order to free space for inserting a new page into the working set. Same as least-recently-used.

LSB *n.*

MINC

The abbreviation for least significant bit. With MINC, the least significant bit is the value associated with the last bit of the A/D input word. In a 12-bit A/D converter, this value is 114096 of the full-scale range. In the case of MINC A/D, this translates to 1.5 mV. Same as least significant bit.

LU *n.*

DECnet

The abbreviation for logical unit. LU is a non-specialized network addressable unit (NAU) corresponding to an application type program in an SNA (systems network architecture) network. Same as logical unit.

LUN *n.*

RSX-11M

LUN is an acronym for logical unit number. A LUN is a number associated with a physical device during a task's I/O operations. Each task can establish its own correspondence between LUNs and physical device units. Same as logical unit number.

LUSTAT *n.*

DECnet

The acronym for logical unit status. LUSTAT is an SNA (systems network architecture) data flow control request used to transfer status information that is not directly related to communications. Same as logical unit status.

lvalue *n.*

VAX C

The abstract value that denotes the location of an object whose contents can be assigned or modified.

machine language *n.*

generic

A set of binary codes that form instructions that can be linked and then executed by the computer.

macro *n.*

DIGITAL-specific

A body of text (statements and instructions) that is substituted for the macro name whenever that name appears in a program.

generic

A statement that generates a set of instructions.

RT-11

An instruction in a source language that is equivalent to a specified sequence of assembler instructions, or a command in a command language that is equivalent to a specified sequence of commands.

VAX C

A text substitution that is defined with the #define preprocessor control line and includes a list of "parameters". The parameters in the #define control line are replaced at compile time with the corresponding arguments from a macro reference encountered in the source text.

VAX/VMS

A statement that requests a language processor to generate a predefined set of instructions.

macrocode *n.*

generic

A system of codes that assembles groups of computer instructions into single code words.

macrograph *n.*

GIGI

A named string that can be recalled and that consists of ReGIS commands.

magnetic tape *n.*

generic

A tape with a magnetic coating on which information is recorded in magnetic polarized areas.

magnetic tape volume list (MVL) *n.*

VAX/VMS

A data structure built by the mount program to describe volumes within a multivolume set. The MVL contains the number of volumes, volume identifiers, relative volume numbers, and the status of all the volumes within the multivolume set. Same as MVL.

mailbox *n.*

VAX/VMS

A software data structure that is treated as a record-oriented device for general interprocess communication. Communication using a mailbox is similar to other forms of device-independent I/O. Senders write to a mailbox, the receiver reads from that mailbox.

main keyboard *n.*

DECWORD

The larger DECWORD keyboard that looks like a typewriter keyboard. See also mini-keyboard.

generic

The largest set of keys on a keyboard.

main keypad *n.*

GIGI

The portion of the keyboard consisting of the alphanumeric characters and other symbols, similar to those on standard typewriter keys.

RGL/FEP

That portion of the VT125 keyboard above the space bar and separated from the auxiliary keypad; it consists of alphanumeric keys and same special-character keys.

main memory *n.*

generic

The primary storage area in a computer, connected directly to the central processing unit, and from which instructions and data can be fetched, manipulated and executed.

VAX/VMS

The memory modules connected to the SBI that are used to store both instructions that the processor can directly fetch and execute and any other data that a processor is instructed to manipulate. Also called main memory. Same as physical memory.

main menu *n.*

DECWORD

DECWORD's central menu, from which a user can choose to create, edit, or print a document, or choose many other options.

main program *n.*

BASIC-PLUS-2, RT-11, and TOPS-10

The module containing the address at which object program execution normally begins. Usually, the main program exercises primary control over the operations performed and calls subroutines to perform specific functions.

generic

The primary section of a computer program or routine that exercises control over other subroutines or subprograms.

main screen *n.*

A-to-Z

A key that, when pressed, returns you to the Main Manager Menu.

MAINT.SYS *n.*

DECsystem-10

The area of the disk reserved for maintenance use only.

maintenance operation protocol (MOP) *n.*

DECnet

A formal set of messages and rules used to load and dump computer memory as well as test a communications link between two adjacent nodes. Same as MOP.

main text buffer *n.*

VAX/VMS

In EDT, the default text buffer for keyboard input and for input files, and the source for output files.

main tree *n.*

VAX/VMS

An overlay tree whose root segment is loaded by the Executive when the task is made active.

management information systems (MIS) *n.*

generic

Batch and online systems for routine business functions that generally have data stored in databases, and thus provide for easier maintenance and change. Same as MIS.

MANAGER *n.*

A-to-Z

An account that allows one person to control and maintain the use of the system.

mandatory member *n.*

VAX DATATRIEVE and VAX DBMS

A record that, upon becoming a member of a set occurrence of a set type, must remain a member of that set type until the record is erased from the database. See also fixed member, optional member, permanent member, and retention class.

mandatory set membership *n.*

VAX DBMS

The specification of a set member (in the schema) such that once the membership of a record occurrence in the set is established, the membership is permanent; it cannot be removed from the set unless it is deleted from the data base.

manual input *n.*

RT-11

The entry of data by hand into a device at the time of processing.

manual loading *n.*

VAX/VMS

The method of loading overlay segments in which the user includes explicit calls in routines to load overlays and handles unsuccessful load requests.

manual member *n.*

VAX DBMS

A record that becomes a member of a given set by direction of the application program. Manual set membership is declared in the schema. See also automatic member and manual set membership.

manual record locking *n.*

VAX/VMS

A capability that allows users to lock multiple records in a file simultaneously. The user has explicit control over the locking and unlocking of records. A lock occurs when the ULK bit is set in the record processing options field on the execution of a $GET, $FIND, or $PUT macro instruction. Once a record is manually locked, it will remain in that state until it is explicitly unlocked by either the free or release service, or until the stream terminates.

manual record unlocking *n.*

VAX/VMS

A VAX RMS capability that allows users to lock multiple records in a file simultaneously. The user has explicit control over the unlocking of records. A lock occurs when the RAB$V_ULK bit is set in the record processing options field on the execution of a Get, Find, or Put service. Once a record is locked when record unlocking is enabled, it will remain locked until it is explicitly unlocked by either the Free or Release service, or until the stream terminates.

manual set membership *n.*

VAX DBMS

A form of set membership in which membership is established by a run-unit by means of the INSERT command. Manual membership of the record occurrence in a set is declared by the database administrator when the schema is set up. See also manual member.

manufacturing costs *n.*

generic

Costs incurred in the manufacturing process during an accounting period, whether or not the goods were completed.

map *n.*

generic

1. A statement that defines how the fields of a record are to be stored in a file.

2. A description of the contents of actual memory location.

3. A hardware circuit that is used in address translation.

DSM-11

A disk storage unit. A map consists of 400 DSM blocks (which are 1024 bytes long). The 400th block of every map is a map block that contains allocation data about the previous 399 blocks in the map, and about itself.

FMS

A description of what data will be moved from form fields to program record fields and/or from program record fields to form fields.

mapped array area *n.*

VAX/VMS

An area of the task's physical memory, preceding the task image, that is used for storage of large arrays. Space in the area is reserved by means of the VSECT keyword or through a mapped array declaration contained in an object module. Access is through the mapping directives issued at run time.

mapped memory *n.*

MicroPower PASCAL

Memory that is divided into segments, or pages, each located separately in (mapped into) physical storage. Mapping translates the 16-bit addresses used with LSI-11 processors into a physical memory space of 18- or 22-bit address size. With the LSI-11/23, up to the equivalent of four 64K byte virtual address spaces can be mapped into non-contiguous 8K-byte segments (18-bit mode) or 64 different spaces (22-bit mode).

mapped system *n.*

generic

A system which uses the hardware memory management unit to relocate virtual memory addresses.

mapping *n.*

FMS

In FMS, mapping refers to both of the following:

1. the process of describing the exchange of data between a field and a program

2. the actual movement of data between a form and a program record by the FMS LEVEL II routines. At run time, when the request definition is read and executed, data conversion is performed.

Terminal Data Management System

The description of the exchange of data between a TDMS (Terminal Data Management System) form and a program record and/or a request.

mapping window *n.*

VAX/VMS

A subset of the retrieval information for a file that is used to translate virtual block numbers to logical block numbers. See also window.

margin *n.*

generic

The difference between revenue and specified expenses.

mark *n.*

GIGI

A displayed symbol used to specify a location.

market value *n.*

generic

The amount for which an asset can be sold in the marketplace.

mask *adj.*

generic

Pertaining to a pattern of bits used to enable or disable functions.

mask *n.*

DECnet

1. A combination of bits that is used to control the retention elimination of portions of any word, character, or byte in memory.

2. On half-duplex circuits, the characters typed on the terminal to make the password unreadable.

generic

A pattern of bits used to enable or disable functions.

RT-11

A combination of bits that is used to manipulate selected portions of any word, character, byte, or register while retaining other parts for use.

mask *v.*

generic

To disable or enable functions by writing specific patterns of bits to a register.

MASSBUS adapter *n.*

VAX/VMS

An interface device between the backplane interconnect and the MASSBUS. Same as MBA.

mass insert *n.*

RSX-11M

An RMS-11 I/O technique for indexed files only by which RMS-11 can extend the primary level 0 bucket by bucket, packing records into the buckets in the order they are written. As each bucket gets full, RMS-11 creates a new one, beginning with the next record inserted, and notes its existence in a primary level 1 index bucket.

mass storage *n.*

DIGITAL-specific

A storage medium on which data can be organized and maintained in both a sequential and nonsequential manner.

mass storage *adj.*

DIGITAL-specific

Pertaining to a device, such as a disk or DECtape, that stores large amounts of data readily accessible to the central processing unit.

generic

Pertaining to a device that can store large amounts of data accessible to the Central Processing Unit.

mass storage control system (MSCS) *n.*

COBOL-74

An input-output control system that directs or controls the processing of mass storage files. Same as MSCS.

mass storage device *n.*

generic

A large capacity peripheral memory device such as a magnetic tape or disk units directly accessible by the central processing unit.

VAX/VMS

An input/output device on which data and other types of files are stored while they are not being used. Typical mass-storage devices include disks, magnetic tapes, and floppy disks.

master file directory (MFD) *n.*

DIGITAL-specific

The file that contains the name of all user file directories (UFDs) on a disk including its own. Same as MFD. See also continued MFD.

generic

A directory file holding the names of all master files found on the structure.

master slave system *n.*

TOPS-10

A specific multiprocessing system involving two processors where one processor has a more important role than the other. Master/slave relationships can also occur between disk, tape, CPU and other computer functions.

master station *n.*

DECnet

A station that has control of a channel at a given instant for the purpose of sending data messages to a slave station.

matching control *n.*

PEARL

A control used to transform a data object during transfer through a DATION (DATA STATION).

matrix *n.*

GAMMA and Medical Systems

In GAMMA a matrix is a two-dimensional array of cells, n rows by n columns, where n is 32, 64, 128, or 256. The matrix represents the surface area of the gamma camera.

generic

1. An array of elements, arranged in rows and columns, that may be worked according to the rules of matrix arithmetic.

2. In computers, an arrangement of dots which represent graphic symbols on CRT screens and line printers.

RT-11

A rectangular array of elements. Any matrix can be considered an array.

maximum cost *n.*

DECnet

The greatest total cost the path to a node may have if the node is to be reachable.

maximum hops *n.*

DECnet

An operator-controllable Transport parameter that defines the point where the routing decision algorithm in a node declares another node unreachable because the length of the shortest path between the two nodes is too long. For correct operation, this parameter must not be less than the network diameter.

maximum node address *n.*

DECnet

The largest node address with which the local node can communicate.

maximum path cost *n.*

DECnet

The routing cost between the two nodes of the network that have the greatest routing cost (where routing cost is the cost of the least cost path between a given pair of nodes).

maximum path length *n.*

DECnet

The routing distance between the two nodes of
the network having the greatest routine distance
(where routine distance is the length of the least-
cost path between a given pair of nodes).

maximum record number *n.*

RSX-11M

RMS-11 will not put a record into a relative file
with a relative record number greater than the
assigned maximum record number (MRN)–unless
MRN is zero. In that case, RMS-11 makes no
check on relative record numbers during put operations. MRN is an attribute of relative files. Same
as MRN.

maximum visits *n.*

DECnet

An operator-controllable transport parameter that
defines the point where the packet lifetime control
algorithm discards a packet which has traversed
too many nodes. For correct operation this
parameter must not be less than the maximum
path length of the network.

VAX/VMS

The maximum number of nodes through which a
packet can be routed before reaching its
destination.

MBA *n.*

VAX/VMS

The abbreviation for MASSBUS adapter. An interface device between the backplane interconnect
and the MASSBUS.

MBZ *n.*

TOPS-20 and VAX/VMS

The abbreviation for must be zero. A field that is
reserved for the future and must be supplied as
zero. If examined, it must be assumed to be
undefined. Same as must be zero.

MCB *n.*

DECnet and RSX-20F

The abbreviation for multifunction communications
base. The software resident in a DN20 that supports DECnet. Same as multifunction communications base.

MCR *n.*

RSX-11M and VAX/VMS

The abbreviation for monitor console routine. The
command interpreter in an RSX-11 and VAX/VMS
system. Same as monitor console routine.

MCS-10 *n.*

COBOL-74

The abbreviation for message control system. A
communication control system that supports the
processing of messages. Same as message control system.

MDB *n.*

generic

The abbreviation for menu database. MDB is a
run-time database containing information derived
from menu definitions. Same as menu database.

MDT *n.*

DECnet

The abbreviation for modified data tag. A bit in
the attribute character of a display field which,
when set, causes that field to be transmitted during a READ MODIFIED operation. Same as modified data tag.

mean-time to repair (MTTR) *n.*

DIGITAL-specific

The average time it takes a field service engineer to isolate and repair a system malfunction. Same as MTTR.

mechanism module *n.*

VAX/VMS

A system module that implements the ability to access (or use) a resource according to the policies set by a policy module.

medium-scale integration *n.*

generic

The accumulation of several circuits (usually less than 100) on a single chip of semiconductor.

member *n.*

VAX PL/I

A data item in a structure that may itself be a structure.

member condition *n.*

VAX DBMS

The verification (for which a truth value can be determined) that a set has members.

member number *n.*

VAX/VMS

The second number in a user identification code. The member number uniquely identifies that code. See also user number.

member record *n.*

VAX DATATRIEVE and VAX DBMS

A record occurrence, other than the owner record, that is included in the set. There may be zero, one, or many member record occurrences in a set occurrence. See also owner record, nonsingular set, and system-owned set.

memory *n.*

generic

1. The physical storage of a computer used to store and recover data.

2. Any device or circuit capable of storing digital information.

VAX/VMS

A series of physical locations into which data or instructions can be placed in the form of binary words. Each location in memory can be addressed and its contents can be altered. Memory should not be confused with mass-storage devices.

memory allocation file *n.*

VAX/VMS

The output file created by the Task Builder that lists information about the size and location of components within a task.

memory cycle overlap *n.*

TOPS-10

The hardware feature on the KL-10 processor that allows a second memory reference to be made before data from the first reference has been received by the processor.

memory hierarchy *n.*

generic

A set of memories with differing sizes and speeds and usually having different cost-performance ratios.

memory image *n.*

MicroPower PASCAL

The file resulting from running the memory image builder (MIB) utility and containing the image of the application program as it will appear in the target system memory. See also run-time module.

RT-11

A replication of the contents of a portion of memory, usually in a file.

memory image builder (MIB) *n.*

MicroPower PASCAL

The MicroPower PASCAL utility program that combines the following components into a memory image file:

1. bootstrap loader (if necessary)

2. kernel

3. relocated process image file (file containing an image of the program as it will appear in its portion of the target system memory). This memory image file is loaded into the target processor.

Same as MIB.

memory interconnect *n.*

VAX/VMS

The internal processor bus for the VAX-11/750.

memory management *n.*

VAX/VMS

The operating system functions that include the hardware's page mapping and protection and the operating system's image activator and pager.

memory mapping *n.*

generic

The process of listing all names, constants, routines, and subroutines, used by the program with their relative addresses, as well as the last location called.

memory mapping enable (MME) *n.*

VAX/VMS

A bit in a processor register that governs address translation. Same as MME.

memory page *n.*

DIGITAL-specific

The physical unit of storage management. It is 512 words long.

memory protection *n.*

DIGITAL-specific

A scheme for preventing read and/or write access to certain areas of storage.

generic

A method that controls access to certain areas in memory that are reserved storage areas.

memory resident *adj.*

VAX/VMS

Pertaining to an entity that resides in memory all the time. The entity, as in the case of memory-resident overlays, may initially reside on disk.

memory-resident overlay *n.*

RSX-11M

An overlay structure or segment maintained in physical memory. The overlay is executed by the task by means of active page registers. See also disk-resident overlay.

memory-resident overlay segment *n.*

VAX/VMS

An overlay segment that shares virtual address space with other segments, but which resides in its own physical memory. The segment is loaded from disk only the first time it is referenced; thereafter, mapping directives are issued in place of disk load request.

memory-time integral *n.*

VAX/VMS

The integration over time of memory-size use.

menu *n.*

A-to-Z

A list of options from which you can choose one at a time. There are two sets of menus: manager and user menus.

DIGITAL-specific

A displayed list of options. The user selects an option by typing the letter or letters shown and pressing RETURN.

generic

1 A list of possible responses to a given request displayed on a video terminal.

2. Any display listing choices that activate programs or subsystems.

VT-11 GRAPHICS

A list of character strings or small pictures, also called light buttons. A user can select an option from a menu by touching the desired character string with the lightpen, or by pressing a programmed keyboard character. Users can display a menu of up to ten light buttons in a single call to the MENU subroutine. By calling MENU repeatedly, users can display as many light buttons as can fit on the desired area of the screen.

menu database (MDB) *n.*

generic

A run-time database containing information derived from menu definitions. Same as MDB.

MERGE *n.*

MicroPower PASCAL

The MicroPower PASCAL utility program that combines two or more object modules, resolving intermodule references if possible, and updating the relocation directories.

merge file *n.*

COBOL-74

A collection of records to be merged by a MERGE statement. The merge file is created and can be used only by the merge function.

message *n.*

DECnet

1. A message consists of one message block, or a series of message blocks, that constitute a logical grouping of information. Each message block is delimited by communications control characters.

2. Specific to ARPANET, a bit stream less than or equal to 8096 bits given to an IMP by a Host for transmission to another Host.

COBOL-74 and TOPS-10

A sequence of characters ended by an EMI (end-of-message indicator) or EGI (end-of-group indicator). See also message indicator.

message control system (MCS) *n.*

COBOL-74

A communication control system that supports the processing of messages. Same as MCS.

message count *n.*

COBOL-74

The number of complete messages that are in the designated message queue.

message datatype *n.*

Rdb/ELN

A VAXELN system datatype that describes data transmitted between processes. A message datum indirectly specifies the sender's message port, the destination port, and the text of a message.

message exchange *n.*

DECnet

The DDCMP component that transfers data correctly and in sequence over a link.

message file *n.*

CTS-300

A file (ERMSG.TXT) in which all the CTS-300 system and utility program messages are stored. Messages in this file are accessed by the program for display.

generic

A file that contains a table of message symbols and their associated text.

message file segment *n.*

CTS-300

A division of the system message file (ERMSG.TXT) that contains all the messages for a given program.

message group *n.*

TOPS-10

A collection of messages ended with EGI (end-of-group indicator). A group is a complete input or output transaction.

message indicators *n.*

COBOL-74 and TOPS-10

Designations that notify the MCS (message control system) that a specific condition exists such as end-of-group, end-of-message, or end-of-segment. There are three types of message indicators: EGI, end-of-group indicator; EMI, end-of-message indicator; and ESI, end-of-segment indicator.

message port *n.*

Rdb/ELN

A first-in/first-out message queue exchanged between processes in a VAXELN system.

message processing program (MPP) *n.*

TOPS-10

A COBOL program that receives transactions from the queue structure and sends messages to destinations. Same as MPP.

message segment *n.*

COBOL-74

Data that forms a logical subdivision of a message normally associated with an end-of-segment indicator.

TOPS-10

Part of a message, ended by an ESI (end-of-segment indicator), EMI (end-of-message indicator), or EGI (end-of-group indicator). If ended by an EMI, the message is complete. If ended by an EGI, the segment completes a transaction.

message switching *n.*

DECnet and VAX PSI

A method of transmission in which there is no direct connection set up between incoming and outgoing lines. The message is received and stored until the proper outgoing line is available, then it is retransmitted.

message type *n.*

CTS-300

A one- or two-character identifier of the nature of a given message in the system file. There are seven categories of message types: error, warning, fatal, non trappable, informational, instructional, and dialog. The message type is stored with the message when it is displayed.

metadata *n.*

DIGITAL-specific

Defines the form of data stored in a database. Metadata can be thought of as "data about data."

metal oxide *adj.*

generic

Made of a binary complex of an element or metal with oxygen.

metering *n.*

TOPS-10

A technique used to do a performance analysis.

MFD *n.*

DIGITAL-specific and VAX/VMS

The abbreviation for master file directory. MFD is the file that contains the name of all user file directories (UFDs) on a disk including its own. Same as master file directory. See also continued MFD.

MFPR *n.*

VAX/VMS

Move From Process Register instruction.

MIC *n.*

DECnet

The abbreviation for middle-in-chain. A 256-byte message element, preceded by a related element marked first-in-chain or middle-in-chain, and followed by a related chain element marked middle-in-chain or last-in-chain. Same as middle-in-chain.

MICRO *n.*

DIGITAL-specific

An account which allows advanced programmers access to Micro/RSX.

microcode *n.*

generic

A system of codes that includes an internal program that controls the execution of computer instructions.

microcode simulation *n.*

generic

The execution of micro instructions in a simulator environment.

microcomputer *n.*

generic

A computer that uses a microprocessor as its CPU (central processing unit) and includes a memory and input/output circuits.

microdiagnostic *n.*

generic

A program written in microcode that is used to diagnose or evaluate the operation of a computer.

microdiagnostic program *n.*

generic

A program, written in microcode, that diagnoses the correctness of a microprocessor.

microfiche *n.*

generic

A sheet of film capable of holding images in an array.

microinstruction *n.*

generic

One word of microcode.

microprocessor *n.*

generic

The control and processing section of a small computer usually made up of a small number of LSI chips.

microprogram *n.*

generic

A program made up of microinstructions used to perform discrete logic operations.

microprogramming *n.*

generic

A method of operating the control part of a computer where each instruction is broken into several small steps (microsteps) that form part of a microprogram.

Micro RSTS *n.*

RSTS/E

A subset of the RSTS/E operating system. DIGITAL has defined this software subset as the most appropriate (in terms of performance and function) for the MICRO/PDP-11 hardware.

MicroVMS *n.*

DIGITAL-specific

A proper subset of VAX/VMS and extends the operating system's capabilities to the MicroVAX I and II processors.

middle-in-chain (MIC) *n.*

DECnet

A 256-byte message element, preceded by a related element first-in-chain or middle-in-chain, and followed by a related chain element marked middle-in-chain or last-in-chain. Same as MIC.

MINC *n.*

MINC

The mnemonic for modular instrument computer: a hardware/software system designed to perform computations in BASIC, produce graphic displays, monitor laboratory processes, control experiments, and acquire data.

minicomputer *n.*

generic

A word for any general-purpose digital computer in the low-to-average price range.

minified display *n.*

Medical Systems

A data analysis process that displays four images of a multiple static or dynamic study on the screen at the same time.

mini-keyboard *n.*

DECWORD

The smaller DECWORD keyboard, containing editing keys. See also main keyboard.

generic

A smaller, alternate set of keys to the extreme right of a main keyboard. Same as minikeypad.

minikeypad *n.*

generic

A smaller, alternate set of keys to the extreme right of a main keyboard. Same as mini-keyboard.

MIS *n.*

generic

The abbreviation for management information systems. MIS are batch and online systems for routine business functions that generally have data stored in databases, and thus provide for easier maintenance and change. Same as management information systems.

MME *n.*

VAX/VMS

The abbreviation for memory mapping enable. A bit in a processor register that governs address translation. Same as memory mapping enable.

mnemonic-name *n.*

VAX-COBOL

A user-defined word associated in the Environment Division with a specific implementor-name.

mode *n.*

DIGITAL-specific

One of a number of possible states of operation. The state may be the result of a user selection or one of an automatic series of operations. Mode can also refer to a facet of program operation or a file access characteristic (such as: output, input, or update mode.) See also executive mode.

model *n.*

CTS-300

A specification of the desired character string for a search operation.

model *n.*

DECSIM

A basic element representing a component in a logic network simulation. It is written in the DECSIM network description language or behavior language. It describes the component's connections to the outside world, and internal structure or behavior.

modem *n.*

generic

1. An acronym for MOdulator-DEmodulator. A device that changes digital signals into analog signals for transmission over long distances, and changes received analog signals to digital signals for use by electronic digital equipment.

2. A device that converts computer signals to signals that can be sent over a telephone line.

modified data tag (MDT) *n.*

DECnet

A bit in the attribute character of a display field which, when set, causes that field to be transmitted during a READ MODIFIED operation. See also MDT.

modify access type *n.*

VAX/VMS

A specific way of accessing characterized by a specified operand of an instruction or procedure being read, and potentially modified and written, during that instruction's or procedure's execution.

modular programming *n.*

MicroPower PASCAL

A method of constructing a program from many small sections, called modules. This method helps segment program concepts so that they can be written either as separate parts of one source program (procedures in MicroPower PASCAL) or as distinct source programs, compiled into separate, cross-referenced object modules to be linked into one load module.

modulation *n.*

generic

The process of changing some feature of a signal.

module *n.*

MicroPower PASCAL

In the MicroPower PASCAL language, an attribute applied to a declaration section of statements.

generic

A separate unit or part of a computer program.

PEARL

An independently compilable unit that may contain a SYSTEM DIVISION and/or a PROBLEM DIVISION.

TOPS-10

The smallest entity that can be loaded by the loader. It is composed of a collection of control sections. In MACRO-10, the code between the TITLE and END statements represents a module. In FORTRAN, the code between the first statements and the END statement is a module. In COBOL, the code between the IDENTIFICATION DIVISION statement and the last statement is a module.

TOPS-20

A collection of one or more routines that are assembled or compiled together and dealt with as an entity.

VAX PSI

A VAX PSI management component. There are three modules: X25-PROTOCOL, X25-SERVER, and X29-SERVER. The X25-PROTOCOL module identifies the PSDN, specifies the local DTE address and maybe user group, and controls the transmission of packets. The X25-SERVER and X29-SERVER modules define destinations for handling incoming calls. The X25-ACCESS module that identifies the multi-host node connected to the PDSN.

VAX/VMS

1. A portion of a program or program library, as in a source module, object module, or image module.

2. A board, usually made of plastic covered with an electrical conductor, on which logic devices (such as transistors, resistors, and memory chips) are mounted, and circuits connecting these devices are etched, as in a logic module.

3. A network management component.

MODULE-LEVEL OBJECT *n.*

PEARL

An object whose declaration in a PROBLEM DIVISION is not enclosed by a PROCEDURE, TASK, or INTERFACE.

module origin *n.*

TOPS-10

The first location occupied by the module in user virtual address space.

modulus *n.*

VAX PASCAL

An integer value that results when one operand, B, is repeatedly subtracted from another operand, A (or repeatedly added, if A is negative), until the difference is less than B. This difference is called the modulus of A with respect to B.

MONEY *n.*

TOPS-10

A program for reading the system's time accounting file and assigning a monetary charge for each user according to the time and resources that each has used on the system.

MONGEN *n.*

TOPS-10

The monitor generator dialogue program that enables the system programmer to define the hardware configuration of his individual installation and the set of software options that the programmer wishes to select for his system.

MONGEN time *n.*

TOPS-10

The time at which the monitor software configuration is being defined or changed. The monitor must then be reloaded with the loader.

monitor *n.*

CTS-300 and RT-11

The master control program that supervises and controls the operation of a computer system. The collection of routines that controls the operation of user and system programs, schedules operations, allocates resources, and performs I/O. The monitor is sometimes called an Executive.

DECnet and DECsystem-10

A logging sink that is to receive a machine-readable record of events for real-time decision-making.

DIGITAL-specific

A video device containing a cathode ray tube (CRT) that the terminal uses to display screen images.

generic

In an operating system, the master control program that checks, controls, or verifies the operation of a computer system. The set of routines that allocates resources, performs I/O, and, in general, controls the operation of user and system programs, schedules and operations.

MicroPower PASCAL

An RT-11 overseer program that controls and tracks system business. The monitor controls, observes, supervises, or verifies actions of the computer system. It is a collection of routines that control the operation of user and system programs, schedule operations, allocate resources, and perform I/O.

monitor call *n.*

DIGITAL-specific

A request to the monitor to perform a specific function during program execution. A monitor call has a predefined symbol, a mnemonic usually indicative of the function to be performed.

monitor call intercept facility *n.*

DECnet and TOPS-20

The series of monitor calls and statements that provide the means for blocking a monitor call in the inferior process before it is executed. The monitoring process then examines the environment in which the call would be executed, and determines the action to be taken. See also JSYS trap.

monitor command *n.*

generic

An instruction issued directly to a monitor from a user.

monitor command mode *n.*

generic

The state of the operating system that allows monitor commands to be entered from the terminal.

monitor console *n.*

generic

The system control terminal.

monitor console routine (MCR) *n.*

generic

An executive routine that allows the user to communicate with the system using an on-line terminal. MCR accepts and interprets commands typed on the terminal keyboard and calls appropriate routines to execute the specified requests.

RSX-11M and VAX/VMS

The command interpreter in an RSX-11 system and in a VAX/VMS system.

MOP *n.*

DECnet

The abbreviation for maintenance operation protocol. A formal set of messages and rules used to load and dump computer memory as well as test a communications link between two adjacent nodes. Same as maintenance operation protocol.

mosaic *n.*

GIGI

A multi-character image created with characters from user-defined character sets. The spacing between characters is decreased.

most significant digit (MSD) *n.*

generic

The farthest digit to the left that is not zero. Same as MSD.

mount *v.*

generic

To put in its correct location or position.

mount a device *v.*

DIGITAL-specific

To assign an I/O device by means of a request to the operator. See also: mount a volume.

mount a volume *n.*

DIGITAL-specific

1. To logically associate a volume with the physical unit on which it is loaded (an activity accomplished by system software at the request of an operator).

2. To load or place a magnetic tape or disk pack on a drive and place the drive on line (an activity accomplished by a system operator). See also: mount a device.

mount count *n.*

TOPS-10

The count of the number of jobs that have a file structure in their active or passive search lists (plus 1 if the structure is in the system search list).

mounting a file structure *n.*

TOPS-10

The process of adding a file structure to a search list. If the file structure is not already defined and mounted, this action is requested of the operator.

mouse *n.*

generic

The user's device for printing to and selecting objects on the screen. When the user moves the device on a hard surface, the pointer on the screen moves. When the user is pointing to an object and presses a button on the device (mouse button), the object is selected.

move mode *n.*

RSX-11M and VAX/VMS

A record I/O access technique in which a program accesses records in its own working storage area. See also locate mode.

VAX DATATRIEVE

The method by which an application program can access records in memory. Move mode requires that a record be copied first to the I/O buffer and then to the program by RMS. Locate mode allows the program to directly access a record in the I/O buffer. See also record transfer mode.

MPP *n.*

TOPS-10

The abbreviation for message processing program. A COBOL program that receives transactions from the queue structure and sends messages to destinations. Same as message processing program.

MPXable device *n.*

TOPS-10

A device that can be connected to an MPX channel: line printers, terminals, paper-tape punches, remote data entry devices, and pseudo-TTYs.

MPX-controlled device *n.*

TOPS-10

A device connected to an MPX channel. A user program connects a device to an MPX channel, when the program issues a CNECT. monitor call.

MRN *n.*

RSX-11M

The abbreviation for maximum record number. RMS-11 will not put a record into a relative file with a relative record number greater than the assigned maximum record number (MRN)–unless MRN is zero. In that case, RMS-11 makes no check on relative record numbers during put operations. MRN is an attribute of relative files. Same as maximum record number.

MSCS *n.*

COBOL-74

The abbreviation for mass storage control system. An input-output control system that directs or controls the processing of mass storage files. Same as mass storage control system.

MSD *n.*

generic

The abbreviation for most significant digit. MSD is the farthest digit to the left that is not zero. Same as most significant digit.

MS™-DOS *n.*

non-DIGITAL product*

A Disk Operating System used widely with personal computers and developed by Microsoft Corporation.
* MS™-DOS is a trademark of Microsoft Corporation.

MSGSER *n.*

TOPS-10

The abbreviation for message service. Part of the monitor that passes messages between a user (such as MCP) and communication devices. Same as message service.

MTAACP *n.*

VAX/VMS

The abbreviation for magnetic tape ancillary control process.

MTTR *n.*

DIGITAL-specific

The abbreviation for mean-time to repair. The average time it takes a field service engineer to isolate and repair a system malfunction. Same as mean-time to repair.

multiaccess channel *n.*

VAX/VMS

A medium (for example, Ethernet) on which many transmitters contend for access.

multi-area file *n.*

RSX-11M

An indexed file with more than one area. See also single-area file.

multi-block count *n.*

RSX-11M

The number of blocks that RMS-11 moves in and out of the I/O buffer during each I/O operation for a sequential file. See also I/O unit.

multicast addressing *n.*

VAX/VMS

An addressing mode in which a given message packet is targeted to a group of logically related nodes.

multicast group address *n.*

VAX/VMS

An address assigned to a number of nodes on an Ethernet and used to send a message to all nodes in the group in a single transmission.

multidimensional array *n.*

PASCAL and VAX PASCAL

An array with elements of an array type; each dimension of such an array has its own subscripts. These subscripts can be of different types. See also dimension

multidrop *n.*

DECnet

A single communications line to which a multiple number of nodes, terminals or control units may be connected. See also multipoint line and multipoint channel.

multifunction communications base *n.*

DECnet and RSX-20F

The software resident in a DN20 that supports DECnet. See also MCB.

multi-host mode *n.*

VAX PSI

A mode of operation where a DECnet node functions both as a DTE (data terminal equipment) and as a Gateway for other hosts. To achieve this, the DECnet node must be configured with VAX PSI (packet switching interface) in multi-host mode.

multikey index file *n.*

VAX DATATRIEVE

An index file that has more than one defined key field. The first defined key is called the primary key; additional defined keys are called alternate keys.

multinational character set *n.*

VAX/VMS

An 8-bit character set containing the set of international alphanumeric characters, including characters with diacritical marks.

multiple branch *n.*

MINC

A program statement that transfers program control to one of several possible locations.

multiple clock-driven sweeps SYN: *n.*

MINC

Two or more sweeps caused by clock overflows and occurring through two or more MNC-series modules operating in parallel. Multiple clock-driven sweeps are possible only if the user installed the REAL/MNC library file that includes facilities for such sweeps. Same as simultaneous sweeps.

multiple line controller *n.*

DECnet

A controller that can manage more than one unit. (DIGITAL multiple line controllers are also called multiplexers.) See also multiplexer.

multiple record access streams *n.*

RSX-11M

The 1 to 255 streams on a relative or indexed file that RSX-11M allows each program to use.

multiple record feature *n.*

DECnet

A feature of certain IBM 2780 remote stations that allows the processing of more than one packet at a time.

multiple-step task *n.*

ACMS

An ACMS/AD task defined in terms of a block step that contains one or more exchange and processing steps.

multiple sweeps *n.*

MINC

Two or more sweeps sampling data (or transferring data) at the same time.

multiple-volume file *n.*

DIGITAL-specific

A file that spans more than one magnetic tape reel.

multiplex *v.*

DECnet

To simultaneously transmit two or more data streams on a single channel. In DNA (DIGITAL Network Architecture), the network services protocol is the only protocol that multiplexes.

multiplexer *n.*

DECnet

A device that manages communications over several lines, connecting them to a computer that may or may not be a stored-program computer. The DV11 line interface is a multiplexer. The KMC11 is a stored-program controller that performs the multiplexing function. See also multiple line controller.

generic

1. A device that sends two or more signals at the same time over a common transmission medium.

2. A device for selecting one of a number of inputs and switching the information to the output.

multiplexing *n.*

generic

The parallel transmission of more than one message over a single line.

MINC

A device that takes signals from two or more channels and selectively routes them to a single channel.

multiplication factor *n.*

GIGI

A number used to multiply the pixels in either a writing pattern or a text cell before displaying the pattern or cell.

multiplicative operator *n.*

VAX/VMS

An operator that performs multiplication (*), division (/), or module arithmetic (%). It performs the usual arithmetic conversions on its operands. The mod operator (%) actually yields the remainder of the division of the first operand by the second.

multipoint channel *n.*

DECnet

A channel connecting more than two stations. Same as multidrop.

multipoint circuit *n.*

VAX/VMS

A circuit connecting two systems, with one of the systems (the control station) controlling the circuit, and the other system serving as a tributary.

multipoint line *n.*

DECnet

A single communications line to which a multiple number of nodes, terminals, or control units may be connected. The use of this type of line usually requires some kind of polling mechanism, addressing each terminal with a unique ID. See also multidrop.

multiport memory *n.*

VAX/VMS

A memory unit that can be connected to multiple processors and that can contain resources such as mailboxes, common event flag clusters, and global sections for use by processes running on different processors.

multiprecision integer *n.*

VAX/VMS

A contiguous sequence of longwords in memory starting on an addressable byte boundary. Only the highest longword contains the sign; the other longwords are treated as unsigned 32-bit quantities.

multiprocess *adj.*

generic

Pertaining to the parallel transmission of more than one message over a single line.

multiprocessing *n.*

generic

The operation of more than one processing unit within a single system. Separate processors may take over communications or peripheral control, for example, while the main processor continues program execution.

multiprogramming *n.*

generic

The parallel processing of more than one routine or program by interleaving them and timesharing the computer system.

MicroPower PASCAL

The simultaneous execution of two or more programs or portions of a program by a single processor. These programs execute instructions alternately in the processor; therefore, more than one program is in progress at any one time.

RT-11

A processing method in which more than one task is in an executable state at any one time, even with one central processing unit.

TOPS-10

A technique that allows scheduling in such a way that more than one job is in an executable state at any one time. TOPS-10 is a multiprogramming operating system in which there are two or more independent instruction streams that are simultaneously active but are not necessarily simultaneously executed.

multi-segment index *n.*

DIGITAL-specific

An index made up of two or more index keys.

multi-tasking *n.*

DIGITAL-specific

Declaring parts of a given application to execute concurrently with each other and with the main program.

multiterminal service *n.*

RSTS/E

A feature that allows one program to interact simultaneously with several terminals on one I/O channel instead of opening each terminal on a separate I/O channel.

multiterminal support *n.*

RT-11

A feature that allows an application program to perform character I/O on up to nine terminals.

multithread *n.*

TOPS-20

A facility that can process multiple requests in parallel.

290

multivolume file *n.*

CTS-300 and VAX DATATRIEVE

A file that exists on more than one volume of a particular hardware storage device.

MUMPS *n.*

DSM-11

The acronym for Massachusetts General Hospital Utility Multi-Programming System.

must be zero *n.*

TOPS-20

A field that is reserved for the future and must be supplied as zero. If examined, it must be assumed to be undefined. Same as MBZ.

mutex *n.*

VAX/VMS

A semaphore that is used to control exclusive access to a region of code that can share a data structure or other resource. The mutex (mutual exclusion) semaphore ensures that only one process at a time has access to the region of code.

mutex semaphore *n.*

DIGITAL-specific

A semaphore that is used to control exclusive access to a shared data base or other resource. It ensures that only one process at a time is within the critical region of code that accesses the resource. See also semaphore.

NAK (negative acknowledgment) *n.*

DECnet

A BYSYNC protocol data-link character used to indicate that the previous transmission block was in error and the receiver is ready to accept a retransmission of the erroneous block. NAK is also the "not ready" reply to station selection (multipoint) or to an initialization sequence (line bid) in point-to-point operation. Same as negative acknowledgment.

naked indicator *n.*

DSM-11

The value of a previous global reference returned so that full references can be constructed from naked references. The naked indicator records the last global reference and its level within the array. See also naked reference.

naked reference *n.*

DSM-11

A feature that provides an abbreviated method for accessing global variables to reduce disk access time. This permits subsequent references to be made to a global reference, simply by specifying an up-arrow (^) followed by one or more subscripts. The variable name is assumed from the last global reference in which a name was explicitly stated. The first subscript in the naked reference replaces the last subscript in the previous reference (either naked or complete). See also naked indicator.

NAM *n.*

VAX/VMS

The abbreviation for name block. An RMS user data structure that contains supplementary information used in parsing file specifications. Same as name block.

name block (NAM) *n.*

VAX/VMS

An RMS user data structure that contains supplementary information used in parsing file specifications. Same as NAM.

named data *n.*

FMS

An ordered collection of information useful to the application program and associated with a specific form, but not displayed on the screen. A named data group consists of (n) constants, each of which can be accessed by a unique name or by its index.

named file *n.*

DECsystem-10

A named ordered collection of 36-bit words (instructions and/or data) whose length is limited only by the available space on the device and the user's maximum space allotment on that device.

name scoping *n.*

VAX COBOL

A term used to describe the methods for resolving references to user-defined words in a contained program environment.

NAND *adj.*

generic

Pertaining to a function of A and B that is true if either A or B is false, pertaining to a completed AND or NOT AND device.

native character set *n.*

COBOL-74

A character set defined by the implementor and specified in the OBJECT-COMPUTER paragraph.

GIGI

The 128 ASCII character set; for GIGI, 95 of these characters are displayable.

native collating sequence *n.*

COBOL-74

A collating sequence defined by the implementor and specified in the OBJECT-COMPUTER paragraph.

native image *n.*

VAX/VMS

An image whose instructions are executed in native mode.

native mode *n.*

VAX/VMS

The VAX processor's primary execution mode in which the programmed instructions are interpreted as byte-aligned, variable-length instructions that operate on the following data types: byte, word, longword, and quadword integers, floating and double floating character strings; packed decimals; and variable-length bit fields. The other instruction execution mode is compatibility mode.

NAU *n.*

DECnet

The abbreviation for network addressable unit. A resource managed by the SNA (systems network architecture) communications system. There are three types of NAUs: SSCP (system services control point), physical units, logical units.

NCB *n.*

VAX PSI

The abbreviation for network connect block. The block that contains the necessary information to set up a virtual circuit or to accept or reject a request to set up a virtual circuit. Same as network connect block.

NCP *n.*

DECnet and VAX/VMS

The abbreviation for network control program. The NCP is the control program that implements the second-level host/host protocol for a specific operations system. The TOPS-20AN NCP is based on TENEX, Released 1.34, with limited modifications necessary for adherence to TOPS-20 coding standards. The NCP for TOPS-20AN is embedded in the TOPS-20AN monitor. Same as network control program.

NCP/VS *n.*

DECnet

The abbreviation for IBM network control program/virtual storage. The control program for the IBM 3704 and 3705 programmable communications controller (CC). In a configuration using the RSX-11M/SNA Protocol Emulator (PE), the CC must be attached to the PE by an SDLC line. Same as network control program/virtual storage.

NCU *n.*

DECnet

The abbreviation for network control utility, a utility that executes network control commands. NCU implements the network information and exchange (NICE) protocol. NCU refers to one of the three major programs of NETCON. Same as network control utility.

negated combined condition *n.*

COBOL-74

The 'NOT' logical operator immediately followed by a simple condition.

negative acknowledgment (NAK) *n.*

DECnet

A BYSYNC protocol data-link character used to indicate that the previous transmission block was in error and the receiver is ready to accept a retransmission of the erroneous block. NAK is also the "not ready" reply to station selection (multipoint) or to an initialization sequence (line bid) in point-to-point operation. Same as NAK.

negative writing *n.*

GIGI

The reversed interpretation of the dot pattern GIGI used for writing.

nested *adj.*

DIGITAL-specific

Contained within, as in a function declared within a procedure or a record that is a field of another record.

generic

Pertaining to the process of including subroutines or bits of data into larger routines or blocks of data.

nested conditional instruction *n.*

Terminal Data Management System

A conditional instruction contained within an outer conditional instruction. TDMS (Terminal Data Management System) executes the inner conditional instruction only if it executes the associates outer conditional instruction.

nesting *n.*

generic

The placement of a block statement inside a block statement, or a subroutine within another subroutine.

NETACP *n.*

VAX/VMS

The abbreviation for network ancillary control process. In SNA (systems network architecture) NETACP is an auxiliary control process that provides the same functions and device support for session control as does the network control program. Same as network ancillary control process. See also ancillary control process.

NETCON *n.*

DECnet

The acronym for a specialized network control task that accepts requests by operator commands and command files. NETCON processes network control requests such as the loading or dumping of communications front end software, the loading or dumping of communications front end synchronous line controllers, the displaying of line statistics for any line, etc. Same as specialized network control task.

NETGEN *n.*

DECnet

NETGEN is the interactive program used to describe the hardware and software during the configuration procedure for a DECnet node.

net income *n.*

generic

The amount by which total revenues exceed total expenses for an accounting period. Same as earnings, "bottom line", and profit.

net loss *n.*

generic

The excess of all expenses and losses for a period over all revenues and gains of the period; negative net income.

net sales *n.*

generic

Sales less returns and allowances, freight, and discounts.

network *n.*

generic

In data communication, a configuration in which two or more terminals or devices are connected to enable information transfer.

VAX/VMS

A collection of interconnected individual computer systems.

network addressable unit *n.*

DECnet

A resource managed by the SNA (systems network architecture) communications system. There are three types of network addressable units: SSCP, physical units, and logical units.

network ancillary control process (NETACP) *n.*

VAX/VMS

In SNA (systems network architecture), NETACP is an auxiliary control process that provides the same functions and device support for session control as does the network control program. Same as NETACP. See also ancillary control process.

network application layer *n.*

DECnet

A layer that provides generic services to the user layer. Service includes remote file access, remote file transfer, remote interactive terminal access, gateway access to non-DNA (DIGITAL Network Architecture) systems, and resource managing programs. This layer contains both user-supplied and DIGITAL-supplied modules.

network connect block (NCB) *n.*

DECnet

The network connect block is a user-generated data structure used in a nontransparent task to identify a remote task and to send user data in calls to request, accept, or reject a logical link connection. Same as NCB.

VAX PSI

A block that contains the information necessary to set up a virtual circuit or to accept or reject a request to set up a virtual circuit. Same as NCB.

VAX/VMS

For DECnet, a user-generated data structure used in a nontransparent task to identify a remote task and optionally send user data in calls to request, accept, or reject a logical link connection.

For VAX PSI, a block that contains the information necessary to set up an X.25 virtual circuit or to accept or reject a request to set up an X.25 virtual circuit.

network control program *n.*

DECnet and VAX/VMS

The block that contains the necessary information to set up a virtual circuit or to accept or reject a request to set up a virtual circuit. Same as NCP.

VAX PSI

A DECnet programthat provides the commands for configuring and monitoring the VAX PSI (packet switching interface) product.

network data structure *n.*

VAX DATATRIEVE

A data structure in which any given element may be related to any other element within the database. Networks show interset relationships. A network structure is a superset of a tree structure.

network dialogue *n.*

DECnet

An exchange of information among interrelated groups of nodes. See also computer network.

network diameter *n.*

DECnet

The network diameter is the maximum diameter over the set of shortest paths between all pairs of nodes in the network.

network earth reference *n.*

Ethernet

Refers to the metallic connection point that has been selected by the system planner as the ground voltage for the Ethernet system.

network file transfer (NFT) *n.*

DECnet

A program that allows users to access or delete files residing on DECnet hosts that provide network file access capabilities. NFT initiates the service requests that will be carried by the FAL program. Same as NFT.

network information and control exchange (NICE) *n.*

DECnet

In the network management layer of DNA (DIGITAL Network Architecture), the protocol used for triggering down-line loading, up-line dumping, testing, reading parameters and counters, setting parameters, and zeroing counters. Same as NICE.

Network Interconnect *n.*

DIGITAL-specific

Digital's name for the Ethernet. Same as NI.

network management layer *n.*

DECnet

A layer that provides user control of and access to operational parameters and counters in lower layers. Network management also performs down-line loading, up-line dumping, remote system control, and test functions. In addition, network management performs event logging functions.

network object *n.*

DECnet and VAX/VMS

A task with a nonzero object type (e.g., programs such as FAL and NML that provide generic services across a network).

network services layer *n.*

DECnet

The layer responsible for the system-independent aspects of creating and managing logical links for network users. End communication modules perform data flow control, end-to-end error control, and segmentation and reassembly of user messages. Same as end communication layer.

network services protocol *n.*

DECnet

A formal set of conventions used in DECnet to perform network management and to exchange messages over logical links.

network status notifications *n.*

DECnet and VAX/VMS

Provide information about the state of both logical and physical links over which two tasks communicate. A nontransparent task can use this information to take appropriate action under conditions such as third party disconnections and a partner's exiting before I/O completion.

network structure n.

VAX DBMS

A general form of data structure in which any given element may be related to any other element in the structure. Networks are used to show interset relationships.

network task n.

DECnet and VAX/VMS

A network task is a nontransparent task that is able to process multiple inbound connection requests (i.e., it has declared a network name or object number).

network virtual terminal protocols n.

DECnet

In the network application layer of DNA (DIGITAL Network Architecture), a family of protocols used for terminal access through the network.

new fields n.

VAX DATATRIEVE

Temporary fields the user can create for reports and the output of PRINT statements by values in elementary fields of one or more rewords.

NEW PAGE mark (or new page marker) n.

DIGITAL-specific

A character that forces all text following it to the top of the next printed page.

next n.

VAX DBMS

A set-ordering criterion requiring that new records be placed immediately after a record occurrence established by the user program.

next record n.

COBOL-74 and VAX DBMS

The record that logically follows the current record of a file.

RSX-11M

The target of a sequential GET that is not immediately preceded by a FIND or a PUT operation. Next record is part of the content of a record access stream.

NFT n.

DECnet

The abbreviation for network file transfer. A program that allows users to access or delete files residing on DECnet hosts that provide network file access capabilities. NFT initiates the service requests that will be carried out by the FAL program. Same as network file transfer.

NI n.

DIGITAL-specific

The abbreviation for Network Interconnect; NI is Digital's name for the Ethernet. Same as Network Interconnect.

nibble n.

DIGITAL-specific

Four contiguous bits of memory; one half of a byte.

NICE n.

DECnet

The acronym for network information and control exchange. In the network management layer of DNA (DIGITAL Network Architecture), the protocol used for triggering down-line loading, up-line dumping, testing, reading parameters and counters, setting parameters, and zeroing counters. Same as network information and control exchange.

NICE protocol *n.*

DECnet

The network information and control exchange (NICE) protocol that enables various DIGITAL computers to access information and control facilities of remote nodes on the same network.

node *n.*

Common Data Dictionary

In the CDD (Common Data Dictionary) message files, the word node is sometimes used as a generic name for dictionary directories, subdictionaries, and objects.

generic

In data communications, the point at which one or more functional units connect transmission lines.

VAX/VMS

An individual computer system in a network that can communicate with other computer systems in the network.

node address *n.*

DECnet

The unique numeric identification of a specific node.

VAX/VMS

The required, unique, numeric identification required of each node in the network.

node identification *n.*

DECnet

Either a node name or a node address. In some cases an address must be used as a node identification. In other cases, a name must be used. A table is maintained for converting one to the other.

node level loopback test *n.*

DECnet

Testing a logical link using messages that flow with normal data traffic through the session control, network services, and transport layers within one node or from one node to another and back. In some cases, node level loopback testing involves using a loopback node name associated with a particular line.

node name *n.*

DECnet

A one- to six-character name uniquely identifying a node within a network. Node names can be any combination of the characters A through Z, and 0 through 9.

VAX/VMS

An optional alphanumeric identification associated with a node address in a strict one-to-one mapping. A node name must contain at least one alphabetic character.

node name mapping table *n.*

DECnet

A table that defines the correspondence between node names and node addresses or channel numbers. Session control uses the table to identify destination nodes for outgoing connect requests and source nodes for incoming connect requests.

node number *n.*

DECnet

A number uniquely identifying a node within a network. Although NSP (network services protocol) allows node numbers of 2 through 240, DECnet-20 nodes may only be assigned numbers 2 through 127.

node specification *n.*

VAX/VMS

The first field in a file specification, which identifies the location of a computer system in a network.

NO ECHO *n.*

generic

A field attribute indicating that any valid character typed by an operator or sent by an application program will not appear on the screen. The attribute is most frequently used to keep passwords private.

noise *n.*

Medical Systems and MSG (SPETS)

An unwanted disturbance of data.

Nonanchored Choice *n.*

ALL-IN-1

When using Recognition, Nonanchored Choice lists all the possible choices for a partial entry.

Nonanchored Recognition *n.*

ALL-IN-1

When using Recognition, Nonanchored Recognition supplies the rest of a partial entry.

non-blocking I/O *n.*

TOPS-10

In buffered modes, a characteristic by which the program does not block while waiting for a buffer to be filled or emptied.

nonbreaking hyphen *n.*

DIGITAL-specific

A hyphen used to join two words that must not be divided at the end of a line, such as the hyphens in a telephone number.

nonbusiness organization *n.*

generic

Municipalities, hospitals, religious organizations, and other organizations that are not operated for the purpose of earning a profit.

noncomputational *adj.*

VAX PL/I

Pertaining to a data item that is not string or arithmetic. The noncomputational data types are entry, file, label, pointer, area, and offset.

nonconductor *n.*

generic

A material that does not transmit heat, electricity, light, sound, and so forth.

noncontiguous file *n.*

generic

A file in which blocks are not necessarily next to each other.

non-directory device *n.*

DIGITAL-specific

A device on the TOPS-10 (such as a magnetic tape or paper tape) that does not contain a file describing the names and layout of data files.

non-directory-structured *adj.*

DIGITAL-specific

Pertains to a storage volume that is sequential in structure and therefore has no volume directory at its beginning. File information (file name, file type, length, and date-of-creation) is provided with each file on the volume. Such volumes include magtape and cassette.

non-displayable characters *n.*

DIGITAL-specific

Characters that cannot be displayed on a terminal or printed on a listing (ASCII characters with a value less than octal 40 and greater than 126). Control characters, for example, are non-displayable characters.

nonfatal *adj.*

CTS-300

Pertaining to an error that does not impair the basic operation of the computer. A nonfatal error can be detected and investigated by a part of the operating system or run-time system and the results can be displayed or used to make a programmed decision. Same as trappable.

non-file-structured device *n.*

DIGITAL-specific

A device such as a paper tape, line printer, or terminal in which data cannot be organized as multiple files.

generic

A device, such as a papertape reader, printer or terminal, in which data is not referenced as a file.

nonkey *adj.*

DIGITAL-specific

Refers to any field that is not used as a key field. See also primary key; alternate key.

nonlocal GOTO *n.*

VAX PL/I

A GOTO statement that results in a transfer of program control to a statement in a previous block.

nonmatching control *n.*

PEARL

A control that, when transferred on the control-channel of a DATION (DATA STATION), changes the internal states of the DATION.

nonnumeric item *n.*

COBOL-74

A data item whose description permits its contents to be composed of a combination of characters taken from the computer's character set. Certain categories of nonnumeric items can be formed from more restricted character sets.

nonnumeric literal *n.*

COBOL-74

A character-string bound by quotation marks. The string of characters can include any character in the computer's character set. To represent a single quotation mark character within a nonnumeric literal, two contiguous quotation marks must be used.

nonoverlaid *adj.*

RSX-11M

Pertaining to a task that does not include overlay segments. All of a nonoverlaid task must fit in the available virtual address space (64KB) and is brought into memory when the task is run.

non-packet-mode DTE *n.*

VAX PSI

A DTE (data terminal equipment) that is unable to handle data in packet form. This DTE must interface through a packet assembly/disassembly (PAD) facility to connect to a PSDN (packet switching data network).

non-PIC *n.*

VAX/VMS

A shortened form of non-position-dependent code, the opposite of position-independent code (PIC). Non-PIC refers to code that cannot execute properly without modification of an address of the virtual address space.

nonprinting character *n.*

VAX/VMS

A character in the computer code set for which there is no corresponding graphic symbol.

nonprivileged *adj.*

DECnet and VAX/VMS

In DECnet-VAX terminology, nonprivileged means no privileges in addition to NETMBX, which is the minimal requirement for any network activity.

DIGITAL-specific

Pertains to having no privileges beyond the minimal requirement for conducting any computer activity.

nonprivileged account *n.*

RSTS/E

An account that allows users to work with their own files but restricts access to system-wide operations.

nonprivileged user *n.*

DIGITAL-specific

Users who have access to most of the system's facilities but cannot alter the system.

nonprivileged user program *n.*

DIGITAL-specific

A program that runs in user mode and does not refer to I/O devices, directly control the memory management unit, or directly access the processor internal registers.

nonprofit organization *n.*

generic

An organization whose profits cannot be distributed to owners.

non-recourse *n.*

USFC/generic

A condition in which a lessor assigns a lease to a funding source and is no longer liable if the lessee defaults.

nonreference object *n.*

PEARL

An object whose content is a value.

nonrouting node *n.*

DECnet

A Phase III DECnet node that contains a subset of routing modules (select process and receive process) and can deliver and receive packets. It is connected to the network by a single line.

generic

A node that can send or receive its information but can not send information received from another node. See also end node.

VAX/VMS

An end node.

non-sharable segment *n.*

TOPS-10

A segment for which each user has his or her own copy. This segment can be created by a CORE or REMAP UUO, or initialized from a file.

nonsingular set *n.*

VAX DATATRIEVE and VAX DBMS

A set that is not owned by the SYSTEM but owned by a user-defined record. See also SYS-TEM-owned set, owner record, and member record.

nonsingular set type *n.*

VAX DBMS

In DBMS, a set type owned by a user-defined record type, not by the SYSTEM record. See also SYSTEM-owned set, member record type, and owner record type.

non-standard default packet size *n.*

VAX PSI

An optional PSDN (packet switching data network) facility that permits a DTE (data terminal equipment) to specify a default packet size that is different from the PSN's default.

non-switched line (or nonswitched line) *n.*

DECnet

A communications link which is permanently installed between two points.

non-transparent mode *n.*

DECnet

Transmission of characters in a defined character format like ASCII or EBCDIC, in which all defined control characters and control character sequences are recognized and treated as such.

nontrappable *adj.*

CTS-300

Pertaining to an error that is of such magnitude that should it occur the system is not capable of reliably performing any logical operation. See also fatal (error).

No-op *n.*

TOPS-10

An instruction that specifically instructs the computer to do nothing. The next instruction in sequence is then executed.

normal flow *n.*

DECnet

The transmission protocol that governs data flow in SNA (systems network architecture). Normal-flow send/receive mode is observed by transmissions in which the value of bit 7, byte 0 in the transmission header is zero.

normalization (of a database) *n.*

DIGITAL-specific

A process used to:

- Reduce a database structure to its simplest form

- Avoid data redundancy

- Identify all data that is dependent on other data

normalize v.

generic

To make an adjustment to the fixed-point part and a corresponding adjustment to the exponent in a floating-point name of a number to make sure that the fixed part is within a limited range, the number represented staying with no changes.

normalized fraction n.

VAX/VMS

The numeric representation patterned for scientific notation, but in which the fraction part of the representation is greater than or equal to 0.5 and less than 1. As a binary form, such a fraction will always begin with a 1 in the leftmost (most significant) bit, unless the number is zero. Because of this, the lead 1 is not stored, and a bit-per-number saving is effected in storage.

normal termination n.

DIGITAL-specific

An error-free completion of a given task. The term DONE is not used because, unlike a DONE flag, a normal termination flag is not set if an error occurs. An error causes the error termination flag to be set.

note payable n.

generic

A liability of an entity.

note receivable n.

generic

An amount owed to an entity.

novalidate mode n.

Terminal Data Management System

The mode in the TDMS (Terminal Data Management System) request definition utility that lets the user create and store a request without checking for correct mappings and references. It creates a request in novalidate mode by using the SET NOVALIDATE command. Validate mode is the default. See also validation.

NSP n.

DECnet and VAX/VMS

The abbreviation for network services protocol. A formal set of conventions used in DECnet to perform network management and to exchange messages over logical links. NSP also refers to the software that implements the NSP protocol. Same as network services protocol.

null n.

VAX DBMS

An attribute associated with currency indicators and data items defined in a subschema. This attribute is independent of the value of the contents of the data items. A null condition indicates that the currency indicator points to no data item or that the data item was not initialized by the run unit.

VAX/VMS

1. The character with the ASCII code 000.

2. An absence of information.

null adj.

generic

Of or pertaining to a mathematical set having no units; pertaining to zero value.

VAX DBMS

Pertaining to that which is not usable, empty, having no meaning or value, or having a value of zero (or zeros).

null device n.

RSTS/E and TOPS-10

A software structure available on all RSTS/E systems for debugging I/O routines and for creating a buffer without tying up a physical device.

null key (characteristic) n.

RSX-11M

A flag associated with an alternate key that indicates whether or not a null key value is defined for the key. For binary, integer, and packed decimal key data types, the null key value is zero expressed in that data type. For the string key data type, users must specify a byte value from 000(8) through 377(8) including ASCII codes. See also change key.

null modem n.

DECnet

A connection box that replaces two modems and their connecting wires to allow devices designed to interact through modems to be locally connected.

generic

A device that replaces a modem in operations in which a modem is usually needed.

null process n.

VAX/VMS

A small system process that is the lowest priority process in the system and takes one entire priority class. The only function of the null process is to accumulate idle processor time.

null string n.

generic

An empty string.

VAX/VMS

A string without content or an empty string represented by adjacent quotation marks.

numeric adj.

generic

Of or pertaining to a number or series of numbers.

numeric literal n.

COBOL-74

A literal composed of one or more numeric characters that also can contain either a decimal point, or an algebraic sign, or both. The decimal point must not be the rightmost character. The algebraic sign, must be the leftmost character.

DSM-11

A literal evaluated mathematically as an integer or decimal number. A numeric literal is one that contains the digits 0 through 9, the decimal point, the unary MINUS operator, the unary PLUS operator, or the letter E. DSM-11 accepts numeric literals with the range plus or minus 10 to the power of plus or minus 26.

generic

An operator specified literal that contains a decimal value.

numeric string n.

generic

A character string composed of an optional plus or minus sign, one or more optional digits (0 through 9), an optional decimal point (.), and more optional digits.

VAX/VMS

A contiguous sequence of bytes representing up to 32 decimal digits (one per byte) and possibly a sign. The numeric string is specified by its lowest addressed location, its length, and its sign representation.

numeric valued expression (nve) n.

DSM-11

A numeric valued expression (nve) is an expression which, when evaluated, produces a numeric result.

numeric variable *n.*

Medical Systems

A computer storage location reserved for a numeric value in the form of a single letter, or a single letter followed by a single digit.

NXM *n.*

RSX-20F

The abbreviation for nonexistent memory. A memory location that does not exist. Same as nonexistent memory.

NXM error *n.*

RSX-20F

An attempt to address a nonexistent memory location.

OA n.

generic

The abbreviation for office automation. OA refers to interactive applications designed to help office workers by simplifying their day-to-day duties and responsibilities, usually includes word processing, electronic mail, and calendar management. Same as office automation.

object n.

DIGITAL-specific

The basic named data definition stored in the CDD (Common Data Dictionary) that forms the end points of the CDD hierarchy branches. Same as dictionary object. See also scalar.

VAX/VMS

1. A DECnet-VAX process that receives a logical link request. It performs a specific network function or is a user-defined image for a special-purpose application.

2. A VAX PSI management component that contains records to specify account information for incoming calls and to specify a command procedure that is initiated when the incoming call arrives.

3. A system resource such as a file, device, or directory.

object code n.

generic

Relocatable machine language code that is output from an assembler or compiler.

object ID n.

Rdb/ELN

The value of a VAXELN system datatype after the datum has been created.

object module n.

generic

The primary unit of output of an assembler or compiler, which can be linked with other object modules and loaded into memory as a program to be executed.

VAX/VMS

The binary output of a language processor such as the assembler or a compiler, which is used as input to the linker.

object time system (OTS) n.

DIGITAL-specific

A collection of procedures that help support a higher level language. Same as OTS. See also run-time procedure library.

generic

The group of modules that is called by compiled code in order to perform many system functions.

MicroPower PASCAL

The MicroPower PASCAL library of object modules that is called by compiled or assembled code to perform predefined operations. Same as OTS.

VAX/VMS

The collection of procedures available to native mode images at run time. These procedures may be used by all native mode images, regardless of the language processor used to compile or assemble the program. These procedures also provide support routines for high-level language compilers. Same as Run-Time Procedure Library.

object type n.

DECnet

A numeric value that may be used for process or task addressing by DECnet processes instead of a process name.

VAX/VMS

A discrete identifier for either a task or DECnet service on a remote node. Object type identifiers can either be 0 plus a name (alternatively, TASK=name), or nonzero without a name (for example, 17= or FAL=).

octal *adj.*

generic

Pertaining to a number system using a base of 8.

octal number *n.*

VAX/VMS

A number in the base-8 numbering system. Only the numerals 0 through 7 are used in this system. If a number includes an 8 or a 9, it cannot be an octal number. Octal numbering is used in computer systems because it is easy to convert to the binary numbers that are actually used by the computer.

octaword *n.*

VAX/VMS

Sixteen contiguous bytes starting on an arbitrary byte boundary. The bits are numbered from the right 0 through 127. An octaword is specified by its address A, the address of the byte containing bit 0. When interpreted arithmetically, an octaword is a two's complement integer with bits of increasing significance going 0 through 126 and bit 127 is the sign bit. The value of the integer is in the range -2 (sup 127) to 2 (sup 127) -1. The octaword data type is not yet fully supported by VAX instructions.

octet *n.*

DIGITAL-specific

A group of 8 bits; a byte.

ODL file *n.*

RSTS/E, RSX-11M, and VAX/VMS

A file containing ODL (overlay description language) statements that describes all or part of the overlay structure for a task. ODL files are control files for the Task Builder.

ODT *n.*

DIGITAL-specific

The abbreviation for on-line debugging technique. An interactive program linked with a user program for finding and correcting errors in the program. All addresses and data are communicated in octal notation. Same as on-line debugging technique.

OEM *n.*

generic

The abbreviation for original equipment manufacturer. A phrase for equipment sold by one company to another for use in its products. Same as original equipment manufacturer.

off balance sheet financing *n.*

USFC/generic

Financing that allows for payment over time and is not shown as a liability on the company's balance sheet.

office automation (OA) *n.*

generic

Interactive applications designed to help office workers by simplifying their day-to-day duties and responsibilities, usually includes word processing, electronic mail, and calendar management. Same as OA.

off-line *adj.*

DIGITAL-specific

Pertaining to equipment or devices not currently under direct control of the computer.

generic

Pertaining to a condition or operation in which a device cannot communicate with or be controlled by the host processor.

offset *n.*

DECnet

The difference between a location of interest and some known base location, i.e., bytes relative to the base of an array.

DIGITAL-specific

A data item whose value represents a displacement from the beginning of an area.

FFE

An FFE editing value that specifies a shift for the character bitmap when printing.

generic

A specific displacement from a starting point.

VAX/VMS

A fixed displacement from the beginning of a data structure. System offsets for items within a data structure normally have an associated symbolic name used instead of the numeric displacement. Where symbols are defined, programmers always reference the symbolic names for items in a data structure instead of using the numeric displacement.

off state *adj.*

DECnet

In the case of a line, a state in which the line is unavailable for any kind of traffic.

Ohm *n.*

generic

A unit of measurement; the unit of electrical resistance through which a potential difference of one volt will maintain a current of one ampere.

OIC *n.*

DECnet

The abbreviation for only-in-chain. A message consisting of 256 or fewer bytes. An OIC is indicated by setting FIC (first-in-chain) and LIC (last-in-chain) in the request response header. Responses are always OIC. In EC (emulator control) and XEC (extended emulator control) modes, OIC messages are marked as such by the PE (protocol emulator) for data flowing from RSX-11M to SNA (systems network architecture). For messages flowing the other way, SNA sets FIC and LIC indicators. This condition specifies only-in-chain. Same as only-in-chain.

once-only time *n.*

TOPS-10

The time at which the operator can change a number of monitor parameters when the monitor is started up (prior to scheduling any jobs).

on condition *n.*

DIGITAL-specific

The process of establishing a condition handler. See also condition.

VAX PL/I

Any one of several named conditions that can interrupt a program and generate a signal, such as a fixed-point or a floating-point overflow.

On-Disk Structure Level 1 (ODS-1) *n.*

VAX/VMS

The original Files-11 structure used by IAS, RSX-11M, and RSX-11D for disk volumes. VAX/VMS supports structure level 1 to ensure compatibility among systems. Same as Files-11 Structure Level 1.

On-Disk Structure Level 2 (ODS-2) *n.*

VAX/VMS

The second generation disk file structure supported by VAX/VMS. Same as Files 11 Structure Level 2.

one's complement *n.*

RT-11, TOPS-10 and VAX/VMS

A number formed by interchanging the bit polarities in a binary number: for example, 1s become 0s, 0s become 1s. See also bit complement.

one-time setting *n.*

DECmate II

The print settings for number of copies (CP), first page printed (FR), and last page printed (TO). They reset to their initial values (CP1, FR1, TO0) after a document is printed or filed.

one-way logical channel incoming *n.*

VAX PSI

An optional PSDN (packet switching data network) facility that prevents a particular logical channel from handling outgoing calls.

on-line (or online) *adj.*

generic

1. Pertaining to a condition in which a unit can communicate with the host processor.

2. Pertaining to equipment or devices directly connected to and under control of the computer.

ON state *n.*

DECnet

A state in which normal line use is allowed. Applied to a node: a state of normal network condition. Applied to a line: a state of availability for normal usage. Applied to logging: a state where a sink is available for receiving events.

ON-unit *n.*

VAX PL/I

PL/I statement or begin block specifying the action to be taken when a specific ON condition is signaled during the execution of a PL/I program.

opcode (or op-code, operations code) *n.*

DIGITAL-specific

The pattern of bits within an instruction that specifies the operation to be performed. Same as operations code.

OPCOM *n.*

TOPS-20 and VAX/VMS

The acronym for operator communication manager. A system process to control communication between a process and the system operator.

open *n.*

TOPS-20

The operation of associating an I/O channel with a particular file.

open accounts *n.*

VAX/VMS

Accounts that do not require passwords.

open control *n.*

PEARL

A non-matching control that can be issued in an open statement.

open curve sequence *n.*

GIGI

A series of points of GIGI used to interpolate a curve whose end points do not meet.

open item *adj.*

generic

Pertaining to an accounting method by which payments and credits are applied against specific invoices.

open mode *n.*

COBOL-74

The state of a file after execution of an OPEN statement for that file, and before the execution of a CLOSE statement for that file. The particular open mode is specified in the OPEN statement as either INPUT, OUTPUT, I/O, or EXTEND.

open subroutine *n.*

TOPS-10

A sequence of code which is inserted into a routine at each place it is used. Very short subroutines are frequently used as open subroutines because they do not warrant the use of the calling sequences required by closed subroutines.

operand *n.*

BASIC-PLUS-2, DSM-11, and RT-11

An expression or expression atom used by an operator to produce a result.

COBOL-74

Any component that is operated upon; any lowercase word (or words) that appears in a statement or entry format can be considered to be an operand and, as such, is a reference to the data indicated by the operand.

DECsystem-10

1. The data accessed when an operation (either a machine instruction or a higher level operation) is executed.

2. The symbolic expression representing that data or the location in which that data is stored, for example, the input data or arguments of a pseudo-op or macro instruction.

operand *adj.*

DIGITAL-specific

Pertaining to that which is or can be operated upon.

operand specifier *n.*

VAX/VMS

The pattern of bits in an instruction that indicates the addressing mode and register, or displacement that identifies an instruction operand.

operand specifier type *n.*

VAX/VMS

The access type and data type of an instruction's operand(s). For example, the text instructions are of read-access type, since they only read the value of the operand. The operand can be of byte, word, or longword data type, depending on whether the opcode is for the TSTB (test bytes), TSTW (test word), or TSTL (test longword) instruction.

operating expenses *n.*

generic

Expenses associated with operating activities.

operating income *n.*

generic

The difference between revenues and operating expenses.

operating system *n.*

generic

1. An integrated collection of programs that controls the execution of computer programs and performs system functions.

2. Software that organizes a central processor and peripheral devices into an active unit for the development and execution of programs.

operation *n.*

generic

The action specified by a single computer instruction.

operational sign *n.*

COBOL-74

An algebraic sign, associated with a numeric data item or a numeric literal, that indicates whether its value is positive or negative.

operation code *n.*

DIGITAL-specific

The pattern of bits within an instruction that specifies the operation to be performed. Same as opcode, or op-code.

operator *n.*

DSM-11

A component of a DSM-11 expression that invokes an algorithm to perform either arithmetic, string, or Boolean manipulations.

generic

1. A person who controls the running or function of a machine or device.

2. The part of an instruction that tells the computer what to do. For example, the plus sign (+) is an operator telling the computer to perform addition.

PASCAL

Symbol used in an expression to cause PASCAL to perform a specific task. PASCAL includes arithmetic, relational, and logical operators.

VAX C

A token that performs an operation on one or more operands.

VAX PL/I

A punctuation symbol that requests or causes PL/I to perform a specific function such as addition or comparison.

VAX/VMS

The person responsible for daily maintenance of the system at a particular installation. The operator does such things as changing ribbons and paper on line printers, rebooting the system, keeping records, and so forth. In small systems, these duties may be combined with those of the system manager or informally divided among several people.

operator communication manager (OPCOM) *n.*

VAX/VMS

A system process that receives input from a process that wants to inform an operator of a particular status or condition, passes a message to the operator, and tracks the message. OPCOM is always active. See also OPCOM.

operator's console *n.*

VAX/VMS

Any terminal identified as a terminal attended by a system operator.

option n.

generic

A choice that can be made from menus.

RT-11

An element of a command or command string that enables the user to select from among several alternatives associated with the command. In the RT-11 computer system, an option consists of a slash character (/) followed by the option name and a colon, and an option value.

optional argument n.

RGL/FEP

An argument that does not have to be specified in a RGL/FEP subroutine call; however, the punctuation that delimits it must be specified.

optional file n.

generic

An input file whose presence is not necessary each time the program executes. The program checks for the presence or absence of the file.

optional member n.

VAX DATATRIEVE

The specification of set membership such that the membership of a record occurrence in a set is not necessarily permanent. Its membership in a set occurrence may be changed without its being deleted from the database. Optional set membership of the record occurrence in a set is declared by the database administrator when the schema is defined.

VAX DBMS

The specification of set membership such that a record occurrence can be disconnected from the set. Its membership in a set occurrence may be changed without its being deleted from the database. See also fixed member, mandatory member, and retention class.

optional set membership n.

VAX DBMS

The specification of set membership such that the membership of a record occurrence in a set is not necessarily permanent.

optional word n.

COBOL-74

A reserved word that is included in a specific format only to improve the readability of the language, and that word is optional when the format in which the word appears is used in a source program.

or n.

generic

A logical operator that compares two expressions. When either expression is true, the logical condition is true.

order code n.

DECnet

A code that may be included in the WRITE data stream transmitted for a display station or printer. It provides additional formatting or definition of the WRITE data. See also buffer control order and printer format order.

order phase n.

FMS

In the Form Editor, a phase in which the order that fields are to be accessed by the Form Driver is established.

ordinal adj.

PASCAL

Pertaining to all nonreal scalar data types; it refers to INTEGER, CHARACTER, and BOOLEAN data types.

ordinal type *n.*

VAX PASCAL

A sequence of values having a one-to-one correspondence with the set of integers. The ordinal types in VAX PASCAL are INTEGER, UNSIGNED, CHAR, BOOLEAN, enumerated types, and subranges of these ordinal types.

OR gate *n.*

generic

A circuit with multiple inputs that provides the wanted output when any or all of the inputs are true.

orientation *n.*

FFE

A font value that specifies the way lines of text are printed across the page, and how characters are aligned in a font.

origin *n.*

FFE

The lowest left pixel of the character, and, therefore, the lower left corner of the Edit Buffer.

original equipment manufacturer (OEM) *n.*

generic

A phrase for equipment sold by one company to another for use in its products. Same as OEM.

originating packet *n.*

DECnet

A packet that began in a particular node's network services layer.

origin location *n.*

RGL/FEP

The location of the first x-coordinate and first y-coordinate. The default origin location is at the bottom left.

oscillator *n.*

generic

A circuit which produces a voltage of current waveform that varies between two values at a set rate.

oscilloscope *n.*

generic

An electronic device that produces a display or a CRT corresponding to some external input voltage as a function of time; the display shows the changes in electric current potential or pulses.

other data messages *n.*

DECnet

The NSP (network services protocol) data request, interrupt request, and interrupt messages. These are all the NSP data messages other than data segment. Because all other data messages move in the same data subchannel, it is useful to group them together.

OTS *n.*

DIGITAL-specific

The abbreviation for object time system. A collection of procedures that help support a higher level language. Same as object time system. See also run-time procedure library.

MicroPower PASCAL

The abbreviation for object time system. The MicroPower PASCAL library of object modules that is called by compiled or assembled code to perform predefined operations. Same as object time system.

outbound connection *n.*

DECnet

Refers to the fact that a task sends logical link connection requests.

VAX/VMS

A task's request for a logical link connection to another node.

Outbox *n.*

DIGITAL-specific

In Electronic Mail, the storage area where messages created by the user reside until they are sent.

outgoing calls barred *n.*

VAX PSI

An optional PSDN (packet switching data network) facility that prevents a DTE (data terminal equipment) from initiating any calls.

out-of-stock costs *n.*

generic

The estimated decrease in future profit as a result of losing customers because of insufficient inventory to meet customer demand.

output *adj.*

generic

Pertaining to the program or device where the results will appear.

output *n.*

generi

1. Information that is produced by a computer program.

2. That which is returned from a program, process, job, or task.

output *v.*

generic

To transfer data from a program or device to another program or device.

output *n.*

generic

Data that has been processed by the computer.

output file *n.*

generic

1. A file that contains the results of a processing operation, for example, a file that has been sorted or edited.

2. A file that is the product of a computer program.

output mode *n.*

COBOL-74

The state of a file after execution of an OPEN statement, with the OUTPUT or EXTEND phrase specified for that file, and before the execution of the CLOSE statement for that file.

output procedure *n.*

PASCAL and VAX PASCAL

A procedure that writes data into a file. Output procedures provided by PASCAL include WRITE, WRITELN, and PUT.

overflow *adj.*

generic

Pertaining to the condition that occurs when the maximum capacity is exceeded.

overflow n.

DIGITAL-specific

A condition that occurs when a mathematical operation yields a result whose magnitude is larger than the space allocated for storing the result.

generic

A condition that occurs when maximum capacity is exceeded.

overflow area n.

CTS-300

In an ISAM (integrated sequential access method) file, an area of size determined by the user in which the ISAM file places records that belong in an existing data group but cannot be placed in that group because it is full.

overhead n.

generic

Any cost not specifically or directly associated with the production or sale of goods and services.

overhead adj

generic

1. Pertaining to a characteristic of a communication device or medium used to project something over a presentor's head onto a viewing surface; generally used in such combinations as overhead projector or overhead transparency.

2. Pertaining to something that exceeds or is in addition to a normal amount, event, sequence, or other characteristic.

overhead bit n.

DECnet

A bit other than an information bit such as a check bit or framing bit.

overlay n.

DIGITAL-specific

1. The technique of repeatedly using the same sections of virtual address space to store different blocks of code and data during different stages of a program. When one routine is no longer needed in storage, another routine can replace all or part of it.

2. One of several blocks of code and data that can potentially occupy the same section of virtual address space.

generic

A process of continually writing over the same areas of internal storage during different phases of a program.

overlay v.

generic

To write over information with new information.

overlay description language (ODL) n.

RSX-11M and VAX/VMS

A set of statements and syntax that the Task Builder can interpret to build the overlay structure for a task. Same as ODL.

overlay runtime routines n.

VAX/VMS

A set of system library subroutines linked as part of an overlaid task that are called to load segments into memory.

overlay segment n.

generic

One of a number of sections of code that can occupy the same storage location at different times during execution.

RSX-11M

A section of a task treated as a unit that can overlay and be overlaid by other overlay segments.

RT-11

A section of code treated as a unit that can overlay code already in memory and be overlaid by other overlay segments when called from the root segment or another resident overlay segment. See also segment.

VAX/VMS

A segment that shares virtual address space with other segments, and is loaded when needed.

overlay structure *n.*

DIGITAL-specific

A system of overlays defined by one or more ODL (overlay description language) files. The structure consists of a root segment and optionally, one or more overlay segments.

generic

A system of overlays made up of a main segment with the option of one or more overlay segments.

overlay tree *n.*

VAX/VMS

A tree structure consisting of a root segment and optionally one or more overlay segments.

overlay writing *n.*

GIGI

A writing method in which the overlaid object (the object defined with the overlay setting) is displayed over the existing object. The overlaid object appears to cover the existing object.

RGL/FEP

A writing mode that provides a user with a transparent overlay of two intersecting graphic objects.

overstrike *v.*

DECWORD

To superimpose the current character on top of the preceding character by pressing Gold DEAD KEY.

overstrike mode *n.*

generic

The mode that causes a character typed on the keyboard to replace the character at the current cursor position on the screen. Overstrike mode moves the cursor to the right but does not cause other characters on the line to be shifted to the right.

overtype mode *n.*

PRO/Diskette System

The way PROSE handles what the user types in a file unless the <INSERT HERE> key is used. In overtype mode, PROSE deletes existing text if the user types over it.

overwrite *v.*

DECmate II and DECWORD

To put text in a document, replacing whatever text was there before. When a user files a document at the end of an editing session, DECWORD overwrites the previous version of the document.

owned area *n.*

RSX-20F

An area in the communications region that is for the use of the related processor. The related processor can READ and WRITE to and from this area.

owner *n.*

DIGITAL-specific and VAX/VMS

An owner (in the context system, owner, group, world) is the particular member of a group to which a file, global section, mailbox, or event flag cluster belongs.

owner process *n.*

VAX/VMS

The process or subprocess that creates a subprocess.

owner record *n.*

VAX DATATRIEVE and VAX DBMS

The head of a group of records that make up a set. There can be only one record type as the owner for each set and one owner record occurrence for each set occurrence. See also member, nonsingular set, and system-owned set.

owner record type *n.*

VAX DBMS

In DBMS, the record types that access entry points to the set occurrences. There can be only one record type as the owner for each set type and one owner record occurrence for each set occurrence. See also member record, nonsingular set, and system-owned set.

owner's equity *n.*

generic

The interest of owners in the assets of a business.

P0 *n.*

VAX/VMS

The lower-addressed half of process address space (P0 region). The program region contains the image currently being executed by the process and other user code called by the image. Same as program region.

P0BR *n.*

VAX/VMS

The processor register, or its equivalent in a hardware process control block, that contains the base virtual address of the page table entry for virtual page number 0 in a process program region. Same as Program Region Base Register.

P0LR *n.*

VAX/VMS

The processor register, or its equivalent in a hardware process control block, that contains the number of entries in the page table for a process program region. Same as Program Region Length Register.

P1 *n.*

VAX/VMS

The higher-addressed half of process space (the P1 region). Control region virtual addresses refer to the process-related information used by the system to control processes such as the kernel, executive, and supervisor stacks; the permanent I/O channels; exception vectors; and dynamically used system procedures (such as the command interpreter). The user stack is normally found in the control region. Same as control region.

P1BR *n.*

VAX/VMS

The processor register, or its equivalent in a hardware process control block, that contains the base virtual address of a process control region page table. Same as Control Region Base Register.

P1LR *n.*

VAX/VMS

The processor register, or its equivalent in a hardware process control block, that contains the number of nonexistent page table entries for virtual pages in a process control region.

P1 through P8 *n.*

VAX/VMS

1. A value passed to a command procedure equated to a symbol ranging from P1 through P8. See also command parameter.

2. An entry in the volatile or permanent database for a network management component.

Same as parameter.

pacing indicator (PI) *n.*

DECnet

A field in the request/response header. If set in a request header, PI indicates that the sender will expect a pacing response. If set in a response header, PI indicates the sender is ready to receive additional normal-flow RUs (request unit/response unit). Same as PI.

pack *v.*

generic

To compress data for more efficient storage or use.

TOPS-10

To compress data in memory or on a peripheral storage medium by taking advantage of known characteristics of the data so that the original data can be recovered.

pack *n.*

generic

A data storage medium made up of two or more magnetic disks. See also disk pack.

pack cluster *n.*

RSTS/E

The minimum number of blocks that the RSTS/E monitor allocates to all files on a particular disk. The pack cluster size is set when the disk is initialized; its minimum value is the device cluster size for the disk type.

RSX-11M

A single- or multi-block unit of disk storage assignment whose size is characteristic of a type of device. See also device cluster.

packed *adj.*

PASCAL and VAX PASCAL

Pertaining to that which is stored as densely as possible in the computer's memory. See also signed integer.

packed decimal *n.*

DIGITAL-specific

A method of representing a decimal number by storing a pair of decimal digits in 1 byte, taking advantage of the fact that only 4 bits are required to represent the number 0 through 9.

VAX/VMS

A method of representing a decimal number by storing a pair of decimal digits in 1 byte, taking advantage of the fact that only 4 bits are required to represent the numbers 0 through 9.

packed decimal key *n.*

RSX-11M

An indexed file key data type where a half-byte represents a decimal digit. See also two-byte signed integer, four-byte signed integer, string, two-byte unsigned binary, and four-byte unsigned binary.

packed decimal string *n.*

VAX/VMS

A contiguous sequence of up to 16 bytes interpreted as a string of 4-bit fields. Each field represents a digit except low-order 4 bits of the highest addressed byte, which represents the sign. The packed decimal string is specified by its lowest addressed location and the number of digits.

packet *n.*

DECnet

A group of bits, comprising data and control information, that is transmitted as a composite whole over a physical link. The data, control, and possibly error information are arranged in a specific format.

generic

A group of bits, including control and data elements, that is transmitted as a unit.

VAX PSI

The unit of data switched through a PSDN (packet switching data network); normally a user data field accompanied by a header carrying destination and other information.

VAX/VMS

A unit of data to be routed from a source node to a destination node; for VAX PSI, the unit of data switched through a PSDN. Normally a user data field accompanied by a header carrying destination and other information.

packet assembly/disassembly (PAD) facility *n.*

VAX PSI and VAX/VMS

A device at a PSDN (packet switching data network) node that allows access from an asynchronous terminal such as an LA36. The terminal connects to the PAD and the PAD puts the terminal's input data into packets (assembles) and takes the terminal's output data out of packets (disassembles).

packet control *n.*

VAX PSI

The functions concerned with the correct routine and reception of individual packets through the network.

packet lifetime control *n.*

DECnet

The Transport component that monitors lines to detect if a line has gone down, and prevents excessive looping of packets that have exceeded the maximum visit limit.

packet-mode DTE *n.*

VAX PSI

A DTE (data terminal equipment) that can handle data in packet form including the capability to assemble and disassemble packets. A computer is one type of packet-mode DTE.

packetnet system interface (PSI) *n.*

VAX PSI

The collective name for the hardware and software products that allow various DIGITAL operating systems to participate in a packet switching environment. Same as PSI.

packet receive sequence number (P(R)) *n.*

VAX PSI

The P(R) number indicates that all packets up to number −1 have been received. The P(R) number thus authorizes the transmission of further packets by updating the lower window edge.

packet send sequence number (P(S)) *n.*

VAX PSI

The P(S) number specifies the position of a packet in a sequential stream. The number starts at zero for the first packet and increases by one for each successive packet sent on one logical channel in one direction. The P(S) number may be either modulo 8 or modulo 128, although modulo 8 is the default for all PSDNs. A packet can be transmitted only if its P(S) is greater than or equal to the lower window edge and less than the upper window edge.

packet switching *n.*

DECnet

The directing of packets from source nodes to destination nodes by one or more intervening nodes. Routing nodes permit route-through. Same as route-through.

generic

A data transmission process using addressed packets, where a channel is occupied only for the duration of transmission of the packet.

VAX PSI

A data transmission process, utilizing addressed packets, in which a channel is occupied only for the duration of transmission of the packet. In certain data communication networks the data may be formatted into a packet or divided and then formatted into a number of packets (either by the data terminal equipment or by equipment within the network) for transmission and multiplexing purposes.

VAX/VMS

A data transmission process, utilizing addressed packets, whereby a channel is occupied only for the duration of transmission of the packet.

packet switching data network (PSDN) *n.*

VAX/VMS

A set of equipment and interconnecting links that provides a packet switching communications service to subscribers.

packet switching exchange (PSE) *n.*

VAX PSI

The equipment in PSS (packet switching service) that is responsible for accepting and routing packets and ensuring their correct arrival. Same as PSE.

packet switching interface (PSI) *n.*

DECnet

The collective name for the hardware and software products that allow various DIGITAL operating systems to participate in a packet switching environment. Same as PSI.

pad *v.*

DIGITAL-specific

To fill the remaining empty data positions in a field with one or more occurrences of a specific character. See also FILL CHARACTER, BLANK FILL, and ZERO FILL.

pad character *n.*

DECnet

Characters included in message streams to ensure complete transmission or reception of the first and last significant character of each transmission. This character consists of all 1-bits and, like the synchronous idle (SYN) character, is stripped off upon receipt and is not included in the received transmission.

padding *n.*

DIGITAL-specific

The process of adding characters to data to achieve a required length. In disk sequential files, RMS-11 adds a null byte (all bits 0) to user data record whose length is an odd number of bytes. Additionally, when users do not allow records to span disk blocks, RMS-11 writes null bytes in the gap between the last record in a block and the end of a block. However, on tape, RMS-11 uses circumflexes (^) to pad blocks. See also word aligned.

page *n.*

DECWORD

The part of a document that will be printed on one sheet of paper.

generic

In a text file, any number of lines terminated by a form feed character.

GIGI

Each image within a picture. A picture can contain one or many pages or images. A new page is created with the ERASE key.

RT-11

That portion of a text file delimited by form feed characters and generally 50 to 60 lines long. Corresponds approximately to a physical page of a program listing.

VAX DATATRIEVE

A fixed-length block of data transferred to and from storage.

VAX DBMS

A fixed-length block of data transferred to and from storage that is maintained by the DBMS-11 I/O routines.

VAX/VMS

1. A set of 512 contiguous byte locations beginning at an even 512-byte boundary used as the unit of memory mapping and protection.

2. The data between the beginning of file and a page marker, between two markers, or between a marker and the end of a file.

page *v.*

DIGITAL-specific

To selectively remove parts of a user's program from core memory.

page address registers (PAR) *n.*

MicroPower PASCAL

Registers containing the base addresses of one- to eight- 8KB blocks of memory. Same as PAR.

page breaking *v.*

DECWORD

To divide the text of a document into pages either manually, or automatically using DECWORD.

page descriptor register (PDR) *n.*

MicroPower PASCAL

A register containing access information about the 8KB pages of memory whose base is described by the corresponding PAR (page address register). Same as PDR.

page fault *n.*

VAX/VMS

An exception generated by a reference to a page that is not mapped into a working set.

page fault cluster size *n.*

VAX/VMS

The number of pages read in on a page fault.

page frame number (PFN) *n.*

VAX/VMS

The address of the first byte of a page in physical memory; the high-order 21 bits of the physical address of the base of a page. Same as PFN.

page frame number mapping (PFN mapping) *n.*

VAX/VMS

The process of mapping a section to one or more pages in physical memory or I/O space (as opposed to mapping it to a disk file). See also connect-to-interrupt. Same as PFN mapping.

page header *n.*

VAX DBMS

A fixed-length section of the page that contains page and storage area information. See also database pages.

page marker *n.*

DIGITAL-specific

A character or characters (generally a form feed) that separates pages in a file that is processed by a text editor.

VAX/VMS

A character or characters (generally a form feed) that separates pages in a file processed by a text editor.

322

pager n.

VAX/VMS

A set of kernel mode procedures that executes as the result of a page fault. The paper makes the page for which the fault occurred available in physical memory so that the image can continue execution. The pager and the image activator provide the operating system's memory management functions.

page table n.

VAX/VMS

A memory management data base used to account for virtual pages. See also system page table, process page table, and global page table.

page table entry (PTE) n.

DIGITAL-specific

An entry in the process page table that describes the location and status of a process page. In a global page table, a PTE describes the location and status of a page of a global section. In the system page table, a PTE describes the status and location of a page of the operating system. Same as PTE.

VAX/VMS

The data structure that identifies the physical location and status of a page of virtual address space. When a virtual page is in memory, the PTE contains the page frame number needed to map the virtual page to a physical page. When it is not in memory, the page table entry contains the information needed to locate the page of secondary storage (disk). Same as PTE.

page throw n.

generic

The British term for form feed.

pagination n.

generic

The division of a document into pages.

paging n.

generic

The separation of a program and data into fixed blocks, often 1,000 words, so that transfers between disk and core can take place in page units rather than as entire programs.

VAX/VMS

The action of bringing pages of an executing process into physical memory when referenced. When a process executes, all of its pages are said to reside in virtual memory. Only the actively used pages, however, need to reside in physical memory. The remaining pages can reside on disk until they are needed in physical memory. In VMS, a process is paged either when it references more pages than it is allowed to have in its working set or when it first activates an image in memory. When the process refers to a page not in its working set, a page fault occurs. This causes the operating system's pager to read in the referenced page if it is on disk (and, optionally, other related pages depending on a cluster factor), replacing the least recently faulted pages as needed. This system only pages a process against itself. The operating system's pager does not read in a referenced page if that page is on the free or modified list.

paintbrush n.

A-to-Z

The graph design function that allows you to ''paint'' the graph with four available colors.

PA keys *n.*

DECnet

In IBM 3270 applications, a type of program attention key that may be defined to solicit application program attention without requiring that input data be transmitted to the program. Only the attention identification (AID) character is transmitted to the program to identify the key that was pressed. Same as program access keys.

paper form *n.*

FMS

A printed document with spaces to be filled in, such as an employment application.

papertape *n.*

generic

A continuous, narrow paper or plastic about one inch wide on which data is represented by punched holes.

PAR *n.*

MicroPower PASCAL

The abbreviation for page address registers. Registers containing the base addresses of one- to eight- 8KB blocks of memory. Same as page address registers.

paragraph label *n.*

DECWORD

A way of numbering the paragraphs in the text by pressing Gold-number-PARA MARKER, where the number is any number from 0 to 9. The paragraphs will be labeled consecutively, and the type of labeling will depend on the number specified.

paragraph marker *n.*

DECWORD

An invisible character producing double spacing between paragraphs. Any new text entered begins at the left margin of the next line. Inserted by typing Gold PARA MARKER.

parallel data transmission *n.*

DECnet

A data communication technique in which more than one code element (for example, bit) of each byte is sent or received simultaneously.

parameter *n.*

DECnet

A volatile or permanent data base entry for a network management component.

generic

A variable that is given a specific value that is passed to a program before execution.

VAX C

A variable declared in an external function definition, between the function name and the body of the function.

VAX/VMS

1. A value passed to a command procedure equated to a symbol ranging from P1 through P8. See also command parameter.

2. An entry in the volatile or permanent database for a network management component.

parameters *n.*

DECnet

DNA (DIGITAL Network Architecture) values to which network management has access for controlling and monitoring purposes.

parent *n.*

Common Data Dictionary

A name applied to a dictionary or subdictionary in the CDD (Common Data Dictionary) that immediately precedes a directory, subdictionary, or object in the CDD hierarchy. The preceding directory or subdirectory is called the parent. The parent is said to own its children. A parent may have many children, but each dictionary directory, subdictionary, and object in the CDD may have only one parent. For example, given CDD$TOP and CDD$TOP.MANUFACTURING, CDD$TOP is the parent and CDD$TOP.MANUFACTURING is the child. CDD$TOP owns CDD$TOP.MANUFACTURING. See also child and descendant.

DSM-11

For any node in an array, the ancestor on the next higher level of an array. See also descendant and directory hierarchy.

TOPS-10

The node logically above (and schematically to the left of) the node on the same branch.

parity *n.*

generic

A method of checking if binary numbers or characters are correct by counting the ONE bits. In odd parity, the total number of ONE bits must be odd; in even parity, the total number of ONE bits must be even.

parity bit *n.*

generic

A binary digit added to a group of bits that checks to see if there are errors in the transmission.

parity check *n.*

DIGITAL-specific

A method of detecting errors when data is sent over a communications line. With even parity, the number of ones in a set of binary data should be even. With odd parity, the number of ones should be odd.

parse *v.*

DIGITAL-specific

To break a command string into its elements in order to interpret it. A PRINT command without a filespec, or with illegal characters in the filespec, will not parse correctly.

generic

To break a string of characters into primary components for the purpose of translation.

parsing *n.*

DECsystem-10

The systematic ordering of the elements in a command or line of coding. For example, parsing a FORTRAN command places the elements in standard form for the compiler.

VAX/VMS

1. Breaking a command string into its elements to interpret it.

2. Interpreting a file specification, as is done by RMS.

partial key lookup *n.*

CTS-300

A condition by which only part of a key is used by QUILL for a search. The part, however, must start at the beginning of the key and be contiguous from that beginning.

partial path name *n.*

Common Data Dictionary and Terminal Data Management System

The shortened form of a dictionary path name. It includes only the parts of the path name that follow the default CDD (Common Data Dictionary) directory name. Use either the full path name or the relative path name to refer to directories, subdictionaries, and objects in the CDD. See also relative path name.

partition *n.*

DSM-11

The memory area in which a job resides. A partition contains both routine and logical variable storage areas, as well as program state information necessary for the timesharing operation.

generic

A contiguous area of memory within which tasks are loaded and executed.

RSX-11M

A predetermined, contiguous area in memory in which tasks are loaded and executed. Each partition has the following characteristics:

1. a name

2. a defined size

3. a fixed starting address.

PASCAL function *n.*

MicroPower PASCAL

A PASCAL program unit that returns a value when executed. A function consists of a heading that includes the function's name, result variable type, and a block.

PASCAL procedure *n.*

MicroPower PASCAL

A PASCAL program unit that consists of a procedure heading and a block; when called, the procedure is executed as a unit.

pass *v.*

DIGITAL-specific

To send, as in "pass an argument." During a call, the application program passes (sends) an argument to a subroutine to set the value of that variable in the function or procedure to be performed.

pass *n.*

generic

One complete reading of a set of data and/or instructions.

passive search list *n.*

TOPS-10

An unordered list of the file structures that have been in the job's active search list but have been removed without ever having been dismounted. Device DSK is not defined by this list. See also active search list.

passive side *n.*

DECnet

With regard to MOP (maintenance operation protocol) loopback tests, the node that loops back the test messages.

password *n.*

DIGITAL-specific

A string of characters that in conjunction with other information, such as the user identification, uniquely confirms the user's identity to the system.

passwords *n.*

VAX/VMS

Character strings that users provide at login time to validate their identity and as a form of proof of their authorization to access the account. There are two kinds of passwords—system passwords and user passwords. User passwords include both primary and secondary passwords.

paste *v.*

DECmate II

To insert the contents of a paste area into the document being typed or edited by pressing PASTE. Users must first cut text into a paste area.

DECWORD

To insert a word that users supply when they log in to DECWORD. It is not seen on the display. Users can only gain access to an account if they know the password associated with it.

paste area *n.*

DIGITAL-specific

The storage location where the most recently cut text is kept. Its contents remain unchanged until another cut is made. Same as paste buffer.

pasteboard *n.*

VAXstation Display System

A finite Cartesian coordinate system used to define both the spatial relationships of virtual displays and the position of a window into the pasteboard.

paste buffer *n.*

DECWORD

The temporary storage area that holds text after it has been cut from a document. Same as paste area.

VAX/VMS

The default text buffer for cut-and-paste operations.

patch *n.*

generic

A change applied to the binary code instead of the source program.

patch *v.*

generic

To modify a program by inserting code.

patch level *n.*

RSX-11M

A number specifying the number of times an RMS-11 utility has been patched.

patch panel *n.*

generic

A board with temporary electrical connections and movable wires.

path *n.*

DECnet

The route a packet takes from source node to destination node. This can be a sequence of connected nodes between two nodes. See also directory path.

VAX/VMS

A route that is traced from one segment in the overlay tree to another segment in that tree.

path cost *n.*

DECnet

The sum of the line costs along a path between two nodes. See also line cost.

327

VAX/VMS

The sum of the circuit costs along a path between two nodes.

path-down *n.*

VAX/VMS

A path toward the root of the tree.

path length *n.*

DECnet

The number of hops along a path between nodes. See also hop.

VAX/VMS

The number of hops along a path between two nodes; that is, the number of circuits a packet must travel along to reach its destination.

path-loading *n.*

VAX/VMS

The technique used by the autoload method to load all segments on the path between a calling segment and a called segment.

path name *n.*

Common Data Dictionary and Terminal Data Management System

A unique designation that identifies a dictionary directory, subdictionary, or object in the CDD (Common Data Dictionary) hierarchy. The full path name joins the given names of directories and objects, beginning with CDD$TOP, ending with the given name of the object or directory users want to specify, and including the given names of the intermediate subdictionaries and directories. The names of the directories and objects are separated by periods.

FMS

The path name provides a unique designation for every directory and object in the CDD (Common Data Dictionary) hierarchy. It is a concatenation of the given names of all the directories passed through by a path traced from CDD$TOP to the particular dictionary directory or object users wish to specify.

path-up *n.*

VAX/VMS

A path away from the root of the tree.

pattern *n.*

generic

The visual texture that represents data values such as the filled section of a bar in a bar graph or the lines in a line graph.

pattern verification *n.*

DSM-11

Pattern verification is a feature that permits evaluation of text strings for the occurrence of desired combinations of alphabetic, numeric and punctuation characters. Pattern verification is specified by the ''?'' operator followed by pattern specification codes (PSC).

payroll taxes *n.*

generic

Taxes levied because salaries or wages are paid.

PC *n.*

VAX/VMS

The abbreviation for program counter. General register 15 (R15). At the beginning of an instruction's execution, the PC normally contains the address of a location in memory from which the processor will fetch the next instruction it will execute.

PCB *n.*

VAX/VMS

The abbreviation for process control block. A data structure used to contain the process context. The hardware PCB contains the hardware context. The software PCB contains the software context, which includes a pointer to the hardware PCS. Same as process control block.

PCB *n.*

generic

The abbreviation for printed circuit board. A circuit wired or etched on a phenolic or fiberglass material complete with all necessary components for performing a specific function. Same as printed circuit board.

PCBB *n.*

VAX/VMS

Process Control Block Base Register

PDR *n.*

MicroPower PASCAL

The abbreviation for page descriptor register. A register containing access information about the 8KB pages of memory whose base is described by the corresponding PAR. Same as page descriptor register.

PEARL task *n.*

PEARL

A separately executable process, several of which can run concurrently. See also task.

pel *n.*

generic

An acronym for pixel. Pel is a picture element: the smallest unit of information or data in a screen display. Same as pixel.

pen mode *n.*

FFE

An FFE editing value that specifies the effect of FFE drawing commands and cursor-moving functions.

PERFORMANCE *n.*

DIGITAL-specific

A command that invokes SPM tools on VAX/VMS systems. The PERFORMANCE verb with its parameters and qualifiers allows you to collect and report on system-wide and per-process performance statistics and to collect and analyze application program tuning data.

peripheral *adj.*

generic

A hardware device that is not a functional part of the CPU.

peripheral devices *n.*

generic

Any unit, distinct from the CPU and physical memory, that can provide the system with input or accept any output from it. Terminals, line printers, and disks are peripheral devices.

permanent data base *n.*

DIGITAL-specific

A file containing information about system components.

VAX/VMS

A file containing information about network management components. See also volatile database and configuration database.

permanent member *n.*

VAX DBMS

A record that, upon becoming a member of a set occurrence of a set type, must remain a member of that or some other occurrence of that set type until the record is erased from the database. Mandatory set membership is declared in the schema. See also fixed member, optional member, and mandatory member.

permanent virtual circuit (PVC) *n.*

DECnet and VAX PSI

A permanent logical association between two DTEs (data terminal equipment), which is analogous to a leased line. Transmission of packets on a PVC needs no call set up or call clearing by the DTE. Packets are routed directly by the network from one DTE to the other. Same as PVC.

VAX/VMS

A permanent logical association between two DTEs, which is analogous to a leased line. Packets are routed directly by the network from one DTE to the other.

per-process address space *n.*

VAX/VMS

The lowest-addressed half of virtual address space, where process instructions and data reside. Process space is divided into a program region and a control region. Same as per-process address space and process address space.

personal dictionary *n.*

DECWORD

A special dictionary that users create in a file named WORD.WPS. This dictionary acts as a user's personal default dictionary: DECWORD automatically looks for it unless another dictionary name is specified. See also dictionary.

PF key(s) *n.*

DECnet

In 3270 applications, a program attention key that may be defined to solicit application program attention that usually requires data to be read from the display buffer, along with the attention identification (AID) character.

DIGITAL-specific

The four keys along the top row of the keypad, marked PF1, PF2, PF3, and PF4 used to perform specific subroutines. Same as programmable function keys; program function keys.

PFN *n.*

VAX/VMS

The abbreviation for page format number. The actual number of a page in physical memory; the high-order 23 bits of a physical address. Same as page frame number. See also PFN data base.

PFN data base *n.*

VAX/VMS

The abbreviation for page frame number data base. The data base maintained by memory management to account for physical pages of memory. See also page frame number.

PFN mapping *n.*

VAX/VMS

The abbreviation for page frame number mapping. Mapping a section to one or more pages in physical memory or I/O space (as opposed to mapping it to a disk file). Same as page frame number mapping. See also connect-to-interrupt.

phantom n.

generic

A model of a wire. In open collector, open emitter, tristate, and MOS circuits, several gate (or transistor) outputs can be wire-tied together. In the network description, the outputs to be connected are given the same name.

A phantom is inserted because a wire was wire-tied or had a PULLUP or PULLDOWN declaration. The declarations WIREOR, WIREAND, WIREMOS, and TRISTATE govern the type of phantom inserted. In the command language, each phantom input has a special name for easy access. These names are discovered through the use of the EXAMINE/FANIN command.

phantom value n.

DIGITAL-specific

The result of two transactions making a calculation, then storing the same value for two different records.

phase n.

generic

The relationship shown in angles between current and voltage in an alternating-current circuit.

phase III end node n.

DECnet

A Phase III node that has implemented a subset of Phase III capabilities. A small routine node can send messages to and receive messages from adjacent nodes only. It has no "route-through" capability, and must rely on an adjacent full routine node for communication with nonadjacent nodes.

phoneme n.

generic

A base or functional sound in a natural language necessary in distinguishing different meanings of words.

photo-optic memory n.

generic

A memory that uses an optical medium for storage. For example, a laser might be used to record on photographic film.

photovoltaic adj.

generic

Pertaining to something that is capable of generating a voltage using light as input.

physical address n.

VAX/VMS

1. The address used by hardware to identify a location in physical memory or on directly addressable secondary storage devices such as disk. A physical memory address consists of a page frame number and the number of a byte within the page. A physical disk block address consists of a cylinder or track and sector number.

2. The unique address value associated with a given system on an Ethernet circuit. An Ethernet physical address is defined to be distinct from all other physical addresses or an Ethernet.

physical address space n.

DIGITAL-specific and VAX/VMS

The set of all possible 30-bit physical addresses that can be used to refer to locations in memory (memory space) or device registers (I/O space).

generic

The set of actual memory locations where information can be stored.

physical block *n.*

generic

An actual area on a mass storage device.

RSX-11M, VAX DATATRIEVE, and VAX/VMS

A block on a mass storage device, identified by its physical address. Physical blocks are device-oriented rather than volume-oriented or file-oriented. See also logical block number, virtual block number, and sector.

physical block number *n.*

VAX/VMS

A physical (device-oriented) address for identifying a block on a mass storage device. This is in contrast to the block's logical (volume-relative) address and its virtual (file-relative) address.

physical connectivity *n.*

DECnet

The condition of nodes being attached to each other by active lines.

physical device *n.*

generic

An I/O or peripheral storage device for a computer configuration.

physical inventory *n.*

generic

The amount of inventory currently on hand, obtained by making a physical count.

physical I/O functions *n.*

VAX/VMS

A set of I/O functions that allows access to all device level I/O operations except maintenance mode.

physical I/O operation *n.*

RSX-11M

The actual transfer of data between memory and disk, involving the positioning of the disk heads and the electrical flow of data. See also I/O operation.

physical link *n.*

DECnet

A communications path between two adjacent nodes. The physical link can be in the form of a dial-up line, leased line, radio, satellite link, or a channel-to-channel connector such as a DTE (data terminal equipment).

VAX/VMS

A signal-carrying medium that links two nodes in a network. Contrast with logical link.

physical mapping *v.*

VAX DATATRIEVE

The transformation of logical information to physical information; i.e., transforming the virtual block numbers in a file to physical addresses on a storage device.

physical memory *n.*

VAX/VMS

The memory modules connected to the SBI that are used to store both instructions that the processor can directly fetch and execute and any other data that a processor is instructed to manipulate. Also called main memory.

physical node *n.*

DECnet

A physical node consists of the hardware comprising a node. See also logical node.

physical page *n.*

RSX-11M

A physical page is the part of the printer form between one perforation and the next perforation. Standard line-printer paper has a physical page length of 66 lines. Each time the line printer encounters a form-feed character (CTRL/L), the line printer moves the paper to the top of the next physical page.

physical record *n.*

generic

The largest unit of data that an I/O device can transmit or receive in a single I/O operation.

TOPS-10

A record identified from the standpoint of the manner or form in which it is stored and retrieved; that is, one that is meaningful with respect to access. A block.

VAX DATATRIEVE

The largest unit of data that the read/write hardware of an I/O device can transmit or receive in a single I/O operation. The length of a physical record is device dependent. For example, a punched card can be considered the physical record for a card reader and is 80 bytes long. The physical record for an RP06 disk is a block, which is 512 bytes long.

physical screen coordinates *n.*

RGL/FEP

The coordinates the terminal uses to define how the screen is addressed.

physical unit name *n.*

TOPS-10

The name of a specific peripheral unit. It is a SIXBIT name consisting of three to six characters. Examples: FHA0, FHA1, DPA0, DPA7, LPT, DTA3.

physical UUOs *n.*

TOPS-10

A short form of physical unimplemented user operations. A physical UUO is used to ignore any logical names assigned by the user by specifying the OPEN and CALL UUOs with the request "physical only." This is used in response to the /PHYSICAL switch. It is also used when the logical-to-physical correspondence has already been made, for example, when the device was returned from the SYSSTR UUO. Same as physical unimplemented user operations.

PI *n.*

DIGITAL-specific

The abbreviation for priority interrupt. An interrupt that usurps control of the computer from the program or monitor and jumps to an interrupt service routine if its priority is higher than the interrupt currently being serviced. Same as priority interrupt.

PI *n.*

DECnet

The abbreviation for pacing indicator. A field in the request/response header. If set in a request header, PI indicates that the sender will expect a PACING response. If set in a response header, PI indicates the sender is ready to receive additional normal-flow RUs. Same as pacing indicator.

PIC *n.*

VAX/VMS

The abbreviation for position independent code. A technique of coding such that the code can be executed without alteration at any address of the virtual address space. Same as position independent code.

picture *n.*

FMS

The appearance of a field as specified by its field characters. The picture describes both the valid contents of a field and its screen format. For example, the picture for a telephone number would describe a 3-digit area code enclosed in parentheses, followed by a 3-digit exchange, a hyphen, and a 4-digit phone number. This picture can be represented by the following field characters: (999)999-9999.

VAX PL/I

A specification of the character-string representation of an arithmetic value. The specification is given as a character-string constant that defines the position of a decimal point, zero suppression, sign conventions, and so on. A data type for which fixed-point decimal values are stored internally as character strings, in accordance with a picture specification.

picture element *n.*

generic

The smallest unit of information or data in a screen display. Same as pixel.

picture object *n.*

RGL/FEP

Any graphic object except graphic text, for example, lines, arcs, polygons, circles.

PID *n.*

VAX/VMS

The abbreviation for process identification. A 32-bit binary value that uniquely identifies a process. Each process has a process identification and a process name. Same as process identification.

piggybacking *n.*

DECnet

The process of sending an acknowledgment within a returned data message.

pin *n.*

generic

1. A thin, round section of metal on the backplane on which wires are wrapped.

2. An area on a module that is a physical and electrical part of the backplane wiring.

3. The electrical connector of an active circuit component.

PIP *n.*

DIGITAL-specific

The abbreviation for peripheral interchange program. The PIP transfers data files from one standard I/O device to another and performs simple editing functions. PIP performs sequencing, trailing blank suppression, compressing blanks into tabs, and magnetic tape control functions. Same as peripheral interchange program.

pipelining *n.*

DECnet

The process of sending messages without waiting for individual acknowledgment of each successive message.

pitch *n.*

DECmate II and DECWORD

The setting in the print menu specifying the number of characters printed per horizontal inch. Typical settings are PI 10 and PI 12.

generic

The auditory property of a sound that enables a listener to place the sound on a scale going from low to high. A pitch is the auditory equivalent of the acoustic parameter FREQUENCY.

pixel *n.*

generic

The density of one picture element; the smallest displayable unit on a monitor screen. Same as pel; see also dot.

placement control *n.*

RSX-11M

The ability to specify a logical block, device cluster, or virtual block number where the file processor should begin an area. On VAX/VMS, the user can also specify a related file as a guide to placement.

placement mode *n.*

VAX-11/DBMS

The storage method by which the Database Control System determines the data base key values associated with record occurrences. Placement mode is declared in the storage schema. See also SCATTERED SET Option and CLUSTERED VIA SET option.

playback *n.*

Medical Systems

A data analysis process that allows users to display movie-like images.

Plenum *n.*

generic

A compartment or chamber to which one or more compartments are connected in a building ventilation system, used only for the carriage of environmental air.

plotter *n.*

MINC

A device to construct visual representations of data by means of an automatic pen or pencil. Plotters can also receive plotting coordinates from digital computers.

PLU *n.*

DECnet

The abbreviation for primary logical unit. In an SNA (systems network architecture) configuration, application programs running the host S/370 are the primary logical units. An application running in a 3790 communication system is an example of a secondary logical unit (SLU). In a configuration using protocol emulator, the SNA (systems network architecture) side of the network always contains PLUs and the PE (protocol emulator) provides support for the SLUs. Same as primary logical unit.

plural entity *n.*

DECnet

A set of entities classified as known or active, or loop.

PMD *n.*

RSX-11M

The abbreviation for post mortem dump. Refers to a dump after the execution has terminated. Same as post mortem dump.

PME *n.*

VAX/VMS
Performance monitor enable bit in PCB.

point *n.*

GIGI
A single location on the monitor screen.

pointer *n.*

DBMS
A place marker that identifies a record's address in a storage area.

generic
A variable or data element that indicates the location of an item of data.

VAX C
A variable that contains the address of another variable or function. A pointer is declared with the unary asterisk operator.

pointer array *n.*

RSX-11M
A series of record pointers stored in each SIDR (secondary index data record) for an alternate key where duplicates are allowed. Each pointer indicates a user data record containing the key value represented by the SIDR. See also duplicate pointer array.

point size *n.*

generic
The standard way of measuring printable characters: one point equals approximately 1/72 of an inch.

point source *n.*

Medical Systems and MSG (SPETS)
A small amount of concentrated radioactive material with a constant level of energy. SPETS software uses point sources for alignment or calibration.

point-to-point channel *n.*

DECnet
A channel connecting only two stations.

point-to-point circuit *n.*

VAX/VMS
A circuit that connects two nodes, operating over a single line.

point-to-point connection *n.*

DECnet
A network configuration in which a connection is established between two, and only two, terminal installations. The connection may include switching facilities. See also multipoint line.

polarity *n.*

generic
An electrical or magnetic condition of the electrodes of something as a result of the flow of current.

polarization *n.*

generic
An electrical or magnetic condition of the electrodes of something as a result of the flow of current.

policy module *n.*

VAX/VMS

A module in the system that establishes a policy for the use or access to a resource. It typically does its work by setting parameters to a mechanism module.

poll *n.*

DECnet

The process of inviting a station to transmit data. A poll may be either general or specific. A general poll invites any of the devices on a station to transmit data, while a specific poll invites a particular device on a station. See also selection.

polling *n.*

DECnet and VAX/VMS

The activity that the control station performs with a multipoint line's tributaries.

generic

The checking regularly of each device that shares a common communication line.

polling mode *n.*

MINC

An operating method of a digital-input module (MNCDI). By this method, the system reads data on the 16 external lines each time a digital-input subprogram requests such a reading.

pool *n.*

RSX-11M

The dynamic storage (DSR) that is part of the Executive's partition in memory. The pool contains the Executive's data base.

TOPS-10

One or more logically complete file structures that provide file storage for the users and that require no special action on the part of the user.

pooled resource *n.*

TOPS-10

Refers to multiple copies of a resource. Users can specify that a resource is to be a pooled (multiple-copy) resource.

pop *v.*

generic

To remove the top entry from a push-down stack.

pop *adj.*

generic

1. Pertaining to an expansion clip.

2. Pertaining to a specific instruction.

populate *v.*

generic

To build a circuit board by attaching jelly beans.

population *n.*

RSX-11M

The process of inserting a large burst of records into a file after it has been created and before it is made available for normal processing.

port *n.*

generic

The name of the socket or connector at the back of the computer to which a terminal, printer, or other communication devices are connected.

TOPS-10

A device that passes messages between the monitor and one or more terminals.

VAX PSI

A logical route for data in or out of a PPI (protocol processing images). A port, in use, contains one or more channels all of which carry the same type of information.

portrait *n.*

generic

One of two kinds of orientation: landscape and portrait. In portrait orientation, lines of text are printed parallel to the short dimension of the paper. Conceptually, characters in portrait fonts are aligned in the conventional, upright position.

ports *n.*

DECSIM

Input and output "stubs" or pins that connect to the outside environment. They are defined by the model header connection list. By using the PORT declaration within the behavior model, you can assign modifiers to ports.

P/OS *n.*

PRO/Diskette System

The abbreviation for the Professional's operating system. An operating system is the set of internal programs that runs a computer.

position-dependent code *n.*

VAX/VMS

Code that can execute properly without modification whenever it is located in virtual address space, even if its location is changed after it is linked. Generally, this code uses addressing modes that form an effective address relative to the PC.

positioner *n.*

generic

The mechanical device that moves something, usually read/write heads.

position-independent code (PIC) *n.*

generic

Code that can execute correctly from any part of memory.

VAX/VMS

Code that can execute properly without modification wherever it is located in virtual address space, even if its location is changed after it has been linked. Generally, this code uses addressing modes that form an effective address relative to the PC (program counter). Same as PIC.

positioning operation *n.*

DIGITAL-specific

On the KL-10, the operation of moving the read-write heads of a disk to the proper cylinder prior to a data transfer. This operation requires the control for several micro-seconds to initiate activity, but does not require the channel or memory system.

position of key in record *n.*

RSX-11M

The number of the byte(s) where a segment or segments of the key begin. Numbering begins with 0; therefore, the first byte in a record is referred to as byte 0. See also key field and segmented key.

postconditional expression *n.*

DSM-11

A truth-valued expression appended to a command or argument that makes the execution of that command or argument dependent on the truth value of the expression. If the postconditional expression is false, DSM-11 does not execute the command or argument. If the postconditional expression is true, DSM-11 does execute the command or argument.

posting n.

generic

The process of transferring transactions from the journal to the ledger.

post mortem dump (PMD) n.

VAX/VMS

Refers to a dump after execution has terminated. Same as PMD.

poststimulus-time (PST) mode n.

MINC

A method of time-data sampling. By this method, the time intervals between the firing of Schmitt-Trigger 1 (ST1) and a series of firings of Schmitt-Trigger 2 (ST2) are measured and stored. The sweep of time-interval samples continues until a clock overflow stops the clock, or until ST1 signals the occurrence of another external event and restarts the clock. Same as PST.

potentiometer n.

generic

A variable resistor.

power down v.

generic

To do a step or sequence of steps that stops the flow of electrical current to a device or system.

power dump n.

generic

The removal of electrical energy, usually not planned, from a computer system or components.

power up v.

generic

To do a step or sequence of steps that starts the flow of electrical current to a device or system.

PPI n.

VAX PSI

The abbreviation for protocol processing images. A software module that is controlled by LES. Several PPIs provide the X.25 and X.29 user interfaces, the VAX PSI Management functions and trace facilities, and control the handling of virtual circuits. Same as protocol processing image.

PPN n.

TOPS-10

The abbreviation for project-programmer number. PPN consists of two numbers separated by a comma (,) that identify the user and the user's file storage area on a file structure. Same as project-programmer number.

PRAGMAT n.

PEARL

A form of comment in a program that affects the action of the compiler.

preamplifier n.

generic

An amplifier used to prepare low-level signals for more voltage.

MINC

A laboratory module that amplifies or attenuates the output of external devices that are producing signals with levels too low or too high for direct A/D conversion. With MINC and REAL systems, a preamplifier is an amplifier connected to a low-level signal source in order to provide gain (amplify signals) so that the signal can be processed further. An example of a preamplifier is the MNCAG.

precedence *n.*

PEARL

The priority order in which operators in an expression are evaluated.

precedence rules *n.*

VAX PASCAL

Rules applied to the order of evaluation of operations in an expression. An operation with higher precedence is performed before an operation with lower precedence.

precision *n.*

DIGITAL-specific

The quality of being exactly or sharply defined or stated. A measure of the precision is frequently the number of significant digits or bits it contains.

MINC

The resolution of a number's representation by a computer. MINC's precision extends to 6 significant digits for real numbers and to 4 (plus) digits for integers.

predecessor value *n.*

PASCAL and VAX PASCAL

A value that immediately precedes a given value in any ordinal type. The PRED function returns the predecessor value.

prefix *n.*

VAX DBMS

A group of data items called pointers that precede record occurrences stored \ in the database. They describe the record's set linkage.

prefix operator *n.*

VAX PL/I

One of the operators = or − that precedes a variable or constant to indicate or change its sign.

preprocessing data *n.*

DIGITAL-specific

The act of manipulating information to ready it for processing.

preprocessor control lines *n.*

VAX C

Lines of text in a VAX C source file that change the order or manner of subsequent compilation.

prestaging *v.*

TOPS-10

The operator's mounting of volumes that a user has not yet requested.

prevailing mode *n.*

GAMMA

A data-analysis mode that remains in effect until GAMMA is commanded to change the mode.

primary *n.*

generic

The winding in a transformer that carries the input current, in contrast to the secondary, which carries the output current.

primary dictionary *n.*

DIGITAL-specific

A dictionary that is defined to have one or two other dictionaries related to it.

primary expression *n.*

VAX/VMS

An expression that contains only a primary-expression operator, or no operator. Primary expressions include previously declared identifiers, constants, strings, function calls, subscripted expressions, and references to structure or union members.

primary expression operator *n.*

VAX/VMS

A C operator that qualifies a primary expression. The set operators consist of paired brackets (to enclose a single subscript), paired parentheses (to enclose an argument list or to change the associativity of operators), a period (to qualify a structure or union name with the name of a member), and an arrow (to qualify a structure or union member with a pointer or other address-valued expression).

primary file *n.*

DIGITAL-specific

A file described by a primary dictionary.

primary index *n.*

RSX-11M

The structure providing the logical access paths for the primary key. See also alternate index.

primary I/O device *n.*

DECnet

The keyboard terminal that initiated the job. This is the device to which an error message is directed for output.

primary key *n.*

RSX-11M

The portion of each user data record whose value determines the position of that record within level 0 of the primary index. RMS-11 constructs the primary index from the primary key values of records inserted into the file. Users must define a primary key for each indexed file. See also segmented key.

VAX DATATRIEVE

The index key whose value determines the order of records in an indexed file. Users cannot modify or erase the value in a primary key field.

VAX/RMS

The mandatory key within the data records of an indexed file; used by VAX-11 RMS to build a primary index. See also key and alternate key.

VAX/VMS

The mandatory key within the data records of an indexed file; used by VAX RMS to determine the placement of records within the file and to build the primary index. See key (indexed files) and alternate key.

primary lock *n.*

VAX DATATRIEVE

An attribute that the database administrator specifies in the subschema to prevent an application from performing certain operations on an area, record, or set.

primary logical unit (PLU) *n.*

DECnet

In an SNA (systems network architecture) configuration, application programs running the host S/370 are the primary logical units (PLU). An application running in a 3790 communication system is an example of a secondary logical unit (SLU). In a configuration using a protocol emulator, the SNA side of the network always contains PLUs and the protocol emulator (PE) provides support for the SLUs. Same as PLU.

primary ODL file *n.*

RSX-11M

The overlay description language (ODL) file referenced by the indirect file users supply to the Task Builder. Users can also supply the name of the primary ODL file directly in a Task Builder command line. See also secondary ODL file.

primary password *n.*

VAX/VMS

A type of user password that is the first user password requested from the user. Systems may optionally require a secondary password as well. As a user password, this password must be the password that is associated with the user name that is supplied with it.

primary processor *n.*

VAX/VMS

The main processor in a VAX-11/782. The primary processor handles I/O, scheduling, paging, and all other system management functions. Contrast with attached processor.

primary protocol *n.*

DECnet

The protocol used between the console front end and the central processor. This protocol is not used until the central processor comes up. See also secondary protocol.

primary root *n.*

RSX-11M

The single bucket that is the entry point for processes following the primary index. See also root.

primary run-time system *n.*

RSTS/E

The run-time system that is permanently resident on a RSTS/E system, and controls system startup and shutdown.

primary timeout category *n.*

DECnet

One of two BSC (binary synchronous communications) timeout categories; each of two communicating systems must be assigned to different timeout categories. See also secondary timeout category.

primary vector *n.*

VAX/VMS

A location that contains the starting address of a condition handler to be executed when an exception condition occurs. If a primary vector is declared, that condition handler is the first handler to be executed.

prime record key *n.*

COBOL-74

A key whose contents uniquely identify a record within an indexed file.

prime RIB *n.*

TOPS-10

The first retrieval information block (RIB) of a file. This block contains all of the user arguments. See also extended RIB.

primitive *n.*

generic

An element that is not defined in relation to another element.

MicroPower PASCAL

A fundamental operation performed by the kernel when requested by a process in the application. Primitive operations are indivisible and must complete; they do not block themselves. In the Micro-Power PASCAL language, primitives are invoked implicitly by calls to predefined real-time procedures and by real-time extensions to the language.

VT-11 GRAPHICS

A basic display element, such as a point, vector, or character string, that can be defined in a single subroutine call and stored in the display file.

principal device *n.*

DIGITAL-specific

The device on which the system conducts all I/O operations in the absence of contrary commands such as specific OPEN and USE or ZUSE commands. For interactive users, the principal device is the terminal on which they logged into the system.

DSM-11

The terminal at which users log in. Although each terminal has a unique device number associated with it, DSM-11 always interprets device 0 to mean the principal device.

printable group *n.*

generic

A report group that contains at least one print line.

printable item *n.*

COBOL-74

A data item, the extent and contents of which are specified by an elementary report entry. This elementary report entry contains a COLUMN NUMBER clause, a PICTURE clause, and a SOURCE, SUM, or VALUE clause.

printed circuit board (PCB) *n.*

generic

A circuit wired or etched on a phenolic or fiberglass material complete with all necessary components for performing a specific function. Same as PCB.

printer control block *n.*

DECWORD

The keywords and text held between two printer control markers.

printer control command *n.*

DECWORD

A facility that instructs DECWORD to insert certain repetitive text on every page of a document.

printer control keyword *n.*

DECWORD

A word indicating the nature of the printer control command, frequently specifying where the command is to take effect. For example, the keyword TOP specifies a header.

printer control markers *n.*

DECWORD

Two markers users insert into the document to distinguish between special-purpose text (for example headers), and normal text.

printer margin *n.*

DECWORD

Spaces added to the left margin of a page when a document is printed, moving the document further to the right on the paper. Specified by the PM setting in the print menu.

printer number *n.*

DIGITAL-specific

An arbitrary number that A-to-Z assigns to each printer. This number is not the same as the port number.

print list *n.*

VAX DATATRIEVE

One or more valued expressions (including the names of elementary and group fields) whose values users want DATATRIEVE to display. A print list can also include optional formatting specifications.

printout *n.*

generic

The document produced by a computer system printer.

print processor *n.*

DIGITAL-specific

A device that enables the orderly printing of files; the print processor is handled by the queue manager. Same as despooler. See also spooler.

print queue *n.*

DIGITAL-specific

The list of documents waiting to be printed.

print settings *n.*

DECWORD

Settings that control the manner in which a document is printed, such as the print margin and pitch. The print menu lets the user see and change these settings.

print wheel *n.*

generic

A wheel in the letter quality printer that produces the print. To print a character, the printer rotates the print wheel to the correct position and strikes one of its spokes with a hammer.

print zones *n.*

generic

1. Blocks of characters.

2. An assumed subdivision of the terminal screen.

3. Positions in which printed items are displayed.

prior *n.*

VAX DBMS

A set-ordering criterion that defines that new records immediately precede a record occurrence established by the user program.

priority *n.*

generic

The value given to a task that determines when that task will receive system resources.

VAX/VMS

A rank assigned to a process to determine its precedence in obtaining system resources.

priority interrupt *n.*

generic

A scheme that ensures that the processor is always attending the most important task.

priority interrupt (PI) *n.*

DIGITAL-specific

An interrupt that takes control of the computer from the program or monitor and jumps to an interrupt service routine if its priority is higher than the interrupt currently being serviced. Same as PI.

privacy key *n.*

VAX DBMS

A key whose contents are used by the DBCS (Database Control Systems) to determine if a locked resource is to be made available to the run unit that specified that privacy key value.

privacy lock *n.*

VAX DBMS

A value, known to the DBCS (Database Control Systems), that is associated with a locked resource.

private delimiter *n.*

RSTS/E

A character used as a delimiter within a specific RSTS/E program.

private line *n.*

DECnet

A communications link that is permanently installed between two points without inter-exchange switching arrangements. See also leased line and nonswitched line.

private section *n.*

VAX/VMS

An image section of a process that is not sharable among processes. Same as process section. See also global section.

privilege *n.*

DIGITAL-specific

The level of system access allowed to a user. See also process privilege, user privilege, and image privilege.

generic

A characteristic assigned to a user or program that determines what operations that user or program can perform.

privileged *adj.*

DECnet

Pertaining to any user privileges in addition to NETMBX and TMPMBX.

DECWORD

Pertaining to a type of account that allows users to use all system facilities. For example, users can start up and shut down the system, access any user account, and create new accounts. See also account and project number.

RSX-11M

Pertaining to commands or tasks that are allowed to perform operations normally considered the domain of the monitor or Executive or that can affect system operations as a whole. There are privileged tasks, privileged users, and privileged terminals.

VAX DATATRIEVE

A characteristic of a user that controls that user's ability to access a file or other resource for a certain purpose. Fourteen privileges have been defined to control access to the CDD (Common Data Dictionary). Five of these privileges are specific to VAX DATATRIEVE; the remaining nine are VAX CDD access privileges. See also access control list.

VAX/VMS

Generally refers to instructions, images, or accounts intended for use by the operating system, specific system programs, or a subset of the system users.

privileged account *n.*

DIGITAL-specific

An account that allows a user complete access to system-wide operations.

privileged front end *n.*

RSX-20F

A PDP-11 attached to a KL by means of a DTE-20 that can use the diagnostic bus and do unprotected deposits. A privileged front end can crash the KL.

privileged instructions *n.*

VAX/VMS

Any instructions intended for use by the operating system or privileged system programs. In particular, instructions that the processor will not execute unless the current access mode is kernel mode (for example: HALT, SVPCTX, LDPCTX, MTPR, and MFPR).

privileged process *n.*

MicroPower PASCAL

In mapped target systems, a process with access to kernel and device register areas of memory.

privileged program *n.*

TOPS-10

1. Any program running under project number 1, programmer number 2.

2. A monitor support program executed by a monitor command that has the JACCT (job status) bit set, for example, LOGOUT.

privileged task *n.*

VAX/VMS

A task that has privileged memory access rights. A privileged task can access the Executive and the I/O page in addition to its own partition and referenced shared regions.

privileged user *n.*

DIGITAL-specific

A user who can alter the operating system through the use of privileged commands.

privileges *n.*

VAX/VMS

A means of protecting the user of certain system functions that can effect system resources and/or integrity. System managers grant privileges according to user's needs and deny them to users as a means of restricting their access to the system. See also process privileges, user privileges, and image privileges.

PRK *n.*

DIGITAL-specific

The abbreviation for program request key. PRK is a set of keys on a terminal keyboard or keypad that the user can define in a request to allow the terminal operator to communicate with the application program at run time. Same as program request key.

PRO/BASIC *n.*

PRO/Diskette System

The BASIC programming language designed specifically for the Professional.

problem division *n.*

PEARL

The problem-specific part of a PEARL module. It contains all the code and data used in the program.

procedure *n.*

VAX DATATRIEVE

1. A general purpose routine, entered by means of a call instruction, that uses an argument list passed by a calling program and uses only local variables for data storage. A procedure is entered from and returns control to the calling program.

2. A fixed sequence of DATATRIEVE commands, statements, clauses, or arguments that users create, name, and store in the CDD (Common Data Dictionary).

See also step procedure, initialization procedure, and termination procedure.

VAX/VMS

A routine entered by means of a call instruction. See also command procedure.

procedure block *n.*

VAX PL/I

A sequence of statements headed by a PROCE-DURE statement and terminated by an END statement. A procedure block is entered when its name is specified in a CALL statement or a function reference. When a procedure block is entered, a block activation is created for it and for the internal variables declared within it.

procedure call *n.*

PASCAL and VAX PASCAL

A statement that invokes a procedure. A procedure call consists of the name of a procedure and its actual parameter list (when required).

procedure file *n.*

CTS-300

Any file which is the output of the LOG command. It contains QUILL commands which are inserted into the file when it is created with QUILL.

procedure heading *n.*

PASCAL and VAX PASCAL

The specification of the name and optional formal parameters of a procedure in a declaration.

procedure server *n.*

ACMS

One of two types of servers that handle processing work for ACMS tasks. Procedure servers do processing work for step procedures called in tasks defined with ACMS/AD.

procedure server image *n.*

ACMS

The image that is loaded into a procedure server process when the process is started by the ACMS execution controller. The procedure server image is created when all the procedures handled by the server are linked together with the procedure server transfer module for that server.

procedure server transfer module *n.*

ACMS

The object module created for a procedure server as a result of building an ACMS task group definition. When a task group is built, the Application Definition Utility produces a procedure server transfer module for each server defined in the task group.

process *n.*

DIGITAL-specific and VAX/VMS

The basic entity scheduled by the system software that provides the context in which an image executes. A process consists of an address space and both hardware and software context.

process address space *n.*

VAX/VMS

The lowest-addressed half of virtual address space, where process instructions and data reside. See also process space.

process context *n.*

VAX/VMS

The definition of the current status of a process by the hardware and the operating system.

Process Context *n.*

ACMS

The information local to a server process, such as record locks and file pointers.

process control block (PCB) *n.*

MicroPower PASCAL

The activation record of a MicroPower PASCAL process. The process control block preserves the software and hardware context of the process and reflects the stage of the process (see process states). The PCB contains:

1. hardware context of the process (including general registers contents, FPU registers contents, and PSW (processor status word) contents)

2. process priority

3. software context of the process (contents of associated flags and pointers maintained by kernel operations)

4. state code

5. state queue pointers.

VAX/VMS

A data structure used to contain process context. The hardware PCB contains the hardware context. The software PCB contains the software context, which includes a pointer to the hardware PCB. Same as PCB.

processed event *n.*

DECnet

An event in final form, after local processing.

process header *n.*

VAX/VMS

A data structure that contains the hardware PCB, accounting and quota information, process section table, working set list, and the page tables defining the virtual layout of the process.

process header slots *n.*

VAX/VMS

That portion of the system address space in which the system stores the process headers for the processes in the balance set. The number of process header slots in the system determines the number of processes that can be in the balance set at any one time.

process identification (PID) *n.*

VAX/VMS

A 32-bit binary value that uniquely identifies a process. Each process has a process identification and a process name. Same as PID.

process index *n.*

MicroPower PASCAL

A 16-bit value (identification number) that identifies a process to the kernel and is assigned by the kernel when the process is created.

Processing Step *n.*

ACMS

One of three kinds of steps that define the work of a task defined with ACMS/AD. The work of a processing step is handled by a server and can consist of computations, data modification, file and database access.

processing time *n.*

generic

The time required to perform a particular function.

process I/O channel *n.*

VAX/VMS

1. A logical path connecting a user process to a physical device unit. A user process requests the operating system to assign a channel to a device so the process can communicate with that device. See also controller data channel.

2. A means of transmission over a packet switching data network. For VAX PSI, a logical path between a DTE and DCE over which data is transmitted. Each channel is identified by a unique reference number called a logical channel number (LCN). Same as channel.

process I/O segment *n.*

VAX/VMS

That portion of a process control region that contains the permanent RMS internal file access block for each open file, and the I/O buffers, including the command interpreter's command buffer and command descriptors.

process name *n.*

MicroPower PASCAL

A six-character alphanumeric string that identifies a process. When a process is created, the user specifies its name, which is stored in the kernel's system name table.

VAX/VMS

A one- to 15-character ASCII string that can be used to identify processes executing under the same group number.

processor *n.*

generic

A functional section of hardware in a computer that changes instructions into a form the computer understands, and executes these instructions.

VAX DBMS

A program similar in function to a compiler in that it translates higher-level statements into another machine-usable form, but lacks the size, scope, and power of a compiler.

processor binding *n.*

DIGITAL-specific

The specification that a process can only be executed on a specific processor.

processor option *n.*

DIGITAL-specific

An implementation technique whereby a particular processor is designed to provide customers with the ability to purchase additional hardware to provide some or all of the omitted instructions or features, or to improve performance.

processor register *n.*

DIGITAL-specific and VAX/VMS

A part of the processor used by the operating system software to control the execution states of the computer system. Processor registers include the system base and length registers, the program and control region base and length registers, the system control block register, and the software interrupt request register.

processor status longword (PSL) *n.*

VAX/VMS

A privileged processor register consisting of a word of privileged processor status and the PSW (processor status word). The privileged processor status information includes: the current IPL (interrupt priority level), the previous access mode, the current access mode, the interrupt stack bit, the trace trap pending bit, and the compatibility mode bit. Same as PSL.

processor status word (PSW) *n.*

RT-11

A register in the PDP-11 that indicates the current priority of the processor, the condition of the previous operation, and other basic control items. Same as PSW.

VAX/VMS

The low-order word of the processor status longword. Processor status information includes: the condition codes (carry, overflow zero, negative), the arithmetic trap enable bits (integer overflow, decimal overflow, floating underflow), and the trace enable bit. Same as PSW.

process-own *n.*

VAX/VMS

A resource that is unique to the process. An example is the stack.

process page tables *n.*

VAX/VMS

The memory management data base used to account for the virtual pages of a process. The P0 page table contains entries for the virtual pages in the program region. The P1 page table contains entries for virtual pages in the control region.

process permanent file *n.*

VAX/RMS

A file opened or created through VAX/RMS in supervisor of Executive mode. The internal data structures of a process permanent file are allocated such that the file may be open across image activations; a restricted subset of allowable operations is available to "indirect" accessors.

process priority *n.*

VAX/VMS

The priority assigned to a process for scheduling purposes. The operating system recognizes 32 levels of process priority, where 0 is low and 31 is high. Levels 16 through 31 are used for time-critical processes. The system does not modify the priority of a time-critical process (although the system manager or process itself may). Levels 0 through 15 are used for normal processes. The system may temporarily increase the priority of a normal process based on the activity of the process. See also software priority.

process privileges *n.*

VAX/VMS

The privileges granted to a process by the system; these privileges are a combination of user privileges and image privileges. See also image privileges.

process section *n.*

VAX/VMS

An image section of a process that is not sharable among processes. Same as private section. See also global section.

process section table *n.*

VAX/VMS

A table maintained and used by memory management to interpret the image file of the image currently executing in a process. Each process has a section table located in the process header.

process space *n.*

VAX/VMS

The lowest-addressed half of virtual address space, where process instructions and data reside. Process space is divided into a program region and a control region. Same as process address space.

process synchronization *n.*

MicroPower PASCAL

In MicroPower PASCAL, coordinating the execution of processes. Semaphores and ring buffers are basic mechanisms that synchronize MicroPower PASCAL processes.

PRO/Communications *n.*

PRO/Diskette System

A P/OS application that enables the user to use the Professional to communicate with DIGITAL PDP-11 and VAX host computers. The user can transfer files to and from the host and use the Professional as if it were a terminal on the host computer.

Professional Specific Subsystem *n.*

ALL-IN-1

A menu option provided in the ALL-IN-1 Office Menu and Extended packages. A user adds personal computer programs in this area.

Profile *n.*

DECnet

The characteristics of an SNA (systems network architecture) session. Each session observes two Profiles: a transmission system (TS) Profile, concerned primarily with transmission control and recovery management, and a function management (FM) Profile, concerned primarily with data-flow control and the manner in which data is presented to the receiving NAU (network addressable unit). FM Profiles 3 and 4/TS Profiles 3 and 4 specify rules to be observed in LU-LU sessions. See also transmission subsystem.

profit *n.*

generic

The amount by which total revenues exceed total expenses for an accounting period. Same as net income, ''bottom line'', and earnings.

profit and loss statement *n.*

generic

A statement of revenues and expenses, and the difference between them. Same as income statement.

program *n.*

generic

1. A set of instructions that a digital computer must execute to get a specific result.

2. A complete sequence of instructions and data with which the computer can solve a problem.

MicroPower PASCAL

In the MicroPower PASCAL language, an attribute applied to a code unit composes of a declaration section and an executable section. When acted on by the MicroPower PASCAL utilities, a program results in a static process within the application.

VAX/VMS

A series of instructions aimed at a particular result. Programming languages are a means of describing procedures so that they can be performed by a computer. See also image.

program access (PA) keys *n.*

DECnet

In 3270 applications, a type of program attention key that may be defined to solicit application program attention without requiring that input data be transmitted to the program. Only the attention identification (AID) character is transmitted to the program to identify the key that was pressed. Same as PA keys.

program attention keys *n.*

DECnet

In 3270 operations, program attention keys are keys on the keyboard that are used to solicit application program action (attention) by setting a condition that causes the 3271 control unit to respond to the next poll received from the host. The 3271 responds as an implicit (hardware generated) READ command. The keys are the CLEAR key, ENTER key, TEST REQ key, CNCL key, program function keys, and program access keys.

program counter (PC) *n.*

DIGITAL-specific

The general register that at the beginning of an instruction's execution, normally contains the address of a location in memory from which the processor will fetch the next instruction it will execute. Same as PC.

program development *n.*

generic

The process of writing, entering, translating, and debugging source programs.

program function key; programmable function key (PF key or PF keys) *n.*

DECnet

In 3270 applications, a program attention key that may be defined to get application program attention that usually requires data to be read from the display buffer, along with the attention identification (AID) character. See also PF.

The four keys along the top row of the keypad, marked PF1, PF2, PF3, and PF4. used to perform specific subroutines. Same as PF key(s).

program interface *n.*

Common Data Dictionary and VAX DATATRIEVE

A set of callable CDD (Common Data Dictionary) routines. Users can use the CDD program interface to build software products that use CDD functions. See also call interface.

program line *n.*

generic

A single line of instructions and data within a program.

program locality *n.*

VAX/VMS

A characteristic of a program that indicates how close or far apart are the references to locations in virtual memory over time. A program with a high degree of locality does not refer to many widely scattered virtual addresses in a short time.

programmable gain *n.*

MINC

A signal gain that is defined by setting the gain-selector switch on a preamplifier (such as the MNCAG) to P (for programmable). In this mode, the gain is controlled by the program running in the computer.

programmable read-only memory (PROM) *n.*

DIGITAL-specific

A type of read-only memory on a silicon chip that is manufactured in the blank state (zeros or ones). Users give the desired bit pattern for an application program by formatting (programming, blasting) the chip in a PROM formatter. The bit pattern is permanent. Same as PROM.

programmed operators *n.*

TOPS-10

Instructions that, instead of performing a hardware operation, cause a jump into the monitor system or the user area at a predetermined point and perform a software operation. The monitor (or special user code) interprets these entries as commands from the user program to perform specified operations. See also UUO and unimplemented user programs.

programmed request *n.*

generic

A program instruction used to call up a service from the monitor.

RT-11

A directive issued by a user program that requests a monitor service.

programmer access code (PAC) *n.*

DSM-11

A three-character code, created at system generation time, that allows the terminal user to enter command mode. There is only one PAC for a system.

programmer number *n.*

DIGITAL-specific and VAX/VMS

The second number in a user identification code that uniquely identifies that code. See also member number and project number.

programming *n.*

generic

The process of planning, writing, testing, and correcting the steps required for a computer to solve a problem or perform an operation.

program origin *n.*

TOPS-10

The location assigned by the linker to relocatable zero of a program.

program region *n.*

VAX/VMS

The lower-addressed half of process address space (PO region). The program region contains the image currently being executed by the process and other user code called by the image.

program region base register (POBR) *n.*

VAX/VMS

The process register, or its equivalent in a hardware process control block, that contains the base virtual address of the page table entry for virtual page number 0 in a process program region. Same as POBR.

program region length register (POLR) *n.*

VAX/VMS

The processor register, or its equivalent in a hardware process control block, that contains the number of entries in the page table for a process program region. Same as POLR.

program request key (PRK) *n.*

DIGITAL-specific

A set of keys on a terminal keyboard or keypad that the user can define in a request to allow the terminal operator to communicate with the application program at run time. Same as PRK.

program section *n.*

generic

A section of memory specifically reserved for either code or data.

MicroPower PASCAL

One of four named units created by the Micro-Power PASCAL compiler from PASCAL source code. These units are used to apportion the target system memory into sections for:

1. executable code

2. memory space for stack and heap

3. storage for constants

4. storage for global variables.

See also PSECT.

RT-11

A named, contiguous unit of code (instructions or data) that is considered an entity and that can be relocated separately without destroying the logic of the program.

VAX/VMS

A section of memory that is a unit of the total allocation. A source program is translated into object modules that consist of program sections with attributes describing access, allocation, relocatability, and others.

program trap *n.*

TOPS-10

One of the non-hardwired operation codes that, when decoded by the processor, causes the next instruction to be executed from a specified address.

project number *n.*

DIGITAL-specific

The first number segment of an account number that identifies an authorized user logging into a system. See also group number, account number, member number, and programmer number.

VAX/VMS

The first number in a user identification code (UIC). See also group number.

project operation *n.*

Rdb/ELN

A procedure that selects and presents only the unique values for a field in a relation.

project-programmer number (PPN) *n.*

DECsystem-10

Two octal numbers, separated by commas, that, when considered as a unit, identify the user and his file storage area on a file structure. Same as PPN.

RSTS/E

A unique number that identifies a user on the RSTS/E system. A project-programmer number (PPN) consists of two decimal numbers separated by a comma. The first number identifies the user's project group; the second identifies the user within a project group. Each number can range from 0 to 254. Same as PPN.

prologue *n.*

RSX-11M

The first blocks of a relative or indexed file where RMS-11 maintains file attributes that cannot fit in the file directory.

PROM *n.*

generic

The acronym for programmable read-only memory. A type of read-only memory on a silicon chip that is manufactured in the blank state (zeros or ones). Users give the desired bit pattern for application programs by formatting (programming, blasting) the chip in a PROM formatter. The bit pattern is permanent. Same as programmable read-only memory.

promissory note *n.*

generic

A written acknowledgment of the amount that a borrower owes a creditor.

prompt *n.*

generic

Text displayed that requests information from the user; also the symbol representing specific information that the user should supply such as the $, command prompt.

DIGITAL-specific

A word or symbol the system uses as cues to assist a user's response. The nature of the prompt also indicates what program the user is in; for example, the $ prompt is for VAX/VMS DCL.

prompting expression *n.*

VAX DATATRIEVE

An expression that directs DATATRIEVE to ask the user to supply a value when a statement is executed.

prompting screen *n.*

generic

A screen containing prompts for information about a file such as the filename and comment to be assigned to the file.

prong *n.*

generic

A pin, also called a base pin, on a connector or plug.

Protected Examines/Deposits *n.*

RSX-20F

An examine or deposit that is range-checked by the KL. The relocation and protection for the examine operation is separate from that for the deposit operation. A privileged front end can override the protection checks; a restricted front end cannot override the protection checks. See also relative address.

protected field *n.*

DECnet

A display field in which data cannot be entered, modified, or deleted.

protected location *n.*

TOPS-10

A storage location reserved for a special purpose in which data cannot be stored without undergoing a screening procedure to establish suitability for storage therein.

protected update mode *n.*

VAX DBMS

A specified usage mode that gives a run unit the capability to make changes to an area of the database while other run units concurrently retrieve data.

protected usage mode *n.*

generic

The state of a realm in which its database records cannot be modified by another run unit.

protection *n.*

DIGITAL-specific

The mechanisms and policies that are concerned with the integrity of the computer system and with ensuring that hardware and software do not fail.

protection address *n.*

TOPS-10

The maximum relative address that the user can reference.

protection code *n.*

DIGITAL-specific

A code in each file that indicates who may and may not access the file.

protection kernel *n.*

VAX/VMS

The mechanism modules in the Executive that implement the controls over the ability for processes to access various system resources such as memory and devices. Same as kernel.

protocol *n.*

generic

The conventions or rules for the format and timing of messages sent and received.

protocol, first-level *n.*

DECnet and TOPS-10

As used by ARPANET, the Host/IMP protocol. First-level protocol is the lowest-level protocol of concern to the programmer. The lower-level IMP/IMP protocol is transparent to the user, and considered as a subnet.

protocol, second-level *n.*

DECnet and TOPS-10

As used by ARPANET, the Host/Host protocol. Second-level protocol is the lowest-level protocol that provides for communication between Hosts. Second-level protocol is implemented by the NCP.

protocol, third-level *n.*

DECnet and TOPS-10

As used by ARPANET, includes all function oriented protocols such as TELENET, FTP, RJE, and NGP.

protocol processing image (PPI) *n.*

VAX PSI

A software module that is controlled by LES (layered environment services). Several PPIs provide the X.25 and X.29 user interfaces, provide the VAX PSI management functions and trace facilities, and control the handling of virtual circuits. Same as PPI.

prototype context *n.*

DIGITAL-specific

The information associated with an image that allows the system to establish an instance of the image in a process.

prototype ODL file *n.*

RSX-11M

A heavily commented version of the ODL (overlay description language) file for the RMS-11 9KB overlay structure. Users can modify this prototype to select only those RMS-11 functions required by a program and to optimize the overlay structure. See also standard ODL file.

PSDN *n.*

VAX PSI

The abbreviation for packet switching data network. A set of equipment and interconnecting links that provides a packet switching communications service to subscribers within a particular country. Same as public packet switching network.

PSE *n.*

VAX PSI

The abbreviation for packet switching exchange. PSE is the equipment in PSS (packet switching service) that is responsible for accepting and routing packets and ensuring their correct arrival. Same as packet switching exchange.

PSECT *n.*

MicroPower PASCAL

The acronym for program section. A compiler-generated structure containing program elements to be stored in one of four separate memory types. Same as program section.

VAX/VMS

A section of memory that is a unit of the total allocation. A source program is translated into object modules that consist of program sections with attributes describing access, allocation, relocatability, and others. Same as program section.

pseudo device *n.*

DECnet

A logical entity treated as an I/O device by the user or the system, but which is not actually any particular physical device; it can be redirected by an operator or within an application program to another physical device unit.

generic

An I/O device, accessible by the user or system, that is not associated with an actual device.

RSX-11M

An entity treated as an I/O device by the user or system, although it is not any particular physical device. It is a forwarding address through which actual physical devices can always be reached. This contention makes it possible to refer to a device without knowing its physical name and number.

pseudodisk *n.*

MINC

A temporary storage volume that MINC-23 and MINC/DECLAB-23 provide. The logical name for pseudodisk is VM.

pseudo interrupt system *n.*

DECnet

A highly structured set of procedures that allows a user to specify certain conditions within an executing program that will result in a transfer of control from the normal program sequence to a specified routine. The procedures include supplying an interrupt-processing routine, setting up channel and priority tables, and use of the monitor calls SIR, EIR and AIC. See also software interrupt system.

pseudo keyboard (also pseudokeyboard) *n.*

DIGITAL-specific

A logical device that has the characteristics of a terminal but has no terminal associated with it. Pseudo keyboards let one job control other jobs on the system, and are especially useful for batch operations.

pseudo-op *n.*

DIGITAL-specific

An operation that is not part of the computer's operation capability as realized by hardware and is therefore an extension of the set of machine operations. In MACRO, pseudo-ops are directions for assembly operations.

pseudo-text *n.*

generic

A sequence of text words, comment lines, or the separator space in a source program, bounded by, but not including, pseudo-text delimiters.

pseudo-text delimiter *n.*

generic

Two contiguous equal sign characters (==) used to delimit pseudo-text.

pseudovariable *n.*

VAX PL/I

A built-in function that can be used on the left-hand side of an assignment to give a special meaning to the assignment.

PSI *n.*

DECnet

The abbreviation for packet switching interface. The collective name for the hardware and software products that allow various DIGITAL operating systems to participate in a packet switching environment. Same as packet switching interface.

VAX PSI

The abbreviation for packetnet system interface. The collective name for the hardware and software products that allow various DIGITAL operating systems to participate in a packet switching environment. Same as packetnet system interface.

PSISER *n.*

TOPS-10

The module in the monitor that allows software interrupts to be accepted as well as hardware interrupts.

PSL *n.*

VAX/VMS

The abbreviation for processor status longword. A system programmed processor register consisting of a word of privileged processor status and the PSW (processor status word). The privileged processor status information includes: the current IPL (interrupt priority level), the previous access mode, the current access mode, the interrupt stack bit, the trace trap pending bit, and the compatibility mode bit. Same as processor status longword.

PST *n.*

MINC

The abbreviation for poststimulus-time mode. A method of time-data sampling. By this method, the time intervals between the firing of Schmitt-Trigger 1 (ST1) and a series of firings of Schmitt-Trigger 2 (ST2) are measured and stored. The sweep of time-interval samples continues until a clock overflow stops the clock, or unit ST1 signals the occurrence of another external even and restarts the clock. Same as poststimulus-time mode.

PSW *n.*

VAX/VMS

The abbreviation for processor status word. The low-order word of the processor status longword. Processor status information includes: the condition codes (carry, overflow, 0, negative), the arithmetic trap enable bits (integer overflow, decimal overflow, floating underflow), and the trace enable bit. Same as processor status word.

PTE *n.*

DIGITAL-specific

The abbreviation for page table entry. An entry in the PTE that describes the location and status of a process page. In a global page table, a PTE describes the location and status of a page of a global section. In the system page table, a PTE describes the status and location of a page of the operating system. Same as page table entry.

VAX/VMS

The abbreviation for page table entry. The data structure that identifies the physical location and status of a page of virtual address space. When a virtual page is in memory, the PTE contains the page frame number needed to map the virtual page to a physical page. When it is not in memory, the page table entry contains the information needed to locate the page of secondary storage (disk).

PTT *n.*

generic

An abbreviation for the Post, Telegraph and Telephone Administrations which usually operate as common carriers for telecommunications in Europe.

public disk pack *n.*

DIGITAL-specific

A disk pack belonging to the storage pool and whose storage is available to all users who have quotas on it. Same as public structure.

public disk structure (public disk structures) *n.*

generic

The disk or disk volume used as a general storage area available to any users having quotas.

public mode *n.*

TOPS-10

The user submode on the KL-10 processor. This mode corresponds to user mode on the KA10 processor.

public packet switching network (PPSN) *n.*

VAX PSI

A set of equipment and interconnecting links that provides a packet switching communications service to subscribers within a particular country. Same as PPSN.

public structure *n.*

DIGITAL-specific

The disk or disks that all users can access on a RSTS/E system. Same as public disk pack.

pulse *n.*

generic

A sudden, short change from the steady state level of current or voltage.

purchase option *n.*

USFC/generic

The option which the lessee has to buy the equipment at a stated time.

purchase order *n.*

generic

A document authorizing a seller to deliver goods with payment to be made later.

pure code *n.*

generic

Code that is never modified during execution.

TOPS-10 and VAX/VMS

Code which is never modified in the process of execution. Therefore, it is possible to let many users share the same copy of a program. Same as re-entrant code.

push *v.*

generic

To place an entry into a push down stack.

push down *adj.*

generic

Pertaining to a last-in, first-out method of queuing.

pushdown list *n.*

TOPS-10

A list that is constructed and maintained so that the item to be retrieved is the most recently stored item in the list (last-in-first-out; first-in-last-out). Same as a FILO list.

push down stack *n.*

generic

A sequential storing arrangement in which the last entry to be written is the first entry to be read.

pushup list *n.*

TOPS-10

A list that is constructed and maintained so that the next item to be retrieved and removed is the oldest item in the list (first-in-first-out). Same as a FIFO list.

PVC *n.*

VAX PSI

The abbreviation for permanent virtual circuit. A permanent logical association between two DTEs (data terminal equipment) which is analogous to a leased line. Transmission of packets on a PVC needs no call set up or call clearing by the DTE. Packets are routed directly by the network from one DTE to the other. Same as permanent virtual circuit.

pyramid *n.*

RSX-11M

A figurative way of representing an index.

q

QC n.

DECnet

The abbreviation for QUIESCE COMPLETE. An SNA (systems network architecture) data flow control request used to acknowledge suspension of data transmission following receipt of QEC command. Same as QUIESCE COMPLETE.

QEC n.

DECnet

The abbreviation for QUIESCE AT END OF CHAIN. An SNA (systems network architecture) data flow control request used to request suspension of data transmission by the receiver. This is an expedited command that may be issued by the PLU (primary logical unit) or SLU (secondary logical unit) in an FM (frequency modulation) Profile 4 session. Same as QUIESCE AT END OF CHAIN.

QI/O n.

VAX/VMS

The abbreviation for queue input/output. Queue I/O is the VAX/VMS system service that services $QIO and $QIOW requests. The Queue I/O Request system service prepares an I/O request for processing by the driver and performs device-independent preprocessing of the request. This system service also calls driver FDT (function decision table) routines. Same as queue input/output.

QMANGR n.

DECsystem-10

The abbreviation for batch queue manager. QMANGR is called by BATCON to schedule jobs by computing and dynamically revising job priorities.

QMG adj.

RSX-11M

The abbreviation for queue manager. QMG pertains to a system program that provides for the orderly processing of print and batch jobs. Same as queue manager.

QMG batch job n.

RSX-11M

A QMG (queue manager) batch job is a chain of one or more user batch jobs to be processed. The SUBMIT command defines a QMG batch job. User jobs within the QMG batch job run serially on the same batch processor without interruption from other batch jobs. The QMG batch job has a name derived from the name of the first file in the job or from a name given in the SUBMIT command.

QMG print job n.

RSX-11M

A QMG (queue manager) print job consists of one or more files to be printed at the same time. Jobs in a QMG print job go to the same line printer in the order they were listed and without interruption. The print job has a name derived from the name of the first file in the job or from a name given in the PRINT command.

quadruple precision n.

VAX PASCAL

Precision of approximately 33 significant digits and a range from $10^{**}-4932$ for a floating-point real number; the type QUADRUPLE provides quadruple precision.

quadruple type n.

VAX PASCAL

A predefined scalar type that has quadruple-precision real numbers as values.

quadword *n.*

VAX/VMS

Four contiguous words (64 bits) starting on any addressable byte boundary. Bits are numbered from right to left, 0 to 63. A quadword is identified by the address of the word containing the low-order bit (bit 0). When interpreted arithmetically, a quadword is a 2's complement integer with significance increasing from bit 0 to bit 62. Bit 63 is used as the sign bit. The value of the integer is in the range -2 (63 sup) to 2 (63 sup)-1.

qualified data-name *n.*

COBOL-74

An identifier that is composed of a data-name followed by one or more sets consisting of either one of the connectives, OF or IN, followed by a data-name qualifier.

qualifier *n.*

COBOL-74

1. A data-name that is used in reference together with another data-name at a lower level in the same hierarchy.

2. A section-name that is used in a reference together with a text-name associated with that library.

3. A library-name that is used in a reference together with a text-name associated with that library.

generic

A parameter, specified in a command string, that modifies the command.

VAX/VMS

A portion of a command string that modifies a command verb or command parameter by selecting one of several options. A qualifier, if present, follows the command verb or parameter to which it applies and is in the format: /qualifier[=option]. For example, in the command string PRINT filename /COPIES=3, the COPIES qualifier indicates that the user wants three copies of a given file printed.

quantity discount *n.*

generic

A reduction in purchase price as the quantity ordered on purchased increases.

quantizing error *n.*

MINC

An analog-to-digital (A/D) conversion error. Because converted values must be expressed in quantum steps with a size of one least significant bit (LSB), any conversion that does not fall exactly at a quantum boundary will be skewed by as much as one least significant bit. A MINC A/D LSB is equal to 2.5 millivolts; therefore, any reading may be in error by as much as 2.5 millivolts.

quantum *n.*

MINC

The amount of an increment as a result of subdividing a range of values.

VAX/VMS

The minimum amount of time that a process can remain in memory; also the maximum amount of time that a process can be the executing process. A specified amount is deducted from the quantum whenever a process enters a wait state.

quantum time *n.*

TOPS-10

The run time given to each job when it is assigned to run.

quasi-differential mode *n.*

MINC

A method of input of certain amplifiers in which the signal to be acted upon gives the appearance of being a differential mode signal but is actually a single-ended mode signal. Instead of sampling the difference between two signals at a given instant (as in differential mode), the A/D converter (MNCAD) first samples one signal, and then a short time later samples the other signal.

que *n.*

DIGITAL-specific

The system-wide name defining the location of the spooling and operator work-request queues.

query *n.*

TOPS-10

A collection of source statements written in English language sentences that IQL (interactive query language) uses to generate one or more reports. The statements in a query are not carried out until the RUN or EXECUTE assistance command is used.

query header *n.*

VAX DATATRIEVE

A substitute column header that replaces the field name when DATATRIEVE displays values from a field on a terminal. The user cannot use query headers as query names.

query language *n.*

DIGITAL-specific

An interactive database utility that can be used to make inquiries, to prototype applications with minimum programming, to enter and modify data, and to perform other functions.

query mode *n.*

RSX-11M

A feature of RMSBCK and RMSRST: the utility prints a detailed error message on a terminal, allowing the user to decide whether to continue processing. See also extended diagnostic messages.

query name *n.*

VAX DATATRIEVE

A synonym for a field name, usually a shorter word to make input easier to type and remember. For example, users can type LOA (for LENGTH-OVER-ALL), BUILDER (for MANUFACTURER), and DISP (for DISPLACEMENT) to refer to fields in DATATRIEVE's sample domain YACHTS.

query/report writer *n.*

DIGITAL-specific

Reports to a program that can search for particular records in a file and output those records in a report format.

queue *n.*

generic

A list of items to be processed in a certain order.

VAX/VMS

A line of jobs to be processed, for example, a batch job queue or a printer job queue. Processing occurs primarily in FIFO order, but does reflect the priority of the process that submitted the job. See also state queue and system queue.

queue *v.*

VAX/VMS

To make an entry in a list or table, perhaps using the INSQUE instruction.

queue elements *n.*

MicroPower PASCAL

Areas of data managed by the kernel, allocated from the kernel pool, and used for communication between processes.

queue file *n.*

RSX-11M

A disk file used by the queue manager for storage of control information and entries for all batch and print processors, all jobs and files to be processed, and all queues. On RSX-11M this file is LB0:[1,7]QUEUE.SYS and on RSX-11M-PLUS the file is SP0:[1,7]QUEUE.SYS. Since this information is retained on disk, the job will not be lost should the system stop operating.

queue manager (QMG) *n.*

DIGITAL-specific

A system program that provides for the orderly processing of print and batch jobs. Same as QMG.

queue priority *n.*

VAX/VMS

The priority assigned to a job placed in a spooler queue or a batch queue. Same as software priority. See also process priority.

queue semaphore *n.*

MicroPower PASCAL

An extension of counting semaphores. In addition to its own integer value, a queue semaphore has queue elements associated with it. The number of queue elements equals the value of the semaphore. Whenever a process signals the queue semaphore, it increments the semaphore by 1 and adds one element to the queue. Whenever a process waits on the queue semaphore, it removes one queue element and decrements the semaphore. If the semaphore is 0 (and the associated queue is empty), the waiting process blocks itself and cannot resume until another process signals the semaphore and adds an element to the queue.

queue structure *n.*

DECsystem-10

A hierarchical queue used to store input messages. It is logically tree-shaped and has relationships like those in a tree (nodes, leaves, branches).

Quick Draw *n.*

DECSIM

A schematics entry system that interfaces with DECSIM through CHAS.

QUIESCE AT END OF CHAIN (QEC) *n.*

DECnet

An SNA (systems network architecture) data flow control request used to request suspension of data transmission by the receiver. This is an expedited command that may be issued by the PLU (primary logical unit) or SLU (secondary logical unit) in an FM Profile 4 session. Same as QEC.

QUIESCE COMPLETE (QC) *n.*

DECnet

An SNA (systems network architecture) data flow control request used to acknowledge suspension of data transmission following receipt of QEC command. Same as QC.

quiet point *n.*

VAX DBMS

A time when a run unit is not accessing any database areas. Quiet points occur between transactions. See also transaction.

QUILL *n.*

CTS-300

A query/report writer available on CTS-300. QUILL allows users to search through data for specific records and to create reports from those records.

QUOLST *n.*

DECsystem-10

A program that prints the user's quotas for each file structure in his search list and the number of free blocks available in each file structure.

quota *n.*

TOPS-10

The number of transactions that will be stored in core memory.

VAX/VMS

The total amount of a system resource, such as CPU time, that a job is allowed to use in an accounting period, as specified by the system manager in the user authorization file. See also limit.

RAB *n.*

VAX/VMS

The abbreviation for record access block. An RMS user control block allocated at either assembly or run time to communicate with VAX-11 RMS. The control block describes the records in a particular file and associates with a file access block to form a record access stream. A RAB defines the characteristics needed to perform record-related operations, such as UPDATE, DELETE, or GET. Same as record access block.

race condition *n.*

VAX/VMS

A situation in which two entities (for example, two processes) are competing for the same resource and the system has no mechanism to detect which entity is serviced first. Therefore, the results are not predictable since the system cannot ensure that data will be processed correctly.

RAD-50 (Radix-50) *n.*

RT-11

A method of formatting data in which three valid characters are packed into 16 bits. Valid characters include: the letters A through Z, the numbers 0 through 9, space, period, and dollar sign.

radial serial protocol (RSP) *n.*

MicroPower PASCAL

A particular prearranged sequence of signals on a communication line. The TU58 device communicates with its device handler process using radial-serial protocol over the serial line that connects it to the processor. Same as RSP.

RT-11

A software communications protocol that controls data transmission between an SB11 and a TU58, or between an SB11 and a host RT-11 system. Same as RSP.

radian *n.*

generic

An angle whose arc length is equal to the radius of the circle.

radius *n.*

generic

The distance from the center of a circle to any point on its circumference.

radix *n.*

generic

The base of a number system; binary is radix 2, octal is radix 8.

rainbow *adj.*

A-to-Z

Refers to an icon that allows users with color output devices to select font colors with which they may paint the graph.

RAM *n.*

DIGITAL-specific

The abbreviation for random access memory. A read/write memory device. Application programs that require storage space for variables and buffers can write data into RAM locations, as well as read the contents of the RAM locations. Same as random access memory.

random access *n.*

DIGITAL-specific

Data access in which the location from which the data will be obtained is not dependent on the location of previously obtained data. Types of random access include hashing, keyed, relative record number, and record file address; used with relative file organization.

generic

1. Pertaining to access that is not sequential. The access to data does not depend on previously accessed data.

2. An access mode in which the program-specified value of a key data item identifies the logical record in a relative or indexed file.

random access block (RAB) *n.*

VAX/VMS

An RMS user control block allocated at either assembly or run time to communicate with VAX-11 RMS. The control block describes the records in a particular file and associates with a file access block to form a record access stream. A RAB defines the characteristics needed to perform record-related operations, such as UPDATE, DELETE or GET. Same as RAB.

random access by hashing *n.*

VAX DATATRIEVE

The retrieval or storage of a record by the transformation (through a hashing algorithm) of a user-specified value into a location within the file.

random access by key *n.*

VAX DATATRIEVE

The retrieval or storage of a record by specification (on retrieval) or presence (for storage) of the contents of a particular field (the key field) of the record.

VAX/RMS

1. For indexed files: Retrieval of a data record in an indexed file by the primary (or optionally, alternate) key within the data record. See also key (indexed files).

2. For relative files or sequential files with 512-byte fixed-length records: Retrieval of a data record in a relative file by the relative record number of the record.

See also key (relative files).

VAX/VMS

The retrieval or storage of a record by specifying the key value. This method of record retrieval and storage applies only to indexed files.

random access by record file address *n.*

VAX/RMS

The retrieval of a record by the record's unique address that VAX-11 RMS returns to the user. This record access mode is the only means of randomly accessing a sequential file containing variable-length records. The record file address remains the same for the life of the file.

VAX/VMS

The retrieval of a record by its unique address, which is provided to the program by RMS upon successful $GET or $FIND operations. The record's file address can subsequently be used to randomly access that same record.

random access by relative record number *n.*

VAX DATATRIEVE and VAX/VMS

The retrieval or storage of a record by specifying its position relative to the beginning of the file. This method of record storage and retrieval applies only to sequential files with fixed-length records and relative files.

VAX/VMS

The retrieval of a record by specifying the record's number relative to the beginning of the file. For relative files, random access by relative record number is synonymous with random access by key. See also random access by key (relative files only).

random access memory (RAM) *n.*

DIGITAL-specific

A read/write memory device. Application programs that require storage space for variables and buffers can write data into RAM locations, as well as read the contents of RAM locations. Same as RAM.

random access storage device *n.*

RT-11

A storage device in which data is addressed by direct reference rather than by a serial search of files or words.

range specification *n.*

VAX/VMS

Used with EDT line editor to define the link(s) to be affected by the editing command.

raster *n.*

generic

The bright area produced by the scanning lines on a cathode ray tube when no signal is being accepted.

raster unit *n.*

MINC

A linear measurement unit used in determining bar width for MINC bargraphs. The MINC terminal screen measures 240 by 512 raster units.

VT-11 GRAPHICS

The smallest resolvable distance between two adjacent points. There are 1024 × 1024 raster units in the viewing area of the VT-11 display screen.

raw event *n.*

DECnet

A logging event as recorded by the source process, incomplete in terms of total information required.

RCB *n.*

VAX/VMS

The abbreviation for result control block. Constructed by a command interpreter to represent the command in a form convenient to the program. Same as result control block.

RCI *n.*

DIGITAL-specific and Rdb/ELN

The abbreviation for relational call interface. In DSRI, one of the three nested protocols that together describe how local and remote programs communicate with a relational database management system. Same as relational call interface.

RDB *n.*

DECnet

The abbreviation for receive data buffer. RDBs are large data buffers used by the RSX-11/3271 Protocol Emulator (PE) and DECnet for receiving data. When the PE receives data from the host, it places the data in an RDB. The PE's BSD (binary synchronous device) module accumulates all the RDBs that make up the message being received. If no errors are detected, the BSD module moves the data to an RSX user application program's receive buffer(s). Same as receive data buffer.

RDU *n.*

Terminal Data Management System

The abbreviation for request definition utility. The utility that the definer uses to translate the request definition text and the library definition text into stored CDD (Common Data Dictionary) definitions. This utility is also used to create the request library files that are accessed by application programs at run time. Same as request definition utility.

RDU commands *n.*

Terminal Data Management System

The commands users issue to operate the TDMS (Terminal Data Management System) request definition utility, including commands to process (create, modify, copy, delete, and so on) a request or a request library definition. See also RDU and request definition utility.

reachable node *n.*

DECnet

A node to which the executor node's transport process determines it has a usable communication path.

VAX/VMS

A node to which the local node has a usable communications path.

read *v.*

generic

To transfer information from a peripheral device into core memory or into a register in the CPU.

VAX/VMS

The act or capability of an image to accept data. For example, when a TYPE command is issued, the system reads the designated file from the disk and writes it to the terminal. See also write.

read access type *n.*

VAX/VMS

An instruction or procedure operand attribute indicating that the specified operand is only read during instruction or procedure execution.

read modified operation *n.*

DECnet

In 3270 operations, an operation in which only those display fields that are operator-modified are transferred.

read-only memory (ROM) *n.*

generic

A memory that cannot be altered in normal use of the computer. Usually a small memory that contains often-used instructions such as microprograms or system software as firmware. Same as ROM.

read sharing *n.*

RSX-11M

The process of allowing more than one task to open a file for read access and allowing other tasks to perform read-type operations.

ready mode *n.*

VAX DBMS

A realm status condition that signifies the realm can be accessed by the run unit that issued the READY statement.

ready prompt *n.*

PRO/Diskette System

The message on the Professional screen that tells the user to insert an application or service diskette and press <RESUME>. It is displayed after the system startup and after exiting an application or service.

ready to receive (RTR) *n.*

DECnet

An SNA (systems network architecture) data flow control request used to indicate that an attempt to start a bracket will be accepted. In EC mode, RTR is issued by the PE (protocol emulator) if a BID, issued by the PLU, is accepted. Same as RTR.

realm *n.*

VAX DBMS

In DBMS, one or more areas grouped to allow sub-schema access. Realms are specified in a sub-schema entry. See also area.

realm currency indicator *n.*

VAX DBMS

The place marker used by the DBCS (Database Control System) to indicate the most recently referenced record occurrence in a specific realm.

real number *n.*

PASCAL

In PASCAL-36, the floating-point internal representation of a number that may be of any size; however, each will be rounded to fit the precision of 27 bits (7 to 9 decimal digits). The value 0.0 is also included.

real-time *adj.*

generic

Pertaining to computer actions controlled by external conditions and actual times.

real-time process *n.*

VAX/VMS

A process assigned to a software priority level between 16 and 31, inclusive. The scheduling priority assigned to a real-time process in never modified by the scheduler, although it can be modified by the system manager or the process itself.

real-time processing *n.*

generic

The method of processing in which an event causes a given reaction within an actual time limit.

RT-11

Computation performed while a related or controlled physical activity is occurring so that the results of the computation can be used in guiding the process.

real-time statement *n.*

PEARL

A statement that affects the state of a PEARL task.

real time system (or real-time system) *n.*

DIGITAL-specific

A system performing computation during the actual time the related physical process transpires, so that the results of the computation can be used in guiding the process.

REAL type *n.*

PASCAL and VAX PASCAL

Predefined scalar type that has the single-precision real numbers as values. Same as SINGLE type.

reassembly *n.*

DECnet

The placing of multiple, received data segments by NSP (network service protocol) into a single session control receive buffer.

receive data buffer (RDB) *n.*

DECnet

Large data buffers used by the RSX-11/3271 Protocol Emulator (PE) and DECnet for receiving data. When the PE receives data from the host, it places the data in an RDB. The PE's BSD (binary synchronous device) module accumulates all the RDBs that make up the message being received. If no errors are detected, the BSD module moves the data to an RSX user application program's receive buffer(s). Same as RDB.

receive sequence number N(R) *n.*

VAX PSI

This number contains the expected sequence number of the next information frame to be received. Prior to the transmission of an information or supervisory frame, N(R) is set equal to V(R). N(R) indicates that the DTE or DCE transmitting N(R) has correctly received all frame numbers up to N(R)−1.

receive state variable V(R) *n.*

VAX PSI

This variable denotes the sequence number of the next in-sequence information frame to be received. V(R) is incremented by 1 upon receipt of an error free, in-sequence information frame whose N(S) equals V(R).

receptacle *n.*

generic

An electrical fitting that accepts a plug or prongs.

Recognition *n.*

ALL-IN-1

An ALL-IN-1 function that lets the user enter part of a word. Recognition completes the rest of the word, or provides a list of words that completes the partial entry.

reconfiguration *n.*

A-to-Z

The process by which A-to-Z gathers information on the terminals and printers hooked up to the computer.

generic

The action, process, or result of changing the logical, electrical, or physical characteristics of a system.

record *n.*

generic

A collection of related data items treated as a unit. A record contains one or more fields.

record access block (RAB) *n.*

VAX/VMS

The abbreviation for record access block. An RMS user control block allocated at either assembly or run time to communicate with VAX-11 RMS. The control block describes the records in a particular file and associates with a file access block to form a record access stream. A RAB defines the characteristics needed to perform record-related operations, such as UPDATE, DELETE, or GET. Same as RAB.

record access mode *n.*

DIGITAL-specific and VAX/VMS

The method used in RMS for retrieving and storing records in a file. Access is by one of four methods: sequential, random by key, random by record's file address, and random by relative record number.

record access mode switching *n.*

VAX/VMS

Term applied to the switching from one type of record access mode to another while processing a file.

record access stream *n.*

VAX DATATRIEVE

A serial sequence of record operation requests. Multiple record access streams may be established for relative and indexed files, allowing several independent record access streams to be processed in parallel. See also stream.

record access type *n.*

VAX/VMS

1. The way in which the processor accesses instruction operands.

2. The way in which a procedure accesses its arguments. Same as access type.

record area *n.*

COBOL-74

A storage area allocated for processing the record described in a record description entry in the file section.

record blocking *n.*

VAX/VMS

The technique of grouping multiple records into a single block. On magnetic tape an IRG is placed after the block rather than after each record. This technique reduces the number of I/O transfers required to read or write the data; and, in addition (for magnetic tape), increases the amount of usable storage area. Record blocking also applies to disk files.

record cell *n.*

VAX/RMS and VAX/VMS

A fixed-length area in a relatively organized file that is used to contain one record.

record collection *n.*

VAX DATATRIEVE

A subset of a domain. A collection may consist of no records (in which case it is a null collection), one record, and up to all records in the domain.

record definition *n.*

FMS

A description of a record. The record is stored in the CDD (Common Data Dictionary) and copied into an application program; if the language used doesn't support the CDD, the user must define the record in the program as well as the CDD. The request definition uses the record definition to define mapping between form and the program.

VAX DATATRIEVE

The description of a record's structure that includes the data type, and length of each field. ACMS, TDMS, DATATRIEVE, and DBMS all store record definitions in the CDD (Common Data Dictionary).

record description entry *n.*

COBOL-74

The total set of data description entries associated with a particular record.

record file address (RFA) *n.*

DIGITAL-specific

The unique address of a record in a file that allows records to be retrieved randomly regardless of file organization. The RFA of any particular record remains constant throughout the life of the file. Same as RFA.

record format *n.*

RSX-11M

The shape or form by which RMS-11 recognizes and processes each record in a file. Format dictates how RMS-11 determines a record's size. See also fixed-length, stream, variable-length, variable-with-fixed-control, and undefined.

VAX DATATRIEVE

A file format that has information about record length. See also fixed-length record format, variable-length record format, variable-with-fixed-control record format, and stream record format.

VAX PL/I

The properties of the records in a specific file, including the record length and variability.

VAX/RMS and VAX/VMS

The way a record physically appears on the recording surface of the storage medium. The record format defines the method for determining record length.

record format overhead *n.*

RSX-11M

The control bytes added to user data that RMS-11 requires to support a record format. See also bucket header and record header.

record gap *n.*

TOPS-10

An area on a data medium between consecutive records. It is sometimes used to indicate the end of a block or record.

record header *n.*

RSX-11M

Seven bytes of control data that RMS-11 appends to every user data record in an indexed file. See also bucket header and record format overhead.

record id access *n.*

VAX PL/I

The specification of a record by its internal file identification.

record identifier *n.*

VAX DBMS

A number defined in the schema DDL (data description language) that is used for internal communications with the Database Control System and uniquely identifies one record.

record instance *n.*

VAX DATATRIEVE and VAX DBMS

A user-stored instance of a record type. A record instance is the physical data representation of a single record in the database but not its definition. Same as record occurrence. See also data item occurrence and record type.

record I/O *n.*

VAX DATATRIEVE

That service of a record management system that accepts/delivers logical records to user application programs.

record key *n.*

COBOL-74

A key, either the prime or an alternate, whose contents identify a record within an indexed file.

record layout *n.*

generic

The way in which a record is organized.

record length *n.*

VAX/RMS and VAX/VMS

The size of a record, expressed as a number of bytes.

record-length field *n.*

RSX-11M

A unit of data appended to every VFC (variable-with-fixed-control) or variable-length record, regardless of file organization. The field contains the length of the record to which it is attached.

record location mode *n.*

VAX DATATRIEVE

The access method by which the Database Control System determines the database key values associated with record occurrences. See also direct mode, calc mode, via mode, and location mode.

record locking *n.*

VAX/VMS

The ability to control operations being performed on relative and indexed files that are being simultaneously accessed by more than one program and/or more than one record stream. Record locking makes certain that when a program is adding, deleting, or modifying a record on a given stream, another program or stream is not allowed to access the same record or record cell. See also automatic record locking and manual record locking.

record management services (RMS) *n.*

DIGITAL-specific

Record management services (RMS) is the more sophisticated of two sets of routines (supplied on RSX-11M-PLUS Systems) that are used to open and close files, read from files, write to files, and extend and delete files. RMS supports three forms of file organization and three forms of file access. Same as RMS. See also FCS.

VAX/VMS

A set of operating system procedures that is called by programs to process files and records within files. RMS allows programs to issue GET and PUT requests at the record level (record I/O) as well as read and write blocks (block I/O). VAX RMS is an integral part of the system software; its procedures run in executive mode.

record manager *n.*

DIGITAL-specific

The facility that implements the record access primitives. It provides the record level structure for each file. See also file manager.

record-name (or record name) *n.*

VAX DBMS

A DBA-defined (database administrator) word that names a record type described in a record description entry or in the record section of a subschema and schema.

record occurrence *n.*

VAX DATATRIEVE

A user-stored instance of a record type. A record occurrence is the physical data representation of a single record in the database, but not its definition. Same as record instance. See also data item occurrence and record type.

VAX DBMS

A group of related data item occurrences that is the basic unit for accessing data in a database. In DBMS, the definition of a record occurrence is the record type. See also data item occurrence and record type.

record operation *n.*

RSX-11M

A processing technique involving a record access stream, including: connect, delete, disconnect, find, flush, get, put, rewind, truncate, update.

record-oriented device *n.*

VAX/VMS

A device such as a terminal, line printer, or card reader, on which the largest unit of data a program can access in one I/O operation is the device's physical record.

record position *n.*

VAX DATATRIEVE

A fixed-length area in a relatively organized file that is used to contain one record.

record reference vector (RRV) *n.*

RSX-11M

A copy of a record header that is left in the record's original position when the record is moved during a bucket splitting operation. The RRV preserves access by record file address and facilitates alternate key access. Same as RRV.

record segment *n.*

DIGITAL-specific

That part of a spanned record that is contained in any one block. The segments of a record do not have segments of other records interspersed.

record selection expression (RSE) *n.*

VAX DATATRIEVE

A phrase defining specific conditions individual records must meet before they are included in a DATATRIEVE record stream. Same as RSE.

VAX DBMS

A word or group of contiguous words in a DML (data manipulation language) source program that specifies the selection criteria to be used by the DBCS (Database Control System) to identify a specific database record. Same as RSE.

record's file address (RFA) *n.*

VAX/VMS

The unique address of a record in a file that allows previously accessed records to be accessed randomly at a subsequent time. This access occurs regardless of file organization. Same as RFA.

record storage cell *n.*

RSX-11M

A fixed-length logical division of a relative file. Records are stored in cells; however, not all cells must contain records.

record stream *n.*

VAX DATATRIEVE

A temporary group of related records formed by a record selection expression. This group lasts only during the execution of the statement that forms it.

record transfer mode *n.*

DIGITAL-specific

The method by which an application program can access records in memory. Move mode requires that a record by copied first to the I/O buffer and then to the program by RMS. Locate mode allows the program to directly access a record in the I/O buffer. See also locate mode and move mode.

record type *n.*

VAX DATATRIEVE

The definition of a collection of records.

VAX DBMS

A group of related data item types that defines a record occurrence. In DBMS, record types are specified by a schema entry and modified in the subschema. See also data item type and record occurrence.

record type currency indicator *n.*

VAX DBMS

The place marker used by the DBCS (Database Control System) to indicate the most recently referenced occurrence of a specific record type.

recourse *n.*

USFC/generic

A condition in which the lender has a general claim against the borrower if the equipment's underlying value (collateral) is insufficient to repay the loan.

recovery *n.*

VAX DBMS

In DBMS, the process of restoring a database to a known condition after a system or program failure. In ACMS, users can define recovery as a characteristic for a multiple-step task that uses VAX DBMS. See also after-image journal, before-image journal, journal file, journaling, and transaction.

recovery unit *n.*

VAX DBMS

The logical grouping of a series of DML (data manipulation language) statements that begins with the execution of the first DML statement and ends with the execution of a COMMIT or ROLLBACK statement. The first DML statement can be the first of a run unit or the first after another transaction ends. There can be many transactions in the course of a run unit. Same as transaction.

recovery-unit journal *n.*

VAX DBMS

The VAX DBMS facility that supports transaction rollback. VAX DBMS does recovery-unit journaling automatically. The recovery-unit journal keeps a record of all database updates that have not yet been committed or rolled back. Same as before-image journaling.

rectifier *n.*

generic

A device that permits current to flow in only one direction.

recursive *adj.*

generic

Pertaining to a process in which each step makes use of the results of earlier steps.

recursive procedure *n.*

DIGITAL-specific

A procedure that may invoke itself.

recursive routine *n.*

generic

Any process that can call itself. See also recursive subroutines.

redirection table *n.*

VAX DBMS

A file maintenance by the database administrator that the DBCS (Database Control System) reads to determine which database a run unit should access.

redundancy *n.*

DECnet

In a protocol, the portion of the total characters or bits that can be eliminated without any loss of information.

generic

The characteristic of having more identical circuits or records to increase dependability.

re-entrant *adj.*

DIGITAL-specific

Pertaining to a program composed of a sharable segment of pure code and a nonsharable segment that is the data area.

generic

Pertaining to a program or routine that can be shared at the same time by more than one task.

re-entrant code *n.*

DIGITAL-specific

Code that is never modified during execution. It is possible to let many users share the same copy of a procedure or program written as re-entrant code.

re-entrant program *n.*

DIGITAL-specific

A program consisting of sharable code that can have several simultaneously independent users.

re-entry *n.*

TOPS-20

The resumption of the execution of a process at a predefined point.

referable object *n.*

PEARL

An object whose location can be the content of another object.

reference *n.*

VAX PL/I

The appearance of an identifier in any context except the one in which it is declared.

reference designators *n.*

generic

The location labels on a PC board, or the gate number in a gate array.

reference format *n.*

COBOL-74

A format that provides a standard method for describing COBOL source programs.

reference object *n.*

PEARL

An object whose content is the location of another object.

reference vector *n.*

VAX/VMS

A pointer to an object, formerly referred to as a transfer vector.

reflexive join *n.*

Rdb/ELN

An operation that combines records in the same relation with themselves. For example, the EMPLOYEES relation contains information about both supervised employees and their supervisors. Because each supervisor is also an employee and appears as a record in the relation, the user can retrieve certain information by matching the values of one field (SUPERVISOR_ID) with a second field (EMP_ID) of the same relation. Same as self-join.

reformat *v.*

TOPS-10

To write new headers on a disk pack using the DCRPC diagnostic program.

refresh *v.*

TOPS-10

To remove all files from a file structure and to build the initial set of files based on information in the home block.

refreshing the screen *n.*

VT-11 GRAPHICS

The result of the cyclic action of the display processor as it loops through the active display list. Because the display processor cycles through the list many times a second, the images on the screen appear constant.

region *n.*

VAX/VMS

A contiguous block of physical addresses in which a driver, a task, a resident common, or library resides.

region of interest (ROI) *n.*

Medical Systems

A specific region of the displayed matrix that users define for analysis. The two types of ROIs are regular and irregular. Same as ROI.

ReGIS *n.*

GIGI and RGL/FEP

The acronym for the Remote Graphics Instruction Set. ReGIS is the set of internal commands used by subroutines to draw pictures and plot data.

register *n.*

generic

A circuit for the storage of data for a short period of time.

VAX/VMS

A storage location in hardware logic other than main memory. See also general register, processor register, and device register.

register deferred indexed mode *n.*

VAX/VMS

An indexed addressing method in which the base operand specifier uses register deferred mode addressing.

register deferred mode *n.*

VAX/VMS

A method of addressing in which the contents of the specified register are used as the address of the actual instruction operand.

register mode *n.*

VAX/VMS

An addressing mode in which the contents of the specified register are used as the actual instruction operand.

related data file *n.*

DIGITAL-specific

The data file described by a particular dictionary.

related dictionary *n.*

DIGITAL-specific

A dictionary specified in a primary dictionary as a second or third dictionary.

relation *n.*

DIGITAL-specific

A tabular array of data items consisting of rows and columns. Columns have unique names and divide rows into a set of fields. For a single field in a row, there is only one data item.

VAX DATATRIEVE

A two-dimensional array of data elements.

relational call interface (RCI) *n.*

DIGITAL-specific and Rdb/ELN

In DSRI, one of the three nested protocols that together describe how local and remote programs communicate with a relational database management system. Same as RCI.

relational database *n.*

DIGITAL-specific

A database comprised of a series of tables, called relations. A relation is comprised of records and fields. Fields contain a single data item. Relations are associated with one another according to field values in the relation.

relational data model *n.*

DIGITAL-specific

Defines the logical structure of data in a relational database. The relational data model is characterized by the representation of data in a tabular format. A relational database is a series of tables, called relations. Each table consists of rows and columns, called records and fields, respectively.

relational expression *n.*

generic

An expression composed of relational operators and specified values that determine the relationship between operator specified fields and values.

relational operation *n.*

DIGITAL-specific

A method used to retrieve records from a relational database. Relational operations are included in programs to replace substantial amounts of user-written code.

relational operator *n.*

COBOL-74

A reserved word, a relation character, a group of consecutive reserved words, or a group of consecutive reserved words and relation characters used in the construction of a relation condition. The permissible operators and their meanings are: IS [NOT] GREATER THAN meaning greater than or not greater than; IS [NOT] > IS [NOT] LESS THAN meaning less than or not less than; IS [NOT] , IS [NOT] EQUAL TO IS [NOT] = meaning equal to or not equal to. See also relation condition.

DSM-11

An operator that produces a truth-values result based on the relationship of its operands. If the relationship expressed by the operator and its operands is true, it produces a value of true (1). If the relationship expressed by the operator and its operands is false, it produces a value of false (0).

generic

A symbol used to compare two values. A relational operator shows a condition that may be either true or false.

PASCAL and VAX PASCAL

A symbol that tests the relationship between two values, the result of which is one of the Boolean values, FALSE or TRUE. PASCAL's relational operators are $<$, $>$, $\leq$, $\geq$, and $<>$.

VAX DATATRIEVE

A symbol or phrase to compare values. For example, in the DATATRIEVE statement FIND YACHTS WITH BEAM > 10, the phrase "BEAM > 10" is a Boolean expression containing the Boolean operator ">" (greater than).

VAX PL/I

One of the punctuation symbols ($>$, $<$, $=$, $\leq$, $\geq$, $\wedge$, $\wedge>$, or $\wedge=$) that states a relationship between two expressions between two expressions and results in a 1-bit Boolean value indicating whether the relationship is true or false. Same as comparison operator.

VAX/VMS

One of the operators $<$, $>$, $\leq$, or $\geq$. The result (type INT) is 0 or 1, indicating a false or true relation, respectively. The usual arithmetic conversions are performed on the two operands. Relational operators group from left to right.

relation condition *n.*

COBOL-74

A condition in which a truth value can be determined that the value of an arithmetic expression or data item has a specific relationship to the value of another arithmetic expression or data item. See relational operator and truth value.

relative accuracy *n.*

MINC

The degree to which digital-to-analog (D/A) output uniformly reflects changes in digital input and, conversely, the degree to which analog-to-digital (A/D) output reflects changes in analog input.

relative address *n.*

generic

The number that specifies the difference between the base address and the actual address.

TOPS-10

The address before hardware or software relocation is added.

RSX-20F

An address specified by the PDP-11 software on a Protected Examine or Deposit. The address specified by the PDP-11 is relative to the Examine or Deposit region, and runs from 0 to the maximum relative address (which is kept by the KL in the executive process table, EPT. See also Examine region, Deposit region, EPT, and Protected Examines/Deposits.

RT-11

The number that specifies the difference between the actual address and a base address.

relative file *n.*

DIGITAL-specific

A record file in which each record occupies a fixed-length, numbered cell. Records in the file are individually accessed by specifying the number of a cell, relative to the first record in the file. The first cell in the file is numbered 1. See also relative organization.

relative file organization *n.*

VAX/VMS

The arrangement of records in a file in which each record occupies a cell of equal length within a bucket. Each cell is assigned a successive number, which represents its position relative to the beginning of the file.

relative key *n.*

COBOL-74

A key whose contents identify a logical record in a relative file.

relative location *n.*

GIGI and RGL/FEP

A point on the screen whose coordinates are based on its distance from the current graphic location rather than from the origin location. The coordinates' units are defined by the user. See also absolute location.

relative organization (or relative file organization) *n.*

DIGITAL-specific

The permanent logical file structure in which each record is uniquely identified by an integer value greater than zero that specifies the record's logical ordinal position in the file. See also relative file.

relative path name *n.*

Common Data Dictionary

The shortened form of a dictionary path name. It includes only the parts of the path name that follow the default CDD (Common Data Dictionary) directory name. Use either the full path name or the relative path name to refer to directories, sub-dictionaries, and objects in the CDD. See also given name, path name, and partial path name.

relative point *n.*

VT-11 GRAPHICS

A point on the display screen that is defined in relation to the current beam position. See also absolute point.

relative record number *n.*

RSX-11M

Each record in a relative file is stored in a cell. Each cell can be addressed randomly by a number relative to its distance from the beginning of the file. This number is called the creative record number.

VAX DATATRIEVE

A number representing a relative position that identifies a record in a relative file. Used in random access to relative files.

VAX PL/I

1. The position of a specific record in a relative file.

2. The key by which a record in a relative file is accessed randomly.

VAX/RMS and VAX/VMS

An identification number that specifies the position of a record cell relative to the beginning of the file; used as the key during random access by key mode to relative files.

relative time *n.*

generic

A positive future time reference with respect to the current simulator time.

relative value *n.*

FFE

In FFE commands, a parameter or argument specified as a signed number or signed coordinate, indicating an increase or decrease from the current setting.

relative vector *n.*

VT-11 GRAPHICS

A line segment drawn from the current beam position to a coordinate position relative to the beam position.

relative volume table (RVT) *n.*

VAX/VMS

A table containing information needed to associate the volumes of a multivolume set with the address of the UCB (unit control block) of the drive on which each volume is mounted. The relative volume table contains the number of volumes and a list of the UCBs used. Same as RVT.

relay *n.*

generic

A switch that is operated by electricity instead of by hand.

RELEASE QUIESCE (RELQ) *n.*

DECnet

An SNA (systems network architecture) data flow control request used to allow resumption of data transmission by a "quiesced" receiver. RELQ is an expedited request that may be issued by the PLU (primary logical unit) or SLU (secondary logical unit) in a Profile 4 session. Same as RELQ.

REL file *n.*

TOPS-10

A file containing one or more relocatable object modules.

relocatable *adj.*

generic

Pertaining to the routine, module, or program that can be run regardless of its physical memory location.

relocatable addresses *n.*

RSX-11M and TOPS-10

The provisional memory addresses assigned by the assembler or compiler for object modules. These addresses are assigned as if the resulting task would have the computer to itself. The Task Builder changes these relocatable addresses into addresses that the system can use when the object modules are linked.

relocatable control section *n.*

RT-11 and TOPS-10

A control section whose addresses have been specified relative to zero. The control section can be placed into any area of core memory for execution.

relocatable object module *n.*

RT-11

An object module that has a control section whose address constants can be changed by the linker. The ability to change the address constants allows the object module to be loaded anywhere in memory.

relocate *v.*

generic

To move a routine, module, or program and to adjust address constants so that the routine module, or program, can be executed.

TOPS-10

1. To move a routine from one portion of storage to another and to adjust the necessary address references so that the routine can be executed in its new location.

2. To convert a relocatable binary module to an absolute binary module.

MicroPower PASCAL

To associate each program section in a merged object module to a specific set of virtual addresses. That is one step in the process of linking a MicroPower PASCAL application program. The RELOC utility performs this function and produces a process image file.

RT-11

In programming, to move a routine from one portion of storage to another and to adjust the necessary address references so that the routine, in its new location, can be executed.

relocation counter *n.*

TOPS-10

1. The number assigned by the linker as the beginning address of a control section. This number is assigned in the process of loading specific control sections into a saved file or a core memory and is transformed from a relocatable quantity to an absolute quantity.

2. The address counter that is used during the assembly of relocatable code.

relocation factor *n.*

TOPS-10

The contents of the relocation counter for a control section. This number is added to every relocatable reference within the control section. The relocation factor is determined from the relocatable based address for the control section (usually 0 and 400000) and the actual address in user virtual address space at which the module is being loaded.

RELQ *n.*

DECnet

The acronym for RELEASE QUIESCE. SNA (systems network architecture) data flow control request used to allow resumption of data transmission by a "quiesced" receiver. RELQ is an expedited request that may be issued by the PLU (primary logical unit) or SLU (secondary logical unit) in a Profile 4 session. Same as RELEASE QUIESCE.

REMACP *n.*

VAX/VMS

Remote I/O ACP.

remote access *n.*

TOPS-10

Refers to communication with a data processing facility by one or more stations that are distant from that facility.

remote batch *n.*

TOPS-10

A feature of the computing system that allows data I/O and job control of batch processing from a distant terminal over a synchronous communication link.

remote command terminal *n.*

VAX/VMS

A terminal that is logically connected to another node by means of a network, in a way that a command terminal is physically connected to a node by means of a dial-up line.

remote database *n.*

generic

A database stored on one computer, called the remote node, and accessed by a program on another, called the host node.

remote device *n.*

VAX/VMS

A device that is not directly connected to the local node, but is available through the VAXcluster.

remote DTE (data terminal equipment) *n.*

VAX PSI and VAX/VMS

Any DTE (data terminal equipment) within the network other than the one at which the user is located.

Remote Graphics Instruction Set (ReGIS) *n.*

GIGI and RGL/FEP

A set of internal commands used by subroutines to draw pictures and plot data. Same as ReGIS.

remote job entry (RJE) *n.*

DECnet

1. Submission of jobs through an input device that has access to a computer through a communications link.

2. The mode of operation that allows input of a batch job by a card reader at a remote site and receipt of the output by means of a line printer or card punch at a remote site.

Same as RJE.

generic

Input of jobs through a device with access to a computer via a communications connection.

remote node *n.*

DECnet

Any other node in a network that is not a user's local node.

generic

Any node other than the local node.

VAX/VMS

Any node in the network other than the one at which the user is located. See also adjacent node, local node, and executor node.

remote NSP (network services protocol) *n.*

DECnet

Refers to the NSP (network services protocol) executing in a remote node.

remote patching *n.*

CTS-300

The ability to make changes in a source file from a remote terminal while the XMTSD run-time system is operating.

remote peripherals *n.*

TOPS-10

The I/O devices and other data processing equipment, with the exception of the central processor, located at the site of the remote batch terminal.

remote repeater *n.*

Ethernet

An Ethernet repeater designed to link Ethernet cable segments separated by up to 1 kilometer. A fiber optic cable is an integral part of the remote repeater (see repeater).

remote server *n.*

VAX DATATRIEVE

The part of DATATRIEVE that lets users access data on other computers. When the user, using the computer VACKS1, types READY PERSONNEL AT VACKS2, DATATRIEVE logs on to an account on VACKS2. The remote server processes statements at the remote computer VACKS2.

remote station *n.*

DECnet

A station, other than a control station, on a multiport line. Same as tributary station.

remote task *n.*

DECnet

A task executing in a remote node.

remote virtual terminal *n.*

VAX PSI

A terminal connected to a packet assembly/disassembly (PAD) facility. This is also called an X.29 terminal.

384

removal class *n.*

VAX DBMS

That characteristic of a record type in a set that determines whether or not a record occurrence of that type may be disconnected from membership in an occurrence of the set.

remove *v.*

RSX-11M

To take the name and address of a task out of the system task directory (STD), thus removing the task. A task must have been installed before it can be removed.

rendition *n.*

VAXstation Display System

The text attribute that specifies whether characters are displayed in some combination of bold, italic, inverse, blinking, and underlined.

reorganization *n.*

VAX/VMS

A record-by-record copy of an indexed file to another indexed file with the same key attributes as the input file.

repeater *n.*

The interconnecting link between two Ethernet cable segments. The repeater provides a means of extending Ethernet networks beyond the 500 meter limit of a single Ethernet coaxial cable.

repeating group *n.*

VAX DBMS

A group data item whose description contains an OCCURS clause, or a group data item subordinate to a data item whose description contains an OCCURS clause.

repetitive statement *n.*

PASCAL and VAX PASCAL

A statement that causes an action to be performed repeatedly. PASCAL's repetitive statements are FOR, REPEAT, and WHILE.

replace *v.*

DECWORD

To make DECWORD delete selected text in a document and insert the text in the paste buffer in its place.

replace writing *n.*

GIGI and RGL/FEP

The mode of writing that causes the object or text string to be written on the screen and to replace any other object that has been written in the same location.

reply line *n.*

MINC

A line on the digital-output module (MNCDO) used by laboratory instruments to indicate to the digital-output module that data has been received.

report clause *n.*

COBOL-74

A clause in the Report Section of the Data Division that appears in a report description entry or a report group description entry.

report description entry *n.*

COBOL-74

An entry in the Report Section of the Data Division that is composed of the level indicator RD followed by a report name, followed by a set of report clauses, as required.

report file *n.*

COBOL-74

An output file whose file description entry contains a REPORT clause. The contents of a report file consist of records that are written under control of the report writer control system.

report footing *n.*

COBOL-74

A report group that is presented only at the end of a report.

report generator *n.*

DIGITAL-specific

A computer program that processes data and combines it into a specified format, such as a report.

report group *n.*

COBOL-74

In the Report Section of the Data Division, an 01 level-number entry and its subordinate entries.

report group description entry *n.*

COBOL-74

An entry in the Report Section of the Data Division that is composed of the level-number 01, the optional data-name, a TYPE clause, and an optional set of report clauses.

report header *n.*

VAX DATATRIEVE

The heading of a DATATRIEVE report writer report, consisting of these optional elements: a centered report-name and, at the top-right corner of the report, a date and a page number.

report heading *n.*

COBOL-74

A report group that is presented only at the beginning of a report.

report level *n.*

TOPS-10

The report level is the level that IQL (interactive query language) enters when the RUN or EXECUTE assistance command is issued to generate a report.

report name *n.*

COBOL-74

A user-defined word that names a report described in a report description entry within the Report Section of the Data Division.

report section *n.*

COBOL-74

The section of the Data Division that contains one or more report description entries and their associated report group description entries.

report specification *n.*

VAX DATATRIEVE

A series of report writer statements creating a report and specifying its format.

report writer *n.*

VAX DATATRIEVE

A subsystem of DATATRIEVE that lets users create reports displaying data in an easy-to-read format.

report writer control system (RWCS) *n.*

COBOL-74

An object-time control system provided by the implementor that constructs reports. Same as RWCS.

report writer logical record *n.*

COBOL-74

A record that consists of the report writer print line and associated control information necessary for its selection and vertical positioning.

request *n.*

Terminal Data Management System

A set of TDMS (Terminal Data Management System) instructions, created in the request definition utility and stored in the CDD (Common Data Dictionary), that describe an exchange of data between a program record and a form. A request includes references to one or more form and record definitions and instructions for mapping data between a form and a program record. A request is passed as a parameter in the TSS$REQUEST call. ACMS tasks use requests to display forms on a terminal and gather information from a terminal user.

request call *n.*

FMS

The call in an application program that activates the request definition. This call causes the display of the form, data collection, data mapping, and data conversion.

Terminal Data Management System

The call in a TDMS (Terminal Data Management System) application program that executes a request.

request count *n.*

DECnet

This term has two definitions in NSP (network services protocol).

1. Variables that NSP uses to determine when to send data.

2. Values sent in link service (data request and interrupt request) messages.

The flow control mechanism adds the request counts received in data request and interrupt request messages to the request counts it maintains to determine when to send data.

request definition *n.*

FMS

A set of instructions stored as an object in the CDD (Common Data Dictionary). These instructions describe an exchange of data between an application program and a form. Includes reference to a form definition, record definition, and instruction for data mapping between form and program. It is named in the request library and the TSS$REQUEST call. Provides the link between the data entry operator and the program.

request definition file (RDF) *n.*

FMS

The VAX/VMS file that contains the request definition text. Same as RDF.

request definition text *n.*

FMS

The series of instructions before the RDU (request definition utility) translates them into a binary request definition. These instructions describe an exchange of data between an application program and a form. The definer types the request definition text directly into redundancy RDU, or into a "request definition file" (RDF) which is passed to RDU for translation.

387

request definition utility (RDU) *n.*

DIGITAL-specific

The TDMS (Terminal Data Management System) utility used to process (create, modify, replace, and so on) requests and request library definitions and to store them in the CDD (Common Data Dictionary). Use this utility to build request library files, which are accessed by an application program at run time. Same as RDU.

request event *n.*

FMS

Both the act of evaluating a request definition or a request segment and the resulting action that FMS2 tabs when it reads and executes the instruction in a segment of a request definition. An EVENT includes all the action resulting from the time an application program calls the FMS2$REQUEST routines until the request action is terminated and control is returned to the application program.

request handle *n.*

DIGITAL-specific

A host variable that lets the user explicitly reference a request.

request header (RH) *n.*

DECnet

A 3-byte field used in SNA (systems network architecture) transmissions to specify certain control functions to be exercised with respect to the accompanying request unit (RU). Same as RH and response header.

request instructions *n.*

Terminal Data Management System

The statements in a TDMS (Terminal Data Management System) request that describe the exchange of data between a program record and a form. These statements can:

- identify the form and record definitions between which data is to be transferred

- provide instructions for transferring the data.

The request instructions are executed when the TDMS application program issues a TSS$REQUEST call.

request library definition *n.*

Terminal Data Management System

A definition, stored in the CDD (Common Data Dictionary), that lists the names of related requests to use in a particular TDMS (Terminal Data Management System) application. A request must be named in a request library definition before users can build a request library file. The program uses the request library file to access requests.

request library file (RLB) *n.*

DIGITAL-specific

The VAX/VMS file that contains all the request and form definitions and all the record references used by an application program at execution time. Before a program can use a request definition, a channel and a request library file must be opened. The request definition utility (RDU) creates this file by extracting the form, request, and record definitions from the CDD (Common Data Dictionary) according to instructions in the CDD library definition.

request library instructions *n.*

Terminal Data Management System

The statements in a TDMS (Terminal Data Management System) request library definition that identify the requests used in a TDMS application. These instructions also give the name of the request library file where these requests and their associated form and record definitions are to be stored.

request recovery *n.*

DECnet

An SNA (systems network architecture) session control request, issued by the protocol emulator in emulator control and extended emulator control modes if it receives a negative response to a sequence number in the TH of a transmission to the PLU (primary logical unit). The command requests a sequence number resynchronization with the PLU.

request segment *n.*

FMS

A piece of a request definition that FMS2 reads and executes during a request event. A request definition may contain one or many such executable pieces.

REQUEST SHUTDOWN *n.*

DECnet

An SNA (systems network architecture) data flow control request used by the SLU to request an orderly session termination. Typically, the PE (protocol emulator) will issue a RSHUT upon receipt of a DSC (disconnect) macro from RSX-11M application. Same as RSHUT.

request to send (RTS) *n.*

RSX-20F

A signal sent from the data terminal equipment (in this case the DTE-20) to the DCE (data communications equipment) to condition the DCE for transmission. Since all terminal communication is full-duplex, the local modem should always be ready to transmit when a user is dialed in. Thus, RTS should always be asserted by the PDP-11 for active dial-up lines. Same as RTS.

request unit *n.*

DECnet

User-created data in SNA (systems network architecture) that accompanies a request header.   The request unit cannot exceed 256 bytes.

rescue *n.*

generic

A formatted dump of data only.

reserved *adj.*

DIGITAL-specific

The description of a field or value that is not to be used. It is specified as either:

1. reserved for DIGITAL, in which case it is reserved for any future extension of the standard architecture; or

2. reserved for CSS/customers, in which case it is to be used for any non-standard applications.

reserved words *n.*

generic

Words defined by the computer to have only one meaning. Reserved words may not be used as field names.

reset *n.*

VAX PSI

The capability of a DTE (data terminal equipment) to re-initialize a virtual circuit by resetting the lower window edge and P(S) and P(R) numbers to zero. All data and interrupt packets that may be in the network are discarded.

resident *adj.*

generic

Pertaining to data or instructions that are stored permanently in main memory.

resident common *n.*

VAX/VMS

A shared region in which data resides and that can be shared by two or more tasks.

resident library *n.*

RSX-11M

A set of memory-resident routines that can be shared by multiple tasks, but are part of none of them. When a task uses a routine in the library, the operating system maps the library segment containing the routine into the task's address space with active page registers.

VAX/VMS

A shared region in which single copies of commonly used subroutines reside that can be shared by two or more tasks.

resident monitor *n.*

DIGITAL-specific

A group of programs that includes terminal service, operating system error handling, system device handlers, EDT processor, and system tables.

residual value *n.*

generic

The amount for which a company expects to be able to sell a fixed asset at the end of its service life. Same as salvage value and scrap value.

resignal *n.*

VAX PL/I

The mechanism by which a condition handler, or ON-unit, indicates that a signal is still active.

resistance *n.*

generic

That characteristic that works against the flow of electric current through material.

resistor *n.*

generic

An electric circuit element used to provide resistance.

resolution *n.*

MINC

The smallest analog change that can be discriminated. In the context of A/D converters; resolution is equivalent to the analog value of the LSB (least significant bit) of the successive approximation register.

resonance *n.*

generic

The phenomenon whereby a system tends to vibrate at a particular frequency when externally excited.

resource *n.*

generic

An available part of the computer's hardware or software.

VAX/VMS

A physical part of the computer system such as a device or memory, or an interlocked data structure such as a mutex. Quotas and limits control the use of physical resources.

resource monitoring display (RMD) *n.*

RSX-11M

The resource monitoring display is invoked by the SHOW MEMORY command. RMD displays the current contents of memory, currently active task, and other system information. Same as RMD.

resource-sharing *n.*

generic

The common use of one central processor by several users as well as by several peripheral devices.

resource wait mode *n.*

VAX/VMS

An execution state in which a process indicates that it will wait until a system resource becomes available when it issues a service request requiring a resource. If a process wants notification when a resource is not available, it can disable resource wait mode during program execution.

response header (RH) *n.*

DECnet

A 3-byte field used in SNA (systems network architecture) transmissions to specify certain control functions to be exercised in respect to the accompanying response unit (RU). Same as RH and request header.

response time *n.*

DECnet

The elapsed time between the generation of the last character of a message at a terminal and the receipt of the first character of the reply. It includes terminal delay, network delay, and service node delay.

generic

The time it takes the system to answer a query from a terminal.

response unit (RU) *n.*

DECnet

Data in SNA (systems network architecture) that accompanies a response header. It cannot exceed 256 bytes, and is generally less than 8 bytes. Same as RU.

restart *v.*

generic

To put or go into motion, operation or activity again.

restart address *n.*

generic

The address at which a program can be restarted.

restarting *n.*

generic

The process of turning on the computer and preparing it for use.

restore *n.*

generic

The process by which you copy files from a diskette or tape to an area on the fixed disk.

restore v.

DIGITAL-specific

To copy back-up data to recover the contents of a file.

restricted front end n.

RSX-20F

A PDP-11 that is attached to a KL by means of a DTE-20 and that cannot crash the KL if the KL hardware and software are working correctly. A restricted front end cannot use the diagnostic bus and cannot read KL memory unless the KL has first set up the interrupt system to allow that to happen.

restricted state n.

DECnet

A node state where no new logical links from other nodes are allowed.

restriction clause n.

VAX DATATRIEVE

A statement allowing users to specify the maximum length of a record stream.

result control block (RCB) n.

VAX/VMS

A block constructed by a command interpreter to represent the command in a form convenient to the program. Same as RCB.

result file descriptor (RFD) n.

VAX/VMS

A descriptor constructed by the command interpreter. Same as RFD.

result option descriptor n.

VAX/VMS

A descriptor constructed by the command interpreter. Same as ROD.

resume n.

VAX/VMS

To activate a suspended process. Contrast with wake.

retaining n.

VAX DBMS

In DBMS, an option on the DML COMMIT statement. The COMMIT RETAINING statement:

- does not empty keeplists

- retains all currency indicators

- does not release realm locks

- releases all record locks.

retention class n.

VAX DBMS

An attribute of member records that describes when and how the member record occurrence can be removed from a set. See also fixed member, mandatory member, and optional member.

retransmission n.

DECnet

The resending of NSP (network services protocol) or DDCMP (Digital Data Communications Message Protocol) data messages that have not been acknowledged within a certain period of time. This is part of NSP's and DDCMP's error control mechanisms.

retrieval information block (RIB) *n.*

TOPS-10

The block that contains pointers to all the groups in a specific file. Each file has two copies of the RIB, one in the first block of the first group, and the second in the block following the last data block in the last group of the file. Same as RIB.

retrieval lock *n.*

generic

An integrity lock that prevents a record from being changed in any way by a concurrent run unit.

retrieval pointer *n.*

RSX-11M

Data associated with a file that specifies blocks on disk. From the structure and content of a retrieval pointer, the file processor can equate virtual blocks to logical blocks. See also window and virtual-to-logical block mapping.

retrieval usage mode *n.*

VAX DBMS

The state of a realm during which its records may be read but cannot be modified.

retry count *n.*

TOPS-10

The number of times an operation is tried, in addition to the first time.

return *n.*

DECWORD

An invisible character that forces all following text to the next line. Sometimes called a carriage return, initiated by pressing RETURN.

DIGITAL-specific

1. The set of instructions at the end of a subroutine that transfers control to the proper point in the calling program.

2. The point in the calling program to which control is returned.

return *v.*

FMS

To send back, as in "return to value." An FDV (Form Driver) subroutine called by an FMS application program returns a value to the program as the result of the function or procedure performed in the subroutine. FDV subroutines can return string values for output arguments, such as current field name, field value, and named data; subroutines can also return numeric values that represent status codes.

return descriptor *n.*

VAX PL/I

A set of attributes describing the data type of the return value of a function.

return status code *n.*

VAX/VMS

A longword value that indicates the success or failure of a specific function. For example, system services always return a status code in R0 upon completion. Same as status code.

revenue *n.*

generic

The increase in owner's equity resulting from operations during a period of time, usually from the sale of goods or services.

reversal (reversing) entry *n.*

generic

An entry in which all debits and credits are the credits and debits, respectively, of another entry, and in the same amounts.

reverse charging *n.*

VAX PSI

An optional PSDN (packet switching data network) facility that allows a DTE (data terminal equipment) to request that the remote DTE is charged for a particular call.

reverse interrupt (RVI) *n.*

DECnet

In binary synchronous communications (BSC), a control character sequence sent by a receiving station instead of ACK1 or ACK0 to request premature termination of the transmission in progress. Same as RVI.

reverse video *n.*

DIGITAL-specific

A feature of the terminal that reverses the default video contrast. (If black figures upon a white background is the default, reverse video displays white upon black.) Used with some editors to highlight a range of text.

rewind (record operation) *v.*

DIGITAL-specific

To reset the context of a stream to the logical beginning of the file.

RFA *n.*

RSX-11M and VAX/VMS

The abbreviation for record file address. RFA is the unique address of a record in a file that allows records, previously accessed, to be accessed randomly at a subsequent time. This occurs regardless of file organization. Same as record file address.

RFD *n.*

VAX/VMS

The abbreviation for result file descriptor. A descriptor constructed by the command interpreter. Same as result file descriptor.

RGL/FEP *n.*

RGL/FEP

The ReGIS graphics library for the FORTRAN enhancement package, Version 2.

RH *n.*

DECnet

The abbreviation for request header or response header. RH is a 3-byte field used in SNA (systems network architecture) transmission to specify certain control functions to be exercised with respect to the accompanying request unit (RU). Same as request header and response header.

RIB *n.*

DECsystem-10 and FMS

The abbreviation for retrieval information block. The block that contains pointers to all the groups in a specific file. Each file has two copies of the RIB, one in the first block of the first group, and the second in the block following the last data block in the last group of the file. Same as retrieval information block.

right-aligned tab *n.*

DECWORD

A column in which tabbed text is aligned on the right. Indicated by > in the ruler.

right-justified attribute *n.*

generic

A field attribute specifying that the data entered is to be aligned with the right-most data position.

right-linked pointer *n.*

DSM-11

A pointer stored in a block used by globals and routine files that specifies the address of a related block.

rights database *n.*

VAX/VMS

The collection of data the system maintains and uses to define identifiers and associate identifiers with the holders of the identifiers.

rights list *n.*

VAX/VMS

The list associated with each process that includes all the identifiers the process holds.

ring buffer *n.*

MicroPower PASCAL

A system data structure designed primarily for character-oriented data communication between processes. Both input and output operations can be performed simultaneously on the same ring buffer.

RJE *n.*

DECnet

The acronym for remote job entry.

1. Submission of jobs through an input device that has access to a computer through a communications link.

2. The mode of operation that allows input of a batch job by a card reader at a remote site and receipt of the output via a line printer or card punch at a remote site.

Same as remote job entry.

RMD *n.*

RSX-11M

The abbreviation for resource monitoring display. The resource monitoring display is invoked by the SHOW MEMORY command. RMD displays the current contents of memory, currently active task, and other system information. Same as resource monitoring display.

RMS *n.*

DIGITAL-specific

The abbreviation for record management services. RMS is the more sophisticated of two sets of routines that are used to open and close files, read from files, write to files, and extend and delete files. RMS supports three forms of file organization and three forms of file access. Same as record management services. See also FCS.

RMS-11 *n.*

VAX/VMS

A set of routines that are linked with compatibility mode programs, and provide similar functional capabilities to VAX RMS. The file organizations and record formats used by RMS-11 are very similar to those of VAX RMS.

RNO *n.*

DIGITAL-specific

The abbreviation for RUNOFF. A DIGITAL document formatter used to prepare and highlight printed documents and manuscripts. To convert RUNOFF documents to DECWORD documents, select WR from the option menu. Same as RUNOFF.

rocker switch *n.*

generic

A type of switch having a control arm in its center and operated by pushing either end.

ROD *n.*

VAX/VMS

The abbreviation for result option descriptor. A descriptor constructed by the command interpreter. Same as result option descriptor.

rollback (or roll-back) *n.*

DIGITAL-specific

A data manipulation statement used to restore a database to an original state. Rollback terminates a transaction and negates all changes made to a database during that transactions.

generic

A system that will restart the running program after a system failure. Snapshots of data and programs are stored at periodic intervals and the system rolls back to restart at the last recorded snapshot.

VAX DBMS

1. In DBMS, the process of using a before-image journal to restore a database to an earlier known state. This process negates updates to the database made by the transaction or recovery unit being rolled back.

2. In ACMS, an application definition utility keyword used when defining multiple-step tasks with recovery.

See also commit.

roll-forward *n.*

VAX DBMS

In DBMS, the process of using an after-image journal to restore a database to known state. This process replaces updates to the database that were lost because a system or program failure required the installation of backup media. See also recover.

rolling out *n.*

DIGITAL-specific

The process by which the Executive makes memory space and processor time available to tasks according to their priority. If a higher-priority task is ready to run and no memory is available, then lower-priority tasks will be temporarily removed, or checkpointed, to make room for the higher-priority task. The lower-priority tasks are saved on the disk exactly as they were when interrupted. When memory is available, the tasks are returned to memory and take up exactly where they left off. The user's task can be checkpointed without his knowledge. If the task seems slow or refuses to accept input, it may be checkpointed. Checkpointing is an automatic process. Same as checkpointing.

rollup *n.*

DIGITAL-specific

In accounting, the act or result of combining together a number of similar items; hence, a summary or total.

ROM *n.*

generic

The acronym for read only memory. A ROM is memory in which information is permanently stored at the time of production and is not alterable by computer instructions. Same as read-only memory.

root *n.*

DSM-11

The first, unscripted name level of an array.

RSX-11M

The highest level in an index. The root is a single-bucket entry point to the index for random accesses using the associated key. See also primary root.

VAX DBMS

The initial segment of a fragmented record.

root caching *n.*

RSX-11M

An I/O technique by which the user supplies virtual address space for more than the two I/O buffers required by RMS-11 for an indexed file. If the file is not being write shared, RMS-11 uses the extra buffers to cache the root buckets of indexes it uses for random access operations. See also multiple buffers.

root dictionary directory *n.*

Common Data Dictionary

The directory at the top of the VAX-11 CDD (Common Data Dictionary) hierarchy. The root directory is named CDD$TOP. Every dictionary directory, subdictionary, and object in the CDD is a descendant of CDD$TOP.

root segment *n.*

CTS-300

The module that is the main part of the program and that calls the external subroutines. It is associated with external subroutines and library modules by the linking process.

generic

The segment of a tree of an overlay structure on which other segments basically depend.

RT-11 and VAX/VMS

The segment of an overlay structure that, when loaded, remains resident in memory during the execution of a program.

rotational speed *n.*

generic

The speed at which data may be exchanged with the central processor, expressed in thousands of bytes per second.

round robin *adj.*

generic

Pertaining to a sequential allocation of computer resources.

round robin n.

VAX/VMS

A form of time sharing that gives images of equal priority equal access to the CPU. The VAX/VMS operating system uses round-robin scheduling for each of the sixteen software priority levels. Each process at a given software priority level executes in turn before any other process at that level (a FIFO queue).

round-robin scheduler n.

RSX-11M

A form of time sharing that gives tasks of equal priority equal access to the CPU (central processing unit). The Executive tends to give CPU time to the first task in the system task directory (STD). The round-robin scheduler rotates the entries in the STD. The round-robin scheduler also causes a significant event after a given time interval. The significant even causes the Executive to search the STD for a task that is eligible to run. The first task in the STD gains access to the CPU. After a time interval, the round-robin scheduler again rotates the entries in the STD and causes another significant event. The new first task in the STD gains access to the CPU and so forth. In this way, tasks of the same priority have an equal share of CPU time.

router n.

VAX/VMS

A node that can send and receive packets, and route packets from one node to another.

router server n.

DECnet

A Phase IV DECnet node that performs routing functions only. The router server connects with the local area network cable on one side and with host nodes or other communications servers on the other.

route-through n.

DECnet

The directing of packets from source nodes to destination nodes by one or more intervening nodes. Routine nodes permit route-through. See also packet switching.

routine n.

generic

A set of instructions that perform as operation.

routine buffer n.

DSM-11

One of five major sections of a partition. The routine buffer stores the lines of a DSM-11 routine. As the routine buffer fills, it grows toward the high end of the partition's memory. As the routine buffer empties, it shrinks toward the low end of the partition's memory.

routine line n.

DSM-11

One or more statements input to DSM for later execution as part of a routine. Users must precede the statements in a routine line with a TAB character. Users can precede the TAB with an optional line label.

routine name n.

COBOL-74

A user-defined word that identifies a procedure written in a language other than COBOL.

DSM-11

An identifier that is associated with a particular routine. System library routine names must use the percent symbol (%) as the first character.

routing *v.*

DECnet

Directing data message packets from source nodes to destination nodes.

VAX/VMS

The network function that determines the path along which data travels to its destination.

routing algorithm *n.*

DECnet and TOPS-20

Specific to ARPANET, the procedure used by the nodes to determine which of the several possible paths through the network will be taken by a packet. ARPANET uses adaptive routine in which routes selected vary according to conditions on the network.

routing layer *n.*

DECnet

Modules in the routing layer used to route user data (called a datagram) to its destination. Such routing modules also provide congestion control and packet lifetime control. Same as transport layer.

routing node *n.*

DECnet

A Phase III DECnet node that contains the full set of transport modules, and can deliver, receive, and route through packets.

generic

A node that can transfer information from one node to another node.

routing protocol *n.*

DECnet

In the routing layer, the protocol that handles routing and congestion control.

row *n.*

MINC

On a terminal screen, the horizontal strip in which a line of text can be displayed. The MINC terminal can display up to 24 rows. With MINC, text coordinates are given in rows and columns; graph coordinates use X and Y.

row-major order *n.*

VAX PL/I

The order of storage of an array's elements, and the order of assignment of values to an array. In row-major order, the rightmost subscript varies the most rapidly.

RPB *n.*

VAX/VMS

The abbreviation for result parameter block. Constructed by the command interpreter. Same as result parameter block.

RQR *n.*

DECnet

The abbreviation for request recovery. SNA (systems network architecture) session control request, issued by the protocol emulator in emulator control and extended emulator control modes if it receives a negative response to a sequence number in the TH of a transmission to the PLU (primary logical unit). The command requests a sequence number resynchronization with the PLU. Same as request recovery.

RRV *n.*

RSX-11M

An abbreviation for record reference vector. A copy of a record header that is left in the record's original position when the record is moved during a bucket splitting operation. The RRV preserves access by record file address and facilitates alternate key access. Same as record reference vector.

RSE *n.*

VAX DBMS

An abbreviation for record selection expression. A word or group of contiguous words in a DML (data manipulation language) source program that specifies the selection criteria to be used by the DBCS to identify a specific database records. Same as record selection expression.

RSHUT *n.*

DECnet

The abbreviation for REQUEST SHUTDOWN. SNA (systems network architecture) data flow control request used by the SLU (secondary logical unit) to request an orderly session termination. Typically, the PE (protocol emulator) will issue a RSHUT upon receipt of a DSC (disconnect) macro from RSX-11M application. Same as REQUEST SHUTDOWN.

RSP *n.*

RT-11

The abbreviation for radial serial protocol. A software communications protocol that controls data transmission between an SB11 and a TU58, or between an SB11 and a host RT-11 system. Same as radial serial protocol.

RSTS/E *n.*

DIGITAL-specific

The acronym for Resource-Sharing Timesharing System/Extended. A DIGITAL operating system for the PDP-11 series of computers.

RT-11 *n.*

DIGITAL-specific

A real time operating system for PDP-11 computers. The basic operating system for CTS-300.

RTR *n.*

DECnet

The abbreviation for ready to receive. SNA (systems network architecture) data flow control request used to indicate that an attempt to start a bracket will be accepted. In EC (emulator control) mode, RTR is issued by the PE (protocol emulator) if a BID, issued by the PLU (primary logical unit), is accepted. Same as ready to receive.

RTS *n.*

DECnet and RSX-20F

The abbreviation for request to send. A signal sent from the data terminal equipment (in this case the DTE-20) to the data communications equipment (DCE) to condition the DCE for transmission. Since all terminal communication is full-duplex, the local modem should always be ready to transmit when a user is dialed in. Thus, RTS should always be asserted by the PDP-11 for active dial-up lines. Same as request to send.

CTS-300

The abbreviation for run-time system. A group of programs, including an interpreter and facilities for handling input/output, that loads a save program into memory and handles error conditions. Each instruction in the save program is sequentially interpreted to machine code and executed. Same as run-time system.

RU *n.*

DECnet

The abbreviation for response unit. RU refers to data in SNA (systems network architecture) that accompanies a response header. It cannot exceed 256 bytes and is generally less than 8 bytes. Same as response unit.

rub out *v.*

DECWORD

To erase any characters to the left of the cursor by pressing RUB CHAR OUT, RUB WORD OUT, Gold RUB LINE, or Gold RUB SENT.

ruler n.

generic

The marker that defines the margins, tabs, indents, and vertical line spacing of all test following it. Any number of rulers may be placed in a document.

run n.

generic

A single execution of a job on a computer.

run v.

DIGITAL-specific

To transfer a save file from a device into memory and begin program execution.

generic

To execute a program in a computer.

runaway tape condition n.

VAX/VMS

A situation in which a tape spins unceasingly on the drive. A runaway tape condition usually occurs because an operation does not incur a timeout condition. The only way to recover from a runaway tape condition is to take the drive off line.

run burst n.

RSTS/E

The length of time, measured in ticks, that a job is allowed to run uninterrupted under timesharing.

run mode n.

DSM-11

A mode of system operation in which the statements of a stored routine are executed. In this mode of operation, commands cannot be entered from the terminal and routines cannot be created or modified.

runnable adj.

PEARL

Pertaining to the state of a TASK activity in which all schedules are satisfied. The activity can execute but is not necessarily currently executing.

runnable task n.

VAX/VMS

A task that has a header and stack and that can be installed and executed.

running data base n.

DECnet

The system image currently in memory. See also permanent data base and system image file.

running rate n.

USFC/generic

The annualized percentage rate on the lease payments stream, exclusive of advance payments or purchase options.

RUNOFF (RNO) n.

DIGITAL-specific

A program that facilitates the preparation of typed or printed manuscripts by performing formatting, case shifting, line justification, page numbering, titleing, and indexing. Same as RNO.

runtime (or run time) n.

generic

The time required for a program to be carried out.

run-time (or runtime) adj.

DIGITAL-specific

Pertaining to the time required for a program to be carried out.

run-time environment *n.*

RT-11

Refers to the factors influencing the operation of a run-time system, such as the size of memory and the types of peripherals.

run-time procedure library *n.*

VAX/VMS

The collection of procedures available to native mode images at run time. These procedures may be used by all native mode images, regardless of the language processor used to compile or assemble the program. These procedures also provide support routines for high-level language compilers. Same as object time system.

run-time system *n.*

DIGITAL-specific

An operating system that controls the execution of a user program. See also RTS.

RSTS/E

System software that manages part of the RSTS/E system. For example, the BASIC-PLUS run-time system manages the BASIC-PLUS programming environment.

run-unit (or run unit) *n.*

VAX DATATRIEVE and VAX DBMS

A program that accesses the database. One or more object programs that interact and function at object time as an entity.

RVN *n.*

VAX/VMS

Relative volume number.

RVT *n.*

VAX/VMS

The abbreviation for relative volume table. A table containing information needed to associate the volumes of a multivolume set with the address of the UCB of the drive on which each volume is mounted. The relative volume table contains the number of volumes and a list of the UCBs (unit control blocks) used. Same as relative volume table.

RWED *n.*

VAX/VMS

The abbreviation for READ, WRITE, EXECUTE, DELETE. Refers to a series of functions or commands for a particular system.

S

77-level-description-entry *n.*

COBOL-74

A data description entry that describes a noncontiguous data item with the level-number 77.

salary *n.*

generic

A form of compensation for personal services.

sale and leaseback *n.*

USFC/generic

A procedure in which a company sells its assets to a leasing company and then leases them back from the buyer.

sales allowances *n.*

generic

A reduction in the originally agreed price for goods or services, usually because the item is not fully satisfactory.

sales discount *n.*

generic

A reduction in the stated selling price, usually as a reward for prompt payment.

sales return *n.*

generic

A reduction from sales revenue arising from goods returned by the buyer.

sales revenue *n.*

generic

Revenue from the delivery of goods or the performance of services.

salvage value/scrap value *n.*

generic

The amount for which a company expects to be able to sell a fixed asset at the end of its service life. Same as residual value.

sampling sweep *n.*

MINC

A process in which data samples are transferred from a laboratory instrument through an MNC-series module as input to a user's program, or transferred as output from a user's program through an MNC-series module to a laboratory instrument. The samples make up a logical stream of data that may use one or more buffers. Same as sweep. See also buffer sweep.

sanity check *n.*

DIGITAL-specific

A software test on system integrity. It requires successful operation of the peripherals, memories, and processors. Sanity check is associated primarily with startup and restart situations.

satellite node *n.*

DECnet

With regard to MOP (maintenance operation protocol) functions, the node being loaded, dumped, tested, or restarted. A satellite node is dependent on its host for such functions.

save *n.*

generic

The process by which you copy files from an area on the fixed disk to a diskette or tape.

saved graph file *n.*

A-to-Z

A file containing a complete graph that consists of the combined data and design files.

save image file *n.*

RSTS/E and RT-11

A program in a form that can be executed on a computer.

save image library (SIL) *n.*

RSTS/E and RT-11

A file format used to store RSTS/E monitor, run-time system, and resident library code. Same as SIL.

save program *n.*

CTS-300

An executable module that is the result of a previous linking process.

SBI *n.*

VAX/VMS

The abbreviation for synchronous backplane interconnect. That part of the hardware that interconnects the processor, memory controllers, MASSBUS adapters, and the UNIBUS adapter. Same as synchronous backplane interconnect.

SBR *n.*

VAX/VMS

The abbreviation for system base register. A hardware register containing the physical address of the system page table. Same as system base register.

scalar *adj.*

DIGITAL-specific

Pertaining to a data item that is neither an array nor a structure. See also object and dictionary object.

scalar type *n.*

PASCAL and VAX PASCAL

Refers to a type in which the values are unique and indivisible units of data. The values of a scalar type follow a particular order. Predefined scalar types include INTEGER, REAL, CHAR, and BOOLEAN.

scale factor *n.*

VAX PL/I

The number of fractional digits for a fixed-point decimal data item.

SCALING *n.*

VT-11 GRAPHICS

The process of defining a user window in which physical distances and locations on the screen are measured according to a nonunit scale.

SCAN *n.*

DECsystem-10

A module that accepts a user's command line, interprets it for correct syntax, and stores it in core in binary.

scattered set option *n.*

VAX DBMS

A record placement option in which records are evenly distributed throughout database pages, based upon data values in the record. SCATTERED mode is declared in the storage schema. See also placement node.

scatter/gather *adj.*

VAX/VMS

Pertaining to the ability to transfer in one I/O operation data from discontiguous pages in memory to contiguous blocks on disk, or data from contiguous blocks on disk to discontiguous pages in memory.

SCB *n.*

VAX/VMS

The abbreviation for system control block. The data structure in system space that contains all the interrupt and exception vectors known to the system. Same as system control block.

SCBBR *n.*

VAX/VMS

The abbreviation for system control block base register. A processor register containing the base address of the system control block. Same as system control block base register.

schedule mode *n.*

ALL-IN-1

The normal state for entering and viewing calendar entries in Calendar Management.

scheduler *n.*

TOPS-20

A process that performs software scheduling based on the priority of executable processes in the balance set.

schedule to master lease agreement *n.*

USFC/generic

An attachment to a master lease that spells out detailed terms pertaining to the equipment listed on the schedule.

scheduling *n.*

MicroPower PASCAL

Determining which process will be allocated control of the processor after a significant event. In MicroPower PASCAL applications, scheduling is performed by the kernel, based on the priorities of the currently eligible (read-active) processes and the running process.

schema *n.*

DIGITAL-specific

The logical description of a data base, including data definitions and data relationships. The schema is written using the schema data definition language (schema DDL).

schema data definition entry *n.*

VAX DBMS

In DBMS, the entry of the data definition language (DDL) used to define the logical structure of a database.

schema data description language (schema DDL) *n.*

VAX DBMS

The language used to describe the logical structure of a database. Same as schema DDL.

schema DDL *n.*

VAX DBMS

The language used to define the logical structure of a database. Same as schema data description language.

schematic *n.*

generic

A diagram of the electrical design of a circuit, with components represented by graphic symbols.

Schmitt Trigger (ST1, ST2) *n.*

MINC

A logic device included in the real-time clock module (MNCKW) that responds to voltage levels rather than voltage transitions. Schmitt-Trigger devices respond once, and only once, when a certain voltage threshold is reached. Schmitt Triggers respond differently than common transistor-transistor logic (TTL) devices which respond to the leading or trailing edge of a rapid voltage shift. With REAL-11/MINC, each real-time clock contains two Schmitt Triggers, called ST1 and ST2. The Schmitt Triggers can act independently of, or interactively with, the clock itself.

Schmitt-Trigger-driven sweep *n.*

MINC

A sweep that is caused, or driven, by the firing of one of the Schmitt Triggers. Same as trigger-driven sweep.

scintillate *v.*

GAMMA and MSG (SPETS)

To emit light or energy; for example, photoemission.

scintillation *n.*

GAMMA

A flash of light produced in a phosphor by an ionization event.

scope *n.*

MicroPower PASCAL, PASCAL, VAX C, VAX PASCAL, VAX PL/I, and VAX/VMS.

The portion of a program in which a particular name has meaning. The scope of names declared in external definitions extends from the point of the definition's occurrence to the end of the compilation unit in which it appears.

scope of an object *n.*

PEARL

The areas in a PEARL program where it is possible to access an object.

scratch *adj.*

generic

Pertaining to a temporary storage area or media.

scratch tape *n.*

DIGITAL-specific

A tape that has been initialized and that contains only volume labels (if a labeled tape), and tape marks, but no user data.

screen *n.*

generic

The display surface of a video terminal.

screen refresh *v.*

FMS

To rewrite the information displayed on a video terminal. Screen refreshing restores information that may have been destroyed by a broadcast from the system manager or by noise on a communication line.

screen refresh *n.*

DIGITAL-specific

Refers to the process of rewriting the information displayed on a video terminal by pressing CTRL/R. Screen refreshing restores to the screen information that may have been interrupted or distorted by a message or by noise on a communication line.

screen width *n.*

VAX/VMS

The number of character positions that can be displayed on a line.

SCRIPT *n.*

DECsystem-10

A program that sends predetermined sequences of characters over multiple pseudo-TTYs in order to simulate a load on the system for testing, measurement, and analysis.

scroll *v.*

generic

To move a display image up or down within a window to make room at the bottom or top of the window.

scroll *n.*

generic

A feature of moving upward or downward the lines of information that are displayed on the screen.

scrolled area *n.*

FMS

An area of a form consisting of identical lines. These lines can move upward or downward within the scrolled area without affecting the remainder of the form, whose position on the screen is fixed.

scrolled form array *n.*

Terminal Data Management System

A list of elements in a scrolled region on a TDMS (Terminal Data Management System) form, all of which have the same name and the same length and data type. The form definer does not specify the number of elements in the scrolled region, and the request definer can map up to 32767 elements of data.

scrolled region *n.*

Terminal Data Management System

An area, specified on the TDMS (Terminal Data Management System) form definition, that permits the terminal operator to move through many lines on a field and view or enter data, although only a few lines appear at one time on the screen.

scrolling *n.*

DIGITAL-specific

A feature of a video terminal that allows the display of more than one screenfull of text by vertical movement.

VAX/VMS

A feature of a video terminal that allows the display of more than one screenfull of text by vertical movement. For example, when the TYPE command is issued, new output appears at the bottom of the screen and eventually disappears off the top.

scrolling region *n.*

generic

A region on the screen in which data is displayed: data is entered on the last line of the scrolling region, the data already being displayed moves up one line in that area defined as the scrolling region and the top line is "lost" out of the top of the region.

SDLC *n.*

DECnet

The abbreviation for synchronous data-link control. SDLC is IBM's bit-level, transparent line discipline used to control half-duplex, full-duplex, point-to-point, or multi-point communication lines. The SDLC module of the protocol emulator (PE) participates in the transmission/reception processing of data frames built by or input to the SNA (systems network architecture) module of the PE. Same as synchronous data-link control.

SDT *n.*

DECnet

The abbreviation for start data traffic. SNA (systems network architecture) session control request used to request data exchange after a BIND or CLEAR command. Same as start data traffic.

search *n.*

DIGITAL-specific

1. The process of locating an object by examining each object in the set to determine if it is the desired object or if the desired object exists.

2. The process by which the controller reads sector heads to find the correct sector.

MINC

The keypad editor's examination of a file, or part of a file, for a designated string.

search and select *v.*

DECWORD

To make DECWORD find a search phrase in a document, place a select marker at the beginning of the phrase and the cursor at the end.

search list *n.*

TOPS-10

An ordered list of file structures.

VAX/VMS

A logical name in which the equivalence name has multiple values, instead of a single value. A common use of a search list is to examine multiple file locations to locate a file.

search model *n.*

MINC

The string that users type as the object of a search.

search path *n.*

TOPS-10

The path that the operating system uses when looking for a file through two or more directories.

search speed *n.*

generic

The maximum tape speed attainable when searching for a specific information unit.

search string *n.*

VAX/VMS

A group of characters defined in a command as the object of a search operation.

secondary index data record (SIDR) *n.*

RSX-11M

A record occupying level 0 of each alternate index. SIDRs contain an alternate key value and one or more pointers to use data records in the primary level 0 that contain the key value. Same as SIDR.

secondary key *n.*

RSX-11M

A series of bytes in a data record that can be used to identify the record for access. Alternate key value does not affect the position of the user data record in the file. Same as alternate key. See also segmented key.

secondary logical unit (SLU) *n.*

DECnet

In an SNA (systems network architecture) configuration, a cluster controller,such as the 3790 Communication System, contains one or more SLU's.
The host S/370 contains the PLUs. In a configuration using the RSX-11M/SNA Protocol Emulator
(PE), the PE represents the SLU (in respect to the
SNA side of the network). From an applications
point of view, the program in RSX-11M is the SLU.
Same as SLU.

secondary ODL file (secondary overlay description language file) *n.*

RSX-11M

An ODL file indirectly referenced by the primary
ODL file. See also primary ODL file.

secondary password *n.*

VAX/VMS

A user password that may be required at login
time, immediately after the primary password has
been correctly submitted. Primary and secondary
passwords can be known by separate users, to
ensure that more than one user is present at the
login. A less common use is to require a secondary password as a means of increasing the password length so that the total number of combination of characters makes password more time
consuming.

secondary pool *n.*

RSX-11M

On RSX-11M-PLUS systems only, some data for
Executive functions is moved from the pool to a
secondary pool. This data includes the task control blocks (TCBs) for protective tasks, some data
used by devices and the file system, and accounting information. See also pool, DSP, DSR, and
dynamic storage region.

secondary protocol *n.*

DIGITAL-specific

The bootstrap protocol used between the central
processor and the console front end. System
shutdown forces the front end to use the secondary protocol. See also primary protocol.

secondary storage *n.*

DIGITAL-specific

Random access mass storage. System storage
implemented on devices such as disks and
drums.

generic

Mass storage other than main memory.

VAX/VMS

Random access mass storage.

secondary timeout category *n.*

DECnet

One of two BSC (binary synchronous communications) timeout categories; each of two communicating systems must be assigned to different
timeout categories. See also primary timeout
category.

secondary vector *n.*

VAX/VMS

A location that identifies the starting address of a
condition handler to be executed when a condition occurs and

1. the primary vector contains 0 or,

2. the handler to which the primary vector points,
   chooses not to handle the condition.

second dictionary *n.*

DIGITAL-specific

The first related dictionary in a primary dictionary.

second normal form *n.*

DIGITAL-specific

The state of a relation when all non-full functional dependencies have been removed from it. A non-full functional dependency occurs if a field in a relation is dependent on only part of the relation's key.

section *n.*

COBOL-74

A set of zero, one, or more paragraphs or entries, the first of which is preceded by a section header. Same as section body.

DECnet

A group of one or more screen fields that are referred to by a single name (the section number).

Medical Systems

A row of matrix elements that is equivalent to a horizontal slice.

VAX/VMS

A portion of process virtual memory that has common memory management attributes (protection, access, cluster factor, etc.) It is created from an image section, a disk file, or as the result of a create virtual address space system service. See also global section, private section, image section, and program section.

section body *n.*

COBOL-74

A set of zero, one, or more paragraphs or entries, the first of which is preceded by a section header. Same as section.

section header *n.*

COBOL-74

A combination of words followed by a period and a space that indicates the beginning of a section in the Environment, Data, and Procedure Division.

section name *n.*

COBOL-74

A user-defined word that names a section in the Procedure Division.

sector *n.*

DIGITAL-specific

A physical portion of a mass storage device. See also physical block.

generic

That part of a track on a magnetic disk or disk pack that can be accessed by the heads in the course of a displacement of the device.

secure terminal server *n.*

VAX/VMS

A piece of VAX/VMS software designed to ensure that users can only login to terminals that are already logged out. When the user presses the BREAK key on a terminal, the secure server (if enabled) responds by first disconnecting any logged in process and then initiating a login. If no process is logged in at the terminal, the login can proceed immediately.

security *n.*

generic

The ability to prohibit access to a database record by unauthorized means.

security alarm *n.*

VAX/VMS

A message sent to operator terminals that are enabled as security operators. Security alarms are triggered by the occurrence of an event previously designated as worthy of the alarm because of its security implications.

security operator terminal *n.*

VAX/VMS

A class of terminal that has been enabled to receive messages sent by OPCOM to "security operators." These messages are security alarm messages. Normally such a terminal is a hardcopy terminal in a protected room, so that the output provides a log of security-related events and details that identify the source of the event.

segment *n.*

CTS-300

A physical division on a disk. Each track on a disk is divided into the same number of segments. Data is stored and accessed by the device handler in relation to segments.

DECnet

The data carried in a data segment message. NSP (network services protocol) divides the data from session control transmit buffers into numbered segments for transmission by Transport.

generic

1. The executable part of a program that may be stored in main memory at any one time.

2. A length of coaxial cable made up of one or more coaxial cable sections, and coaxial connectors, terminated in its characteristic limpedance at each end. A segment may contain up to 1640 feet (500 meters) of coaxial cable.

RT-11

A section of code treated as a unit that can overlay code already in memory and be overlaid by other overlay segments when called from the root segment or another resident overlay segment. See also overlay segment.

TOPS-10

An absolute control section. A logical collection of data, either program data or code, that is the building block of a program. The monitor keeps a segment in core memory and/or on the swapping device.

segment *v.*

generic

To divide a program into segments and to store them on a mass storage device to be brought into memory as needed.

segmentation *n.*

DECnet

The division of normal data from session control transmit buffers into numbered segments for transmission over logical links.

segmented key *n.*

RSX-11M

A primary or alternate string key that consists of separate sections, or segments, in different parts of the record. RMS-11 concatenates the specified segments before it performs any operations that involve key value comparisons. The concatenated version of the key is also stored in index records and SIDRs (for alternate keys). See also key, indexed file, and position of key in record.

segmented string *n.*

DIGITAL-specific

An application-defined datatype (such as graphics and digitized voice) useful for storing large pieces of unformatted data in a database.

segment resident block *n.*

TOPS-10

A block that contains all the information that the monitor requires for a particular segment.

select *v.*

DECWORD

To put a marker in a document by pressing the SEL key.

selected record n.

VAX DATATRIEVE

In a collection, a record marked by the SELECT statement and available for display or change without specifying a record selection expression.

selected records n.

generic

Those records included in a collection.

selection n.

DECnet

A process of inviting another station or node to receive data. A 3271 PE (protocol emulator) station is selected by the host system to demand that the station receive a message. See also poll.

SELECTION n.

PEARL

A component of a structure.

selection code n.

DIGITAL-specific

The one or two letter code of an option. You can type the selection code to select any option.

selection lock n.

generic

An integrity lock that prevents a database record from being erased, modified, connected, or disconnected by a concurrent run unit.

selection specification document n.

DECWORD

A list processing that tells DECWORD which records from the list document to use.

select marker n.

DECWORD

A small rectangular block that shows where the cursor was when the SEL key was pressed.

select range n.

FMS

A rectangular area that defines the extent of an operation or a video attribute assignment performed with the Form Editor in its LAYOUT phase.

self-join n.

Rdb/ELN

An operation that combines records in the same relation with themselves. For example, the EMPLOYEES relation contains information about both supervised employees and their supervisors. Because each supervisor is also an employee and appears as a record in the relation, the user can retrieve certain information by matching the values of one field (SUPERVISOR_ID) with a second field (EMP_ID) of the same relation. Same as reflexive join.

self-paced adj.

generic

Pertaining to something that is controlled by the speed of a person in completing an activity.

selling and administrative expenses n.

generic

An overall category for all expenses other than those related to production.

semaphore n.

DECnet

A common data structure used to control the exchange of signals between concurrent processes. See also mutex semaphore.

MicroPower PASCAL

A nonnegative integer variable on which two types of operations, wait and signal, are defined. Processes use semaphores to coordinate their concurrent execution and to protect shared resources from destructive alteration.

SEMAPHORE *n.*

PEARL

An object used to synchronize execution of concurrent tasks.

semiconductor *n.*

generic

Any of the many solid crystalline materials, such as silicon or germanium, that conduct electricity better than insulators do, but not as well as conductors.

semiconductor memory *n.*

generic

A memory whose storage medium is a semiconductor circuit.

semijustified margin *n.*

DECWORD

A right margin that is less ragged than an ordinary right margin, but is only partially justified. See also justify.

send-all *n.*

RSX-20F

Data that is sent to every active line on the system that has not refused it.

send sequence number N(S) *n.*

VAX PSI

The number that contains the sequence number of transmitted frames. Before transmission of an Information frame, N(S) is set equal to V(S).

send state variable (V(S)) *n.*

VAX PSI

This variable denotes the sequence number of the next in-sequence information frame to be transmitted. V(S) takes the values 0 through 7 and is incremented by 1 with each successive information frame transmission. The value of V(S), at the DCE, cannot exceed N(R) of the last received information frame by more than the maximum number of outstanding frames.

sentinel file *n.*

generic

The last file on a cassette tape. This file indicates the logical end of tape.

sequence control commands *n.*

RSX-11

Special batch commands, such as IF and ON, that control the batch job when errors are encountered. They provide a means of programming error response into the batch job when used with the commands STOP, CONTINUE GOTO, and SET [NO]ON.

sequence number *n.*

TOPS-10

The number given to an entry in the system event file.

sequence number field (SNF) *n.*

DECnet

A field in transmission header. Same as SNF.

sequential access *adj.*

generic

Pertaining to a data access method in which records or files are organized one after another.

sequential access *n.*

generic

An access mode in which logical records are obtained from or placed into a file in consecutive sequence.

sequential access mode *n.*

DIGITAL-specific

A mode of record access where the organization of the file establishes the order where records are processed. Each record access depends on the previous record used. successive operations in the sequential access mode access records in their logical order according to the file organization. See also access by record file address and random access mode.

VAX/VMS

The retrieval or storage of records in which a program reads or writes records one after the other in the order in which they appear, starting and ending at any arbitrary point in the file.

sequential data structure *n.*

VAX DATATRIEVE

A data structure in which each element in the structure, except the first and last, is related only to the element preceding it and the element following it.

sequential file *n.*

generic

A file in which records are accessed one after another in the order in which they appear in the file.

sequential file organization *n.*

DIGITAL-specific and VAX/VMS

A file organization in which records appear in the order in which they were originally written. The records can be fixed length or variable length. Sequential file organization permits sequential record access and random access by record file address. Sequential file organization with fixed-length records also permits random access by relative record number. See also relative file organization, indexed file organization, and sequential organization.

sequential organization *n.*

DIGITAL-specific

The permanent logical file structure in which a record is identified by a predecessor-successor relationship established when the record is placed into the file. See also sequential file organization.

sequential record access mode *n.*

VAX/RMS

The retrieval or storage or records starting at a designated point in the file and continuing to access additional records in the order in which they logically appear.

sequential structure *n.*

VAX DBMS

A data structure in which each element in the structure is related to the element preceding it and to the element following it. A form of sequential structure is used to show intraset relationships in DBMS.

sequential write operations *n.*

RSX-11M

The requirement that PUT operations in sequential access mode must be performed within file organization restrictions.

serial line unit (SLU) *n.*

MINC

One of the four ports on the back of the support chassis (one of the units holding and supporting electronic devices) that is dedicated to hookups with serial line devices such as the terminal and printers. Same as SLU.

serial mode *n.*

MINC

A method of data transmission in which the components of each data word are transmitted according to a prescribed protocol, one after another (serially) along a single pair of lines from a sending device to a receiving device.

serial transmission *n.*

DECnet

A method of transmission in which each bit of information is sent sequentially on a single channel rather than simultaneously as in parallel transmission.

serif *n.*

generic

A short line or cross-stroke in the design of some typefaces, typically at the end of a line or curve, to improve the legibility of the characters.

served device *n.*

VAX/VMS

A device whose local node makes it available to other nodes in the VAXcluster.

server *n.*

generic

A hardware and software device designed to perform a specific function for many users.

server command *n.*

ACMS

The string passed by the ACMS execution controller to a server process at the start of processing step. The string identifies what work the server is to perform.

server image *n.*

ACMS

A VMS image that the ACMS run-time system loads into a server process. There are two types of server images: DCL (Digital Command Language) server image and procedure server image.

server process *n.*

ACMS

A VMS process created according to the characteristics defined for a server in an ACMS application and task group definition.

server task *n.*

DECnet

An alternate designation for a task that has declared itself willing to accept a network connection, usually to provide some system service.

service life *n.*

generic

The time over which an asset is estimated to be of service to an entity.

service password *n.*

DECnet

The password required to permit triggering of the node's bootstrap ROM.

service slave mode *n.*

DECnet

A mode in which the processor is taken over and the adjacent executor node is in control (usually for execution of a bootstrap program for downline loading or for upline dumping).

service state *n.*

DECnet

A line state in which operation such as downline load, upline dump, or line loopback are performed. This state allows direct access to the line by network management.

servo *n.*

generic

(A form of servometer.) A closed system for controlling mechanical position or motion using feedback from the mechanical part of the device as an input.

session *n.*

DECnet

An SNA (systems network architecture) term for a logical connection between two network addressable units. Communication within a session is governed by the FM and TS Profiles.

A-to-Z

The time since the user last requested to run Business Graphics from the A-to-Z menu, until the user exits from Business Graphics.

session control layer *n.*

DECnet

A layer that defines the system-dependent aspects of logical link communication. A logical link is a virtual circuit on which information flows in two directions. Session control functions include name to address translation, process addressing, and, in some systems, process activation and access control.

session control protocol *n.*

DECnet

In the session control layer of DNA (DIGITAL Network Architecture), the protocol used for functions such as sending and receiving logical link data, and disconnecting and aborting logical links.

set *n.*

PASCAL

A collection of nonreal scalar elements, called members.

VAX DATATRIEVE

A defined relationship among records in a database.

VAX DBMS

A defined relationship among records in a database. A set contains an owner record, one or more member record types, and zero or more member record occurrences. See also set occurrence and set type.

VAX PASCAL

A collection of elements of an ordinal type.

set and test sequence numbers (STSN) *n.*

DECnet

An SNA (systems network architecture) session control request used to resynchronize message sequence numbers. Same as STSN.

set member *n.*

VAX DATATRIEVE and VAX DBMS

A record stored in a database as a nonowner participant in a particular set.

set mode *n.*

VAX DBMS

The method of accessing the data in a set. DBMS supports CHAIN mode.

set occurrence *n.*

VAX DATATRIEVE

A collection of one or more (logically) related record occurrences. Set occurrence is the actual data in the set, not its definition, which is the set type.

VAX DBMS

In DBMS, an occurrence of a set type. A set occurrence consists of one record occurrence from an owner record type and one record occurrence from zero, one, or more different member record types.

set order *n.*

VAX DBMS

The declaration of the logical order of the member record occurrences to be maintained within each set occurrence.

set-ordering criterion *n.*

VAX DBMS

The argument used by the DBCS (Database Control System) to determine the position of a record within a set.

set owner *n.*

generic

A database record whose existence establishes the existence of a specific set.

set type *n.*

VAX DATATRIEVE

A specific named set that has been defined in the schema data definition language (schema DDL). It is the definition of a collection of sets that have identical characteristics.

VAX DBMS

In DBMS, a definition of a relationship that exists among record types in a database. A set type contains an owner record type, and one or more member record types. See also set occurrence.

set type currency indicator *n.*

VAX-COBOL

A currency indicator associated with a particular database set type. A set type currency indicator identifies a particular set of the set type and a particular record and/or position in that set.

VAX DBMS

A place marker used by the DBCS (Database Control Systems) to indicate the last referenced record occurrence of a specific set type.

SET-UP key *n.*

DIGITAL-specific

The key on the main VT100-series keyboards that allows the user to change the characteristics of the terminal.

set-up mode *n.*

GIGI

An operating mode in which set-up parameters can be changed.

set-up parameter *n.*

DIGITAL-specific

Terminal characteristics that can be changed in set-up mode to adapt the terminal to the operating environment.

severe error *n.*

RSX-11M

An exit status code that is usually returned when one or more fatal errors are encountered or a task is aborted.

SFD *n.*

TOPS-10

The abbreviation for sub-file directory. A directory pointed to by a UFD (user file directory) or a higher-level SFD (sub-file directory). Each user has a UFD containing as many SFDs as the user wants. Same as sub-file directory. See also continued SFD.

shade character *n.*

RGL/FEP

A user-selected character that the terminal uses when it shades picture objects.

shade line *n.*

RGL/FEP

The y-coordinate that delimits the area to be shaded during a write operation.

shade pattern *n.*

RGL/FEP

The line pattern or character the terminal uses during a write operation when a shading option is enabled.

sharable image *n.*

generic

An image that has all of its internal references resolved, but that must be linked with one or more object modules to produce an executable image. A sharable image cannot be executed. A sharable image file can be used to contain a library of routines. A sharable image can be used to create a global section by the system manager.

sharable program *n.*

generic

A copy of a program that can be used by many users at the same time.

sharable segment *n.*

DIGITAL-specific

A (high) segment that can be used by several users at a time.

shared access *n.*

DIGITAL-specific

Refers to more than one task, file access block, or record access stream maintaining simultaneous access paths to the same file. See also exclusive access to a file.

shared code *n.*

DIGITAL-specific

Pure code residing in a shared segment.

shared device *n.*

DIGITAL-specific

Equipment shared by users (such as disks, diskettes, and printers).

shared memory *n.*

DIGITAL-specific

A memory unit that can be connected to multiple processors and that can contain resources (for example, mailboxes, common event flag clusters, and global sections) for use by processes running on different processors. Same as multiport memory.

shared-peripheral operations on line (SPOOL) *n.*

DIGITAL-specific

The process of sending output to a peripheral device, particularly a line printer, in an orderly fashion. Same as SPOOL.

shared read access *n.*

VAX DATATRIEVE

A method by which multiple user programs gain concurrent access to a file for read-only purposes.

shared region *n.*

DIGITAL-specific

A shared region is a block of data or code that resides in physical memory and can be used by any number of tasks. A shared region is built and installed separately from the task.

shared update *n.*

VAX DBMS

The state of a realm in which its records can be modified by concurrent run units. See also concurrent update.

shared write access *n.*

VAX DATATRIEVE

A method by which multiple user programs gain concurrent access to a file for input and output record operations.

shareholder equity *n.*

generic

The owner's equity section of a corporation's balance sheet.

shareholders *n.*

generic

The owners of a corporation; also referred to as stockholders.

sharer's group *n.*

TOPS-10

A subset of those jobs desiring shared ownership of a particular resource.

sharing specification in access programs *n.*

RSX-11M

A condition in which a program, when it opens a file, must declare the record operations it intends to perform on the file and the type of record operations it will allow other programs to perform on the file.

shell process *n.*

VAX/VMS

A predefined process that the job initiator copies to create the minimum context necessary to establish a process.

shift *n.*

generic

A movement of a sequence of bits to the left or right.

shift *v.*

generic

To move register contents right or left. In a shift left, the right most end of the register is filled with zeros. In a shift right, the left most end of the register is filled with zeros.

shift operator *n.*

VAX/VMS

One of the binary operators << or >>. Both operands must have integral types. The value of E1<<E2 is E1 (interpreted as a bit pattern) left-shifted by E2 bits. The value of E1>>E2 is E1 right-shifted by E2 bits.

short read *n.*

DECnet

In 3270 operations, a READ MODIFIED command sent in reply to pressing the CLEAR, CNCL, or a program access key at the keyboard. Only an AID (attention identification) character is transferred to the host.

short vector *n.*

VT-11 GRAPHICS

A vector stored in a format in which it occupies one memory word; such format is called a short-vector format.

shrink working set *n.*

VAX/VMS

An alternative available to the swapper process to obtain pages in physical memory. The swapper will shrink the size of the working set of selected processes to obtain pages in physical memory. See also swapping.

shunt *n.*

generic

Any part connected or the action of connecting a part in parallel with another part.

SHUTC *n.*

DECnet

The abbreviation for SHUTDOWN COMPLETE. SHUTC is an SNA (systems network architecture) data flow control request used by an SLU (secondary logical unit) to acknowledge suspension of transmission and to indicate that impending session termination is acceptable. Same as SHUTDOWN COMPLETE.

SHUTD *n.*

DECnet

The abbreviation for SHUTDOWN. SNA (systems network architecture), a command used by PLU (primary logical unit) to quiesce traffic from an SLU (secondary logical unit) as part of an orderly session termination sequence. Same as

shutdown *n.*

generic

The process by which you can turn off the system without losing any user's information.

SHUTDOWN *n.*

DECnet

An SNA (systems network architecture) data flow control command used by PLU (primary logical unit) to quiesce traffic from an SLU (secondary logical unit) as part of an orderly session termination sequence. Same as SHUTD.

SHUTDOWN COMPLETE (SHUTC) *n.*

DECnet

An SNA (systems network architecture) data flow control request used by an SLU to acknowledge suspension of transmission and to indicate that impending session termination is acceptable. Same as SHUTC.

shut state *n.*

DECnet

A node that in which existing logical links are undisturbed, but new ones are prevented.

sibling *n.*

DECsystem-10 and DSM-11

For any node in an array, all nodes that have the same immediate ancestor (parent). Siblings have the same number of subscripts and differ only in the last subscript.

SIDR *n.*

RSX-11M

The abbreviation for secondary index data record. Records occupying level 0 of each alternate index. SIDRs contain an alternate key value and one or more pointers to use data records in the primary level 0 that contain the key value. Same as secondary index data record.

signal *n.*

DECnet

An SNA (systems network architecture) data flow control command used to request a Change Direction on a half-duplex flip/flop session.

TOPS-20 and VAX/VMS

1. An electrical impulse conveying information.

2. The software mechanism used to indicate that an exception condition was detected.

VAX PL/I

A mechanism by which PL/I indicates that an error or other special condition occurred.

SIGNAL *n.*

PEARL

A PEARL object used to administer synchronous events. The action that initiates a synchronous event is also called a signal.

signal channel *n.*

PEARL

The channel associated with a DATION along which signals that the DATION generates are transferred.

signal integer (key) *n.*

RSX-11M

A key data type that can represent certain decimal integer values. See two-byte signed integer, four-byte integer, packed decimal, two-byte unsigned binary, four-byte unsigned binary, and string.

sign bit *n.*

generic

A bit used to indicate whether a value is positive or negative.

sign condition *n.*

generic

A test to determine whether the algebraic value of a data item or an arithmetic expression is either less than, greater than, or equal to zero.

significant event *n.*

generic

A specific occurrence identified by some systems that permits the executive program to consider the priorities of active tasks.

MicroPower PASCAL

A change in the state of a running or ready-active process that affects its ability to take control of the CPU resource. A significant event may occur synchronously with process execution (a primitive operation) or asynchronously (an external interrupt). Examples are:

- occurrence or clock interrupt
- creating or deleting a process
- a process blocking itself by waiting on a semaphore
- resuming a suspended process
- signaling a semaphore on which a process is waiting
- suspending a running or ready-active process.

In other words, any change in a process state involving either the run or ready-active queues is a significant event.

RSX-11M

A state that is declared whenever there is a change in system status. Whenever there is a significant event, the Executive reviews the eligibility of tasks to execute, because the change that caused the significant event to be declared may mean that a priority task that was blocked is no longer blocked. For instance, a significant event is declared when a task completes its execution or when a task cannot continue I/O because of the unavailability of an output device. The round-robin scheduler causes a significant event to occur regularly.

SIL *n.*

RSTS/E

The abbreviation for save image library. A file format used to store RSTS/E monitor, run-time system, and resident library code. Same as save image library.

silicon *n.*

generic

An element which can be used as a semiconductor.

silo *n.*

generic

A storage area (buffer) in which the first item stored is the first item output (FIFO).

simple condition *n.*

generic

Any single condition from the set:

    relation condition

    class condition

    condition-name condition

    switch-status condition

    sign condition

    tenancy condition

    member condition

    database key condition

    success/failure condition

    simple-condition (in parentheses)

simple record array *n.*

DIGITAL-specific

A field that contains several elements referenced in a request by the same name and having the same characteristics (length, data type, and so on). Same as array.

simulate *v.*

generic

To represent certain features of the operation of a device, system, or program.

SIMULATE *n.*

DECnet

A command to D60SPL that is synonymous with EMULATE. (Note that this does not coincide with the generic definition of simulation.)

simulation ratio *n.*

generic

An indication of the efficiency of a simulator. It is the quotient of CPU runtime divided by elapsed simulated time.

simultaneous clock-driven sweeps *n.*

MINC

Two or more sweeps caused by clock overflows that are occurring through two or more MINC-series modules operating in parallel. See also multiple clock driven sweeps.

simultaneous update *n.*

TOPS-10

Allowing more than one cooperating job to update a file.

VAX DBMS

The capability to update or retrieve data while another run-unit updates or retrieves data in the same area.

single access *n.*

TOPS-10

The status of a file structure that allows only one particular job to access that file structure. This job is the one whole project number matches the project number of the owner of the file structure.

single-area file *n.*

RSX-11M

An indexed file with one area, whether by default or definition. Sequential and relative files also consist of one area for purposes of placement control. See also multi-area file.

single-ended mode *n.*

MINC

An input method in which the signal to be acted upon at any instant is defined as the difference between an input terminal and ground. With MINC, the input requires only one active terminal; therefore twice as many such channels can be accommodated by a given multiplexor than could be accommodated in differential mode.

single key index file *n.*

VAX DATATRIEVE

An index file with only a primary key defined, allowing access on one key only.

single precision *n.*

PASCAL and VAX PASCAL

Precision of approximately seven significant digits for a floating-point real number; the types SINGLE and REAL provide single precision.

single precision floating datum *n.*

DIGITAL-specific

Four contiguous bytes (32 bits) starting on an arbitrary byte boundary. The value of a floating datum is in the approximate range, $.29 \times 10^{-38}$ through 1.7×10^{38}. The precision of a floating datum is approximately one part in 2^{23}, typically seven decimal digits. Same as floating datum.

single-server *n.*

ACMS

An ACMS server in which the server image
processes only one task instance at a time.

single-step task *n.*

ACMS

An ACMS task that has only a single processing
step. Single-step tasks can be defined in a task
group or a separate task definition.

single-stream batch *n.*

generic

A method of batch processing in which only one
flow of batch commands is processed.

single thread *n.*

DIGITAL-specific

A facility that completes one request before starting another.

single type *n.*

PASCAL and VAX PASCAL

A predefined scalar type that has the single-precision real numbers as values. Same as REAL type.

single user access *n.*

generic

The protection status of a disk or disk volume that
allows only one user to access the file structure.

singular entity *n.*

DECnet

A specific circuit entity such as a line, a logging
sink type, or a node.

singular set *n.*

Terminal Data Management System and VAX DBMS

In DBMS, a set type owned by the SYSTEM
record rather than by a record type selected by
the user. A SYSTEM-owned record has only one
occurrence in the database, but can be the owner
of many member record types. It allows unassoci-
ated record types to be used as entry points into
the database. See also member record, owner
record, nonsingular set and system-owned set.

sink *n.*

DECnet

1. The point of usage of data in a network.

2. A data terminal installation that receives and
   processes data from a connected channel.

3. A place where a copy of an event is to be
   recorded.

See also logging sink.

sink node *n.*

DECnet and VAX/VMS

A node where logging sink types are actually
located. These types include a file or a console.

SIXBIT code *n.*

TOPS-10

A 6-bit code in which textual information is
recorded. It is a compressed form of the ASCII
character set, and thus not all of the characters in
ASCII are available in SIXBIT, notably the nonprint-
ing characters and the lowercase letters are omitted. The range of SIXBIT code is 00 to 77 (octal),
which is equal to 40 through 137 (octal) in ASCII.

size validators *n.*

Terminal Data Management System

A field validator on a TDMS (Terminal Data Management System) form definition that determines the field datatype and sets a predefined range for numeric fields. At run time, size validators prevent the operator from entering data that is not within that range. The form definer assigns size validators in the assign phase.

skew *n.*

generic

A motion characteristic on a magnetic tape that is the angle speed between the gap center line and a line vertical to the tape center line.

skip *n.*

DIGITAL-specific

The process by which an instruction, macro, or subroutine causes control to bypass one instruction and proceed to the next instruction.

generic

The ignoring of one or more logical instructions in a sequential procedure.

slave *n.*

DECnet

A system or terminal that responds only to remotely generated requests.

generic

A component in a system that operates under the control of another system component.

slave station *n.*

DECnet

A tributary station that can send data only when polled or requested to by a master control station. In some multiplex situations a tributary can act as both slave and master.

slave terminal *n.*

RSX-11M and VAX/VMS

A terminal from which the user cannot issue commands to the command interpreter; it is a terminal allocated to application software.

sleep state *n.*

RSTS/E

A RSTS/E job state in which the job is suspended for a specific interval. The program that is executing specifies this time interval, but certain system activities can cause the job to resume execution before the time is up.

slew rate *n.*

MINC

The ability of the input or output of an analog circuit to respond to voltage, or change its voltage, in a given time.

slice *n.*

Medical Systems and MSG (SPETS)

A horizontal or vertical strip or the image that varies in width from one to nine rows of the matrix.

slide *n.*

generic

A mnemonic for serial line in demand everywhere (used for manufacturing check-out).

sliver *n.*

generic

A 32 word area of memory.

slope *n.*

generic

A linear change of voltage in reference to time.

SLP *n.*

RSX-11M

The abbreviation for source language input program. Most programming languages are source languages. These languages describe the procedure users wish the computer to follow. They are the source of the task that is actually run on the computer. Same as source language input program.

SLR *n.*

VAX/VMS

The abbreviation for system length resister. A processor register containing the system page table in longwords. Same as system length register.

SLU *n.*

DECnet

The abbreviation for secondary logical unit. In an SNA (systems network architecture) configuration, a cluster controller, such as the 3790 communication system, contains one or more SLUs. The host S/370 contains the PLUs. In a configuration using the RSX-11M/SNA Protocol Emulator (PE), the PE represents the SLU (in respect to the SNA side of the network). From an applications point of view, the program in RSX-11M is the SLU. Same as secondary logical unit.

SLU *n.*

MINC

The abbreviation for serial line unit. One of the four ports on the back of the chassis (one of the units holding and supporting electronic devices) that is dedicated to hookups with serial line devices such as the terminal and printers. Same as serial line unit.

small buffer *n.*

RSTS/E

A 16-word storage area located in the monitor area of RSTS/E memory. The monitor uses small buffers as temporary storage for data transfers, file processing requests, interjob messages, and other similar operations.

small buffer pool *n.*

RSTS/E

The area of RSTS/E monitor memory that contains general small buffers.

small process *n.*

VAX/VMS

A process, with abbreviated context and no program region, that is scheduled using the normal process scheduling algorithm.

smoothing *n.*

Medical Systems and MSG (SPETS)

A data analysis process that increases image clarity and removes image noise.

SNA gateway access protocol *n.*

DECnet

In the network application layer of DNA (DIGITAL Network Architecture), a protocol that allows a node, which is not connected directly to an IBM SNA network, access to the facilities of the SNA (systems network architecture) network for terminal access and remote job entry.

snapshot *n.*

generic

A picture of what is occurring at a particular instant within a file, system, process, and so forth.

TOPS-10

The information gathered by the operating system immediately after recovering from a crash.

SNF *n.*

DECnet

The abbreviation for sequence number field. The field in the transmission header. Same as sequence number field.

socket *n.*

DECnet and TOPS-20

Specific to ARPANET, a 32-bit main-space field that identifies the end-entity of a connection. A socket is either a receiver (female) or sender (male) but not both. Connections are made between a male socket in one Host and a female socket in another (or the same) Host. A two-way exchange of information requires that two pairs of sockets be connected.

soft error *n.*

TOPS-10

A recoverable error.

soft return *n.*

DIGITAL-specific

A type of carriage return automatically placed in a document to accomplish word wrap. Same as word wrap return.

software *n.*

generic

Programs, routines, codes, and other information for use with computers or other types of hardware.

software bootstrap *n.*

DIGITAL-specific

A bootstrap that is activated by manually loading the instructions of the bootstrap and specifying the appropriate load and start address.

software clock *n.*

MINC

A memory location that is incremented by 1 each time a clock overflow interrupt occurs in the secondary real-time clock (MNCKW). The software clock is available only with MNC-series systems that include two real-time clocks. The CLOCKB subprogram controls the software clock.

software context *n.*

VAX/VMS

The context maintained by the VAX/VMS to describe a process. See also software process control block (PCB).

Software Event Logger (SWL) *n.*

Terminal Data Management System

The TDMS (Terminal Data Management System) process that records ACMS and TDMS software events that occur during the running of an application program. In order to see the events logged by the SWL, a user must use the Software Event Logger Utility Program. Same as SWL. See also Software Event Logger Utility Program.

Software Event Logger Utility Program (SWLUP) *n.*

Terminal Data Management System

The TDMS (Terminal Data Management System) utility used to list selected events that were logged by the Software Event Logger. Same as SWLUP.

software installation n.

DIGITAL-specific

Activities performed to prepare a copy or copies of software so that the system can be used.

software interrupt n.

VAX/VMS

An interrupt generated on interrupt priority levels 1 through 15, and that can be requested only by software.

software interrupt system n.

TOPS-10 and TOPS-20

A highly structured set of procedures that allows a user to specify certain conditions within an executing program that will result in a transfer of control from the normal program sequence to a specified routine. See also pseudo interrupt system.

software modules n.

DIGITAL-specific

Program units that are discrete and identifiable for compiling, combining with other units, and loading.

software PCB n.

VAX/VMS

The abbreviation for software process control block. The data structure used to contain a process's software context. The operating system defines a software PCB for every process when the process is created. The software PCB includes the following kinds of information about the process: current state; storage address if it is swapped out of memory; unique identification of the process; and address of the process header (which contains the hardware PCB). The software PCB resides in system region virtual address space. It is not swapped with a process. Same as software process control block. See also software context.

software priority n.

VAX/VMS

The priority assigned to a job placed in a spooler queue or a batch queue. Same as queue priority. See also process priority.

software process control block (software PCB) n.

TOPS-20 and VAX/VMS

The data structure used to contain a process software context. The operating system defines a software PCB for every process when the process is created. The software PCB includes the following kinds of information about the process: current state; storage address if it is swapped out of memory; unique identification of the process; and address of the process header (which contains the hardware PCB). The software PCB resides in system region virtual address space. It is not swapped with a process. Same as software PCB. See also software context.

Software Product Description (SPD) n.

DIGITAL-specific

Defines the function of a product and minimum hardware needed to support it. It describes software, components, and service. Same as SPD.

Software Services n.

DIGITAL-specific

DIGITAL software specialists based throughout the world who provide information and support for systems. Software specialists are responsible for pre-sales information, system installation, and after-sales assistance.

software updating package (SOUP) n.

DECsystem-10

A package that consists of a set of programs for facilitating the update of system files or user source files. Same as SOUP.

SOH *n.*

DECnet

The abbreviation for start-of-header. A BISYNC protocol data-link character used at the beginning of a sequence of characters that constitute a status information or a machine-sensible address. Such a sequence is referred to as a header. Same as start-of-header.

solid-state *adj.*

generic

Pertaining to circuits and components having semiconductor devices.

sort *v.*

DECWORD

In list processing, to examine a list document and rearrange it into a new order based on the contents of one or more of the fields in each record. For example, a list of names and telephone numbers sorted in alphabetical order might be rearranged into number order.

DIGITAL-specific

An option from the document and transfer utilities menu allowing users to rearrange account indexes. Users can order an index according to document number, name, or last edit date.

SORTED *n.*

VAX DBMS

A set-ordering criterion, based on the collating sequence of the data types of the sort keys, that determines record placement by a user-specified key.

sorted set *n.*

VAX DBMS

A sorted set in which a tree-structured index is used to access specific records quickly. This is declared in the storage schema definition language. See also INDEX mode set.

sorting *n.*

VAX/VMS

The ordering of records in a prescribed sequence.

sort key *n.*

DECWORD

In list processing, the order or organization pattern by which lists are sorted.

VAX DATATRIEVE

A field that forms the basis for sorting. For example, users can rearrange the records in DATA-TRIEVE's sample domain YACHTS according to size by using the sort key LENGTH-OVER-ALL.

SOUP *n.*

DECsystem-10

The abbreviation for the software updating package that consists of a set of programs for facilitating the update of system files or user source files. Same as software updating package. Same as software updating package.

source *n.*

DECnet

1. The point of entry of data in a network.

2. A data terminal installation that enters data into a connected channel. Data entry may be under operator or machine control.

source (point or line) *n.*

Medical Systems

A small amount of concentrated radioactive material with a constant level of energy. Point or line sources are used for alignment or calibration.

source code n.

DIGITAL-specific

Text, usually in the form of an ASCII format file, that represents a program. Such a file can be processed by an appropriate system program.

source deck n.

TOPS-10 and TOPS-20

A card deck that constitutes a computer program in symbolic language.

source diskette n.

DECmate II

The document diskette that contains the documents to be copied.

source file n.

DIGITAL-specific

A source file is a text file containing material suitable for translation into an object module by an assembler or compiler. Such files cannot be run or task built. The Task Builder turns object modules into task image files. See also text file.

VAX/VMS

A text file containing material suitable for translation into an object module by an assembler or compiler. Such files cannot be run or linked.

source form file n.

FMS

A file containing a single form description consisting of Form Language statements in source format. See also form description.

source item n.

COBOL-74

An identifier designated by a SOURCE clause that provides the value of a printable item.

source language n.

DIGITAL-specific

The original form in which a program is prepared prior to its processing by the computer to produce the object-language program.

generic

The system of symbols that a programmer uses to record a procedure that a computer can translate into object code.

source language program (SLP) n.

DIGITAL-specific

The original, untranslated version of a program written in a high-level language (such as FOR-TRAN, COBOL, or MACRO). A translator (assembler, compiler, or interpreter) is used to perform the mechanics of translating the source program into a machine language program that can be run on the computer. Source programs, when translated, produce object modules as their primary output. A program may exist as a source program, an object module, and a runnable core image. Same as SLP.

source node n.

DECnet

The node at which the request for a connection is initiated or from which a message is transmitted.

source program n.

COBOL-74

A syntactically correct set of COBOL statements beginning with an Identification Division and ending with the end of the Procedure Division. In contexts where there is no danger of ambiguity, the word "program" alone can be used in place of the phrase "source program."

CTS-300

A\ program written in a high-level language converted later to machine language by a compiler. In CTS-300 a source program is written in the DIBOL-11 language.

generic

The computer program written in the source language.

TOPS-10 and TOPS-20

A computer program written in a language designed to express procedures or problem formulations to users. A translator (assembler, compiler, or interpreter) is used to perform the mechanics of translating the source program into an object- or machine-language program that can be run on a computer.

source task *n.*

DECnet and VAX/VMS

In a task-to-task communication environment, the source task is the one that initiates a logical link connection request.

SP *n.*

VAX/VMS

The abbreviation for stack pointer. SP is general register 14 (R14). SP contains the address of the top (lowest address) of the processor-defined stack. Reference to SP will access one of the five possible stack pointers, kernel, executive, supervisor, user, or interrupt, depending on the value in the current mode and interrupt stack bits in the processor status longword (PSL). Same as stack pointer.

spanned record *n.*

TOPS-10

A record contained in a file in which each record may begin in one block and end in another.

VAX/VMS

A record that can cross block boundaries. A spanned record consists of one or more data segments. The position of a segment within the record and the length of the segment is denoted by the segment control word, the first five characters of each segment.

sparse array *n.*

DSM-11

An array that need not be predefined to its maximum size.

SPD *n.*

DIGITAL-specific

The abbreviation for Software Product Description. SPDs define the function of a product and minimum hardware needed to support it. They describe software, components, and service. Same as Software Product Description.

special dictionary *n.*

DECWORD

In spelling error detection, a dictionary for finding spelling mistakes in documents with a specialized vocabulary. For example, if users are writing a document in French, they could create a special dictionary containing French vocabulary. See also dictionary.

special key function *n.*

DECWORD

A function in which the Gold-number-SFK tells DECWORD to insert an invisible character, which designates a function that is to be performed while a document is printing. For example, it may specify non standard paper movements.

special variable *n.*

VAX DBMS

A variable that is permanently defined within the operating system. Such variables provide system and control information to all routines.

specification *n.*

PEARL

A definition of an object that creates an access function for an existing object.

speech recognition *n.*

generic

The act of enabling a computer to recognize utterances of a natural language.

speech synthesis *n.*

generic

The synthetic replication of human speech by computer.

spelling error detection *n.*

DECWORD

The S option from the main menu that enables users to find spelling mistakes in documents. DECWORD checks a document against a dictionary stored on disk. Any words in the document that are not listed in the dictionary are classed as spelling mistakes.

SPM *n.*

DIGITAL-specific

The abbreviation for Software Performance Monitor. SPM is a set of tools that collects and reports performance statistics for VAX/VMS and RSX-11M systems. System-wide and per-process statistics can be collected, as well as data for tuning application programs.

spool *v.*

generic

To store input from, or output to, a slow device on a faster device until the data is ready for processing.

SPOOL *n.*

DIGITAL-specific

The acronym for shared-peripheral operations on line. It refers to the process of sending output to a peripheral device, particularly a line printer, in an orderly fashion. Same as shared-peripheral operations on line.

spooled *n.*

generic

Indicates whether or not files sent to a busy printer are saved for later printing. A spooled printer automatically puts print requests in a waiting line and prints the files one after the other.

spooled device *n.*

DIGITAL-specific

A spooled device is a line printer or other output device under control of the queue manager. Spooled devices are initialized with certain attributes.

spooler *n.*

DIGITAL-specific

A program enabling many users to share the printing devices of a system without interfering with each other. The DECWORD spoolers are also responsible or formatting documents, and for printing text as specified in printer control block.

generic

A program that temporarily stores data on disk or tape until the data is ready for processing or printing.

spooling *n.*

DIGITAL-specific and VAX/VMS

The technique of using a high-speed mass storage device to buffer data passing between low-speed I/O devices and high-speed memory.

1. Output spooling: The method by which output to a low-speed peripheral device (such as a line printer) is placed into queues maintained on a high-speed device (such as disk) to await transmission to the low-speed device.

2. Input spooling: The method by which input from a low-speed peripheral (such as the card reader) is placed into queues maintained on a high-speed device (such as disk) to await transmission to a job processing that input.

generic

The way in which output to slow devices is placed into queues on faster devices to wait for transmission to the slower devices.

spool queue *n.*

VAX/VMS

The list of files supplied by processes that are to be processed by a symbiont. For example, a line printer queue is a list of files to be printed on the line printer. See also device queue.

spread sheet *n.*

generic

A work sheet organized in a matrix that provides a two-way classification of accounting data.

SPRINT *n.*

DECsystem-10

The batch input stacker. SPRINT reads any sequential input stream, sets up the job's control file and data files, and enters the job into the batch input queue.

SPT *n.*

DIGITAL-specific and VAX/VMS

The abbreviation for system page table. The data structure that maps the system region virtual addresses, including the addresses used to refer to the process page tables. The system page table (SPT) contains one page table entry (PTE) for each page of system region virtual memory. The physical base address of the SPT is contained in a register called the system base register (SBR). Same as system page table.

SRP *n.*

VAX/VMS

Short request packet.

S/S bytes *n.*

DECnet

The abbreviation for status and sense bytes. Two bytes used in 3270 communications to record all remote status and sense conditions. Status and sense conditions are recorded by the 3271 control unit for each device. The conditions include device busy, device ready, detected errors, etc. The RSX-11/3271 Protocol Emulator (PE) supports the device end, device offline, and command reject status and sense conditions. Same as status and sense bytes.

SSCP *n.*

DECnet

The abbreviation for system services control point. A network addressable unit (NAU) responsible for startup, control, and shutdown of an SNA network. The protocol emulator (PE) communicates with the SSCP in a session governed by FM Profile 0, TS Profile 1 protocols. Same as system services control point.

SSP *n.*

VAX/VMS

Supervisor Mode Stack Pointer.

stack n.

DIGITAL-specific

An area of memory set aside for temporary storage, or for procedure and interrupt service linkages. A stack uses the last-in-first-out (LIFO) concept. As items are added to ("pushed on") the stack, the stack pointer decrements. As items are retrieved from ("popped off") the stack, the stack pointer increments.

generic

A block of storage locations one after the other which is accessible on a last-in first-out condition (LIFO).

stack frame n.

VAX-11

A data structure built on the stack in conformance with the VAX-11 procedure call standard. Same as frame.

VAX/VMS

A standard data structure built on the stack during a procedure call, starting from the location addressed by the FP to lower addresses, and popped off during a return from procedure. See also call frame.

stack pointer (SP) n.

VAX/VMS

General register 14(R14). SP contains the address of the top (lowest address) of the processor-defined stack. Reference to SP will access one of the five possible stack pointers, kernel, executive, supervisor, user, or interrupt, depending on the value in the current mode and interrupt stack bits in the processor status longword (PSL). Same as SP.

stack processing n.

generic

The ability through machine instructions to access sequentially-nested data.

stall I/O queue n.

VAX/VMS

A queue created by the MTAACP to record I/O requests to a blocked process. The stall I/O queue is part of the volume virtual page. Except for a cancel I/O request, all other I/O requests to a blocked process will be placed in the stall I/O queue until the blocked process is unblocked.

stand-alone or standalone adj.

DIGITAL-specific

Pertaining to a system or piece of equipment that is capable of doing its job without being connected to anything else.

stand-alone system n.

VT-11 GRAPHICS

A hardware/software configuration in which the VT-11 display processor is connected to the PDP-11 central processor by the UNIBUS. Stand-alone systems have the advantage of higher speed compare with host-satellite systems, at the expense of dedicating computer hardware more or less totally to graphic programming. A stand-alone system can use either an RT-11 or RSX-11M operating system.

standard file structure and interface n.

RSX-11M

Refers to the capability of RMS-11 to operate on most PDP-11 operating systems as well as VAX/VMS. The files it creates are identical and can be used on any system within the confines of on-disk structures. The RMS-11 interface with user programs is also standard and identical on all systems (subject to system-specific limitations). VAX/RMS uses the same disk structure for files as RMS-11 and an interface that parallels RMS-11s.

start data traffic (SDT) *n.*

DECnet

An SNA (systems network architecture) session control request used to request data exchange after a BIND or CLEAR command. Same as SDT.

start element *n.*

VAX PSI

A single 0-bit that marks the start of a character in start-stop transmission.

starting criterion *n.*

TOPS-10

The number of transactions that must be in a leaf or the leaves under a node before an MPP will be started. Same as threshold.

start I/O routine *n.*

VAX/VMS

The routine in a device driver that is responsible for obtaining necessary resources (for example, the controller data channel) and activating the device unit. Same as driver start I/O routine.

start of header (SOH) *n.*

DECnet

A BISYNC protocol data-link character used at the beginning of a sequence of characters that constitutes a status information or a machine-sensible address. Such a sequence is referred to as a header. Same as SOH.

start of text (STX) *n.*

DECnet

A communication control character that precedes a sequence of characters that is to be treated as an entity and entirely transmitted through to the ultimate destination. Such a sequence is referred to as text. Same as STX.

star topology *n.*

DECnet

A network configuration in which one central node is connected to more than one adjacent, end node. A star can be a subset of a larger network.

start-stop mode DTE *n.*

VAX PSI

A DTE (data terminal equipment) that is unable to handle data in packet form. This DTE must interface through a packet assembly/disassembly (PAD) facility to connect to a PSDN (packet switching data network).

start/stop transmission *n.*

VAX PSI

Asynchronous transmission in which a group of bits corresponding to a character is preceded by a start element and is followed by a stop element.

state *n.*

DIGITAL-specific

The functions that are currently valid for a given network component. States include line, circuit, local node, module, DTE, and logging.

statement *n.*

BASIC-PLUS-2 and CTS-300

An expression or instruction written in a source language.

COBOL-74

A syntactically valid combination of words and symbols written in the Procedure Division and beginning with a verb.

generic

1. An instruction in a source language.

2. A reserved word that operates under the control of a command and specifies certain details relevant to the functioning of the command.

MicroPower PASCAL

A line of PASCAL code. A statement is delimited in PASCAL by a semicolon (;). Note that a compound statement consists of more than one PASCAL statement delimited by the PASCAL-reserved words BEGIN and END.

PASCAL

A sequence of reserved words, identifiers, operators, expressions, and special symbols describing a program action or altering the flow of program execution.

VAX DATATRIEVE

A string of characters that a user or program transmits to a software product to execute a function. In DATATRIEVE, a statement is distinct from a command. A statement performs query, report, or data manipulation functions. Two or more statements can be joined, while a command must stand alone. See also command.

VAX PASCAL

Sequence of reserved words, identifiers, operators, expressions, and special symbols describing a program action or altering the flow of program execution.

VAX PL/I

A sequence of PL/I keywords, user-specified identifiers, and punctuation marks that specifies an executable instruction or data declaration in a program.

VAX/VMS

The language elements that perform the action of a function. Statements include expression statements (an expression followed by a semicolon), a null statement (the semicolon by itself), several kinds of compound statements, and an assortment of statements identified by keywords (such as RETURN, SWITCH, DO).

state queue *n.*

VAX/VMS

A list of processes in a particular processing state. The scheduler uses state queues to keep track of processes' eligibility to execute. They include: processes waiting for a common event flag, suspended processes, and executable processes. See also system queue.

static allocation *n.*

MicroPower PASCAL

Dedicating a resource to the process that allocated it. Static allocation occurs during system building, compiling, and linking. See also storage schema.

VAX DBMS

In DBMS, the default allocation option of the record statement of the storage schema entry. It is used to specify the amount of physical storage users want to dedicate to a particular data item type. Users make the specification during the definition of the database, but the actual allocation does not occur until the creation of the database. See also dynamic allocation, storage schema, and storage schema data definition entry.

static dump *n.*

TOPS-10

A dump that is performed at a particular instant with respect to a machine run, frequently at the end of a run.

static process *n.*

MicroPower PASCAL

A process that exists in the application after initialization (is always present after power is on or system-reset processing is completed). A static process corresponds to a PASCAL main program. In MACRO-11, a static process is defined by the DFSPC$ macro.

static study *n.*

Medical Systems

A matrix study that contains one image or a group of separate but related images. GAMMA collects a static study for a specified number of light events (counts) or for a specified amount of time.

static variable *n.*

VAX PL/I

A variable whose storage is allocated for the entire execution of a program.

station *n.*

DECnet

A physical termination of a line, having both a hardware and software implementation, that is, a controller and/or a unit. A station is part of a circuit identification.

Ethernet

Computer or intelligent device that is served by a transceiver drop cable, and can transmit and receive packets on the Ethernet communications system. Also called workstation, or node. A station typically used by a single user rather than being dedicated to common (global) use like a file server. Usually it consists of a controller, display, keyboard, one or more disks, and an interface to the network.

status *n.*

DECnet

Dynamic information relating to entities, such as their state. Status is a network management information type. Also, a message indicating whether or not an NCP command succeeded.

generic

The relative condition or state of something.

VAX/VMS

A display type for the NCP commands SHOW and LIST. Status refers to dynamic information about a component that is kept in either the volatile or permanent database.

status and sense bytes (S/S bytes) *n.*

DECnet

Two bytes used in 3270 communications to record all remote status and sense conditions. Status and sense conditions are recorded by the 3271 control unit for each device. The conditions include device busy, device ready, detected errors, etc. Same as S/S bytes.

status code *n.*

VAX/VMS

A longword value that indicates the success or failure of a specific function. For example, system services always return a status code in R0 upon completion. See also return status code.

STATUS code *n.*

FMS

A decimal value returned to the application program representing the success or failure of a Form Driver call.

VAX DBMS

A value that indicates the database exception condition that most recently occurred in a run unit or DBCS (Database Control System) or indicates that no database exception condition occurred.

STD *n.*

RSX-11M

The abbreviation for system task directory. The STD is a list of all the tasks installed on the system. Users can display the STD through the DCL SHOW TASKS/INSTALLED command. Same as system task directory.

step *n.*

generic

A part of a task definition that identifies one or more operations to be performed.

step action *n.*

ACMS

The part of a step definition that tells ACMS what to do after completing the work for that step. These instructions can consist of a single unconditional action or a series of conditional actions based on the value of a field in a workspace.

step label *n.*

ACMS

A name assigned to a step in a multiple-step ACMS task.

stepping *n.*

MicroPower PASCAL

The procedure for stopping a process after each statement or instruction of the process executes.

step procedure *n.*

VAX DATATRIEVE

A fixed sequence of DATATRIEVE commands, statements, clauses, or arguments that are created, named, and stored in a CDD (Common Data Dictionary). See also procedure.

step work *n.*

ACMS

The part of an ACMS step definition that describes terminal interactions, processing, or both.

stimulus mode *n.*

MINC

A method of operating a digital-input module (MNCDI) in which the assertion of each of the 16 lines on the module is treated as an external event. When one of the lines is asserted, the system reads the data on that line. The programmer sets this mode in the arguments of the MDISET subprogram.

stockholders *n.*

generic

The owners of a corporation; also referred to as shareholders.

stop bit *n.*

PRO/Communications

A bit that is used to indicate the end of a transmitted character.

stopcode *n.*

TOPS-10

A message containing a three-letter code printed at the CTY indicating that a serious error has occurred in the operating system's data base.

stop element *n.*

VAX PSI

Either one or two 1-bits that mark the end of a character in start-stop transmission.

stopped *adj.*

MicroPower PASCAL

Pertaining to a process state in which a process can be forced to reenter itself at its termination sequence entry point when it or another process performs the STOP function or the STPC$ macro. Either action stops the subject process.

storage n.

generic

A place for keeping information.

storage allocation n.

DIGITAL-specific

The assignment of space to a file on the recording medium.

storage allocation table n.

DIGITAL-specific

A file reflecting the status of every addressable block on the disk.

storage class n.

VAX DBMS

That characteristic of a record type that determines under which conditions the record of a particular record type becomes a member of a set type.

VAX PL/I

The attribute of a variable that describes how its storage is allocated and released by PL/I. The storage classes are automatic, static, based, defined, and parameter.

VAX/VMS

The attribute that, with its type, specifies C's interpretation of an identifier. The storage class determines the location and lifetime of an identifier's storage. Examples are static, external, and auto.

storage reference n.

DSM-11

A name symbolic representation of a storage location that has the value of the contents of that location. DSM recognizes four types of storage reference: local variables, global variables, special variables, and naked references.

storage schema n.

DIGITAL-specific

A description of the physical storage of data in a database. The storage schema is written using the storage schema data definition language (storage schema DDL). See also storage schema data definition entry and static allocation.

storage schema data definition entry n.

VAX DBMS

In DBMS, the entry of the data definition language (DDL) used to define the physical organization of a database. See also storage schema.

storage schema DDL (data definition language) n.

VAX DBMS

The language used to define the physical organization of the database. See also storage schema.

stored print settings n.

DIGITAL-specific

A complete set of print settings stored for later use. A document's print settings may be stored under a number from 0–9 by using the SS option in the Print Menu; stored print settings may be recalled with the RS option in the Print Menu.

stored ruler n.

DIGITAL-specific

Ruler settings saved for later use. A stored ruler is assigned a number from 0–9 and can be retrieved by typing its number when the current ruler is being displayed.

store through *n.*

VAX/VMS

A cache management technique in which data from a write operation is copied in both cache and main memory. Cache and main memory data are always consistent. Same as write through.

stream *n.*

RSX-11M

A series of contiguous characters that make up each record in a file. RMS-11 detects the end of a stream record only by the presence of specific terminators. See also fixed-length, variable-length, variable-with-fixed-control, undefined, record format, and record access stream.

VAX/VMS

An access window to a file associated with a record access control block, supporting record operation requests.

stream I/O *n.*

VAX PL/I

The transmission and interpretation of input or output data in terms of sequences of ASCII characters that are delimited by spaces, tabs, commas, or fields defined by format items.

stream record format *n.*

VAX DATATRIEVE

A file format in which records are variable in size and delimited by special characters. The file is treated as a stream of ASCII characters. This format is used for file interchange with non-RMS application programs in sequential file organization.

VAX/RMS and VAX/VMS

The property of a file specifying that the data in the file is interpreted as a continuous sequence of bytes, without control information. Stream record format applies to sequential files only.

string *n.*

DIGITAL-specific

A set of contiguous items of similar type; a connected sequence of characters. See also signed integer.

generic

A series of consecutive characters, words, or other elements connected in logical or physical order.

VAX/VMS

1. An array of type CHAR.

2. A constant consisting of a series of ASCII characters enclosed in quotation marks. Such a constant is declared implicitly as an array of CHAR, initialized with the given characters, and terminated by a NUL character (ASCII 0, C escape sequence \0).

string (key) *n.*

RSX-11M

An indexed file key data type where each byte is interpreted by its binary contents. Permissible values are not limited to valid ASCII codes. See also packed decimal key, two-byte signed integer, four-byte signed integer, two-byte unsigned binary, four-byte unsigned binary.

string constant *n.*

Medical Systems and MINC

One or more characters, words, or other elements (enclosed in quotations) that maintain their value. Same as string literal.

PASCAL and VAX PASCAL

A character string used as a literal constant in the program.

string data *n.*

DSM-11

Any set of between 0 and 255 characters taken as a string data entry and referenced by a local or global variable.

string descriptor *n.*

Terminal Data Management System

A data structure that specifies the address, length, and data type of a string. String descriptors are passed as arguments to subroutines.

STRING DESCRIPTOR *n.*

FMS

Used as an argument in FMS calls to indicate length, data type, and location of the string.

string expression *n.*

DSM-11

An expression to which DSM-11 does not give a special (numeric or logical) interpretation.

string literal *n.*

DSM-11, Medical Systems, and MINC

A string of characters enclosed in double quotation marks within the context of a line. The value of a string literal is a function of its spelling. Same as string constant.

string search buffer *n.*

VAX/VMS

A buffer used to store the string being searched for.

string valued expression *n.*

DSM-11

An expression that produces a string result upon evaluation.

string variable *n.*

Medical Systems and MINC

A variable used for an ordered collection of numeric, alphabetic, and special characters. An alphabetic letter followed by a dollar sign ($) or a letter and a number followed by a $ designate a string variable.

PASCAL and VAX PASCAL

Variable of type PACKED ARRAY [1..N] OF CHAR, where N represents an integer constant.

strip chart mode *n.*

MINC

The dynamic display of data in graphic form. This is a MINC feature that allows users to view a large number of points plotted in a continuous flow across the screen, resembling the action of a strip chart.

strobe *n.*

generic

A signal that allows a circuit to accept data on its input lines, or send data on its output lines.

strong definition *n.*

VAX/VMS

Definition of a global symbol that is explicitly available for reference by modules linked with the module in which the definition occurs. The linker always lists a global symbol with a strong definition in the symbol portion of the map. The librarian always includes a global symbol with a strong definition in the global symbol table of a library.

strong reference *n.*

VAX/VMS

A reference to a global symbol in an object module that requests the linker to report an error if it does not find a definition for the symbol during linking. If a library contains the definition, the linker incorporates the library module defining the global symbol into the image containing the strong reference.

structure *n.*

MicroPower PASCAL

Refers to system data structure; a process control block, semaphore, ring buffer, or packet.

VAX PL/I

A hierarchical arrangement of related data items, called members, that need not have the same data type.

VAX/VMS

An aggregate type consisting of a sequence of named members. Each member may have any type. A structure member may also consist of a specified number of bits, called a field.

STRUCTURE *n.*

PEARL

A compound data object with elements of different types.

structured type *n.*

MicroPower PASCAL

A definition of a type that contains several data types. This structured type can be attributed to a structured variable. In this way, one structured variable may be composed of several types of data items.

PASCAL

A collection of related data components. The components can be of the same type (as for arrays and files) or of different types (as for records).

VAX PASCAL

Subset of an existing scalar type, defined for use as a type. A subrange must be a continuous range of values, and is described by its upper and lower bounds separated by the .. symbol.

structured variable *n.*

MicroPower PASCAL

A group of variables collected under one variable name. The parts of the structured variable may be different data types.

STRUCTURE field description statement *n.*

Common Data Dictionary

In CDDL (common data definition language), STRUCTURE field description statements define fields that are subdivided into one or more subordinate fields. The top-level field description statement for a record is ordinarily a STRUCTURE field description statement.

structure ID *n.*

MicroPower PASCAL

A 48-bit value assigned to a structure when the structure is created. This value consists of the structure index and structure serial number.

structure-qualified reference *n.*

VAX PL/I

The naming of a member of a structure by specifying each higher-level name within the structure and separating the names with periods.

structure reference *n.*

VAX PL/I

A variable reference denoting an entire structure (as opposed to a member of a structure).

STSN *n.*

DECnet

The abbreviation for set and test sequence numbers. STSN is an SNA (systems network architecture) session control request used to resynchronize message sequence numbers. Same as set and test sequence number. See also set and test sequence numbers.

STX *n.*

DECnet

The abbreviation for start of text. A communication control character that precedes a sequence of character that is to be treated as an entity and entirely transmitted through to the ultimate destination. Such a sequence is referred to as text. Same as start of text.

subblock *n.*

DECSIM

A subblock, found inside a model definition, describes the same logical block of a model in a different modeling style or level.

subcell *n.*

RGL/FEP

A subdivision in a graph's axis. A subcell boundary is displayed as a short tickmark or a dotted line across a graph. See also cell.

subchannel *n.*

DECnet

A logical communications path within a logical link that handles a defined category of NSP data messages. Because data segment messages are handled differently from other data messages, the two types of messages can be thought of as traveling in two different subchannels.

subcommand *n.*

RSX-11M

In EDT, the DEC Editor, commands entered in character mode are called subcommands to distinguish them from commands entered in command mode.

subdictionary (or sub-dictionary) *n.*

Common Data Dictionary and FMS

In the CDD (Common Data Dictionary) hierarchy, subdictionaries function almost exactly as if they were dictionary directories, but they exist as physically separate dictionary files.

subdirectory *n.*

TOPS-10

A continued subfile directory.

VAX PL/I and VAX/VMS

A directory file cataloged in a higher-level directory that lists additional files belonging to the owner of the directory.

subexpression *n.*

DSM-11

An expression element that consists of any legitimate expression enclosed in parentheses.

sub-file directory (SFD) *n.*

TOPS-10

A directory pointed to by a UFD (user file directory) or a higher-level SFD (sub-file directory). Each user has a UFD containing as many SFDs as the user wants. Same as SFD. See also continued SFD.

subject of entry *n.*

VAX COBOL

An operand or reserved word that appears immediately after the level indicator or level-number in a Data Division entry.

sublist *n.*

DECWORD

A list containing selected records from a list processing list document.

subpicture *n.*

VT-11 GRAPHICS

A unit composed of several primitive definitions. A subpicture is analogous to a subroutine. See also TAG.

subprocess *n.*

VAX/VMS

A subsidiary process created by another process. The process that creates a subprocess is its owner. A process and its subprocesses share a pool of quotas and limits. When an owner process is removed from the system, all its subprocesses (and their subprocesses) are also removed.

subprogram *n.*

DIGITAL-specific

A program or a sequence of instructions that can be called to perform the same task (though perhaps on different data) at different points in a program, or even in different programs. See also subroutine.

sub-queue *n.*

COBOL-74

A logical hierarchical division of a queue.

subrange type *n.*

PASCAL and VAX PASCAL

A subset of an existing scalar type, defined for use as a type. A subrange must be a continuous range of values, and is described by its upper and lower bounds separated by the .. symbol.

subroutine *n.*

DIGITAL-specific

A routine designed to be used by other routines to accomplish a specific task. See also subprogram.

generic

A set of instructions used to perform a secondary function in the main program.

VAX/VMS

A subsidiary routine that executes when called by another program. A subroutine is often called repeatedly until a certain condition is met.

subschema *n.*

generic

A user view of a database. The subschema can include everything in the corresponding schema or any part thereof.

VAX DBMS

In DBMS, a tailored, user-oriented view of a database. A view may be tailored to meet the needs of a particular programming language or to focus the kind of data a program can access to that specifically required to perform an end user task. The subschema can include everything in the corresponding schema or any part of the schema. The subschema is written using the subschema data definition entry. See also subschema data definition entry.

subschema data definition entry *n.*

VAX DBMS

In DBMS, the entry of the data definition language (DDL) used to define user-oriented views of a database.

subschema data description language *n.*

VAX DBMS

The language used to define the user view of a database. See also subschema.

subschema object *n.*

VAX DBMS

A file of machine language instructions that describes that portion of a database known to a program.

subscript *n.*

DIGITAL-specific

A subscript is a numeric or string valued expression or expression element that is appended to a local or global variable name and that uniquely identifies specific elements of an array. Subscripts are enclosed in parentheses. Multiple subscripts must be separated by commas and can be used in global references only.

generic

1. A character printed one-half line below line level.

2. A symbol or a number used to specify one element of an array in certain programming languages.

3. An integer whose value identifies a table element.

subscripted data-name *n.*

COBOL-74

An identifier that is made up of a data-name followed by one or more subscripts enclosed in parentheses.

subscripted variable *n.*

DIGITAL-specific

A variable name followed by one or more subscripts in parentheses.

subsettable instructions *n.*

VAX/VMS

The instructions that a processor implementor may choose to include as an option, to include always, or to omit.

substate *n.*

DECnet

An intermediate line state that appears as a tag on a line-state display.

VAX/VMS

An intermediate circuit state that is displayed for a circuit state display when the NCP commands SHOW or LIST are issued.

substitute buffer *n.*

VAX/VMS

A buffer used to store the string to be substituted for the search string.

substitution directive *n.*

VAX DATATRIEVE

An expression in a command or statement passed to DATATRIEVE from a calling program. The substitution directive is replaced by parameters given in the program.

substring *n.*

DSM-11 and MINC

Any contiguous part of a larger string.

subsystem *n.*

VAX/VMS

A collection of mechanism and policy modules that implement a particular facility in the system. Examples include the file subsystem and the batch subsystem.

subtend *v.*

RGL/FEP

To be opposite to and to delimit. For example, the side of a triangle subtends the opposite angle.

success *n.*

RSX-11M

An exit status code.

successive approximation *n.*

MINC

A method of converting an analog level into a digital equivalent by a series of approximations, each with twice the resolution of its predecessor. The MINC A/D implements its successive approximation by iterating a specific algorithm 12 times, once for each bit in the successive approximation register (SAR).

successor value *n.*

PASCAL and VAX PASCAL

A value that succeeds a given value in any nonreal scalar type.

SUD *n.*

CTS-300

The abbreviation for single-user DIBOL. SUD is a run-time system that supports one user and uses the SJ, F/B, or XM monitor. Same as single-user DIBOL.

summary *n.*

DIGITAL-specific

The default display type for the SHOW and LIST commands. Summary refers to the most useful information for a component, selected from the status and characteristics information.

VAX/VMS

The default display type for the NCP commands SHOW and LIST. A summary includes the most useful information for a component, selected from the status and characteristics information.

summary lines *n.*

CTS-300

Lines that summarize or total the data in a QUILL report and are produced with an AT statement.

VAX DATATRIEVE

Information users can display in a DATATRIEVE report with the AT TOP and AT BOTTOM statements.

summary listing *n.*

RSX-11M

A series of messages that serve as an audit trail of the processing performed by an RMS-11 utility. Normally, a summary listing can be printed on a user's terminal or written into a specified file.

super-cluster *n.*

TOPS-10

A contiguous set of one or more clusters introduced to compress the file pointer for large units into 18 bits. Refer to compressed file pointer.

superscript *n.*

generic

A character printed one-half line above line level.

Super-USETI *n.*

DECsystem-10

A style of reading a disk unit of file structure by giving absolute addresses rather than locations within a file.

supervisor *n.*

DIGITAL-specific

A privileged program that is not part of the kernel.

supervisor mode *n.*

DECsystem-10

The executive submode of the KL10 processor. Similar to public mode; however, code executed in supervisor mode is able to access, but not alter, concealed mode code.

VAX/VMS

The third most privileged processor access mode (mode 2). The operating system's command interpreter runs in supervisor mode.

supervisor-mode library *n.*

VAX/VMS

A library of routines that uses the supervisor-mode memory management APRs (active page registers) to map to both the task and its own routines.

Supervisor Only attribute *n.*

FMS

A field attribute indicating that the field is considered to be displayed only when this attribute is enabled for a terminal. The application program enables and disables supervisor-only mode at run time.

supervisory programs *n.*

RT-11

Computer programs that have the primary function of scheduling, allocating, and controlling system resources, rather than processing data to produce results.

supported *adj.*

DIGITAL-specific

Pertaining to the obligations that DIGITAL has to its customers. Systems allow for many variations of hardware and software. While a particular item of hardware or software may not be present on every system, that hardware or software is considered supported if it is possible to include it without a special effort. The Software Product Description (SPD) for the system identifies what is supported. Supported also refers to the assistance the installation gets from DIGITAL in setting up and operating the system. Support of this sort is defined at the time the system is purchased.

support mode *n.*

DECnet

The use of software/hardware combination that enables a DECSYSTEM-20 to be seen by a remote 2780/3780-like station as an IBM 370. Same as termination.

suspension *n.*

VAX/VMS

A state in which a process is inactive, but known to the system. A suspended process becomes active again only when another process requests the operating system to resume it. See also hibernation.

SVA *n.*

VAX/VMS

The abbreviation for system virtual address. A virtual address identifying a location mapped by an address is system space. Same as system virtual address.

SVC *n.*

DECnet and VAX PSI

The abbreviation for switched virtual circuit. A temporary logical association between two DTEs (data terminal equipment) connected to a PSDN (packet switching data network). An SVC is set up only when there is data to transmit and is cleared when the data transfer is complete. Same as switched virtual circuit.

swap *v.*

DECmate II

To exchange or transpose the character at the cursor with the one to its right.

DIGITAL-specific

To remove a process from memory to secondary storage and to return it to memory at a future time.

swap file *n.*

RSTS/E

A special file that stores a RSTS/E job image after it is moved from memory to disk.

swap mode *n.*

VAX/VMS

A process execution state that determines the eligibility of a process to be swapped out of the balance set. If process swap mode is disabled, the process working set is locked in the balance set.

swapper *n.*

VAX/VMS

The process that performs system-wide memory scheduling. The swapper writes modified pages to secondary storage, creates a shell for new processes, shrinks the physical size of inactive processes, removes processes from the balance set, and brings processes waiting for execution into the balance set.

swapping *n.*

DIGITAL-specific and VAX/VMS

The method for sharing memory resources among several processes by writing an entire working set to secondary storage (swap out) and reading another working set into memory (swap in). For example, a process's working set can be written to secondary storage while the process is waiting for I/O completion on a slow device. It is brought back into the balance set when I/O completes. Contrast with paging.

generic

A process that transfers the contents of an area of main storage to or from auxiliary storage.

RSTS/E

The transfer of a job from memory to disk or vice versa. Swapping lets the system run more jobs than its memory can hold at any one time.

swapping class *n.*

TOPS-10

A category of swapping units distinguished from other categories of swapping units according to speed.

swapping device *n.*

DIGITAL-specific

Secondary storage that is suitable for swapping, usually a high-speed disk or drum.

generic

A mass storage device with a fast transfer rate.

sweep *n.*

MINC

A process in which data samples are transferred from a laboratory instrument through an MNC-series module as input to a user program, or transferred as output from a program through an MNC-series module to a laboratory instrument. The samples make up a logical stream of data that may use one or more buffers. Same as sampling sweep. See also buffer sweep.

sweep-information array *n.*

MINC

A 40-word INTEGER*2 array that is the general status area for a sweep subprogram.

sweep-status word *n.*

MINC

The first word of a sweep-information array. The sweep-status word contains codes that indicate the current status of the sweep.

switch *n.*

DIGITAL-specific

1. The part of a file specification that is preceded by a slash.

2. One of several physical controls on the operator's console.

3. A flag that is used to control the path of execution within programs.

generic

A method that controls the flow of functions and operations in software.

VAX/VMS

A portion of a command string that modifies a command verb or command parameter by selecting one of several options. A qualifier, if present, follows the command verb or parameter to which it applies and is in the format: /qualifier[=option]. For example, in the command string PRINT filename /COPIES=3, the COPIES qualifier indicates that the user wants three copies of a given file printed. Same as qualifier.

switched line *n.*

DECnet and VAX PSI

A communications link for which the physical path may vary with each use. The dial-up telephone network is an example of a switched line.

switched virtual circuit (SVC) *n.*

DECnet, VAX PSI, and VAX/VMS

A temporary logical association between two DTEs (data terminal equipment) connected to a PSDN (packet switching data network) (analogous to connection by a dial-up line). An SVC is set up only when there is data to transmit and is cleared when the data transfer is complete. Same as SVC.

switch-status condition *n.*

generic

The proposition that an external switch has been set to an "on" or "off" status.

SWL *n.*

Terminal Data Management System

The abbreviation for Software Event Logger. The TDMS (Terminal Data Management System) process that records ACMS and TDMS software events that occur during the running of an application program. In order to see the events logged by SWL, a user must use the Software Event Logger Utility Program. Same as Software Event Logger.

SWLUP *n.*

Terminal Data Management System

The abbreviation for Software Event Logger Utility Program. The TDMS (Terminal Data Management System) utility used to list selected events that were logged by the software event logger. Same as Software Event Logger Utility Program.

symbiont *n.*

DIGITAL-specific and VAX/VMS

A full process that transfers record-oriented data to or from a mass storage device. For example, an input symbiont transfers data from card readers to disks. An output symbiont transfers data from disks to line printers.

generic

A process that transfers data to or from a mass storage device.

symbiont manager *n.*

DIGITAL-specific and VAX/VMS

The function (job controller) that maintains spool queues, and dynamically creates symbiont processes to perform the necessary I/O operations.

symbol *n.*

DIGITAL-specific

A symbol is a representation of something by reason of relationship, association, or convention. In a programming context, a symbol (sometimes called a variable) is an entity that must be defined, or given a meaning, so that it can be used.

VAX/VMS

An entity that when defined will represent a particular function or entity (for example, a command string, directory name, or file name) in a particular context. See local symbol, global symbol, and universal symbol.

symbol binding *n.*

TOPS-10

The process of resolving references in one module to symbols that are defined (assigned a value) in another module.

symbol definition file *n.*

VAX/VMS

The output object file created by the Task Builder that contains the global symbol definitions and values and sometimes program section names, attributes, and allocations in a format suitable for reprocessing by the Task Builder. Symbol definition files contain linkage information about shared regions.

symbol file *n.*

MicroPower PASCAL

A file containing a symbol table.

symbolic *adj.*

DIGITAL-specific

Pertaining to dumps and to objects that are given as names rather than as a binary, octal, or hexadecimal format.

symbolic address *n.*

TOPS-10

An address used to specify a storage location in the context of a particular program. Symbolic addresses must then be translated into relocatable (or absolute) addresses by the assembler.

symbolic-character *n.*

generic

A user-defined word that specifies a user-defined figurative constant.

symbolic constant *n.*

DIGITAL-specific

An identifier assigned a constant value by a define control line. A symbolic constant may be used wherever a literal is valid.

symbolic debugger *n.*

MicroPower PASCAL

A program residing in the RT-11 host system that allows the user to examine or deposit memory locations or PASCAL variables, set breakpoints, and examine kernel structures in application storage. PASDBG is the symbolic debugger used with the MicroPower PASCAL application.

VAX/VMS

A program that aids a programmer in finding errors in other programs.

symbol table *n.*

DIGITAL-specific

A table containing entries and binary values for each symbol defined or used within a module. This table generally contains additional information about the way in which the symbol was defined in the module.

SYN *n.*

DECnet

The abbreviation for synchronous idle. A BISYNC protocol data-link character used to help synchronize communications between the sending and receiving stations. The RSX-11/3271 Protocol Emulator (PE) may use from 3 to 15 consecutive SYN characters to establish synchronization. SYN characters may also be embedded in the transmitted text by the host for time-fill to maintain synchronization (the PE does not use SYN characters in this way). The SYN characters are deleted from the message by the receiving station and are not included in the BCC (block character check) computation at either station. Same as synchronous idle.

synchronize *v.*

generic

To cause two or more things to occur in the correct relation to each other.

synchronizer *n.*

Medical Systems

A circuit that causes an event to occur at a particular time or rate.

SYNCHRONIZER *n.*

PEARL

An object that permits time-ordered selection of interacting activities.

synchronous *adj.*

DIGITAL-specific

Pertaining to related events where all changes occur simultaneously or in definite timed intervals.

generic

Pertaining to a method of data transmission which allows each event to operate in relation to a timing signal.

synchronous backplane interconnect (SBI) *n.*

VAX/VMS

The part of the hardware that interconnects the processor, memory controllers, MASSBUS adapters, and the UNIBUS adapter. Same as SBI.

synchronous call *n.*

Terminal Data Management System

A call to a TDMS (Terminal Data Management System) subroutine that performs the entire requested action before a program can continue running. Thus, a program continues only after the completion of the called subroutine. Most calls are synchronous calls. See also asynchronous calls.

synchronous data-link control (SDLC) *n.*

DECnet

SDLC is IBM's bit-level, transparent line discipline used to control half-duplex, full-duplex, point-to-point, or multipoint communication lines. The SDLC module of the protocol emulator (PE) participates in the transmission/reception processing of data frames built by or input to the SNA (systems network architecture) module of the PE. Same as SDLC.

synchronous disconnect *n.*

DECnet

The terminating of I/O operations by nontransparent tasks over a logical link without deassigning the channel. Thus, the task can use the channel for subsequent I/O operations with the same or a different remote task.

VAX/VMS

The disconnect that occurs when a nontransparent task can issue a call to terminate I/O operations over a logical link without deassigning the channel. Thus, the task can use the channel for subsequent I/O operations with the same or a different remote task.

synchronous idle (SYN) *n.*

DECnet

A BISYNC protocol data-link character used to help synchronize communications between the sending and receiving stations. The RSX-11/3271 Protocol Emulator (PE) may use from 3 to 15 consecutive SYN characters to establish synchronization. SYN characters may also be embedded in the transmitted text by the host for time-fill to maintain synchronization (the PE does not use SYN characters in this way). The SYN characters are deleted from the message by the receiving station and are not included in the BCC (block character check) computation at either station. Same as SYN.

synchronous line *n.*

DECnet

A line (cable) over which synchronous transmissions occur. Such lines are used to connect processors. Synchronous transmission is data transmission in which time intervals between transmitted characters are of equal length. Synchronous transmission is typically done at relatively high rates of speed. See also synchronous transmission.

synchronous operation *n.*

RSX-11M

Any operation where RMS-11 returns control to a user program only after all processing associated with the operation is finished. File operations are always synchronous. Record operations can be asynchronous.

synchronous record operation *n.*

VAX DATATRIEVE and VAX/VMS

A mode of record processing in which a user program issues a record read or write request and then waits until that request is fulfilled before continuing to execute.

synchronous serial data transmission *n.*

DECnet

A data communication technique in which the information required to determine when each byte begins is sent at the beginning of a group of bytes (the sync bytes). The time interval between successive bytes in the group is zero. The time interval between successive groups of bytes is unspecified.

synchronous system trap *n.*

generic

A system condition which occurs as a result of an error or request for service within the executing task.

synchronous transmission *n.*

DECnet, TOPS-10, and VAX PL/I

Transmission in which the data characters and bits are transmitted at a fixed rate with the transmitter and receiver synchronized. This eliminates the need for start-stop elements, thus providing greater efficiency. See also synchronous line.

SYNC pattern *n.*

DECnet

A character pattern essential to the block and control-sequence formats in BSC (binary synchronous communication) operations. The SYNC pattern causes the transmitter and the receiver to operate in step with each other. It always precedes a transmission and establishes bit and character synchronization between the transmitter and the receiver. This action ensures the complete transmission and reception of the first significant character of each file transfer (or message). The leading SYNC character is stripped upon receipt and does not appear in the received message.

syndrome *n.*

generic

The result of a comparison between a calculated ECC (error correction code) value and a stored ECC value.

syntax *n.*

DIGITAL-specific

The rules governing statement structure in a computer language: the structure of a language.

generic

1. The formal structure of a statement or a command string.

2. The arrangement of characters and groups of characters and their relation to one another regardless of their specific meanings.

VAX/VMS

The particular form of a command, including spelling and the order of qualifiers and parameters. Misspelled words are the most common syntax errors.

SYS *n.*

TOPS-10

A system-wide logical name for the system library. This is the area where the standard programs of the system are maintained.

SYSGEN *n.*

DIGITAL-specific

The acronym for system generation. System generation is the process of tailoring an operation system for a particular hardware configuration with modifications and additions to the software configuration as well. Same as system generation.

SYS search list *n.*

TOPS-10

The file structure search list for device SYS. This is also used for several of the ersatz devices because it is a constant, well-ordered list.

SYSTAT *n.*

DECsystem-10

A program that outputs to the user's terminal status information on the system as a whole, on selected aspects of the system, or on a selected job or set of jobs.

system *n.*

generic

A group of related elements that are interactive to form a complete thing that performs a specific function.

VAX/VMS

In the context "system, owner, group, world," system refers to the group numbers that are used by operating system and its controlling users, the system operators, and system manager.

system address space *n.*

VAX/VMS

The higher-addressed half of virtual address space. See also system space and system region.

system base register (SBR) *n.*

DIGITAL-specific and VAX/VMS

A processor register that contains the physical address of the base of the system page table. Same as SBR.

system base time *n.*

DIGITAL-specific

Refers to the actual date and time that a system uses as an absolute beginning time (time zero). All times, then, needed to be referenced or "read" by a system will use this absolute beginning time to "measure" all subsequent times since then.

Many Digital systems use Smithsonian Astronomical Base Time, midnight, November 17, 1858. That is the exact moment that Smithsonian first exposed astral photographic plates.

system-buffered I/O *n.*

VAX/VMS

An I/O operation, such as terminal or mailbox I/O, in which an intermediate buffer from the system buffer pool is used instead of a process-specified buffer.

system build procedure *n.*

RT-11

A procedure in system generation in which conditional files and command files are used to assemble and link the operating system produced by the system generation process.

system command *n.*

DIGITAL-specific

An instruction to the system to perform an operation.

system communication locations *n.*

VAX DBMS

Locations in core provided by DBMS for run-unit/DBCS interaction.

system configuration *n.*

DIGITAL-specific

The combination of hardware and software that makes up a usable computer system.

system control block (SCB) *n.*

VAX/VMS

The data structure in system space that contains all the interrupt and exception vectors known to the system. Same as SCB.

system control block base register (SCBBR) *n.*

VAX/VMS

A processor register containing the base address of the system control block. Same as SCBBR.

system default ruler *n.*

DECWORD

DECWORD is distributed with 10 stored rulers known as system default rulers. When users create documents, DECWORD displays system default ruler 0.

system-defined identifier *n.*

VAX/VMS

One of three classes of identifiers. System-defined identifiers are provided by the system to identify groups of users according to their usage of the system. For example, all users who access the system by dialing up receive the DIALUP identifier.

system device *n.*

DIGITAL-specific and VAX/VMS

The random access mass storage device unit on which the volume containing the operating system software resides.

generic

The device on which the operating system is stored.

system disk *n.*

RSTS/E

The disk that is required by the RSTS/E monitor to start the system and thereafter to allow the system to run properly under timesharing. The system disk is part of the public structure.

system division *n.*

PEARL

The operating system and installation-dependent part of a PEARL program.

system dynamic memory *n.*

VAX/VMS

Memory reserved for the operating system to allocate as needed for temporary storage. For example, when an image issued an I/O request, system dynamic memory is used to contain the I/O request packet. Each process has a limit on the amount of system dynamic memory that can be allocated for its use at one time.

system event file *n.*

TOPS-10

The file where the operating system records hardware and software events.

system file *n.*

RT-11

A file containing a component of the MRRT operating system, such as MRRT monitor or device handlers

system function call *n.*

RSTS/E

A call to the RSTS/E monitor that lets a BASIC-PLUS or BASIC-PLUS-2 program perform special I/O functions, set terminal characteristics, establish special job characteristics, and request other operations from the monitor.

system generation (SYSGEN) *n.*

DIGITAL-specific

System generation is the process of tailoring an operating system for a particular hardware configuration with modifications and additions to the software configuration as well. Same as SYSGEN.

generic

The process of building an operating system with software configuration adjustments on or for a specific hardware configuration.

system identification register *n.*

VAX/VMS

A processor register that contains the processor type and serial number.

system image *n.*

VAX/VMS

The image that is read into memory from disk when the system is started up.

system image file *n.*

DECnet

The data base that contains a binary image of the RSX-11 operating system, including an RSX-11/3271 Protocol Emulator (PE) software. If the PE is co-resident with DECnet, the system image file may optionally contain an image of a local RSX DECnet system. The system image file can be modified by use of the VNP utility. See also permanent data base and running data base.

system length register (SLR) *n.*

VAX/VMS

A processor register containing the length of the system page table in longwords, that is, the number of page table entries in the system region page table. Same as SLR.

system library *n.*

DIGITAL-specific

All the relocatable routines used by the operating system are defined in the system library. These routines perform various common functions, such as a converting binary numbers to decimal, saving the contents of registers, formatting input and output, and managing memory. System library routines can also be called by user tasks.

system maintenance diskettes *n.*

PRO/Diskette System

Diskettes provided with the Professional that diagnose hardware problems.

system manager *n.*

generic

The person responsible for the policies, procedures, and the daily operation of a computer system.

system monitor *n.*

generic

A program that controls functions that occur with the operating system.

SYSTEM-owned set *n.*

VAX DBMS

A set type owned by the SYSTEM record rather than by a record type users have selected. SYSTEM-owned sets have only one occurrence in the database and are used for relationships with large numbers of memory occurrences or as entry points into the database. See also member record, owner record, nonsingular set, and singular set.

system page table (SPT) *n.*

DIGITAL-specific and VAX/VMS

The data structure that maps the system region virtual addresses, including the addresses used to refer to the process page tables. The system page table (SPT) contains one page table entry (PTE) for each page of system region virtual memory. The physical base address of the SPT is contained in a register called the system base register (SBR). Same as SPT.

system password *n.*

VAX/VMS

A password required by a terminal before login can be initiated at the terminal.

system process *n.*

MicroPower PASCAL

A process supplied as part of the MicroPower PASCAL package for inclusion in user-created applications. System processes furnish commonly needed services and are usually privileged in mapped targets.

system program *n.*

DIGITAL-specific

A program that performs system-level functions. Any program that is part of or supplied with the basic operating system.

generic

A program that resides on system disk as part of the operating system.

system programmer *n.*

generic

A person who designs and/or writes operating systems, or who designs and writes procedures or programs that provide general purpose services for an application system.

system prompt *n.*

generic

The prompt that indicates system commands may be executed.

system protection (code) *n.*

RSX-11M

A file attribute that dictates how the operating system restricts access to a file based on account number and type of operation.

system queue *n.*

DIGITAL-specific

A queue used and maintained by operating system procedures to control the allocation of system resources. See also state queue.

VAX/VMS

A queue used and maintained by operating system procedures. See also state queue.

system region *n.*

VAX/VMS

The third quarter of virtual address space (the lower-addressed half of system space). Virtual addresses in the system region are sharable between processes. Some of the data structures mapped by system region virtual addresses are system entry vectors, the system control block (SCB), the system page table (SPT), and process page tables. See also system space and system address space.

system services *n.*

VAX/VMS

Procedures provided by the operating system that can be called by user images. See also directive.

system services control point (SSCP) *n.*

DECnet

A network addressable unit (NAU) responsible for startup, control, and shutdown of an SNA (systems network architecture) network. The protocol emulator (PE) communicates with the SSCP in a session governed by FM Profile 0, TS Profile 1 protocols. Same as SSCP.

system space *n.*

VAX/VMS

The higher-addressed half of virtual address space. Same as system virtual space. See also system region and system address space.

system task *n.*

RSX-11M

A task that performs system-level functions is called a system task. Thus, a system task is any task that is part of the basic operating system, such as an editor or other system utility. See also applications task.

system task directory (STD) *n.*

RSX-11M

A list of all the tasks installed on the system. Users can display the STD through the DCL SHOW TASKS/INSTALLED commands. Same as STD.

system unit *n.*

PRO/Diskette System

The part of the Professional system that contains the diskette drive, option modules, power supply, and the computer itself. The system unit is the main component of the Professional.

system virtual address (SVA) *n.*

VAX/VMS

A virtual address identifying a location mapped by an address in system space. Same as SVA.

system virtual space *n.*

VAX/VMS

The higher-addressed half of virtual address space. Same as system space. See also system region.

system-wide dictionary *n.*

DECWORD

A multipurpose dictionary containing 10,000 words for general use. Also known as the system default dictionary. DECWORD checks a document against this dictionary if a user account does not contain a personal dictionary or if there is no group dictionary. See also dictionary.

system workspace *n.*

ACMS

A task workspace whose record definition is provided by ACMS/AD.

t

10-K report *n.*

U.S. Government

The name of the report required by the SEC (Securities and Exchange Commission) from all publicly traded companies. It is similar to a company's annual report.

tabbed text *n.*

DECWORD

Text typed after the TAB key is pressed.

table *n.*

generic

An arrangement of data identified by a label for easy reference.

table-driven control file *n.*

DECWORD

A file containing information that tells DECWORD how to control the printers.

table element *n.*

generic

A data item that belongs to the set of repeated items comprising a table.

tab mark *n.*

generic

An invisible character that forces the next character forward to the next tab position. Inserted by pressing the TAB key.

tab position *n.*

generic

One of the locations to which a tab mark or tabulation key may move text.

tachometer *n.*

generic

A device used to measure speed, usually the speed of revolutions.

TAG *n.*

VT-11 GRAPHICS

A unique name assigned to a subpicture.

tag variable *n.*

Common Data Dictionary

An optional variable in CDDL VARIANTS field description statements. The run-time value of the tag variable determines the current VARIANT. See also VARIANTS field description statement.

tap *n.*

generic

An electrical connection fixed to a specified position on a delay line, potentiometer, etc.

tape *n.*

generic

A removable cassette that can store information.

tape mark *n.*

VAX/VMS

A delimiter that consists of the single character block device control character DC3 (which translates to a CTRL/S) that is used to indicate the boundaries between label groups and a file section.

target bucket *n.*

RSX-11M

The data bucket where RMS-11 determines it should perform the specified operation.

target directory *n.*

TOPS-10

A disk directory that is included by a wildcard.

target node *n.*

DECnet and DECsystem-10

The node that receives a memory image during a downline load, generates an upline dump, or loops back a test message. See also server task.

VAX/VMS

The node that receives a memory image from another node during a downline load; a node that loops back a test message.

target processor *n.*

MicroPower PASCAL

A microcomputer in which the MicroPower PAS-CAL application program is intended to run, once developed, on the host (RT-11) processor.

target system *n.*

VAX/VMS

The system on which a task executes.

target system environment *n.*

DIGITAL-specific

A computer that runs dedicated applications.

target task *n.*

DECnet and VAX/VMS

In a task-to-task communication environment, the target task is the one that receives and processes a logical link connection request. See also server task.

tariff *n.*

VAX PSI

A published rate for telecommunications service.

task *n.*

A-to-Z

On the Show Current Users display, an indication of how much work the computer is doing for users.

DECnet

An image running in the context of a process.

generic

A basic unit of executable code.

PEARL

A separately executable process, several of which can run concurrently. See also PEARL task.

RSX-11M

The fundamental, executable programming unit. It may include one or more routines taken from a library or routines written for a particular purpose. Many DCL (DIGITAL Command Language) or MCR (monitor console routine) commands that a user enters are tasks. Any utility invoked is also a task.

VAX/VMS

An RSX-11/IAS term for a process and image bound together.

Task Builder (TKB) *n.*

RSTS/E and RSX-11M

A system utility that converts and combines object modules into a task image. The Task Builder also arranges task segments according to an overlay structure defined in an ODL (overlay description language) file. Same as TKB.

task control block (TCB) *n.*

RSX-11M

Each installed task has a TCB in the dynamic storage region (pool). The TCB contains all the information needed to run the task. The TCB is created when the task is installed and eliminated when the task is removed. The system task directory (STD) consists of TCBs. Same as TCB.

task debugger *n.*

ACMS

A debugging tool, provided by ACMS/AD, that is primarily for debugging multiple-step tasks that use procedure servers.

task group *n.*

ACMS

One or more ACMS tasks with similar processing requirements, gathered together so they can share resources.

task group database (TDB) *n.*

A run-time database containing information derived from task and task group definitions. Same as TDB.

task image *n.*

RSX-11M

The disk file containing the executable code that comprises the task. RMS-11, a task image, is the product of the Task Builder utility. When a task image is executed, it is called a task.

task image file *n.*

RSX-11M

The contiguous file containing a runnable image of a task. This file is built from one or more object modules by the Task Builder.

VAX/VMS

The output file created by the Task Builder that contains the executable portion of the task.

task instance *n.*

ACMS

The occurrence of the processing of a task. Each selection of a task is a task instance.

TASK LEVEL OBJECT *n.*

PEARL

An object that is declared within a PEARL task but is not enclosed within an inner block.

task selection string *n.*

ACMS

The string of characters a terminal user types, in addition to the selection keyword or number, when making a selection from a menu.

task specifier *n.*

DECnet and VAX/VMS

Information provided to DECnet-VAX software that enables it to complete a logical link connection to a remote task. This information includes the name of the remote node on which the target task runs and the name of the task itself.

task state *n.*

RSX-11M

One of two possible conditions of a task:

1. dormant–installed, but not yet requested to run

2. active–requested to run. It remains active until it exits, terminates, or is aborted.

See also active task and dormant task.

task workspace *n.*

ACMS

A workspace used mainly to pass information between steps in a multiple-step ACMS task.

taxable income *n.*

generic

The amount of income subject to income tax, computed according to the rules of the IRS (Internal Revenue Service).

TCAM *n.*

DECnet

The abbreviation for telecommunications access method (IBM software). A queued access method that extends the techniques of the logical IOCS to the communications system environment. Same as telecommunications access method.

TCB *n.*

VAX/VMS

The abbreviation for termination control block. The block used for termination handling. Same as termination control block.

TCB *n.*

RSX-11M

The abbreviation for task control block. Each installed task has a TCB in dynamic storage region (pool). The TCB contains all the information needed to run the task. The TCB is created when the task is installed and eliminated when the task is removed. The system task directory (STD) consists of TCBs. Same as task control block.

TDB *n.*

The abbreviation for task group database. TDB is a run-time database containing information derived from task and task groups definitions. Same as task group database.

TDMS *n.*

Terminal Data Management System

The abbreviation for Terminal Data Management System. A VAX-11 product that uses forms to collect and display information on the terminal. TDMS provides facilities for interactively creating customized forms that have different kinds of field and text characteristics, as well as several video features (such as bolding and reverse video). TDMS provides data independence by allowing data used in an application to be separated from the application program. ACMS/AD multiple-step tasks use TDMS services to manage terminal input and output. Same as Terminal Data Management System.

TECO *n.*

DIGITAL-specific

A sophisticated text editor and corrector program that allows simple editing requests, character string searches, complex program editing, command repetition, and text block movement. TECO editing is performed on files consisting of ASCII characters.

telecommunications *n.*

generic

The activity in which data is transmitted and received over distances using electromagnetic or light signals.

telecommunications access method (TCAM) *n.*

DECnet

Telecommunications access method (IBM Software) is a queued access method that extends to the techniques of the logical IOCS to the communications system environment. Same as TCAM.

TELENET *n.*

generic

A packet switching network available in the U.S.A.

temporary area *n.*

VAX DBMS

An area not shared among concurrent run units. A run unit that references a temporary field is used in form documents, enabling list processing to perform more complex operations, such as calculations.

temporary field *n.*

DECWORD

A list processing field that has a fixed name and variable value. A temporary field is used in form documents, enabling list processing to perform more complex operations, such as calculations.

DIGITAL-specific

A field defined by the operator that is valid only for the command with which it is executed.

temporary text delay (TTD) *n.*

DECnet

In binary synchronous communications, a control character sequence (STX ENQ) sent by a transmitting station to either indicate a delay in transmission or to initiate an abort of the transmission in programs. Same as TTD.

tenancy condition *n.*

VAX DBMS

The proposition for which a truth value can be determined that the current record is a member of a specific set.

tenant *n.*

generic

A database record that is either the owner or a member of a specific set.

tenant record *n.*

generic

An owner or member record of a set.

VAX DBMS

Any record that participates in a set, whether a member or owner.

TENEX *n.*

DECnet and TOPS-20

A time-shared operating system developed by BB&N (Bolt Beranak and Newman Inc.) to run on a DEC PDP-10 processor augmented with paging hardware.

term *n.*

generic

Each of the quantities separated by an operator in an equation or series.

terminal *n.*

DIGITAL-specific

The general name for peripheral devices that have keyboards and video screens or printers. Under program control, a terminal enables users to type commands and data on the keyboard and receive messages on the video screen or printer. See also video terminal.

generic

An interactive input/output device used in computer systems or networks.

VAX/VMS

The general name for peripheral devices that have keyboards and video screens or printers. Under program control, a terminal enables users to type commands and data on the keyboard and receive messages on the video screen or printer. Examples of terminals are the LA36 DECwriter hardcopy terminal and VT100 video display terminal.

terminal control area *n.*

FMS

An area in memory set aside for a terminal to be used in an FMS application.

terminal control subsystem *n.*

ACMS

A set of ACMS-controlled processes that control terminal user access to ACMS.

Terminal Data Management System (TDMS) *n.*

Terminal Data Management System

A VAX-11 product that uses forms to collect and display information on the terminal. TDMS provides facilities for interactively creating customized forms that have different kinds of field and text characteristics, as well as several video features (such as bolding and reverse video). TDMS provides data independence by allowing data used in an application to be separated from the application program. ACMS/AD multiple-step tasks use TDMS services to manage terminal input and output. Same as TDMS.

terminal emulation *n.*

Personal Computer Products

The mode of operation in which the Professional is logged on to a host computer and appears to the host as a VT102 terminal.

terminal IMP *n.*

DECnet and TOPS-20

The short form for terminal interface processor (TIP). The terminal IMP is essentially an IMP (interface message processor) with flexible terminal-handling capability for users who have no facilities of their own to contribute to the resource pool. TIPS are at a site with no host computer or at a site with a computer not equipped to handle direct interface to an IMP. The primary hardware features that distinguish the TIP from the IMP are an additional 8K to core memory and a multiline controller (MLC). Same as TIP and terminal interface processor.

terminal interface processor (TIP or terminal IMP) *n.*

DECnet and TOPS-20

The terminal interface processor is essentially an IMP (interface message processor) with flexible terminal-handling capability for users who have no facilities of their own to contribute to the resource pool. TIPS are at a site with no host computer or at a site with a computer not equipped to handle direct interface to an IMP. The primary hardware features that distinguish the TIP from the IMP are an additional 8K of core memory and a multiline controller (MLC). Same as TIP and terminal IMP.

terminal server *n.*

DECnet

A Phase IV DECnet node that connects up to 32 terminals with the network.

generic

A system part that connects terminals to services on nodes in a local area network; users have the same capability that they would have if they were connected to the node by direct lines.

VAX DATATRIEVE

The part of DATATRIEVE that gives the user access to DATATRIEVE's interactive data management services.

terminal subsystem controller *n.*

ACMS

The process in the terminal control subsystem that controls which terminals have access to ACMS.

terminate self (TERMS) *n.*

DECnet

An SNA (systems network architecture) network services request used by a SLU to request an orderly or forced session termination. TERMS is issued by the PE (protocol emulator) to the SSCP (system services control point).

termination (of a remote station) *n.*

DECnet

The use of a software/hardware combination that enables a DECSYSTEM-20 to be seen by a remote 2780/3780-like station as an IBM 370.

termination control block (TCB) *n.*

VAX/VMS

The block used for termination handling. Same as TCB.

termination point *n.*

MicroPower PASCAL

The location within a process where execution begins when that process is stopped. A termination point is not required for every process.

termination procedure *n.*

VAX DATATRIEVE

A general purpose routine, entered by means of a call instruction, that uses an argument list passed by a calling program and uses only local variables for data storage. A procedure is entered from and returns control to the calling program. See also procedure.

TERMS *n.*

DECnet

The acronym for terminate self. An SNA (systems network architecture) network services request used by an SLU (system logical unit) to request an orderly or forced session termination. TERMS is issued by the PE (protocol emulator) to the SSCP (system services control point). Same as terminate self.

test phase *n.*

FMS

A Form Editor phase in which a form is displayed on the screen as it would appear in an application program. During the test phase, data can be entered into fields to verify that the fields accept data as intended.

TEST REQUEST READ *n.*

DECnet

In 3270 operation a READ MODIFIED command that results from the operator pressing the TEST REQ key to allow entry of a predefined test request data format.

text *n.*

DECnet

1. A sequence of characters forming part of a transmission that is sent from the data source to the data receiver and that contains the information to be conveyed. It may be preceded by a header and followed by an EOT (end-of-transmission) signal.

2. In ASCII, as well as in general communications usage, a sequence of characters treated as an entity if preceded by a STX and followed by an EOT control character.

GIGI

An operating mode in which GIGI operates as a VT100- or VT52-compatible system terminal.

text buffer *n.*

VAX/VMS

An EDT storage area for text (either terminal input or file input).

text cursor *n.*

RGL/FEP

A VT100 cursor that indicates the terminal is in text mode and also indicates where on the screen that text will be displayed.

text file *n.*

PASCAL and VAX PASCAL

A file that has components of type CHAR and is implicitly divided into lines.

RSX-11M

Files written in ASCII code that can be read by both humans and by software. See also source file.

text mode *n.*

FMS

The mode in the Form Editor LAYOUT phase that allows creation and modification of background text in a form.

RGL/FEP

One of the two operating modes of a VT125 terminal that RGL/FEP uses. In text mode the terminal operates as a standard ASCII text terminal.

THEME *n.*

DECmate II

The word used to select proportional spacing from the Print Menu.

thermal *adj.*

generic

Pertaining to using or producing heat.

thermistor *n.*

generic

A semiconductor device whose resistance varies with temperature.

thermocouple preamplifier *n.*

MINC

A laboratory module that collects thermal data from a thermocouple probe. A thermocouple preamplifier also provides programmable signal conditioning and differential amplification for eight thermocouple channels.

thermocouple probe *n.*

MINC

An external device that provides analog temperature data to the thermocouple preamplifier module.

thickness *n.*

generic

The width in pixels of lines and circles.

third dictionary *n.*

DIGITAL-specific

A second related dictionary defined in a primary dictionary.

third normal form *n.*

DIGITAL-specific

The state of a relation when all fields are fully functionally-dependent on the key of the record to which they belong; that is, all transitive dependencies have been removed.

thread *n.*

RSX-20F

The link word in a node.

threshold *n.*

GAMMA

A setting of a level above which or below which data is not displayed, analyzed, etc.

Medical Systems

A setting that defines the intensity levels for display or analysis. Data is not displayed or analyzed below or above the lower and upper threshold setting.

TOPS-10

The number of transactions that must be in a leaf or in leaves under a node before an MPP will be started. See also starting criterion.

throughput *n.*

DECnet and TOPS-20

1. The total useful information processed or communicated through a device or system.

2. Specific to ARPANET, the sum of the message bits entering and leaving the IMP (interface message processor) each second. Throughput has been measured to be approximately 700 kilobits per second.

generic

The rate of processing computer computations.

throughput class negotiation *n.*

VAX PSI

An optional PSDN (packet switching data network) facility that indicates the maximum data rate for a particular virtual circuit. The facility allows a DTE (data terminal equipment) to request a higher or lower data rate depending on the throughput of the packets.

TI: *n.*

RSX-11M

The abbreviation for the terminal input pseudo device. TI: is a terminal a user can use in place of the terminal's device name (TTn:) in commands. Same as terminal input pseudo device.

Tickler items *n.*

ALL-IN-1

Personal notes the user inserts in the calendar in Calendar Management.

tickler mode *n.*

ALL-IN-1

The state you enter to view the Tickler items in Calendar Management.

tied account *n.*

VAX/VMS

A type of VAX/VMS account that limits the activities of the user. Typically, the user is restricted to using certain command procedures and/or commands. The user may not be allowed to use the CTRL/Y key. (This type of account is synonymous with a turnkey or tied account.) Same as captive account.

tied terminal *n.*

DSM-11

A terminal that can run only preselected routines and access only preselected globals. When a user logs in at a tied terminal, DSM-11 forces the automatic and protected startup of the application to which the terminal is tied.

time-data sampling *n.*

MINC

A sweep that measures the time between external events. A time-data sampling can occur in interstimulus-interval (ISI) mode or in poststimulus-time (PST) mode. Same as time-data sweep.

time-data sweep *n.*

MINC

A sweep that measures the time between external events. A time-data sweep can occur in interstimulus-interval (ISI) mode or in poststimulus-time (PST) mode. Same as time-data sampling.

time mark *n.*

Medical Systems

An external clock pulse. With the NCV-11 interface, a 0 is recorded in the memory location (as a list study) to indicate that a clock pulse occurred.

time of millennium *n.*

VAX/VMS

A time and date indicator that has a range and precision such that times never duplicate or repeat.

timeout *n.*

DSM-11

An integer-valued expression preceded by a colon that can be appended to the argument of an OPEN, LOCK, READ, or ZJOB command. The integer specifies the number of seconds DSM-11 is to try to complete the operation the command specifies before resuming execution.

VAX/VMS

The expiration of the time limit in which a device is to complete an I/O transfer.

time quantum *n.*

generic

In timesharing, a unit of time allocated to each user by the monitor.

timer *n.*

DIGITAL-specific and VAX/VMS

Two system processes: one that maintains the time of day and the date, and another that scans for device timeouts and performs time-dependent scheduling upon request. The timer interrupt service routine creates the timer process.

time-shared *adj.*

generic

Refers to a system that supports more than one user at a time.

time-shared DIBOL (TSD) *n.*

CTS-300

The TSD run-time system supports multiple users and uses the SJ, F/B, or XM monitor. Same as TSD.

time sharing (or timesharing) *n.*

DIGITAL-specific

A method of allocating resources to multiple users so that the computer, in effect, processes a number of programs concurrently.

generic

A method that applies, in an interleaving way, the time or use of a device to two or more programs.

time-sharing (or timesharing) *adj.*

generic

Pertaining to a system in which multiple-user programs get, in turn, equal time or use of a computer or computer device.

time slice *n.*

DIGITAL-specific

The period of time allocated by the operating system to process a particular partition's routine. See also time sharing, round robin scheduler, and real time.

generic

The period of time allocated by the operating system to process a specific program.

timing fault *n.*

DECSIM

A fault type in which a device timing parameter falls outside the acceptable maximum and minimum limits.

TIP *n.*

DECnet and TOPS-20

The acronym for terminal IMP or terminal interface processor. The TIP is essentially an IMP (interface message processor) with flexible terminal-handling capability for users who have no facilities of their own to contribute to the resource pool. TIPS are at a site with no host computer or at a site with a computer not equipped to handle direct interface to an IMP. The primary hardware features that distinguish the TIP from the IMP are an additional 8K of core memory and a multiline controller (MLC). Same as terminal IMP and terminal interface processor.

TKB *n.*

RSTS/E and RSX-11M

The abbreviation for Task Builder. A system utility that converts and combines object modules into a task image. The Task Builder also arranges task segments according to an overlay structure defined in an ODL file. Same as Task Builder.

toggle *v.*

generic

To cause a change from one of two states to the other.

RT-11

To use switches on the computer operator's console to enter data into the computer memory.

tokens *n.*

VAX/VMS

The fundamental elements making up the text of a C program. Tokens are identifiers, keywords, constants, strings, operators, and other separators. White space (such as spaces, tabs, new lines, and comments) is ignored except where it is necessary to separate tokens.

tolerance *n.*

generic

The allowed difference from a specified value or standard.

tone *n.*

DIGITAL-specific

An audible signal emitted by the MINC whenever an editor operation fails, or when users type to the end of a line.

top hat *n.*

generic

A passive cooling device attached to integrated circuit packages. The device consists of a cylinder of heat radiating material topped with a circle whose diameter is larger than the cylinder, similar in total shape to a top hat.

top margin *n.*

generic

An empty area that precedes the page body.

469

topology *n.*

DECnet

The physical arrangement and relationship of inter-connected nodes and lines in the network. A legal topology satisfies all DNA (DIGITAL Network Architecture) requirements.

generic

A physical or logical configuration.

TOPS-10 *n.*

DIGITAL-specific

A timesharing operating system. TOPS-10 manages all hardware and software resources.

TOPS-20 *n.*

DIGITAL-specific

A timesharing operating system. TOPS-20 manages all hardware and software resources.

TOPS-20AN *n.*

DIGITAL-specific

The timesharing system with ARPANET interface supported on the 1090T, 2040T, and 2050T by Digital Equipment Corporation. TOPS-20AN is a superset of TOPS-20.

total system *n.*

DIGITAL-specific

An operational combination of component software products, component hardware products, and a number of component services.

total user core *n.*

DIGITAL-specific

The amount of physical core that can be used for locked and unlocked jobs. This is all of the physical core minus the core size of the monitor.

trace *n.*

DECnet

A function performed by software that allows the user or system manager to see how messages appear on the communications line. Trace is useful for program and line debugging.

generic

The pattern appearing on the screen of a cathode-ray tube by an electron beam.

traceback *n.*

VAX/VMS

The system facility that examines and displays the status of the user call stack when an image terminates abnormally.

trace facility *n.*

Terminal Data Management System

The facility that helps users debug a TDMS (Terminal Data Management System) application by letting them monitor the action of a TDMS application program at run time.

tracepoint *n.*

MicroPower PASCAL

A particular report used when a certain program statement is executed, but it does not cause PASDBG to halt the application.

tracing *n.*

DIGITAL-specific

The act of recording the history of flow of control through a process.

track *n.*

generic

A path on a storage media that has information.

VAX/VMS

A collection of blocks at a single radius on one recording surface of a disk.

tracks *n.*

generic

The number of bits (7 or 9) that may be recorded and read within each frame. Each frame represents one information unit (byte) plus a parity bit.

trade discount *n.*

generic

A discount from a list price offered to all customers of a given type.

trade-in *n.*

generic

An asset that is given in part payment for another asset.

trailing spaces *n.*

generic

Spaces used to fill out the length of a left-justified field.

transaction *n.*

generic

1. The logical grouping of a series of COBOL DML statements that begins with the execution of the first DML statement and ends with the execution of a COMMIT or ROLLBACK. The first DML statement can be the first of a run unit or the first after another transaction ends. There can be many transactions in the course of a run unit. Compare with Quiet Point.

2. An action or process between two or more things that produces a response.

3. An event that is recorded in financial accounting records.

VAX DBMS

A set of operations on a recoverable resource such as a database. The operations in a transaction are treated as a group; either all of them are completed at once, or none of them are completed. In DBMS, a transaction group is a series of DML statements that perform a task. It normally begins with a READY statement and ends with a COMMIT or ROLLBACK statement. However, a transaction may begin with any DML statement, other than READY, if the previous transaction in the run unit ended with a COMMIT statement that contained a RETAINING clause. See also commit, quiet point, recovery, and rollback.

transaction code *n.*

TOPS-10

The part of a transaction that specifies the action required. This determines the leaf into which the transaction will be placed. The transaction code must be in the first segment of a transaction.

transaction handle *n.*

DIGITAL-specific

A host variable that specifies the name of a transaction so it can be uniquely identified.

transaction processing n.

generic

A technique for organizing multi-user, high volume, on-line applications that provides control over user access and updates of databases.

transaction processor n.

generic

The software that processes a transaction.

transceiver n.

generic

1. A device or circuit that transmits and receives signals or data.

2. The device that connects directly to the coaxial cable to provide both the electronics to send and receive the encoded signals and to detect collisions or clear channel on the cable and the required electrical isolation. It is the coupling device that links the user device to the coaxial cable.

transceiver attachment mark n.

Ethernet

An indicator (or ring) around the circumference of the coaxial cable every 2.5 meters (8.2 feet) to indicate a point where transceivers are to be connected. Same as annular ring.

transducer n.

generic

A device that changes energy from one form to another.

transfer address n.

VAX/VMS

The address of the location containing a program entry point (the first instruction to execute).

TRANSFER CONTROL n.

PEARL

A control issued with a data transfer statement that defines how data is to be transferred.

transfer data n.

generic

The speed at which data may be exchanged with the central processor, expressed in thousands of bytes per second.

transfer operation n.

TOPS-10

The hardware operation of connecting a channel to a controller and a controller to a unit for passing data between the memory and the unit. The transfer operation involves verification, search, and actual transfer.

transfer statement n.

PEARL

A PEARL statement issued by a PEARL task to initiate the transfer of data items on a previously opened dataway.

transfer vector n.

VAX/VMS

The obsolete term for reference vector which is a pointer to an object.

transformation n.

FFE

An editing operation in which the appearance of a character is altered independent of the current pen mode.

transformer *n.*

generic

An electrical device that transfers electrical energy from one or more circuits to one or more other circuits at the same frequency, but usually at a different voltage or current value.

transient member *n.*

VAX DBMS

A record that can be removed from a given set.

transistor *n.*

generic

A semiconductor device used for performing functions such as amplification, rectification, and switching.

transistor-transistor logic (TTL) *n.*

MINC

A digital logic family with well defined operating characteristics and generally available in integrated-circuit form. Some examples of TTL operating characteristics are current, input and output voltages, and drive characteristics. Same as TTL.

transitive dependency *n.*

DIGITAL-specific

A dependency in which a field is actually dependent on another field in the same record rather than on the record key itself.

transit packet *n.*

DECnet

A packet arriving at a node from a source node and destined for another node.

translate *v.*

DIGITAL-specific

To compile or assemble a source program into a machine language program, usually in the form of an (relocatable) object module.

translation *n.*

FMS

The process by which RDU (request definition utility) scans a definition text checking for syntax and logic errors, creates a binary representation of that definition, and stores it in the CDD (Common Data Dictionary).

translation buffer *n.*

DIGITAL-specific and VAX/VMS

An internal processor cache containing translations for recently used virtual addresses.

translator *n.*

DIGITAL-specific

That which translates a DCL (DIGITAL Command Language) command into the appropriate MCR (monitor console routine) or utility command.

generic

A program or series of programs that changes statements from one machine language into another.

transmission subsystem (TS) *n.*

DECnet

The characteristics of an SNA (systems network architecture) session. Each session observes two Profiles: a transmission subsystem (TS) Profile, concerned primarily with transmission control and recovery management, and a function management (FM) Profile, concerned primarily with data-flow control and the manner in which data is presented to the receiving NAU. FM Profiles 3 and 4/TS Profiles 3 and 4 specify rules to be observed in LU-LU sessions. Same as TS. See also Profile.

transparency *n.*

DECnet and VAX PSI

A property of a communications medium to pass within specified limits a range of signals having one or more defined properties; for example, a channel may be code transparent, or a device may be bit pattern transparent.

transparent *adj.*

DIGITAL-specific

Pertaining to a function that a user can use without seeing it. For example, when a command is issued, the command interpreter parses the command string and invokes the appropriate system software. The user sees only the result of the processing, not the processing itself.

transparent data *n.*

DECnet

Binary data transmitted with the recognition of most control characters suppressed. DDCMP (Digital Data Communications Message Protocol) provides data transparency because it can receive, without misinterpretation, data containing bit patterns that resemble DDCMP control characters.

transparent mode *n.*

DECnet

Transmission of binary data with the recognition of most control characters suppressed. In binary synchronous communications, entry to and exit from the transparent mode is indicated by a sequence beginning with a special data-link escape (DLE) character.

transparent spooling *n.*

RSX-11M

The procedure of substituting the device name of a spooled output device for a file specification in any system task or user-written task that creates an output file.

transportable *adj.*

generic

Movable from one computer system to another without modification.

transport layer *n.*

DECnet

Modules in the routing layer used to route user data (called a datagram) to its destination. Such routing modules also provide congestion control and packet lifetime control. Same as routing layer.

trap *n.*

DECnet, TOPS-20, and VAX/VMS

An exception condition that occurs at the end of the instruction that caused the exception. The PC (program counter) saved on the stack is the address of the next instruction that would normally have been executed. All software can enable and disable some of the trap conditions with a single instruction.

generic

The process of branching or jumping to a subroutine that provides the desirable operation when a specific condition occurs.

MicroPower PASCAL

An exception condition caused by executing a specific trap instruction. Trap instructions include the EMT, TRAP, BPT, and IOT instructions. Trace traps (T-bit traps) are also included. The exception, which occurs after execution of the trap instruction, is therefore synchronous with the process.

RT-11 and TOPS-10

An unprogrammed conditional jump to a known location, automatically activated by a side effect of executing a processor instruction. The location from which the jump occurred is then recorded. It is distinguished from an interrupt that is caused by an external event.

trap *v.*

generic

To branch or jump to a subroutine when a specific condition occurs.

trap enables *n.*

VAX/VMS

Three bits of the processor status word (PSW) that control the processor's action on certain arithmetic exceptions. Same as exception enables.

trappable *adj.*

CTS-300

Pertaining to an error that does not impair the basic operating of the computer. A trappable error can be detected and investigated by a part of the operating system or run-time system and the results can be displayed or used to make a programmed decision. See also nonfatal.

trap servicing routines *n.*

TOPS-10

Routines that allow programs to handle errors while a program is running. Some of the errors that can be handled in this manner are illegal memory reference and pushdown list overflows.

tray files *n.*

GIGI

Files that contain the names of one or more picture files.

tree *n.*

DIGITAL-specific

1. A method of linking data in which each element may be related to any number of elements at the level below it (schematically to its right), but to only one element above it (schematically to its left).

2. A diagram with a branching form like that of a tree.

tree data structure *n.*

VAX DATATRIEVE

A data structure in which each element may be related to any number of elements at a level below it, but to only one element above it in the hierarchy. Hierarchical structure shows interset relationships. Same as hierarchical data structure.

tree structure *n.*

DSM-11

The structure of DSM-11 arrays. The tree structure is drawn like a family tree with the root (name) at the top and the nodes arranged below by their depth of subscripting. All nodes with one subscript are on the first level, all nodes with two subscripts are on the second level, and so forth. The tree structure is only a logical picture of an array; it does not reflect how DSM-11 physically stores the array. For example, the tree structure shows all pointer nodes and defined data nodes. DSM-11 does not store such pointer nodes, but does recognize their logical existence.

VAX DBMS

A hierarchical structure in which each element may be related to any number of elements at any level below it, but to only one element above it in the hierarchy. Tree structures are used to show interest relationships.

trend line *n.*

A-to-Z

A line that appears when the user selects the scatter graph that has the trend line graph type. This line shows the mathematical trend of the data.

trial balance *n.*

generic

A listing of account balances to check the accuracy of previous entries.

tributary *n.*

DECnet

A physical termination on a multipoint line that is not a control station. Part of the line identification for a multipoint line.

VAX/VMS

A physical termination on a multipoint circuit that is not a control station.

tributary address *n.*

DECnet and VAX/VMS

A numeric address that the control station uses to poll a tributary.

tributary station *n.*

DECnet

A station, other than a control station, on a multipoint line. Same as remote station.

generic

A site on a central network which can communicate only with the control site when polled or selected by the control site.

trigger *v.*

generic

To start action in a circuit or circuit device by using a pulse.

trigger-driven sweep *n.*

MINC

A sweep that is caused, or driven, by the firing of one of the Schmitt Triggers. Same as Schmitt-Trigger-driven sweep.

Trojan horse program *n.*

VAX/VMS

A program that gains access to otherwise secured areas through its pretext of serving one purpose when its real intent is far more devious and potentially damaging.

troubleshoot *v.*

generic

To isolate and correct errors in computer programs or hardware.

true lease *n.*

USFC/generic

A lease defined by the IRS in which the lessor is deemed to be the owner, and the tax benefits of ownership may be passed on to the lessee in the form of lower payments or directly in the case of investment tax credit.

truncate (record operation) *v.*

RSX-11M

To logically delete the current record and all records following it in the file by establishing a new end-of-file position at the first byte of the current record (for sequential files only in RMS-11).

truncation *n.*

generic

The process of removing one or more characters from the left or right of a number or string.

truth table *n.*

generic

A table that lists all possible input states and corresponding output states of a logical function.

truth value *n.*

COBOL-74

The representation of the result of the evaluation of a condition in terms of one or two values: true, false.

generic

The result of determining whether a condition is true or false.

truth-valued expression *n.*

DSM-11

An expression whose result is a truth-value. A false expression produces a result of zero. A true expression produces a result of one.

TSD *n.*

CTS-300

The abbreviation for time-shared DIBOL. TSD is a run-time system that supports multiple users and uses the SJ, F/B, or XM monitor. Same as time-shared DIBOL.

TTD *n.*

DECnet

The abbreviation for temporary text delay. In binary synchronous communications, TTD is a control character sequence (STX ENQ) sent by a transmitting station to either indicate a delay in transmission or to initiate an abort of the transmission in progress. Same as temporary text delay.

TTL-driven sweep *n.*

MINC

A sweep caused or "driven" by transistor-transistor logic (TTL) signals that are transmitted directly to the appropriate MINC-series module, without involving a clock.

tube *n.*

DIGITAL-specific

A video terminal is sometimes called a tube. See also terminal.

tuning *n.*

DIGITAL-specific

The act of collecting and reporting on system, process, or application program tuning data for the purpose of improving performance.

tuple *n.*

VAX DATATRIEVE

A group of related fields.

turnaround time *n.*

DECnet

In communications, the actual time required to reverse the direction of transmission from sender to receiver, or vice versa, when using a two-way alternate circuit. Time is required by line propagation effects, modem timing, and computer reaction.

generic

The elapsed time between entering a job and receiving results.

turnkey *adj.*

DIGITAL-specific

Pertaining to a computer system sold in a ready-to-use state.

generic

Pertaining to a computer system that is ready to be used immediately.

turnkey account *n.*

VAX/VMS

A type of VAX/VMS account that limits the activities of the user. Typically, the user is restricted to using certain command procedures and/or commands. The user may not be allowed to use the CTRL/Y key. (This type of account is synonymous with a turnkey or tied account.) Same as captive account.

turnover *n.*

generic

The number of times that inventory or accounts receivable is replaced during the year.

two-byte signed integer (key) *n.*

RSX-11M

A key data type that can represent the decimal integer value −32,768 through +32,767. See also four-byte signed integer, two-byte unsigned binary, four-byte unsigned binary, packed decimal key, and string.

two-byte unsigned integer (key) *n.*

RSX-11M

A key data type that can represent the decimal integer values 0 through +65,535. See also four-byte unsigned integer, two-byte signed binary, four-byte signed integer, packed decimal key, signed integer, and string.

two-dimensional array *n.*

DIGITAL-specific

An array requiring two subscripts, commonly shown as a matrix.

generic

An arrangement of data consisting of rows and columns.

two's complement *n.*

DIGITAL-specific

A number used to represent the negative of a given value in many computers. This number is formed from the given binary value by changing all 1s to 0s and all 0s to 1s and then adding 1.

VAX/VMS

A binary representation for integers in which a negative number is one greater than the bit complement of the positive number.

two-way alternate operation *n.*

DECnet

A mode of operation of data links in which data may be transmitted in both directions, one way at a time. Also called half-duplex operation.

two-way associative cache *n.*

VAX/VMS

A cache organization that has two groups of directly mapped blocks. Each group contains several blocks for each index position in the cache. A block of data from main memory can go into any group at its proper index position. A two-way associative cache is a compromise between the extremes of fully associative and direct mapping cache organizations that takes advantage of the features of both.

two-way simultaneous operation *n.*

DECnet

A mode of operation of a data link in which data may be transmitted simultaneously in both directions over two channels. One of the channels is equipped for transmission in one direction while the other is equipped for transmission in the opposite direction. Same as full-duplex and duplex.

two-wire *adj.*

DECnet

Pertaining to a channel consisting of one pair of wires. Such a channel can be made to operate in duplex mode by sharing bandwidth.

type *n.*

Common Data Dictionary

A characteristic of each element in the CDD (Common Data Dictionary). Directories and subdictionaries are dictionary types, and there are several types of dictionary objects (for example, CDD$RECORD, DTR$DOMAIN, and DBM$SCHEMA).

PASCAL

A set of values usually named with an identifier, for which certain operations are defined. Some types are defined by PASCAL: INTEGER, REAL, SINGLE, DOUBLE, BOOLEAN, and CHAR. Others are defined by the programmer.

VAX/VMS

The attribute that, with its storage class, specifies C's interpretation of an identifier. The type determines the meaning of the values found in the identifier's storage. Types include the integral and floating types, pointers, enumerated types, and the derived types array, function, structure, and union.

type-ahead *adj.*

RSTS/E and VAX/VMS

Pertaining to a terminal handling technique in which the user can enter commands and data while the software is processing a previously entered command. On RSTS/E, characters are echoed as the user types them. On VAX/VMS, the commands typed ahead are not echoed on the terminal until the command processor is ready to process them. They are held in a type-ahead buffer.

type-ahead *n.*

VAX/VMS

A terminal handling technique in which the user can enter commands and data while the software is processing a previously entered command. The commands typed ahead are not echoed on the terminal until the command processor is ready to process them. They are held in a type-ahead buffer.

type face *n.*

generic

The font attribute that describes the general style of characters in a font, such as Kitter.

type name *n.*

VAX/VMS

The declaration of an object of a given type that omits the name of the object. A type name is used as the operand of the case and size of operators.

type size *n.*

generic

The font attribute that specifies the height of the characters.

UBA *n.*

VAX/VMS

UNIBUS adapter; an interface between the back-plane interconnect to the VAX-11/780 and the UNIBUS.

UBI *n.*

VAX/VMS

UNIBUS interconnect; an interface between the backplane interconnect to the VAX-11/750 and the UNIBUS.

UCB *n.*

DIGITAL-specific and VAX/VMS

The abbreviation for unit control block. A structure in the I/O data base that describes the characteristics of and current activity on a device unit. The unit control block also holds the fork block for its unit's device driver; the fork block is a critical part of a driver fork process. The UCB also provides a dynamic storage area for the driver. Same as unit control block.

UCI *n.*

DSM-11

The abbreviation for user class identifier. A three-character code used at terminal login to permit access to a group of routines and global files. Same as user class identifier and data record.

UDK *n.*

DIGITAL-specific

The abbreviation for user-defined key (or user defined key). A key in which a sequence of keystrokes is stored by the user. The user then needs only to press that single key at any time to initiate the stored sequence.

UETP *n.*

DIGITAL-specific

The acronym for user environment test package. UETP is a collection of programs, data files, and batch control files designed to allow the user to verify the integrity of the operating system. UETP acts as an interface between the user and the batch system by allowing the user to selectively access, enable, and run tests in the form of batch control files. UETP is used during installation, verification, and certification procedures. Same as user environment test package.

VAX/VMS

The abbreviation for user environment test package. A collection of routines that verifies that the hardware and software systems are complete, properly installed, and ready to use.

UFD *n.*

DIGITAL-specific

The abbreviation for user file directory.

1. A file whose entries are the names of files existing in a given project-programmer number area within a file structure.

2. The top-level directory for each user, and the top-level directory for the ersatz devices that appear as one directory.

VAX/VMS

The abbreviation for user file directory. A file that briefly catalogs a set of files stored on disk or tape. The directory includes the name, type, and version number of each file in the set, as well as a unique number that identifies the file's actual location and points to a list of its attributes. Same as directory.

UIC *n.*

DIGITAL-specific

The abbreviation for user identification code. UIC is the pair of numbers assigned to users and to files, global sections, common event flag clusters, and mailboxes that specifies the type of access (read and/or write access; and in the case of files, execute and/or delete access) available to the owners, group, world, and system. The UIC consists of a group number and a member number separated by a comma and enclosed within square brackets. Same as user identification code.

VAX/VMS

The abbreviation for user identification code. A 32-bit value assigned to users and to files, global sections, common event flag clusters, and mailboxes that specifies the type of access (read and/or write access; and in the case of files, execute and/or delete access) available to the system, owner, group, and world. A UIC has two formats: numeric and alphanumeric. The numeric UIC consists of a group identifier and a member identifier separated by a comma and enclosed within square brackets. These identifiers may appear as alphanumeric characters. The alphanumeric UIC consists of a member name and, optionally, a group name.

unadjusted trial balance *n.*

generic

The trial balance before the adjusting and closing entries are made at the end of a period.

unary operator *n.*

DIGITAL-specific

An operator that takes a single operand. In C, some unary operators can be either prefix or postfix. The set includes the asterisk (indirection), ampersand (address of), minus (arithmetic unary minus), exclamation (logical negation), tilde ([~] one's complement), double plus (increment), double minus (decrement), cast (force type conversion), and size of (yields size, inbytes), its operand.

generic

A plus (+) or a minus (−) sign that precedes a variable or left parenthesis in an arithmetic expression. It has the effect of multiplying the expression by +1 or −1.

unattended operation *n.*

DECnet

The automatic features of a station's operation that permit the transmission and reception of messages without human intervention.

generic

A mode of system operation in which operator action is not needed.

UNBIND session *n.*

DECnet

An SNA (systems network architecture) session control request used to terminate a LU-LU session.

unblocked record *n.*

TOPS-10 and VAX/VMS

A record contained in a single block with no other records or parts of records contained in that block.

unbundled *adj.*

DIGITAL-specific

Pertaining to software that is not supplied as part of the basic RSX-11M-PLUS operating system. The high-level languages, such as FORTRAN or COBOL, are unbundled software, and must be purchased under a separate license.

uncollectible account *n.*

generic

An account receivable that an entity believes will not be paid and, therefore, is written off as an expense; sometimes called a bad debt.

unconditional branch *n.*

generic

An instruction that diverts a program from its normal sequence of operations to perform another operation.

unconditional transfer *n.*

TOPS-10

An instruction that transfers control to a specified location.

unconsolidated subsidiary *n.*

generic

An entity whose accounts are not included in a consolidated financial statement, either because the parent company does not own more than 50% or because the subsidiary is in an unrelated business.

undefined (record format) *adj.*

RSX-11M

Pertaining to records that are not defined for the file. RMS-11 reads only blocks, and the program must interpret the contents of each block (used with block I/O only). See also fixed-length, stream, variable-length, variable-with-fixed-control and record format.

underflow *n.*

DIGITAL-specific

A condition that occurs when a mathematical operation yields a result whose magnitude is smaller than the space allocated for storing the result. For unsigned arithmetic: a result that is negative.

generic

1. A condition that occurs when a quantity is decremented below its minimum value.

2. A condition that occurs when an operation results in a numerical value smaller than the program can handle.

unformatted display *n.*

DECnet

A screen display in which no attribute character (and, therefore, no display field) has been defined. An unformatted display is used in a free-form manner. The location of the data to be input in relation to the display screen is unimportant. See also formatted display and display field.

UNIBUS adapter *n.*

VAX/VMS

An interface between the backplane interconnect to the VAX-11/780 and the UNIBUS.

uniform commercial code *n.*

USFC/generic

A system adopted by nearly all stated to protect secured parties', or assignees', security interests in personal property.

unimplemented user operations (UUO) *n.*

TOPS-10

Instructions that, instead of performing a hardware operation, cause a jump into the monitor system or the user area at a predetermined point and perform a software operation. The monitor (or special user code) interprets these entries as commands from the user program to perform specified operations. Same as UUO. See also programmed operators.

union n.

VAX/VMS

An aggregate type. It can be considered a structure all of whose members begin at offset 0 from the base, and whose size is sufficient to contain any of its members.

unipolar analog signal n.

MINC

An analog signal whose polarity does not change; the polarity remains either negative or positive.

unique name n.

generic

A designation assigned to a component, such as a task, that is used to identify that component within and across definitions.

uniqueness n.

VAX/VMS

A property of the names used for certain structure and union members. A name is unique if either one of the following conditions is true:

1. The name is used only once.

2. It is used in two or more different structures (or unions), but each use denotes a member at the same offset from the base and of the same data type. The significance of uniqueness is that a unique member name can be used to refer to a structure in which the member name was not declared (although a warning message is issued).

unit n.

DECnet

A part of a line identification. A unit together with the controller forms a station.

DIGITAL-specific

The smallest portion of a device that can be positioned independently from all other units. Several examples of units are: a disk, a disk pack, or a drum.

unit control block (UCB) n.

DIGITAL-specific and VAX/VMS

A structure in the I/O data base that describes the characteristics of and current activity on a device unit. The unit control block also holds the fork block for its unit's device driver; the fork block is a critical part of a driver fork process. The UCB also provides a dynamic storage area for the driver. Same as UCB.

unit initialization routine n.

VAX/VMS

The routine that readies controllers and device units for operation. Controllers and device units require initialization after a power fail and during the driver loading procedure.

unit record device n.

DIGITAL-specific

A type of device that deals with individual records. Typically used to refer to card readers and line printers.

VAX/VMS

A device such as a card reader or line printer.

unit-scaled coordinates n.

VT-11 GRAPHICS

Coordinates in the default (unscaled) coordinate system, in which adjacent positions on an axis are separated by a single raster unit; coordinates in a system in which one numerical unit equals one raster unit.

universal device index (UDX) *n.*

DIGITAL-specific

A number used to identify any device on the system. The monitor assigns the device a UDX when a program issues the appropriate monitor call. Same as UDX.

universal symbol *n.*

VAX/VMS

A global symbol in a sharable image that can be used by modules linked with that sharable image. Universal symbols are typically a subset of all the global symbols in a sharable image. When creating a sharable image, the linker ensures that universal symbols remain available for reference after symbols have been resolved.

unmapped memory *n.*

MicroPower PASCAL

Contiguous physical memory that is not managed by memory-management hardware; unmapped virtual and physical addresses are identical.

unmapped system *n.*

generic

Any software system that does not have a unit for hardware memory management available to relocate virtual addresses.

unprotected field *n.*

DECnet

A display field into which the operator or application program can enter, modify, or delete data.

unreachable node *n.*

DECnet

A node to which a routing node has determined that the path exceeds the maximum hops of the network.

unsigned 16-bit integer *n.*

MINC

Binary numbers that use all 16 bits of a word to represent a positive number.

unsigned number *n.*

DIGITAL-specific

A datum whose values are positive. The values range from 0 through a specified upper limit.

unsigned type *n.*

VAX PASCAL

A predefined scalar type that has an extended set of nonnegative integers as values.

unsolicited data *n.*

VAX PSI

Data that arrives for a process without a request being issued for it that is placed in the process's mailbox. It can be an incoming call, an interrupt, a reset, or a clear.

unspanned record *n.*

TOPS-10

A record contained in a file in which each record by design ends in the same block in which it begins.

unsuccessful execution *n.*

generic

The attempted execution of a statement that does not result in the execution of all its operations. The unsuccessful execution of a statement does not affect any data referenced by that statement. However, it can affect status indicators.

unwind the call stack *v.*

VAX/VMS

To remove call frames from the stack by tracing back through nested procedure calls using the current contents of the FP (frame pointer) register and the FP register contents stored on the stack for each call frame.

update *n.*

DIGITAL-specific

A software release that corrects faults in a software product and may contain enhancements. The software product remains within the growth constraint set forth in the SPD (Software Product Description), and retains identical external interfaces.

update level *n.*

TOPS-10

The level that IQL (interactive query language) enters when the user issues the UPDATE assistance command to IQL to read or change a data file.

update lock *n.*

generic

An integrity lock that prevents a record from being used in any way in a concurrent run unit.

update usage mode *n.*

VAX DBMS

The state of a realm during which its records may be both accessed and modified.

up-line dump (or upline dump) *v.*

DECnet

To send a copy of a target node's memory image up a line to a file at the host node.

VAX/VMS

A DECnet-VAX function that allows an adjacent RSX-11S node to dump its memory to a file on a VAX/VMS system.

up-line dumping (or upline dumping) *n.*

DECnet

The process of transmitting a copy of a computer's memory over a logical link and storing it in a file on another node.

upward compatible *adj.*

generic

Pertaining to that which is designed for use on small machines, but capable of running without change on larger machines.

urgent interrupt *n.*

TOPS-20 and VAX/VMS

An interrupt received on interrupt priority levels 24 through 31 that can be generated only by the processor for the interval clock, serious errors, or power failures.

usage mode *n.*

DIGITAL-specific

The combination of the DML READY statement's allow mode and the access mode. The usage mode describes how a realm you have readied can be accessed. The six usage mode combinations are CONCURRENT RETRIEVAL, CONCURRENT UPDATE, PROTECTED RETRIEVAL, PROTECTED UPDATE, EXCLUSIVE RETRIEVAL, and EXCLUSIVE UPDATE. See also access mode and allow mode.

VAX DBMS

In DBMS, usage mode is the combination of the DML READY statement's allow mode and the access mode. It describes how a readied realm can be used. The eight usage mode combinations are: batch update, protected update, concurrent update, exclusive update, batch retrieval, protected retrieval (default), concurrent retrieval, and exclusive retrieval. See also access mode and allow mode.

user *n.*

DIGITAL-specific

The person who is directly using the computer, either by terminal or batch input.

user action routine *n.*

FMS

A routine in the application program that is associated with a particular field (or form) and that is called when the operator signals completion of a field (or form) by pressing a terminator key. Same as action routine.

user action routine *n.*

FMS

A routine associated with a particular field or form and that is invoked by FMS when the operator completes a field or a form by pressing a terminator key or by requesting help.

user authorization file *n.*

DIGITAL-specific and VAX/VMS

A file containing an entry for every user that the system manager authorizes to gain access to the system. Each entry identifies the user name, password, default account, UIC (user identification code), quotas, limits, and privileges assigned to individuals who use the system.

user batch job *n.*

RSX-11M

A complete terminal session consisting of commands to be processed, each preceded by a dollar sign ($). The user batch job begins with $JOB, which logs the job in, and ends with $EOJ, which logs the job out. A file can contain only one user batch job. Batch processing is available in RSX-11M-PLUS systems only.

user buffer *n.*

RSX-11M

The memory allocated within a program's portion of a task to store one record.

user class identifier (UCI) *n.*

DSM-11

A three-character code used at terminal login to permit access to a group of routines and global files. Same as UCI and data record.

user data record *n.*

RSX-11M

The record the program provides in its user buffer plus RMS-11 overhead: the logical unit of data actually stored in a file. See also index record.

user default device *n.*

RSX-11M

A pseudo device that can be located on any number of different physical devices.

user-defined key (or user defined key) (UDK) *n.*

DIGITAL-specific

A key in which a sequence of keystrokes is stored by the user. The user then needs only to press that single key at any time to initiate the stored sequence.

user-defined type *n.*

VAX PASCAL

An identifier created by the programmer to denote a program, constant, type, variable, procedure, or function.

user-defined word *n.*

COBOL-74 and VAX DBMS

A COBOL word that must be supplied by the user to satisfy the format of a clause or statement.

user definition file *n.*

ACMS

A file, created and maintained with the user definition utility, that contains a list of users authorized to access ACMS.

user definition utility *n.*

ACMS

The ACMS tool for authorizing ACMS users and defining characteristics of those users.

user environment test package (UETP) *n.*

VAX/VMS

A collection of routines that verifies that the hardware and software systems are complete, properly installed, and ready to use. Same as UETP.

user file directory (UFD) *n.*

DIGITAL-specific and VAX/VMS

A directory is a file that briefly catalogs a set of files stored on disk or tape. The directory includes the name, type, and version number of each file in the set as well as a unique number that identifies that file's actual location and points to a list of its file attributes. See MFD (master file directory) and UFD (user file directory) for definitions of the two main types of directories. The DIRECTORY command displays directory information for specified files. Same as UFD. See also directory.

user identification *n.*

DIGITAL-specific

A string used to identify a user to the system and to other users. A password is not a user identification; a password confirms the user's identity.

user identification code (UIC) *n.*

DIGITAL-specific

The pair of numbers assigned to users and to files, global sections, common event flag clusters, and mailboxes that specify the type of access (read and/or write access; and in the case of files, execute and/or delete access) available to the owners, group, world, and system. The UIC consists of a group number and a member number separated by a comma and enclosed within square brackets. Same as UIC. See also account.

VAX/VMS

A 32-bit value assigned to users and to files, global sections, common event flag clusters, and mailboxes that specifies the type of access (read and/or write access; and in the case of files, execute and/or delete access) available to the system, owner, group, and world. A UIC has two formats: numeric and alphanumeric. The numeric UIC consists of a group identifier and a member identifier separated by a comma and enclosed within square brackets. These identifiers may appear as alphanumeric characters. The alphanumeric UIC consists of a member name and, optionally, a group name.

generic

The number or set of numbers that identifies a specific account, including owner of the file, in certain multiple user systems.

user identifier n.

PASCAL and VAX PASCAL

An identifier created by the programmer to denote a program, constant, type, variable, procedure, or function.

user I/O mode n.

TOPS-10

The central processor mode that allows a user program to be run with automatic protection and relocation in effect as well as the normal execution of all defined operation codes (including I/O instructions).

user layer n.

DECnet

The layer that contains most of the user-supplied functions. It also contains the network control program, a network management module that gives system managers interactive terminal access to lower layers.

user library n.

TOPS-10

Any user file containing one or more relocatable binary modules of which some or all can be loaded in library search mode.

user mode n.

TOPS-10

A central processor mode during which instructions are executed normally except for all I/O and HALT instructions, which return control to the monitor. This makes it possible to prevent the user from interfering with other users or with the operation of the monitor. Memory protection and location are in effect.

DSM-11

In this hardware mode, certain instructions cannot be executed. This mode is used to prevent one user in a multi-user system from altering data in other partitions, or in the operating system itself.

VAX/VMS

The least privileged processor access mode (mode 3). User processes and Run-Time Library Procedures run in user mode.

user name n.

DIGITAL-specific

The name that a user types on a terminal to log on to the system. See also password.

generic

A designation assigned to a user to identify that user.

user number n.

DIGITAL-specific

The second number in a user identification code. The user number uniquely identifies that code. Same as member number.

VAX/VMS

The second number in a user identification code. The member number uniquely identifies that code. Same as member number.

user password *n.*

VAX/VMS

A password that is associated with a user. This password must be correctly supplied when the user attempts to log in so that the user is authenticated for access to the system. The two types of user passwords are primary and secondary.

user privileges *n.*

DIGITAL-specific and VAX/VMS

The privileges granted a user by the system manager. See also process privileges.

user profile *n.*

ALL-IN-1

A data file provided by the system manager that allows a person to access a system. A user profile tells the computer what privileges the user has.

user queue *n.*

MINC

A list of the numbers of buffers that have been processed in a data transfer.

user's program *n.*

TOPS-10

All of the data and code running in a user virtual address space.

user task *n.*

RSX-11M

An application task that performs a specific job for the user. In general, the term refers to any task that is not part of the operating system or of a programming language. Same as applications task.

user utility *n.*

ACMS

The ACMS tool for authorizing ACMS users.

user virtual address space *n.*

TOPS-10

A set of memory addresses within the range of 0 to 256K words. These addresses are mapped into physical core memory by the paging or relocation-protection hardware when a program is executed.

user volume *n.*

MINC

The storage medium reserved for user files and the HELP text file.

user working area (UWA) *n.*

VAX DBMS

An area of core memory where all data provided by the DBCS (Database Control System), in response to a call for data, is delivered, and where all data to be picked up by DBCS must be placed. Same as UWA.

user workspace *n.*

generic

A workspace, defined as an attribute of a task group, that holds information about a terminal user.

usual arithmetic conversions *n.*

VAX/VMS

The set of rules that govern the conversion of operands in arithmetic expressions. The rules are applied in the following order:

1. any operands of type CHAR or SHORT are converted to INT, and any of type FLOAT are converted to DOUBLE

2. then, if either operand is DOUBLE, the other is converted to DOUBLE, and that is the type of the result

3. otherwise, if either operand is UNSIGNED, the other is converted to UNSIGNED and that is the the the type of the result

4. otherwise, both operands must be INT, and that is the type of the result.

utility *n.*

DIGITAL-specific

A program that provides a set of related general purpose functions, such as a program development utility (an editor, a linker, etc.), a file management utility (file copy or file format translation program), or operation management utility (disk quotas, diagnostic program, etc.). Same as utility program. See also utility routine.

generic

A software program that provides basic services and functions.

utility program *n.*

DIGITAL-specific

A program that provides a set of related general purpose functions, such as a program development utility (an editor, a linker, etc.), a file management utility (file copy or file format translation program), or operation management utility (disk quotas, diagnostic program, etc.). Same as utility. See also utility routine.

utility routine *n.*

DIGITAL-specific

This term refers to any general-purpose routine that is included in an operating system to perform common functions. See also utility and utility program.

UUO *n.*

TOPS-10

The abbreviation for unimplemented user operations. Instructions that, instead of performing a hardware operation, cause a jump into the monitor system or the user area at a predetermined point and perform a software operation. The monitor (or special user code) interprets these entries as commands from the user program to perform specified operations. Same as unimplemented user operations. See also programmed operators.

UWA *n.*

VAX DBMS

The abbreviation for the user working area. An area of core where all data provided by the DBCS (Database Control System) in response to a call for data is delivered and where all data to be picked up by DBCS must be placed. Same as user working area.

validate mode *n.*

Terminal Data Management System

The process of checking data on entry to ensure that it meets pre-established requirements. Same as validation. See also valid request, valid request library definition, and novalidate mode.

validation *n.*

FMS

The process by which RDU (request definition utility) checks the external references in a request definition or a library definition and marks the request and/or library definition "valid". Same as validate mode.

Terminal Data Management System

The process of checking data on entry to ensure that it meets pre-established requirements. Same as validate mode. See also valid request, valid request library definition, and novalidate mode.

validation expression *n.*

DIGITAL-specific

Checks the validity of a field when the field is stored or modified.

valid definition *n.*

FMS

- A request definition in the CDD (Common Data Dictionary) with the following characteristics:

    form and record definitions named in the definition have existing matching form and record definitions in the CDD

    field names referenced in the request definition have matching record fields and form fields in the CDD form and record definitions.

- The data types of fields mapped to each other are compatible.

- The length of fields mapped to each other are compatible.

- The structure of records mapped to each other are compatible.

valid request *n.*

Terminal Data Management System

A TDMS (Terminal Data Management System) request in the CDD (Common Data Dictionary) with the following characteristics:

- The form and record definitions named in the request are stored in the CDD.

- The record field and form field names used in mapping instructions are the same as those contained in the form and record definitions.

- According to TDMS mapping rules, the following are compatible:

    the data types of fields mapped to each other

    the lengths of fields mapped to each other

    the types (for example, simple, group, array) of fields mapped to each other.

value expression *n.*

VAX DATATRIEVE

A string of symbols that specifies a value DATATRIEVE can use when executing statements.

value initialization *n.*

VAX PASCAL

A VAX PASCAL extension that allows a programmer to assign a constant value to a variable in the program's declaration section.

value match *n.*

RSX-11M

A criterion used by RMS-11 during a random read-type operation on an indexed file. A user program must specify whether the key value in a record must be greater than or equal to (or either) the value specified when the operation was initiated.

value parameter *n.*

VAX PASCAL

A formal parameter that represents an actual parameter expression whose value is used as input to a subprogram.

value return registers *n.*

VAX/VMS

The general registers R0 and R1 used by convention to return function values. These registers are not preserved by any called procedures. They are available as temporary registers to any called procedure.

variable *n.*

CTS-300

A quantity that can assume any one of a set of values.

DIGITAL-specific

The symbolic representation of a logical storage location. Specific types include: local, global, simple and subscripted variables. Variables are symbolically referenced by means of identifiers.

generic

That which can assume any of a given set of values.

TOPS-10

A numeric working item generated by IQL (interactive query language) for reading and writing a value. Names of variables must start with X or ZZ, can be up to thirty characters long, and contain alphanumeric characters and dashes. Variables for IQL contain thirteen integer and five decimal places.

VAX DATATRIEVE

In DATATRIEVE, a variable is a value expression created in a declare statement.

VAX/VMS

An identifier used as the name of an object.

variable cost *n.*

generic

An element of cost that changes approximately in proportion to changes in volume.

variable-length (record format) *n.*

RSX-11M

The records in the file can be any length, up to the maximum record size associated with the file. For each record, RMS-11 maintains a record-length field specifying the number of data bytes in the record. See also fixed-length, stream, variable-with-fixed-control, and undefined.

variable-length bit field (VBF) *n.*

VAX/VMS

A set of 0 to 32 contiguous bits located arbitrarily with respect to byte boundaries. A variable bit field is specified by four attributes:

1. the address A of a byte

2. the bit position P of the starting location of the bit field with respect to bit 0 of the byte at address A

3. the size, in bits, of the bit field

4. whether the field is signed or unsigned.

Same as VBF.

variable-length record *n.*

DIGITAL-specific

A file format in which the records are not necessarily the same length. Same as variable-length record format.

variable-length record format *n.*

DIGITAL-specific

A file format in which records are not necessarily the same length. Same as variable-length record.

VAX/RMS

The property of a file specifying that records of variable-length contain an additional fixed control area capable of storing data that may have no bearing on the other contents of the record. Variable with fixed-length control record format is not applicable to indexed files.

VAX/VMS

A file format in which records may be of different lengths.

variable-occurrence data item *n.*

VAX DBMS

A data item that is repeated a varying number of times. Such an item must contain an OCCURS DEPENDING clause in its record description entry or be subordinate to such an item.

variable parameter *n.*

PASCAL and VAX PASCAL

Formal parameter that represents an actual parameter variable whose value can change as a result of the execution of a subprogram.

variable reference *n.*

VAX PL/I

A reference to all or part of a variable. The reference may include qualification by member names and subscripts.

variables *n.*

generic

Words or symbols that can have different values at different times.

variable spacing *n.*

FFE

One of two kinds of spacing in LN01 font files: fixed and variable. In variable spaced fonts, characters may have different widths, and the spacing between characters is usually proportional to the widths of the characters.

variable-with-fixed-control (record format) (VFC) *n.*

RSX-11M

A format in which each record in the file consists of a fixed control area whose length is the same for all records and a variable area that can vary from zero to the maximum record size associated with the file. Same as VFC. See also fixed-length, stream, variable-length, undefined, and record format.

variable with fixed-length control *n.*

VAX DATATRIEVE, VAX/RMS and VAX/VMS

A file format in which records of variable length contain an additional fixed-length control area. The control area may be used to contain file line numbers and/or print format controls. See also VFC and variable-length.

variance *n.*

generic

The difference between an actual amount and a standard or budget amount.

VARIANTS field description statement *n.*

Common Data Dictionary

A CDDL statement defining a set of two or more fields that provide alternative descriptions for the same portion of a record. The function of the VARIANTS field description is similar to that of the REDEFINES clause in VAX/VMS, COBOL and VAX DATATRIEVE. See also tag variable.

varistor *n.*

generic

A passive resistor whose resistance is a function of the current through it or the voltage across it.

varying character string *n.*

VAX/PASCAL

A sequence of ASCII characters whose length changes according to its current value.

VAX *n.*

DIGITAL-specific

A computer made by the Digital Equipment Corporation. VAX is a high-performance, multiprogramming computer system based on a 32-bit architecture. VAX stands for Virtual Address Extension.

VAX-11 record management services *n.*

VAX/RMS

The file and record access system for the VAX/VMS operating system. VAX-11 RMS allows programs to issue requests at the record and block level.

VAX/VMS *n.*

DIGITAL-specific

The abbreviation for Virtual Address Extension/Virtual Memory System. VAX/VMS is the virtual memory operating system that runs on the entire range of VAX (32-bit) processors.

VBF *n.*

VAX/VMS

The abbreviation for variable-length bit field. A set of 0 to 32 contiguous bits located arbitrarily with respect to byte boundaries. A variable bit field is specified by four attributes:

1. the address A of a byte

2. the bit position P of the starting location of the bit field with respect to bit 0 of the byte at address A

3. the size, in bits, of the bit field

4. whether the field is signed or unsigned.

Same as variable-length bit field.

VBN *n.*

RSX-20F

The abbreviation for virtual block number. A number used to identify a particular block within a file on a storage device. Virtual blocks in a file are sequentially numbered beginning with virtual block number. A virtual block number is file-oriented rather than volume-oriented or device-oriented. Same as virtual block number.

VCB *n.*

DIGITAL-specific

The abbreviation for volume control block. A data structure that contains the information needed to control access to a volume. It is created when the volume is mounted. Same as volume control block.

VDH *n.*

DECnet and TOPS-20

The abbreviation for very distant Host. Specific to ARPANET. A combination of Host and IMP (interface message processor) where the Host is more than 2000 feet from the IMP. The VDH has an entirely different interface to the IMP. It saves the IMP (interface message processor) at the expense of more complex software. Same as very distant Host.

vector *n.*

BASIC-PLUS-2

A horizontal or vertical list. Also, an array with only one dimension.

FFE

In drawing lines with FFE, the imaginary line from the current position to the coordinates you specify for the end of the line. Each pixel that the vector passes through is drawn or erased (according to the current pen mode) to form the line.

generic

1. A quality or line that has both magnitude and direction.

2. An address that usually tells a processor to use a service routine.

GIGI and RGL/FEP

A directed line, specified by a magnitude and a direction. The numbers (x,y) are components of the vector.

RT-11

A pair of locations in memory that contain the entry address of a service routine and processor status word for a particular peripheral device interrupt request or processor trap.

VAX/VMS

A storage location known to the system that contains the starting address of a procedure to be executed when a given interrupt or exception occurs. The system defines separate vectors for each interrupting device controller and for classes of exceptions. Each system vector is a longword. Same as exception vector and interrupt vector.

VT-11 GRAPHICS

A line segment extending from one coordinate position to another on the display screen. The length of a relative vector cannot exceed 1023 raster units.

vendor *n.*

generic

A supplier from whom the entity acquires goods and services.

verification *n.*

TOPS-10

1. A process in which the controller reads sector headers to determine if the mechanical parts of the system have correctly positioned the arm; the first step in the transfer operation.

2. A second pass, often following a copy operation, during which the original and copied information are read back and verified that they are identical.

verification procedure *n.*

DECnet

A DECnet procedure that ensures that the appropriate DECnet-20 software modules have been installed. The verification process checks for the existence of each required module and for the correct version of each required module.

VERIFY (VFY) *n.*

RSX-11M

A file-structure verification utility. Same as VFY.

version number *n.*

DIGITAL-specific

Numeric component of a file specification. When a file is edited, its version number is increased by one.

VAX/VMS

1. The field following the file type in a file specification. It begins with a semicolon (;) or period (.) and is followed by a number which generally identifies it as the latest file created of all files having the identical file specification but for version number.

2. The number used to identify the revision level of program.

version skew *n.*

DIGITAL-specific

Having incompatible versions of two facilities or a facility and the operating system.

vertically indexed field *n.*

FMS

A field with multiple occurrences below it on consecutive lines of a form; the second and subsequent occurrences of the field have the same name as the initial occurrence and they are accessed by index value rather than by name. Note that the concept of vertically indexed fields has changed from Version 1 of RMS to Version 2; it no longer indicates the order in which fields will be accessed.

very distant host *n.*

DECnet and TOPS-20

Specific to ARPANET. A combination of Host and IMP (interface message processor) where the Host is more than 2000 feet from the IMP. The VDH has an entirely different interface to the IMP. It saves the IMP at the expense of more complex software.

vestigial job data area *n.*

TOPS-10

The first ten (octal) locations of the high segment used to contain data for initializing certain locations in the job data area. These locations are usually 400000-400007 (octal) inclusive.

VFC *n.*

RSX-11M

The abbreviation for variable-with-fixed-control. Each record in the file consists of a fixed control area whose length is the same for all records and a variable area that can vary from zero to the maximum record size associated with the file. Same as variable-with-fixed-control. See also fixed-length, stream, variable-length, undefined, and record format.

VFY *n.*

RSX-11M

The abbreviation for VERIFY. VFY is a file-structure verification utility. Same as VERIFY.

VIA mode *n.*

VAX DATATRIEVE

Allows access to a record using owner-member relationships; retrieval is simplified by placing members near owners.

VAX DBMS

The location mode in which the user specified that the record is stored near other records that participate in a set. The set is specified in the location mode clause of the record definition.

VID *n.*

TOPS-10

The acronym for visual identification. VID is the visual identification label, the physical label that is affixed to a magnetic tape reel. Same as visual identification.

video attribute *n.*

generic

A characteristic assigned to areas of a form, indicating a video feature, such as bolding, underlining, or blinking, that is to be activated.

Terminal Data Management System

A characteristic of a TDMS (Terminal Data Management System) form that provides one or more of the following special visual effects to an area of a form:

- reverse video (light background, dark text)

- bolding

- blinking

- underlining

- double-height characters

- double-width characters.

Video Graphics Utility *n.*

Digital-specific

This utility is the component of VAX SPM which collects performance data and dynamically displays its output to a VT240 or other REgis-compatible terminal. Different displays show load balance (Kiviat graph), system and working set statistics.

video terminal *n.*

VAX/VMS

A terminal with a video screen for accessing output. See terminal.

view *n.*

MSG (SPETS)

A set of ray sums created by a series of transmission measurements during a linear scan.

Rdb/ELN

A subset of the database defined by a single relation, or by combining fields from two or more relations (or other views) into a single "virtual" relation.

VAX DATATRIEVE

A particular cross section of a domain.

view *v.*

DECtype

To make DECtype display text in a way that shows characters that are normally invisible, such as carriage returns.

view domain *n.*

VAX DATATRIEVE

A special type of DATATRIEVE domain that allows users to select some (or all) fields in some (or all) records from one or more domains.

viewing area *n.*

VT-11 GRAPHICS

The 9.25-inch by 9.25-inch area of the screen in which images can be displayed. The viewing area consists of 1024 raster units along the x-axis and 1024 along the y-axis.

view marker *n.*

DECWORD

A symbol that represents an invisible character.

viewport *n.*

VAXstation Display System

A rectangle that contains the image defined by a window into a pasteboard. Users control the visibility and placement of viewports on the physical screen.

A-to-Z

A section of the terminal screen.

virtual *adj.*

generic

Pertaining to occurring in effect, or simulated, but not true in actual fact or form.

virtual address *n.*

MicroPower PASCAL

A value in the range octal 0 to 177777; a 16-bit address within a program's (maximum) 64K-byte address space. In unmapped systems virtual addresses and physical addresses have a one-to-one relationship. In mapped systems with multiple address spaces, virtual addresses and physical addresses have a one-to-many relationship.

VAX/VMS

A 32-bit integer identifying a byte location in virtual address space. The memory management hardware translates a virtual address to a physical address. The term virtual block number (VBN) refers to the address used to identify a virtual block on a mass storage device.

virtual addresses *n.*

VAX/VMS

The addresses within the task. Task addresses can range from 0 through 177777 (8) depending on the length of the task.

virtual address space *n.*

generic

A set of memory addresses that is mapped to physical memory addresses by the system.

TOPS-20

The address space provided for each process. The space is actually a "window" into physical storage and for this reason is called virtual.

VAX/VMS

The set of all possible virtual addresses that an image executing in the context of a process can use to identify the location of an instruction or data. The virtual address space seen by the programmer is a linear array of 4,294,967,296 (2(32 sup)) byte addresses.

virtual array *n.*

generic

1. Any file structure that is considered an array.

2. An array stored as a disk file but accessed as though it were in memory.

virtual array file *n.*

MINC

A file appearing in the program as an array even though it is a file stored on a volume. A virtual array file contains information directly accessible by MINC. The system can retrieve any piece of data without having to examine the information preceding it.

RSTS/E

An array stored on disk. Each record in a vertical array file is one array element, and the array can contain real, integer, or string data. One file can contain several arrays.

virtual block *n.*

generic

A block numbered in sequence according to its relative position within a file instead of by its physical location on disk.

VAX DATATRIEVE

One of a collection of blocks that make up a user file. The block is virtual only in that its address, VBN (virtual block numbers), refers to a position within a file regardless of file placement on a storage medium.

VAX/VMS

A block on a mass storage device referred to by its file-relative address rather than its logical (volume-oriented) or physical (device-oriented) address. The first block in a file is always virtual block 1.

virtual block number (VBN) *n.*

RSX-11M

The number assigned to each virtually contiguous block. The file processor treats each file as a device containing virtually contiguous blocks, numbered serially from 1. See also logical block.

VAX/VMS

The file-relative address of a block on a mass storage device. The first block in a file is always virtual block 1. Contrast with logical block number and physical block number.

VAX DATATRIEVE

A number used to identify a particular block within a file on a storage device. Virtual blocks in a file are sequentially numbered beginning with virtual block number. A virtual block number is file-oriented rather than volume-oriented (see logical block number) or device-oriented. See also physical block. Same as VBN.

VAX/RMS

The number assigned to a block of a file. This number refers to the position of the block relative to other blocks in the same file, instead of to its position relative to other blocks on the volume (logical blocks). Virtual block numbers are assigned to the blocks of a file beginning with 1. The file header provides relocation information for mapping the file's virtual block numbers to the volume's logical block number. See also logical block number.

virtual circuit *n.*

DECnet

An independent logical path between two end-entities for the purpose of exchanging data. The concept of a virtual circuit is common to packet switching networks, but the terminology is far from stable. The virtual circuit is variously referred to as a connection (ARPA), a liaison (CYCLADES), a session (IBM), and a logical link (DECNET), as well as a virtual circuit (TELENET, TRANSPAC).

VAX PSI and VAX/VMS

An association between two DTEs (data terminal equipment) connected to a PSDN (packet switching data network) which makes it seem as if a specific circuit were dedicated to them throughout the transmission. In reality, only a logical connection is established: actual, physical circuits are allocated according to criteria such as route availability and overload conditions. Refer to SVC and PVC, the two types of virtual circuit. See also circuit.

virtual communications access method (VTAM) *n.*

DECnet

VTAM is IBM software that serves as a link between application programs and terminals or other applications in a communications network. Same as VTAM.

virtual core *n.*

DECnet

The space on secondary storage (disk or drum) where the monitor keeps a copy of the job's core image to be used when the job has to be swapped out of core in order to make room for other jobs.

virtual disk *n.*

VAX/VMS

A dedicated portion of disk space allocated for storing console files when performing save or restore operations on console media. Virtual disks eliminate the need to create a disk/directory for the console media. Also, because the command procedure that handles the task invokes EXCHANGE, the conversion of the file format from RT-11 to Files-11 is done automatically.

virtual display *n.*

VAXstation Display System

A virtual output device that has the properties of a physical screen, but is not necessarily visible on a physical screen.

virtual I/O functions *n.*

VAX/VMS

A set of I/O functions that must be interpreted by an ancillary control process.

virtual keyboard *n.*

VAXstation Display System

A virtual input device associated with a pasteboard. When users select a window into a pasteboard with a virtual keyboard, the physical keyboard is directed to the virtual keyboard and can be read by a program.

virtual memory *n.*

DIGITAL-specific and VAX/VMS

The set of storage locations in physical memory and on disk that is referred to by virtual addresses. From the programmer's viewpoint, the secondary storage locations appear to be locations in physical memory. The size of virtual memory in any system depends on the amount of physical memory available and the amount of disk storage used for nonresident virtual memory.

virtual page number (VPN) *n.*

VAX/VMS

The virtual address of a page of virtual memory. Same as VPN.

virtual program section *n.*

VAX/VMS

A program section that has virtual memory allocated to it, but not physical memory. Virtual address space is mapped into physical memory at run time by means of the mapping directives.

virtual relation *n.*

Rdb/ELN

A temporary relation resulting from a relational operation (select, join, and project). A virtual relation is not actually stored in the database.

virtual telecommunications access method *n.*

DECnet

IBM software that serves as a link between application programs and terminals or other applications in a communication network. Same as VTAM.

virtual terminal (VT) *n.*

DECnet

An imaginary but well-defined terminal. The network virtual terminal used in the ARPANET TELENET protocol provides a standard, netwide intermediate representation of a terminal that attempts to strike a balance between simplicity (restricting Hosts with state-of-the-art terminals) and complexity (penalizing Hosts with modest terminals). The Hosts are then free to negotiate options to use a more elaborate set of conventions or to accept the default value provided by the NVT (network virtual terminal). Same as VT.

RSX-11M

A virtual terminal is a software terminal created by the Executive to pass commands and data to the operating system, as from batch jobs. As far as the system is concerned, a virtual terminal has the same behavior as a physical terminal. Virtual terminals are supported on RSX-11M-PLUS only. Same as VT.

virtual-to-logical-block mapping *n.*

RSX-11M

The file processor translates the virtual block number supplied by RMS-11 to the logical block number that the processor must provide to the device driver during a disk access operation. See also retrieval pointer and window.

visual identification (VID) *n.*

TOPS-10

A visual identification label; the physical label that is affixed to a magnetic tape reel. Same as VID.

VMS *n.*

DIGITAL-specific

The operating system for a VAX computer. VMS stands for Virtual Memory System.

VNP20 *n.*

DECnet

The program that creates the communication front-end system image during the configuration procedure for a DECnet node.

volatile data base *n.*

DECnet and VAX/VMS

A memory image containing information about network management components.

TOPS-10

A temporary data base that consists of dynamic values currently in memory. Parameters can be states, such as line or node states, or characteristics, such as CPU type or time values, and remain constant until cleared or reset. Volatile data base values are lost when the system shuts down.

voltage *n.*

generic

The quantity of electrical pressure measured in volts.

volume *n.*

DIGITAL-specific and VAX/VMS

1. A mass storage medium such as a disk pack or reel of magnetic tape.

2. The largest logical unit of the file structure.

generic

A logical unit of data storage made up of one or more devices that must be mounted as a set.

volume control block (VCB) *n.*

DIGITAL-specific

A data structure that contains the information needed to control access to a volume. It is created when the volume is mounted. Same as VCB.

volume set *n.*

DIGITAL-specific and VAX/VMS

The file-structured collection of data residing on one or more mass storage media.

volume switch *n.*

TOPS-10

The process of removing a volume from a tape drive and mounting the next volume of the set.

voucher *n.*

generic

A document that serves to recognize a liability and authorize the disbursement of cash.

VPN *n.*

VAX/VMS

The abbreviation for virtual page number. The virtual address of a page of virtual memory. Same as virtual page number.

VT *n.*

RSX-11M

The abbreviation for virtual terminal. A virtual terminal is a software terminal created by the Executive to pass commands and data to the operating system, as from batch jobs. As far as the system is concerned, a virtual terminal has the same behavior as a physical terminal. Virtual terminals are supported on RSX-11M-PLUS only. Same as virtual terminal.

VTAM *n.*

DECnet

The abbreviation for virtual telecommunications access method. VTAM is IBM software that serves as a link between application programs and terminals or other applications in a communication network. Same as virtual communications access method.

WACK *n.*

DECnet

The acronym for wait-before-transmitting-positive-acknowledgement. In binary synchronous communications, a DLE (data-link escape) is sent by a receiving station to indicate that it is temporarily not ready to receive. Same as wait-before-transmitting-positive-acknowledgement.

wafer *n.*

generic

A "slice" of semiconductor material used in the manufacture of integrated circuits.

wage *n.*

generic

An amount earned for personal services rendered.

wait *v.*

DIGITAL-specific

To become inactive. A process enters a process wait state when the process suspends itself, hibernates, or declares that it needs to wait for an event, resource, mutex, and so forth.

VAX/VMS

To become inactive. A process enters a process wait state when the process suspends itself, hibernates, or declares that it needs to wait for an event, resource, mutex, and so forth.

wait-before-transmitting-positive-acknowledgement (WACK) *n.*

DECnet

In binary synchronous communications, a DLE (data-link escape) is sent by a receiving station to indicate that it is temporarily not ready to receive. Same as WACK.

wait-for-interrupt request *n.*

VAX/VMS

A request made by a driver's start I/O routine after it activates a device. The request causes the driver fork process to be suspended until the device requests an interrupt or the device times out.

waiting *n.*

MicroPower PASCAL

A process in the wait state. A process waits on a ring buffer or semaphore, unable to change states and resume execution until the ring buffer or semaphore has been signaled by another process.

wake *v.*

DIGITAL-specific and VAX/VMS

To activate a hibernating process. A hibernating process can be awakened by a time-scheduled, wake-up call.

generic

To change or to cause to change from an inactive state to a running state.

warm start *n.*

DIGITAL-specific

The rebootstrapping of a running system.

generic

A restart of a system so that the system begins operations at the point where it stopped.

watchpoint *n.*

MicroPower PASCAL

Stops execution when a certain memory location is modified.

wave *n.*

generic

An oscillation that passes from point to point in a medium or an energy field.

waveform *n.*

generic

A graphic drawing of electrical or electromagnetic amplitude change on a time base.

WCB *n.*

VAX/VMS

The abbreviation for window control block. A data structure that stores access control information for a file. It is created when a file is accessed on a volume. It is deleted when the file is deaccessed. Same as window control block.

WCC *n.*

DECnet

The abbreviation for write control character. WCC is a character used in conjunction with a 3270 write-type command to specify that a particular operation, or combination of operations, is to be performed at a display station or printer. Same as write control character.

WCS *n.*

VAX/VMS

Writeable control store.

WDCS *n.*

VAX/VMS

Writeable diagnostic control store.

weak definition *n.*

VAX/VMS

The definition of a global symbol that is not explicitly available for reference by modules linked with the module in which the definition occurs.

weak reference *n.*

VAX/VMS

A reference to a global symbol that requests the linker not to report an error or to search the default library's global symbol table to resolve the reference if the definition is not in the modules explicitly supplied to the linker. Weak references are often used when creating object modules to identify those global symbols that may not be needed at run time.

weight *n.*

generic

The particular style of a font used for textual emphasis or some other typographic purposes.

Wheel *n.*

TOPS-20

Refers to a privileged user.

wide-area network *n.*

DECnet

A public or private data communications system in which transmission are carried primarily over telephone lines.

wide document *n.*

DECWORD

A document that is up to 131 characters wide instead of the normal 79 characters wide.

generic

A document containing a wide ruler.

wide line *n.*

DECWORD

A line where a wide ruler is in effect.

wide ruler *n.*

DECWORD

A ruler where the right margin (R, S, or J) is set beyond column 79.

generic

A ruler where the right margin (R or J) is set beyond column 80.

width *n.*

generic

A character value that specifies the width (in pixels) of a character cell in printing.

wildcard *n.*

generic

1. A symbol that represents either a variable character or a variable string.

2. Something that can represent part of a filename in a command.

wild card (or wild-card, wildcard) *adj.*

generic

Pertaining to a symbol that indicates that any variable information may be substituted for that character.

wild card character (or wild-card character, wildcard character) *n.*

generic

A symbol, such as an asterisk or percent sign, that is used within or in place of a file name, file type, directory name, or version number in a file specification to indicate ''all'' for the given field.

wildcard construction *n.*

DECsystem-10

A technique used to designate a group of files without enumerating each file separately.

wildcard operation *n.*

RT-11

A shorthand method of referring to all files with a specific characteristic in their name.

Winchester disk *n.*

generic

A hard disk installed into the computer system. It can store 25 or more times the information of a diskette, and gives much faster response times.

window *n.*

generic

An area within a display image; commonly used in computer graphics to reference a specifically defined segment of the terminal screen.

MINC and VT-11 GRAPHICS

A segment of a terminal screen on which graphic images can be displayed. A window is a specifically defined segment of the terminal screen through which a user can view a portion of an x/y coordinate space.

RGL/FEP

The part of the user's picture that RGL/FEP displays. When RGL/FEP is entered, the window is set to be the same as the screen's coordinates; the window is the full screen.

RSX-11M

The set of retrieval pointers the operating system maintains in memory for each open file for mapping virtual block numbers to logical block numbers. See also retrieval pointer and virtual-to-logical block mapping.

VAX PSI

A sequence of consecutively numbered data packets that are authorized to cross the DTE/DCE interface. Windowsize is the total number of packets that can cross (typically, seven).

VAX/VMS

A continuous virtual address space that can be moved to allow the task to examine different parts of a region or different regions. See also mapping window.

window block *n.*

VAX/VMS

A structure defined by the Task Builder that describes a range of continuous virtual addresses.

window control block (WCB) *n.*

VAX/VMS

A data structure that stores access control information for a file. It is created when a file is accessed on a volume. It is deleted when the file is deaccessed. Same as WCB.

window position *n.*

FFE

An FFE editing value that specifies the location of the Editing Window relative to the character in the Edit Buffer.

window turning *n.*

RSX-11M

The process of changing the retrieval pointers in memory until the window contains pointers covering the specified virtual blocks.

wiper *n.*

generic

The moving element that makes contact with a terminal in a relay or switch; in a potentiometer, the contact that moves the length of the element, dividing the resistance according to its mechanical arm.

withholding *n.*

generic

An amount deducted by the employer from an employee's gross earnings and remitted to the IRS (Internal Revenue Service) as advance payment on an employee's income tax. It also applies to amounts deducted from interest or dividend payments for a similar purpose.

word *n.*

COBOL-74

A character string of not more than 30 characters that forms a user-defined word, a system name, or a reserved word.

DECnet, DECsystem-10, and DECSYSTEM-20

A set of contiguous bits or bytes of a specific size determined by the hardware and/or software. Whatever the length of a word used by a specific machine, a word is usually of a length equal to one addressable location unit. DECSYSTEM-20, TENEX, and DECsystem-10 use 36-bit words.

DECWORD

In DECWORD, a word is any group of visible characters separated by one of the following: a space, a return, a tab, a paragraph marker, a page marker, or a new page marker.

DIGITAL-specific and VAX/VMS

Two contiguous bytes (16 bits) starting on an addressable byte boundary. Bits are numbered from the right, 0 through 15. A word is identified by the address of the byte containing bit 0. When interpreted arithmetically, a word is a 2s complement integer with significance increasing from bit 0 to bit 14. If interpreted as a signed integer, bit 15 is the sign bit. The value of the integer is in the range −32,768 to 32,767. When interpreted as an unsigned integer, significance increases from bit 0 through bit 15 and the value of the unsigned integer is in the range 0 through 65,535.

generic

A character string or a bit string considered as a logical group.

MINC

The number of characters treated as a unit in a workspace. MINC words can contain two characters, one integer, or one half of a real number.

word aligned *n.*

RSX-11M

A convention by which each record in a sequential file starts and ends on a word boundary; that is, each record is stored as an even number of bytes. RMS-11 uses this convention to maintain structural compatibility with FCS-11 sequential files. See also padding.

word processing *n.*

generic

A computer program that is used for document creation and text production.

word wrap *n.*

Digital-specific

A feature that automatically drops to the next line any word a user types if it extends past the right margin of the text.

word wrap indent *n.*

DECmate II

The column to which text is indented when there is a W in the ruler. A word that follows a word wrap return is indented to this column, so all lines except the first line in the paragraph are indented.

word wrap return *n.*

DIGITAL-specific

A type of carriage return automatically placed in a document to accomplish word wrap. It is a temporary marker that the system deletes and inserts as necessary as the line endings change. See also hard return and soft return.

working capital *n.*

generic

The difference between current assets and current liabilities.

working set *n.*

DIGITAL-specific and VAX/VMS

The set of pages in process space to which an executing process can refer without incurring a page fault. The working set must be resident in memory for the process to execute. The remaining pages of that process, if any, are either in memory and not in the process working set or they are on secondary storage.

generic

The set of pages in the address space of a process to which an active job is referring.

working set list *n.*

VAX/VMS

A memory management data base maintained for each process to indicate those pages of the process that are in the process's working set.

working set swapper *n.*

TOPS-20 and VAX/VMS

A system process that brings process working sets into, and removes them from the balance set.

work-in-process inventory *n.*

generic

The costs incurred to date on products for which production has begun but has not yet been completed.

work sheet *n.*

A tabular schedule for convenient summary of adjusting and closing entries.

workspace *n.*

FMS

The scratch area or "buffer" in memory used by the Form Driver when it displays a particular form; the workspace maintains context from one Form Driver call to the next for the same form. The workspace is called the impure area in FMS Version 1.

MINC

MINC's storage area for temporarily holding a program and its associated values.

Workspace Symbol Module *n.*

ACMS

An object module, produced as a result of building a task group definition, that contains a main routine and debug symbol table used by the ACMS Task Debugger to examine workspaces.

world *n.*

VAX/VMS

In the context system, owner, group, or world, world refers to all users, including the system operators, the system manager, and users both in an owner's group and in any other group.

world coordinates *n.*

RGL/FEP

The user-specified coordinate range that defines how the screen is addressed.

WPS *n.*

DIGITAL-specific

The abbreviation for word processing system, referring to any one of DIGITAL's word processing products such as WPS-PLUS.

wrap-around *v.*

generic

To continue on the next line, a text line that is too long for the screen.

wrap symbol *n.*

MINC

The two-character symbol displayed by the keypad editor whenever a file line is longer than a screen row. The wrap symbol indicates that the preceding line does not end with a line terminator.

write *v.*

generic

To record data on a medium.

VAX/VMS

The act or capability of an image to send data. For example, when a PRINT command is issued, the specified file is read from wherever it is stored and written to the line printer.

write access *v.*

DIGITAL-specific

To open a file to perform PUT, UPDATE, or DELETE operations, as well as GET or FIND operations.

write access type *n.*

VAX/VMS

The specified operand of an instruction or procedure is only written during that instructor's or procedure's execution.

write allocate *n.*

VAX/VMS

A cache management technique in which cache is allocated on a write miss as well as on the usual read miss.

write back *n.*

VAX/VMS

A cache management technique in which data from a write operation to cache is copied into main memory only when the data in cache must be overwritten. This results in temporary inconsistencies between cache and main memory.

write control character (WCC) *n.*

DECnet

A character used in conjunction with a 3270 WRITE-TYPE command to specify that a particular operation, or combination of operations, is to be performed at a display station or printer. Same as WCC.

write-enabled *adj.*

DIGITAL-specific

Pertaining to the condition of a volume that allows transfers that would write information on it.

write-off *v.*

generic

To remove an asset from the accounts.

write parameters *n.*

PASCAL and VAX PASCAL

Expressions that are specified as parameters to the WRITE or WRITELN procedure, which writes them in the specified file.

write-protected *adj.*

DIGITAL-specific

Pertaining to the condition of a volume that is protected against transfers that would write information on it.

write sharing *n.*

RSX-11M

The process of more than one task opening a file for write access and allowing other tasks to perform write-type operations.

write through *n.*

VAX/VMS

A cache management technique in which data from a write operation is copied in both cache and main memory. Cache and main memory data are always consistent. See also store through.

write-type (record operation) *v.*

RSX-11M

To DELETE, PUT, or UPDATE.

X.25 *n.*

VAX PSI and VAX/VMS

A CCITT recommendation that specifies the interface between data terminal equipment (DTEs) and data circuit-terminating equipment (DCEs) for equipment operating in the packet mode on public data networks.

X.25 Gateway Access Protocol *n.*

DECnet

In the network application layer of DNA (DIGITAL Network Architecture), a protocol that allows a node which is not connected directly to a public data network to access the facilities of that network through an intermediary gateway node.

X.25 Protocol *n.*

DECnet

In the data link layer of DNA (DIGITAL Network Architecture), the protocol that implements the X.25 packet level (level 3) and X.25 frame level (level 2) of the CCITT X.25 recommendation for public data network interfaces.

X.28 *n.*

VAX PSI and VAX/VMS

A CCITT recommendation that specifies the DTE/DCE (data terminal equipment/data circuit-terminating equipment) interface for a start-stop mode DTE accessing the packet assembly/disassembly (PAD) facility in a public data network situated in the same country.

X.29 *n.*

VAX PSI and VAX/VMS

A CCITT recommendation that specifies procedures for the exchange of control information and user data between a packet-mode DTE and a packet assembly/disassembly (PAD) facility.

X.29 Terminal *n.*

VAX/VMS

A terminal connected to a packet assembly/disassembly (PAD) facility.

X.3 *n.*

VAX PSI and VAX/VMS

A CCITT recommendation that specifies the packet assembly/disassembly (PAD) facility in a public data network.

X.75 *n.*

VAX PSI

The CCITT recommendation that specifies the procedures for communicating between PSDNs (packet switching data networks).

XAB *n.*

VAX/VMS

The abbreviation for extended attribute block. An RMS user data structure that contains additional file attributes beyond those expressed in the file access block (FAB), such as boundary types (aligned on cylinder, logical block number, and virtual block number) and file protection information. Same as extended attribute block.

X axis *n.*

generic

The horizontal line of a graph.

X axis label *n.*

generic

The text identifying the data represented on the X axis of a graph.

XBUF *n.*

RSX-11M

The abbreviation for extended buffer pool. In RSTS/E, a portion of a computer's physical memory that is reserved for use by the operating system. Message send/receive, the DECnet/E package, the RSTS/2780 package, the FIP buffering module, and the data caching module use this reserved memory; if none is available, they use small buffers. Same as extended buffer pool.

RSTS/E

The abbreviation for extended buffer pool. An area of user memory reserved for extended buffers, which can range in size from 32 words to the maximum size of the extended buffer pool. The extended buffer pool is used for data caching, directory caching and other system functions. Same as extended buffer pool.

XDELTA *n.*

VAX/VMS

A tool for debugging operating systems and drivers.

XEC mode *n.*

DECnet

The abbreviation for extended emulator control mode. In sessions where management of SNA (systems network architecture) protocol is shared by the applications and the protocol emulator (PE), those sessions are said to be operating in extended emulator control (XEC) mode. The RSX-11M application uses the CON$ macro to specify extended protocol options, which provide some of the functions available to what IBM defines as "type 2" interactive sessions. Protocol options available in EC mode are also available in XEC mode. Same as extended emulator control mode.

XMTSD *n.*

CTS-300

The abbreviation for extended memory time-shared run-time system. This system supports multiple users and requires the XM monitor to allow upper memory access.

XON/XOFF *n.*

PRO/Communications

The abbreviation for transmitter on/transmitter off. An item on the line characteristics menu used to synchronize data transmission between the Professional and a host.

XSS - Executive Support Systems *n.*

DIGITAL-specific

Systems that provide access to information to high level managers. Most commonly, those referred to as "status access", where the manager views information rather than input it or manipulate it.

X value *n.*

generic

The text or value plotted on the X axis of a graph.

Y axis *n.*

generic

The vertical line of a graph.

Y axis label *n.*

generic

The text identifying the data represented on the Y axis of a graph.

Y value *n.*

generic

The numeric value of data which is plotted on the Y axis of a graph.

ZAP *n.*

RSX-11M

A utility used to patch task images.

zero compression *n.*

TOPS-10

The technique of compressing a core memory image by eliminating consecutive blocks of zeros and replacing them with an indication of the number of words of zeros that were removed.

zero fill *n.*

FMS

A field attribute specifying that field values returned to the application program are to be padded with ASCII zeros. See also fill character, PAD, and RIB.

zero fill attribute *n.*

generic

A field attribute specifying that field values returned to the application program are to be padded with zeros.

zero-length module *n.*

TOPS-10

A module containing symbol definitions but no instructions or data words.

zoom mode *n.*

Medical Systems and MSG (SPETS)

A software value that magnifies an image area.

ABBREVIATIONS, ACRONYMS, MNEMONICS, AND EXPANSIONS

ABBREVIATIONS, ACRONYMS, MNEMONICS, AND EXPANSIONS

The DIGITAL Dictionary Committee has compiled this list as a handy reference. Although the Committee made a thorough search throughout DIGITAL for such terms, this list is not complete.

The Committee welcomes suggested additions. Please refer to the Reader's Comment page at the front of this Dictionary.

AAAI American Association for Artificial Intelligence

AAS advanced application system (DEC)

AASP ASCII asynchronous support package

ABC applications, basics, and concepts
automatic bandwidth control

ABCDIC auto baud control dictionary

ABD ancillary control process buffer descriptor
ACP buffer descriptor

ABM asynchronous balance mode
automatic batch mixing

ABO advanced byte-oriented

ABS absolute

ABSL absolute loader

ABSLDR absolute loader

ABT abort

A BUS I/O adapter bus

AC accumulator (see also ACC)
alternating current
automatic computer

ACA	asynchronous communications adaptor	**ACR**	abandon call and retry (networks) access control register address compare register automatic call and retry (networks)
ACB	action control block		
ACC	accumulator (see also AC)		
ACCR	accelerator maintenance register	**ACS**	access
ACCS	accelerator control/status register	**ACT**	active
		ACTLU	activate logical unit
ACD	automatic call distributor	**ACTPU**	activate physical unit
ACF	access control field	**ACU**	arithmetic control unit automatic calling unit (networks)
ACI	access control information asynchronous communications interface automated check in		
		A/D	analog to digital
ACIA	asynchronous communications interface adapter	**ADA**	automatic data acquisitions
		ADALINE	adaptive linear element
		ADAM	a data management system
ACK	acknowledgment/affirmative (or positive)	**ADB**	application diskette builder (PRO 350) application database
ACL	access control link access control list	**ADC**	analog to digital converter
ACMS	Application Control and Management System	**ADCCP**	advanced data communication control procedure (ANSI)
ACMS/AD	Application Control and Management System/Application Development	**ADDAR**	automatic digital data acquisition and recording
ACP	ancillary control process (VAX term) ancillary control processor ancillary control program auxiliary control process	**ADE**	advanced data entry (system) a software layered product (RSTS/E and VAX/VMS); formerly, the acronym for application development environment

ADL	active device list
	application development language
ADU	application definition utility
ADO	ampex digital optics
ADP	adapter control block (VAX term)
	automatic data processing
ADPC	automatic data processing center
ADPE	automatic data processing equipment
ADPS	automatic data processing system
	automatic display and plotting system
ADR	address data register
ADRS	address
ADS	address data strobe
	application development systems
	automatic distribution system
ADSS	advanced software system
ADT	application design tool
ADU	application definition utility
ADX	automatic data exchange
AED	ALGOL extended for design
AEDS	automated engineering design system
AESC	American Engineering Standards Committee (now ANSC)

AESOP	an evolutionary system for on-line processing
AF	audio frequency
AFC	automatic frequency control
AFCAL	Association Francaise de Calcul (A French computer association)
AFCALTIC	a French association for computing and data processing
AFG	analog function generator
AFNOR	French standards organization
AFT	automatic fine tuning
AFTN	aeronautical fixed telecommunication network
AGC	automatic gain control
AHD	audio high density (type of compact audio disc)
AI	artificial intelligence
AIB	ACP I/O buffer
	ancillary control process I/O buffer
AIC	applications and industry channels (Digital)
AID	algebraic interpretive dialogue
	attention identification
AIDS	automated information and diagnosis system (Digital field services)
	automatic input distribution system

AIE	ada integrated environment	**AL/X**	advice language/X (artificial intelligence language)
AIEE	American Institute of Electrical Engineers	**AM**	address mark
AIEEE	American Institute of Electrical and Electronics Engineers		amplitude modulation associative memory
		A/M	auto-manual
AIP	access in progress applications interchange program	**AMAR**	automatic measurement, analysis, and reporting system
AIS	advanced information services (Digital)	**AMBIT**	algebraic manipulation by identity translation
AISB	artificial intelligence and simulation of behavior	**AMC**	automatic message counting automatic modulation control
AIU	autonomous interface unit		
ALC	arithmetic and logic circuits automatic level control	**AME**	applications migration executive (VAX term)
ALD	automatic logic diagnosis	**AM-DBS**	amplitude modulation-double side band
ALE	address latch element		
ALGDDT	ALGOL dynamic debugger	**AML**	amplitude modulated link
ALGOL (or IAL)	Algorithmic Oriented Language	**AMP**	ampere (unit of electrical current) amplifier asymmetric multiprocessing system
ALIC	analog-line interface circuit		
ALLOC	allocations	**AMR**	automatic message registering
ALM	area logistics manager assembly library module	**AMS**	administrative management systems
ALNMT	alignment		
ALS	Ada language system	**AM-SSB**	amplitude modulation-single side band
ALT	alternate mode or escape key	**AMT**	amplitude modulated transmitter automated module test
ALU	arithmetic library unit arithmetic logic unit		

AMTRAN	automatic mathematical translation	**A/P**	accounts payable
AMU	alterable microcomputer unit (AMI)	**APA**	arithmetic processing accelerator
ANACOM	analog computer	**APAS**	adaptable programmable assembly system (Westinghouse)
ANATRON	analog translator		
ANC	advanced numerical control	**APC**	actual product cost automatic phase control automatic power control
AND	a Boolean operator		
ANI	automatic number identification	**APD**	angular position digitizer avalanche photo diode
ANL	analog loop	**APEC**	automated procedures for engineering consultants
ANLG	analog	**APF**	active page field
ANS	American National Standard	**APL**	Advanced Programming Language
ANSC	American National Standards Committee	**APP**	auxiliary power plant applications
ANSI	American National Standards Institute	**APR**	active page register
ANSI-SPARC	American National Standards Institute - Systems Planning and Research Committee	**APRXLY**	approximately
		APS	accounts payable system
		APST	automatic power supply test
ANT	antenna	**APT**	automated process and test system automatically programmed tools automatic picture transmission automatic product test
AO	amplifier output		
A-O AMPL	and-or amplifier		
AOC	automatic output control		
AOI	and/or invert area of interest		
		APU	Auxiliary processing unit
AOS	add or subtract	**APUHS**	automatic program unit, high speed
AP	argument pointer (VAX term) attached processor		
		APULS	automatic program unit, low speed

AQ	any quality	**ARQ**	automatic repeat request - retransmit data blocks with errors
AQB	ancillary control process queue header block	**ARS**	accounts receivable system
AQL	acceptable quality level	**ART**	automatic reporting telephone
AQP	ACP queue header block		
AQS	automated quote system	**ARU**	audio response unit
AR	address register arithmetic register	**AS**	add subtract
A/R	accounts receivable	**ASA**	American Standards Association (now ANSI)
AR11	analogue real-time subsystem	**ASAP**	as soon as possible
ARAM	analog random access memory	**ASBLR**	assembler
ARC	automatic ratio control automatic relay calculator automatic remote control	**ASC**	advanced scientific computer (Texas Instruments) ALGOL source conversion ASCII file extension automatic synchronized control
ARCH	architecture automatic remote cassette handler	**ASCII**	American Standard Code for Information Interchange
ARITH	arithmetic	**ASD**	application systems development group automatic synchronized discriminator
ARL	acceptable reliability level authorized returns list		
ARLC	auto reload and count	**ASECT**	absolute address section
ARM	access arm asynchronous response mode automated route management	**ASF**	automatic sheet feed
		ASITFT	amorphous silicon thin-film transistor
ARPANET	ARPA Network (packet switching)	**ASK**	amplitude shift keying applications software kit (DIGITAL)
ARPS	automatic reliability prediction system	**ASL**	arithmetic shift left

ASLT	advanced solid logic technology
ASM	advanced systems manufacturing
ASN	average sample number
ASP	attached support processor automatic servo plotter automatic switching panel
ASQ	asynchronous trap queue
ASR	arithmetic shift right automatic send/receive
ASRA	automatic stereophonic recording amplifier
ASSIST-11	a directory assistance system
AST	asynchronous system trap
ASTLVL	asynchronous system trap level (VAX term)
ASTRO	asynchronous synchronous transmitter receiver
ASV	automatic self verification
ASYNC	asynchronous
ASYNCH	asynchronous
A&T	acquisition and test group (Digital)
A/T	action time
ATA	asynchronous terminal adaptor
ATSM	asynchronous time division multiplexing
ATE	automated test equipment

ATG	applied technology group automated test generation
ATL	active task list application terminal language
ATS	applicant tracking system automatic test system
ATTN	attention
AU	angstrom unit
AUTO	automatic
AUTOPIC	automatic personal identification code
AUX	auxiliary
AV	Audiovisual
AVC	automatic volume control
AVD	alternate voice data
AVDU	alphanumeric visual display unit
AVE	automatic volume expansion
AVG	average
AVL	available
AVM	application virtual machine
AVO	advanced video option (DEC VT-100)
AVR	automatic volume recognition
AVS	assembly verification system
AWG	American wire gauge
AX	automatic transmission

AXE	VAX-11 and MicroVAX architecture	**BB**	beginning of block
B	bit or byte (varies from system to system, and company to company)	**BBA**	BIT BLT accelerator
		BBCCI	branch on bit clear and clear interlock
BA	batch processor device binary add buffered address bus arbitrator	**BBD**	bucket brigade device
		BBI	begin bracket indicator
		BBL	bug back list
BAC	BASIC compiled program file binary asymmetric channel	**BBS**	bulletin board systems
		BBSSI	branch on bit set and set interlock
BACE	basic automatic checkout equipment	**BBSY**	bus busy
BAD	bad block locator utility	**BBU**	battery back-up unit
BADC	binary asymmetric dependent channel	**BC**	binary code byte counter
BAI	bus address increment	**BCB**	buffer control block
BAP	band amplitude product	**BCC**	block check character binary check character branch if clear
BAR	backup address register buffer active register buffer address register bus address register		
		BCD	binary coded decimal
		BCD/B	binary coded decimal/binary
BAS	BASIC program source BASIC source file	**BCDIC**	binary coded decimal information code
BASIC	Beginner's All-purpose Symbolic Instruction Code (a computer language)	**BCD/Q**	binary coded decimal/quaternary
		BCFSK	binary code frequency shift keying
BAT	bad allocation table batch file	**BCH**	batch
BATMAN	bulk autonomous transfer manager	**BCI**	binary coded information broadcast interference
BATS	backplan automatic test systems	**BCL**	batch command language

BCO	binary coded octal	**BE**	band elimination
BCP	Bar Code/Block Character (software) Package (RSX-11M)	**BEQ**	branch if equal
		BER	binary error rate bit error rate
BCPL	basic computer programming language	**BETB**	between brackets
BCRT	bright cathode ray tube	**BEX**	broadband exchange
BCTR	byte count register	**B/F**	background/foreground
BCW	buffer control word	**BFG**	binary frequency generator
BD	block diagram buffered data	**BFO**	beat frequency oscillator
		BFR	buffer
BDA	BI disk adaptor	**BG**	bus grant
BDAM	Basic Direct Access Method (a file organization)	**BGE**	branch if greater or equal
BDBE	basic database environment	**BGR**	beginner
BDC	binary decimal counter	**BGT**	branch if greater than
BDD	binary-to-decimal decoder	**BHI**	branch if higher
BDL	basic design language business definition language	**BHIS**	branch if higher or same
		BI	backplan interconnect batch input device blanking input
BDL/CS	basic design language for cycle simulation		
BDMS	basic data management system	**BIC**	bit clear
		BIDEC	binary-to-decimal
BDOS	basic disk operating system	**BIM**	beginning of information marker
BDP	buffered data path business data processing		
		BIMD	biomedical series of computer programs
BDMS	basic data management system	**BIN**	binary binary file extension
BDS	behavioral DECSIM business definition system		
		BINAC	Binary Automatic Computer
BDU	basic display unit	**BIOS**	basic input/output system

BIPCO	built-in-place components	**BLISS**	Basic Language for Implementation of System Software
BIS	batch input stream		
BISAD	business information systems analysis and design	**BLK**	block
		BLKI	block in
BISAM	basic indexed sequential access method (a file organization)	**BLKO**	block out
		BLNK	blank
BISYNC	binary synchronous communications protocol (also BSC)	**BLOS**	branch if lower or same
		BLR	binary language representation
BIT	binary digit built-in test	**BLT**	block transfer branch if less than
BITBLT	bit block transfer	**BLU**	basic line unit basic logic unit
BITN	bilateral iterative network		
BIS	bit set	**BM**	buffer module
BIT	bit test	**BMC**	bubble memory controller
BIU	basic information unit bus interface unit	**BMD**	biomedical series of computer programs
BIVAR	bivariant function generator	**BMI**	branch if minus
BIX	binary information exchange	**BMS**	business management system
BKP	backup	**BN**	binary number system block number
BKSP	backspace		
BL	blanking	**BNDR**	binder
BLA	branch logistics administrator	**BNE**	branch if not equal buffer not empty
BLC	branch logistics coordinator	**BNF**	Backus-Naur Form Backus Normal Form - formal method for defining language syntax
BLDER	builder		
BLE	branch if less or equal		
BLF	bubble lattice file		

BO	back ordered beat oscillator byte offset		**BPUS**	binary program update service
BOA	base operand address (VAX term)		**BPV**	bound procedure value (data type)
BOF	Birds Of a Feather (DECUS)		**BR**	branch request break request bus request
BOI	branch output interrupt			
BOOT	bootstrap (see also BTSP)		**BRAM**	battery-powered random access memory (battery back-up)
BORAM	block oriented random access memory		**BRC**	branch conditional
BOS	basic operating system Business and Office Systems (Digital)		**BRD**	bus register data magnetic tape read binary
			BRIE	bus request interrupt enable
BOSE	Business and Office Systems Engineering (Digital)		**BRM**	binary rate multiplier
			BROMAR	backup ROM address register
BOSM	Business and Office Systems Marketing (Digital)		**BRRVR**	buffer selection verification register bus request receive vector register
BOSS	batch operating subsystem			
BOT	beginning of tape		**BRS**	bibliographic retrieval services break request signal
BP	bandpass batch pseudo device			
BPF	bandpass filter		**BRSVR**	buffer selection verification register
BPI	bits per inch		**BRU**	backup and restore utility branch unconditional
BPL	branch if plus			
BPO	booking purposes only		**BS**	back space binary subtract bit shift block schematic buffer state
BPS	bits per second			
BPSK	binary phase-shift keying			
BPSS	basic packet-switching service		**BSAM**	basic sequential access method

BSB	backspace block	**BTL**	business transaction language
BSC	BASIC (a computer programming language) BASIC message switching center binary synchronous communications	**BTSP**	bootstrap (see also BOOT)
		BTST	busy-tone start lead
		BUBA	buffered UNIBUS address
BSC/DV	bisynchronous communications driver	**BUF**	buffer
		BUIC	back-up interceptor control
BSD	based binary synchronous device	**BUPI**	batch user program interface
BSDC	binary symmetric dependent channel	**BUS**	basic utilities system business
BSF	backspace file	**BVC**	branch if overflow clear
BSI	branch and store instructions British Standards Institute	**BVM**	Boolean vector machine
		BVS	branch if overflow set
BSIC	binary symmetric independent channel	**BW**	bandwidth
		BWR	bandwidth ratio
BSSG	Base Systems Software Group	**BYSYNC**	binary synchronous communication
BSP	back space	**BYTE**	binary element string (usually 8 bits)
BSR	back space record bus shift register	**CA**	cost accounting
BST	beam switching tube	**CAD**	compact audio disc computer aided design
BSY	busy	**CADC**	Cambridge Computer Aided Design Centre
BTA	BI tape adapter		
BTAM	Basic Telecommunications Access Method (a file organization) (IBM)	**CADCAP**	computer aided design capture
BTDL	basic-transient diode logic	**CADD**	computer aided design and drafting
BTE	buffer transfer error		

CADEG	computer aided design environment group (Digital)	**CAMT**	coexistence architecture, methods and tools
CADSE	Computer Aided Design Systems Engineering (Digital)	**CAP**	capacity
		CAPP	computer-aided process planning
CAE	computer aided engineering	**CAPPS**	creating application systems
CAEM	Computer Aided Engineering and Manufacturing (Digital)	**CAPS**	cassette programming system
			Centralized Applications and Product Support (US Area Software Services)
CAFS	content addressable file store		Corporate Application Support Group (Digital Software Services)
CAI	computer aided instruction computer analog input computer assisted instruction	**CAPS-11**	Cassette Programming System-11
CAI/OP	computer analog input/output	**CAR**	capitol appropriation request command address register computer aided retrieval contents of the address register - used in LISP cylinder address register
CAM	central address memory communications access manager (networks) communication link access module (IBM) computer aided manufacturing content address memory	
		CARAM	content addressable random access memory
		CARP	computer anatomical reconstruction package
CAMA	centralized automatic message accounting	**CARR**	carriage
CAMEO	CNP autonomous maintenance emulating organizer	**CAS**	column address strobe commercial applications systems competitive analysis system (Digital database) courseware authoring system (Digital)
CAMP	computer-aided mask preparation common access monitor program	
CAMPS	computer-aided manufacturing process sheets system	**CAS-11**	construction accounting system

529

CASA	Computer and Automated Systems Association CASA/SME Computer and Automated Systems Association of SME	**CBT**	computer-based training console boot terminator
CASTE	course assembly system and tutorial environment	**CC**	carriage control channel control command code condition code connecting circuit
CAT	computer aided testing computer aided tomography computerized axial tomography (physical x-section using x-rays)	**CCA**	Central Computer Agency
		CCB	channel control block (VAX term) communications control block communication control buffer
CATO	compiler for automatic teaching operations (for PLATO)	**CCC**	copy control character
CATS	commercial application/terminal support	**CCD**	charge coupled device (an analog IC) complementary coded decimal Corporate Component Engineering
CAW	channel address word		
CB	channel buffer circuit breaker coated back		
		CCEG	Central Commercial Engineering group
CBBS	computer based business system	**CCETT**	Centre Commun d'Etudes de Television et de Telecommunications (Common Research Center of the French PTT and the French Broadcasting Agency)
CBE	computer based education		
CBI	compound batch identification computer based instruction control bus in		
		CCF	console carrier facility consolidation control file
CBL	COBOL input file extension computer based learning	**CCG**	computer communications group
CBO	control bus out		
CBR	console bus request	**CCIA**	Computer and Communications Industry Association
CBS	communications system base		

CCITT	Comite Consultatif International de Telegraphique et Telephonique (International Telegraph and Telephone Consultative Committee)		**C-DAD**	compact-digital audio disc
			CDB	cartographic data base
			CDC	Control Data Corporation code directing character corporate data center
CCL	concise command language concise control language console command language		**CDCE**	central data conversion equipment
CCP	character controlled protocol console carrier protocol console command processor		**CDD**	Common Data Dictionary
			CDDL	common data definition language
CCR	console carrier requestor		**CDE**	complex data entry compound document editor
CCS	common channel signaling communications control system computer control store configuration control switch console carrier server		**CDDL**	common data definition language (utility)
			CDH	command and data handling
CC&S	central computer and sequencer		**CDH-LOC**	constricted double heterojunction – large optical cavity injection diode laser
CCSS	comprehensive computing systems and services		**CDI**	collector diffused isolation
CCT	circuit		**CDL**	computer design language
CCTA	Central Computer and Telecommunications Agency		**CDK**	channel data check
			CDMS	commercial data management system
CCTV	closed circuit television		**CDP**	card punch communications data processor
CCU	command charge unit communications control unit			
			CDR	contents of the decrement register – used in LISP
CCW	channel control word			
CD	check digit clock driver		**CD-ROM**	compact disc – read only memory
CDA	core dump analyzer utility crash dump analysis utility		**CDSL**	connect data set to line

CDT	control data terminal		**CGB**	convert gray to binary
CDU	central display unit		**CGI**	computer generated images
CE	channel end compiler environment		**CGL**	core graphics library (graphics standard used in PRO 300 series)
CEC	Commission for the European Communities		**CHAMP**	call handling and management planning (Digital Field Service)
CEF	common event flag (VAX term)		**CHAR**	character
CEO	chief executive officer		**CHG**	change
CEP	circular error probability		**CHILL**	CCITT high-level language
CEPA	civil engineering programming applications		**CHIP**	configurable, highly parallel computer
CEPT	Conference of European Post and Telecommunications Administration		**CHM**	charge mode
			CHNL	channel
CET	callable PROSE text editor (PRO 350)		**CHRG**	charge
			CHSE	Commercial Hardware Systems Engineering
CEX	Communications Executive			
CF	current frame pointer (VAX term)		**CI**	call indicator circuit interpreter computer images computer interconnect bus (Digital) console input (pseudo) device
CFB	coated front and back			
CFCB	communications file control block			
CFE	configuration file editor		**C/I**	carrier-to-interference ratio
CFL	control file language compiler		**CIA**	computer interconnect adapters
CFR	castatrographic failure rate		**CIB**	COBOL information bulletin console interface board
CFS	common file system software (Digital)		**CICS**	customer information control system (IBM)
CG	character generator computer graphics		**CIF**	central index file

CIG	computer image generation	**CIU**	communications interface unit computer interface unit
CICS/VS	customer information control system/virtual storage		
		CK DIG	check digit
CII	Compagnie Internationale pour l'Informatique	**CKO**	checking operator
CIL	core image library computer instrumentation limited	**CKQ**	clock queue
		CKSM	checksum
CILS	Corporate Information and Library Services (Digital)	**CKT**	circuit
CIM	computer input from microfilm Computer Integrated Manufacturing	**CL**	central line closing console listing (pseudo) device control logic conversion loss
CIO	central input/output multiplexer	**CLA**	communication line adapters
CIOCS	communications input/output control system	**CLAS**	computerized library acquisition systems (Lukak Data Systems) customer level accounting system
CIR	circuit		
CIS	Corporate Information Services corporate information systems	**CLASSIC**	classroom interactive computer
		CLAT	communication line adapters for teletypewriter
CISC	complex instruction set computer	**CLC**	cellular logic computer (used for logic processing) communications link controller (networks) current location counter
CIT	call in-time COBOL intermediate temporary (data type) command language interpreter table component incoming test		
		CLCS	current logic, current switching
		CLD	called line central log desk
CITEL	Inter-American Telecommunications Commission	**CLEM**	communications line error management

CLG	calling	**CMC**	communications mode control
CLI	calling indicator command language interpreter command line interpreter	**CMCT**	communicate
		CMC7	MICR fount standard

CLIP	cellular logic image
	  processor
	compiler language for
	  information processing
		CMD	central money disk
			command

		CMDR	command reject (bit protocol control)
CLK	clock	**CMF**	cross modulation factor customer master file
CLM	closed loop manufacturing		

CLP	command list pointer	**CMI**	Comet (11/750) memory
			  interconnect
			computer managed
			  instruction

CLR	clear computer language recorder CUPID link region		
CLS	Calls COBOL language subcommittee	**CML**	commercial current mode logic
		CMN	common

CLSC	CODASYL Language
	  Structure Committee
		CMOS	complimentary metal oxide
			  semiconductor

CLT	communication line terminal
	computer language
	  translator
		CMP	compatibility mode bit (VAX
			  term)
			computer
			Corporate Materials and
			  Planning (Digital)
			file compare utility

CLU	central logic unit		
CLUST	cluster		
CM	centimeter central memory channel mask communications multiplexer compatibility mode computer module control mark corrective maintenance	**CMPLX**	complex
		CMPR	compare
		CMPT	computer
		CMR	command mode rejection common mode rejection
CMA	circular mil area (wire gauge)	**CMRR**	command mode rejection ratio

CMS	code management system (VAX-11 DEC/CMS – similar to UNIX SCCS)	**CNR**	carrier-to-noise power ratio
		CNS	communications network simulator Corporate Network Services
CMS-11	classified advertising management system – PDP-11/70		
		CNSL	console
CMT	computerized module test	**CNT**	counter
CMV	common mode voltage	**CNTRL**	central
CMX	communications multiplexer	**CNU**	compare numeric unequal
C/N	carrier/noise ratio	**CNVT**	convert
CNA	communications network architecture	**CO**	close-open console output (pseudo) device
CNC	computerized numerical control	**C/O**	checkout
CNCP	a Canadian data network	**COAX**	coaxial cable
CNCT	connect	**COB**	COBOL source program complementary off-set binary
CND	condition could not duplicate		
CNE	compare numerical equal	**COBDDT**	COBOL dynamic debugging technique
CNF	contract notification form configuration (VAX)	**COBOL**	Common Business Oriented Language
CNFGR	CNF register	**CODASYL**	conference on data systems languages
CNFIE	CNF interrupt enable		
CNL	circuit net loss	**CODEC**	coder-decoder
CNP	communications network processor	**CODIC**	computer-directed communications
CNPGU	communications network processor generation utilities	**COED**	computer operated electronic display
		COEM	Commercial Original Equipment Manufacturer
CNPR	console non-processor request	**COG**	Corporate Operations Group (of Software Services)

COGENI	compiler and generalized translator	**COMPROSL**	compound procedural scientific language
COGO	computer language for solving problems in plane COordinate GeOmetry	**COMSAT**	a communications satellite corporation
		COMSEC	communications security
COHO	coherent oscillator	**COMTEX**	communications oriented multiple terminal executive
COL	computer oriented language		
COLINGO	compile on line and go	**CONC**	concentrated
COLP	collided page (VAX term)	**CONFIG**	configuration
COLT	computerized on-line testing	**CONGEN**	control generator
COM	computer output microfilm computable (VAX term)	**CONI**	conditions in
		CONO	conditions out
COMB	combine	**CO/NO**	current operator-next operator
COML	commercial language		
COMLIB	callable communications facility (PRO 350)	**CONS**	carrier operator noise suppression console
COMM	communication(s)	**CONV**	conversion converter
COMMCEN	communications center		
COMMSWITCH	communications failure detecting and switching equipment	**COP**	console operator package call originating packet (networks) computer optimization package
COMMZ	communications zone		
COMP	comparator composition	**COPE**	communications oriented processing equipment
COMPACT	computerized optimization of microwave passive and active circuits	**COR**	CORAL source program
		CORAL	Computer On-line Real-time Application Language
COMPL	complete	**CORE**	core graphics system
COMPOOL	communications pool		

COS	communications operating system	**CPL**	computer programming language
	commercial operating system		conversational programming language
	class of service (IBM's System Network Architecture)		cross products line (Digital)
		CPLD	coupled
COSBA	a computer services and bureau association	**CPLMT**	complement
		CPM	cards per minute
COSMON	component open/short monitor		8-bit microprocessor operating system
COSTAR	computer stored ambulatory record		Corporate Products Management (Digital)
CP	card punch		control program/microprocessor (used in Digital's ROBIN)
	central processor		critical path method
	clock phase	**CP/M**	control program for microprocessors (used in Digital's ROBIN)
	clock pulse		
	communications processor		
	control panel		
CPA	control bus parity	**CPM**	control program monitor
			cycles per minute
CPC	card-programmed calculator		
	ceramic-wafer printed circuit	**CPR**	certified paths of restraint
	computer process control	**CPRNT**	callable print services (PRO 350)
CPDD	command post digital display		
		CPRS	compress
CPE	central processing element	**CPS**	central processing system
	central programmer and evaluator		characters per second
	control parity error on MASSBUS		circuit pack system
			Computer Performance Products Services group (Digital)
CPEUG	computer performance evaluation users group		Contract Programming Services
CPG	commercial products group		conversational program system
	current pulse generator		Corporate Product Support
CPI	characters per inch		cycles per second
		CPT	compatibility

CPTY	capacity		**CRF**	carrier-frequency telephone repeater
CPU	central processing unit			cross-reference program (MACRO-11)
CQA	corporate quality assurance			cross-reference lister (IAS)
CQG	Corporate Quality Group (Digital)		**CRG**	Corporate Research group
CQT	correct		**CRIL**	CORAL intermediate language
CR	call request		**CRIC**	channel read in counter
	card reader		**CRM**	control RAM memory
	carriage return command register		**CRMR**	continuous-reading meter relay
	command return core		**CRO**	cathode ray oscilloscope
	count reverse		**CROC**	channel read out counter
CRA	Corporate Research and Architecture (Digital)		**CROM**	control read only memory
	control RAM address cyclic response area		**CRP**	capacity requirements planning
CRAM	card random access memory		**CRR**	customer response representative (Digital Field Service)
	card random access method			
CRB	channel request block		**CRS**	command retrieval system
CRC	carriage return contact		**CRT**	cathode ray tube
	control and reporting center cyclic redundancy code		**CRTOG**	cartography
	cyclic redundancy check		**CRTU**	combined receiving and transmitting unit
CRCC	CRC character		**CRYPTO**	cryptographics
CRD	customer runnable diagnostics		**CRYPTONET**	crypto-communications network
CREF	cross-reference table cross reference utility program		**C/S**	characters per second

CS	check sorter circuit schematic (revision or documentation) control signal cycles shift		**CSN**	cartridge serial number
			CSO	chained sequential operation
			CSP	commercial subroutine package
CSA	computing services association Canadian Standards Association		**CSR**	communications status register (VAX) control/status register channel status register customer service representative
CSB	complementary straight binary			
CSC	COBOL source converter CODASYL systems committee		**CSRA**	control and status register address (VAX term)
CSD	constant speed drives		**CSS**	circuit switching service computer special systems
CSE	Central Software Engineering Control Systems Engineering		**CSSE**	Customer Service Systems Engineering
			CSSL	continuous system simulation language
CSECT	control section			
CSG	Commercial Systems group		**CSST**	computer systems sales training
CSI	command string interpreter common systems integration control sequence introducer		**CST**	channel status table core status table
			CSTL	COBOL syntax table language
CSL	computer sensitive language computer simulation language		**CSTSS**	common scheduling telephone status system
CSM	Computer System Manufacturing CSMA carrier sense multiple access		**CSW**	channel status word
			CT	computerized tomography configuration table counter
CSMA/CD	carrier sense multiple access with collision detection		**CTAS**	computer time accounting system

CTC	complementary two's complement counter time circuit	**CTY**	console terminal
		CU	close up control unit
CTCA	Channel and Traffic Control Agency	**CUE**	control unit end
CTE	configuration table entry	**CUG**	closed user group
CTISLS	Corporate Technical Information Systems and Library Services	**CUP**	communications utility program (Tandem)
CTL	checkpointable task list commercial and technical languages complementary transistor logic computer technology limited	**CUPID**	CNP user program I/O directives
		CUR	complex utility routine current
		CUSP	commonly-used system program
CTNE	Compania Telefonica Nacional de Espana	**CUST**	customer
CTOD	controller to drive	**CUSYS**	credit union system
CTP	Creative Typeset and Publishing (Digital, Merrimack) communications test program	**CU WKG**	control unit working
		CV	common version
		CVSD	continuously variable slope delta (modulation technique)
CTRL	control key	**CVSN**	conversion
CTRLR	controller	**CVT**	constant-voltage transformer
CTS	clear to send commercial transaction operating system (CTS-300) communication technology satellite	**CVU**	constant voltage unit
		CW	calls waiting carrier wave clockwise continuous wave control word
CTSS	compatible time-sharing system	**CWP**	communicating word processor
CTT	central trunk terminal		
CTU	central terminal unit	**CWV**	continuous wave video

CX	character transfer	**DAME**	data acquisition and monitoring equipment
CVT	constant voltage transformer	**DAMS**	data access management system (DEC database)
CYBORG	cybernetic organism		
CYCLADES	a French data network	**DAP**	data access protocol
CYC	cycle	**DAR**	data address register
	cyclorama		device address register
CYC-O	cycle ordering	**DART**	direct access remote terminal
DA	data acquisition		
	device adapter	**DAS**	data acquisition system
	differential analyzer		digital analog simulator
	distribution amplifier		digital attenuator system
D/A	digital to analog	**DASD**	direct access storage device
DAA	data access arrangement		
	direct access arrangement	**DAT**	data file
			dynamic address translation
DAC	design augmented by computer	**DATACOM**	data communications
	digital arithmetic center	**DATAI**	data in (see also DATI)
	digital-to-analog converter		
	dynamic amplitude control	**DATAO**	data out (see also DATO)
DACS	data acquisition and control system	**DATAPAC**	a public data network in Canada
	digital access and cross-connect system		packet switching network of the computer communications group of TCTS (Trans-Canada Telephone System)
DACTLU	deactivate logical unit		
DACTPU	deactivate physical unit		
DAFT	dump and fix technique	**DATATRIEVE**	interactive, query, report and data maintenance system
DAGC	delayed automatic gain control		
DAL	DIGITAL authoring language (DIGITAL)	**DATEX-P**	public packet network–West Germany
	DIMENSION authoring language (DIGITAL)	**DATEXP**	latest implementation of DATAPAC
DAM	direct access module	**DATI**	data in (see also DATAI)

DATO	data out (see also DATAO)	**DBRT**	directed beam refresh tube
DATRAN	data transmission corporation (USA)	**DBS**	direct broadcast satellite
		DBTG	data base task group
DAV	data valid	**DBX**	digital branch exchange
DAVFU	direct address vertical format advance unit (part of line printer)	**DC**	data collection data control digital comparator direct current
DB	data base data buffer decibel Deutsche Bundespost (German network) device busy (general networks)	**DCA**	DIGITAL Computers Association distributed communications architecture
		DCAS	data collection and analysis system
dB	decibel	**DCB**	data control block define control block device control block
DBA	data base administrator		
DBC	data byte count		
DBCR	data byte count register	**DCBD**	define control block dummy
DBCS	Data Base Control System	**DCC**	DIGITAL certified courseware
DBD	database description		
DBG	debugging	**DCCU**	data communications control unit
DBGR	debugger	**DCD**	data carrier detected Diode-Capacitor-Diode (gate)
DBL	double		
Dbkey	database key	**DCDR**	decoder
DBM	data base manager	**DCE**	data circuit-terminating equipment data communications equipment
DBMS	data base management system		
DBN	digital business network		
		DCF	document control file
DBO	database operation utility (VAX-11 DBMS)	**DCG**	DIGITAL components group
DBQ	data base query		

DCI	data communications interrogate DIGITAL communications interface	**DCU**	decimal counting unit device control unit digital counting unit disk control unit
DCK	data check	**DCUTL**	direct-coupled unipolar transistor logic
DCL	DIGITAL command language digital control logic	**DCW**	data communication write
DCLN	direct coupled loop network	**DCWV**	direct current working volts
DCN	DIGITAL control number	**DD**	data definition (card) decimal divide digital display double density double diffused dual density
DCNA	data communications network architecture (Japan)		
DCON	Diagnostic CONsole Program		
DCP	dedicated control program device control program digital communications process digital communications protocol (American Bell)	**DDA**	digital differential analyzer
		DDAS	digital data acquisition system
		DDB	device data block
		DDCE	digital data conversion equipment
DCPS	digitally controlled power source	**DDCMP**	Digital Data Communications Message Protocol
DCR	design change recommendation digital conversion receiver	**DDD**	direct distance dialing
DCS	data collection system data control system device control string diagnostic control store DIGITAL classified software	**DDG**	digital display generator
		DDL	data definition language (VAX-11 DBMS) data description language
		DDM	device driver module
DCTL	direct-coupled transistor logic	**DDMF**	distributed data manipulation facility (Datatrieve)
DCTS	data communication terminal system	**DD NAME**	data definition name

DDP	direct data path
	device data block
	device data path
	digital data processor
	distributed data processing
	distributed data processor
DDS	data dictionary system
	data-phone digital service
	digital display scope
DDT	DIBOL debugging technique
	digital data transmitter
	driver data table
	driver dispatch table (VAX term)
	dynamic debugging technique
	dynamic debugging tool
DDX	a Japanese public data network
DE	data entry
	device end
	digital element
DEC	decimal
	decrement
	Digital Equipment Corporation
DECAL	DEC computer assisted instruction authoring language
DEC/CMS	Digital Equipment Corporation/Code Management System
DECnet	DEC networking software
	DIGITAL's Distributed Systems (data network)
DECO	diagnostic engineering change order
DECR	decrement

DECUS	Digital Equipment Computer Users Society
DED	data element dictionary
	double error detection
DEBD	data entry database
DEFT	dynamic error-free transmission
DEL	delay
	delete
DEM	demodulator
DE-ME-DRIVE	decoding memory drive
DEMENTER	design methodology and environment (CMU)
DEMOD	demodulator
DENS	density
DEP	data entry products
	deposit
DEPO	diagnostic engineering patch order
DEPSK	differential-encoded phase shift keying
DEQ	double ended queue
DEQUE	double-ended queue
DEREP	DIGITAL Equipment's Ethernet Repeater
DES	data encryption standard
	data entry sheet
	differential equation solver
	digital expansion system
DESEL	deselect
DET	detection

DETAB	decision table programming language	**DI**	device interconnect dielectric isolation digital input
DEU	data exchange unit	**DIAG**	diagnostic(s)
DEUNA	DIGITAL Equipment UNIBUS Adapter	**DIAL**	digital idle asset listing (DEC database)
DEV	deviation code device	**DIAMAG**	an on-line extension of ALGOL
DF	displacement field fixed head (RF11) disc	**DIAMON**	diagnostic monitor
D-F	direct flow	**DIANE**	a European data network
DFA	digital fault analysis	**DIB**	displacement in block
DFC	disk file check disk file controller display file compiler	**DIBOL**	DIGITAL Business Oriented Language
DFCU	disk file control unit	**DIBS**	DIGITAL integrated business systems
DFG	diode function generator discrete frequency generator	**DIC**	directive identification code (RSX-20F)
DFM	double frame mode	**DICAM**	data interactive communications access method
DFR	disk file read		
DFSU	disk file storage unit	**DICOMP**	DIBOL compiler
DFT	discrete fourier theorem discrete fourier transform	**DICS**	digital information communication system
DFW	disk file write	**DIGICOM**	digital communication system
DG	diode gate	**DIGRM**	digit/record mark
DGT	digit	**DIGRMGM**	digit/record mark group/mark
DGTL	digital		
DHE	data handling equipment	**DIG**	digital image generation
DHSFT	dynamic high speed functional tester	**DIGS**	DIGITAL interest groups

DII	device independent interface (re: graphics standard)	**DIX**	DIGITAL, Intel, Xerox (Ethernet standard)
DIIC	dielectrically isolated integrated circuit	**DJ11**	asynchronous fixed multiplexor
DIL	data interchange library	**DK**	RK05 cartridge disk RK11 disk
DILIC	dual in-line integrated circuit	**DKED**	DIBOL keypad editor
DIMATE	depot installed maintenance automatic test equipment	**DK-NF**	domain key normal form
DIN	national standards organization (Germany)	**DL11**	single line asynchronous interface
DIOB	digital input/output buffer	**DL**	data link delay line diode logic disjunctively linear (logical nets)
DIP	dual in-line package		
DIR	defect investigation report directory file		
DIS	design information system DIBOL instruction set DIGITAL information systems	**DLART**	DL-type asynchronous receiver/transmitter
		DLC	data-link control (module) data-link control (protocol)
DISC	disconnect (bit protocol control)	**DLCC**	data link control chip
DISE	distributed information systems evaluation (DEC)	**DLE**	data-link escape direct line executive
DISG	distributed information systems group (DEC, Merrimack)	**DLI**	data line interface
		DLIMP	descriptive language implemented by macro processor
DISSPLA	display integrated software system and plotting language	**DLL**	down-line (system) loader
		DLM	data link mapping
DIST	distribution	**DLP**	data-link protocol
DIU	data interchange utility	**DLT**	device load table
DIV	divider	**DLX**	direct line access
		DLYNCT	delay count

DM	delta modulation disconnect mode RK06 disk drive	**DMS**	data management software data management system diagnostic mode set dynamic mapping system

DM11	asynchronous
	  programmable multiplexor
	line adaptor or modem
	  control
		DMSS	data multiplex subsystem

		DMT	design maturity test
DMA	direct memory access direct memory address	**DMU**	dictionary management utility
DMAC	direct memory access control	**DMUX**	demultiplex
		DN	down
DMA-INPUT	direct memory access	**DN1**	public data network (Holland)

DMASG	design manufacturing
	  automation steering group
	  (Digital)
		DNA	data not available (VAX)
			DIGITAL Network
			  Architecture
			distributed network
			  architecture

DMC	digital microcircuit		
DMCL	device/media control language		
		DNIC	data network identification code

DME	direct machine environment
	distance measuring
	  equipment
		D-NIM	data-network interface
			  module

DMED	digital message entry device	**DO**	digital output dolly out

DME/P	precision distance
	  measuring equipment
		DOC	data optimizing computer
			drop out compensator
			  (circuit in a VTR or TBC)

DMF	disk management facility		
DML	data manipulation language	**DOCUS**	display oriented computer usage system
DMM	digital multi-meter		
		DOF	degrees of freedom

DMOS	discrete metal oxide
	  semiconductor
	double-diffusion metal oxide
	  semiconductor
		DO/IT	digital output/input
			  translator

		DOL	DEC-O-Log (DIGITAL field service)
DMP	file dump utility	**DOP**	direction of projection

DOS	disk operating system	**DPSS**	data processing subsystem
DP	RP02/3 disk RP02/3/4 disk data processing draft printer dynamic programming	**DPST**	double pole single throw
		DPT	driver-prologue table
		DPU	data processing unit defects per unit
DPAT	device product acceptance test	**DQ11**	full/half duplex synchronous NPR interface
DPB	directive parameter block	**DQM**	data quality monitors
DPCM	differential pulse code modulation	**DR**	data recorder digital resolver drive RM03 disk
DPD	documentation products directory (DIGITAL)		
DPDT	double pole double throw	**D/R**	direct or reverse
DPE	data parity error on MASSBUS data path executive data processing equipment	**DRAM**	dynamic random access memory
		DRAT	device rotational access table
DPG	data processing group digital pattern generator	**DRAW**	direct-read-after-write videodisc
DPL	diagnostic program listing (Digital field service)	**DRC**	design rule checking
		DRG	DECnet review group
DPLX	duplex	**DRI**	database remote interconnect data recording instrument data reduction interpreter
DPM	data path module digital panel meter display processor module		
DPMS	data processing management system	**DRICO**	data recording instrument company
DPN	discrete project number	**DRO**	digital readout
DPR	data position register	**DRS**	diagnostic runtime service
DPS	data processing system	**DRT**	diode recovery tester
DPSK	differential phase shift keying	**DRV**	data recovery vehicle

DRVR	driver	**DSP**	dynamic storage region-pool
DS	RS03/4 disk data set data synchronization data systems	**DSPCH**	dispatch
		DSPLY	display terminal input/output handler
DSA	define symbol address DIGITAL storage architecture – clusters	**DSR**	data set ready (networks) device status register Digital Standard Runoff (text processing utility) dynamic storage region (RSX-11M)
DSB	double sideband		
DSC	disk save and compress		
DSDA	digital switch data service (Bell)	**DSS**	decision support system distributed system
DSDL	data storage description language	**DST**	debug symbol table
DSE	data switching exchange data storage equipment	**DSU**	data synchronization unit device switching unit
DSET	dataset limited	**DSW**	data status word device status word directive status word
DSG	data set group		
DSI	DATATRIEVE security interface	**DT**	data transmission DECtape
DSK	disk-like devices Dvorak's Simplified Keyboard	**DTE**	data terminal equipment DEC Ten/Eleven interface dumb terminal emulator
DSKETS	diskettes	**DTG**	data time group
DSKL	dataskil limited	**DTI**	data terminal interface
DSL	data sublanguage DIGITAL simulation language	**DTL**	data terminal equipment-20 list data terminal loop diode transistor logic
DSM	DIGITAL standard MUMPS	**DTM**	delay timer multiplier
DSME	distributed systems maintainability engineering	**DTMF**	dual-tone multifrequency
		DTN	DIGITAL telephone network
DSN	data set name	**DTP**	directory tape processor

DTR	data terminal ready data transfer rate Datatrieve dead track register digital telemetering register		**DX**	document exchange document transmission duplex floppy disk
DTS	data test data transmission system		**DXC**	data exchange control
			DYANA	dynamics analyzer
DTTU	data transmission terminal unit		**DYSAC**	digitally simulated analog computer
DU11	full/half duplex synchronous interface		**DYSTAL**	dynamic storage allocation language
DUAL	fixed decimal and floating decimal computing system		**E13B**	MICR fount standard (British)
DUDE	development utilities and debugging environment		**EA**	effective address
			EAE	extended arithmetic element
DUP	device utility program diagnostic utilities program (for VAXcluster) duplication		**EAROM**	electrically alterable read only memory
			EAS	external application software
DUT	device under test		**EASL**	external application software library
DV	decimal overflow			
DV11	synchronous multiple line communication processor		**EAT**	editor audit trail
			EAU	erase all unprotected
DVG	digital vector generator		**EBCDIC**	extended binary coded decimal interchange code
DVM	digital voltmeter			
DVST	direct-view storage tube		**EBI**	end-bracket indicator equivalent background input
DVT	design verification test device table		**EBO**	extended bit-map option
DV	digital voice exchange (Wang)		**E BOX**	logic part of CPU (instruction execution unit)
DW	data word buffer		**EBPA**	electron beam parametric amplifier
DWB	designer's workbench			
			EBR	electron beam recording exec base register

EC	emulator control engineering changes error correcting	**ECTL**	emitter-coupled transistor logic
ECAP	electric circuit analysis program	**ED**	edit electronic digital analyzer expansion direction
ECB	event control block exit control block (VAX)	**EDAC**	error detection and correction
ECC	error checking and correction error correcting character error correction circuitry error correction code	**EDC**	error detection code
		EDCW	external device control word
		EDDT	executive dynamic debugging technique
ECDC	electrochemical diffused- collector transistor	**EDG**	European Development Group
ECL	emitter coupled logic	**EDGE**	electronic data gathering equipment
ECLO	emitter-coupled logic operator	**EDHE**	electronic data handling equipment
ECM	electronic countermeasure	**EDI**	Editor (line text) electron diffraction instrument
ECMA	European Computer Manufacturers Association		
ECME	electronic countermeasures equipment	**EDLC**	Ethernet data link control
ECN	Engineering change notice	**EDP**	electronic data processing
ECO	engineering change order (DIGITAL)	**EDPM**	electronic data processing machine
ECOM	electronic computer originated mail	**EDPS**	electronic data processing system
ECPG	error correction pattern generator	**EDS**	exchangeable disc store electronic documentation system (Digital database)
ECR	error correction register	**EDT**	Editor (DIGITAL)
ECS	extended core storage	**EDU**	electronic display unit
ECT	emission computer tomography	**EDVAC**	electronic discrete variable automatic computer

EE	employee expenses	**EKS**	electrocardiogram simulator
EEPROM	electrically erasable programmable read only memory	**ELAN**	Elementary Linguistic Analysis (Gilmour)
EF	extended format	**ELF**	extremely low frequency
EFL	emitter-follower logic	**ELI**	error logging interface
EFN	event flag number	**ELM**	execution level modules (sub-level of a larger system)
EFP	engineers' function processor	**EM**	electronic mail
EFPH	equivalent full power hours		electron microscopy end of medium (or end-of-medium)
EHF	extremely high frequency		
EHQ	European Headquarters	**EMF**	electromotive force
EHV	extra high voltage	**EMMS**	electronic mail and message systems
EIA	Electronic Industries Association	**EMOD**	extended multiply and integerize
EIAJ	Electronic Industries Association of Japan	**EMP**	electromagnetic power electromagnetic pulse
EIES	electronic information exchange system (computer network)	**EMS**	electronic mail system
		EMS-11	editorial management system - PDP-11/70
EIN	European Informatics Network	**EMT**	emulator trap
EIRP	effective incident radiated power	**EMUL**	emulator
EIRS	electronic information retrieval system	**ENA**	enable
		ENGRG	engineering
EIS	end interruption sequence European Information Systems extended instruction set	**ENQ**	end-of-poll/select sequence enquiry
		ENVIR	environment
EJCC	Eastern Joint Computer Conference	**EOA**	end of address

EOB	end of block end of buffer (or end-of-buffer)	**EPLS**	Engineering product library system (DIGITAL)
		EPM	Ethernet protocol manager
EOC	end of conversion	**EPMP**	exec page map page
EOD	end of data (or end-of-data)	**EPO**	emergency power off
EOE	errors and ommissions excepted	**EPP**	electrostatic plotter/printer
EOF	end of file (or end-of-file)	**EPR**	error pattern register
EOH	end of header	**EPROM**	electrically programmable read only memory erasable programmable read-only memory
EOJ	end of job (or end-of-job)		
EOL	end of life (reliability term) end of line (or end-of-line)	**EPS**	European Purchasing System
EOM	end of medium end of message (or end-of-message)	**EPSS**	experimental packet switching system
		EPT	executive page table executive process table
EON	end of number	**EPU**	electrical power unit
EOP	end output	**EQ**	equalizer
EOR	end of run (or end-of-run)	**ER**	error register
EOT	end of tape end of transmission (or end-of-transmission)	**ERA**	error recording area
		ERG	erase gap
EOV	end of volume (or end-of-volume)	**EROM**	erasable read only memory
EP	end of program even parity	**ERP**	effective radiated power
		ERR	error
EPAM	elementary perceiver and memorizer	**ERX**	electronic remote switching
EPC	electronic program control	**ES**	electromagnetic storage
EPD	electrophoretic display	**ESC**	escape or ALT-mode key
EPIC	electronic printer image construction	**ESD**	electronic storage development (DIGITAL)

ESD&P	Educational Service Development & Publishing		**EV**	electron volt
			EVC	network event collector
ESDC	European Software Distribution Centre		**EVL**	event logger
ESE	European Software Engineering		**EXP**	exponent
			EX	execute
ESG	electronic sweep generator		**EXC**	exception
ESI	externally specified indexing		**EXD**	external device
ESP	electrosensitive programming Euronet switching protocol executive mode stack pointer		**EXEC**	TOPS-20 command processor
			EXPLOR	explicitly-defined patterns, local operations, and randomness
ESR	effective signal radiated environment specific routine exception service routine		**EXPN**	expansion
			EXTND	extended data transfer
ESS	electronic switching system		**E/Z**	equals zero
ESSU	electronic selective switching unit		**F11ACP**	Files-11 Ancillary Control Process (VAX term)
EST	estimate		**FA**	formatted ASCII
ESU	electrostatic unit		**F&A**	finance and administration
ETB	end of block test end of transmission block		**FAB**	file access block (VAX term)
			FABS-II	Fast Access B-Tree Structure (data retrieval program for CP/M)
ETIM	elapsed time			
ETL	etched by transmitted light			
ETM	elapsed time meter		**FAC**	facility code file access channel
ETS	electronic transfer system			
ETX	end of text		**FACS**	field administrative and control systems
EUA	erase unprotected to address		**FACT**	fully automatic compiling technique
EURONET	the European data network		**FAL**	file access listener

FAM	fast access memory	**FCP**	file control primitive
FAMOS	floating gate avalanche injection metal ozide semiconductor		file control support Files-11 Ancillary Control Processor (PRO P/OS)
FAP	FORTRAN assembly program	**FCS**	file control services file conversion system first customer ship (DIGITAL) frame checking sequence (polynomial)
FAR	failure analysis report false alarm rate fixed assets registers		
FA&T	final assembly and test	**FCTN**	function
FAX	facsimile	**FCTNL**	functional
FB	foreground/background formatted binary	**FD**	file description frequency divider functional dependency
F/B	foreground/background		
FBC	fully buffered channel	**FDB**	file data block file descriptor block
F BOX	logic part of CPU (floating point)	**FDC**	factory data collection floppy disk controller
FCA	fixed control area	**FDL**	file definition language (DIGITAL)
FC&A	frequency control and analysis	**FDM**	frequency division multiplexing factory data collection
FCB	file control block		
FCC	Federal Communications Commission FCD functional class description functional code descriptor	**FDS**	fixed disc store
		FDT	function decision table (VAX term)
FCDR	failure cause data report	**FDU**	form definition utility
FCI	flux changes per inch	**FDV**	Form Driver
FCO	field change order (DIGITAL) frequency controlled oscillator	**FDX**	full duplex
		FE	format effector framing error (networks)
		FED	Form Editor

FEDS	fixed exchangeable disc store	**FILEX**	file exchange program
FEP	FORTRAN enhancement package front end processor	**FILO**	first in/last out
		FILSYN	filter synthesis program
FET	field-effect transistor	**FIN**	finance
FETP	front end transaction processing	**FINAR**	financial analysis and reporting
FF	form feed	**FIP**	file processor buffering
F-F	flip-flop	**FIS**	floating instruction set
FFT	fast fourier transform	**FIUO**	for internal use only
FG	function generator	**FLBIN**	floating-point binary
FGI	finished goods inventory	**FLDEC**	floating-point decimal
FGN	file generation number	**FLECS**	FORTRAN language with extended control structures
FHDS	fixed head disc store		
FI	fixed interval	**FLK**	first line kit
FIB	file information block focused ion beam equipment	**FLP**	frame level protocol
		FLPL	FORTRAN-compiled list processing language
FIC	first in chain (or first-in-chain)	**FLTG**	floating
FICS	factory information collection system	**FLX**	file transfer utility (VAX/VMS)
FID	Federation International de Documentation field identifier file identification number	**FM**	field merged (FA&T) frequency modulation function management
		FMAINT	file maintenance
FIDIC	International Federation of Consulting Engineers	**FME**	frequency measuring equipment
FIFO	first-in-first-out	**FMEVA**	floating-point means and variance
FILDDT	file dynamic debugging technique		

FMFB	frequency modulation with feedback	**FOSDIC**	film optical sensing device for input to computers
FMS	Forms Management System	**FOT**	fiber optic transceiver
FMS/FDV	forms driver of FMS	**FOT/D**	fiber optic transceiver/double function
FMS/FED	forms editor of FMS		
FMT	format	**FOT/S**	fiber optic transceiver/single function
FMTR	formatter	**FOTP**	file oriented transfer program
FMU	Form Management Utility		
FNB	filename block	**FP**	frame pointer (VAX term) function processor
FO	flash override fiber optic	**FPA**	floating-point accelerator
FOB	free on board	**FPD**	first part done
FOCAL	formula calculator - DIGITAL programming language	**FPG**	free page wait (VAX term)
		FPLA	field programmable logic array
FOCUS	forum of control data users	**FPLS**	field programmed logic sequencer
FOL	fiber optic link		
FOP	flexible option plan	**FPP**	floating-point processor
FOPT	fiber optical photo transfer	**FPROM**	field-programmable read-only memory
FOR	FORTRAN source program		
FOROTS	FORTRAN object time system	**FPS**	floating-point status register
FORMAC	formula manipulation compiler	**FR**	flux reversal
		FRAC	fraction
FORLIB	FORTRAN library	**FREQ**	frequency
FORT	file-oriented transfer program (DEC OS-8) FORTRAN	**FR KIT**	microfiche kit
		FRMR	frame reject
FORTRAN	Formula Translation Language	**FRU**	field replaceable unit

FS	field service fast select floating sign		**FTQ**	file transfer queuer
			FTS	file transfer spooler
FSA	field search argument		**FTSDEQ**	file transfer spooler dequeuer
FSB	forward space block			
FSC	FORTRAN source converter		**FTSQUE**	file transfer spooler request queue
FSCAN	FORTRAN source conversion aid program		**FTU**	file transfer utility
			FU	floating underflow
FSC	FORTRAN source converter		**FUE**	first user evaluation
FSCI	field service contracts invoicing system		**FUNC**	function
FSD	full scale integration		**FUT**	form utility
FSF	forward space file		**FUU**	form upgrade utility
FSI	full system integration		**FVS**	first volume ship
FSK	first site kit frequency shift keying		**FXBIN**	decimal to fixed binary translation
FSL	field service logistics		**FYI**	for your information
FSM	finite state machine		**FY**	fiscal year
FSR	feedback shift register file storage region		**GAR**	group address register
			GASP	general activity simulation program
FT	field test		**GAT**	generalized algebraic translator
FTB	file transfer protocol			
FTC	frequency time control		**GCD**	global common directory
FTH	Federal Institute of Technology		**GCLISP**	Golden Common List Processing language (for DIGITAL Rainbow)
FTL	fixed task list			
FTM	frequency time modulation		**GCML**	get command line
FTN	FORTRAN IV source file extension FORTRAN source file		**GCP**	graphics control processor
			GCR	group code recording

GCS	graphics compatability system	**GIDIS**	general image display instruction set
GCT	Greenwich Civil Time	**GIGI**	graphics image generator and interpreter
GD	gate driver grown diffused	**GIGO**	garbage in garbage out
GDE	general data entry	**GIOS**	graphics input/output system
GDI	graphics design/illustrator	**GIPSY**	general information processing system
GDO	grid-dip oscillator		
GDOS	graphics disk operating system (for CP/M)	**GIS**	general information systems government information systems
GDS	graphic data system		
GDU	graphics display unit	**GKG**	gold key groups (local DIGITAL WPS users groups)
GECOM	generalized compiler		
GEMS	a semi-automated process of digitizing printed circuit layout	**GKS**	graphical kernel system (graphics standard)
		GLIDE	graphical language for interactive design
GEORGE	general organizational operating environment	**GLOBECOM**	global communications
GFD	group file directory	**GLOSS**	a graphical design language
GFI	general format identifier	**GN**	get next
GFS-11	a general financial system	**GND**	get network data
GHZ	Gigahertz (a billion cycles per second)	**GNP**	get next within parent (IMS)
GIA	General International Area (DIGITAL)	**GOR**	general operational requirement
		GP	general purpose
GIDE	Guide to Instructional Development and Evaluation	**GPAC**	general purpose analog computer
GIDEP	government-industry data exchange program	**GPC**	general peripheral controller general purpose computer

GPDC	general purpose digital computer	**GTS**	Global Telecommunications System
GPIB	general purpose interface bus	**GTWY**	gateway (DECnet interface to other network)
GPI/O	general purpose input/output	**GU**	guide unique (IMS)
GPL	generalized programming language	**GUIDE**	guidance for users of integrated data-processing equipment
GPM	general purpose macrogenerator	**GUP**	graphics utility package
GPO	graphics processor option (DEC VT-100)	**GZ KIT**	a documentation kit
		HA	half add
GPR	general purpose registers	**HAL**	house-programmed array logic
GPSS	general purpose simulation system	**HAR**	head address register
GRAF	graphic additions to FORTRAN	**HASP**	Houston Automatic Spooling Program
GRAIL	Greeley's Authoring Language	**HB**	high band
		HC	handling capacity
GRASP	graphical scheduling prototype	**HCP**	hard copy printer
GSAM	generalized sequential access method	**HD**	high definition high density
GSD	global section descriptor	**HDA**	head/disc assembly (as in Winchester disc)
GSI	grand scale integration	**HDAM**	hierarchical direct access method
GST	global symbol table (VAX term)		
GSX	graphics software extension (Digital Research Inc.)	**HDDS**	high density data system
		HDI	head to disk interference
GT	graphics terminal gate	**HDLC**	high-level, data-link control (bit protocol)
GTP	general test program	**HDLG**	handling

HDR	header	**HLSE**	high level, single ended
HDW	hardware	**HLT**	halt
HDX	half duplex	**HMOS**	high density or high speed metal oxide semiconductor
HEM	hybrid electromagnetic wave	**HNDBK**	handbook
HEMT	high-electron-mobility transistor	**HNDLR**	handler
HEP	heterogeneous element processor (Denelcor)	**HO**	high order
		HOL	high order language
HEX	hexadecimal (numbering system - base or radix 16)	**HOP**	routing layer - logical distance between two adjacent nodes
HI	human interface (VAXstation)	**HOSS**	home office software support
HIB	hibernate (VAX term)	**HP**	Hewlett-Packard high pass filter host to printer
HICS	hardware inventory control system		
HIDAM	hierarchical indexed direct access method	**HPCB**	hardware process control block (VAX term)
HIM	host interface module	**HPF**	highest possible frequency
HIP	host interface processor	**HS**	half subtract high speed
HIPO	hierarchical input-process-output (an IBM documentation method)	**HSAC**	high speed analog computer
		HSAM	hierarchical sequential access method
HISAM	hierarchical indexed sequential access method	**HSC**	hierarchical storage controller
HLD	host task loader		
HLI	hold last image (VAX term)	**HSCCU**	high-speed cluster control unit
HLL	high-level language	**HSDA**	high-speed data acquisition
HLR	handler	**HSI**	hardwired serial interface
HLS	high-level scanner		

HSM	high-speed memory	**IAS**	interactive application system
HSP	high-speed printer		
HSR	high-speed reader	**IASCOM**	time-sharing data structures library
HSS	high-speed scanner	**IBG**	installed base group (DIGITAL Sales) inter-block gap
HT	horizontal tabulator		
HTDVR	host terminal driver	**IBM**	International Business Machines
HTL	high threshold logic		
HTTL	high power transistor-transistor logic	**I BOX**	logic part of CPU (instruction address area)
HV	high voltage	**IC**	input circuit instruction counter insert cursor integrated circuit
HVPS	high voltage power supply		
HVRC	header vertical redundancy check	**I&C**	installation and checkout
HW	hardware	**ICA**	international computer association
HY	Henry (unit of electrical inductance)	**ICAPS**	integrated composition and pagesetting system
HYCOTRAN	hybrid computer translator (language)	**ICB**	ionized cluster beam (IC manufacturing technique)
HZ	hertz (cycles per second)	**ICC**	International Computer Center
I	symbol for electrical current		
IA	indirect addressing international alphabet	**ICCC**	International Computer Communications Conference
IADR	invalid address		
IAL (or ALGOL)	international algebraic language	**ICCE**	International Council for Computers in Education
IAM	indexed access method	**ICCN**	industrial computer controller networks
IAOR	international abstracts in operations research	**ICCS**	intercomputer communication switch (same as CI)
IAR	instruction address register		

ICD	IVIS course development	**IDC**	integrated disk controller
ICE	in-circuit emulator input checking equipment integrated communications executive (networks)	**IDEA**	interactive design and engineering analysis
		IDECUS	internal DEC users society
ICF	intercommunication flip-flop	**IDF**	integrated data file
ICFC	Industrial and Commercial Finance Company	**IDFT**	inverse discrete Fourier transform
ICIP	International Conference on Information Processing	**IDI**	improved data interchange
		IDMS	integrated data base management system
ICL	International Computers Limited	**IDN**	integrated digital network
ICON	a programming language	**IDP**	integrated data processing
ICOT	Institute for New Generation Computer Technology (Japan)	**IDS**	image display system integrated data store
ICP	installation certification procedure installation checkout procedure	**IDT**	intelligent diagnostic tool
		IE	industrial engineering
		IEC	International Electrotechnical Commission
ICT	in-circuit tester	**IEE**	Institution of Electrical Engineers (Britain)
IC/T	integrated computer/telemetry	**IEEE**	Institute of Electrical and Electronics Engineers
ICW	interrupted continuous wave		
ID	identification	**IF**	intermediate frequency
IDA	interconnect device arrangement	**IFAB**	internal file-access block
IDACS	industrial data acquisition and control system	**IFIP**	International Federation for Information Processing
IDB	index descriptor block interrupt data block interrupt dispatch block	**IFL**	indexed file load
		IFR	internal function register
IDBM	internal database management	**IFRU**	interference rejection unit

IGES	initial graphics exchange specification (or system)	**IMS**	information management system
IGFET	insulated gate field-effect transistor	**IMS/VS**	information management system/virtual storage
IGU	image generator unit	**INB**	intermediate buffering switch
IHF	inhibit halt flip-flop	**INCRMTL**	incremental
IHS	information handling service	**INCYTE**	in-process, computer-aided, yield, tracking and evaluation (process control system)
IHU	intelligent head unit		
IIL	integrated injection logic		
ILD	injection laser diodes	**INDAC**	industrial data acquisition language
ILE	interface latch element		
ILF	illegal function	**INFINET**	integrated factory information network (a factory data collection system developed from MEIS)
ILOG	intelligent logistics assistant		
ILR	illegal register		
ILS	insertion loading system		
ILSW	interrupt level status word	**INFO**	information
IM	intermodulation distortion	**INIT**	initialize input/output
IMACS	intelligent management assistance for computer systems (DIGITAL)	**INITS**	initialize self
		INQ	inquire
		INST	installation
IMC	image motion compensation	**INSTL**	installation
IMD	instructional media development	**INSTR**	instructor
		INT	interrupt
IMDD	instructional media design and development	**INTA**	interactive
		INTCON	international connection
IMIS	integrated management information system	**INTEC**	interference
IMP	image memory processor interface message processor (ARPAnet)	**INTELSAT**	International Telecommunications Satellite Consortium

INTELPOST	international electronic post	**IOX**	input/output executive
INTG	integrated INTL internal	**IPA**	ICCS port adapter intermediate power amplifier
INTPR	interpreter	**IPB**	inter-processor buffer
INTRO	introduction	**IPC**	industrial process control information processing center
INV	inverter		
INWG	inter-network working group	**IPCF**	inter-process communication facility
I/O	input/output	**IPD**	insertion phase delay
IOB	input/output buffer	**IPE**	interpret parity error
IOC	input/output controller	**IPG**	International Products Group (DIGITAL)
IOCB	input/output control block		
IOCC	input/output control center	**IPL**	information processing language initial program loading inter processor link interrupt priority level (VAX term)
IOCS	input/output control system		
I/OM	input/output multiplexer		
IOO	input/output operation		
IOP	input/output processor	**IPL/V**	information processing language V
IOPS	input/output programming system	**IPM**	impulses per minute incidental phase modulation
IOR	input/output register	**IPR**	impostor pass rate
IORB	I/O request block	**IPS**	inches per second
IOREQ	input/output request	**IPSS**	international public switched service
IOSB	input/output status block		
IOT	input/output transfer input/output trap	**IPSSB**	information processing systems standards board
IOTA	information overload testing apparatus	**IQL**	interactive query language
		IR	information retrieval instruction register intervention required
IOU	immediate operation use		

IRAB	internal record access block	**ISDN**	integrated services digital network
IRC	international record carrier	**ISECT**	image section (VAX term)
IRG	interrecord gap	**ISG**	information systems group
IRIA	Institut de Recherche d'Informatique et d'Automatique	**ISI**	internally specified index interstimulus-interval mode (method of time-data sampling)
IRIS	interactive real-time information system		
IRL	information retrieval language	**ISIT**	intensified silicon intensifier target
IRM	information and record management	**ISL**	integrated Schottky logic interactive system language
IRP	input/output request packet (VAX term)	**ISM**	intermediate storage module
		ISO	International Standards Organization individual system operation
IRQ	input/output queue		
IR	internal rate of return	**ISP**	interrupt stack pointer (VAX term) instruction set processor
IRS	interchange record separator		
IRUS	independent RSTS users society	**ISR**	interrupt service routine (VAX term) information storage and retrieval
IS	interrupt stack (VAX term) information systems		
ISA	interrupt storage area integrated systems architecture intelligent scheduling assistant (DIGITAL)	**ISS**	internal special systems (DIGITAL)
		ISSG	internal software support group
		ISTAB	international systems technical advisory board (of ANSI)
ISAM	indexed sequential access method integrated switching and multiplexing		
		ISW	initial storage write (block)
ISD	image section descriptor instructional systems design	**ISWS**	internal software services (DIGITAL)
IS&D	integrate sample and dump		

IT	internal translator - early language for math computations	**JDC**	job description card
ITA	international telegraph alphabet	**JEDEC**	Joint Electronic Devices Engineering Council
ITB	intermediate text block	**JEIDA**	Japan Electronics
ITI	interactive terminal interface	**JEPIA**	Japan Electronic Parts Industry Association
ITP	interactive terminal protocol	**JDM**	Jackson design method
ITPD	interconnect technology and process development (DIGITAL)	**JFET**	junction field-effect transistor
ITS	interactive troubleshooting simulator (DIGITAL)	**JGN**	junction gate number
		JI	junction isolation
ITT	International Telephones and Telecommunications	**JIAC**	Joint Automatic Control Conference (ISA, IEEE, AIAA)
ITU	International Telecommunications Union	**JIS**	Japanese Industrial Standard job information station
ITX	intermediate text block	**JOD**	COBOL journal of development
IV	integer overflow		
IVIS	interactive video information system	**JOHNNIAC**	John von Neumann's Integrator and Automatic Computer
IVP	installation verification procedure	**JOVIAL**	Jules' (Schwartz) own version of international algebraic language
I&W	installation and warranty		
JA	jump address	**JPW**	job processing word
JAWS	Josephson Atto-Weber Switch (superconducting logic gate)	**JTIDS**	joint tactical information distribution system
		JUG	joint users group
JCL	job control language	**JV**	journal voucher
JCS	job control sheet		
JD	join dependency		

K	kilo (1000) kilo (1024 when referring to memory) Kelvin	**KIPS**	knowledge information processing systems
		KLAD	KL acceptance diagnostic
KA	Kanata Backplane Manufacturing (Ontario, Canada)	**KL COMP**	KL 10 compatibility
		KLDCP	KL 10 diagnostic console program
KB	keyboard	**KLDDT**	KL 10 dynamic debugging technique
KBD	keyboard		
KBL	keyboard listener	**KLNIK**	KL integrated network for investigation and correction
KBS	Knowledge Based Simulation (CMU)		
KC	kilocycle	**KL REV**	KL 10 revision control
KCB	kilo-core tick	**KMON**	keyboard monitor
KCC	keyboard common contact	**KMS**	keysort multiple selectors (telephone term)
KC/S	kilocycle per second	**KP**	key pulsing
KCS	1000 characters per second	**KPC**	keyboard priority controller
KDA	KMX microcode dump analyzer	**KRL**	knowledge representation language
KDD	Kokusai Denshin Denwa Co. Ltd (Japan networks)	**KS COMP**	KS 10 compatibility
		KS REV	KS 10 revision control
KDS	key display system	**KSP**	kernel mode stack pointer
KDSS	key-to-disk subsystem	**KSR**	keyboard send/receive keyboard send/receive hardcopy terminal
KE11-A	extended arithmetic element		
KE11-E	extended instruction set option	**KT11-D**	memory management unit
KE11-F	floating-point option	**KTR**	keyboard typing reperforator
KED/EDT	keypad mode of EDT	**KV**	kilovolt
KEYB	keyboard	**KW**	kilowatt
KHZ	kilohertz	**KW11**	clock

KWIC	keyword in context	**LBR**	labor
			librarian utility
KWOC	keyword out of context		library management utility
L	inductance	**LC**	level control
			line connector
LA	link allotter		local currency
			location counter (IBM)
LAB	laboratory		logical channel (networks)
LADS	local area data service	**LCB**	line control block
LADT	local area data transport	**LCCH**	logical communication channel handler
LAMA	local automatic message accounting (telephone term)	**LCD**	liquid crystal display
		LCDTL	load compensated diode transistor logic
LAN	local area networking		
LAP	link access protocol	**LCEG**	large computer engineering group
LAPB	link access protocol B	**LCG**	large computer group
LAPUT	light-activated programmable unijunction transistor	**LCGN**	logical channel group number
LARCT	last radio contact	**LCN**	logical channel number
			local computer network
LASCAR	light-activated silicon controlled rectifier		low cost Nebula (VAX 11/720)
LASER	light amplification by the stimulated emission of radiation	**LCP**	LAT (local area transport) control program
			logical (laws of) construction of programs
LAT	local area transport (protocol - as in LAT-11)	**LCS**	large capacity storage
			large core storage
LATA	local access transport area (telephone term)		logical (laws of) construction of systems
LB	library file pseudo device	**LCU**	line control unit
	line buffer	**LCV**	last character viewed
LBN	logical block number (VAX term)	**LD**	logic driver

LDB	large data buffer logical database	**LGC**	logic
LDBR	logical database record	**LGN**	line gate number
LDDS	low density data system	**L/H**	low to high
LDE	linear differential equations	**LI**	line item
LD EN	load enable	**LIB**	library
LDF	linear (segmented) display file	**LIC**	last in chain (or last-in-chain) linear integrated circuit
LDP	Laboratory Data Products (DIGITAL)	**LICIL**	linked core image library
LDPE	low density polyethylene	**LICOF**	land lines communications facilities
LDPG	laboratory data products group	**LIF**	line item forecasting
LDR	loader	**LIFO**	last-in-first-out
LDRI	low data rate input	**LIM**	limit
LDT	logic design translator	**LIMS**	laboratory information management system
LDX	long distance xerography	**LIMS/SM**	laboratory information management system/sample management
LEAS	lower echelon automatic switchboard		
LEBC	low end business center (DIGITAL)	**LIMS/IM**	laboratory information management system/instrument management
LED	light emitting diode		
LEF	local event flag (VAX term)	**LIN**	line watcher
LES	layered environment services	**LINAC**	linear accelerator
LET	logical equipment table	**LINC**	laboratory instrument computer
LF	line feed low frequency	**LIOCS**	logical input/output control system
LFU	least frequently used	**LIPS**	logical inferences per second
LG	line generator		

LIS	large interactive surface	**LOTIS**	logic, timing, sequencing – programming language
LISP	list processing language		
LKR	linker	**LOU**	level of urgency
LLC	logical link control (module)	**LP**	line printer linear programming
LLDPE	linear low density polyethylene	**LPC**	linear predictive coding linear power controller
LLL	low-level logic	**LPD**	layered environment services process descriptor
LLTV	low light level television		
LM/F	low and medium frequency	**LPE**	local procedure error
LMLR	load memory lockout register	**LPG**	laboratory products group
LN	line	**LPL**	local processor link
LNA	low noise amplifier	**LPM**	lines per minute
LNK	linker	**LPS**	laboratory peripheral system lines per second
LNT	logical name table	**LPT**	line printer
LO	local oscillator	**LPTTL**	low-power transistor-transistor logic
LOC	location		
LOCAL	load on call	**LPTV**	low power television
LOC/MS	location code/mail stop	**LPU**	line protocol unit
LOG	logarithm	**LQP**	letter quality printer
LOGANDS	logical commands	**LR**	level recorder limited release
LOGRAM	logical program		
LOLITA	language for the on-line investigation and transformation	**LRC**	longitudinal redundancy check
		LRCC	longitudinal redundancy check character
LOO	loopback tester		
LOS	level of service level of support loss of signal	**LRD**	long range data
		LRIM	long range input monitor

LRP	long range planning	**LTPD**	lot tolerance percent defective
LRS	long range search		
LRU	least recently used	**LTTL**	low power transistor-transistor logic
LS	LASER System line spacing	**LTU**	line termination unit
LSA	line-sharing adaptor	**LU**	logical unit (IBM's SNA)
LSB	least significant bit left side bearing	**LUB**	line unit bus
		LUG	logical users group
LSBY	least significant byte	**LUN**	logical unit number
LSC	least significant character	**LUSTAT**	logical unit status
LSD	large systems diagnostics least significant digit lost servo data	**LUT**	logical unit table look up table
		LV	low voltage
LSG	large systems group	**LVCD**	least voltage coincidence detection
LSI	large scale integration		
LSI/SEG	Large Scale Integration/Semiconductor Engineering Group	**LWR**	loop write to read
		M	mega memory meter 1000
LSM	large systems marketing		
LSN	TLK servier (listen) utility	**MA**	memory address
LSP-11	Laboratory Subroutine Package	**MAC**	multi access computing MACRO assembler MACRO source program MACRO-11 assembly call
LSR	line service routines		
LSS	low speed scanner		
LSSB	local storage skew buffer	**MACREL**	DIGITAL Macro Assembler Language (produced relocatable modules for PDP-8)
LSSG	laboratory systems support group (DIGITAL)		
LST	listing file	**MACRO**	macroinstruction
LT	LINC tape	**MACRO-10**	assembly language for DECsystem-10/20
LTC	line time clock		

MACRO-11	assembly language for PDP-11	**MB**	megabyte memory buffer mother board
MAD	multiaperature device	**M-B**	make-break
MADT	microalloy diffused base transistor	**MBA**	MASSBUS adaptor
MAG	magnetic	**MBB**	make before break
MAGCARD	magnetic card	**MBC**	MASSBUS controller
MANIAC	mechanical and numerical integrator and computer	**MBE**	molecular beam epitaxy (IC microfabrication tool)
MANOP	manual operation	**MBI**	MASSBUS interface
MAP	macro arithmetic processor manufacturing automation program mathematical analysis without programming memory access processor message acceptance pulse memory allocation map	**MBM**	magnetic bubble memory
		M BOX	logical part of CPU (cache and paging)
		MBQ	modified binary code
		MBR	memory buffer register
		MBR-E	memory buffer register-even
MAPPS	Management and Project Planning System	**MBR-O**	memory buffer register-odd
MAR	a MACRO-32 source program memory address register	**MBUSS**	MASSBUS
		MBZ	must be zero (VAX term)
MARS	memory address register storage	**MC**	megacycle
MARTEC	Martin thin-film electronic circuit	**MCA**	Motorola Macro Cell Array (Motorola Corp.)
MAS	manufacturing applied systems	**MCB**	module control block multifunction communication bus (networks) multifunction communication base
MAST	modular approach to system test		
MAT	marketing acceptance test microally transistor	**MCC**	multi-component circuits
		MCCU	multi-channel communications control unit

MCD	Micro Systems Development	**MDG**	market development group (DIGITAL)
MCH	machine check handler	**MDIOC**	multi device input/output channel
MCI	Microwave Communications Inc. (USA)	**MDL**	Maynard definition language (DIGITAL)
MCIS	Marlboro Cluster Information Systems	**MDIOC**	multi device input/output channel
MCIU	multi-channel interface unit		
MCMP	Multichip Micropackaging Project (DIGITAL)	**MDP**	Medical Data Products (DIGITAL)
MCP	macrocode control program master control program	**MDR**	memory data register multichannel data recorder
MCR	master control routine magnetic character reader monitor console routine (VAX/VMS)	**MDS**	microprocessor development system minimum discernible signal modular data system
MCS	master control system message control system multipurpose communications and signaling	**MDSG**	micro development systems group (DIGITAL)
		MDT	modified data tag microprogram debugging tool mean down time
MCU	microprogram control unit		
MCW	modulated continuous wave	**MDTI**	multi-stream data transmission interface
MD	memory date message data micro diagnostic dispatcher multi density	**MDTS**	modular data transaction system
		ME	molecular electronics
M-D	modulation-demodulation	**M&E**	manufacturing and engineering
MDAC	multiplying digital-to-analog converter	**MED**	medium
MDC	manufacturing distribution control	**MEDLARS**	Medical Literature Analysis and Retrieval System
MDE	microcomputer development environment	**MEDLINE**	MEDLARS On-Line System

MEEP	microprogrammed emulation environment package	**MFS**	magnetic tape field search
MEG	maintainability engineering group	**MFSK**	multiple frequency-shift keying
MEIS	manufacturing engineering information systems	**MFT**	1000 ft. multiprogramming with a fixed number of tasks
MEM	memory	**MHL**	microprocessor host loader
MEMISTOR	memory resistor storage device	**MHZ**	megahertz (1 million cycles per second)
MEPS	monotone electronic prepress systems	**MI**	memory interconnect
MER	minimum energy requirements	**MIB**	memory image builder
MESFET	metalized semiconductor field effect transistor	**MIC**	middle in chain (or middle-in-chain) macro interpretive commands microwave integrated circuit
MESUCORA	Association for Measurement, Control, Regulation and Automation	**MICR**	magnetic ink character recognition
MEV	Manufacturing Engineering Videotext (DIGITAL database)	**MICRO**	one millionth microcomputer
MF	medium frequency	**MIDAC**	Michigan Digital Automatic Compiler
MFC	magnetic-tape field scan microfunctional circuit	**MIL**	one thousandth of an inch
MFD	master file directory microfarad (unit of electrical capacitance)	**MIMD**	multi-instruction multiple data stream multiprocessor
MFG	manufacturing	**MIMIC**	a major simulation package
MFKP	multifunctional key pulsing	**MIMR**	magnetic-ink mark recognition
MFM	modified frequency modulation	**MIN**	minimum
MFPR	move from process register (VAX term)	**MINC**	calculator system (scientific) modular instrument computer

MINI	minicomputer	**MLR**	memory lockout register
MINMAX	minimum value of CORMAX	**MM**	magnetic tape (TU16, TE16, TU45) millimeter main memory
MIPS	million instructions per second		
MIR	memory information register	**MMA**	multiple module access
MIS	management information systems medical information systems metal insulator semiconductor	**MMD**	moving map display
		MME	memory mapping enable (VAX term)
		MMG	Mini-Micro Group (DIGITAL)
MISAR	finance and administration system	**MMIC**	monolithic microwave integrated circuits
MISC	miscellaneous	**MMS**	manufacturing management system module management system (VAX-11 DEC/MMS – part of UNIX; UNIX is a trademark of Bell Labs)
MISG	Management Information Services Group		
MK	manual clock		
MKS	meter kilogram second		
ML	mailing list memory location machine language	**MMU**	memory management unit
		MNC	MINC
		MNOS	metal-nitride-oxide semiconductor
MLA	microprocessor language assembler		
MLB	multilayer board	**MNT**	module name table
MLC	multiline controller	**MO**	message output pseudo device master oscillator
MLD	microprogram loader		
MLE	microprocessor language editor	**MOCVD**	metal-organic chemical vapor deposition
MLI	marker light indicator	**MOD**	modulation module
MLP	Maynard list price		
MLPWB	multilayer printed wiring board	**MODAM**	module amender
		MODEM	modulator demodulator
		MODLIST	module lister

MOE	measure of effectiveness
MOF	master order form
MOL	machine oriented language
MONOS	monitor out of service
MONSTR	monitor for software trouble reporting
MOP	multiple on-line programming maintenance operation protocol (DECnet)
MOPA	master oscillator power amplifier
MOPB	manually operated plotting board
MOREPS	monitor station reports
MOS	metal oxide semiconductor
MOSAIC	Motorola oxide self-aligned implanted circuit (Motorola Corp.)
MOSFET	metal oxide semiconductor field-effect transistor
MP	mathematical programming memory parity microprocessor
MPA	multipartition adaptor
MPC	multi-project chips
MPG	microprocessor products group microwave pulse generator
MPOE	multi-programming overlaid executive

MPP	massively parallel processor message processing program
MPS	micro processing systems megabytes per second
MPT	microprogramming tools
MPU	microprocessor unit
MPX	multiplex
MQ	multiplier quotient
MQR	multiplier quotient register
MR	memory register
MRG	medium range
MRL	memory required list memory request list
MRN	maximum record number
MRP	materials requirement planning
MRP II	manufacturing resource planning
MRU	most recently used
MS	mean square memory system millisecond
MSB	most significant bit mark sense batch
MSBY	most significant byte
MSC	mass storage control
MSC/ NASTRAN	general purpose finite element analysis program
MSCP	mass storage control protocol

MSCS	mass storage control system	**MTBI**	mean-time between incidents
MSD	mass storage device most significant digit modem sharing device (networks)	**MTCU**	magnetic tape control unit
		MTD	mass tape duplicator/verifier month-to-date
MSDB	main storage database	**MTDP**	magtape diagnostic package
MS/DOS	microsoft disk operating system	**MTE**	multi track error
MSG	medical systems group message	**MTH**	multiple terminal handler
MSGMESH	mesh generating program	**MTICA**	multi-terminal integrated communications adaptor
MSGREC	message and recovery	**MTIOC**	multi-terminal input/output channel
MSGSER	message service	**MTL**	merged transistor logic
MSI	medium scale integration	**MTP**	modular terminal processor
MSK	mask	**MTPR**	move to process register (VAX term)
MSM	message switching multiplexer	**MTR**	mean-time of recovery
MSS	medium speed scanner	**MTS**	message transport service multi-terminal system
MST	macro symbol table		
MSW	machine status word	**MTT**	magnetic tape terminal
MT	magnetic tape	**MTTD**	mean-time to diagnose
MTAC	mathematical tables and other aids to computation	**MTTF**	mean-time to failure
		MTTI	mean-time to install mean-time to isolate
MTAACP	magnetic tape ancillary control process (VAX term)	**MTTR**	mean-time to repair
MTBB	mean-time between breakdowns	**MTU**	multiplexer and terminal unit
		MTUP	message text update
MTBC	mean time between calls	**MU**	machine unit
MTBF	mean-time before failure mean-time between failure	**MUF**	maximum usable frequency

MUG	MUMPS user group	**NBA**	narrow band allocation
MUL	message usage list	**NBCD**	natural binary-coded decimal
MUMPS	Massachusetts General Hospital Utility Multi-Programming System	**NBCH**	natural binary-coded hexadecimal
MUTEX	mutual exclusion semaphore	**NBFM**	narrow band frequency modulation
MUX	multiplexer multi-terminal emulator	**NBS**	National Bureau of Standards
MUX-ARO	multiplex-automatic error correction	**NC**	no connection
MV	millivolt	**N/C**	numerical control
MVL	magnetic tape volume list	**NCA**	non-contiguous array (data type)
MVS	multiple virtual storage	**NCB**	network connect block
MVT	multiprogramming with a variable number of tasks	**NCC**	network control centre (networks) National Computer Centre
MW	megawatt milliwatt	**NCM**	node control module
MWI	message waiting indicator	**NCP**	network control processor network control program
MXCU	multiplexor channel control unit	**NCP/VS**	network control program/virtual storage
MXR	mask index register	**NCR**	National Cash Register
N	nano (1 × 10E-9)	**NCU**	network control utility
NACK	negative acknowledgement	**ND**	no detect
NAK	negative acknowledgement	**NDA**	network crash dump analyzer
NAL	new assembly language	**NDC**	normalized device coordinates
NAM	name block (VAX term)		
NAND	Not AND (Boolean Operator)	**NDC**	normalized device coordinates
NAU	network addressable unit (IBM's SNA)	**NDCS**	normalized device coordinate space
NB	narrow band		

NDE	nonlinear differential equations	**NFT**	network file transfer
NDN	Nordic Data Network	**NG**	no good
NDRO	nondestructive readout	**NI**	Network Interconnect (Ethernet) network inferface
NDT	nondestructive testing		
NEC	national electrical code	**NIA**	network interface adaptor
NEG	negative	**NIB**	noninterference basis
NELIAC	Navy Electronics Laboratory International ALGOL Compiler	**NIC**	not in contact
		NICE	network information and control exchange
NES	not elsewhere specified	**NIM**	network interface module
NET	network	**NIPO**	negative input positive output
NETACP	network ancillary control process (VAX term)	**NL**	new line
NETEX	network exerciser	**NLP**	natural language processor
NETPAN	network panic dump routine	**NLR**	noise load ratio
NETS	networks	**NLS**	no load speed
NEXM	non-existant memory	**NM**	not measured
NEXT	near end crosstalk loss	**NMC**	network measurement centre
NEXUS	synchronous backplane interconnect interface logic	**NMDVR**	network measurement device driver
NF	normal frequency	**NME**	noise measuring equipment
NFAR	network file access routine	**NML**	network management listener
NFB	negative feedback		
NFG	not first grade	**NMM**	network management module
NFP	not file protected	**NMOS**	N-channel metal oxide semiconductor
NFQ	night frequency		
NFRU	non-field replaceable unit	**NMR**	nuclear magnetic resonance

NMS	network management system	**NR**	noise ratio
NMVACP	network management volatile ACP	**NRC**	NRZI read clock
		NR KIT	update microfiche kit
NO	normally open	**NRL**	new relocatable language
NOE	network operating environment	**NRZ**	non-return to zero
		NRZ-C	non-return to zero-change
NONSTD	non standard	**NRZI**	non-return to zero indiscrete non-return to zero inverted
NOP	no operation		
NO-OP	no operation	**NRZ-M**	non-return to zero-mark
NOR	normalize Not OR (Boolean Operator)	**NS**	nanosecond
		NSA	non-sequenced acknowledgement (bit protocol control)
NOS	not otherwise specified		
NOT	inverting gate (Boolean Operator)	**NSC**	network switching centre noise suppression circuit
NP/1	new program language	**NSD**	no significant difference
NPG	non processor grant	**NSDVR**	network services driver
NPH	nine-thousand remove protocol handler	**NSEC**	nanosecond
NPL	a datagram (networks) National Physical Laboratory	**NSI**	non-sequenced information (bit protocol control)
NPM	counts per minute	**NSP**	network services protocol
NPN	a type of transistor with N-type and P-type silicon areas	**NSR**	nine-thousand remove service routine
		NSV	nonautomatic self-verification
NPR	non-processor request		
NPS	counts per second	**NT**	no transmission
NPU	natural processing unit	**NTD**	network display utility
NPV	net present value net present volume	**NTDEMO**	network display server task
		NTI	noise transmission impairment

NTR	nine-thousand remove	**OBJ**	object object module file
NTS	network test system		
NTSC	National Television System Committee	**OBM**	OFIS base machine
		OC	operation check
NTT	Nippon Telegraph and Telephone Public Service - Japan	**O/C**	open circuit
		OCAL	on-line cryptanalytic aid language
NTU	network termination unit		
NUI	network user identification	**OCF**	operator communications file
NVDRV	network virtual terminal driver	**OCO**	open-close-open contact
NVE	numeric valued expression	**OCP**	operator control panel order code processor output control pulses
NVM	nonvolatile memory		
NVP	network verification program utility	**OCR**	optical character recognition
		OCT	octal
NVR	nonvolatile memory	**OD**	outside diameter
NVRAM	nonvolatile random access memory	**ODL**	overlay description language
		ODS	on-disk structure (system) output data strobe
NVT	network virtual terminal		
NXDRV	network direct line access driver	**ODT**	on-line debugging technique on-line debugging tool
NXF	nonexecutable function	**OEM**	original equipment manufacturer other equipment manufacturer
NXM	nonexistent memory		
NZDOM	New Zealand Department of Health (software)		
		OF	operational fixed
OA	office automation order administration	**OFAL**	OFIS authoring language
		OFC	optimising FORTRAN compiler
OAI	order administration accounting interface		
		OFIS	DIGITAL office architecture
OAS	order administration system	**OFLNE**	off-line

O/H	overhead	**OPP**	opposite
OIC	only in chain (or only-in-chain) OIS office information systems	**OPR**	operator command language optical pattern recognition
OL	overlap	**OPRG**	operating
O/L	operations/logistics	**OPS**	on-line process simulator operations option panel space
OLA	on-line assistance		
OLB	object library file extension	**OPS COMM**	operations committee
OLBS	on-line budgeting system	**OPSUM**	optional summary (DIGITAL)
OLC	outgoing line circuit	**OPT**	option
OLRT	on-line real time	**OPTCL**	optical
OM	operations maintenance	**OPTUL**	optical pulse transmitter using LASER
O&M	organization and methods	**OR**	Boolean Operator operations research
OMNIBUS	synchronous bus for PDP-8s		
OMR	optical mark reader	**O/R**	on request
ONLNE	on-line	**ORACLE**	on-line inquiry and report generator
OOPS	off-line operating simulator	**ORD**	optical rotary dispersion
OP	odd parity operation optical	**ORDVAC**	ordinance variable automatic computer
OPAL	operational performance - analysis language	**OROM**	optical read only memory
OPCOM	operator communication manager (VAX term)	**ORP**	optional response poll (bit protocol control)
OPM	operations per minute operations programming method	**ORT**	on-going reliability testing
		OS	operating system
OPN	open	**OSAM**	overflow sequential access method
OPND	operand	**OSC**	oscillator

OSI	open system interconnection (ISO network model)	**PA**	physical address
		PAB	professional application builder (PRO 300 series)
OSO	optoelectronics systems operations	**PAC**	programmer access code
OSP	office systems programs	**PAD**	packet assembler/disassembler facility
OSS	operating system sector		
OS/S	operating system for PDP-8	**PAES**	purchase and vendor evaluation system
OSSL	operating system specific subroutine library	**PAF**	page address field
OTL	on-line task loader	**PAIGEN**	pattern driven text generation program
OTS	object time system	**PAL**	phase alternation line (Brit. & Ger. TV, 625 line, 50 Hz) programmed-array logic programming assembly language
OUT	output		
OVFLO	overflow		
OVLP	overlap		
P0BR	program region base register (VAX term)	**PALAF**	phase alternate line alternate field (new TV standard)
P0LR	program region length register (VAX term)	**PALE**	phase alternating line encoding
P0PT	program region page table	**PAM**	protocol assist module pulse amplitude modulation
P1BR	control region base register (VAX term)		
		PAN	panel mounted
P1LR	control region length register (VAX term)	**PANTT**	PERT and GANTT program
P1PT	control region page table	**PAR**	page address register parabolic aluminized reflector parity positive acknowledgement retransmit program-aid routine
P	pico (1 × 10E-12)		
P(R)	packet receive sequence number		
P(S)	packet send sequence number	**PARAM**	parameter

PARCOR	partial autocorrelation	**PCBB**	process control block base
PAS	program address storage	**PCC**	program controlled computer
PAT	file patch utility (VAX/VMS) object module patch utility path analysis technique	**PCF**	professional communications facility (PRO 350)
PAX	physical address extension	**PCG**	personal computer group (DIGITAL)
PB	parity bit peripheral buffer	**PCH**	professional call handling
PBD	project base data	**PCI**	Packet Communications Inc. (networks) pattern correspondence index
PBI	process branch indicator		
PBN	price book number (European Information Services) physical block number		
		PCL	parallel communications link printed circuit lamp
P0BR	program region P0 base register	**PCM**	pulse code modulation plug compatible mainframe plug compatible manufacturer
P1BR	program region P1 base register		
PBP	push button panel	**PCR**	program control register
PBT	permeable base transistor	**PCS**	patchable control store (VAX 11/750) process control systems project control system planning control sheet program counter store
PC	parity checker personal computer photo conductor process control program counter printed circuit		
		PCU	peripheral control unit
P-C	process controller	**PD**	potential difference
PCA	printed circuit assembly	**PDA**	probability distribution analyzer pulse distribution amplifier
PCB	process control block program communication block printed circuit board		
		PDB	physical database
		PDBR	physical database record
PCBA	printed circuit board assembly	**PDC**	parallel data controller

PDCS	physical device coordinate space	**PEC**	photoelectric cell
PDE	partial differential equation	**PEL**	picture element (pixel)
PDF	probability distribution function processor defined function	**PEM**	photoelectromagnetic
		PENCIL	pictorial encoding language
PDG	product development group	**PEPR**	precision encoding and pattern recognition
PDL	program description language program design language programmable data logger	**PERCOS**	performance coding system
		PERDEF	percent defective
		PERF	performance
PDM	pulse duration modulation	**PERIPH**	peripheral
PDM	precedence diagramming method	**PERT**	parametric expander of texts program evaluation and review technique
PDP	Programmable Data Processor	
PDQ	programmed data quantizer	**PES**	photoelectric scanning
PDR	page descriptor register	**PET**	position-event-time positron emission tomography
PDS	program development system power distribution system (DIGITAL)	**PETE**	parametric expander of texts
PDT	programmable data terminal	**PF**	picofarad (measure of capacitance) power factor power fail program function
PDV	Computer Process Control Project (Germany) process descriptor vector (networks)	
		P/F	poll/final
PE	parity error phase encoded (or encoding) processing element protocol emulator	**PFCC**	print file control character
		PFK	programmed function keyboard
		PFM	pulse frequency modulation
PEARL	Process and Experiment Automation Real-time Language	**PFN**	page frame number (VAX term)

PFR	programmed film reader system pulse frequency	**PIN**	P Insulated N channel (as in PIN diode) positive intrinsic negative (as in PIN diode)
PFT	professional file transfer (VAX to PRO to VAX file transfer utility)	**PINO**	positive input-negative output
PFW	page fault wait (VAX term)	**PIO**	precision iterative operation
PG	parity generator pattern generator or generation program generated pulse generator	**PIP**	peripheral interchange program programmable integrated processor
		PIPS	pattern information processing systems (Japan)
P/G	product group		
PGF	page fail	**PIR**	program interrupt request register
PGR	precision graphic recorder		
PHA	pulse height analysis	**PISW**	process interrupt status word
PHIGS	Programmers' Hierarchical Interactive Graphics Standard (ANSI)	**PIV**	peak inverse voltage (diode rating)
PHT	product hardware test phototube	**PIXEL**	picture element
		PJ-NF	projection join normal form
PI	priority interrupt pacing indicator	**P/L**	product line
PIA	peripheral interface adapter priority interrupt active	**PL/1**	programming language one
		PLA	programmable logic array
PIC	position independent code priority interface adapter	**PLACE**	positioner layout and cell evaluator
PID	process identification (VAX term)	**PLC**	CODASYL programming language committee
PIE	parallel interface element	**PLF**	page length field
PIL	precision in-line (color electron gun assembly)	**PLI**	port to link interconnect packet level interface
		PLL	phase locked loop

PLM	pulse length modulation	**PMG**	permanent-magnet generator
PL/M	programming language for micros	**PMOS**	P-channel metal oxide semiconductor
PLMGEN	a documentation generation program	**PMS**	Pantone matching system processor-memory-switch
PLO3	a small-business application system	**PMT**	process maturity test
PLOTX	PERTX graphics utility	**PNMR**	phosphorus nuclear magnetic resonance
PLP	packet level protocol		
PLS	programmed logic sequencer	**PNP**	a type of transistor with P-type and N-type silicon areas
PLT	plotter	**PNT**	point
PLTR	plotter	**PNX**	Private Network Exchange
PLU	primary logical unit	**PO**	purchase order
P0LR	program region P0 length register	**POC**	process operator console
P1LR	program region P1 length register	**POE**	port of entry
PM	phase modulation	**POL**	problem oriented language procedure oriented language
PMA	physical memory address Professional Tool Kit MACRO-11 Assembler (PRO 350)	**PORT**	photo-optical recorder tracker
PMAC	priority memory access controller	**P0PT(E)**	process region P0 page table (entry)
PMC	pre molded carrier	**P1PT(E)**	process region P1 page table (entry)
PMD	post mortem dump	**P/OS**	Professional's operating system
PME	performance monitor enable (VAX) performance measurement and evaluation package	**POS**	positive
		POT	positive off track potentiometer
		POW	power

POWU	post office work unit	**PRBS**	pseudorandom binary sequence
PP	paper tape punch peripheral processor	**PRD**	printer dump
P-P	peak-to-peak	**PRESRV**	media backup utility
PPI	plan-position indicator programmable peripheral interface protocol processing image	**PRETTY**	BLISS automatic formatting program
		PRF	pulse repetition frequency
PPL	peripheral processor link (Ranyan) Polymorphic Programming Language program production library	**PRGMG**	programming
		PRGMR	programmer
		PRI	priority
PPM	parts per million pulse position modulation	**PRIP**	pattern recognition and image processing
PPN	project-programmer number	**PRISM**	problem reporting information and solution management
PPS	page printing system parallel processing system pulses per second	**PRK**	program request key
PPSN	public packet switching network	**PROG**	program
		PROGR	programmer
PPT	post-telephone-telegraph administration (European reg. agency)	**PROLOG**	programming in logic (language)
PPU	peripheral processing unit	**PROM**	programmable read only memory
PR	paper tape reader print register	**PROSE**	text editor for PROFESSIONAL 300 series personal computers
P(R)	packet receive sequence number	**PRO/SORT**	callable sorting task (PRO 350)
PRACL	page-replacement algorithm and control logic	**PROVIDE**	PRO/VAX integrated data extract system (DIGITAL's NEAS Management Center)
PRAM	programmable random access memory		
		PRP	pseudorandom pulse

PRR	pulse repetition rate	**PSDN**	packet sharing data network packet switched data network public and private switching data networks
PRS	pattern recognition system		
PRT	program reference table		
PRTIL	Professional Real-Time Interface Library (PRO 350)	**PSE**	packet switching exchange
PRV	peak reverse voltage	**PSEC**	picosecond
PRW	percent rated wattage	**PSECT**	program section
PS	packet switch (networks) parity switch processor status word picosecond positive switch	**PSI**	packet switching interface (networks) packetnet system interface (networks) program software interface
P-S	pressure sensitive	**PSI/CAN**	packet switching interface/Canada
P(S)	packet send sequence number	**PSI/FR**	packet switching interface/France
PS/8	programming system for PDP-8	**PSK**	phase shift keying
PSA	problem statement analyzer	**PSL**	processor status longword (VAX term)
PSAR	programmable synchronous/asynchronous receiver	**PSN**	public switched network
		PSR	processor state register
PSAT	programmable synchronous/asynchronous transmitter	**PSS**	packet switching service public packet network (UK)
PSB	partition status byte program specification block	**PST**	permanent symbol table poststimulus-time
PSC	product service center programmable systolic chip (CMU)	**PSTN**	private switched telephone network (UK) public switched telephone network
PSCD	product schedule control document	**PSTS**	power supply test systems
PSD	product specification document port sharing device	**PSW**	processor status word (VAX term) program status word

PT	page table program tab	**PVR**	precision voltage reference
PT11	paper tape reader/punch	**PVT**	product validation test
PTD	process technology development group (DIGITAL)	**PW**	pulse width
		PWB	printed wire board
PTE	page table entry	**PWC**	parametric waveform coding pulse width coded
PTF	program temporary fix	**PWD**	pulse width descriminator
PTI	packet type identifier	**PWE**	pulse width encoder
PTH	plated through hole (in printed circuit board)	**PWM**	pulse width modulation
PTM	pulse time modulation	**Q**	merit of a coil or a capacitor
PTP	paper tape punch point-to-point	**QA**	quality assurance
PTR	paper tape reader paper tape recorder	**QAM**	quadrature amplitude modulation
PTS	paper tape software paper tape system	**QAR**	quality assurance report
PTT	program test tape postal telegraphic and telephone authority	**QC**	quality control QUIESCE COMPLETE (networks)
		QCB	queue control block
PU	physical unit (IBM's SNA)	**QDA**	quantity discount agreement
PUD	physical unit directory physical unit device table	**QDPSK**	quaternary differential phase shift keying
PUP	peripheral unit processor	**QE**	quality evaluation
PUSART	programmable universal asynchronous synchronous receiver transmitter	**QEC**	QUIESCE AT END OF CHAIN (networks)
		QIO	queue an input/output request
PUT	programmable unijunction transistor	**QI/O**	queue input/output
PVC	permanent virtual circuit polyvinyl chloride (a type of plastic)	**QIP**	quad in-line package
		QLSA	queuing line sharing adaptor

QMANGR	batch queue manager	**RAM**	random-access memory
QMG	queue manager	**RAMAC**	random access method of accounting and control
QMQB	quick make, quick break		
QNT	quantizer	**RAMP**	reliability, availability, maintainability program
QRA	quality reliability assurance		
QSAM	queued sequential access method	**RAMP-UP**	bring to production
		RAPPI	random access plan position indicator
QT	queueing theory	**RAS**	row address strobe
QTD	quarter-to-date	**RB**	read buffer
QTY	quantity	**RBI**	ripple blanking input
QUAD	quadruplex video recording	**RBO**	ripple blanking output
QUEL	query language (INGRES)	**RBT**	resistance bulb thermometer
QUIKTRAN	quick FORTRAN	**RC**	read and compute remote control
QUILL	a query/report writer		
QY	query	**RCB**	result control block
R	register DC resistance	**RCC**	read channel continue remote communications complex
RA	repeat to address		
RAB	record access block	**RCD**	record
RAD	radiation dose calculator rapid access disk	**RCE**	rapid circuit etch
		RCEEA	Radio Communications and Electric Engineering Association
RADAR	radio detection and ranging		
RADAS	random access discrete address	**RCF**	recall finder
		RCI	relational call interface read channel initialize
RADAT	radio data transmission system		
		RCLK	receiver clock
RAE	register access error	**RCO**	remote control oscillator
RALU	register arithmetic logic unit		

RCP	reseau a commutation par paquets (French computer network)	**RDU**	request definition utility
		RDY	ready
RCR	reader control relay	**REACT**	remote access test system
RCS	records communications switching system	**REC**	receive
		RECAP	repeat call action prompter (DIGITAL Field Service)
RCV	receive		
RCVR	receiver	**RECOMP**	recomplement
RD	read remote diagnostics	**RED**	reliability exercise diagnostic
		REF	reference
R & D	research and development	**REG**	register
RDB	receive data buffer	**ReGIS**	Remote Graphics Instruction Set
RD CHK	read check		
RDB	receive data buffer	**REI**	return from exception or interrupt
RDC	remote diagnostic console (DIGITAL Field Service)	**REJ**	reject (bit protocol control)
RDCP	remote data communications package	**REL**	release reload
RDD	random digit dialing	**RELIAB**	reliability
RDF	radio direction finder request definition file	**RELOC**	relocatable
		RELQ	RELEASE QUIESCE
RDI	request for design investigation	**REMACP**	remote I/O ancillary control process
RDL	remote digital loop	**REN**	remote enable
RDM	remote diagnostics module	**REP**	reply to message number (in computer communications)
RDMS	relational data management system		
RDS	relational data system (System R)	**REPERF**	reperforator
		REP-OP	repetitive operation
RDT	remote data transmitter	**REQ**	request

RES	reset	**RIF**	reliability improvement factor
RET	return		
RETD	a virtual call service	**RIFI**	radio interference field intensity
REV CON	revision control	**RIM**	read in mode
REV LEVEL	revision level	**RIP**	raster image processor
REW	rewind	**RIRO**	roll in roll out (or roll-in, roll-out)
RF	radio frequency		
RFA	record file address (VAX term)	**RIS**	reduced instruction set
RFD	ready for data result file descriptor	**RISC**	reduced instruction set computer
RFR	reject failure rate	**RISOP**	rapid interval scan operation
RFS	ready for sending	**RITE**	ReGIS illustrated text editor
RG	reverse gate	**RJE**	remote job entry
RGL	ReGIS graphics library	**RJF**	remote job facility
RGL/FEP	ReGIS graphics library for FORTRAN enhancement package	**RL**	relay logic
		RLY	relay
RH	request header response header	**RM**	record mark
		RMC	rod memory computer
RHM	remote hardware monitoring	**RMD**	resource monitoring display
RI	radio interference reliability index robotics international	**RMI**	radio magnetic indicator
		RMM	read mostly memory
RIA	Robotics Institute of America	**RMM**	read-mostly mode
		RMR	register modification refused
RIB	retrieval information block	**RMS**	Record Management Services root mean square
RIC	read-in clock restructurable integrated circuit		
		RMS-11K	Record Management Services-11 keyed access

RMSE	root-mean-square error	**ROTR**	receiving-only typing reperforator
RMT	remote remote command terminal facility	**RP**	reception poor
		RPB	result parameter block
RMXX	rotating memory drive (number)	**RPC**	remote position control
RNA	request node address	**RPCNET**	REEL project computer network (IBM networks)
RNDM	random	**RPE**	remote procedure error
RNO	RUNOFF	**RPG**	report program generator
RNR	receive not ready (bit protocol control)	**RPL**	running program language
RNV	radio noise voltage	**RPM**	revolutions per minute
RO	read only receive only	**RPMI**	revolutions per minute indicator
ROC	read-out clock	**RPS**	revolutions per second rotational position sensing
ROD	result option descriptor	**RPT**	report
ROI	region of interest	**RPXX**	rotating pack - controller/drive (number)
ROL	request on line (bit protocol control)	**RQI**	request for initialization (bit protocol control)
ROM	read only memory (or read-only memory)	**RQR**	request recovery
ROM ACC	ROM access error	**RQS**	request to send
ROMAR	ROM address register	**RQT**	reliability qualification test
ROMON	receiving-only monitor	**RR**	receive ready (bit protocol control) repetition rate
ROMSL	ROM sense latches		
ROPP	receive-only page printer	**RRN**	relative record number
ROS	read-only storage	**RRV**	record reference vector
ROT	rate of turn	**RS**	remote station
ROT	rotating		

RS-232	standard signal interface for remote communications	**RT2**	Subset of RT-11
RSA	remote station alarm	**RT**	real-time foreground/background system
RSE	record selection expression (DBTG)		run time
RSET	receiver signal element timing	**RTA**	reliability test assembly
R/S GEN	Reed/Solomon generator	**RTAM**	remote terminal access method
RSHUT	request shutdown	**RT/C**	real time/computation (software systems)
RSI	reschedule interval	**RTC**	reader tape contact
RSL	requirements statement language	**RTD**	resistance temperature detectors
RSP	radial serial protocol	**RTE**	real time executive remote terminal equipment
RSS	range safety system		
RST	reset restore	**RTF**	radiotelephone
		RTI	real time interface (PRO350)
RSTS	resource sharing timesharing system	**RTL**	resistor-transistor logic register transfer level (simulator) run-time library
RSTS/E	resource sharing timesharing system/extended		
		RTP	remote transfer point
RSV	reserve	**RTR**	ready to receive
RSX	real-time resource sharing executive resources executive operating system (real-time)	**RTS**	rapid transmission and storage real-time system remote terminal scanning system request to send return to service run-time system
RSX-11	real-time resource sharing executive (operating system for PDP-11)		
		RTT	Regie des Telegraphes et des Telephones (Belgium)
RT-11	Real-Time system (most compact operating system for PDP-11)		

RTTY	radio teletypewriter communications	**SAC**	store access controller systems and clusters group (DIGITAL)
RTU	remote terminal unit	**SACO**	select address and contract operate
RTVS	real time visual system		
RU	request unit/response unit response unit	**SAD**	serial analog delay
		SADT	structured analysis and design technique
RUSH	remote use of shared hardware	**SAEM**	Scanning Auger Electron Microanalysis
RVI	reverse interrupt	**SAGE**	semi-automatic ground environment simulation of asynchronous gate elements
RVT	relative volume table		
R/W	read/write		
RWC	read, write and compare		
RWCS	report writer control system	**SAID**	speech autoinstruction device
RWED	read, write, execute, delete (VAX)	**SAINT**	symbolic automatic integrator
REWD	read, write, extend, delete (RSX)	**SAM**	scanning auger microprobe analysis sequential access method
RWI	read, write, initialize		
RX	receive (data transmission)	**SAMM**	source and message manager
RXD	received data		
RX01	single density floppy diskette	**SAR**	sector address register
		SARM	set asynchronous receive mode
RX02	double density floppy diskette		
		SAS	sales accounting system
RY	relay	**SAT**	storage allocation table
RZ	return to zero (coding)	**SAV**	saved file system image file
SA	successive approximation		
		SBA	set buffer address
SABM	set asynchronous balanced mode	**SBB**	system building block (re: VAX)

SBC	single board computer small business computer	**SCCB**	system control base
SBI	synchronous backplane interconnect	**SCCP**	system services control point (IBM's SNA)
SBR	system base register (VAX term)	**SCCS**	source code control system (part of UNIX)
SBS	silicon bilateral switch	**SCCU**	single channel communications control unit
SBT	surface barrier transistor		
SC	semiconductor	**SCDSB**	suppressed carrier double sideband
S/C	short circuit	**SCE**	single cycle execute
SCA	subchannel adapter synchronous communications adaptor	**SCI**	station concentration interface system control and interface program system control interface
SCAD	shift count adder		
SCADA	supervisory control and data acquisition	**SCIP**	system control and interface program
SCAM	synchronous communications access method	**SCL**	system control language
		SCOM	system communication area
SCAN	command line scanner	**SCPC**	single channel per carrier
SCB	stream control block (networks) system control block (VAX term)	**SCR**	scanning control register silicon controlled rectifier
		SCS	scientific character set specification control systems (DIGITAL)
SCBB	system control block base (VAX term)		
SCBBR	system control block base register (VAX term)	**SCT**	subroutine call table system compatibility test
		SCTL	short circuited transmission line
SCC	specialized common carriers storage connecting circuit (teletypewriter term)	**SD**	sample delay

SDA	source data automation	**SEG/CAD**	Semiconductor Engineering Group Computer Aided Design
	system display architecture (DIGITAL VAXstation)		
	system dump analyzer (VAX term)	**SEL**	systems engineering laboratories
SDB	small data buffer	**SEM**	scanning electron microscope
SDC	signal data converter	**SEQ**	sequence
	Software Distribution Center (DIGITAL)	**SER**	series
SDF	structured display file	**SERDES**	serializer/deserializer
SDI	source data information	**SETDIA**	set diagnose
	standard drive interface	**SEU**	smallest executable unit
SDL	software design language	**SF**	start field
SDLC	synchronous data-link control	**S/F**	store and forward
SDM	space division multiplexing	**SFC**	sectioned file controller shop floor control
SDP	sequential disk processor	**SFD**	sub-file directory
SDS	share data set	**SFD-ALGOL**	system function description - ALGOL
SDT	software development policy (DIGITAL)	**SFK**	special function key
	start data traffic	**SFM**	set file mask
SEC	single error correction	**SG**	scanning gate
SECAM	Systeme Electronique Couleur Avec Memoire (FR. TV, 625 lines, 50 Hz) (sequential color with memory)		screen grid
			symbol generator
		SGA	shared global area
		SGN	scan gate number
SECO	sequential control	**S/H**	sample and hold
SED	software engineering development	**SHF**	super high frequency
SEER	a computerized software support system	**SHF CNT**	shift counter
	software maintenance tool		
SEF	software engineering facility		

SHISAM	simple hierarchical indexed sequential access method	**SIMEON**	simplified control
SHSAM	simple hierarchical sequential access method	**SIMM**	single in-line memory module
		SIMULA	simulation language
SHUTC	SHUTDOWN COMPLETE	**SIN**	symbolic integrator
SHUTD	SHUTDOWN	**SIO**	start input/output
SI	sample interval storage interconnection bus (DIGITAL) Systeme International d'Unites	**SIP**	short irregular pulses single in-line package system image preservation program
S/I	signal-to-intermodulation ratio	**SIPO**	system installation productivity options
SIAM	Society for Industrial and Applied Mathematics	**SIPP**	save image patch program
		SIR	special investigation report
SIC	semiconductor integrated circuits	**SIRC**	signal integrity reference cable
SID	serial input line	**SIRUS**	a software performance report monitoring tool
SIDR	secondary index data record		
SIE	single instruction execute	**SISD**	single instruction single data stream processor
SIFT	share internal FORTRAN translator	**SIT**	silicon intensifier tube
SIG	special interest group (of DECUS)	**SITA**	Societe Internationale de Telecommunications Aeronautiques (International Airlines Reservation Network)
SIL	save image library speech interference level		
SILO	hardware buffer (first in/first out)	**SITGO**	compile-load-go FORTRAN
		SIT-REP	situation report
SIM	set initialization mode (bit protocol control)	**SIXEL**	six pixels (picture elements)
		SJ	single job
SIMD	single instruction multiple data stream array processor	**SJCC**	spring joint computer conference

SJV	standard journal voucher	**SMDR**	station message detail recorder
SLAM	scanning laser acoustic microscope	**SMF**	system management facilities
SLC	straight-line capacity	**SMG**	screen management (VMS V4.0)
SLD	satellite task loader		
SLDC	Software Literature Distribution Centre	**SML**	symbolic machine language system macro library file extension
SLI	suppress length indication	**SMP**	session main processor shared memory processor symmetrical multi-processing
SLIC	simulator of integrated circuits		
SLIP	symmetric list processor		
SLIPER	Source Language Input Program and Editor	**SMR**	statement marketing requirements
SLM	signal level meter	**SMS**	self maintenance service for software standard modular system
SLP	Source Line/Language Input Program		
SLR	system length register	**SN**	serial number
SLRAP	standard low frequency range approach	**S/N**	signal-to-noise
		SNA	systems network architecture (IBM)
SLRN	select read numerically		
SLT	solid logic technology system line table	**SNAFU**	situation normal, all fouled up
SLU	secondary logical unit serial line unit	**SNAPS**	standard network access protocol specification
SMA	structured memory access architecture	**SNF**	sequence number field
		SNI	sequence number indicator
SMAC	store multiple access controller	**SNOBOL**	string oriented symbolic language (a string processing and pattern matching language)
SMBU	standard MUMPS backup and utility system		
SMD	storage module drive	**SNR**	signal-to-noise ratio

SNRM	set normal response mode (bit protocol control)	**SPAR**	subsystem program for analysis and repair
S/O	send only	**SPC**	small peripheral controller
SOA	state of the art	**SPCC**	Southern Pacific Communications Company
SOAP	symbolic optimizer and assembly program symbolic optimum assembly programming	**SPD**	Software Product Description (DIGITAL) system programming division
SOD	serial output line		
S/OFF	sign off	**SPE**	stored program element
SOH	start of header	**SPEAR**	standard package for error analysis and reporting (DIGITAL)
SOI	silicon on insulator (technique used for 3-D integrated circuits)	**SPETS**	single photom emission tomography software single photom emission tomography system
SOL	simulation oriented language		
SOM	start of message	**SPF**	system programming facility
SONAR	sound navigation and ranging	**SP/GR**	specific gravity
S/ON	sign on	**SPL**	sound pressure level
SOP	standard operating procedures	**SPM**	software performance monitor (VAX-11)
SOS	Silicon On Sapphire standard operating system	**SPOC**	specs-on-computer
SOS MOS	Silicon On Sapphire Metal Oxide Semiconductor	**SPOOL**	shared-peripheral operations on line
SOUP	software updating package	**SPOOLING**	simultaneous peripheral operations on line
SP	shift pulses spooling device stack pointer structured programming	**SPR**	Software Performance Report (DIGITAL) spooled output file extension spooler program
SPAM	spool file allocation manager		

SPS	software performance summary software product services symbolic programming system	**SSB**	single sideband stream status block
SPT	system page table (VAX term)	**SSCP**	system services control point
SPTE	system page table entry	**SSD**	storage systems development
SPU	switching processor unit	**SSDA**	synchronous serial data adapter
SQL	structured query language	**SSE**	silicon systems engineering (DIGITAL)
SQM	software quality management (DIGITAL)	**SSEC**	selective sequence electronic calculator
SQUID	superconducting quantum interface device	**SSI**	small scale integration subsystem integration
SR	shift register	**SSLC**	synchronous single line controller
S/R	subroutine	**SSM**	solid state memory matrix
SRA	stored record address	**SSOU1**	system output unit 1
SRAM	static random access memory	**SSP**	supervisor mode stack pointer (VAX term)
SRC PT	source paper tape	**SSP-11**	scientific subroutine package
SRCCOM	source compare	**SST**	synchronous system trap
SRL	scheme representation language (CMU)	**ST**	segment table
SRQ	send/receive queue	**STA**	status
SRT	sort work file extension	**STAM**	sequential thermal anhysteric magnetization (hi speed dup. of vid. tape)
SS	solid state		
SSA	segment search argument system software assurance	**STAR**	self-test and repair (computer)
SSAH	shared subchannel attachment handler	**STAT**	static

STB	symbol table file extension
STC	single track correction
	standard transmission code
STD	standard
	subscriber trunk dialing (networks)
	system task directory
STDM	synchronous time division multiplexing
STE	system timing element
STEP	system for tracking the evolution of programs
STI	standard tape interface
STP	standard terminal port
STR	synchronous transmitter-receiver
STRESS	structural engineering systems solver
STRUDL	structural design language
STS	static test stand
STSN	set and test sequence numbers
STUDD	simulator and tester usage for design and diagnostics
STX	start of text
SU	system unit
SUB	subroutine
SUBTR	subtract
SUD	single-user DIBOL
SUM	summary

SUP	suppress
SUPPL	supplement
SURGE	sorting, updating, report generating
SUS	silicon unilateral switch
SUVAX	single user VAX
SVA	system virtual address (VAX term)
SVC	switched virtual circuit
SVET	software validation executing trials
SW	short wave
	software
SWAB	swap byte
SWIFT	Society for Worldwide Interbank Financial Telecommunication
SWL	Software Event Logger
SWLUP	Software Event Logger Utility Program
SWR	standing wave ratio
SWS	Software Services (DIGITAL)
SYM	symmetrical
SYN	synchronous idle
SYNC	synchronize
	synchronizing sequence
SYS	system
	system file
	system library
SYSERR	system error report

SORCERER	system error	**TC**	transmission control
SYSGEN	system generation	**T&C**	terms and conditions
SYSLIB	system library	**TCAM**	telecommunications access method
SYSOP	system operator		
SYSOUT	system output	**TCB**	task control block termination control block
SZ	size	**TCL**	remote task control utility
TAB	tabulate switch task administration box	**TCLK**	transmitter clock
TABS	typesetting applications business system	**TCM**	terminal-to-computer multiplexer
TAC	TELENET access controller transistorized automatic control	**TCO**	trunk cutoff
		TCP	timesharing control primitives transmission control program (networks)
TACH	tachometer		
TAG	temporary assistance group	**TCR**	card reader
TAM	terminal access module test area management	**TCTS**	Trans-Canada Telephone System
TAP	terminal application package	**TCU**	terminal control unit
TAS	terminal address selector	**TCW**	time code word
TASC	terminal area sequence and control transformation arithmetic scene converter	**T**	time delay timing diagram tunnel diode
TASI	time-assigned speech interpolation	**TDB**	task group database
		TDDL	time division data link
TB	translation buffer	**TDF**	two degrees of freedom
TBC	time base corrector	**TDG**	test data generation
TBL	table building language	**TDM**	time division multiplexing
TBMT	transmitter buffer empty	**TDMA**	time division multiple-access
T BUS	the bus (BI)		

TDMS	Terminal Display Management System	**TI**	pseudo device-input terminal tape indicator terminal interface
TDR	transmission domain reflectometry	**TIA**	terminal interface architecture
TDS	time division switching Tiny-11 (microprocessor) development system	**TIC**	TELENET interface controller transfer in channel
TDTL	tunnel diode transistor logic	**TICCIT**	time-shared, interactive computer-controlled information television
TDXX	tape deck – controller (number)		
TE	testing envelope	**TID**	tuple identification (System R – INGRES)
TECO	Text Editor and Corrector (Editor)	**TIE**	track in error
TEGAS	test generation and simulation program	**TIES**	total integrated engineering system
TELCO	telephone company product line	**TIG**	telecommunications industry group
TELENET	a public data network (USA)	**TIM**	terminal intelligence module (PDT-11) terminal interface module
TELEX	Western Union world-wide teletypewriter exchange		
TEM	T-11 evaluation module (DIGITAL)	**TIN**	tangent intersection
		TIP	terminal IMP (interface message processor) terminal interface processor
TERMS	terminate self		
TFR	transfer	**TIS**	thermal imaging system
TFT	thin-film technology thin-film transistor	**TK**	teletype keyboard
		TKB	Task Builder (RSX-11M)
TG	transmission group (IBM's SNA)	**TKTN**	task termination notification routine
TGHA	the great heuristic algorithm		
THR	test handling routine	**TL**	time limit transmission level
		TLC	total laboratory computing

TLK	terminals communications utility (DECnet)	**TODS**	test-oriented disk system
TLP	line printer	**TOEM**	technical original equipment manufacturer group
TLR	toll line release	**TOF**	top of file top of form
TLSA	transport line sharing adapter	**TOMS**	ACM transactions on mathematical software
TLZ	transfer on less than zero	**TOPLAS**	ACM transactions on programming languages and systems
TM	tape mark transverse magnetic		
T-M	time and materials	**TOPS**	time-shared operating systems T Operating System
TMC	magnetic cassette		
TMG	timing	**TOPS-10**	DECsystem-10 operating system for single processor
TMP	temporary file		
TMR	triple modular redundancy	**TOPTS**	test oriented paper tape system
TMS	text management system transfer micro store		
		TOS	tape operating system
TMS-11/ CMS-11	text management system/classified management system	**TOT**	total
		TOY	time of year (CPU clock)
TMT	transmit	**TP**	teletype printer terminal processor (networks) trace trap pending (VAX term) transaction processing
TMXX	tape magnetic controller (number)		
TNF	transfer on no overflow		
T-NIM	telephone-network interface module	**TPA**	transient program area
		TPB	teletype printer buffer
TNZ	transfer on non-zero	**TPD**	task partition directory
TO	pseudo device-output terminal	**TPG**	terminal products group
TOC	table of contents	**TPI**	tracks per inch (on disk memory)

TPM	tape preventative maintenance	**TSET**	transmitter signal element timing
TPS	terminals per station transaction processing systems	**TSF**	ten statement FORTRAN
		TSI	technical sales instruction
TPSG	terminal products service group	**TSK**	task image file
		TSL	three-state logic
TPU	text processing utility	**TSN**	tape serial number terminal switching network time sharing network
TR	transfer request transmit and receive		
TRA	trace capture task transient program area	**TSO**	time sharing option
		TSS	time sharing system
TRAC	text reckoning and compiling	**TSSN**	a timesharing null task
TRAFFIC	transaction routing and form formatting in COBOL	**TST**	transaction step task
		TT	terminal device
TRANS	transaction	**TTC**	typewriter console
TRANSPAC	a public data network (France)	**TTD**	temporary text delay
		TTL	transistor - transistor logic
TRAX	transaction processing system	**TTMS**	telephoto transmission measuring set
TRI	trace interrupt task	**TTR**	tape trigger register
TRL	transistor resistor logic	**TTS**	teletypesetter
TRU	transmit-receive unit	**TTSCA**	thirty-two-seventy communications adaptor (or 3270 communications adaptor)
TS	terminal server (DECnet/Ethernet terminal connection) time sharing transmission subsystem		
		TTW	teletypewriter
TSAR	time series analysis and reduction	**TTY**	teletypewriter equipment or terminal
TSD	time-shared DIBOL	**TU**	tape unit transmission unit

TUMS	register transfer level simulator	**UC**	unit check uppercase
TWAIT	terminal wait	**UCB**	unit control block (VAX term)
TWP	talking word processor (DECtalk)	**UCC**	uniform commercial code
TWT	traveling-wave tube	**UCI**	user class identifier
TWX	Teletypewriter Exchange Service (USA)	**UCK**	unit check
TX	transmit transmitter	**UCL**	user command linkage
		UCODE	micro-code
TXT	text	**UCS**	user control service
TYP	typeset	**UD**	unit description
TYPOUT	typewriter output routine	**UDA**	UNIBUS disk adaptor
UA	unformatted ASCII (RSX) UNIBUS address unnumbered acknowledgment	**UDB**	unit data block
		UDC	universal digital controller
		UDK	user-defined key
UAF	user authorization file	**UDL**	unified database language
UAP	user application program	**UDLC**	universal data link control
UART	universal asynchronous receiver/transmitter	**UDR**	universal document reader
		UDU	user data unit user defined units
UB	unformatted binary		
UBA	UNIBUS adaptor user base address	**UDX**	universal device index
		UESL	universal external subroutine library
UBC	universal buffer controller	**UET**	UNIBUS exercise terminator
UBI	UNIBUS interface	**UETP**	user environment test package
UBR	user base register		
UBUS	UNIBUS	**UFB**	undefined file buffer
UBW	UNIBUS window	**UFD**	user file directory (VAX term)

UFI	user friendly interface	**URCLK**	universal receiver clock
UG	unigraphics	**US**	unit separator
UHF	ultra-high frequency	**USAH**	unshared subchannel attachment handler
UIC	user identification code		
UIT	united integrated and test user identification table	**USART**	universal synchronous asynchronous receiver/transmitter
UJN	user job node	**USASCII**	USA Standard Code for Information Interchange
ULF	ultra-low frequency		
UMC	universal memory module	**USFC**	U.S. Customer Finance
UMR	UNIBUS memory registers	**USI**	user system interface
UN1004	UNIVAC 1004 terminal emulator	**USP**	user mode stack pointer (VAX term)
UNA	UNIBUS network adapter UNIBUS to NI adapter	**USR**	user service routine
		USRT	universal synchronous receiver transmitter
UNCOL	universal computer oriented language	**UST**	user symbol table
UNI	univac	**UTC**	coordinated universal time
UNIBUS	asynchronous information bus for the PDP-11 universal basic utilities system	**UTCLK**	universal transmitter clock
		UTF	universal transmission format
UNIX	operating system developed by Bell Labs (UNIX is a trademark of Bell Labs) user interface for operating instructions	**UTIL**	utility
		UTL	user task list
		UTN	user terminal node
UOV	units of variance	**UUO**	undefined user operation unimplemented user operations
UPD MCRF	update microfiche		
UPS	uninterrupted power supply	**UUT**	unit under test
UPT	user page table	**UWA**	user working area
UPU	user protocol unit		

V	version volt		**VDG**	voice driven graphics
			VDH	very distant host
VA	video amplifier virtual address volt amperes		**VDI**	virtual device interface (graphics standard)
			VDM	virtual device metafile (part of VDI graphics standard)
VAB	voice answer back			
VAC	value added counter		**VDS**	VAX diagnostic supervisor
VAM	virtual access method		**VDSS**	VAXstation display services software
VAX	Virtual Address Extension			
VAX-IMA	VAX information management architecture		**VDT**	video display terminal visual display terminal
VAXSIM	VAX system integrity monitor		**VDU**	visual display unit
			VDH	very distant host
VAX/VMS	Virtual Address Extension/Virtual Memory System		**VEC**	vector
			VEL	velocity verified encoded logging
VBF	variable-length bit field (VAX term)		**VERA**	vision electronic recording apparatus
VBN	virtual block number			
VC	videocassette virtual circuit voltage comparator		**VET**	vertical electron transistor
			VF	voice frequency
VCB	volume control block (VAX term)		**VFC**	variable frequency control variable-with-fixed-control
VCD	variable center distance variable capacitance diode virtual circuit descriptor		**VFM**	virtual file manager
			VFO	variable frequency oscillator
			VFT	voice-frequency carrier telegraph terminal
VCF	voltage-controlled filter			
VCO	voltage-controlled oscillator		**VFU**	vertical format unit
VCW	valid control word		**VFY**	VERIFY (a utility program) verify
VD	video disc			
VDA	video distribution amplifier		**VGA**	variable gain amplifier

VHD	video high density (capacitance video disc)	**VM**	virtual machine virtual memory
VHF	very high frequency	**VMA**	virtual memory address
VHLL	very high level language	**VMCS**	VAX manufacturing control system (DIGITAL)
VHO	very high output		
VHP	very high performance	**VME/B**	virtual memory environment (B operating system)
VHSIC	very high speed integrated circuit	**VME/K**	virtual memory environment (K operating system)
VIA	VAX information architecture	**VMOS**	V-groove metal oxide semiconductor
VIAS	voice interference analysis set	**VMR**	virtual MCR loader
VIBA	virtual instruction buffer address	**VMS**	virtual memory storage virtual memory system
VICE	VAX integrated commercial environment	**VNL**	via-net-loss
VID	visual identification label	**VNP**	virtual network processor
VIDAT	visual data acquisition	**VO**	voice over
VIL	vertical injection logic	**VOC**	variable output circuit
VIPS	voice interruption priority system	**VODACOM**	voice data communications
VIS	visual instrumentation subsystem	**VOL**	volume
		VOS	voice operated switch
VISSR	visible/infrared spin-scan radiometer	**VOX**	voice operated control
VLCS	voltage-logic, current, switching	**VPE**	vertical parity error (magtape)
VLF	very low frequency	**VPN**	virtual page number (VAX term)
VLS	VAX layout system (internal CAD system)	**VPT**	virtual packet terminal
		VPW	VAX professional workstation
VLSI	very large scale integration	**VR**	voltage regulator

VRAM	video random access memory	**W BUS**	write bus
VRC	vertical redundancy check visible record computer	**WC**	word count write and compute
VRP	view reference point	**WCB**	window control block (VAX term)
VS	virtual storage	**WCC**	write control character write control check
VSAM	virtual sequential access method	**WCE**	word count error
VSCF	variable speed constant frequency	**WCF**	white cathode follower
VSMF	visual search microfilm	**WCP**	worst case patterns
VSP	voice synthesis processor	**WCR**	word control register
VSVP	VAX system verification package	**WCS**	writable control store
		WD	word
VSWR	voltage standing-wave ratio	**WDCS**	writable diagnostic control store (VAX term)
VT	video terminal vertical tabulator virtual terminal	**WDR**	word data register
		WE	write enable
VTAM	virtual telecommunications access method (IBM)	**WED**	Western European Division
VTEM	virtual terminal emulator package (VAXstation)	**WF**	write forward
		WFM	waveform monitor
VTP	virtual terminal protocol	**WGA**	workstation graphics architecture
VU	volume unit		
VXO	variable crystal oscillator	**WIP**	work in process
W	watt	**WISE**	a college administrative system on the PDP-11
WABT	wait before transmitting	**WK**	work file pseudo device
WAC	write address counter	**WL**	wavelength write list
WACK	wait acknowledge		
WATS	wide area telephone service	**WM**	word mark

WMG	world marketing group	**XDELTA**	tool for debugging operating systems and drivers (VAX term)
WMMG	worldwide manufacturing and maintenance group		
		XDT	executive debugging tool
WMO	World Meterological Organization	**XEC**	extended emulator control mode
WO	write out	**XEDT**	extended VAX/VMS EDT editor (DIGITAL)
WP	word processing		
WP/AS	word processing/administrative support	**XFER**	transfer
		XFT	X.25 file transfer
WP/OS	word processing/office system	**XIC**	transmission interface converter
WPM	words per minute	**XIO**	execute input/output
WPS	word processing system	**XLSI**	extreme large-scale integration
WR CHK	write check	**XLT**	translated
WR EN	write enable	**XM**	extended memory
WRKSTAN	work station	**XMIT**	transmit
WS	working storage	**XMTR**	transmitter
WTM	write tape mark	**X-OFF**	transmitter off
WTS	word terminal synchronous	**X-ON**	transmitter on
XAB	extended attribute block	**XON/XOFF**	transmitter on/transmitter off
XBM	extended basic mode	**XOR**	exclusive OR (Boolean operator)
XBUF	extended buffer pool		
XCON	expert configuration system expert systems product configurator (DIGITAL)	**XPN**	external priority number
		XREF	cross reference
XD	indexed	**XREP**	auxiliary report
XDCSP	X.25 DCI sub-protocol	**XSS**	executive support systems
		XTA	X.25 trace analyzer

XTAL	crystal	**ZAP**	a program patch utility
XUI	X.25 user interface	**ZD**	zero defect
XUT	X.25 utility task	**ZFB**	signals fading badly
XWAT	executive wait time module	**ZIF**	zero insertion force
XXDP	diagnostics package software for PDP-11	**ZMOS**	a custom MOS integrated circuit
YTD	year to date (or year-to-date)	**ZOE**	zero-energy
ZA	zero and add		

APPENDIX A

READABILITY/ TRANSLATABILITY

Premise

This Section of the DIGITAL Dictionary is a guide for writers, editors, translators, and course developers for producing easily readable, easily translatable information about DIGITAL products.

The members of the DIGITAL Dictionary Committee produced this Section on the premise that READABILITY has a direct causal relationship with TRANSLATABILITY. If written information is easy to understand in American English, then it is easy to translate into most foreign languages.

Readability and Translatability

Effective writing is a craft.

To produce understandable sentences and paragraphs, a writer must use the main tools of the craft—the elements of readability. These elements have been recommended by educators and writing professionals for many years. Since 1976, many publication groups in DIGITAL have established writing guidelines containing various readability elements. In this Section, The DIGITAL Dictionary Committee recommends 25 of those elements as valuable tools for writing technical and general information. The Committee has compiled the 25 elements primarily from three DIGITAL publications:

Writing Quality Checklist, Software Publications Methods, 1977.

DEC English Program, DEC Writing Rules, Educational Services, 1980.

Writing for the Reader, Software Publications, 1976.

This Appendix should be looked upon as a guide and checklist for all persons at DIGITAL involved in the transfer of information to assure that their writing is easy to understand and easy to use. Such easily readable writing will assure more easily translatable information.

The 25 Elements of Readability

The Dictionary Committee defines readability as that which has understandability and usability.

No one element of readability in this list should be considered more important than any other element. For example, the understandability of an otherwise well written document may be seriously affected by poor visual impact. Similarly, a document of exceptional visual quality may be difficult to understand because of excessive use of passive voice or poor organization of ideas. However, the value of one element can exceed the value of another depending upon the variable considerations for a particular writing. One important variable that tends to make some elements more essential than others is audience level. For example, the element CLEAR, UNDERSTANDABLE TERMS, properly applied, is probably the most helpful element in effectively targeting your writing to a particular audience.

The Dictionary Committee recommends that particular emphasis be given to using the element CLEAR, UNDERSTANDABLE TERMS. Here, the Committee is recommending avoiding the use of big words. Such careful, considerate selection and use of terms has proven to be one of the best aids to achieving readability of text and, thus, helping translators of technical information. The Committee, therefore, has included in Appendix B of this dictionary a list of terms recommended for use in producing written information about DIGITAL products. This list is sometimes called DEC English. The Committee recognizes that DEC English is not only an aid to readability and our human translation efforts, but can also be an aid to producing an effective computer-aided translation data base.

The quality of human communication, written or oral, is the responsibility of the sender, not the audience. Such quality can be measured and, therefore, controlled. The degree of quality is directly proportionate to what the participants possess in common, and is inversely proportionate to the amount of burden placed upon the receiver (audience). The application of these 25 elements of readability can avoid burdening the audience with annoyance, interruption, or confusion when reading information about DIGITAL products.

The appendix of this Second Edition will be as much in process of change as is the craft of writing. As the needs of DIGITAL writers and our audiences change, so will the contents of the DIGITAL Dictionary. The Dictionary Committee welcomes your comments and suggested changes, particularly regarding the 25 elements of readability. Please refer to the Reader's Comment page at the front of this dictionary.

The 25 elements of readability are presented here in three parts:

- a list of the 25 elements
- the reader value of the 25 elements
- an editing checklist patterned in the order of the 25 elements

The List of 25 Elements of Readability

Elements of Organization

1. Logical, simple, sentence structure
2. Correct parallel form for parallel ideas
3. Unified and coherent paragraphs
4. Properly ordered sections and chapters
5. Appropriate links: the use of transitional terms, sentences, and paragraphs
6. Appropriate audience-level pace (minimal density of ideas)

Elements of Writing Style

7. Correct grammar, spelling, punctuation, capitalization
8. Clear, understandable terms
9. Consistent use of terms
10. Minimal use of abbreviations and acronyms
11. Elimination of abstract terms
12. Elimination of deadwood
13. Minimal use of foreign terms
14. Minimal negative constructions
15. Discreet use of passive voice
16. Close positioning of modifiers to modified elements
17. Elimination of long strings of modifiers
18. Clear pronoun relationships

Graphic Elements

19. Pleasing, comfortable visual impact
20. Clear, easy-to-understand graphic elements
21. Appropriately placed graphic elements

Other Elements to Aid the Reader

22. Complete, clear Table of Contents (when needed)
23. Appropriate introductory material to define audience and scope
24. A well-designed Glossary (when appropriate)
25. A complete, accurate, easy-to-use Index (when appropriate)

The Reader Value of the 25 Elements of Readability

Elements of Organization

1. Logical, Simple Sentence Structure

The basic structure of the American-English sentence is subject-verb-complement, in that order. The closer a sentence is to that order, the more understandable it is. Subject-verb-complement structure provides the following:

- direct expression of ideas
- avoidance of embedded clauses
- closeness of related ideas.

2. Correct Parallel Form for Parallel Ideas

Parallel structure is the use of similar grammatical elements to express similar ideas. Proper parallel structure stresses the equality of ideas and assures smoothness of reading. Faulty parallel structure can confuse the reader and interrupt the reader's concentration.

3. Unified and Coherent Paragraphs

A well-organized paragraph has:

- *unity.* The first sentence (topic sentence) of the paragraph should briefly describe the main idea of that paragraph. All other sentences in that paragraph should discuss and support that main idea.
- *coherence.* The sentences in the paragraph should be smoothly connected; the writer should provide a smooth flow of thought for the reader. Coherence is accomplished by providing information in logical order, and by connecting that information with transitional terms. (See Readability Element 5.)

A paragraph that is neither unified nor coherent is often called a "haystacked paragraph". It contains lists of technical facts that the writer has failed to connect for the reader.

4. Properly Ordered Sections and Chapters

In the same way that ideas in an individual sentence or paragraph should be related and expressed coherently, so the information in a document as a whole should be unified and coherent. It should be clear to the reader how each chapter within a document relates to other chapters, and how each section within a chapter relates to other sections.

5. Appropriate Links: The Use of Transitional Terms, Sentences, and Paragraphs

A writer should explicitly link related ideas. The relationship of ideas may not be obvious to the reader; a writer should make those links for him or her. This linking enhances coherence and, consequently, reader comprehension.

Transitional terms help the reader understand the relationship of ideas more clearly. A writer should clearly designate to the reader the end of one idea and the start of another by using transitional terms such as:

thus	similarly
therefore	first
next	finally
because	however

These terms help the reader to distinguish between main ideas and subordinate ideas, and they provide clues to time relationships and causal relationships. They make the document easier to understand.

6. Appropriate Audience-Level Pace (Minimal Density of Ideas)

Density is the bunching together of details so closely that the reader cannot read them at his or her normal reading rate. The writer makes little attempt to articulate the details; the writer merely lays them down side by side. The impression on the reader is that he or she is being fed too rich a diet of information.

Writing is too dense if it contains either of the following:

- too many details in a sentence or paragraph. Paragraphs that contain sentence after sentence of "bunched" details cannot be read easily, especially if there are few transitional terms or sentences to aid the reader in connecting the details.
- unbalanced sentences and paragraphs. Paragraphs that contain some sentences rich in technical detail and other sentences with little or no technical information can keep the reader off balance.

Elements of Writing Style

7. Correct Grammar, Spelling, Punctuation and Capitalization

The mechanical details of writing are as important to readability as the details of organization. Close attention to details such as grammar, spelling, punctuation, and capitalization can prevent inconsistencies that distract the reader and lessen the overall quality of the writing. For references to these details, the Dictionary Committee recommends the following preferred authorities:

The Chicago Manual of Style, 13th ed. The University of Chicago Press, Chicago, 1982.

Webster's New Collegiate Dictionary. G. & C. Merriam Company, Springfield, Mass., 1976.

8. Clear, Understandable Terms

In most writing, a short word, one that has three or less syllables, will do the job as well as or better than a big word (polysyllabic word). Short words are easier for the reader to understand, and they produce more easily translatable sentences for the translator. Most short words are clearer in meaning than big words. The more syllables in a word, the greater the chance for ambiguity, abstraction, and confusion, especially if many big words are grouped in close sequence in a sentence or paragraph. However, some words with three or less syllables also may be considered "big" if they are not commonly used, and, therefore, probably not understood by most readers. A few examples of such words are poignant, hibernate, rapport, kludge, and proscribe.

In many areas of technical writing, a writer cannot avoid using big words, since they carry specific meanings. In such instances, the writer must assure that his audience will easily understand all of the terms used. This can be done by explaining the term the first time it is used, or providing an adequate glossary with the document. However, the overuse of big technical words can confuse and interrupt a reader in the same way that nontechnical big words do, especially when they occur often or in a series within a sentence.

The DIGITAL Dictionary Committee has included in Appendix B a list of such short or commonly understood words. The Committee recommends the use of such words in preference to using big words when communicating information about DIGITAL products. This list is sometimes referred to as "Common English Terms" and "DEC English."

9. Consistent Use of Terms

A writer helps to make writing understandable by using consistent terminology throughout a document. When a writer uses two or more terms to refer to the same thing, or gives two or more meanings to the same term, the writer is switching terms, causing confusion for the reader.

Sometimes, a writer switches terms within a single sentence or within a single paragraph. The reader may be confused if a writer uses "CPU" one time, "computer" the next time, and "processor" another time. The DIGITAL Dictionary is intended as a source for finding the "right" term. Once found, that term should be used consistently to refer to the same thing throughout a document.

10. Minimal Use of Abbreviations and Acronyms

Abbreviations and acronyms are frequently used in technical writing. If the subject matter contains many abbreviations and acronyms, the reader may have to struggle to perform the mental conversions to expand the abbreviations and acronyms.

If a document contains abbreviations or acronyms:

- The reader should be able to tell what they mean the first time they are used. This is normally done by spelling the term out in full the first time it is used, and following it with the appropriate abbreviation or acronym (usually in parentheses).
- The reader should be able to easily recall what they mean each time they are used. This can be done by providing an index or glossary entry that lists the term, the abbreviation or acronym for the term, the meaning of the term, and the page or section in which the term is first used.

Additional help is given if the reader is told that each abbreviation and acronym used in the document has an index entry. Some experienced writers have suggested that all abbreviations and acronyms appear in a document's Glossary, and that the index entry for each term refer the reader to the Glossary.

11. Elimination of Abstract Terms

An abstract term refers to something that does not exist in the physical world, and, therefore, does not have a specific referent against which it can be checked. In a general sense, then, an abstract term may not be specific enough for the reader to readily, clearly understand.

Writing that contains a high percentage of abstract terms has the following faults:

- It is difficult to understand.
- It is inefficient in transferring information from the writer's head to the reader's.
- It is difficult to retain.

Ambiguous terms come under the category of abstract terms. An ambiguous term is one whose meaning is obscured if it is possible for the reader to get two different meanings from it.

12. Elimination of Deadwood

Deadwood refers to words that add nothing to the meaning of a passage; they are "empty" words. They occupy space, making long sentences still longer and detract from the "full" meaning of other words. Deadwood is also the needless repetition of ideas. Deadwood should not merely be avoided; it should be eliminated.

13. Minimal Use of Foreign Terms

Many readers of American English do not know a foreign language. The majority of readers who encounter a foreign term must stop and reread a sentence to discover the meaning of the term; even after rereading, a reader may still not understand a foreign term. Terms such as the following may confuse a reader:

ad hoc	*ibid.*
e.g.	*i.e.*
et al.	*per se*
etc.	*viz.*

14. Minimal Negative Constructions

Negative expressions are more difficult to understand than positive expressions. A reader confronted with many negative expressions must expend additional mental energy to understand what is written. Often, a reader must reread a sentence to decipher its meaning by translating negative expressions to positive expressions.

A writer should especially avoid the combination of negative elements and passive voice (See Element 15). The passive-negative sentence is the most difficult sentence for the reader to understand.

15. Discreet Use of Passive Voice

The passive voice can be an effective communication method. However, overuse or needless use of the passive voice in technical writing can burden the reader; passive voice forces the reader to search for the doer of an action.

In general, active voice is the better method of presentation when the doer of the action is more important to the idea of a sentence than the action or receiver is.

16. Close Positioning of Modifiers to Modified Elements

A modifier adjacent to the word it modifies usually is not misread. However, a modifier that appears near several nouns can be misread. If the reader has to decide to which term the modifier belongs, coherence is lost.

17. Elimination of Long Strings of Modifiers

Placing long strings of modifiers before a modified element adds considerably to sentence length. Sentence length is a basic measure of complexity in a piece of writing. Long strings of modifiers add to the number of relationships that a reader must analyze and associate in order to understand the sentence. What puts an even greater burden on the reader is that he or she cannot begin to accurately analyze or associate ideas until he or she has "reached" the modified element itself.

18. Clear Pronoun Relationships

The pronouns "it," "they," "this," and "these" refer to nouns that precede them in the text. Clear reference to a noun by a pronoun guides the reader in understanding the relationship of ideas. The DIGITAL Dictionary Committee recommends using nouns instead of pronouns, whenever possible.

Graphic Elements

19. Pleasing, Comfortable Visual Impact

The visual impact of a document, its appearance, affects its understand-ability. Even before beginning to read, a reader is impressed, favorably or unfavorably, by what he or she sees. The document's visual appeal, or lack of it, psychologically affects the reader. For example, a reader may be "put off" by a page that is jammed with prose, without white space or graphics to lessen the visual burden. If the reader is not ready to read and understand, the reader will not read and therefore cannot understand.

A page with lots of white space and an appealing layout is more "comfortable" for the reader. The reader approaches the document in a more receptive frame of mind. Furthermore, figures, tables, and visuals show that the writer has written the document with the reader's needs in mind.

20. Clear, Easy-To-Understand Graphic Elements

Graphic elements (figures, photos, tables, examples, and other artwork) aid the reader in understanding ideas that are difficult to express with words alone. Judicious use of graphics also improves the visual impact of a document (see Element 19).

A useful graphic is:

- *clear.* A graphic should contain all the information a reader needs to understand the idea being presented; in other words, a graphic should stand alone as an idea.
- *uncluttered.* A graphic should contain only the information the reader needs to understand the idea; extraneous information in a graphic is similar to "deadwood" in text.
- *clearly titled.* The title should be a brief but coherent description of the information to be found in the graphic.

21. Appropriately Placed Graphic Elements

The graphic element should be physically close to the portion of text that calls it out to the reader. Normally, a graphic should appear on the same page as the call-out, or on the page immediately following. In some cases, when a graphic is large, it should appear on the page facing its call-out. A reader should not have to spend time searching back and forward in a document in order to find related elements such as text and graphics.

Other Elements to Aid the Reader

22. A Complete, Clear Table of Contents (when needed)

The Table of Contents is a reader's first indication of the document's contents and organization. By reading the Table of Contents, the reader determines whether he or she needs the information and how difficult it might be for him or her to use the information.

Basically, a good Table of Contents is a topical outline that shows the structure of the document; that is, the main subjects and the relationship of subtopics to the main subjects.

If a writer fails to show a logical structure through a Table of Contents, the reader can become confused as to what the document is about. This confusion can cause the reader to:

- become discouraged about the document before he or she starts reading
- believe that the document covers a subject that it does not cover
- believe that the document does not cover a subject that it does cover.

23. Appropriate Introductory Material to Define Audience and Sco

An overview and a summary can be effective reader aids. Overviews prepare the reader for the material and the organization that follows. A prepared reader can more easily grasp the material at the first reading. Summaries recall material just read and enhance the learning experience.

24. A Well-Designed Glossary (when appropriate)

A Glossary serves the dual purpose of making the information in a document easier to use and easier to understand. The Glossary should contain all little-known or new terms used in the document. The Glossary should also contain a listing of all abbreviations, acronyms, and mnemonics used in the document, with appropriate expansions of each. If possible, the Glossary should list the pages or sections in which Glossary entries are first used.

An effective Glossary can appear at the beginning of a document (following the Preface) or at the end of a document (preceding the Index). If the document is of a tutorial nature and is meant to be read cover-to-cover, a Glossary may be helpful at the beginning of the document.

25. A Complete, Accurate, Easy-to-Use Index (when appropriate)

An Index is one of the most important elements of a high-quality document, especially a document that is to be used for reference. A useful Index:

- contains entries for every important item or description mentioned in the document
- indicates clearly where each item or description can be found in the document.

In addition to the publications mentioned earlier, the Dictionary Committee recommends the following books for additional information about elements of style and readability:

Clear Technical Writing, John A. Brogan. McGraw-Hill Book Company, New York, 1973.

Software Publication Style Guide, Software Publication Methods, DIGITAL Equipment Corporation, 1980.

The Handbook of Technical Writing, Charles T. Brusaw, Gerald J. Alred, and Walter E. Oliu. St. Martin's Press, 1976.

An Editing Checklist of the 25 Elements of Readability

This checklist is patterned in the order of the 25 elements of readability. The checklist is intended as an aid to those who are editing their own writing, as well as to those who are reviewing the writing of others.

The use of this checklist is also recommended as a pre-writing refresher.

Organization

Is there a clear organizational pattern or outline in the document?

Are sentences generally simple in structure?

Do sentence parts agree in case, number, person, tense, voice, and mood?

Are parallel ideas presented in parallel forms?

Are chapters and sections logically organized?

Are main topics and supporting details presented in logical order?

Is information presented at an easy pace, and is density controlled?

Are paragraphs unified and coherent?

Are organizational paragraphs provided to introduce, connect, and summarize important topics?

Writing Style

Are the basic elements of good writing followed (correct grammar, spelling, punctuation, capitalization)?

Are words clear in meaning?

Are new terms and concepts clearly explained?

Are terms used consistently?

Are abbreviations, acronyms, symbols, and mnemonics clearly explained when used?

Are abstract words and expressions avoided?

Are unnecessary words and expressions ("deadwood") avoided?

Are foreign terms (including Latin abbreviations) avoided?

Are negative constructions avoided?

Is the use of passive voice minimal?

Are modifiers (words, phrases, clauses) close to the elements they are meant to modify?

Are strings of modifiers avoided?

Are antecedents for pronouns clear?

Are transitional terms effective in connecting ideas?

Graphics

Is the overall visual appearance of the document pleasing?

Are graphics clear and easy to understand?

Are tables easy to understand?

Are graphics effectively positioned and called out in text?

Is color used effectively?

Reader Aids

Is the Table of Contents accurate and effective in outlining the content of the manual?

Does the Preface define the intended audience and scope of the manual?

Is the Introduction effective in introducing the content of the manual?

Are references and cross-references accurate and sufficient in number?

Is the Glossary well designed and well written?

Is the Index complete, accurate, and easy to use?

Are there other notable reader aids?

RECOMMENDED COMMON ENGLISH TERMS

Recommended Common English Terms

The DIGITAL Dictionary Committee recommends the use of short, commonly understood terms in preference to using big words when communicating information about DIGITAL products. The use of such terms (Readability element 8, Appendix A) helps to produce clear, understandable English.

In this Appendix, the Committee has included a reference list of short, commonly understood terms, sometimes referred to as "DEC English" or "Common English Terms."

Recommended Common English Terms

a (an)	above	accessible
abbreviate	absence	accessory
abbreviated	absent	according to
abbreviation	accept	accuracy
ability	acceptable	accurate
able	acceptance	accurately
about	access	acknowledge

acknowledgement
acronym
across
action
active
actual
add
addition
additional
adjacent
adjust
adjustable
adjustment
administer
administration
administrator
advance
advancement
advise
affect
after
again
against
agree
agreement
air
alike
all
allow
almost
alphabet
alphabetic
alphabetically
also
alternate
although
altitude

aluminum
always
ambiguous
among
amount
analysis
analyze
and
angle
another
answer
anticipation
any
anything
anywhere
appear
application
apply
appropriate
approval
approve
approximate
approximately
are
area
arm
around
arrange
arrangement
arrive
arrow
as
ask
assemble
assign
assignment
associate

associated
assume
at
attach
attachment
attention
audible
authority
authorize
authorization
automatic
automatically
available
average
away

back
background
backspace
backward
bad
balance
bar
base
basic
basically
be
because
become
before
beginning
behind
bell
below
bend
bent
benefit

beside
better
between
big
bill
billing
binder
blank
blink
block
body
bolt
book
both
bottom
box
branch
break
bright
brightness
brightness
bring
broken
building
bulletin
burn
business
busy
but
buy
by

calendar
call
can
capability
capable

capacity
car
card
cardboard
careful
carefully
careless
carelessly
catalogue
cause
center
certain
chalk
chance
change
chapter
characteristic
check
checklist
checkout
choice
chronological
chronologically
circle
circular
class
clause
clean
cleaner
clear
clearance
clerk
clip
clock
clockwise
close
cloth

cold
collect
color
column
combination
combine
come
comment
committee
common
communicate
communication
company
compare
comparison
compatibility
compete
completely
completion
complex
compute
computer
concept
condition
confidential
connect
connection
consecutive
consider
consideration
constant
contain
container
content
continue
continuity
continuous

continuously
contrast
control
convention
conversational
copy
cord
corner
correct
correction
correctly
corresponding
cost
could
count
counterclockwise
cover
create
creation
critical
cross-reference
cubic
current
curve
customer
cycle

daily
damage
danger
dangerous
dark
date
day
decision
decrease
defect

defective
degree
delay
delete
deletion
department
depend
dependent
dependability
dependable
depth
describe
description
design
desirable
desk
destination
destroy
detach
detail
detailed
detergent
determine
develop
development
device
diagram
dial
dictionary
differ
difference
different
difficult
digit
dim
dimension
direct

direction
directly
dirty
disadvantage
disagree
disagreement
disappear
disassemble
discard
disconnect
discontinue
discuss
discussion
distance
distribute
divide
divisible
division
do
document
documentation
door
double
down
downward
drawer
drawing
drop
dry
dual
duration
during
dust

each
early
earth

easy
edge
edit
editor
educational
effect
effective
efficiency
efficient
efficiently
either
electrician
electrical
electricity
electronic
electronics
element
emergency
employee
empty
enabling
enclose
end
engineer
engineering
enough
enter
entrance
envelope
environment
equal
equally
equipment
equivalent
error
even
event

ever
every
exactly
example
except
exception
expand
expect
experience
expert
explain
explanation
extension
external

face
facility
fact
factory
fail
failure
false
familiar
family
fan
far
fast
fatal
feature
feedback
few
figure
fill
film
final
find
fire

first
fit
fixed
flash
flashing
flat
flexible
floor
flow
focus
follow
following
foot
for
force
forward
fraction
frame
free
frequency
from
front
full
function
functional
fundamental
furniture
future

general
get
give
glass
glue
go
good
government

grease
greatly
group
guarantee
guide

half
hall
halt
hand
handle
hard
have
he
head
hear
heat
heavy
height
help
here
high
history
hold
hole
home
horizontal
horizontally
hot
hour
house
how
however
humidity

I
identical

identification
if
ignore
ignored
illegally
immediately
implied
importance
important
impossible
improve
improvement
in
inactive
inattention
inaudible
inch
include
incomplete
incorrect
incorrectly
increase
indent
independent
independently
indirect
indirectly
individual
industrial
industry
inefficient
inefficiently
inform
information
initial
ink
insert

insertion
inside
instead
instruction
internal
international
interpret
interrupt
intersect
intersection
into
introduction
invalid
inventory
isolate
it
item

job

keep
key
kit
knob
know
knowledge

label
language
large
last
late
leading
leap year
learn
least
leave

left
length
less
lesson
let
letter
level
library
license
life
lift
light
like
limit
limitation
line
lined
link
lint
liquid
list
listing
little
load
local
location
lock
logic
logical
long
look
loosen
lose
lost
loud
low
lower

machine
main
maintain
maintenance
major
make
management
manager
manual
manually
manufacturer
many
margin
mark
marked
market
match
material
maximum
may
mean
meaning
measure
measurement
mechanical
meet
meeting
member
message
metal
meter
method
microscopic
might
minimum
minor
minute

missing
mistake
modern
money
month
more
morning
most
motion
motor
movable
move
movement
much
multiple
multiplication
multiply
must

name
narrow
natural
near
necessary
necessarily
need
never
new
next
night
no
none
normal
normally
not
note
now

number
numeral
nut
nylon

obey
object
objective
obsolete
obvious
occupy
occur
occurrence
odd
odor
of
off
offer
office
often
oil
old
omission
omit
on
once
one
only
open
opening
operate
operator
opposite
option
optional
or
order

ordered
organization
organize
oriented
original
other
otherwise
out of
outside
over
own
owner
ownership

pack
package
page
pair
panel
paper
paragraph
parallel
part
partial
particle
past
pattern
peak
pen
people
per
percent
perfect
perform
performance
permanent
permanently

permit
person
personnel
pertaining to
phase
philosophy
phrase
physical
physically
place
plan
plastic
plate
please
plug
point
pointer
position
possible
possibly
potential
powerful
practical
practice
precede
preceding
preliminary
preparation
prepare
presence
present
press
prevent
preventive
previous
previously
price

primarily
primary
print
priority
private
probable
probably
problem
procedural
procedure
proceed
process
produce
product
production
profit
program
progress
project
proportional
proposal
protect
protection
protective
provide
public
pull
punctuation
purpose
push

qualification
quality
quantity
question
quiet
quota

quote
rack
raise
ramp
random
range
rapid
rate
rating
reach
react
reaction
read
reader
ready
rear
reason
recognition
recognize
recommend
recommended
record
recover
recovery
rectangle
rectangular
refer
reference
regardless of
regular
regularly
reject
rejection
relate
related
relation
relationship

relative
release
remainder
remember
remote
removable
removal
remove
repair
repeat
replace
replacement
report
represent
requirement
reserve
resist
resource
respond
response
responsibility
responsible
rest
restore
restraint
restriction
result
return
reverse
review
right
ring
rod
roll
room
round
routine

row
rub
rule

safe
safety
same
sample
save
say
schedule
screw
seal
second
secondary
secretary
section
see
seldom
select
selection
sell
send
sentence
separate
sequence
sequential
sequentially
series
serious
service
set
share
she
sheet
shelf
shield

shift
shipment
shock
short
should
show
side
sign
similar
similarity
simple
single
site
size
skill
slot
slow
slowly
small
smooth
so
socket
soft
solution
solve
some
something
soon
sound
source
space
spacing
spare
speak
speaker
special
specific

specifically
specification
specify
speed
split
square
stabilize
stable
standard
start
starting
state
statement
stay
steady
step
sticky
stockroom
stop
straight
straighten
strong
structure
student
study
subset
subtract
subtraction
success
successful
successfully
such
sudden
suggestion
sum
summary
supersede

supervisor
supplementary
supplier
supply
support
sure
surface
symbol
symbolic
system

tabular
tabulate
take
technical
technology
telephone
tell
temperature
temporarily
temporary
tendency
term
test
text
than
that
the
their
them
then
theory
there
thereafter
thereby
therefore
these

they
thick
thin
thing
think
this
those
thread
through
tighten
time
times
tip
title
to
today
together
tomorrow
tone
too
tool
top
torn
total
touch
toward
train
training
transaction
translate
translation
transparent
triangle
trouble
true
try
turn

twisted
two-way
type
typical

unacceptable
unauthorized
unbroken
undefined
under
understand
unequal
unique
unit
unless
unload
unlock
unpack
unplug
unrelated
unsafe
unscheduled
unsuccessful
unsure
until
unusable
unusual
up
upper
upright
upward
usable
use
useful
usual
usually

valuable	warning	wide
value	warranty	width
vapor	water	will
variation	way	wire
vendor	we	wiring
verbal	wear	with
version	week	within
vertical	weekly	without
very	weight	word
via	well	work
view	wet	worn
visible	what	wrap
visual	when	write
vocabulary	where	writer
voice	whether	wrong
	which	
wait	while	year
wall	who	yes
want	why	yesterday
		you

Ordering Information

To order additional copies of this book, fill in and mail this form or call the toll-free telephone number below. Orders under $50 must be prepaid by check or charge card; postage and handling are free on prepaid orders. There is a 10 percent discount on orders of two or more copies.

Digital Press/Order Processing
Digital Equipment Corporation
12A Esquire Road
Billerica, MA 01862

QTY.	TITLE	ORDER NO.	PRICE*	TOTAL
	The Digital Dictionary, 2d Ed	EY-3433E-DP	$25.00	

Total	
Discount	
Add state sales tax	
Total remitted	

METHOD OF PAYMENT

_____ Check included (Make checks payable to Digital Equipment Corporation)

_____ Purchase order (Please attach)

_____ MasterCard   _____ VISA

Charge Card Acc't No. _____

Expiration Date _____

Authorized Signature _____

Name _____   Phone _____

Address _____

City _____   State _____   Zip _____

TOLL-FREE ORDER NUMBER

To order books by Master Card or VISA, call 1-800-343-8321, continental U.S. only. For information, call Customer Service (617) 663-4152. Phone lines are open from 8:00 A.M. to 4:00 P.M., Eastern time.

*Price and terms quoted are U.S. only and are subject to change without notice. For prices outside the U.S., contact the nearest office of Educational Services, Digital Equipment Corporation.

The DIGITAL Dictionary

Your comments and suggestions will help us in our continuous effort to improve the quality and usefulness of future editions.

What is your general reaction to this Dictionary?

	Excellent	Very Good	Good	Fair	Poor
Accuracy	☐	☐	☐	☐	☐
Completeness	☐	☐	☐	☐	☐
Organization	☐	☐	☐	☐	☐
Format	☐	☐	☐	☐	☐

What features are most useful? _____

_____

_____

_____

_____

Does the publication satisfy your needs?　　☐ Yes　　☐ No

What errors have you found?
(Designate page number, entry term, text reference, or other) _____

_____

_____

_____

_____

Additional Comments _____

_____

_____

_____

(Attach additional pages, if needed)

Name _____

Title _____

Department _____

Company _____

Address _____

digital

Digital Press
Digital Equipment Corporation
FPO/B9
30 North Avenue
Burlington, MA 01803